Poland

Gdańsk & Pomerania
p303

Warmia & Masuria
p365

Mazovia & Podlasie
p84

Wielkopolska
p279

Warsaw
p46

Silesia
p236

Małopolska
p158

Kraków
p115

Carpathian Mountains
p195

Simon Richmond, Mark Baker, Mark Di Duca,
Anthony Haywood, Hugh McNaughtan, Ryan Ver Berkmoes

Contents

LDAMBIES/SHUTTERSTOCK ©

WILANÓW PALACE P65

EWG3D/GETTY IMAGES ©

TATRA MOUNTAINS P197

Contents

Welcome to Poland

Picturesque cities such as Kraków and Gdańsk vie with energetic Warsaw for your urban attention. Elsewhere, woods, rivers, lakes and hills beckon for some fresh-air fun.

A Thousand Years

Poland's history stretches over a millennium of twists and turns and kings and castles. WWII history buffs are well served – monuments and museums dedicated to that epic, tragic conflict, and to Poland's remarkable survival, can be seen everywhere. There's a growing appreciation, too, of the country's rich Jewish heritage. Beyond the deeply affecting Holocaust memorials, synagogues are being sensitively restored, and former Jewish centres such as Łódź and Lublin have created heritage walking trails.

Castles to Log Cabins

The former royal capital of Kraków is a living museum of architecture through the ages. Its nearly perfectly preserved Gothic core proudly wears overlays of Renaissance, baroque and art nouveau. Fabulous medieval castles and evocative ruins dot hilltops around the country, and the fantastic red-brick fortresses of the Teutonic Knights stand proudly in the north along the Vistula. Simple but finely crafted wooden churches hide amid the Carpathian hills, and the ample skills of the highlanders are on display at the country's many skansens (open-air ethnographic museums).

Heart-Warming Food

Good home cooking, the way your grandmother used to make it, is the basis of Polish cuisine. Local ingredients, such as pork, duck, cabbage, mushrooms, beetroot and onion, are combined simply and honed to perfection. Regional specialities and accomplished chefs keep things from getting dull. As for sweets, it's hard to imagine a more accommodating destination. Cream cakes, apple strudel, pancakes, fruit-filled dumplings and a special mania for *lody* (ice cream) may have you skipping the main course and jumping straight to the main event.

Fresh-Air Pursuits

Away from the big cities, much of Poland feels remote and unspoiled. While large swathes of the country are flat, the southern border is lined with a chain of low-lying but lovely mountains that invite days, if not weeks, of splendid solitude. Well-marked hiking paths criss-cross the country, taking you through dense forest, along broad rivers and through mountain passes. Much of the northeast is covered by interlinked lakes and waterways ideal for kayaking and canoeing – no experience necessary. Local outfitters are happy to set you up for a couple of hours or weeks.

Why I Love Poland

By Simon Richmond, Writer

Family and friend connections first brought me to Poland, nearly 30 years ago. Even in those more challenging times I remember being impressed by the country's effort to rebuild itself, as witnessed in the amazing reconstruction of Warsaw's Old Town and the preservation of historic locations such as Kraków and Gdańsk. Today, Poland is one of Europe's economic star performers. Creative energy is abundant in the urban areas, but progress hasn't come at the expense of the beautiful countryside, which, for adventurous travellers, remains a playground of forests, beaches and mountains.

For more about our writers, see p448

Above: Main Market Square and St Mary's Basilica, Kraków (p119)

Poland

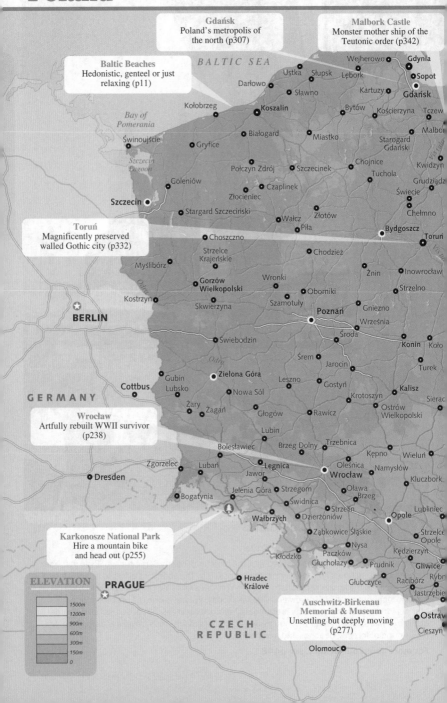

Gdańsk
Poland's metropolis of the north (p307)

Malbork Castle
Monster mother ship of the Teutonic order (p342)

Baltic Beaches
Hedonistic, genteel or just relaxing (p11)

BALTIC SEA

Wejherowo
Gdynia
Sopot

Ustka
Słupsk
Lębork
Kartuzy
Gdańsk

Darłowo
Sławno

Kołobrzeg
Koszalin
Bytów
Kościerzyna
Tczew

Bay of Pomerania

Białogard
Miastko
Starogard Gdański
Malbor

Świnoujście
Gryfice

Szczecin Lagoon

Połczyn Zdrój
Szczecinek
Chojnice
Tuchola
Kwidzyn

Goleniów
Czaplinek
Grudziądz
Świecie

Złocieniec
Chełmno

Szczecin
Stargard Szczeciński
Wałcz
Złotów
Piła

Bydgoszcz
Toruń

Toruń
Magnificently preserved walled Gothic city (p332)

Choszczno

Strzelce Krajeńskie
Chodzież
Żnin
Inowrocław

Myślibórz

Gorzów Wielkopolski
Wronki
Oborniki
Strzelno

Kostrzyn
Skwierzyna
Szamotuły
Gniezno

BERLIN

Świebodzin
Poznań
Września

Środa
Konin
Koło

Zielona Góra
Śrem
Jarocin
Turek

Leszno
Gostyń

GERMANY

Gubin
Lubsko
Nowa Sól
Kalisz

Cottbus
Żary
Żagań
Krotoszyn
Sierac

Głogów
Rawicz
Ostrów Wielkopolski

Wrocław
Artfully rebuilt WWII survivor (p238)

Lubin

Bolesławiec
Brzeg Dolny
Trzebnica

Zgorzelec
Lubań
Kępno
Wieluń

Jawor
Legnica
Oleśnica
Namysłów

Dresden

Jelenia Góra
Strzegom
Oława
Kluczbork

Bogatynia
Świdnica
Brzeg

Strzelin
Lubliniec

Wałbrzych
Dzierżoniów
Opole
Strzelce Opole

Karkonosze National Park
Hire a mountain bike and head out (p255)

Ząbkowice Śląskie
Nysa
Kędzierzyn

Kłodzko
Paczków
Prudnik
Gliwice

Głuchołazy
Racibórz
Rybn

ELEVATION

PRAGUE

Głubczyce
Jastrzębie

Hradec Králové

Auschwitz-Birkenau Memorial & Museum
Unsettling but deeply moving (p277)

Ostraw

1500m
1200m
900m
600m
300m
150m
0

CZECH REPUBLIC

Cieszyn

Olomouc

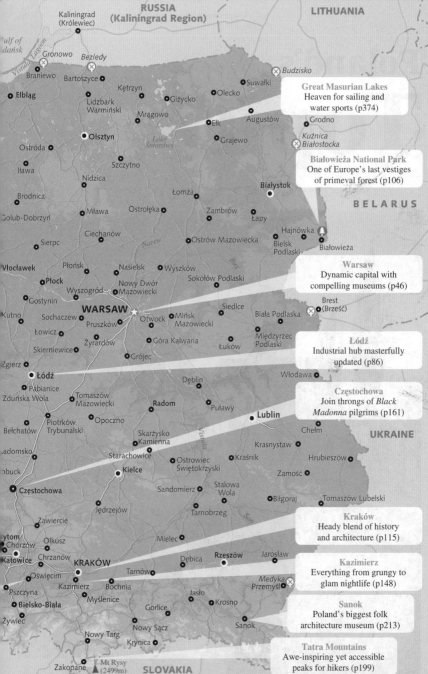

N

0 ——— 50 km
0 ——— 30 miles

RUSSIA
Kaliningrad (Królewiec)
(Kaliningrad Region)

LITHUANIA

Gulf of Gdańsk

Vistula Lagoon

Gronowo
Bezledy
Braniewo
Bartoszyce
Kętrzyn
Budzisko
Suwałki
Elbląg
Lidzbark Warmiński
Giżycko
Olecko
Olsztyn
Mrągowo
Ełk
Augustów
Grodno
Ostróda
Lake Śniardwy
Grajewo
Kuźnica Białostocka
Iława
Szczytno
Nidzica
Brodnica
Łomża
Białystok
BELARUS
Golub-Dobrzyń
Mława
Ostrołęka
Zambrów
Łapy
Sierpc
Ciechanów
Narew
Ostrów Mazowiecka
Hajnówka
Bielsk Podlaski
Białowieża
Włocławek
Płońsk
Nasielsk
Wyszków
Bug
Płock
Nowy Dwór Mazowiecki
Sokołów Podlaski
Gostynin
Wyszogród
Brest (Brześć)
Kutno
WARSAW
Siedlce
Biała Podlaska
Sochaczew
Pruszków
Otwock
Mińsk Mazowiecki
Łowicz
Żyrardów
Góra Kalwaria
Łuków
Międzyrzec Podlaski
Skierniewice
Grójec
Zgierz
Dęblin
Włodawa
Łódź
Pabianice
Zduńska Wola
Tomaszów Mazowiecki
Radom
Puławy
Lublin
Piotrków Trybunalski
Opoczno
Chełm
UKRAINE
Bełchatów
Skarżysko-Kamienna
Radomsko
Starachowice
Kraśnik
Hrubieszów
Obuck
Kielce
Ostrowiec Świętokrzyski
Kraśnik
Zamość
Częstochowa
Sandomierz
Stalowa Wola
Zawiercie
Jędrzejów
Biłgoraj
Tomaszów Lubelski
Tarnobrzeg
San
Bytom
Chorzów
Olkusz
Mielec
Katowice
Chrzanów
KRAKÓW
Dębica
Rzeszów
Jarosław
Oświęcim
Tarnów
Pszczyna
Kazimierz
Bochnia
Medyka
Przemyśl
Bielsko-Biała
Myślenice
Jasło
Krosno
Żywiec
Gorlice
Sanok
Nowy Targ
Nowy Sącz
Krynica
Zakopane
Mt Rysy (2499m)
SLOVAKIA

Great Masurian Lakes
Heaven for sailing and water sports (p374)

Białowieża National Park
One of Europe's last vestiges of primeval forest (p106)

Warsaw
Dynamic capital with compelling museums (p46)

Łódź
Industrial hub masterfully updated (p86)

Częstochowa
Join throngs of *Black Madonna* pilgrims (p161)

Kraków
Heady blend of history and architecture (p115)

Kazimierz
Everything from grungy to glam nightlife (p148)

Sanok
Poland's biggest folk architecture museum (p213)

Tatra Mountains
Awe-inspiring yet accessible peaks for hikers (p199)

Poland's
Top 17

1

Kraków

1 It's easy to see why Kraków (p115) is an unmissable destination. The former royal capital beguiles with its heady blend of history and harmonious architecture. At its heart is the vast Main Market Sq (Rynek Główny), Europe's largest medieval marketplace. Equally magnificent is Wawel Royal Castle (p117; pictured below), on a hill above the Old Town. But that's just the start – every part of the city is fascinating, from the former Jewish district of Kazimierz and its scintillating nightlife to the communist-era concrete structures of Nowa Huta.

Warsaw's Museums & Palaces

2 Warsaw (p46) has a dramatic history, and its best museums reflect that complex past. Start with the Museum of Warsaw, which maps out the city's development. Move on to powerful Warsaw Rising Museum, focusing on the darkest hours of WWII, followed by the award-winning POLIN Museum of the History of Polish Jews (p55; pictured below). Beautiful music can be heard at the Fryderyk Chopin Museum and communist-era eye candy shines bright at the Neon Museum. For stately charm, don't miss Wilanów Palace, or Łazienki Park's lovely Palace on the Isle.

Gdańsk

3 The colossal red-brick St Mary's Church peers down on slender merchants' townhouses, wedged ornately between palaces that line wide, ancient thoroughfares and crooked medieval lanes. A cosmopolitan residue of art and artefacts left behind by a rich maritime and trading past packs whole museums, and tourists from around the world compete with amber stalls and street performers for cobblestone space. This is Gdańsk (p307); once part of the Hanseatic League, it's now in a league of its own.

Wrocław

4 Throughout its history, Wrocław (p238) – the former German city of Breslau – has taken everything invaders could throw at it, and survived. Badly damaged in WWII, it was rebuilt around its beautiful main market square, where you'll find the gothic Old Town Hall (p238; pictured below). Other highlights include the rococo buildings of the University of Wrocław and the Panorama of Racławice, a vast 19th-century painting exhibited in a purpose-built rotunda. The town also has a vibrant nightlife, with plenty of dining and drinking options in the narrow streets of its lively Old Town.

The Great Masurian Lakes

5 Sip a cocktail on the deck of a luxury yacht, take a dip, or don a lifejacket, grab your paddle and slide off into a watery adventure on one of the interconnected lakes (p374) that make up this mecca for Polish sailing and water-sports fans. Make your base one of the lakeside resorts, such as the picturesque Mikołajki (p380; pictured above) where the slap and jangle of masts competes with the clinking of glasses and the murmur of boat talk. Return to the lakes in winter to go cross-country skiing over their frozen surfaces.

Baltic Beaches

6 The season may be brief and the sea one of Europe's nippiest, but if you're looking for a dose of sand, there are few better destinations than the Baltic's cream-white beaches. Many people come for the strands along one of the many coastal resorts, be it hedonistic Darłówko, genteel Świnoujście or the spa town of Kołobrzeg; others opt to flee the masses and head out instead for the shifting dunes of the Słowiński National Park (p350; pictured top right), where the Baltic's constant bluster sculpts mountains of sifted grains.

Malbork Castle

7 Medieval monster mother ship of the Teutonic order, Malbork Castle (p343) is a mountain of bricks held together by a lake of mortar. This Gothic blockbuster was home to the all-powerful order's grand master and later to visiting Polish monarchs. They have all now left the stage of history, but not even the shells of WWII could dismantle this baby. If you travelled to Poland to see castles, this is what you came to see; catch it just before dusk when the slanting sunlight burns the bricks kiln-crimson.

SASHKO/SHUTTERSTOCK © ARCHITECTURE FIRM KWADRAT

Gdańsk's Museum of WWII

8 Not many museums have visitors in a daze when they leave, but you may need a sit down after a few hours in Gdańsk's Museum of WWII (p313). Housed at the northern end of the waterfront, in a painfully angular piece of architecture, this Gdańsk must-see marches choronologically through WWII, with exhibits mostly examining the human suffering the conflict caused. The vast concrete interior, painted almost exclusively in black and grey, creates an oppressive effect. The dark subject and the very fabric of the museum leave few untouched.

Gothic Toruń

9 While many of northern Poland's towns went up in a puff of red-brick dust in WWII's endgame, Toruń (p332) miraculously escaped intact, leaving today's visitors a magnificently preserved, walled Gothic city by the swirling Vistula. Wander through the Unesco–listed Old Town crammed with museums, churches, grand mansions and squares, and when you're flagging, perk up with a peppery gingerbread cookie, Toruń's signature snack. Another treat is the city's Copernicus connections – Poland's most illustrious astronomer allegedly first saw the light of day in one of Toruń's Gothic townhouses.

Folk Architecture

10 'Skansen' in Polish refers to an open-air museum of folk architecture, and Poland offers plenty of them. These great gardens of log cabins and timbered chalets make for a wonderful ramble and are testament to centuries of peasant life across the country. Sanok's Museum of Folk Architecture (p214; pictured above) in the Carpathians is the country's biggest skansen, and includes timber churches, an early-18th-century synagogue and even a fire station. As well as these museums, you'll find remnants of old wooden churches and other buildings sprinkled throughout the mountains.

Jasna Góra Pilgrimage

11 In many parts of Europe, religious buildings are often little more than historical sights or curiosities. In Poland, however, many churches and monasteries remain an integral part of everyday life. Nowhere is this more apparent than at the Jasna Góra monastery (p162; pictured below) in Częstochowa. Every year millions of pilgrims come to pray in Poland's spiritual capital. For the most impressive display of devotion, pay a visit on 15 August, when the Feast of the Assumption sees this relatively small town swamped by hundreds of thousands of worshippers.

Białowieża National Park

12 That bison on the label of a bottle of Żubr beer or Żubrówka vodka starts to make a lot more sense once you've visited this little piece of pristine wood on the Belarus border. The Unesco–listed Białowieża National Park (p106) holds one of Europe's last vestiges of primeval forest, which you can visit in the company of a guide. The bison, which was once extinct outside zoos, has been successfully reintroduced here, although your best bet for seeing these magnificent animals is the nearby European Bison Show Reserve.

Auschwitz-Birkenau Memorial & Museum

13 These Nazi German extermination camps (p277) were the scene of history's greatest genocide, the killing of more than a million people. Now they form a museum and memorial to the victims. Beyond the infamous 'Arbeit Macht Frei' sign at the entrance to Auschwitz are surviving prison blocks that house exhibitions as shocking as they are informative. Not far away, the former Birkenau camp holds the remnants of the gas chambers used for mass murder. Visiting the complex is an unsettling but deeply moving experience.

Cycling in the Karkonosze

14 Slung between Mt Wielki Szyszak (1509m) to the west, and Mt Śnieżka (1602m) to the east, Karkonosze National Park (p255) is not only a treat for hikers. Through its leafy expanse are threaded several mountain-biking trails, covering some 450km, that are easily accessed from the mountain towns of Szklarska Poręba (p258) or Karpacz (p260). Pick up a free bike-trail map from the tourist office, hire a bike and head on out through the trees, passing impressively lofty cliffs carved by ice-age glaciers.

Nightlife in Kazimierz

15 Once a lively blend of both Jewish and Christian cultures, the western half of Kazimierz (p148) is one of Kraków's nightlife hubs. Hidden among its narrow streets and distressed facades are numerous small bars, ranging from grungy to glamorous. The centre of all this activity is Plac Nowy, a small, atmospheric square dominated by a circular central building that was once the quarter's meat market. If Kraków's Old Town is becoming a bit staid for your taste, a night in Kazimierz will revive your spirits.

Hiking in the Tatra Mountainss

16 In many ways, the Tatras (p197) are the perfect mountain range: awe-inspiring yet approachable, with peaks that even ordinary folks – with a little bit of extra effort – can conquer. That doesn't diminish their impact, especially on a summer day when the clouds part to reveal the mountains' stern rocky visage climbing up over the dwarf pines below. The best approach to the peaks is from the mountain resort of Zakopane, where the Tatra Park Nature Education Centre provides a good grounding in the natural history of the mountains.

Łódź

17 Poland's third-largest city (p86) has mastered the knack of transforming former industrial spaces into bold architectural projects, housing cultural, shopping and entertainment areas. For example, EC1, Łódź' first heating and power plant, has been refashioned into a complex with a planetarium, a huge science and technology centre and a range of exhibition spaces. The Manufaktura mall (p86; pictured above) includes the MS2 Museum of Art, a zip line and an artificial beach. And don't miss the remarkable Fabryczna railway station, an architecturally stunning work of art.

Need to Know

For more information, see Survival Guide (p411)

Currency
Polish złoty (zł)

Language
Polish

Visas
Generally not required for stays of up to 90 days.

Money
ATMs widely available. Credit cards widely accepted in hotels and restaurants.

Mobile Phones
Poland uses the GSM 900/1800 system, the same as Europe, Australia and New Zealand, but which is not compatible with most cell phones from North America or Japan. Before bringing your own phone to Poland, check with your service provider to check if it is compatible.

Time
Central European Time (GMT/UTC plus one hour)

When to Go

• Gdańsk
GO Jun–Aug

• Poznań
GO May–Sep

• Warsaw
GO Sep–Oct

• Wrocław
GO May–Sep

• Kraków
GO May–Sep

Warm to Hot Summers, Cold Winters

High Season
(May–Sep)

➡ Expect sunny skies in June and July, but prepare for rain.

➡ Museums, national parks and other attractions are open for business.

➡ You'll find big crowds, especially over holidays and at weekends.

Shoulder
(Mar, Apr & Oct)

➡ Some attractions may be closed or have shorter hours.

➡ April and October are cool, but there'll be some sunny days.

➡ Easter weekend can be very crowded; book in advance.

Low Season
(Nov–Feb)

➡ Snow in the mountains brings skiers to the southern resorts.

➡ The week between Christmas and New Year can be busy.

➡ Museums and castles in smaller towns may be closed.

Useful Websites

Polish Tourism Organisation
(www.poland.travel) National
tourism information site.

Warsaw Tourist Information
(www.warsawtour.pl) Official
Warsaw tourism website.

Magiczny Kraków (www.
krakow.pl) Official Kraków
tourism website.

Culture.pl (www.culture.pl)
Fascinating cultural background features on Poland.

Our Poland (www.ourpoland.
com) General travel guide to the
country.

Lonely Planet (www.lonely
planet.com/poland) Destination
information, hotel bookings,
traveller forum and more.

Important Numbers

Ambulance	☏999
Fire	☏998
Police	☏997
Emergency from mobile phone	☏112
Poland's country code	☏48

Exchange Rates

Australia	A$1	2.68zł
Canada	C$1	2.85zł
Europe	€1	4.28zł
Japan	¥100	3.44zł
NZ	NZ$1	2.54zł
UK	£1	5.03zł
US	US$1	3.82zł

For current exchange rates, see
www.xe.com.

Daily Costs

**Budget:
Less than 200zł**

➡ Low-cost guesthouse or
hostel dorm bed: 50zł

➡ Meals in milk bars and self-
catering: 30zł

➡ Day pass for local transport:
15zł

**Midrange:
200–600zł**

➡ Room in a midrange hotel or
pension: 200–400zł

➡ Lunch and dinner in decent
restaurants: 80–100zł

➡ Museum tickets: 10–30zł

**Top End:
More than 600zł**

➡ Double room in a top hotel:
600–800zł

➡ Meal in a top restaurant:
200–300zł

➡ Opera ticket: 200zł

Opening Hours

Most places adhere to the
following hours. Shopping
centres generally have longer
hours and are open from 10am
to 10pm on weekends. Many
(but not all) museums are
closed on Mondays, and have
shorter hours outside high
season.

Banks 9am–5pm Monday to
Friday, to 1pm Saturday (varies)

Offices 8am–4pm Monday to
Friday (varies)

Post Offices 8am–8pm Monday
to Friday, to 1pm Saturday
(cities)

Restaurants 11am–11pm daily

Shops 8am–6pm Monday to
Friday, 10am–8pm Saturday

Arriving in Poland

Chopin Airport (Warsaw)
Both trains (4.40zł, every
30 minutes to every hour,
20 minutes) and buses (4.40zł,
every 15 minutes, 30 minutes)
run to the city centre. Taxis
cost 35zł to 50zł and take 20
to 30 minutes.

**John Paul II International
Airport** (Kraków) Trains and
buses run from the airport to
the city centre every 30 minutes. An official Kraków Airport
Taxi into the city centre should
cost 70zł to 90zł and take about
30 minutes.

Lech Wałęsa Airport (Gdańsk)
Trains and more frequent buses
run to the main station near
the Old Town (3.80zł, 35 to 40
minutes). For the train, you
normally need to change at
Gdańsk Wrzeszcz. A taxi should
cost around 60zł.

Getting Around

Poland has an extensive and
reasonably priced rail and bus
network, though it's not always
terribly fast or efficient.

Train PKP InterCity trains offer
affordable and fast services
between major cities and on
international routes. Slower
PKP trains run to smaller towns
around the country.

Bus Nationwide FlixBus/Polski
Bus services link big cities and
can be faster than trains on
some routes. Elsewhere, buses
are useful for remote towns and
villages that aren't serviced by
trains.

Car Handy for travelling at your
own pace, but note that some
Polish roads can be narrow and
crowded. Cars can be hired in
many towns and cities. Drive on
the right.

 For much more on **getting around**, see p422

If You Like...

Castles

Wawel Royal Castle The grand-daddy of them all, the mighty Kraków castle is the symbol of the Polish nation. (p117)

Malbork The mind boggles at the millions of red bricks needed to build Europe's biggest medieval fortress. (p343)

Książ Silesia's largest castle is a splendid edifice that holds a curious wartime secret beneath its foundations. (p250)

Krzyżtopór This evocative ruin is what you get when you cross magic, money and a 17th-century Polish eccentric. (p172)

Krasiczyn A picture of Renaissance perfection and the turreted castle of your childhood fairy-tale fantasy. (p212)

Łańcut Poland's largest and richest aristocratic home dates back to the 15th century and is now a museum. (p209)

Museums

National Museum Several centuries of top-quality Polish art and design are gathered in the country's largest museum. (p59)

Schindler's Factory Evocative museum within Oskar Schindler's former enamel factory tells the story of Kraków under German occupation in WWII. (p131)

National Maritime Museum If maritime flotsam and jetsam float your boat, you'll love this museum complex in Gdańsk. (p315)

Fryderyk Chopin Museum A high-tech, interactive homage to Poland's greatest composer. (p52)

POLIN Museum of the History of Polish Jews Impressive multimedia exhibits document 1000 years of Jewish history in Poland. (p55)

Silesian Museum Based in an ingeniously repurposed coal mine, this fascinating museum in Katowice showcases the region's arts and culture. (p271)

Communist Architecture

Kielce's Bus Terminal Check out this flash, Jetsons-style bus station in a country where a handsome bus station is, admittedly, hard to find. (p169)

Palace of Culture & Science Stalin's 'gift' to the Polish people continues to dominate the heart of Warsaw. (p52)

Nowa Huta This sprawling 1950s suburb makes a startling contrast to Kraków's Old Town. (p134)

Forum Przestrzenie In a creative reuse of a 1970s eyesore, this old hotel in Kraków has been repurposed as a trendy bar and events space. (p149)

Monument to the Victims of June 1956 Dramatic monument to the Poznań workers killed in a brutal crackdown. (p286)

Katowice Check out the industrial hub's 1970s-style Rynek (central market square), then cast your glance northward to the monolithic Hotel Katowice. (p271)

Hiking

Zakopane Just outside the door of your hotel, you'll find Poland's highest and most dramatic walks in the Tatras. (p197)

Bieszczady Green, clean and remote. This little corner wedged by Ukraine is as off the beaten track as it gets in Poland. (p213)

Karkonosze National Park Hike the ridge between Mt Szrenica and Mt Śnieżka in this Silesian national park for views of forests and mighty cliffs. (p255)

Góry Stołowe National Park Explore strange and fascinating rock formations in the Sudetes Mountains. (p265)

Wolin National Park Trails running through here provide hiking happiness for a day or two in the bracing Baltic Sea air. (p348)

Top: Hiking in the Tatra National Park (p199).

Bottom: Fryderyk Chopin Museum, Warsaw (p52)

Nightlife

Praga Warsaw's 'right bank' is where the city goes to let down its hair. (p76)

Wrocław Thousands of university students have to have something to do on a Friday night. (p247)

Kazimierz This Kraków district is home to a plethora of cool, small bars, tucked behind attractive old facades in narrow streets. (p148)

Poznań A magnet for business people and local students, the city's Old Town is packed with lively pubs, clubs and eating spots. (p291)

Sopot Get down by the Baltic where the fun spills out of Sopot's many nightspots and onto the balmy beach. (p329)

Folk Culture

Sanok The Museum of Folk Architecture here is the biggest in the country, with some 120 historic buildings. (p214)

Tarnów The Ethnographic Museum specialises in the folk history of the minority Roma. (p204)

Upper Silesian Ethnographic Park Industrial Katowice is the unlikely location of this 20 hectare skansen (open-air ethnographic museum). (p271)

Kashubia This traditional region of drowsy villages and ethnographic museums provides folksy contrast to the brashness of the coast. (p331)

Olsztynek The Museum of Folk Architecture teleports visitors back to a timber past. (p371)

Month by Month

January

New Year's Eve celebrations are held around the country with fireworks and drinking. The country sleeps off its hangover for the next few days then largely retreats indoors as the snow falls.

✦ Kraków New Year

Kraków rings in the New Year with classical music from the Kraków Philharmonic and a series of concerts and fireworks on the Main Market Sq. (p150)

🏃 Ski Season

Poland's festival pulse is barely beating. A better idea is to head south for a bit of skiing, such as to the country's main winter resort of Zakopane.

February

The winter ski season reaches its peak this month at resorts in the southern mountains. The crowds on slopes worsen about mid-month during the winter break, when schoolkids get the week off.

✦ Shanties

A 'shanty' is a traditional sailor's song and Kraków has held this international fest celebrating the ditties since 1981 – in spite of the city's landlocked location! (p136)

March

The first tentative signs of spring are felt towards the end of this month, but you'll still want to wrap up well as temperatures across the country can remain bone-chillingly cold.

✦ Beethoven Easter Festival

Coinciding with Easter (so sometimes in April), this festival sees a series of concerts held across Warsaw celebrating the work of the great German composer.)

April

As the hours of daylight start to lengthen, trees bud and spring flowers appear. The warm, sunny afternoons promise better days ahead. Easter is a big travel weekend.

☆ Remembering the Ghetto Uprising

On 19 April those who died during the Warsaw Ghetto Uprising of 1943 are remembered as flowers are laid at the Ghetto Heroes Monument and paper daffodil badges are distributed around the city.

🍴 Restaurant Week

Your chance to eat from special menus at top restaurants in 30 cities across Poland for bargain prices. This annual event (www.restaurantweek. pl) is usually held in mid-April.

🏃 Cracovia Marathon

Kraków's marathon is a highly popular running event that draws more than 1000 runners to its scenic course, which heads out from the Old Town.

May

The return of reliably decent weather sees flowers in bloom, plus restaurants, cafes and bars setting up their outdoor terraces and the sound of happy students about to be freed from school.

✯ Sacral Music

Częstochowa is known as a Catholic pilgrimage site, but each May it shows off its ecumenical side with the Gaude Mater Festival, highlighting religious music from Christian, Jewish and Islamic faiths. (p163)

✯ Baltic Music

The Probaltica Music & Art Festival of Baltic States in Toruń brings together traditional musicians from across the Baltic region. (p336)

✯ Juvenalia

This carnival in Kraków at the end of the academic year sees students take over the city for four days and three nights of fun involving live music, street dancing and fancy-dress parades. (p137)

✯ Orange Warsaw Festival

Top international pop and rock performers hit the stage for the Orange Warsaw Festival, the city's premier outdoor music fest, usually held at the end of the month.

June

Summer really starts to get rolling as the weather warms up and the kids get out of school.

Festivals marking Corpus Christi (usually June, but sometimes May) can be raucous. The biggest is in Łowicz.

✯ Lajkonik Pageant

A colourful pageant headed by the Lajkonik, a comic figure disguised as a bearded Tatar. Look for it on the first Thursday after Corpus Christi (usually in June, but possibly late May). (p136)

☆ Theatre in Poznań

Poznań's Malta International Theatre Festival is Poland's biggest theatre and dramatic arts event. Expect a week of entertaining street theatre – and thousands of people competing for hotel rooms.

✯ Midsummer's Night

In Warsaw the longest day of the year sees locals indulging in pagan rituals, including the lighting of bonfires, big fireworks displays and the floating of wreaths studded with candles down the Vistula River.

✯ Jewish Culture Festival

Kraków's Jewish Culture Festival, at the end of June and start of July, climaxes with a grand open-air klezmer concert on ul Szeroka in Kazimierz. (p137)

✯ Warsaw Street Art

Starting at the end of June and slipping into July, Warsaw's Street Art Festival brings five days of theatre, open-air art installations and 'happenings', staged in public places. (p67)

July

July is usually hot and sunny but there can also be rain showers. Resorts are crowded, but not as much as they are in August. The music-festival season kicks into high gear.

✯ Open'er Festival

Gdynia's Open'er Festival of pop and indie rock is *the* summer event everyone in the Tri-City talks about. It's held the first week of July at Gdynia-Kosakowo Airport. (p318)

☆ Blues Express

Ride the rails between Poznań and Zakrzewo while enjoying an onboard blues concert with a view of the Polish countryside. (p287)

✯ Warsaw Summer Jazz Days

This series of concerts sees top international jazz stars play alongside local talent. A highlight is the open-air concert in Castle Sq.

August

Expect big crowds at the Baltic beaches as well as lake and mountain resorts, which only worsen at weekends. As compensation, you'll get sunshine and lots of festivals.

✯ Dominican Fair

This top Gdańsk fair has been held since 1260. Launched by Dominican monks as a feast day, the fun has spread to streets all around the Main Town. (p312)

✨ Getting Down with Highlanders

Zakopane's International Festival of Mountain Folklore draws highlanders (mountain folk) from around Europe and the world for a week of music, dance and traditional costume. (p200)

✨ Singer's Warsaw Festival

Held from late August to early September, this major Jewish cultural festival includes theatre, music, films, exhibits and workshops at various city locations. (p68)

September

The first nip of autumn arrives early in the month as kids return to school and life returns to normal. However, the sunshine is fairly good, making this month perfect for enjoying crowd-free resorts.

✨ Four Cultures

Each year, Łódź celebrates its historic role as a meeting place of Polish, Jewish, Russian and German cultures with the suitably named Four Cultures Festival. It includes theatre, music, film and visual arts. (p90)

☆ Wratislavia Cantans

The unforgettably named Wratislavia Cantans is Wrocław's top music and fine-arts confab. The focus is on sacred songs and tunes but there's also classical and folk music. (p244)

✨ Old Jazz Festival

Poznań's Old Jazz Festival features local and international jazz performers, both old and young, at concert venues around town. (p287)

☆ Archaeological Festival

This festival held at Biskupin Archaeological Reserve includes demos of ancient dances, handcrafts and food, as well as colourful re-enactments of battles between Germanic and Slavic tribes. (p298)

October

The tourist season is officially over, and castles and museums revert to winter hours or fall into a deep slumber.

✨ Warsaw Film Festival

The Warsaw Film Festival highlights the world's best films over 10 days in October. There are screenings of Polish films and plenty of retrospectives. (p68)

November

The first significant snowfalls cover the mountains, though the ski season doesn't begin in earnest until December. Elsewhere around the country, brisk temperatures and darkening afternoons herald the coming of winter.

☆ All Souls' Jazz

Cracovians enjoy the week-long All Souls' Day Jazz Festival, which is held around All Souls' Day (2 November). Look for performances all over town in clubs, bars and churches.

✨ St Martin's Day

Polish Independence Day falls on 11 November, but in Poznań it's also St Martin's Day, a day of parades and general merriment, including the scoffing of special St Martin's Day sweet croissants. (p287)

December

The air turns frosty and the ski season in the south begins around the middle of the month. The only thing keeping people going, amid the grey skies, is the coming Christmas and New Year holidays.

🔒 Barbican Christmas Market

Warsaw's main Christmas market starts in late November and hits its stride in December. You can hardly get a more picturesque setting than the red-brick rotunda of the Old Town's Barbican.

◉ Kraków Christmas Cribs

December kicks off an unusual competition to see who can build the most amazing Christmas crèche. The *szopki* (Nativity scenes) are elaborate compositions fashioned in astonishing detail from cardboard, wood and tinfoil. (p137)

Itineraries

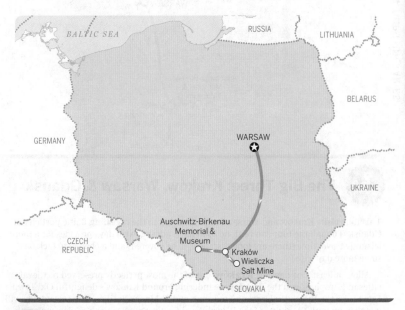

1 WEEK **Essential Poland**

Poland is a big country with lots to see, so travellers with limited time will have to choose their destinations carefully. For first-time visitors, especially, the places to start are the capital, Warsaw, and the country's most popular city, Kraków. For a week-long tour, budget roughly three days in each, and a day for travel.

Warsaw offers a scintillating mix of architectural styles, with mammoth Soviet-era and contemporary buildings standing alongside a lovingly restored Old Town. Leave at least a day for museum-hopping, zoning in on the equally excellent Warsaw Rising Museum, POLIN Museum of the History of Polish Jews, the Museum of Warsaw and the National Museum.

The former royal capital of **Kraków** is smaller than Warsaw but packs in plenty to see. Spend a day in the Old Town and the Wawel Royal Castle, a second day around the former Jewish quarters of Kazimierz and Podgórze, and a third day with a side trip to the **Wieliczka Salt Mine** (if you have kids in tow) or the **Auschwitz-Birkenau Memorial & Museum**.

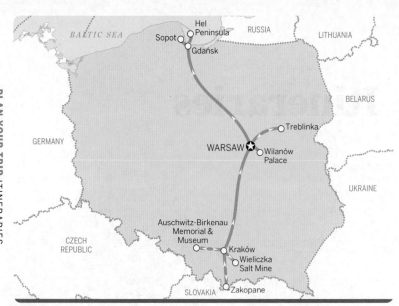

The Big Three: Kraków, Warsaw & Gdańsk

This tour visits Kraków and Warsaw before heading to the ravishing Baltic port city of Gdańsk. Though the tour can be done in 10 days, adding extra days provides for a more leisurely travel time (there are long distances to be covered) and a chance to tack on some more day trips.

Allow at least four days for **Kraków**, one of the most perfectly preserved medieval cities in Europe. Spend the first day meandering around Kraków's delightful Old Town. Don't miss the Rynek Underground museum and St Mary's Basilica. The second day will be taken up with the sights of the Wawel Royal Castle. Spend your third day exploring the former Jewish quarters of Kazimierz and Podgórze. On the last day, make a side trip to either the **Wieliczka Salt Mine** or **Auschwitz-Birkenau Memorial & Museum**. Alternatively, breathe in the mountain air of the Tatras in the resort of **Zakopane**, two hours away by bus.

Fast intercity trains are the best way to get to **Warsaw**, where you should plan to stay put for another three to four days. You'll need that time to do justice to the city's many amazing museums as well as to enjoy the sights of the Old Town. Make sure you also take in the view from the observation deck of the Palace of Culture & Science, and go for a stroll along and across the banks of the Vistula to Praga, where there's a great bar scene. A walk through lovely Łazienki Park is also highly recommended. For day trips consider **Wilanów Palace**, 6km south of the centre, and the former Nazi German extermination camp at **Treblinka**.

From Warsaw, take the train to **Gdańsk** and prepare to be dazzled by the stunningly restored Main Town, which was rebuilt from WWII ruins. Learn all about that conflict at the city's excellent Museum of WWII. Proceed down the Royal Way and don't miss the Amber Museum. Then there's the waterfront district and pretty ul Mariacka.

If the weather is warm, spend your last full day on the water, at either the brash but popular beach resort of **Sopot**, or the quieter, more refined strand on the **Hel Peninsula**.

Along the Vistula

The Vistula is Poland's greatest river, winding its way from the foothills of the country's southern mountain range to the Baltic Sea. It's played a key role in Poland's very identity, as it passes through – or close to – many of its oldest and most important settlements. Ideally suited to roaming, this tour is for visitors who are not on a strict timetable and are looking for an unusual approach to Poland's core. The four-week schedule assumes that you rely on buses, as train services to many of these towns are not as frequent. Naturally, if you have your own wheels, you could cover the terrain in three weeks or even less.

Begin upstream with two or three days at the former royal capital of **Kraków** and take a day tour to **Auschwitz-Birkenau Memorial & Museum** in Oświęcim. From Kraków, make your way by bus to beautiful **Sandomierz**, one of Poland's undiscovered delights, with its impressive architectural variety and position on a bluff overlooking the river. From here, it's worth taking a detour, again by bus, to the Renaissance masterpiece of **Zamość**, a nearly perfectly preserved 16th-century town.

Back on the path along the Vistula, stop in at the former artists' colony – now a popular weekend retreat – of **Kazimierz Dolny**. Set aside several days to do **Warsaw** justice – the Vistula embankments in the capital offer nature, beaches, public art and lively nightlife. Next, call in at **Płock**, home to the finest collection of art nouveau art and architecture in the country. Follow the river into Pomerania and through the heart of medieval **Toruń**, another nicely preserved Gothic town that is also the birthplace of stargazer Nicolaus Copernicus.

Soon after Toruń, the river heads directly for the sea. In former times, the Vistula's path was guarded by one Teutonic Knight stronghold after another. Today, these Gothic gems silently watch the river pass by. You can see the knights' handiwork at **Chełmno**, **Kwidzyn** and **Gniew**, but the mightiest example resides at **Malbork**, on the banks of one of the river's side arms. End your journey in the port city of **Gdańsk**, where the river meets the sea.

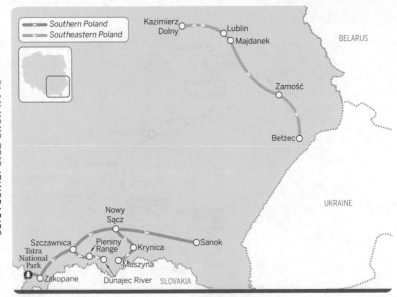

1 WEEK Southern Poland

Poland's southern border, lined with mountains end to end, is ideal for walkers. Though this trip can be done in a week, bus transport can be spotty in parts.

Start in the mountain resort of **Zakopane**, which is easily reached by bus from Kraków. Allow at least a day to see the town's historic wooden architecture and the Museum of Zakopane Style, and another for a walk into the **Tatras** (or more for a longer trek).

From here you'll have to make some tough choices. We like the **Pieniny range**, east of the Tatras. The spa town of **Szczawnica** makes a good base for hikes, as well as biking and the ever-popular rafting ride down the **Dunajec River**.

From Szczawnica, the medium-sized city of **Nowy Sącz** offers urban comforts, or opt for **Krynica** or **Muszyna**, two popular spa resorts and good jumping-off points for more hikes.

A long bus ride from Nowy Sącz brings you to **Sanok**, with its amazing skansen (open-air ethnographic museum) and access to the 70km Icon Trail and its wooden churches.

1 WEEK Southeastern Poland

The southeastern corner of Poland is seldom explored and is a good place to see the country off the beaten path.

Begin in **Lublin**, whose Old Town has been much spruced up in recent years, with some great places to see and dine in. Don't miss Lublin Castle or the chance to clamber up the Trinitarian Tower for a commanding view of the countryside.

Spend a half-day at the enormous **Majdanek** concentration camp on the outskirts of the city. Also use the city as a base for visiting the riverside artists' retreat at **Kazimierz Dolny**, filled with museums and charming galleries. The surrounding fields and forests make for a perfect day out on a bike or on foot.

From Lublin, head south to **Zamość**. This perfectly preserved 16th-century Renaissance town has a lively central square, which hosts summertime concerts and music fests. From Zamość it's an easy drive to **Bełżec**, where the excellent museum and memorial for the former extermination camp is moving without being bombastic.

Cities of the West
Eastern Borderlands

1 WEEK — Cities of the West

Historic and thriving urban centres are the focus of this circuit of western Poland, a region hotly contested between Poland and Germany over the centuries.

Devote at least two days to **Wrocław**, the former German city of Breslau, where the architecture retains a Germanic flavour. After WWII, Wrocław was repopulated by refugees from Poland's eastern lands lost to the Soviet Union, giving the city an added ethnic dimension.

Continue to **Poznań**, a thriving commercial hub where tourists rub shoulders with business people and a large student population in the city's buzzing Old Town square. It was in Poznań that the Polish kingdom got its start a millennium ago and the town offers many historical attractions, too.

The beautifully preserved Gothic town of **Toruń** is a short bus or train ride away from Poznań. It has enchanting red-brick architecture and gingerbread cookies. Finish the tour in either **Gdańsk** or **Szczecin**, the latter adding a gritty contrast to the architectural beauty of the other cities.

3 WEEKS — Eastern Borderlands

Travelling around this relatively remote swathe of Poland will appeal to wanderers who prefer natural splendour to the hustle-bustle of the big city.

Start in **Kraków** for convenience's sake, but head quickly to **Sanok**, with its *skansen* and museum, and then head deeper into the **Bieszczady National Park**. Turn north and take the back roads, via **Przemyśl**, to the Renaissance town of **Zamość**, as well as stopping to see the memorial for the Nazi German extermination camp at **Bełżec**. After a night in Zamość move on to the big-city comforts of **Lublin**.

Strike out north through rural backwaters to **Białowieża National Park** and its primeval forest and bison herd. Head north again to the provincial city of **Białystok** and the hamlet of **Tykocin**, with its unforgettable synagogue.

From here there's a wealth of parklands: the **Biebrza** and **Wigry National Parks**, and beyond, the **Great Masurian Lakes**, all with excellent hiking and boating possibilities.

Plan Your Trip

Outdoor Activities

Poland is a dream destination for an activity-driven vacation. From the Baltic coast to the rugged Carpathian Mountains, you can hire a bike, grab a paddle or put on a pair of walking boots and get some fresh air in beautiful landscapes. There's also skiing in winter.

Best Outdoor Activities

Best Hiking
Tatra Mountains (p199), Pieniny Mountains (p232), Bieszczady Mountains (p215)

Best Kayaking
Krutynia River (p374), Drawa Route (p34), Brda River (p34)

Best Mountain Biking
Bieszczady Mountains (p215), Sudetes Mountains (p254)

Best Skiing
Zakopane (p197), Szklarska Poręba (p258)

Best Water Sports
Great Masurian Lakes (p374), Augustów Canal and around (p109)

Best Time to Go
June to August Summer is ideal for hiking, cycling and kayaking.

May & early September These months can be sunny, with the trails, lakes and waterways less frequented.

November to March The best time for skiing and snowboarding in the mountain ranges of the south.

Cycling

Almost every region of Poland offers well-signposted cycling routes, from short and easy circuits to epic international routes, and the situation is improving by the year. It's possible to restrict yourself to the flatter areas of the country and travel the rest by train, but if you're not deterred by gradients you can cycle some of the more riveting (and relatively unexplored) regions. Maps showing cycling trails can be hard to source outside Poland, but tourist offices can normally supply good cartography.

Where to Cycle
Carpathian Mountains
Some epic bicycle adventures are waiting in the Bieszczady ranges. These tracks will roll you through a montage of deep forest green and rippling meadows, opening up intermittently to postcard-perfect natural and architectural panoramas. Part of the 70km Icon Trail (p215) near the town of Sanok is accessible to cyclists and rewards pedalling with views of old timber churches and castles. The town of Sanok lies astride a sprawling network of bike-friendly roads and pathways that covers hundreds of kilometres in Poland and extends to neighbouring Slovakia and Ukraine.

SAFE CYCLING

➡ Where possible stay on marked cycling trails; sharing national roads with Poland's erratic drivers can be a hair-raising experience.

➡ Motorists in Polish cities are rarely cycle-conscious, so don't expect too much consideration for your space and safety. Ride defensively.

➡ Among the big cities, Kraków offers scenic and safe cycling routes along the river. Warsaw, too, has dedicated cycle paths, including ones alongside the Vistula.

➡ Even small towns have at least one cycle shop selling spare parts and offering a cheap repair service.

➡ Away from major routes, the roads can be poorly maintained – watch out for wheel-swallowing potholes and uneven pavements along the road edges.

➡ Get the best lock you can and always use it, even when storing your bike in buildings and travelling on trains. Better to be safe than cycle-less.

➡ If in doubt, take your bike with you into your hotel room at night. Many hotels have specially locked storage rooms that can accommodate bikes, but some don't.

➡ Check that your accommodation is accessible by bike; some places may not be, owing to street layout, traffic density and road conditions.

➡ Drinking and cycling don't mix: you could be jailed if you ride under the influence.

The region around the Dunajec River in the Pieniny isn't just for rafting. Szczawnica (p233), in particular, is a great cycling centre. It's the starting point for several rewarding rides and is blessed with numerous bike-rental outfits. One of the region's best rides follows the Dunajec River for around 15km all the way to the Slovak town of Červený Kláštor.

Białowieża Forest

There are some enchanting routes (starting near the village of Białowieża) through the northern part of the Białowieża Forest and the large stretches of undisturbed woods that lie to the north and west of Białowieża National Park (p107), including detours into parts of the park itself. Pick up a map from the park's information centre and head off. If you need wheels, try Rent a Bike (p108).

The Northeast

Cycling in the Masuria region is rewarding, and also pretty easy as the terrain is as flat as a board. The town of Węgorzewo (p377) on Lake Mamry is a convenient base from which to access 18 marked routes ranging from 25km to 109km circuits. The Augustów Forest (p113) and the areas around Suwałki (p112) are also great biking territories. There are plenty of bike-rental outfits in Augustów.

Sudetes Mountains

The Sudetes, especially the area around the town of Szklarska Poręba (p258), are a jackpot for mountain bikers. Stretching to the Czech border, Karkonosze National Park (p255) offers myriad marked mountain-biking trails and is popular with Polish extreme-sports enthusiasts. Some of the trails cross over into the Czech Republic. The Szklarska Poręba tourist office (p260) can help with maps and advise on rentals.

Cycling Tours

Most cyclists go it alone in Poland, but if you fancy joining an organised group, two reliable specialist companies (both UK-based) to contact are **Cycling Holidays Poland** (🖉 in the UK +44 1536 738 038; www.cyclingpoland. com) and **Hooked On Cycling** (🖉 in the UK +44 1506 635 399; www.hookedoncycling.co.uk).

Cycling Websites

EuroVelo (www.eurovelo.com) The European Cyclists' Federation has a project to establish a 65,000km European Cycle Network throughout the continent. Six of the 12 routes (not all fully completed) run through Poland. The website has some great maps of the international network as it stands.

Cities for Bicycles (www.miastadlarowerow.pl) Grassroots cycling group promoting safe cycling in cities. Has slightly dated but still useful practical information for cyclists.

TREK SAFE

To ensure you enjoy your walk or hike in comfort and safety, put some thought into your preparations before hitting the trail.

➡ Obtain reliable information about the conditions and characteristics of your intended route from local national-park authorities.

➡ Buy a suitable map from the local bookshop or tourist office.

➡ If possible, always inform someone of your route and when you expect to be back.

➡ Always check the weather forecast with the local tourist office or national-park authority.

➡ Weather conditions can be unpredictable in mountainous areas, so pack appropriate clothing and equipment.

➡ Ensure you are fit enough for and feel comfortable with the walk you choose.

➡ Be aware of the local laws, regulations and etiquette about flora and fauna.

➡ Always be ready to turn back if things start to go wrong.

➡ If planning to overnight in a mountain hut, try to reserve in advance or at least let someone know you're coming. Otherwise you risk not having a place to sleep.

Cycling Holidays Poland (www.cyclingpoland. com) UK-based cycling-tour operator that caters for international tourists.

Central & Eastern European Greenways (www. greenways.by) List of trails and descriptions for the Greenways long-distance cycling and hiking routes that run through Central Europe.

Walking & Hiking

Poland's mountainous areas are a joy to explore on foot and attract thousands of hikers every year and in every season. The country's national parks are riddled with trails, most well marked and well equipped with shelters. Nature's repertoire of heights, gradients, climates and terrains is showcased in Poland: hiking options range from week-long treks for the hardcore hiker to hour-long rambles for the ascent averse. The PTTK (p414), Poland's tourist organisation, has a notoriously wonky website, but it's still a decent resource for hiking and walking in all parts of the country. The website has a list of PTTK-run mountain huts and info centres, and lots of other useful info for planning a trek.

Where to Walk & Hike

The southern mountain ranges are best for exhilarating high-altitude hikes, but low-level walks can be found across the country.

Carpathian Mountains

The Tatra Mountains (p199) in the south are the most notable region for hiking. The West and the High Tatras offer different scenery; the latter is more challenging and as a result more spectacular. One of the most popular climbs in the Tatras is Mt Giewont (1895m). The cross at the peak attracts many visitors, though the steep slopes deter some.

The valleys around Zakopane offer walks of differing lengths (some take less than an hour) for walkers of varying fitness levels. Similarly, trails around the nearby Pieniny (p232) and the Bieszczady (p215) in the east offer exciting hiking experiences – even for those who prefer to stroll. Another great option is Beskid Sądecki (p229), which has convenient paths dotted with mountain hostels. Muszyna and Krynica are popular bases from which to access this region.

The lower Beskid Niski (p224) mountain range offers less arduous walks and less spectacular views.

Your first port of call in each of these areas should be the local tourist information office.

Sudetes Mountains

The Karkonosze National Park (p255) offers a sterling sample of the Sudetes. The ancient and peculiar 'table top' rock formations of the Góry Stołowe (Table

Mountains) are among the highlights of the Sudetes.

The area is easily accessed from the town of Szklarska Poręba at the base of Mt Szrenica (1362m), and there is a choice of walking trails from Karpacz to Mt Śnieżka (1603m). Further south, the village of Międzygórze is another well-kitted-out base for Sudetes sojourns. Tourist offices in Karpacz and Szklarska Poręba stand ready to point you to suitable trails and mountain hostels.

Other Regions

➡ The Augustów Forest (p113) in the Augustów-Suwałki region has 55 lakes and many well-paved roads and dirt tracks. Diverse wildlife can be found in various stretches of the forest. There are numerous bays and peninsulas to explore around nearby Lake Wigry in the Wigry

National Park (p113), and the 63-sq-km Suwałki Landscape Park (p112) offers drop-dead-gorgeous views from its picturesque terrain.

➡ The lowest mountain range in the country is in the Świętokrzyski National Park (p169) in Małopolska, near Kielce. There's an 18km walk here that takes you past an ancient hilltop holy site that's now a picturesque monastery.

➡ **Roztocze National Park** (p193) offers a range of light walks through gentle terrain, and the landscape park surrounding Kazimierz Dolny (p186) offers some easy but worthwhile rambles.

PLAN YOUR TRIP OUTDOOR ACTIVITIES

POLAND'S NATIONAL PARKS

Poland has 23 national parks featuring a wide variety of landscapes. Check national park websites for more information on hiking and cycling routes. Things change, so ask in person before you assume any route is open.

NATIONAL PARK	FEATURES	ACTIVITIES	BEST TIME TO VISIT	WEBSITE
Białowieża (p106)	primeval forest; bison, elk, lynx, wolf	wildlife watching, hiking	spring, summer	www.bpn.com.pl
Biebrza (p103)	river, forest, wetland; elk, great snipe, aquatic warbler	birdwatching, canoeing	spring, summer, autumn	www.biebrza.org.pl
Kampinos (p83)	forest, sand dunes	hiking, mountain biking	summer	www.kampinoski-pn.gov.pl
Karkonosze (p255)	mountains; dwarf pine, alpine flora	hiking, mountain biking	summer, winter	www.kpnmab.pl
Narew (p104)	river, reed beds; beaver, waterfowl	birdwatching, canoeing	spring, autumn	www.npn.pl
Ojców (p160)	forest, caves, rock formations; eagle, bat	hiking	autumn	www.ojcowskiparknarodowy.pl
Roztocze (p193)	forest; elk, wolf, beaver, tarpan	hiking	spring, autumn	www.roztoczanskipn.pl
Słowiński (p350)	forest, bog, sand dunes; white-tailed eagle, waterfowl	birdwatching, hiking	all year	www.slowinskipn.pl
Tatra (p199)	alpine mountains; chamois, eagle	hiking, climbing, skiing	all year	www.tpn.pl
Wolin (p348)	forest, lake, coast; white-tailed eagle, bison	birdwatching, hiking	spring, autumn	www.wolinpn.pl

MOUNTAIN GUIDES

Two commendably practical walking guides for the Tatras are *High Tatras: Slovakia and Poland*, by Colin Saunders and Renáta Nározná (revised edition from 2017), and the excellent *Tatra Mountains of Poland and Slovakia,* by Sandra Bardwell (revised in 2015).

➡ Biebrza National Park (p103) is easy to get to by train and offers great hikes of a couple of hours or more.

➡ There's also Kampinos National Park (p81) just outside Warsaw, with its famed sand dunes, Wielkopolska National Park (Wielkopolski Park Narodowy; www.wielkopolskipn.pl) **FREE** in Wielkopolska, and the compact Wolin National Park (p348) in northwest Poland.

Walking Tours

Many local companies and individual guides operate along the tracks and trails of Poland's wild side. UK-based **Venture Poland** (in the UK +44 20 7558 8179; www.venturepoland.eu) specialises in organised walking tours of the Carpathian Mountains.

Canoeing, Kayaking & Rafting

Choices of where to kayak in Poland flow freely: the lowlands of Masuria, Warmia and Kashubia in Poland's north offer literally thousands of lakes and rivers to choose from. Further to the east is the Augustów Canal (p109), and the lakes and rivers connected to it. Just south of Augustów there's a series of seldom-visited national parks that offer more kayaking opportunities in a protected and isolated environment of river tributaries and bogs.

There's no need to haul your kayak through airports either, as there are plenty of hire centres, where boats, paddles and life jackets can be rented for very reasonable rates, as well as numerous tour companies and guides. Local tourist offices can usually point you in the right direction.

Where to Get Paddling

The Great Masurian Lakes

The town of Olsztyn (p367) is a handy base for organising adventures on water, particularly kayaking. PTTK Mazury here organises trips, equipment and guides. From Olsztyn it's possible to canoe the Łyna River to the border of Russia's Kaliningrad exclave, or spend a couple of laid-back hours floating closer to the city.

The most popular kayaking route in the Great Masurian Lakes area runs along the Krutynia River, originating at Sorkwity, 50km east of Olsztyn, and following the Krutynia River and Lake Bełdany to Ruciane-Nida. Some consider Krutynia the most scenic river in the north and the clearest in Poland. It winds through 100km of forests, bird reserves, meadows and marshes. To get a taste of the river (hopefully not literally), PTTK Mazury in Olsztyn runs kayaking tours at regular intervals from June to August, along the Krutynia, starting at the **Stanica Wodna PTTK** (www.sorkwity. pttk.pl) in Sorkwity. You can also do the trip on your own, hiring a kayak (30zł to 40zł per day) from the Stanica Wodna PTTK in Sorkwity, but check availability in advance.

Augustów-Suwałki Region

Less visited than the renowned Great Masurian Lakes (and arguably cooler than them, too), the lakes of the Augustów-Suwałki region (p109) are not connected, but their waters are crystal clear. The river to paddle in these parts is the Czarna Hańcza, generally from Augustów along the Augustów Canal, all the way to the northern end of Lake Serwy. This route takes in the 180-year-old Augustów Canal, the Suwałki Lake District and the Augustów Forest. Numerous tour operators cover this loop, but it is also possible to do this and other routes independently.

Close to the city of Suwałki, Lake Wigry in the Wigry National Park (p113) offers surprisingly pristine paddling. In the Augustów-Suwałki region, check in with Szot (p111) in Augustów, which offers an excellent selection of short and long trips and English-friendly guides.

Top: Winter hiking in the Tatra Mountains (p199)

Bottom: Kayaking on the Krutynia River (p374)

POSZTOS/SHUTTERSTOCK ©

South of the Masurian Lakes, the Biebrza River runs through the scenic splendour of the Podlasie region and through Biebrza National Park (p103), with its varied landscape of river sprawls, peat bogs, marshes and damp forests. The principal kayaking route here flows from the town of Lipsk downstream along the Biebrza to the village of Wizna, for a distance of about 140km (seven to nine days). While this is longer than most people will have time for, shorter stretches are also possible and camping sites dot the river along the way to allow for overnight stops.

The Narew National Park (p104), further south, is just as interesting as the Biebrza National Park, but not as geared towards visitors. This park protects an unusual stretch of the Narew River that's nicknamed the 'Polish Amazon', where the river splits into dozens of channels. For adventures in this part of Podlasie, try the outfit **Kaylon** (📞502 508 050; http://kajak.nazwa.pl/kajakcompl/index.php; ul Kolejowa 8, Uhowo; kayak rental per day 30zł; ⊙May-Sep) for canoeing and kayaking adventures.

Pomerania

The most renowned kayaking river in Pomerania is the Brda, which leads through forested areas of the **Bory Tucholskie National Park** (www.pnbt.com.pl) and past some 19 lakes.

The Drawa Route, which runs through **Drawa National Park** (www.dpn.pl), is an interesting trip for experienced kayakers. The Drawa Route is believed to have been a favourite kayaking jaunt of Pope John Paul II when he was a young man.

Carpathian Mountains

The organised rafting trip to do in Poland is the placid glide through the Dunajec Gorge (p233) in the Pieniny. The river snakes from Czorsztyn Lake (Jezioro Czorsztyńskie) west between several steep cliffs, some of which are over 300m high. The river is narrow, in one instance funnelling through a 12m-wide bottleneck, and changes incessantly from majestically quiet, deep stretches to shallow mountain rapids. Be advised, however, that this is not a white-water experience but a leisurely pleasure trip. For more details contact the Polish Association of Pieniny Rafters.

Skiing & Snowboarding

If you haven't skied before, Poland is a good place to start, if only because you'll pay less for the privilege here than in many other parts of Europe. Accommodation in ski-resort areas can range from 40zł for a hostel dorm bed up to rooms in more luxurious hotels for 300zł-plus. Ski-lift passes cost around 100zł per day.

Where to Ski

Obviously, the mountain ranges of southern Poland are the places to snap on skis and snowboards, though there's plenty of cross-country skiing in other, flatter locations, especially around (and on) the lakes of Masuria.

Tatra Mountains

The Tatras are the best-equipped skiing area, and the country's winter-sports capital of Zakopane (p197) is the most popular place to slither. The slopes of this region, which peak at Kasprowy Wierch (p199, 1985m), are suitable for all skill levels, and Zakopane has good equipment and facilities. As well as challenging mountains (such as Kasprowy Wierch and Gubałówka (p199), with runs of 4300m and 1500m respectively), the varied terrain around Zakopane offers flat land for beginners and plenty of time to learn, with a generous ski season lasting into April some years.

Sudetes Mountains

Another centre of outdoor action is Szklarska Poręba in Silesia, at the foot of Mt Szrenica (p259) (1362m). The city offers almost 15km of skiing and walking routes, and great cross-country skiing. The nearby town of Karpacz, on the slopes of Mt Śnieżka (1603m), enjoys around 100 days of snow per year. The website of Karpacz' tourist office (p261) has an excellent round-up of downhill and cross-country skiing options, as well as options for snowboarding and snow tubing. The town of Międzygórze also hosts ski enthusiasts, who venture out to the ski centre (p262) at the 'Black Mountain' of Czarna Góra.

Beskid Śląski

The village of Szczyrk, at the base of the Silesian Beskids, has less severe slopes and far shorter queues than elsewhere in the country. Szczyrk is home to the Polish Winter Olympics training centre and has mild enough mountains for novice skiers and snowboarders. Szczyrk's official website (www.szczyrk.pl) has information on ski routes, ski schools, equipment hire and tourist services.

Other Outdoor Activities

Horse Riding

It's worth spending some time in the saddle in Poland – a country that has enjoyed a long and loyal relationship with the horse. National parks, tourist offices and private equestrian centres have become quite proficient in marking routes and organising horse-riding holidays along them.

The PTTK (p414) can assist with organising independent horse riding through its Mountaineering and Horse Riding division. There are many state-owned and private stables and riding centres throughout the country, from rustic agrotourism establishments to luxurious stables fit for a Bond film. It's also possible to organise riding tours of a few hours, or a few days,

through numerous private operators. The cost of undertaking these experiences varies depending on duration and level of luxury. A down-to-earth horse ride on a pony for a week can cost around €800, while a weekend at a fine estate with access to steed-studded stables can cost upwards of €500. Shop around until you find something that suits your taste, ability and budget.

The **Polish Equestrian Association** (PZJ; 22 417 6700; www.pzj.pl) has a lot of information on the local horse scene, but it's in Polish.

Sailing

It's possible to hire yachts or sailing ships complete with their own shanty-singing skipper in Poland. The Baltic coast attracts some craft, but the summer crowds testify to the sailing suitability of the Great Masurian Lakes, which truly live up to their name. This sprawling network of interconnected lakes allows sailors to enjoy a couple of weeks on the water without visiting the same lake twice.

You can hire sailboats in Giżycko, Mikołajki and several smaller villages. In Giżycko, the tourist office (p379) maintains a list of boats and yachts for hire on its website, and also offers good first-hand advice in person.

Boat enthusiasts will get a particular thrill from excursions on the Elbląg-Ostróda Canal (p346) in the Olsztyn

---

WHERE TO RIDE

Białowieża National Park Offers the chance to ride (or use horse-drawn carriages and sleighs in winter) on nondesignated routes through forests. Contact the National Park Information Centre (p108) for details.

The Bieszczady Several bridle paths cross the Bieszczady range, including within Bieszczady National Park. The best place to organise a trip is in the town of Ustrzyki Dolne. The town's helpful tourist office (p218) is a good place to get started.

Lower Silesia Offers the 360km Sudety Horse-Riding Route. The privately operated **Horse Ranch Sudety-Trail** (www.sudety-trail.eu) runs all kinds of equestrian packages, suited to both novices and experienced riders, from May to November.

Masurian Lake District Ride horses around the lakes. The **Old Smithy Inn** (Karczma Stara Kuźnia; www.starakuznia.com.pl), near Giżycko, is housed in a 19th-century Prussian manor house, and offers guided rides as well as meals and overnight stays. UK-based **Farandride.com** (www.farandride.com) offers a seven-day itinerary at **Galiny Palace** (www.palac-galiny.pl/en), a luxurious hotel, restaurant, stud farm and riding school.

GEOCACHING

This GPS-based treasure-hunting game may not be as popular in Poland as it is in other countries such as the UK, but an ever-increasing number of Poles are now finding their way to it. The websites www.opencaching.pl and www.geocaching.pl are good places to start. Also check out the Twitter feed of Geocaching Polska (www.twitter.com/geocachingpl), a great source on current trends and trails. Tweets are normally in Polish but can be deciphered fairly easily with an online translator.

region. The 82km canal is the longest navigable canal still in use in Poland. It's also the most unusual. The canal deals with the 99.5m difference in water levels by means of a unique system of slipways, where boats are physically dragged across dry land on rail-mounted trolleys. The canal follows the course of a chain of six lakes, most of which are now protected conservation areas. From June to September, pleasure boats operated by Żegluga Ostródzko-Elbląska (p346) sail the main part of the canal between Ostróda and Elbląg. Trips of various durations are offered.

Baltic Sea sailing takes place on the bay at Szczecin (p359), shared by Germany and Poland. Sailors can visit Wolin National Park (p348) and Wolin Island when sailing this 870-sq-km bay. The bay in Gdańsk also offers access to sea harbours and quaint fishing towns.

In the Carpathian Mountains, Solina Lake (p219) is the Bieszczady region's most important centre for water sports, including boating and recreation. It's about 30km southwest of Ustrzyki Dolne and accessible by bus. The Solina Lake tourist office (p219), just off Hwy 894 on the way to Lesko, can supply you with all the details.

Climbing & Caving

The Tatras offer opportunities for beginner and advanced climbers. Contact the **Polish Association of High Mountain**

Guides (www.pspw.pl) for further information and a list of qualified guides.

There are more than 1000 caves in the country, but few are ready for serious spelunking. A good one is **Bear's Cave** (www.jaskinianiedzwiedzia.pl), near the village of Kletno, in Silesia, southeast of the city of Kłodzko. It's reachable by car and is situated on the elevation of Śnieżnik Kłodzki, on the right slope of the Kleśnica valley. Check the website for details, and note that you must reserve a tour in advance.

There are two caves in the Kraków–Częstochowa Upland. **King Łokietek Cave** (Grota Łokietka; ☏12 419 0801; www.grotalokietka.pl; Czajowice; adult/child 12/6zł; ⏰9am-6.30pm mid-Apr–Aug, to 5.30pm Sep, to 4.30pm Oct, to 3.30pm Nov) stretches over 270m through several passages and can be visited on a 30-minute tour. Nearby Wierzchowska Górna Cave (p160) is the longest in the region and goes on for nearly 1km.

Hang-Gliding & Paragliding

Hang-gliding and paragliding are taking off in Poland, particularly in the southern mountains, starting around Zakopane and moving eastward. The website www.paraglidingmap.com/sites/Poland maintains a good list of launch sites, complete with pictures and weather forecasts. A popular place from which to start is the top of Kasprowy Wierch (p199), south of Zakopane, though bear in mind that at 1967m, the elevation is high and winds can be strong. For more information, enquire at tourist offices and tour operators in Zakopane.

Windsurfing & Kitesurfing

Windsurfing and kitesurfing are mostly done in the same areas that attract sailors, but the true heartland is Hel – the Gulf of Gdańsk between Władysławowo and Chałupy along the Baltic coast. The arbitrary dance of wind and currents constantly changes the shape of the enticingly named Hel Peninsula (p329). The Great Masurian Lakes may be popular, but there's no place like Hel.

Plan Your Trip

Eat & Drink Like a Local

The traditional ingredients of Polish food, such as potatoes, cucumbers, beets, buckwheat and apples, reflect the country's long agrarian tradition. The necessity of making food last the winter means the cuisine is rich in pickles, preserves, smoked fish and meat. Foraged wild foods, such as mushrooms and berries, add seasonal character to dishes in uniquely Polish ways.

Polish Specialities

Bread

Chleb (bread) has always meant more than sustenance to Poles. It's a symbol of good fortune and is sacred to many; some older people kiss a piece of bread if they drop it on the ground. Traditional Polish bread is made with rye, but bakeries nowadays turn out a bewildering array of loaves, including those flavoured with sunflower, poppy and sesame seeds, and raisins and nuts.

Soup

Every substantial meal in Poland traditionally begins with *zupa* (soup), and Poland has some excellent ones. Rye is a staple ingredient in what will likely become a staple order of yours: *żurek*. This soup is made with beef or chicken stock, bacon, onion, mushrooms and sour cream, and given a distinctive tart flavour through the addition of *kwas* (a mixture of rye flour and water that has been left to ferment for several days). It's often accompanied by a hard-boiled egg or *kiełbasa* (Polish sausage) and is traditionally served inside a hollowed-out loaf of bread.

As Polish as *żurek*, but perhaps not as unique, is *barszcz* (or *barszcz czerwony*), a red beetroot soup known in Russia and Ukraine as borscht. It can also be served

The Year in Food

While many Polish staples are served year-round, each season brings something a little special.

Spring

Strawberries Strawberry season arrives in late spring; look for them layered on ice cream, poured over cakes and stuffed inside pierogi (dumplings).

Summer

Berries The Polish summer yields raspberries, blackberries and blueberries. These national treasures are usually laden over pancakes or stuffed inside pierogi.

Autumn

Mushrooms Poles are crazy about mushrooms, and the cool, damp mornings of early autumn are perfect for picking. Mushrooms are used in soups, as a stuffing for pastries and in sauces.

Winter

Beetroot This deep red root vegetable is a staple of Polish cooking with beetroot soup a cherished part of the traditional Christmas Eve meal.

as *barszcz czysty* (clear borscht), *barszcz z uszkami* (borscht with tiny ravioli-type dumplings stuffed with meat) or *barszcz z pasztecikiem* (borscht with a hot meat- or cabbage-filled pastry).

Pierogi

Pierogi ('Polish ravioli') are square- or crescent-shaped dumplings made from dough and stuffed with anything from cottage cheese, potato and onion to minced meat, sauerkraut and fruit. They are usually boiled and served doused in melted butter.

Pierogi can either be eaten as a snack between meals or as a main course. They're a budget traveller's dream. No matter how fancy a restaurant is, the menu will often have an inexpensive option of pierogi.

They can also be a vegetarian's best friend: many of the more popular versions, especially the ubiquitous *pierogi ruskie* (Russian pierogi), stuffed with cottage cheese, potato and onion, are meatless. Just remember to tell the waiter to hold the bacon bits that may be scattered on top. Popular variations to look for:

pierogi z mięsem – stuffed with spicy minced meat, normally pork

pierogi z serem – with cottage cheese

pierogi z kapustą i grzybami – with cabbage and wild mushrooms

pierogi z jagodami – with blueberries

pierogi z truskawkami – with wild strawberries

Kiełbasa

What would a trip to Poland be without sampling some of the country's signature sausages? *Kiełbasa* is normally eaten as a snack or as part of a light lunch or dinner, served with a side of brown bread and mustard. It's usually made with pork, though other meats, like beef and veal, can be added. The sausages are generally seasoned with garlic, caraway and other spices to create distinctive flavours.

The most popular type, *Wiejska kiełbasa,* is a thick cylinder of pork, spiced with garlic and marjoram, that probably comes closest to the type of *kiełbasa* known outside of Poland. Some other popular varieties:

kabanosy – thin pork sausages that are air-cured and seasoned with caraway seeds

krakowska – as the name implies, these originated in Kraków, though they're found throughout the country; usually thick and seasoned with pepper and garlic

biała – thin white sausages sold uncooked and then boiled in soups like *żurek staropolski* (sour barley soup with white sausage)

Bigos

If there's one dish more genuinely Polish than any other, it might just be *bigos*. Sometimes translated into English as 'hunter's stew', it's made with sauerkraut, chopped cabbage and meat, including one or more of pork, beef, game, sausage and bacon. All the ingredients are mixed together and cooked over a low flame for several hours, then put aside to be reheated a few more times. As with French cassoulet, this process enhances the flavour. The whole operation takes a couple of days and the result can be nothing short of mouth-watering. Every family has its own well-guarded recipe, and you will never find two identical dishes.

Because it's so time-consuming to make, *bigos* does not often appear on a restaurant menu. The version served in cafes and cheap eateries is often not worth its name – though you can find worthy variations at Polish festivals and fairs.

Pork

Polish menus appear to be an egalitarian lot, usually featuring a range of dishes made from beef, chicken and pork, as well as other meats such as turkey and duck. But don't let that fool you. The main event is almost always *wieprzowina* (pork), and Poles have come up with some delicious ways to prepare it:

golonka – boiled pig's knuckle, usually served with horseradish and sauerkraut

kotlet schabowy – breaded pork chops

schab wieprzowy – succulent roast loin of pork

dzik – wild boar, a rare treat but one worth trying if you get the chance

Regional Dishes

There are many regional specialities across the country – freshwater fish dishes in the north, aromatic duck preparations in Wielkopolska, large dumplings called *kluski* in Silesia that are often served with bacon *(kluski śląskie ze słoniną)* – but nowhere are these regional dishes so well defined as in the Podhale at the foot of the Tatras. Among some of the things to try here are *kwaśnica* (sauerkraut soup), *placki po góralsku* (potato pancakes with goulash) and the many types of *oscypek* (smoked sheep's-milk cheese) that come in oblong shapes with distinctive stamps on the rind. Buckwheat groats *(kasza gryczana)* are a delicious side dish – and a nice change of pace from the more common rice or potatoes. They are typically found in rural areas or in simpler restaurants around the country.

Vodka

Poles love their *wódka* (vodka) – only the Russians drink more per capita – and make some of the best in the world. While drinking habits are evolving in Poland, and most Poles normally relax over a glass of beer or wine, vodka remains the drink of choice when it comes to holidays, special occasions, or simply times when only vodka will do.

The most popular type of vodka in Poland, as with much of the rest of the world, is *czysta* (clear) vodka, usually made from rye grain but sometimes wheat or potatoes. Famous brands to look out for include Wyborowa, Żytnia, and Żubrówka, a vodka flavoured with grass from the Białowieża Forest on which bison feed (or as local wags have it, 'on which bison peed').

Among the many other varieties of *wódka* you'll come across are:

myśliwska – meaning 'hunter's vodka' and tasting not unlike gin

pigwówka – flavoured with quince (not too tart, not too sweet)

wiśniówka – flavoured with cherries

cytrynówka – flavoured with lemon

pieprzówka – flavoured with pepper

Generally, clear vodka should be served chilled. Flavoured vodkas don't need as much cooling, and some are best drunk at room temperature.

Traditionally, vodka in Poland was drunk neat and never mixed as cocktails. However, that rule is changing and some local cocktails have proved very popular. Żubrówka vodka and apple juice – known as a *tatanka* (buffalo) – is a match made in heaven.

HOW TO DRINK VODKA IN POLAND

Serious vodka drinking normally follows a few standard rules. Vodka is usually drunk from a 50mL shot glass called a *kieliszek*. It's downed in a single gulp – *do dna* (to the bottom), as Poles say. A small snack (often a pickle or piece of pickled herring) or a sip of mineral water is consumed just after drinking to give some relief to the throat. Glasses are immediately refilled for the next drink and it goes quickly until the bottle is empty. Poles say, 'The saddest thing in the world is two people and just one bottle.'

As you may expect, unless you're a seasoned drinker, at this rate you won't be able to keep up for long. Go easy and either miss a few turns or sip your drink in stages. Though this will be beyond the comprehension of a 'normal' Polish drinker, you, as a foreigner, will be treated with due indulgence. If you do get tipsy, take comfort in the fact that Poles get drunk, too – and sometimes rip-roaringly so. *Na zdrowie!* (Cheers!)

Beer

There are many brands of locally brewed *piwo* (beer); the major brands include Żywiec, Tyskie, Okocim and Lech. Beer is readily available in shops, cafes, bars, pubs and restaurants – virtually everywhere – and is commonly lager, although you will find that the major brewers do also make very good porters.

In recent years craft brewing, or microbrewing, has really taken off and there are now well over 1000 different local *piwo rzemieślnicze* (craft beers) to sample. Among the best-known Polish craft breweries are Pracownia Piwa, AleBrowar, Pinta, Doctor Brew and Profesja.

Don't ask us why, but you'll soon see that Poles (particularly women) like to flavour their beer with fruit juices and syrups. It's then drunk through a straw.

The craft-brewing revolution has seen Polish brewers digging back into historical recipe books to rediscover the 14th-century *grodziskie*. This refreshing style of beer, unique to Poland, is light in alcohol and made with an oak-smoked wheat malt that gives it a distinctive aroma and flavour.

How to Eat & Drink

When to Eat

Poles tend to be early risers and *śniadanie* (breakfast) is taken between 6am and 8am. Polish breakfasts are similar to their Western counterparts and may include *chleb z masłem* (bread and butter), *ser* (cheese), *szynka* (ham), *jajka* (eggs) and *herbata* (tea) or *kawa* (coffee). Hotels and pensions normally offer a *szwedzki bufet* (Swedish-style buffet), consisting of these items as well as slices of cucumber and tomatoes, pickles and occasionally something warm like a pot of scrambled eggs, *kiełbasa*, *parowki* (frankfurters) or pancakes.

Obiad (lunch) normally kicks off a bit later than you might be used to, around 1pm or 2pm, and can stretch to as late as 3pm or 4pm. It's traditionally the most important and substantial meal of the day.

The evening meal is *kolacja* (supper). The time and menu vary greatly: sometimes it can be nearly as substantial as *obiad*, but more often it's just sliced meats with salad or even lighter – a pastry and a glass of tea.

Where to Eat

Normally you'll eat in a *restauracja* (restaurant), a catch-all expression referring to any place with table service. They range from unpretentious eateries where you can have a filling meal for as little as 20zł, all the way up to luxurious establishments that may leave a big hole in your wallet.

The menus of most top-class restaurants are in Polish with English translations, but don't expect foreign-language listings in cheaper eateries (nor waiters speaking anything but Polish).

A cheaper but usually acceptable alternative to a restaurant is a *bar mleczny* (milk bar). This is a no-frills, self-serve cafeteria that offers mostly meat-free dishes at very low prices. The 'milk' part of the name reflects the fact that no alcohol is served, but they also offer many vegetarian dishes. You can fill up for around 20zł.

Milk bars open around 8am and close at 6pm (3pm or 4pm on Saturday); only a handful are open on Sunday. The menu is posted on the wall. You tell the cashier what you want, then pay in advance; the cashier gives you a receipt, which you hand to the person dispensing the food. Once you've finished your meal, return your dirty dishes (watch where other diners put theirs). Milk bars are very popular and there are usually queues.

Menu Advice

Polish menus can be quite extensive and go on for several pages. You'll soon get a general feel, though, for how they're organised, and that doesn't change much from place to place. Menus are normally split into sections, including *zakąski* (hors d'oeuvres), *zupy* (soups), *dania drugie* or *potrawy* (main courses), *dodatki* (side dishes), *desery* (desserts) and *napoje* (drinks). The main courses are often split further into *dania mięsne* (meat dishes), *dania rybne* (fish dishes), *dania z drobiu* (poultry dishes) and *dania jarskie* (vegetarian dishes).

The name of the dish on the menu is accompanied by its price and, in milk bars in particular, by its weight. The price of the main course doesn't normally include side orders such as potatoes, chips and salads; these must be chosen from the *dodatki* section. Only when all these items are listed together is the price that follows for the whole plate of food. Also note that for menu items that do not have a standard

MEMORABLE MEALS

Bez Gwiazdek (p70) Menu inspiration comes from across Poland at this gem of a Warsaw restaurant.

Alewino (p71) Superb seasonal dishes, excellent local wines and a relaxed atmosphere in Warsaw.

Sąsiedzi (p144) High-end Polish restaurant in Kraków's Kazimierz district with a lovely, secluded garden.

Gothic (p344) Situated in Malbork Castle itself, this is one of the north's top restaurants.

Restauracja Jadka (p246) Wrocław treasure offering impeccable modern takes on Polish classics, silver-service table settings and Gothic surrounds.

Quale Restaurant (p92) Classic Polish dishes, exquisitely prepared, in Łódź.

Kaszubska Marina (p322) Sample finely prepared regional dishes at this delightful Gdańsk restaurant.

Restauracja Buda (p225) Excellent traditional Polish cooking and a refined but unstuffy atmosphere in Krosno.

Restauracja Tejsza (p103) This place in Tykocin is home to Poland's best home-cooked kosher – and arguably the best pierogi (dumplings), too.

W Starym Siole (p222) A repurposed peasant's hut in the Carpathian village of Wetlina serving grilled fish and great wines.

Tatiana (p274) Perhaps Katowice's best restaurant elevates the regional dishes of Silesia.

portion size – most commonly fish – the price given is often per 100g. When ordering, make sure you know how big the fish (or piece of fish) is that you're getting.

Etiquette

Dining out in Poland is fairly straightforward and not much different from eating out anywhere else. Many places, particularly outdoor cafes, are self-service, so if no one comes to your table right away, it might be a sign you're expected to fetch your own drinks and make food orders at the counter.

Polish restaurants are not particularly kid-friendly. Children are always welcome, of course, and some places even have special children's menus, but you won't usually find high chairs or even lots of room to push a stroller through in many places.

Tip 10% of the tab for good service (slightly more for an extraordinary experience).

Cook Like a Local

If you'd like to take your appreciation of Polish food to the next level, cooking courses are run in Warsaw, Kraków, Wrocław and Gdańsk by the following companies:

Delicious Poland (p135)

Eat Polska (p135)

Polish Your Cooking (p63)

There are a number of cookbooks that can help you increase your understanding of Polish cooking.

➡ *Rose Petal Jam: Recipes & Stories From a Summer in Poland* by Beata Zatorska & Simon Target

➡ *Polska: New Polish Cooking* by Zuza Zak

Regions at a Glance

Which region of Poland you choose to focus on will depend on whether you prefer an active holiday, centred on hiking, boating and biking, or one involving more urban-based pursuits, such as visiting museums, cafes and clubs.

For the latter, Poland's trilogy of great cities, Kraków, Warsaw and Gdańsk, offers excellent museums, restaurants and other urban amenities. Kraków, in particular, escaped damage in WWII and is an unmissable mix of modern and medieval.

If sports are on the card, consider the regions of Warmia and Masuria, and Mazovia and Podlasie. These areas are Poland's lake country, with abundant kayaking, hiking and biking opportunities. The Carpathian Mountains in the south are covered in hiking paths and the place to go to get away from it all.

Warsaw

History
Drinking & Nightlife
Food

Amazing Museums

History here is not just the stuff of dusty tomes – the past is brought to life in thought-provoking, interactive museums, such as the Warsaw Rising Museum and the Museum of Warsaw.

Coffee, Cocktails & Clubbing

Warsaw's youthful population loves nothing more than whiling away the hours between sundown and sunup at classic dives, cool coffee shops, trendy cocktail bars and happening clubs.

Culinary Capital

Not only are the best modern Polish restaurants in Warsaw, but there's a thriving international food scene too, along with a surprising number of trendy vegetarian and vegan places.

p46

Mazovia & Podlasie

Nature
Water Sports
Architecture

Primeval Forest

Podlasie is home to three of the country's best national parks, including Białowieża, which claims a small patch of Europe's last remaining primeval forest. Birders will appreciate the abundant waterfowl at Biebrza National Park.

River Paddling

The Suwałki region in the extreme northeast is a quieter version of the Masurian Lakes and is home to canals, rivers and lakes that invite hours of canoeing and kayaking.

Revitalised Łódź

The old industrial city of Łódź has been given a splendid makeover, with vibrant public art, renovated textile factories now used for shopping, museums and a great local food scene.

p84

Kraków

Museums
Nightlife
Food

Interpreting the Past

Kraków has plenty of excellent museums, including several on majestic Wawel Hill. Newer, high-tech institutions include the Rynek Underground and Oskar Schindler's old enamel factory.

Kazimierz Crawl

From quiet bars to pumping nightclubs, Kraków has it all. The most distinctive options are its Old Town cellar pubs and the character-packed bars and cafes of Kazimierz.

Street Eats

Kraków has arguably Poland's best street-food scene, complete with late-night sausage stands, an open-faced cheese baguette known as *zapiekanka* (or, tongue in cheek, 'Polish pizza') and the pretzel-bagel hybrid, *obwarzanek*.

p115

Małopolska

Religious History
Heritage
Architecture

Place of Pilgrimage

Częstochowa's Jasna Góra monastery is one of the most important pilgrimage destinations for Catholics, and it retains a feeling of hushed holiness, even for nonbelievers.

Jewish History

Explore Jewish heritage in Lublin and pay your respects to those murdered at the region's notorious Nazi WWII extermination camps. There's an excellent memorial at Bełżec and a new Holocaust museum at Sobibór.

Gothic & Renaissance

Sandomierz has a beautifully preserved Gothic town square, while Zamość calls itself the 'Pearl of the Renaissance' – with good reason.

p158

Carpathian Mountains

Hiking
Architecture
Spas

Tranquil Treks

Walkers are spoiled for choice in the Carpathians. Want drama? Go for the Tatras. Solitude? Head for the Bieszczady. The chance to mix a bit of boating with a hike? The Pieniny.

Wooden Treasures

The Carpathians are sprinkled with old wooden churches and traditional timber architecture of Poland's mountain people. In Zakopane, this architecture was raised to an art form.

Hot Springs

Abundant hot springs in the mountains translate into spa resort towns such as the large and popular Krynica. Szczawnica, on the Dunajec River, is smaller and quieter.

p195

Silesia

Mountains
Nightlife
Architecture

Hiking & Climbing

Bordered by the Sudetes Mountains, Silesia is a hiker's dream. The Karkonosze National Park offers hikes among craggy cliffs, while the Góry Stołowe mountains are dotted with strange rock formations perfect for climbing.

Student Pubs

Silesia's cultural capital, Wrocław, is a major university town, and thousands of students translate into hundreds of bars, pubs and clubs.

Gothic to Modern

Silesia's tumultuous history has left its mark on the diverse built environment, including the bizarre Chapel of Skulls at Kudowa-Zdrój, the grand facades of Wrocław and the modernist lines of Katowice.

p236

Wielkopolska

History
Cycling
Food

Poland's Birthplace

Wielkopolska's deep history is seen everywhere, from the cathedrals of Poznań and Gniezno to the plentiful museums across the region that document events from the Middle Ages to the communist era.

Country Roads

One of the flattest parts of Poland, the region is a great place to hire a bike and hit the road, whether in Poznań or the rural countryside.

Poznań Dining

Poznań's restaurant scene is varied and sophisticated, offering everything from cheapie milkbar survivors to cutting-edge casual dining.

p279

Gdańsk & Pomerania

Architecture
Beaches
Folk Festivals

Medieval Buildings

Poland's north is littered with hundreds of medieval churches, castles, walls and town halls. Even the Red Army couldn't put a dent in this redbrick wealth, and postwar reconstruction restored many buildings to their former glory.

Baltic Bathing

Poland's Baltic sea coast may be chilly, but when the sun shines and the winds abate, there's no better place for a spot of beach fun than the stretches of white sand along the northern coast.

Kashubian Culture

Inland, you'll find the Kashubian culture thriving at festivals, celebrations and the open-air museum in Wdzydze Kiszewskie.

p303

Warmia & Masuria

Lakes
Water Sports
Architecture

Lakeland Adventures

Poland has more lakes than any other country in Europe except Finland – and most are in Masuria, which is also home to the country's biggest body of water, Lake Śniardwy.

Swimming & Rowing

The Great Masurian Lakes are the best places in Poland to don flippers, grab a paddle or hire a yacht for a bit of waterborne R&R.

Castles & Churches

Away from its watery attractions, the region has some remarkable architecture, including the baroque church at Święta Lipka and the red-brick majesty of Lidzbark Warmiński's castle.

p365

On the Road

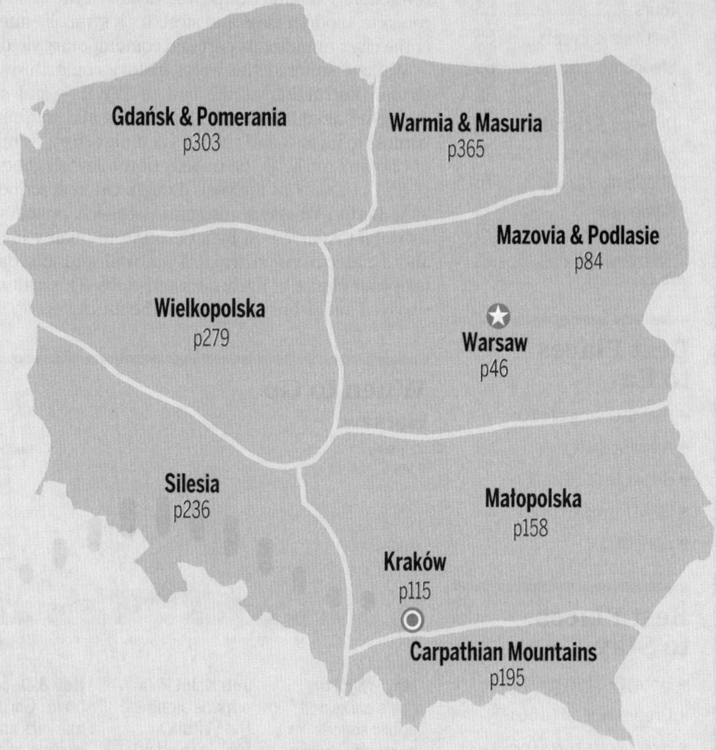

Gdańsk & Pomerania
p303

Warmia & Masuria
p365

Mazovia & Podlasie
p84

Wielkopolska
p279

Warsaw
p46

Silesia
p236

Małopolska
p158

Kraków
p115

Carpathian Mountains
p195

Warsaw

POP 1.76 MILLION

Best Places to Eat

➡ Bez Gwiazdek (p70)
➡ Alewino (p71)
➡ Bibenda (p70)
➡ SAM Powiśle (p69)
➡ Zoni (p71)

Best Places to Stay

➡ Hotel Bristol (p67)
➡ Dream Hostel (p66)
➡ Hotel Warszawa (p67)
➡ Chill Out Hostel (p67)
➡ Autor Rooms (p67)

Why Go?

Once you've travelled around Poland, you realise this: Warsaw is different. Rather than being centred on a traditional market square, the capital covers an architecturally diverse area: reverentially rebuilt Gothic, the dead weight of communist concrete, modern glass and steel. It's a symbolic intersection of the city's tumultuous past and contemporary victories.

Warsaw suffered the worst history could throw at it – virtual destruction at the end of WWII – and survived. Today, its neighbourhoods, landmarks and museums bear witness to its past and share its complex story, from the joys of Chopin's music to the tragedy of the Jewish ghetto.

It's not all about the past, though. Often described as the 'new Berlin', Warsaw's restaurant scene is punching above its weight, spurred on by a devotion to quality ingredients and a nascent vegan trend. Dine well and affordably and take your choice of lively bars and clubs. This gritty city has survived and is busy celebrating the future.

When to Go
Warsaw

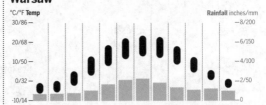

May Watch the city's parks and public spaces burst into greenery and flowers.

Jun & Jul Relax outside along the Vistula at bars, cafes and riverside beaches.

Nov & Dec Wrap up for Christmas markets and skating at outdoor ice rinks.

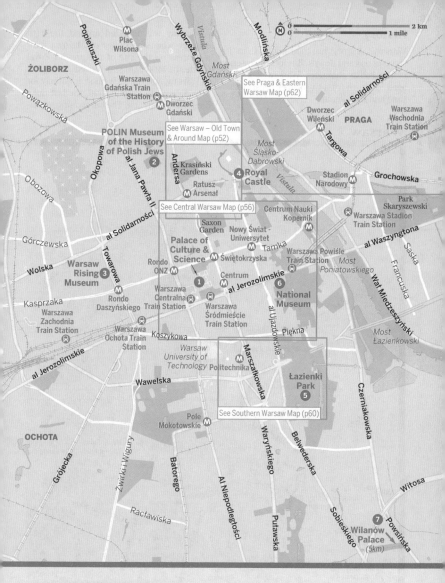

Warsaw Highlights

1 Palace of Culture & Science (p52) Taking in the city skyline from the top of this iconic building.

2 POLIN Museum of the History of Polish Jews (p55) Learning about Poland's Jewish community, past and present.

3 Warsaw Rising Museum (p55) Experiencing the city's doomed 1944 uprising.

4 Royal Castle (p50) Marvelling at the meticulous recreation of this Old Town landmark.

5 Łazienki Park (p59) Strolling through this gorgeous park to the splendidly restored Palace on the Isle.

6 National Museum (p59) Admiring the beautiful works of Polish art and design.

7 Wilanów Palace (p63) Touring this resplendent palace and its surrounding parklands.

History

Warsaw's history has had more than its share of ups and downs. But like the essence of the Polish character, Warsaw has managed to return from the brink of destruction time and time again.

Warsaw was founded around the 14th century when the dukes of Mazovia built a fortress on the site of the present Royal Castle. In 1406 Janusz I moved his capital to Warsaw, and things went swimmingly for over a century until, in 1526, the last duke died without an heir. The burgeoning town –

Warsaw

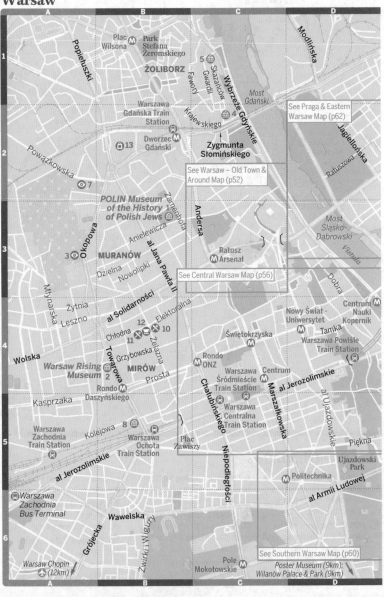

and the whole of Mazovia – fell under the direct rule of the king in Kraków and was incorporated into royal territory.

Warsaw's fortunes took a turn for the better after the unification of Poland and Lithuania in 1569, when the Sejm (the lower house of parliament) voted to make Warsaw the seat of its debates because of its central position in the new, larger country. The ultimate ennoblement came in 1596, when King Zygmunt III Waza decided to move his capital from Kraków to Warsaw.

The Swedish invasion from 1655 to 1660 was not kind to Warsaw, but the city recovered and continued to develop. Paradoxically, the 18th century – a period of catastrophic decline for the Polish state – witnessed Warsaw's greatest prosperity. A wealth of palaces and churches was erected, and cultural and artistic life flourished, particularly during the reign of the last Polish king, Stanisław August Poniatowski.

In 1795 the city's prosperity was again shattered. Following the partition of Poland, Warsaw's status was reduced to that of a provincial town of the Russian Empire. When Napoleon arrived in 1806 on his way to Russia, things started looking up. The warring Frenchman created the Duchy of Warsaw and the city became a capital once more. The celebrations were brief, however, as in 1815 Warsaw, and much of the rest of Poland, fell back under Russian rule.

After WWI Warsaw was reinstated as the capital of newly independent Poland and the urban development and industrialisation begun in the late 19th century continued. By 1939 the city's population had grown to

Warsaw

◎ Top Sights

◎ Sights

⬭ Sleeping

✕ Eating

◎ Drinking & Nightlife

⬛ Shopping

1.3 million. This included 380,000 Jews, who had long been a significant part of Warsaw's population.

German bombs began to fall on 1 September 1939 and a week later the city was besieged; despite brave resistance, Warsaw fell in a month. The conquerors terrorised the local population with arrests, executions and deportations, and a Jewish ghetto was built. The city's residents rebelled against the Germans twice; first came an eruption in the Jewish ghetto in April 1943, followed by the general Warsaw Rising in August 1944. Both revolts were cruelly crushed.

At the end of the war, the city of Warsaw lay in ruins and 800,000 people – more than half of the prewar population – had perished. (By comparison, the total military casualties for US forces in WWII was 400,000, for UK forces 326,000.) A massive rebuilding project was undertaken soon after, including the meticulous reconstruction of the historic Old Town. Despite more than 40 years of Communist rule, the city adapted well to the fall of the regime. As the business centre of Poland, Warsaw became the focus of economic growth and now corporate towers have joined Stalin's Palace of Culture on the city skyline.

◉ Sights

◉ Old Town & New Town

★ Royal Castle   MUSEUM
(Zamek Królewski; Map p52; ☑ 22 355 5170; www. zamek-krolewski.pl; Plac Zamkowy 4, Stare Miasto; adult/concession 30/20zł, free Wed; ☺ 10am-6pm Tue-Thu & Sat, to 8pm Fri, 11am-6pm Sun, closes 4pm Oct-Apr; ᪥ Stare Miasto) This remarkable copy of the original castle blown up by the Germans in WWII is filled with authentic period furniture and original works of art. Highlights are the Great Apartments (rooms

---

ℹ FREE MUSEUMS

Take advantage of the free days at many of the city's main attractions.

National Museum: Tuesdays

Fryderyk Chopin Museum: Wednesdays

Museum of Warsaw (all branches): Thursdays

Łazienki Park (all museums): Thursdays

Warsaw Rising Museum: Sundays

---

1 to 9) including the magnificent Great Assembly Hall and the lavishly decorated Throne Room; King's Apartments (rooms 11 to 20) including the Canaletto Room, hung with 22 paintings by Bernardo Bellotto (1721–80), known in Poland as Canaletto; and the Lanckoroński Collection with two portraits by Rembrandt.

★ Museum of Warsaw   MUSEUM
(Muzeum Warszawy; Map p52; ☑ 22 277 4402; www. muzeumwarszawy.pl; Rynek Starego Miasta 28-42, Stare Miasto; adult/concession 20/15zł, free Thu; ☺ 10am-7pm Tue-Sun; ᪥ Stare Miasto) Occupying 11 tenement houses on the north side of the Old Town Sq, this superb museum tells Warsaw's dramatic history in innovative ways. Start with the Warsaw Data-infographics in the cellar then work your way, in no particular order, through the core exhibition 'Things of Warsaw', which categorises some 7352 objects into 21 themed rooms ranging from photographs and postcards to clothing and patriotic items.

Old Town Square   SQUARE
(Map p52; Rynek Starego Miasta, Stare Miasto; ᪥ Stare Miasto) For those with an eye for historic buildings this is Warsaw's loveliest square, not to mention its oldest having been established at the turn of the 13th century. It's enclosed by around 40 tall houses exhibiting a fine blend of Renaissance, baroque, Gothic and neoclassical elements; aside from the facades at Nos 34 and 36, all were rebuilt after being reduced to rubble by the Germans at the close of WWII.

Monument to the Warsaw Rising   MONUMENT
(Pomnik Powstania Warszawskiego; Map p52; Plac Krasińskich, Nowe Miasto; ᪥ Plac Krasińskich) One of Warsaw's most important landmarks, this dynamic bronze tableau depicts Armia Krajowa (AK; Home Army) fighters emerging ghostlike from the shattered brickwork of their ruined city, while others descend through a manhole into the network of sewers. The monument was unveiled on 1 August 1989, the 45th anniversary of the doomed revolt against German military occupation.

The **Supreme Court of Poland** (Sąd Najwyższy; Map p52; www.sn.pl;), the impressive backdrop to the monument, was designed by Marek Budzynski and the entire ensemble is especially dramatic when illuminated at night.

WARSAW IN...

One Day

Start at the Royal Castle, rebuilt like most of the rest of the Old Town following WWII. Learn about the city's history at the **Museum of Warsaw**. Spend the afternoon at the **POLIN Museum of the History of Polish Jews** (p55) in an amazing contemporary building at the heart of the former ghetto. Attend an early evening Chopin piano recital. After dinner at **Bez Gwiazdek** (p70) or a night at the opera or ballet at **Teatr Wielki** (p75) take a romantic walk around the Old Town's cobblestone streets.

Two Days

Spend the morning immersed in Polish art and cultural treasures at the **National Museum** (p59), then go admire the socialist realist architecture of **Plac Konstytucji** (p60). The market precinct **Hala Koszyki** (p78) is packed with lunch options. In the afternoon, stroll around magnificent **Łazienki Park** (p59) or be transported to the city during WWII at the **Warsaw Rising Museum** (p55).

At dusk head to the 30th-floor observatory deck in the **Palace of Culture & Science** (p52). For dinner try **Alewino** (p71) or **Youmiko Vegan Sushi** (p70), followed by hanging out with Warsaw's cool crowd in **Cafe Kulturalna** (p72) or **BarStudio** (p72).

Adam Mickiewicz Museum of Literature   MUSEUM

(Muzeum Literatury im A Mickiewicza; Map p52; ✓ 22 831 4061; http://muzeumliteratury.pl; Rynek Starego Miasta 20, Stare Miasto; adult/concession 6/5zł; ⊙ 10am-4pm Mon, Tue, Fri, 11am-6pm Wed & Thu, 11am-5pm Sun; 🚊 Stare Miasto) Occupying two historic tenement buildings in the Old Town Sq, this museum does a good job of covering the life and times of Poland's national poet Adam Mickiewicz (1798–1855). The exhibition spans several rooms, includes some original manuscripts and paintings of the romantic poet, and has good English captions.

St John's Cathedral   CATHEDRAL

(Archikatedra św Jana; Map p52; ✓ 22 831 0289; www.katedra.mkw.pl; ul Świętojańska 8, Stare Miasto; crypt 2zł; ⊙ 10am-1pm & 3-5.30pm Mon-Sat; 🚊 Stare Miasto) Considered the oldest of Warsaw's churches, St John's was built at the beginning of the 15th century on the site of a wooden church, and subsequently remodelled several times. Razed during WWII, it regained its Gothic shape through postwar reconstruction. Look for the red-marble Renaissance tomb of the last dukes of Mazovia in the right-hand aisle, then go downstairs to the crypt to see more tombstones, including that of Nobel Prize–winning writer Henryk Sienkiewicz (1846–1916).

Marie Skłodowska-Curie Museum   MUSEUM

(Muzeum Marii Skłodowskiej-Curie; Map p52; ✓ 22 831 8092; www.muzeum-msc.pl; ul Freta 16, Nowe Miasto; adult/concession 11/6zł; ⊙ 10am-7pm Tue-Sun Jun-Aug, 9am-4pm Tue-Sun rest of year; 🚊 Plac Krasińskich) The first woman to win the Nobel Prize, Marie Curie was born in this building in 1867 and lived here for her first 19 years. It is now a small museum chronicling the life and work of the distinguished scientist and displaying items from Marie and her husband Pierre's laboratory as well as other memorabilia. Unfortunately, there are sparse English captions.

◉ Powiśle & Northern Śródmieście

★ Copernicus Science Centre   MUSEUM

(Centrum Nauki Kopernik; Map p56; ✓ 22 596 4100; www.kopernik.org.pl; ul Wybrzeże Kościuszkowskie 20, Powiśle; adult/concession Mon-Fri 31/21zł, Sat & Sun 33/22zł; ⊙ 9am-6pm Mon-Fri, 10am-7pm Sat & Sun, usually closed 1st Mon of month; Ⓜ Centrum Nauki Kopernik) This fully interactive, push-the-buttons-and-see-what-happens museum pulls off that tricky feat of being both hugely fun and educational. With over a million visitors a year, it is also very popular: advance booking of tickets is highly recommended or you may find yourself waiting all day for a slot to enter. Check the website for exact opening times as they vary throughout the year.

Warsaw – Old Town & Around

★ **Palace of Culture & Science**   HISTORIC BUILDING

(PKiN, Pałac Kultury i Nauki; Map p56; ☑ 22 656 7600; www.pkin.pl; Plac Defilad 1, Śródmieście Północne; observation deck adult/concession 20/15zł; ☺ observation deck 10am-8pm; Ⓜ Centrum) For over 60 years this socialist realist palace has dominated central Warsaw. A 'gift of friendship' from the Soviet Union, it was completed in 1955 and is, at 237m high, the tallest building in Poland – a title it will keep until the nearby 53-storey, 320m Varso Tower tops out in 2020. Among the many attractions at PKiN, the one not to be missed is the 30th-floor (115m) observation terrace.

★ **Fryderyk Chopin Museum**   MUSEUM

(Map p56; ☑ 22 441 6251; https://muzeum.nifc. pl/pl; ul Okólnik 1, Śródmieście Północne; adult/ concession 22/13zł, Wed free; ☺ 11am-8pm Tue-Sun; Ⓜ Nowy Świat-Uniwersytet) This multimedia museum within the baroque Ostrogski Palace showcases the work of Poland's most famous composer. You're encouraged to take your time through four floors of displays, including stopping by the listening booths in the basement where you can browse Chopin's oeuvre to your heart's content. Limited visitation is allowed each hour; book your visit in advance online, by phone or at the booking office at ul Tamka 43.

Warsaw - Old Town & Around

Heavens of Copernicus Planetarium   PLANETARIUM

(Niebo Kopernika; Map p56; ☑22 596 4100; www.niebokopernika.pl; ul Wybrzeże Kościuszkowskie 20, Powiśle; adult/concession from 22/16zł; ⊙9am-6.30pm Mon-Thu, until 9.30pm Fri, 10am-8.30pm Sat & Sun; ⓂCentrum Nauki Kopernik) You may well find yourself wanting to make multiple visits to this far from average planetarium. A packed repertoire of films is projected across a 16m-wide spherical screen with headphones providing commentary in a variety of languages. Some screenings are in 3D, for which there's a slightly higher ticket price, as is the case for other events including regular laser shows and the classical music, jazz and kids' music shows.

Tomb of the Unknown Soldier   MONUMENT

(Grób Nieznanego Żołnierza; Map p56; Plac Piłsudskiego 1-3, Śródmieście Północne; ☐Zachęta) Dedicated to the unknown soldiers who have given their lives for Poland, this military memorial occupies the last remnant of the Saxon Palace that stood here until it was destroyed by the Germans in WWII. In a marching ceremony across the square, the pair of soldiers who guard the eternal flame are changed every hour on the hour.

Warsaw University Library   LIBRARY

(Biblioteka Uniwersytecka w Warszawie; Map p56; ☑22 552 5178; www.buw.uw.edu.pl; ul Dobra 56/66, Powiśle; ⊙8am-10pm Mon-Fri, from 9am-9pm Sat, 3-8pm Sun – shorter hours in Jul & Aug; ⓂCentrum Nauki Kopernik) The stunning copper-clad building that houses the university library was awarded top prize by the Association of Polish Architects in 2000. The main facade, curving down ul Dobra, is lined with 7m-high book-shaped slabs, decorated with classical texts in the Sanskrit, Hebrew, Arabic, Greek, Russian Cyrillic and Latin alphabets.

To the rear of the building is the university **garden** (Ogród Biblioteki Uniwersyteckiej; Map p56; ul Dobra 68/70, Powiśle; ⊙8am-8pm, rooftop garden only Apr-Oct) **FREE**, with a ground-level section open year-round and the 2000-sq-m rooftop garden open April to October. Step inside the main entrance corridor to view the interior decoration that includes classic Polish posters, originals and copies of which you can buy from **Galeria Plakatu Polskiego w BUW, Warszawa** (Polish Poster Gallery; Map p56; ☑503 341 328; https://polishpostergallery.com; ⊙12.30-7pm Mon-Fri, to 5pm Sat).

LOCAL KNOWLEDGE

MUSEUMS AT THE WARSAW CITADEL

The Polish government is building two major museums in the grounds of the Warsaw Citadel. The new **Polish History Museum** (http://muzhp.pl) and the relocated and enlarged **Polish Army Museum** (Muzeum Wojska Polskiego; Map p56; ☑ 22 629 5271; www.muzeumwp.pl;al Jerozolimskie 3, Śródmieście Południowe; adult/concession 15/8zł, free Thu; ⊙ 10am-5pm Wed, to 4pm Thu-Sun; ⬚ Muzeum Narodowe) are set to be completed by 2021. The pentagonal-shaped, red-brick Citadel was originally built as an army garrison and political prison in the mid-19th century during imperial Russian rule of Poland.

The **Katyn Museum** (Muzeum Katyńskie; Map p48; ☑ 26 187 8342; www.muzeum katynskie.pl; ul Jana Jeziorańskiego 4, Żoliborz; ⊙ 10am-5pm Wed, to 4pm Thu-Sun; ⬚ Most Gdański, ⬚ Most Gdański) FREE, devoted to the massacre of Polish military officers in the forests of Katyn in 1940, as well as all Polish victims of Soviet aggression during WWII, occupies the southern section of the Citadel. A wing of the old prison has been turned into the interesting **Museum of the X Pavilion of the Warsaw Citadel** (X Pawilon Cytadeli Warszawskiej; Map p48; ☑ 22 839 1268; http://muzeum-niepodleglosci.pl/ xpawilon; ul Skazańców 25, Żoliborz; adult/concession 8/5zł, Thu free; ⊙ 10am-5pm Wed-Sun; ⬚ Cytadela).

Museum on the Vistula   MUSEUM
(Muzeum nad Wisłą; Map p56; ☑ 22 596 4010; https://artmuseum.pl; ul Wybrzeże Kościuszkowskie 22, Powiśle; adult/concession 5/2zł; ⊙ noon-8pm Tue-Thu, to 10pm Fri, 11am-8pm Sat, 11am-6pm Sun; Ⓜ Centrum Nauki Kopernik) Poland's largest painting, measuring 1600 sq m, by Sławomir Pawszak covers the exterior of a pavilion by Austrian architect Adolf Krischanitz. Until the Museum of Modern Art in Warsaw gets its permanent home, the pavilion is being used for regularly changing exhibitions.

Zachęta –
National Gallery of Art   GALLERY
(Zachęta – Narodowa Galeria Sztuki; Map p56; ☑ 22 556 9651; https://zacheta.art.pl; Plac Stanisława Małachowskiego 3, Śródmieście Północne; adult/ concession 15/10zł, free Thu; ⊙ noon-8pm Tue-Sun; ⬚ Zachęta) Specialising in contemporary art, Zachęta organises a variety of temporary exhibitions, which change roughly every three months. A visit to this elegant neo-Renaissance building that celebrated its centenary in 2000 could include shows by Polish as well as Argentinian and Iraqi Kurdish artists in mediums ranging from painting to video installations and photography.

Church of the Holy Cross   CHURCH
(Kościół św Krzyża; Map p56; ☑ 22 826 8910; www.swkrzyz.pl; ul Krakowskie Przedmieście 3, Śródmieście Północne; ⊙ 10-11am & 1-4pm Mon-Sat, 2-4pm Sun; Ⓜ Nowy Świat-Uniwersytet) Of Warsaw's many impressive churches, this is the one most visitors want to see – not so much to admire the fine baroque altarpieces that miraculously survived the 1944 Warsaw Rising reprisals, but to pay homage at the second pillar on the left side of the nave. Adorned with an epitaph to Frédéric Chopin, the pillar enshrines a jar that contains the composer's heart.

St Anne's Church   CHURCH
(Kościół Św Anny; Map p52; ☑ 501 158 477; www.swanna.waw.pl; ul Krakowskie Przedmieście 68, Śródmieście Północne; concert admission 15zł; ⊙ 9am-3pm Mon-Sat, 10am-7pm Sun; ⬚ Stare Miasto) Marking the start of the Royal Way, this is arguably Warsaw's most ornate church. It escaped major damage during WWII, which explains why it sports an original trompe l'oeil ceiling, a rococo high altar and a gorgeous organ, on which a 30-minute concert is played at noon between mid-April and mid-October, except for Sundays and holidays. The largely neoclassical facade dates from 1788 and was designed by the royal architect Piotr Aigner.

Climb the 148 steps of the separate bell tower to reach a **viewing terrace** (Taras Widokowy; adult/concession 6/5zł; ⊙ 10am-6pm Mon-Fri, 11am-8pm Sat & Sun; ⬚ Stare Miasto) providing superb panoramas over the Old Town and its surrounds.

Nożyk Synagogue   SYNAGOGUE
(Synagoga Nożyków; Map p56; ☑ 22 620 4324; www.warszawa.jewish.org.pl; ul Twarda 6, Śródmieście Północne; 10zł; ⊙ 9am-5pm Sun-Thu, to 4pm Fri; Ⓜ Świętokrzyska) The only synagogue in Warsaw to survive WWII was built between 1898 and 1902 in neo-Romanesque style. Its handsomely restored interior features grand metal chandeliers and tall vaulted colonnades. Men should cover their heads on entering.

Ethnographic Museum MUSEUM

(Państwowe Muzeum Etnograficzne w Warszawie; Map p56; ☑ 22 827 7641; http://ethnomuseum. pl; ul Kredytowa 1, Śródmieście Północne; adult/concession permanent exhibitions 12/6zł, Thu free, temporary exhibitions 20/10zł; ☉ 10am-5pm Tue, Thu & Fri, 11am-7pm Wed, 10am-6pm Sat, noon-5pm Sun; Ⓜ Świętokrzyska) Although it's a little complicated to navigate and could do with a bit more in the way of English signage, this museum has a fine assembly of Polish folk art and crafts, as well as fascinating temporary exhibitions. Ask at reception for directions to the traditional costumes gallery, which is a museum highlight.

◉ Muranów, Mirów & Powązki

★ Warsaw Rising Museum MUSEUM

(Muzeum Powstania Warszawskiego; Map p48; www.1944.pl; ul Grzybowska 79, Czyste; adult/concession 25/20zł, Sun free; ☉ 8am-6pm Mon, Wed & Fri, to 8pm Thu, 10am-6pm Sat & Sun; Ⓜ Rondo Daszyńskiego, ☒ Muzeum Powstania Warszawskiego) This exceptional museum, housed in a former tram power station and its surrounding grounds, traces the history of the city's heroic but doomed uprising against the German occupation in 1944 via five levels of interactive displays, photographs, film archives and personal accounts. It's an immersive, overwhelming experience that takes the better part of a day to see, if you're to do everything here justice.

★ POLIN Museum of the History of Polish Jews MUSEUM

(Map p48; ☑ 22 471 0301; www.polin.pl; ul Anielewicza 6, Muranów; adult/concession main exhibition 25/15zł, temporary exhibition 12/8zł, free Thu; ☉ 10am-6pm Mon, Thu & Fri, to 8pm Wed, Sat & Sun; Ⓜ Ratusz Arsenał, ☒ Muranów or Anielewicza) Housed in one of Warsaw's best examples of contemporary architecture, this award-winning museum documents 1000 years of Jewish history in Poland. The multimedia permanent exhibition includes accounts of the earliest Jewish traders in the region through waves of mass migration, progress and pogroms, all the way to WWII, the destruction of Europe's largest Jewish community and the present-day situation.

Railway Museum MUSEUM

(Stacja Muzeum; Map p48; ☑ 22 620 0480; www.stacjamuzeum.pl; ul Towarowa 3, Czyste; adult/concession 12/6zł, free Mon; ☉ 10am-6pm May-Sep, 9am-5pm Oct-Apr; Ⓜ Rondo Daszyńskiego, ☒ Plac Zawiszy) Occupying the former premises of Warszawa Główna, the city's main train station until the opening of Warszawa Centralna in 1975, this open-air museum is a real treat for fans of the iron way and the golden age of railways. After ogling the some 500 historical exhibits inside, including model trains, uniforms and other memorabilia, head outside to the platforms to inspect up close 50 steam, diesel and electrical engines, carriages and rolling stock.

REBUILDING WARSAW

At the end of WWII, about 15% of Warsaw was left standing. So complete was the destruction that there were even suggestions that the capital should be moved elsewhere, but instead it was decided that parts of the prewar urban fabric would be rebuilt. The most valuable historic monuments were restored to their previous appearance, based on original drawings and photographs.

Between 1949 and 1963 work was concentrated on the Old Town, aiming to return it, more or less, to its 17th- and 18th-century appearance – today not a single building in the area looks less than 200 years old. So complete was the restoration that Unesco granted World Heritage status to the Old Town in 1980.

Reconstruction of the Royal Castle began in 1971 and it took until 1984 for the splendid baroque building to be fully resurrected. Here, as elsewhere in the Old Town, many original architectural fragments were incorporated into the walls. For a greater appreciation of the monumental task and community cooperation involved in the reconstruction works drop by the **Heritage Interpretation Centre** (Map p52; ☑ 22 635 3402; www.muzeumwarszawy.pl; ul Brzozowa 11/13, Stare Miasto; adult/concessions 5/3zł; ☉ 10am-7pm Tue-Sun, free Thu; ☒ Stare Miasto).

Central Warsaw

al Solidarności

Andersa

Plac Bankowy

Senatorska

Wierzbowa

Elektoralna

Niecała

14
Plac Piłsudskiego

13

Saxon Garden

Plac Małachowskiego

Królewska

18

36

50 **68**

al Jana Pawła II

71

Kredytowa

6

Grzybowska

Marszałkowska

Plac Dąbrowskiego

Mazowiecka

Próżna

Zielna

28

Świętokrzyska

11

Plac Grzybowski

27

Plac Powstańców Warszawy

47

20

Świętokrzyska M

Jasna

Twarda

Moniuszki

59
Sienkiewicza
52

Rondo ONZ M

Emilii Plater

45

Plac Defilad

Złota

Zgoda

ul Chmielna

Sienna

Palace of Culture & Science **4**

Centrum M

55

Złota

Tourist Office – PKiN

60 **62**

Smolna

73

Warszawa Centralna Train Station

Warszawa Śródmieście Train Station

al Jerozolimskie

7 **19**

Nowogrodzka

al Jerozolimskie

Chałubińskiego

Niepodległości

Emilii Plater

Wspólna

Poznańska

Marszałkowska

Oczki

42 **37**

69
23 **46**

Plac Zawiszy

Hoża

38

22

Wilcza

Koszykowa

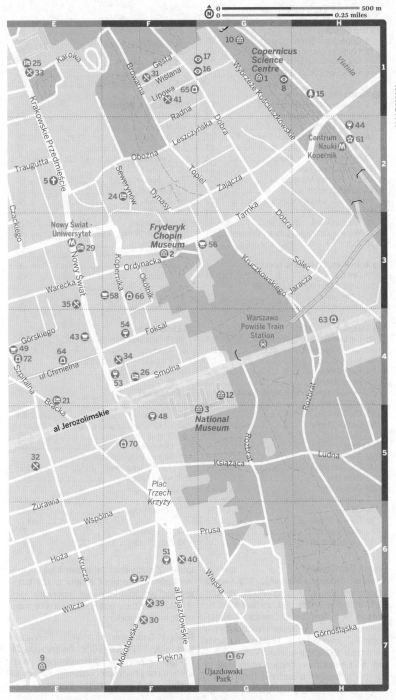

Central Warsaw

◉ Top Sights
1	Copernicus Science Centre	G1
2	Fryderyk Chopin Museum	F3
3	National Museum	G5
4	Palace of Culture & Science	C4

◉ Sights
5	Church of the Holy Cross	E2
6	Ethnographic Museum	D2
7	Fotoplastikon	C5
8	Heavens of Copernicus Planetarium	G1
9	Museum of Life Under Communism	E7
10	Museum on the Vistula	G1
11	Nożyk Synagogue	B3
12	Polish Army Museum	G4
13	Saxon Garden	C2
14	Tomb of the Unknown Soldier	D1
15	Vistulan Boulevards	H1
16	Warsaw University Library	G1
17	Warsaw University Library Garden	G1
18	Zachęta – National Gallery of Art	D2

✪ Activities, Courses & Tours
	Creatours	(see 4)
19	Galeria Bolesławiec & Studio Ceramiki	C5
20	Menora Info Punkt	B3

⊜ Sleeping
21	Between Us Bed & Breakfast	E4
22	Chill Out Hostel	D7
23	H15	D7
24	Hostel Helvetia	F2
25	Hotel Bristol	E1
26	Hotel Indigo Warsaw Nowy Świat	F4
27	Hotel Warszawa	D3
28	Oki Doki City Hostel	D3
29	SixtySix Hotel	E3

✪ Eating
30	Alewino	F7
31	Bez Gwiazdek	F1
32	Bibenda	E5
33	Cafe Bristol	E1
	Charlotte Menora	(see 20)
34	Cô Tú	F4
35	Dawne Smaki	E3
36	Hala Gwardii	A2
37	Kieliszki na Hożej	D7
38	Kuchnia Konfliktu	D7
39	Przegryź	F7
40	Rusiko	F6
41	SAM Powiśle Warszawska	F1 (see 27)
42	Youmiko Vegan Sushi	D6

◉ Drinking & Nightlife
43	A Blikle	E4
44	BarKa	H2
45	BarStudio	C4
46	Beirut	D7
	Cafe Kulturalna	(see 62)
47	Cosmo	B3
48	Cuda na Kiju	F5
49	E Wedel	E4
50	Galeria	A2
51	Klub SPATiF	F6
52	Metropolis	D4
	Między Nami	(see 21)
53	Pawilony	F4
54	PiwPaw Beer Heaven	F4
	Powidoki	(see 10)
55	Smolna	D5
56	Stor	G3
57	Woda Ognista	F6
58	Wrzenie Świata	F3

✪ Entertainment
59	Filharmonia Narodowa	D4
60	Kinoteka	C5
61	Plac Zabaw nad Wisłą	H2
62	Teatr Dramatyczny	C5

◉ Shopping
63	Acephala	H4
64	Cepelia	E4
65	Chrum.com	F1
66	DecoDialogue	F3
67	Desa Unicum	G7
	Galeria Plakatu Polskiego w BUW, Warszawa	(see 16)
68	Hala Mirowska	A2
69	KABAK	D7
70	Mysia 3	F5
71	Porcelanowa	D2
	Tebe	(see 7)
72	TFH Concept	E4
73	Złote Tarasy	B5

Jewish Cemetery CEMETERY
(Cmentarz Żydowski; Map p48; http://warsza
wa.jewish.org.pl; ul Okopowa 49/51, Powązki;
adult/concession 10/5zł; ⊙10am-5pm Mon-Thu,
9am-1pm Fri, to 4pm Sun; ⊡ Cmentarz Żydowski)
Founded in 1806, Warsaw's main Jewish
Cemetery covering 33.4 hectares contains
more than 150,000 tombstones, the largest
and most beautiful collection of its kind in
Europe. Incredibly it suffered little during
WWII. A notice near the entrance lists the
graves of many eminent Polish Jews, including Ludwik Zamenhof, creator of the international artificial language Esperanto. Men
should cover their heads with a hat or a cap
while in the cemetery.

Powązki Cemetery CEMETERY
(Map p48; ☏22 838 5525; Powązkowska 14,
Powązki; ⊙7am-8pm; ⊡Powązkowska) Warsaw's most prestigious cemetery covers 43
hectares and contains the graves of well

over a million souls. Illustrious Poles from all walks of life are buried here and a set of signs in Polish by the main gate lists the notables under their respective professions and areas of interest.

◉ Łazienki Park & Southern Śródmieście

★Łazienki Park   GARDENS
(Park Łazienkowski; Map p60; ☑ 504 243 783; www.lazienki-krolewskie.pl; ul Agrykola 1, Ujazdów; ⊙ 24hr; ⬛ Plac Na Rozdrożu) FREE Pronounced wah-*zhen*-kee, this beautiful park includes manicured gardens, an ornamental lake, wooded glades and strutting peacocks. Once a hunting ground, Łazienki was acquired by King Stanisław August Poniatowski in 1764 and transformed over the centuries to include a couple of palaces, an amphitheatre, museums and various follies. In the park you'll also find the fabulous art nouveau bronze **Chopin Monument** (Map p60) FREE. Such was this bronze statue's symbolic power to Poles that it was blown up by the occupying Germans in 1940. Fortunately, the statue mould survived WWII and the copy was resurrected in Łazienki Park in 1958.

Palace on the Isle   PALACE
(Pałac na Wyspie; Map p60; ☑ 22 506 0024; www.lazienki-krolewskie.pl; ul Agrykola 1, Ujazdów; adult/concession 25/18zł, free Thu; ⊙ 9am-4pm Tue-Sun Oct-Apr, 10am-6pm Tue, Wed, Fri-Sun, to 8pm Thu May-Sep; ⬛ Łazienki Królewskie) Łazienki Park's centrepiece is a delightful neoclassical palace, the former residence of King Stanisław August Poniatowski, which stands on an island in an ornamental lake. Some 140 paintings and works of art from the king's collection are on display here. Architectural highlights include an ornate ballroom and the 17th-century marble reliefs depicting scenes from Ovid's *Metamorphoses* that grace the original bathhouse (*łazienki* in Polish, hence the name), which was the foundation of the palace.

★National Museum   MUSEUM
(Muzeum Narodowe; Map p56; ☑ 22 621 1031; www.mnw.art.pl; al Jerozolimskie 3, Śródmieście Południowe; adult/concession 20/12zł, Tue free; ⊙ 10am-6pm Tue-Thu, Sat & Sun, to 9pm Fri; ⬛ Muzeum Narodowe) Drawing on a collection of some 830,000 works of art, both local and international, this is Poland's largest museum. It will come as a revelation for anyone unfamiliar with Polish creativity through the ages. The diverse exhibits include medieval Coptic Christian paintings rescued by Polish archaeologists from Sudan, gems of Polish design, and superb art from the 19th to 21st centuries.

Fotoplastikon   MUSEUM
(Map p56; ☑ 22 629 6078; http://fotoplastikon warszawski.pl; al Jerozolimskie 51, Śródmieście Południowe; adult/concession 6/4zł, Thu free; ⊙ 10am-6pm Wed-Sun; ⬝ Centrum) This contraption from the late-19th-century will thrill photography enthusiasts. Reputedly the last working example of its kind in Europe, it consists of a large rotating drum that you peer into via individual eyepieces to see stereoscopic 3D photos. The 48 images on display vary fairly often and include ones in colour. Every Sunday the set is of Warsaw in the early 20th century.

THE RINGELBLUM ARCHIVE

Inscribed on Unesco's Memory of the World Register, the Ringelblum Archive (https://onegszabat.org) is a precious collection of around 6000 documents that provide direct testimony about the extermination of Polish Jewry during WWII. It is named after the historian Emanuel Ringelblum (1900–44) who created the organisation Oneg Shabbat (which means 'Joy of the Sabbath' in Hebrew) in November 1940 to gather documentary evidence of what was happening to Jews under German occupation.

Members of Oneg Shabbat met secretly, usually on Saturday, at the building that today houses the **Jewish Historical Institute** (JHI; Żydowski Instytut Historyczny; Map p52; ☑ 22 827 9221; www.jhi.pl; ul Tłomackie 3/5, Śródmieście Północne; adult/concession 12/7zł, Sun free; ⊙ 9am-6pm Mon-Fri, 10am-5pm Sun; ⬝ Ratusz Arsenał). The archive, which includes essays, diaries, drawings, photographs and posters, was secured in metal boxes and milk cans and buried in batches. The collection of material stopped in January 1943 in the final months of the Warsaw ghetto. In September 1946 the first part of the archive was unearthed, but it wouldn't be until December 1950 that another part of it was found by chance. Part of it still remains buried.

The archive has been digitised and preserved at the Jewish Historical Institute, where you can view a remarkable exhibition about the project.

Southern Warsaw

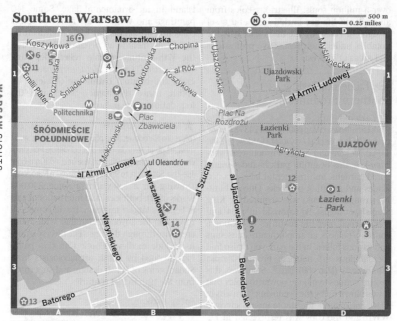

Southern Warsaw

Museum of Life Under Communism MUSEUM
(Muzeum Życia w PRL; Map p56; ☑ 511 044 808; https://czarprl.pl; ul Piękna 28/34, Śródmieście Południowe; adult/concession 10/8zł; ⊗ 10am–6pm Mon-Thu, noon-8pm Fri, noon-6pm Sat & Sun; 🚇 Plac Konstytucji) This small, privately run museum, devoted to the communist period in Poland's history, has found its spiritual home over a KFC that overlooks socialist realist Plac Konstytucji. There's a year-by-year timeline and a focus on different aspects of the People's Republic of Poland (PRL) from politics to fashion. It's all attractively laid out and, by Warsaw standards, not too overwhelming to digest.

Plac Konstytucji SQUARE
(Map p60; Śródmieście Południowe; 🚇 Plac Konstytucji) Completed in 1952, this expansive square is the centrepiece of the Marszałkowska Residential District (MDM). Although contemporary shopfronts, commercial signage and parked cars mar the socialist realist vision of the architecture, wonderful details remain, not least the heroic worker reliefs carved into facades and the giant pair of lamps at the southern end.

DON'T MISS

KONESER REBOTTLED

The handsome 19th-century brick buildings that once were the **Koneser Vodka factory** (Map p62; ☑ 22 128 4444; http://koneser.eu; Plac Konesera, Szmulowizna; Ⓜ Dworzec Wileński) are the star turn in the latest chapter in the hip revamp of industrial Praga. Here you'll find office spaces (hello Google!), the groovy hotel Moxy (p68); the interactive and entertaining **Polish Vodka Museum** (Muzeum Polskiej Wódki; Map p62; ☑ 22 419 3150; https://muzeumpolskiejwodki.pl/en/; pl Koneser 1, Szmulowizna; adult/concession 40/28zł; ☺ 11am-8.30pm Sun-Thu, to 9.30pm Fri & Sat), where entry is by tour (those led by English-speaking guides leave 40 minutes past the hour); the fine dining restaurant Zoni (p71); several other restaurants and bars, including **Bar ¾** (Map p62; ☑ 22 419 3152; www.facebook.com/bartrzyczwarte; pl Konesera 1, Szmulowizna) and **WuWu** (Map p62; ☑ 22 355 3002; https://wuwu.bar; pl Konesera 1, Szmulowizna; ☎) both of which – naturally – specialises in drinks with a vodka base; and a shopping mall with a focus on Polish products.

◉ Praga & Eastern Warsaw

★ **Praga Museum of Warsaw**   MUSEUM
(Map p62; ☑ 22 518 3400; http://muzeumpragi.pl; ul Targowa 50/52, Stara Praga; adult/concession 10/7zł, free Thu; ☺ 10am-6pm Tue, Wed, Fri-Sun, to 8pm Thu; Ⓜ Dworzec Wileński) Occupying three tenement buildings spanning the 18th and 19th centuries, this museum does a fantastic job of covering Praga's rich and varied history. It includes creative displays of art, photos, memorabilia and other artefacts, art installations, restored Jewish prayer rooms and fascinating recordings of locals talking on a wide variety of topics.

A joint ticket (adult/concession 20/15zł) covers here and the main Museum of Warsaw (p50) in the Old Town

★ **Neon Museum**   MUSEUM
(Muzeum Neonów; Map p62; ☑ 665 711 635; www.neonmuzeum.org; ul Mińska 25, Kamionek; adult/concession 13/10zł; ☺ noon-5pm Mon, Tue, Thu & Fri, to 6pm Sat, 11am-5pm Sun; 🚊 Bliska) Situated within the Soho Factory complex of old industrial buildings housing designers and artists, this museum is devoted to the preservation of the iconic neon signs of the pre-WWII and communist era. Inside the museum, around 100 large, fully lit pieces are on display. More salvaged signs are dotted around the complex and are illuminated after dark.

Żabińskis' Villa   HISTORIC BUILDING
(Willa Żabińskich; Map p62; ☑ 603 059 758; https://zoo.waw.pl; ul Ratuszowa 1/3, Nowa Praga; zoo admission plus 5zł; ☺ 11am & 1pm 1st Sun of month & by appointment; 🚊 Park Praski) The incredible true life story of how zoo director Jan Żabiński and his wife Antonia helped save over 70 Jews during WWII has become famous through the book and movie *The Zookeeper's Wife*. The elegant modernist villa, where the Żabińskis lived and risked their lives by hiding Jews, is open for a guided tour, which is well worth doing.

National Stadium   STADIUM
(PGE Narodowy; Map p48; ☑ 22 295 9000; www.stadionnarodowy.org.pl; al Poniatowskiego 1, Kamionek; adult/concession observation point 12/7zł, guided tours 22/15zł; ☺ 9am-9pm; Ⓜ Stadion Narodowy, 🚊 Rondo Waszyngtona) This prominent landmark on the east bank of the Vistula was constructed for the Euro 2012 football championships on the site of a communist-era stadium. Its red-and-white patterning references the Polish flag, and the interior can seat 58,000 spectators for either sporting or entertainment events. Visitors can access an observation point for a view of the interior, or join a daily tour in English; check the website for times and to book tickets.

Warsaw Zoological Gardens   ZOO
(Miejski Ogród Zoologiczny w Warszawie; Map p62; ☑ 22 619 4041; https://zoo.waw.pl; ul Ratuszowa 1/3, Nowa Praga; adult/concession Oct-Mar 20/15zł, Apr-Sep 30/20zł; ☺ 9am-6pm Apr-Sep, to 3.30pm Dec & Jan, to 4pm Feb & Nov, to 5pm Mar & Oct; 🚊 Park Praski) Established in 1928, this well-managed zoo is home to some 3000 animals representing 500 species from across the world, including bears, wolves, hippopotamuses and two male gorillas. There are even sharks and other sea creatures in what is Poland's largest aquarium. The elephant house, where there's also a cafe, is particularly impressive and the leafy grounds make for pleasant wandering throughout the year.

Praga & Eastern Warsaw

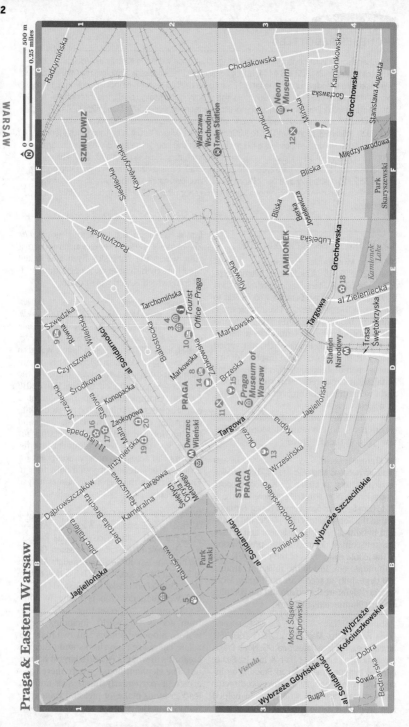

500 m
0.25 miles

SZMULOWIZ

Radzymińska

Kawęczyńska

Siedlecka

Radzymińska

Warszawa
Wschodnia
Train Station

Chodakowska

Neon
Museum 1

Żupnicza

12

Mińska

Kamionkowska

Grochowska

Gocławska

Stanisława Augusta

Międzynarodowa

7

Bliska

KAMIONEK

Bliska

Bełka

Jasielewicza

Lubelska

Grochowska

Park
Skaryszewski

Kłopowska

Kamionek
Lake

Szwedzka

Równa

al Solidarności

Wileńska

Czynszowa

Środkowa

Strzelecka

Stalowa

Konopacka

Zaokopowa

11 Listopada

Inżynierska

16

17

Mała

20

19

Tarchomińska

Białostocka

Tourist
Office – Praga

3 4

10

Markowska

Zabkowska

Markowska

8

14

PRAGA

Brzeska

15

Praga
Museum of
Warsaw 2

11

Dworzec
Wileński

Targowa

Targowa

Targowa

al Zieleniecka

18

Stadion
Narodowy

Trasa
Świętokrzyska

Jagiellońska

Kępna

Okrzei

Wrzesińska

13

Dąbrowszczaków

Bertolta Brechta

plac Hallera

Targowa

Kameralna

Ratuszowa

Świętych
Cyryla i
Metodego

al Solidarności

Kłopotowskiego

Panieńska

STARA
PRAGA

Wybrzeże Szczecińskie

Jagiellońska

Ratuszowa

Park
Praski

6

5

Most Śląsko-
Dąbrowski

Wybrzeże
Kościuszkowskie

Wybrzeże Gdyńskie

al Solidarności

Vistula

Bugaj

Dobra

Sowia

Bednarska

◉ Wilanów

★ Wilanów Palace   PALACE

(Pałac w Wilanowie; ☑ 22 544 2850; www.wilanow-palac.pl; ul Potockiego 10/16, Wilanów; adult/concession route 1, 20/15zł, route 2, 15/10zł, both routes 30/20zł; ☺ 9.30am-6pm Sat-Mon & Wed, to 4pm Tue, Thu & Fri mid-Apr–mid-Oct, 9.30am-4pm Wed-Mon mid-Oct–mid-Apr; ▣ Wilanów) Warsaw's top palace, 10km south of the city centre, was commissioned by King Jan III Sobieski in 1677. It has changed hands several times over the centuries, with each new owner adding a bit of baroque here and a touch of neoclassical there. Restoration of the palace's 2nd floor will continue until 2020, but you can still tour the magnificent ground-floor rooms packed with artistic baubles and treasures. Last entry to the palace is an hour before closing.

Wilanów Park   GARDENS

(Park Wilanowski; www.wilanow-palac.pl; ul Potockiego 10/16, Wilanów; adult/concession 5/3zł, Thu free; ☺ 9am-8pm Apr, to 9pm May & Aug, to 10pm Jun & Jul, to 7pm Sep, to 4pm Oct-Mar; ▣ 116 or 180) This splendid 45-hectare park adjoins Wilanów Palace and contains a variety of landscaping. The central part comprises a manicured, two-level baroque Italian garden, which extends from the palace down to the lake; the south is Anglo-Chinese in design; the northern section is an English landscape park. There's also a Renaissance-inspired rose garden. Last entry is 30 minutes before closing time.

Poster Museum   MUSEUM

(Muzeum Plakatu; ☑ 22 842 2606; www.posternmuseum.pl; ul Potockiego 10/16, Wilanów; adult/concession 10/7zł, Mon free; ☺ noon-4pm Mon, from 10am Tue-Sun; ▣ Wilanów) Polish poster art is outstanding and this museum's collection numbers over 36,000, with an additional 26,000 artistic, advertising and propaganda prints from around the world. Only a fraction of these are shown at any one time, but exhibitions change regularly. There's also a great selection of posters, postcards and books to buy.

✈ Activities & Courses

Galeria Bolesławiec & Studio Ceramiki   ARTS & CRAFTS

(Map p56; ☑ 690 800 184; https://pomaluj.art; al Jerozolimskie 49, Śródmieście Południowe; from 19zł; ☺ noon-8pm Tue-Sat; Ⓜ Centrum) Attached to the showroom for a local ceramics manufacturer is a studio where already-fired pieces of plain pottery await creative decoration. All the glazes and various implements needed are provided. Firing your masterpiece to completion may take up to two weeks, but the finished product can be posted to you.

Polish Your Cooking   COOKING

(Map p52; ☑ 501 598 681; www.polishyourcooking.com; ul Długa 44/50, Muranów; class 199zł; ☺ 10.30am Wed & Sat, 6pm Fri; Ⓜ Ratusz Arsenał) Come to this modern kitchen studio for English lessons in Polish cuisine, during which you'll learn to cook two classic dishes and sample several others.

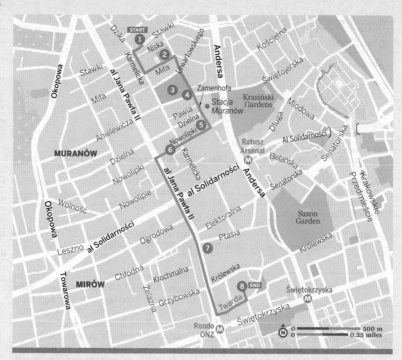

City Walk
Jewish Warsaw

START UMSCHLAGPLATZ
END NOŻYK SYNAGOGUE
LENGTH 3KM; THREE TO FOUR HOURS

This walk traces a route through Warsaw's former Jewish heartland, a location that is inseparable from the infamous ghetto that corralled some 400,000 Jews between 1940 and 1943.

Start at ① **Umschlagplatz**, a monument built on the site of the railway terminus from which Jews were transported to the concentration camp Treblinka. A couple of blocks south down ul Dubois on the corner with ul Miła is ② **Anielewicz's Bunker**. Also known as Miła 18, the memorial mound and obelisk mark what was once a hidden shelter used by ŻOB, a Jewish resistance group. Mordechaj Anielewicz, the leader of the Ghetto Uprising, and several others committed suicide here rather than surrender in 1943.

Muranów was rebuilt during the 1950s following modernist architectural principles.

Nathan Rapoport's sculpted ③ **Ghetto Heroes Monument** was erected in 1948 when all around still lay in ruins. Behind it, inside a park, stands the ④ **POLIN Museum of the History of Polish Jews** (p55).

Nearby, the community-arts group Stacja Muranów (http://stacjamuranow.pl) has commissioned several murals on the sides of buildings and courtyard arches to commemorate the area's most famous personalities, including ⑤ **Ludovik Zamenhof**, inventor of the language Esperanto, and ⑥ **Bohdan Lachert**, the architect who designed part of Muranów.

Either walk or catch a tram for a couple of blocks south along al Jana Pawła II. Get off at the elegant 19th-century market hall ⑦ **Hala Mirowska** (p78). Continue south along Jana Pawła II and turn left on ul Twarda, to find the historic and functioning ⑧ **Nożyk Synagogue** (p54), triumphant proof of the Jewish community's survival against impossible odds.

Menora Info Punkt
COOKING

(Map p56; ☑ 22 415 7926; www.polin.pl/pl/menora; Plac Grzybowski 2, Śródmieście Północne; courses from 200zł; ☺ 10am-5pm Mon-Fri; Ⓜ Świętokrzyska) Inside Charlotte Menora (p68), this information office can advise on all aspects of Jewish Warsaw. A couple of times a month it also organises Jewish cooking classes – places can be booked via the website of POLIN (p55). Culinary tours of Poland are also run in conjunction with the Taube Center for the Renewal of Jewish Life in Poland (www.taubephilanthropies.org).

🧭 Tours

Adventure Warsaw
BUS

(Wycieczki po Warszawie; Map p62; ☑ 515 908 505; https://adventurewarsaw.pl; from 149zł) This long-established company offers offbeat tours of Warsaw in communist-vintage vans and buses. Topics include the communist era, Warsaw by night, Jewish Warsaw and districts 'off the beaten track'. You will be picked up from your hotel.

Chopin Pass
CULTURAL

(☑ 533 493 940; www.chopinpass.co; adult/youth/child 119/99/72zł) Join these bus tours for an easy way to combine visiting the Fryderyk Chopin Museum (p52) and the composer's birthplace in Żelazowa Wola, 54km west of the city. Tickets can be bought online or from the Palace of Culture & Science (p52) from March to October; at other times call the company directly.

Creatours
CULTURAL

(Map p56; ☑ 22 656 6148; http://creatours.pl; Plac Defilad 1, Śródmieście Północne; adult/concession 30/25zł; ☺ 11am-4pm; Ⓜ Centrum) In the building's main lobby, next to the booth selling tickets for the observatory, you can sign up for a 45-minute tour of some of the ornate interiors of the Palace of Culture & Science (p52). The cost includes a ticket for the 30th-floor observatory, which you can visit at your leisure after the tour.

🎆 Festivals & Events

Equality Parade
PARADE

(Parada Równości; www.paradarownosci.eu; ☺ Jun) Held in most years since 2001, this colourful LGBTQ march through the city's streets in mid-June is in support of social equality and diversity. It attracts tens of thousands of spectators and supporters

Mozart Festival
MUSIC

(Festiwal Mozartowski; www.operakameralna.pl) Staged annually from mid-June to the end of July and organised by the Warszawa Opera Kameralna (p75). Features performances across the city of all 26 of Mozart's stage productions, plus a selection of his other works.

Midsummer's Night
FIREWORKS

(Slaska Noc Swietojanska; ☺ Jun) Around the date of the longest day of the year, Warsaw comes over all pagan with midsummer rituals, including the lighting of bonfires, major fireworks displays and the floating of wreaths studded with candles down the Vistula River.

Street Art Festival
THEATRE

(Festiwal Sztuka Ulicy; www.sztukaulicy.pl) Held from late June to early July, this week-long festival features street theatre, open-air art installations and 'happenings' staged in public places such as Old Town Sq, the Royal Way, public parks and even bus stops.

WARSAW FOR CHILDREN

Warsaw does a good job of entertaining children of all ages. The city's tourist information offices offer a colourful, fold-out map aimed primarily at teens and students, but with some hints for younger travellers as well. For more ideas, see Kids in the City (http://kidsinthecity.pl).

The top museum for kids of all ages is the wonderful Copernicus Science Centre (p51), which also includes a Planetarium (p53); note the museum can get very busy on weekends and school holidays - book ahead! Older children might enjoy the visual and sound effects of the highly interactive Warsaw Rising Museum (p55), though parental guidance is recommended in explaining its dark story. POLIN Museum of the History of Polish Jew (p55) has a dedicated children's section.

Parks abound. Łazienki Park (p59) has plenty of space to run, plus peacocks to spot, ducks to feed and a boat trip to take. The Saxon Garden (Ogród Saski; Map p56; http://zielona.um.warszawa.pl; ul Marszałkowska & ul Królewska, Śródmieście Północne; 🚊 Królewska) and Krasiński Garden (Pałac i Ogród Krasińskich; Map p52; http://zielona.um.warszawa.pl; pl Krasińskich 5, Muranów; ☺ park 7am-midnight; Ⓜ Ratusz Arsenał) both have good playgrounds. There are plenty of outdoor enclosures to explore at Warsaw Zoological Gardens (p61).

Singer's Warsaw Festival PERFORMING ARTS
(www.festiwalsingera.pl; ☉ late Aug-early Sep) Held annually since 2004, this Jewish-themed festival includes theatre, music, films, exhibits and workshops at various city locations, including the Nożyk Synagogue, the Jewish Theatre and the Austrian Cultural Forum.

Warsaw Autumn Festival of Contemporary Music MUSIC
(Warszawska Jesień Międzynarodowy Festiwal Muzyki Współczesnej; http://warszawska-jesien.art.pl) This 50-year-old festival, held over nine days in September across a number of venues, is the city's pride and joy. It offers a chance to hear the world's best avante-garde music, including new works by major Polish composers.

Warsaw Film Festival FILM
(Warszawski Festiwal Filmowy; www.wff.pl) Screenings of the year's best international films over 10 days in October, plus Polish film highlights and plenty of retrospectives.

🛏 Sleeping

Accommodation ranges from fun backpacker hostels to luxury boutique hotels, spread widely across the city centre; there are also plenty of centrally located rental apartments. Public transport is excellent so don't be afraid of staying slightly outside the centre to take advantage of lower accommodation rates. Note that many central hotels are geared towards business travellers and are priced accordingly (many offer discounted rates at weekends).

🛏 Old Town & New Town

Oki Doki Hostel Old Town HOSTEL €
(Map p52; ☏ 22 635 0763; http://okidoki.pl/oldtown; Długa 6, Nowe Miasto; dm 50zł, d & tw /225zł; @ 🕈; 🚇 Plac Krasińskich) Oki Doki offers a prime location for both the Old and New Towns. Everything is well done from the pleasant four- to eight-bed dorms and private rooms, to the well-equipped kitchen and inviting lounge and courtyard spaces. It has another branch in Northern Śródmieście.

★ Castle Inn HOTEL €€
(Map p52; ☏ 22 425 0100; http://castleinn.pl; ul Świętojańska 2, Stare Miasto; s/d from 356/376zł; @ 🕈; 🚇 Stare Miasto) This 'art hotel' is housed in a 17th-century townhouse, one of the few that was not totally destroyed during WWII. All 20 rooms overlook either Castle Sq or St John's Cathedral, and come in a range of creative designs, such as 'Viktor', named for a reclusive street artist, complete with tasteful graffiti and a gorgeous castle view.

Dom Literatury HOTEL €€
(Map p52; ☏ 22 635 0404; https://domliteratury.com.pl; ul Krakowskie Przedmieście 87/89, Stare Miasto; s/d 275/435zł; 🕈; 🚇 Stare Miasto) This old-fashioned small hotel has a wonderful location and without doubt the slowest elevator in Warsaw (staff even joke about it). The views from 3rd-floor rooms, sporting wood-beamed ceilings and formal decor, over the Old Town are stunning. Breakfast is 20zł per person extra.

Mamaison Hotel Le Regina HOTEL €€€
(Map p52; ☏ 22 531 6000; www.leregina.com; ul Kościelna 12, Nowe Miasto; r from 541zł; P @ 🕈; 🚇 Plac Krasińskich) Housed in a lovely arcaded 18th-century-style palace, the Regina manages a successful combination of traditional architecture and contemporary design. Rooms are light and airy, and decorated in shades of chocolate and vanilla, with lots of polished walnut, gleaming chrome and marble in the more expensive rooms.

🛏 Powiśle & Northern Śródmieście

★ Dream Hostel HOSTEL €
(Map p52; ☏ 22 419 4848; https://dream-hostels.com; Krakowskie Przedmieście 55, Śródmieście Północne; dm/tw from 51/200zł; @ 🕈; 🚇 Plac Zamkowy) This large and lively hostel, one in a chain that's well established across Eastern Europe, is just steps from the Old Town and has everything going for it. Expect comfy beds, clean bathrooms, well-equipped kitchens, a choice of dorms (some women only) or private rooms, a friendly on-site bar and helpful staff.

Oki Doki City Hostel HOSTEL €
(Map p56; ☏ 22 828 0122; www.okidoki.pl; Plac Dąbrowskiego 3, Śródmieście Północne; dm/d from 38/168zł; 🕈; Ⓜ Świętokrzyska) One of Warsaw's most popular hostels and certainly one of the best, each of its bright, large rooms is individually named and decorated. Accommodation is in three- to eight-bed dorms, with a special three-bed dorm for women only. The management are wise to the needs of backpackers, providing a kitchen and a laundry service. Breakfast available (15zł).

Hostel Helvetia HOSTEL €
(Map p56; ☏ 22 826 7108; www.hostel-helvetia.pl; ul Sewerynów 7, Śródmieście Północne; dm/d/apt from 50/160/250zł; 🕈; Ⓜ Nowy Świat-Uniwersytet)

Hostel with spick-and-span rooms, painted in warm, bright colours, with wooden floors and a good amount of space. Choose from three- to eight-bed dorms or good-value private singles and doubles. Laundry and kitchen facilities are in top order, and with a limited number of beds, it's best to book ahead in summer.

★ **Hotel Indigo**
Warsaw Nowy Świat HOTEL €€
(Map p56; ☑ 22 418 8900; http://indigowarsaw. com; ul Smolna 40, Śródmieście Północne; r from 415zł; ❋ @ ☜; ☖ Muzeum Narodowe) A dazzling light fixture made from 900 coloured glass baubles hangs above the atrium lobby of this fine 2017 addition to Warsaw's stock of stylish business hotels. Rooms with double-height ceilings are classily decorated with teal velvet sofas and other plush furnishings, and have pristine-white bathrooms.

SixtySix Hotel BOUTIQUE HOTEL €€
(Map p56; ☑ 22 826 6111; www.hotelsixtysix.com; ul Nowy Świat 66, Śródmieście Północne; d from 560zł; ❋ ☜; Ⓜ Nowy Świat-Uniwersytet) The 18 rooms at this contemporary design hotel are very chic with sapphire-blue curtains and upholstered chairs providing a pop of colour in otherwise oh-so-cool monotone rooms. There's a stylish wine bar and a restaurant on the ground floor, and plenty more places to wine and dine around the neighbourhood.

Between Us Bed & Breakfast GUESTHOUSE €€
(Map p56; ☑ 603 096 701, 10am-11pm 22 828 5417; www.between-us.eu; ul Bracka 20, Śródmieście Północne; d from 365zł; ☜; Ⓜ Centrum) Offering three individually and tastefully decorated double rooms with wooden floors, Between Us is a charming guesthouse in a 19th-century central Warsaw apartment block. There's a small kitchen area but otherwise breakfast is taken downstairs in its stylish cafe-bar Między Nami (p73), which is where you check in.

★ **Hotel Bristol** HOTEL €€€
(Map p56; ☑ 22 551 1000; www.hotelbristolwarsaw. pl; ul Krakowskie Przedmieście 42/44, Śródmieście Północne; r from 665zł; ❋ ☜ ☒; ☖ Hotel Bristol) Established in 1899 and restored to its former glory, the Bristol is Warsaw's most historic hotel and the address at which VIPs and celebs have stayed through the decades. Its neoclassical facade conceals original art nouveau features. The 206 rooms and suites are big and comfortable, and attentive staff cater to every whim.

ⓘ APARTMENT RENTALS

Warsaw is awash with good-value, short-term rental apartments, such as those offered by Airbnb and local agencies like **ApartmentsApart** (☑ 22 887 9800; www.apartmentsapart.com; apt from 200zł; ☜). If you're planning to stay longer than a couple of days, they are an excellent option. Short-term rentals allow you to self-cater and often there's a washing machine, a handy solution to the city's lack of laundromats. There's often no reception desk, so you'll usually have to confirm how to get access to the apartment when you book online.

Hotel Warszawa DESIGN HOTEL €€€
(Map p56; ☑ 22 470 0300; https://warszawa. hotel.com.pl; Plac Powstańców Warszawy 9, Śródmieście Północne; d from 800zł; ❋ @ ☜ ☒; Ⓜ Świętokrzyska) What many Varsovians know as the Prudential Building, an iconic pre-WWII tower block, has been transformed into this swoon-worthy hotel. The radical makeover both respects (and reveals) the building's concrete bones, adding lustre through judicious natural materials, including copper, marble, granite and fine-grained wood. Some may find it stark, we find it incredible.

⛺ Łazienki Park & Southern Śródmieście

★ **Chill Out Hostel** HOSTEL €
(Map p56; ☑ 22 409 9881; www.chillouthostel.pl; ul Poznańska 7/5, Śródmieście Południowe; d from 170zł, dm/s/d without bathroom from 43/129/156zł; ☖ Plac Konstytucji) An elegant pre-WWII building (thus no lift) on vibrant ul Poznańska houses this fine hostel. All rooms are pleasantly decorated in a cool, Scandi style with pops of colour provided by the furniture and wall tiles of the comfy and well-equipped communal kitchen and lounge.

★ **Autor Rooms** DESIGN HOTEL €€
(Map p60; ☑ 797 99 27 37; https://autorrooms.pl; ul Lwowska 17/7, Śródmieście Południowe; d from 434zł; ☜; ☖ Plac Konstytucji) Contemporary Polish design, art and products are given a spotlight at this quartet of individually styled rooms. There are no TVs in the rooms, but rates include breakfast, which is served in the spacious lounge and dining room.

H15 BOUTIQUE HOTEL €€€

(Map p56; ☑ 22 553 8700; www.h15boutique
apartments.com; ul Poznanska 15, Śródmieście
Południowe; r/apt from 540/1250zł; P✳❄;
⧏Hoża) Set in a gorgeous late-19th-century
apartment block that once housed the Soviet Union's embassy, this is one of Warsaw's
most luxurious hotels. Modern art and designer furniture vie for your attention in
spacious parquet-floored rooms, which are
quirky and individual. The location is bang
in the middle of the city's coolest district.

🛏 Praga & Eastern Warsaw

★ Lull Hostel HOSTEL €

(Map p48; ☑ 608 031 743; http://lullhostel.pl; ul
Jakubowska 4, Saska Kępa; dm/r from 55/150zł;
❄; ⧏) More of a home than a hostel, Lull
is based in one of Saska Kępa's modernist
houses. The light-filled rooms with exposed
brick walls, graphic art by local artists
and contemporary furnishings are highly
appealing. There's also a pleasant lounge-
dining room and a small kitchen.

Aparthostel Warszawa HOSTEL €

(Map p62; ☑ 511 063 553; www.aparthostel
warszawa.pl; ul Ząbkowska 23/25, Stara Praga;
dm/tw from 50/250zł; ❄; Ⓜ Dworzec Wileński)
Rooms in this characterful hostel have a
contemporary Scandi design feel and are
decorated with graphic wallpaper. A few of
the private rooms share a bathroom. There's
a nice cafe by the reception to hang out in
and have breakfast. The location is also ideal
for cruising the bars of ul Ząbkowska.

Moxy Warsaw Praga DESIGN HOTEL €€

(Map p62; ☑ 22 279 6699; http://moxy-hotels.
marriott.com/en; ul Ząbkowska 29, Szmulowizna;
d/tw from 313zł; P✳@❄; Ⓜ Dworzec Wileński)
Moxy is the kind of hotel where the cafe-bar
doubles as the reception. The public areas feel
like a romper room for adults with games,
toys and cool, colourful decor – perfect for Instagram snaps. The rooms sport a more sober
and soothing design.

★ Arthotel Stalowa 52 BOUTIQUE HOTEL €€

(Map p62; ☑ 22 618 2732; http://stalowa52.pl;
ul Stalowa 52, Nowa Praga; d from 500zł; @❄;
⧏ Szwedzka, ⧏ Czynszowa) A showcase for
local artists, this chic hotel offers 19 guest
rooms that are super-tastefully furnished
in a contemporary style with a retro edge,
thanks to wooden floors and antique-style
rugs. A great perk is that every room comes
with a smart phone that's free to use during
your stay.

🍽 Eating

Warsaw is one of the most polished performers on the European culinary scene with
creative chefs working with top-quality produce to create dishes that please their customers and earn Michelin stars. The city's
food scene is a democratic one embracing
hipster food halls, revamped milk bars (self-
serve canteens), and a superb selection of
vegetarian and even vegan eateries.

🍽 Old Town & New Town

★ Warszawski Sznyt STEAK €€

(Map p52; ☑ 22 829 2050; https://warszawskisznyt.
pl; ul Senatorska 2, Stare Miasto; mains 22-79zł;
🕑 8am-11pm; ⧏ Stare Miasto) With a dress-
circle view of Plac Zamkowy and the Royal
Castle, this stylish, multilevel place is great
for all-day dining. It specialises in steaks
and burgers and also does a mean pastrami
sandwich.

Enoteca POLISH €€€

(Map p52; ☑ 882 048 012; www.restauracjaenoteka.
pl; Rynek Nowego Miasta 13/15, Nowe Miasto; mains
59-89zł; 🕑 10am-10pm Sun-Thu, to 11pm Fri & Sat;
⧏ Plac Krasińskich) Classy, chic spot for good
Polish and Italian food or a glass of wine,
with a view onto the New Town's central
square. In warmer months it has outdoor
tables.

U Fukiera POLISH €€€

(Map p52; ☑ 22 831 1013; http://ufukiera.pl;
Rynek Starego Miasta 27, Stare Miasto; mains
56-105zł; 🕑 noon-midnight; ❄; ⧏ Stare Miasto)
Polish cuisine is served simply but elegantly in this choice, antique Old Town spot,
one in the stable of celeb restauranteur
Magda Gessler. The main dining room is
all wood panelling and vaulted ceilings.
There's also a cosy wine cellar and a lovely internal courtyard for dining in warmer
weather.

🍽 Powiśle & Northern Śródmieście

Charlotte Menora BAKERY €

(Map p56; ☑ 668 669 137; http://bistrocharlotte.
pl; Plac Grzybowski 2, Śródmieście Północne;
mains 10-19zł; 🕑 7am-midnight Mon-Thu, to 1am
Fri, 8am-1am Sat, 8am-10pm Sun; Ⓜ Świętokrzyska) This second Warsaw branch of the fine
bakery-cafe Charlotte has a Jewish lilt to its
menu, taking inspiration from its location in
the former Jewish heartland of the city.

MILK BARS

Warsaw's milk bars (*bar mleczny*) – dirt-cheap, self-service canteens from communist times – serve hearty Polish food, mainly vegetarian or dairy-based, hence the name. Though their ranks have thinned since their glory days, there are several popular survivors across the city, some of which have given their proletarian decor a contemporary makeover.

Prasowy (Map p60; ☑ 666 353 776; https://prasowy.pl; ul Marszałkowska 10/16, Śródmieście Południowe; mains 6-19zł; ⊙ 9am-8pm Mon-Fri, 11am-7pm Sat & Sun; ☑; ⧉ Plac Unii Lubelskiej) Epitomises the best of self-serve, milk-bar culture with its classy twist on a retro interior and a democratic menu of hearty Polish staples.

Bar Mleczny Pod Barbakanem (Map p52; ☑ 22 831 4737; http://barpodbarbakanem.pl; ul Mostowa 27, Nowe Miasto; mains 7-10zł; ⊙ 8am-4pm Mon-Fri, 9am-5pm Sat & Sun; ☑; ⧉ Plac Krasińskich) Don't be put off by the faded decades old exterior; this New Town spot is ideal for budget pierogi (dumplings) and pork chops.

Gdański Bar Mleczny (Map p52; ☑ 22 831 2962; www.facebook.com/gdanski.bar.mleczny; ul Andersa 33, Muranów; mains 8-10zł, set meals 18-20zł; ⊙ 9am-8pm Mon-Fri, 11am-7pm Sat & Sun; ⧉ Muranowska) This smartly updated 'milk bar' offers a fresh, modern interior and an English menu to choose from – line up at the hatch to place your order.

Cô Tú

ASIAN €

(Map p56; ☑ 22 826 8339; Pavillion 21, ul Nowy Świat 22/28a, Śródmieście Północne; mains 15-23zł; ⊙ 11am-9pm Mon-Fri, from noon Sat, noon-7pm Sun; ⧉ Foksal) The wok at this simple Asian diner never rests as hungry Poles can't get enough of the excellent dishes coming from the kitchen. The menu is enormous, covering all the main bases (seafood, vegetable, beef, chicken, pork), and you'll never have to wait more than 10 minutes for your food.

Accessed via the archway at ul Nowy Świat, find it at the rear of the **Pawilony** (http://pawilonynowyswiat.pl) complex of bars and cafes.

★ SAM Powiśle

CAFE €€

(Map p56; ☑ 600 806 084; www.sam.info.pl/; ul Lipowa 7a, Powiśle; mains 29-39zł; ⊙ 8am-10pm Mon-Fri, from 9am Sat & Sun; ☑; Ⓜ Centrum Nauki Kopernik) A large communal table dominates this slick bakery, deli and cafe that aims to use organic produce from local farmers and suppliers in its dishes. It's very popular for breakfast or lunch – make sure you book early in the week for a slot at the weekend or you may find yourself waiting in line for a while.

Warszawska

POLISH €€

(Map p56; ☑ 532 745 367; https://warszawa. hotel.com.pl; Plac Powstańców Warszawy 9, Śródmieście Północne; mains 15-71zł; ⊙ 7am-11pm; Ⓜ Świętokrzyska) Occupying two basement levels of Hotel Warszawa (p67), the design of this fabulous restaurant and bar conjures up the sleek lair of a James Bond villain. Chef Darek Baranski prepares a very tasty

selection of small plates that you can mix and match to create the perfect meal. You can't go wrong with a selection of charcuterie from their house-cured meats.

Cafe Bristol

CAFE €€

(Map p56; ☑ 22 551 1828; www.cafebristol.pl; Krakowskie Przedmieście 42/44, Śródmieście Północne; breakfast from 27zł, mains 35-43zł; ⊙ 8am-8pm; ☎; ⧉ Hotel Bristol) Exemplifying the grand style of European cafe society since 1901, this is an elegant location for a posh breakfast or a light meal to set up a day's sightseeing, as well as a delightful pit stop for coffee with an expertly executed pastry or cake.

Dawne Smaki

POLISH €€

(Map p56; ☑ 22 465 83 20; http://dawnesmaki.pl; ul Nowy Świat 49, Śródmieście Północne; mains 35-69zł; ⊙ noon-midnight Mon-Thu, to 1am Fri & Sat, to 11pm Sun; ☎) An excellent restaurant to try Polish specialities, such as herring in cream, stuffed cabbage rolls, pierogi (dumplings) and all the rest. The interior is traditional white walls, wood and lace, without being overly hokey. Try the good-value lunch specials.

Elixir by Dom Wódki

POLISH €€

(Map p52; ☑ 22 828 2211; www.domwodki.pl/elixir. html; ul Wierzbowa 9/11, Śródmieście Północne; mains 49-67zł; ⊙ noon-midnight; Ⓜ Ratusz Arsenał) Every dish at this stylish restaurant comes with a suggested pairing of Polish vodka, honey mead or a local liqueur. It's an inspired way to enjoy classics such as beef tartar and roasted duck, all of which are beautifully presented.

★ **Bez Gwiazdek** POLISH €€€
(Map p56; ☑ 22 628 0445; www.facebook.com/
bezgwiazdek; ul Wiślana 8, Powiśle; set menus 100-
180zł; ⊙ 6pm-midnight Tue-Sat, 1-4pm Sun; ☎;
Ⓜ Centrum Nauki Kopernik) 'Without Stars' is
a supremely successful expression of contemporary Polish cooking. Each month chef
Robert Trzópek takes inspiration from a different province of Poland for his set menus,
which include four to six courses and can
be enjoyed with wine pairings. For creative,
beautifully presented dishes in a relaxed environment this restaurant cannot be beat.

✖ Muranów, Mirów & Powązki

★ **Kur & Wiino** CHICKEN €€
(Map p52; ☑ 570 580 180; www.facebook.com/
kurwino; ul Andersa 21, Muranów; whole/half/
quarter chicken 38/24/16zł; ⊙ noon-10pm;
🚇 Muranów) The 'chicken and wine' restaurant is a contemporary rotisserie serving
succulent free-range, corn-fed chickens and
barbecue-sauce-basted guinea fowl. Veggies,
sides, sauces and breads are all extra. The
house wine, on tap at just 8zł a glass, washes
it all down very nicely.

Czerwony Wieprz POLISH €€
(The Red Hog; Map p48; ☑ 22 850 3144; www.czer-
wonywieprz.pl; ul Żelazna 68, Mirów; mains 26-65zł;
⊙ noon-11pm; 🚇 Hala Mirowska, 🚇 Chłodna) The
menu at this touristy but fun communist-
era-themed restaurant, set in an outsized log
cabin, is split between dishes for dignitaries
such as Polish duck and those fit for the pro-
letariat (dumplings).

★ **Winosfera** INTERNATIONAL €€€
(Map p48; ☑ 22 526 2500; http://winosfera.pl; ul
Chłodna 31, Mirów; mains 67-129zł; ⊙ noon-11pm
Mon-Sat; ☎; 🚇 Chłodna) As the name suggests,
there's a focus on wine at this restaurant
aimed squarely at business-account holders.
In an industrial-styled space with exposed
brick walls, tasty, seasonally inspired dishes
are presented with flair. There's a good-value
lunch Monday to Friday (two/three courses
49/59zł) and a wine shop.

✖ Łazienki Park & Southern Śródmieście

Kuchnia Konfliktu VEGAN, VEGETARIAN €
(Map p56; www.facebook.com/kuchniakonfliktu;
ul Wilcza 60, Śródmieście Południowe; mains 22zł;
⊙ 1-8pm Tue, Wed & Sat, to 10pm Thu-Sat; ☎;
🚇 Koszykowa) Refugees and new immigrants

to Poland are given a leg up by being em-
ployed by this mainly vegan cafe, decorated
with greenery. The menu chalked on the
blackboard changes daily and staff should
be able to translate. A three-course meal for
just 30zł is brilliant value and portions are
huge – so come hungry.

★ **Youmiko Vegan Sushi** SUSHI €
(Map p56; ☑ 22 404 6736; www.facebook.com/
youmiko.vg; ul Hoża 62, Śródmieście Południowe;
sushi from 8zł, mains 25zł; ⊙ noon-10pm Mon-Thu,
to 11pm Fri & Sat, 1-9pm Sun; ☑; 🚇 Hoża) Once
you've sampled Youmiko's freshly made vegan takes on sushi, including toppings made
from edamame beans, sweet potato and
jackfruit, you may never feel like going back
to the fish version again. Put yourself in the
chefs' hands and treat yourself to the degus-
tation feast (69zł).

★ **Bibenda** POLISH €€
(Map p56; ☑ 502 770 303; www.bibenda.pl; ul
Nowogrodzka 10, Śródmieście Południowe; mains
29-65zł; ⊙ noon-midnight Tue-Sat, 10am-10pm
Sun; ☑; 🚇 Krucza) If this is modern Polish
cooking, we love it. The beef cheeks doused
in a 'magic' sticky sauce is a superb comfort
dish. Or there's burnt sweet potato in a pea-
nut sauce with a zing of lime, just one of several very good vegetarian options. The space
combines a bar with a casual restaurant
and feels contemporary and welcoming –
no wonder it's popular.

Rusiko GEORGIAN €€
(Map p56; ☑ 22 629 0628; www.rusiko.pl; al
Ujazdowskie 22, Śródmieście Południowe; mains 27-
39zł; ⊙ restaurant noon-11pm Tue-Sun, wine bar from
3pm Tue & Wed, to midnight Thu & Fri, noon-midnight
Sat, noon-11pm Sun; 🚇 Plac Trzech Krzyży) Consistently tapped as Warsaw's best Georgian
restaurant, Rusiko serves very authentic
dishes such as freshly baked cheese and egg-
filled breads and creamy nutty dips, as well
as wines and brandies from the region. If the
restaurant is full (reservations are recommended), try the neighbouring wine bar.

Przegryź EUROPEAN €€
(Map p56; www.facebook.com/przegryz; ul Mokotowska 52, Śródmieście Południowe; mains 29-38zł;
⊙ 9am-10pm Mon-Fri, from 11am Sat & Sun; ☎ 🍴;
🚇 Plac Trzech Krzyży) Original paintings by
top Polish artist Marcin Maciejowski and
colourfully patterned tiles create a warm,
quirky atmosphere at this fab all-day bistro.
Breakfast dishes are served until noon, after
which you can choose between items like

free-range chicken, beef cheeks, or potato dumplings. The coffee is excellent, and there is even a menu for your pooch.

★Alewino INTERNATIONAL €€€
(Map p56; 📞22 628 3830; www.alewino.pl; ul Mokotowska 48, Śródmieście Południowe; mains 56-65zł; ⊙5-11pm Mon, from noon Tue-Sat; 🛜; 🚊Plac Trzech Krzyży) A series of rustically chic rooms wrapped around a courtyard house one of Warsaw's best restaurants and wine bars. The wine selection is excellent and features some top Polish labels. The creative cooking uses seasonal produce and includes more than the usual throwaway vegetarian option. Service is relaxed and friendly.

Kieliszki na Hożej POLISH €€€
(Map p56; 📞22 404 2109; http://kieliszkinahozej. pl; ul Hoża 41, Śródmieście Południowe; mains 44-89zł; ⊙noon-10pm Mon-Wed, to 11pm Thu & Fri, 2-11pm Sat; 🚊Hoża) The availability of 160 wines by the glass is reason enough to swing by 'Glasses on Hoża', but there's also its accomplished contemporary Polish cooking to take into account. Small but perfectly formed dishes include starters such as pickled cherries and a splendid beef tartare, and mains of cloudlike cottage cheese dumplings in an umami mushroom broth.

🍴 Praga & Eastern Warsaw

Coś na ZĄBkowskiej EASTERN EUROPEAN €
(Map p62; 📞22 618 1579; www.facebook.com/ cosnazabkowskiej; ul Ząbkowska 9, Stara Praga; bagel sandwiches 21-24zł; ⊙noon-10pm, to 11pm Fri & Sat; Ⓜ Dworzec Wileński) A log-burning stove keeps it cosy at this convivial cafe-bar where dishes include goose goulash and herring on rye bread with seaweed. It also offers a tempting range of homemade bagel sandwiches.

ArtBistro Stalowa 52 POLISH €€
(Map p62; 📞22 252 0503; https://artbistro.pl; ul Stalowa 52, Nowa Praga; mains 39-65zł; ⊙7am-10pm Mon-Fri, from 8am Sat & Sun; 🚊Szwedzka, 🚊Czynszowa) It's worth making the trip out to the edges of Praga to sample chef Dariusz Tomczyk's contemporary Polish cuisine. He uses the best seasonal produce for dishes such as pheasant broth and dumplings and beef stuffed with speck at this relaxed bistro sharing premises with an excellent boutique hotel.

★Zoni POLISH €€€
(Map p62; 📞22 355 3001; https://zoni.today; pl Konesera 1, Szmulowizna; mains 68-160zł, tasting menu from 260zł; ⊙noon-11pm; 🛜; Ⓜ Dworzec

Wileński) Chef Aleksander Baron pulls out all the stops with his contemporary take on old Polish dishes, such as Ruthenian pierogi (dried pike roe dumplings) and *zraz* (an aged beef roulade). Produce is seasonal and the presentation beautiful. The industrial chic setting, incorporating the five giant vodka stills of the old factory, is very impressive.

Warszawa Wschodnia MODERN EUROPEAN €€€
(Map p62; 📞22 870 2918; www.mateuszgessler. com.pl; Soho Factory, ul Mińska 25, Kamionek; mains 58-78zł, tasting menu 150zł; ⊙24hr; 🛜; 🚊Bliska) In a huge industrial building, and taking its name from the neon sign salvaged from the nearby train station of the same name, this visually impressive place is in the stable of restaurants run by celeb chef Mateusz Gessler. It serves decent modern interpretations of Polish cuisine with French influences.

🍷 Drinking & Nightlife

Varsovians are generally up for a lively night's drinking and dancing whatever the day of the week, although you'll find more clubbing options on Friday and Saturday nights. There's also little to distinguish between places that serve coffee and those that serve alcohol. Most places do both, starting the day pushing caffeine and ending it selling beer and cocktails.

🍷 Old Town & New Town

★Same Fusy TEAHOUSE
(Map p52; 📞22 635 9014; www.samefusy.pl; ul Nowomiejska 10, Stare Miasto; ⊙1-11pm; 🚊Stare Miasto) This brick-vaulted basement offers a romantic, candle-lit atmosphere in which to enjoy some 120 different types and flavours of tea and infusions.

Maryensztadt CRAFT BEER
(Map p52; 📞791 522 406; www.restauracja maryensztadt.pl; ul Szeroki Dunja 11, Stare Miasto; ⊙noon-11pm Sun-Thu, to midnight Fri & Sat; 🚊Stare Miasto) This award-winning craft brewery based in Zwoleń, a small town near Warsaw, offers 15 of its beers on tap (plus a guest beer) and many more by the bottle. It's also a good place to eat a variety of Polish dishes (25zł to 59zł) that you can pair with its beers.

Same Krafty CRAFT BEER
(Map p52; 📞793 802 523; www.facebook.com/ samekrafty; ul Nowomiejska 10, Stare Miasto; ⊙2-11pm Mon, from 1pm Tue & Wed, until midnight Thu & Sun, until 1am Fri & Sat; 🚊Stare Miasto) Split

PARTY BY THE VISTULA

Running for around 5km along the west bank of the river between the Poniatowski and Gdańsk bridges, the **Vistulan Boulevards** (Bulwary Wiślane; Map p56; Powiśle) have been brilliantly landscaped and designed to become an attractive riverside promenade with terraces, pavilions, public art, artificial beaches and plenty of spots to eat, drink or just watch the world go by. Popular seasonal options include **BarKa** (Map p56; www.facebook. com/planbarka; Skwer im Tadeusza Kahla, Powiśle; ⊗ 11am-2am Sun-Thu, to 6am Fri & Sat Apr-Sep) on a floating pontoon and **Plac Zabaw nad Wisłą** (Map p56; www.facebook.com/placza bawnadwisla; Wybrzeże Kościuszkowskie, Powiśle; ⊗ Mar-Nov) where live concerts and other events are held. Open year round is **Powidoki** (Map p56; www.facebook.com/powidoki.bistro; Wybrzeże Kościuszkowskie 22, Powiśle; ⊗ noon-9pm Tue-Thu, to 3am Fri, 11am-3am Sat, 11am-8pm Sun), which has a terrace with a view across the river. The nearest metro stop is Centrum Nauki Kopernik.

across two locations facing each other on opposite sides of the street, Same Krafty is a convivial spot to sample a wide variety of Polish craft beers accompanied by slices of pizza.

Pożegnanie z Afryką

CAFE

(Map p52; ☑ 501 383 091; www.facebook.com/ pozegnaniezafrykawawa; ul Freta 4/6, Nowe Miasto; ⊗ 10am-7pm Mon-Fri, to 5pm Sat & Sun; ▣ Plac Krasińskich) 'Out of Africa' is a cosy cafe that offers little beyond coffee – but what coffee! Choose from around 50 varieties, served in little pots, and a range of tempting cakes.

🍴 Powiśle & Northern Śródmieście

★ E Wedel

CAFE

(Map p56; ☑ 22 827 2916; www.wedelpijalnie.pl; Szpitalna 8, Śródmieście Północne; ⊗ 8am-10pm Mon-Fri, from 9am Sat, 9am-9pm Sun; Ⓜ Centrum) The Austrian Wedel family set up their first Warsaw chocolate factory in this handsome building in 1865. Varsovians have been flocking here for the luscious hot chocolate and sweet treats ever since. The classic drink is the one without sugar and milk (15zł). There is also plenty available to eat including savoury dishes – it's a good breakfast choice.

★ PiwPaw Beer Heaven

CRAFT BEER

(Map p56; ☑ 534 734 945; www.piwpaw.pl; ul Foksal 16, Śródmieście Północne; ⊗ noon-11pm Sun-Tue, to 1am Wed & Thu, to 3am Fri & Sat; 🛜; ▣ Foksal) We'll leave it up to you how many merry evenings you spend here working your way through the nearly 80 on tap beers, plus over a hundred more bottled ones. Suffice to say this is a superior craft-beer pub, where seemingly every inch of wall is covered in mosaics made from bottle tops.

BarStudio

BAR

(Map p56; ☑ 603 300 835; www.barstudio.pl; Plac Defilad 1, Śródmieście Północne; ⊗ 10.30am-1am Sun & Mon, to 2am Tue-Thu, to 5am Fri & Sat; 🛜; Ⓜ Świętokrzyska) Hit the dance floor at Warsaw's most entertaining venue, doubling as the lobby bar and cafe of Studio Teatrgaleria. Depending on the DJs, you could be bopping along to a disco version of *Anarchy in the UK* or to video images from *The Big Lebowski* and then segueing from a Disneytheme tune sing-a-long to rocking out to *Highway to Hell*.

Cafe Kulturalna

BAR

(Map p56; ☑ 22 656 6281; www.kulturalna.pl; Plac Defilad 1, Śródmieście Północne; ⊗ noon-midnight; 🛜; Ⓜ Centrum) The best place for a casual drink and something to eat within the Palace of Culture & Science (p52), Kulturalna occupies a spacious hall off the main lobby of the Teatr Dramatyczny (p76). The atmosphere is always relaxed and exudes cool sophistication.

Stor

COFFEE

(Map p56; ☑ 22 290 5190; www.stor.cafe; ul Tamka 33, Powiśle; ⊗ 8.30am-9.30pm; Ⓜ Nowy Świat-Uniwersytet) One of Warsaw's best third-wave coffee havens, Stor drips with potted-plant greenery and has appealing bakes and snacks to go with its drinks. Browse a copy of the *Coffee Spots Polska* guidebook that's published by the cafe's owner and is on sale here.

Cosmo

COCKTAIL BAR

(Map p56; www.cosmobar.pl; ul Twarda 4, Śródmieście Północne; ⊗ 5pm-midnight Mon-Wed, to 1am Fri & Sat; Ⓜ Świętokrzyska) 🍸 Not only is Cosmo one of Warsaw's most sophisticated and creative cocktail bars, it also aims for sustainability with a minimal-waste policy. Straws and napkins are biodegradable, and used citrus is turned into syrups and cordials to flavour drinks. The menu changes seasonally and the waiters will talk you through the delicious options.

Między Nami BAR

(Map p56; ☑22 828 5417; www.miedzynamicafe.com; ul Bracka 20, Śródmieście Północne; ⊙10am-11pm Mon-Thu, to midnight Fri & Sat, 2-11pm Sun; 🐾; 🅼Centrum) 'Between Us' attracts a trendy set with its designer furniture, cool art hanging on whitewashed walls, excellent drinks list and supremely friendly vibe.

Smolna CLUB

(Map p56; www.smolna38.com; ul Smolna 38, Śródmieście Północne; admission 30-40zł; ⊙11pm-8am Fri & Sat; 🅼Muzeum Narodowe) Unless you look hip and cool, you can expect to be turned away from Warsaw's coolest club. This doesn't stop locals lining up for the all-night techno and electronic music events that take place at this historic tenement building with two dance floors, a chill-out room, three bars and a patio.

Wrzenie Świata CAFE

(Map p56; ☑22 828 49 98; http://wrzenie.pl; ul Gałczyńskiego 7, Śródmieście Północne; ⊙9am-10pm, from 10am Sat & Sun; 🐾; 🅼Nowy Świat-Uniwersytet) This peaceful, arty bookshop and coffee house. It draws journalists and those interested in Polish and world affairs and is located on a quiet backstreet behind ul Nowy Świat.

A Blikle CAFE

(Map p56; ☑669 609 706; www.blikle.pl; ul Nowy Świat 33, Śródmieście Północne; ⊙9am-10pm; 🐾; 🅼Foksal) The mere fact that A Blikle

has survived two world wars and the challenges of communism makes it a household name locally. But what makes this legendary cafe truly famous is its rose jam doughnuts, for which people have been queuing up for generations.

🍴 Muranów, Mirów & Powązki

Fat White COFFEE

(Map p52; ☑570 096 017; www.facebook.com/fatwhitecoffee; ul Andersa, Muranów; ⊙7am-8pm Mon-Fri, 8am-5pm Sat; 🐾; 🅼Muranów) Coffee lovers will be impressed by this compact, cute cafe that offers coffee prepared either by the Chemex, Aeropress or drip method, as well as the usual steam-based espresso style. It's connected to the hipster barbers Ferajna (www.ferajna.pro) in case you need a hair or beard trim.

Chłodna 25 CAFE

(Map p48; ☑506 045 827; www.facebook.com/pg/chl25; ul Chłodna 25, Mirów; ⊙9am-11pm Mon-Fri, from 10am Sat & Sun; 🐾; 🅼Chłodna, 🅼Hala Mirowska) This arty, bohemian haunt has been a touchstone of the area for several years. Concerts, films, debates and lectures feature regularly in the basement space in the evenings. Coffee, wine, beer and home-made cakes are available all day upstairs.

🍷 Łazienki Park & Southern Śródmieście

★Klub SPATiF CLUB

(Map p56; ☑22 625 1498; http://klubspatif.pl; al Ujazdowskie 45, Śródmieście Południowe; admission depending on event; ⊙6.30pm-late Wed-Sat; 🅼Plac Trzech Krzyży) In the mid-20th century, this club-bar in an elegant tenement

---

LGBTQ WARSAW

Warsaw's City Hall is committed to supporting LGBTQ rights and initiatives. There are LGBTQ bars and clubs in Warsaw and they're not too difficult to find. That said, many Poles are conservative and not accepting of gay culture, so use caution in showing same-sex affection in public.

The Equality Parade (p65), which has been held in most years since 2001, passes through the city's streets in mid-June in support of social equality and diversity.

Revolution (www.facebook.com/revolutionwarsaw) is an occasional gay dance night held at different venues across the city.

Metropolis (Map p56; ☑576 000 845; www.facebook.com/metropoliswarszawa; ul Sienkiewicza 7, Śródmieście Północne; admission 10zł; ⊙11pm-5am Fri & Sat; 🐾; 🅼Świętokrzyska) Muscled, topless bar staff and drag queens keep it glam at this weekend gay dance club.

Galeria (Map p56; www.clubgaleria.pl; Plac Mirowski 1, Śródmieście Północne; admission free, Sat 10zł; ⊙9pm-5am Tue-Sun; 🅼Hala Mirowski) Long running, gay-friendly bar and DJ club beneath Hala Mirowska.

building was a hang-out for Warsaw's arty and theatrical set. Revived, it has bounced back better than ever, playing host to a cool crowd who love to dance at events such as regular live concerts by the Mała Orkiestra Dancingowa, playing 1930s Polish pop.

★Gram
BAR

(Map p60; www.facebook.com/grammarszalkow ska; ul Marszałkowska 45/49, Śródmieście Południowe; ⊙4pm-1am Sun-Tue, to 2am Wed, to 3am Thu & Fri, 2pm-3am Sat; 🔊 Plac Zbawiciela) Play pinball and old-school arcade computer games at this cute, circus-themed bar where the beers go for a bargain 10zł. On your way up from the bigger and rowdier Warmut bar on the ground floor, admire and perhaps take a selfie against the super-cool backdrop of 3D models of Warsaw landmark buildings hanging from the ceiling.

Plan B
BAR

(Map p60; ✆503 116 154; www.planbe.pl; al Wyzwolenia 18, Śródmieście Południowe; ⊙11am-late; 🔊 Plac Zbawiciela) A legendary Warsaw watering hole, this grungy, upstairs bar on Plac Zbawiciela invariably draws a crowd. Find some couch space and relax to smooth beats from regular DJs. On warm summer evenings the action spills out onto the street, giving the square the feel of a summer block party.

CLUBBING AT UL 11 LISTOPADA 22

This cool street art decorated courtyard in Nowa Praga is home to a trio of popular bars and live music venues. **Chmury** (Map p62; ✆505 849 386; www.facebook.com/pg/kawiarniachmury; tickets from 10zł; ⊙4-11pm Sun-Thu, to 3am Fri & Sat; 🔊 Inżynierska) is a homage to the TV series and movie *Twin Peaks* with an intimate performance space and bar that's a nice spot to hang out regardless of whether there's a concert on. **Hydrozagadka** (Map p62; ✆502 070 916; www.hydrozagadka.waw.pl; ⊙6pm-midnight, to 3am Fri & Sat; 🔊 Inżynierska) has room for around 400 people and hosts indie bands and singers from all over Europe and the US, while **Skład Butelek** (Map p62; ✆505 849 386; www.skladbutelek.pl; ⊙6pm-midnight, to 3am Fri & Sat; 🔊 Inżynierska) offers a jam session every Thursday and more live acts on other nights.

Coffee Karma
CAFE

(Map p60; ✆22 875 8709; www.facebook.com/coffeekarma.warszawa; Plac Zbawiciela 3/5, Śródmieście Południowe; ⊙7.30am-10pm Mon-Fri, from 10am Sat & Sun; 🔊; 🔊 Plac Zbawiciela) Laid-back Coffee Karma has an enviable perch on Plac Zbawiciela, with comfy couches and a light menu. The warmly lit interior hung with art is a fine place to work through a morning-after slump with the aid of caffeine.

Cuda na Kiju
CRAFT BEER

(Map p56; www.facebook.com/cudanakijumulttitap bar; ul Nowy Świat 6/12, Śródmieście Południowe; ⊙noon-1am Mon-Thu, to 2am Fri & Sat, to midnight Sun; 🔊 Muzeum Narodowe) There are some 16 different draft ales on tap at this popular multilevel bar. A big draw is that its seats spill out on the huge paved courtyard within the city's former Communist Party HQ, making it one of the coolest inner-city hangouts in warm weather.

Woda Ognista
COCKTAIL BAR

(Map p56; ✆22 258 1441; www.wodaognista.com; ul Wilcza 8, Śródmieście Południowe; ⊙5am-midnight Sun-Thu, to 2am Fri & Sat; 🔊; 🔊 Plac Trzech Krzyży) Colourful characters and auspicious events from Poland's nightlife from the 1920s and '30s inspire the seasonal cocktails at 'Fire Water'. Everything is professionally prepared by friendly bartenders who work at a handsome bar beneath a pressed-tin ceiling.

Beirut
BAR

(Map p56; www.facebook.com/beiruthummusbar; ul Poznańska 12, Śródmieście Południowe; mains 10-25zł; ⊙noon-2am; 🔊; 🔊 Hoża) Hip and informal, this super-popular Lebanese-style drinking den bills itself as a 'hummus & music bar'. Most customers appear content to focus on the alcoholic beverages, but the creamy hummus and other Middle Eastern bites are attention worthy. It can get crowded, but DJs keep the mood bubbling along nicely.

🍺 Praga & Eastern Warsaw

★W Oparach Absurdu
BAR

(Map p62; ✆660 780 319; www.facebook.com/woparachabsurdu; ul Ząbkowska 6, Stara Praga; ⊙noon-3am, to 5am Fri & Sat; Ⓜ) It's best to make a reservation if you want to be sure of getting a table at the eternally popular 'In the Fumes of Absurdity' bar. Old carpets and an eclectic bric-a-brac interior make for a cosy atmosphere, and it has a great choice of local beers, other drinks and comfort food.

LISTEN TO CHOPIN

There's no excuse for not listening to a little Chopin while in Warsaw. Each evening intimate piano recitals are given at both the **Best of Chopin Concerts** (Map p52; 534 188 708; www.chopinconcerts.pl; Warsaw Archdiocese Museum, ul Dziekania 1, Stare Miasto; adult/concession 45zł; 6.30pm; Stare Miasto) or **Time For Chopin** (Map p52; 501 127 125; https://timeforchopin.eu; ZPAF Old Gallery, Plac Zamkowy 8, Stare Miasto; 60zł; 6pm; Stare Miasto); the performers are virtuosos who have played at major venues around the world. The recitals last an hour including a short break.

On most Thursdays at 6pm between January and June, free piano concerts are performed by talented young musicians at the Fryderyk Chopin Museum (p52). A fixture on Warsaw's summer calendar are the free outdoor piano concerts held beside the Chopin Monument (p59).

Also download the free Chopin in Warsaw and Selfie With Chopin apps (http://en.chopin.warsawtour.pl) to help locate the 15 public benches scattered across Warsaw that play a snippet of Chopin at the touch of a button.

★Centrum Zarządzania Światem LOUNGE
(Map p62; 22 618 2197; www.centrumswiata.com; ul Stefana Okrzei 26, Stara Praga; 8am-11pm Mon-Thu, to midnight Fri, 10am-midnight Sat, 10am-11pm Sun; ; Dworzec Wileński) If the TV series *Friends* were to be reset in Warsaw, Centrum could double for Central Perk. Friends do gather in comfy chairs around low tables at this cosy cafe-bar to sip coffee, drink inventive cocktails (try the bacon-laden twist on a Bloody Mary) and munch on crispy *tarte flambée*.

Galeria Sztuki CAFE
(Map p62; 22 619 8109; http://caffee.stanowski.pl; ul Ząbkowska 13, Stara Praga; 9am-11pm Mon-Thu, to midnight Fri, from 10am Sat, to 10pm Sun; ; Dworzec Wileński) This cosy antique-style cafe-bar is a great place to rest your feet while exploring Praga. It serves some of the best coffee in town, along with delicious cakes and wines by the glass, and does breakfast (mostly egg-based) until noon.

☆ Entertainment

Warsaw's entertainment options are the best in the country. The city is home to many classical music, opera and performing arts venues. Polish theatre has long been enthusiastically supported in the capital, and the theatres stage top-class productions that are worth making time to see. Film is also well represented at both mainstream and arthouse cinemas.

Classical Music, Dance & Opera

★Teatr Wielki OPERA
(National Opera; Map p52; 22 826 5019; www.teatrwielki.pl; Plac Teatralny 1, Śródmieście Północne; tickets 60-260zł; box office 9am-7pm Mon-Fri, from 11am Sat & Sun; Ratusz Arsenał) Dating from 1833, destroyed in WWII and rebuilt to Antonio Corazzi's original design in 1965, this magnificent building is home to the Polish National Opera and Ballet companies. The principal 1768-seat Moniuszko Auditorium, one of the world's largest opera stages, is used for a quality repertoire of classic and new works by Polish and international composers.

★Filharmonia Narodowa CLASSICAL MUSIC
(National Philharmonic; Map p56; 22 551 7130; www.filharmonia.pl; ul Jasna 5, Śródmieście Północne; tickets from 60zł; box office 10am-2pm & 3-7pm Mon-Sat; Świętokrzyska) Home of the world-famous National Philharmonic Orchestra and Choir of Poland, the National Philharmonic was founded in 1901. Destroyed during WWII, it was rebuilt in 1955 to house a concert hall (enter from ul Sienkiewicza 10) and a chamber-music hall (enter from ul Moniuszki 5), both of which stage regular concerts.

Warszawa Opera Kameralna OPERA
(Warsaw Chamber Opera; Map p52; 22 625 7510; www.operakameralna.pl; al Solidarności 76b, Muranów; tickets from 30zł; box office 11am-7pm Mon-Fri, 3hr before performance Sat & Sun; Ratusz Arsenał) Performs a repertoire ranging from medieval mystery plays to contemporary works, but is most famous for its performances of Mozart's operas.

Royal Theatre THEATRE
(Teatrem Królewskim; Map p60; 22 511 5900; https://operakrolewska.pl; ul Agrykola 1, Ujazdów; adult/concession 60/30zł; Plac Na Rozdrożu) Polska Opera Królewska regularly perform

concerts and operas in this intimate and authentic 18th-century court theatre featuring beautiful stucco and *trompe l'oeil* decoration. The only performance space of its kind in Poland, it was designed by Domenico Merlini, court architect to King Stanisław August Poniatowski.

Live Music

Stodoła
LIVE MUSIC

(Map p60; ☑ 22 825 6031; www.stodola.pl; ul Batorego 10, Śródmieście Południowe; ☺ box office 9am-9pm Mon-Fri, to 2pm Sat; Ⓜ Pole Mokotowskie) One of Warsaw's biggest and longest-running live-music stages, Stodoła is a great place to catch local and touring singers and bands. It started out in 1956 showcasing jazz but has since branched out into all genres of music and other live performances.

12on14 Jazz Club
JAZZ

(Map p60; ☑ 22 635 4949; http://12on14club.com; ul Stanisława Noakowskiego 16, Śródmieście Południowe; tickets 100zł; ☺ 6-1pm Tue-Sat; ☒ Plac Politechniki) Head to this respected jazz club early if you want to bag a table and seat for the concerts. The sound system is excellent and the atmosphere cosy.

Cinemas

Kinoteka
CINEMA

(Map p56; ☑ 22 551 7070; www.kinoteka.pl; Plac Defilad 1, Śródmieście Północne; tickets from 25zł; Ⓜ Centrum) There are eight auditoriums, several of them quite grand, at this multiplex cinema housed in the Palace of Culture & Science (p52). A good range of films are screened here. The entrance faces al Jerozolimskie.

Muranów Cinema
CINEMA

(Map p52; ☑ 22 635 3078; www.muranow.gutekfilm.pl; ul Andersa 1, Muranów; tickets 12-23zł; Ⓜ Ratusz Arsenał) This vintage-style cinema screens mainly art-house films in its two main halls and two smaller rooms. There's a cafe in the foyer and a shop selling DVDs.

Theatres

Teatr Dramatyczny
THEATRE

(Map p56; ☑ 22 656 6844; www.teatrdramatyczny.pl; Plac Defilad 1, Śródmieście Północne; tickets 40-90zł; ☎; Ⓜ Centrum) This storied-theatre company, based in a wing of the Palace of Culture & Science (p52), is at the vanguard of the dramatic arts in Warsaw. On the two stages – the grand main auditorium and a studio space – a mixed repertoire of shows ranging from contemporary Polish to Shakespeare and hit musicals – some with English subtitles.

★ Teatr Powszechny
THEATRE

(Map p62; ☑ 22 818 2516; www.powszechny.com; ul Zamojskiego 20, Kamionek; tickets from 60zł; Ⓜ Stadion Narodowy, ☒ Stadion Narodowy) With three auditoriums of different sizes, this repertory theatre company stages an impressive range of works from both international and local playwrights. Contact them to see which shows have English subtitles.

TR Warszawa
THEATRE

(Map p60; ☑ 22 480 8008; http://trwarszawa.pl; ul Marszałkowska 8, Śródmieście Południowe; ☒ Plac Unii Lubelskiej) Styling itself as a home to all kinds of artistic experiments, TR Warszawa is one of the city's most interesting theatre companies, staging new Polish works and international plays. Some performance have English translations.

🛍 Shopping

🛍 Old Town & New Town

★ Dom Sztuki Lodowej
GIFTS & SOUVENIRS

(Map p52; ☑ 22 831 1805; www.epolart.pl; Rynek Starego Miasta 10, Stare Miasto; ☺ 10am-6pm Mon-Fri, to 4pm Sat, noon-4pm Sun; ☒ Stare Miasto) One of the best and certainly the most colourful collections of Polish folk-art souvenirs in the Old Town. Across two floors you'll find good examples of everything from painted wood carvings to traditional costumes and pottery.

Lapidarium
ANTIQUES

(Map p52; ☑ 509 601 894; www.lapidarium.pl; ul Nowomiejska 15/17, Stare Miasto; ☺ 10am-9pm; ☒ Stare Miasto) Every square inch of this Aladdin's Cave of a shop is packed with antiques and curios, including jewellery, folk and religious art, military medals, badges and uniforms, and tons of vintage postcards and photos.

Polish Poster Gallery
ART

(Galeria Plakatu; Map p52; ☑ 516 830 525; www.poster.com.pl; ul Piwna 28/30, Stare Miasto; ☺ 10am-8pm Sun-Thu, to 9pm Fri & Sat; ☒ Stare Miasto) Living up to its name, the Polish Poster Gallery stocks a broad collection of locally produced posters, both originals and cheaper new prints. A touchscreen catalogue of its wares makes it easy to browse the options, which includes movie, theatre, circus and music posters.

Powiśle & Northern Śródmieście

★ Chrum.com
FASHION & ACCESSORIES

(Map p56; ☑ 22 415 5224; www.chrum.com; ul Dobra 53, Powiśle; ◷ 11am-7pm Mon-Fri, noon-6pm Sat; Ⓜ Centrum Nauki Kopernik) Leonardo's *Lady with a Piglet*? Just one of the cheeky, quirky and colourful print T-shirts and other fashion accessories stocked by this porcine-loving brand that is constantly coming up with new designs. The T-shirts are hand-printed and made from good-quality Polish cotton.

Acephala
FASHION & ACCESSORIES

(Map p56; ☑ 661 772 666; https://acephalafashion.com/acs; al 3 Maja 14, Powiśle; Ⓡ Warszawa Powiśle) With collections inspired by women's-rights campaigners and the likes of French avant-garde photographer and writer Claude Cahun, Monika Kędziora's designs stand out from the crowd. The brand's flagship concept store also stocks menswear from Amsterdam-based Delikatessen, eyewear by Sirène, accessories and indie style mags and books.

DecoDialogue
ARTS & CRAFTS

(Map p56; ☑ 510 133 163; https://decodialogue.pl; ul Kopernika 8/18, Śródmieście Północne; ◷ 11am-7pm Mon-Fri, to 4pm Sat; Ⓜ Nowy Świat-Uniwersytet) Specialising in homewares by Polish craftspeople, DecoDialogue has enthusiastic staff who are delighted to chat about their carefully selected range of ceramics, linens, furniture and other decorative objects.

Porcelanowa
CERAMICS

(Map p56; ☑ 501 569 444; http://porcelanowa.com; ul Kredytowa 2, Śródmieście Północne; ◷ 11am-7pm Mon-Fri, to 3pm Sat; Ⓡ Królewska) At this gallery you can admire and buy ceramics by some of Poland's leading contemporary potters and artists. Items include gorgeous hand-painted vases by Malwina Konopacka (http://malwina konopacka.com) and tea sets by Marek Cecuła (https://modusdesign.com).

Cepelia
ARTS & CRAFTS

(Map p56; ☑ 22 827 0987; www.cepelia.pl; ul Chmielna 8, Śródmieście Północne; ◷ 11am-8pm Mon-Fri, to 2pm Sat; Ⓡ Foksal) Established in 1949, Cepelia is dedicated to promoting Polish arts and crafts, stocking woodwork, pottery, sculpture, fabrics, embroidery, lace, paintings and traditional costumes. The selection at this branch is particularly impressive.

Galeria Art
ART

(Map p52; ☑ 22 828 5170; www.galeriaart.pl; ul Krakowskie Przedmieście 17, Śródmieście Północne;

LOCAL KNOWLEDGE

MULTIMEDIA PARK FOUNTAIN

Cap a summer's evening stroll along the Old and New Town's cobbled lanes by attending the impressive sound and light shows at the **Multimedia Fountain Park** (Multimedialny Park Fontann; Map p52; http://park-fontann.pl; skwer I Dywizji Pancernej, Nowe Miasto; ◷ 8.30am-10.30pm; Ⓡ Sanguszki) **FREE**. Arrive early to grab a good viewing spot – from mid-May to mid-August the shows start at 9.30pm, at other times 9pm – although it's best to check online as shows are weather dependent. There are also shorter, winter light shows held Friday to Sunday at 4pm, 5pm and 6pm from early December until the end of January.

◷ 11.30am-7pm Mon-Fri, to 5pm Sat; Ⓡ Hotel Bristol) Owned by the Association of Polish Artists and Designers, this excellent gallery sells a broad range of original contemporary Polish art by its members, as well as postcards and books.

TFH Concept
FASHION & ACCESSORIES

(Map p56; ☑ 502 488 348; www.tfhkoncept.com; ul Szpitalna 8, Śródmieście Północne; ◷ 11am-8pm Mon-Sat, noon-6pm Sun; Ⓜ Centrum) If you're looking for contemporary streetwear courtesy of young Polish designers, you've come to the right place. Clothes and accessories feature upstairs in this attractive boutique, while downstairs you can browse retro items.

Złote Tarasy
MALL

(Map p56; ☑ 22 222 2200; www.zlotetarasy.pl; ul Złota 59, Śródmieście Północne; ◷ 9am-10pm Mon-Sat, to 9pm Sun; 🛜; Ⓜ Centrum, Ⓡ Warszawa Centralna) The popular 'Golden Terraces' mall hosts major local and international chains, including Zara, H&M, Sephora and the Empik book and CD store. It also has many places to eat and a multiplex cinema.

Muranów, Mirów & Powązki

Arkadia
MALL

(Map p48; ☑ 22 323 6767; www.arkadia.com.pl; al Jana Pawła II 82, Muranów; ◷ 10am-10pm Mon-Sat, to 9pm Sun; Ⓡ Rondo Radosława) One of Poland's largest shopping malls, Arkadia offers some 240 shops, plus 30 cafes and restaurants and a 15-screen multiplex under one roof.

DON'T MISS

HISTORIC MARKET HALLS

Despite much of its main hall having been converted into a modern supermarket, **Hala Mirowska** (Map p56; Plac Mirowski 1, Śródmieście Północne; ⊘ most stalls 6am-6pm Mon-Sat; 🚃 Hala Mirowska) is worth visiting for its splendid architecture. The ornate red-brick pavilion of this late-19th-century marketplace is in exceptional condition. Surrounding the main hall are traditional stalls selling fresh flowers, fruit, vegetables and other produce.

Next door is the art nouveau **Hala Gwardi** (Map p56; https://halagwardii.pl; Plac Żelaznej Bramy 1, Śródmieście Północne; mains 15-25zł; ⊘ 9am-1am Fri & Sat, 10am-11pm Sun; 🚃 Hala Mirowska), offering both food and souvenir stalls plus street-food style outlets, bars and coffee spots. It's very relaxed with a youthful edge and has something for everyone – from freshly baked pizza to sushi and craft beer. After WWII the hall was used as a bus depot, then later hosted boxing matches – hence the blown-up black and white photos that hang from the walls.

Lovely art nouveau architecture is also a draw at **Hala Koszyki** (Map p60; www.koszyki.com; ul Koszykowa 63, Śródmieście Południowe; mains 10-50zł; ⊘ 9am-9pm Mon-Sat, to 8pm Sun; 🚃 Plac Konstytucji) an artfully converted early-20th-century market hall now stacked with a wide variety of grazing options from sushi and tapas bars to craft-beer stations and artisan chocolate shops.

🔒 Łazienki Park & Southern Śródmieście

★ Tebe
FOOD & GIFTS

(Map p56; ☏ 693 528 671; www.tebe.waw.pl; al Jerozolimskie 51; ⊘ 10am-6pm Mon-Fri, to 2pm Sat; Ⓜ Centrum) To say that Tebe sells traditional Polish gingerbread does it a disservice. The edible and decorative pieces created here by Teresa Bilska are mini works of art and make for light, portable and sweet souvenirs. Coffee is also served in gingerbread cups that you can eat afterwards.

★ Pan tu nie stał
FASHION & ACCESSORIES

(Map p60; ☏ 887 887 772; https://pantuniestal.com; ul Koszykowa 34/50, Śródmieście Południowe; ⊘ 11am-7pm Mon-Sat; 🚃 Plac Konstytucji) Worth a visit as much for its quirky interior design as its products, this fashion brand started in Łódź in 2009. Some of its prints on T-shirts, socks, underwear and other accessories are derived from Polish cultural products from the mid-20th century. It's a fun spot to pick up a nonstandard Polish souvenir or gift.

Desa Unicum
ART

(Map p56; ☏ 22 163 6600; https://desa.pl; ul Piękna 1a, Śródmieście Południowe; ⊘ 11am-7pm Mon-Fri, to 4pm Sat; 🚃 Piękna) In the northwest corner of Park Ujazdowski, surrounded by government offices and embassies, this long-established gallery and auction house opened its new home in 2018. The glass box building strikes a contemporary note sitting in an excavated plot. There's already a bookshop and plans to add a cafe and a restaurant. A short walk away, its branch facing **Plac Konstytucji** (Map p60; ☏ 22 621 6669) sells reprints of works by famous Polish artists and illustrators, such as Rafał Olbiński and Edward Dwurnik. Some of the images are transferred to mugs, ties and scarves making for unusual gifts.

Mysia 3
MALL

(Map p56; ☏ 603 767 574; https://mysia3.pl; ul Mysia 3, Śródmieście Południowe; ⊘ 10am-8pm Mon-Sat, noon-6pm Sun; 🚃 Muzeum Narodowe) International brands such as Cos and Muji form part of this compact boutique mall that has a swirling line of neon decorating its facade. Rummage around **Nap** to find artisan Polish ceramics and tableware, and check out what's showing at the **Leica 6×7 Gallery**.

KABAK
FASHION & ACCESSORIES

(Map p56; ☏ 693 794 092; https://kabak.com.pl; ul Hoża 51, Śródmieście Południowe; ⊘ 10am-7pm Mon-Fri, noon-4pm Sat; 🚃 Hoża) Super-colourful Polish design socks in lots of fun patterns, plus scarves, belts and other fashion accessories, are sold by this brand whose philosophy is based on fair trade principles.

🔒 Praga & Eastern Warsaw

★ Look Inside
VINTAGE

(Map p62; ☏ 668 405 284; https://lookinside.pl; ul Wileńska 21, Nowa Praga; ⊘ 11am-7pm Mon-Fri, noon-4pm Sat; Ⓜ Dworzec Wileński) In an area well endowed with antique and vintage stores, Look Inside stands out for its cool selection and attractive displays. It also has contemporary items including fine porcelain by Ćmielów Design Studio and works by local artists and printers.

★ Cafe Melon VINTAGE

(Map p62; ☑792 925 982; https://vintagekolektyw.pl; ul Inzynierska 1, Nowa Praga; ☺10am-7pm Mon-Fri; Ⓜ Dworzec Wileński) Worth searching out if you're in the market for some vintage Polish glass, crystal, china and stoneware. The cafe (which serves excellent coffee) also stocks postcards and some books.

ⓘ Information

DANGERS & ANNOYANCES

Overall Warsaw is a safe place to visit, but you should take precautions while walking at night.

Watch your possessions on public transport and in other crowded places.

Bikes are particularly at risk; try not to leave your bike out of sight for too long, and always lock it firmly with the strongest lock you can find.

MEDICAL SERVICES

For an ambulance call 999, or 112 from a mobile phone. English-speaking dispatchers are rare, however, so you're probably better off phoning a medical centre with multilingual staff.

For nonurgent treatment, you can go to one of the city's many *przychodnia* (outpatient clinics). Your hotel or embassy can provide recommendations.

There are plenty of pharmacies where you can get medical advice; look or ask for an *apteka*.

Damian Medical Centre (Centrum Medyczne Damiana; ☑22 566 22 53; www.damian.pl; ul Foksal 3/5, Śródmieście Północne; ☺7.30am-8pm Mon-Fri, 8am-3pm Sat; ⓖ Muzeum Narodowe) Reputable private outpatient clinic with hospital facilities.

DOZ Apteka (www.doz.pl; al Jerozolimskie 54, Śródmieście Północne; ☺7am-11pm) All-night pharmacy at Warszawa Centralna train station.

EuroDental (☑22 540 5600; www.eurodental. pl; ul Śniadeckich 12/16, Śródmieście Południowe; ☺8am-8pm Mon-Fri; ⓖ Plac Konstytucji) Private dental clinic with multilingual staff.

Lux Med (☑22 332 2888; www.luxmed.pl; Marriott Hotel Bldg, al Jerozolimskie 65/79, Śródmieście Południowe; ☺7am-8pm Mon-Fri; ⓖ Warszawa Centralna) Private clinic with English-speaking specialist doctors and its own ambulance service; carries out laboratory tests and arranges house calls.

POST

Main Post Office (Poczta Główna Warszawa; Map p56; ☑22 505 3534; www.poczta-polska.pl; ul Świętokrzyska 31/33, Śródmieście Północne; ☺24hr; Ⓜ Świętokrzyska)

Post Office (Map p62; ul Targowa 73, Stara Praga; ☺24hr; Ⓜ Dworzec Wileński)

TOURIST INFORMATION

Tourist Office – Old Town (Map p52; www. warsawtour.pl; Rynek Starego Miasta 19/21, Stare Miasto; ☺9am-8pm May-Sep, to 6pm Oct-Apr; ☏; ⓖ Stare Miasto)

Tourist Office – PKiN (Map p56; www.warsaw tour.pl; Plac Defilad 1, Śródmieście Północne; ☺8am-7pm May-Sep, to 6pm Oct-Apr; ☏; Ⓜ Centrum, ⓖ Warszawa Śródmieście) Warsaw's official tourist information organisation provides maps, leaflets and plenty of friendly advice. There's no phone number, so visit in person.

Tourist Office – Praga (Map p62; Plac Koneser, Szmulowizna; ☺11am-7pm)

USEFUL WEBSITES

City of Warsaw (www.um.warszawa.pl) Official website of the city.

Warsaw in Your Pocket (www.inyourpocket. com/warsaw) Highly opinionated and often amusing reviews.

Warszawa Warsaw (https://warszawawarsaw. com) Local insight into what's best about the city.

ⓘ Getting There & Away

AIR

Warsaw Chopin Airport (p420), 9km south of the city centre, handles most domestic and international flights.

Warsaw Modlin Airport (p420) 39km north of the city is used by budget carriers, including Ryanair, for flights to and from the UK.

BUS

FlixBus (https://global.flixbus.com) operates buses to cities across Poland and beyond from Młociny bus station north of the city centre

Warszawa Zachodnia bus terminal (Dworzec Autobusowy Warszawa Zachodnia; Map p48; ☑22 823 62 00, 24hr 703 403 403; www.dawz. pl; al Jerozolimskie 144, Czyste; ☺information & tickets 5.30am-10pm), west of the city centre, handles the majority of international and domestic routes from Warsaw, run by various operators.

Wilanowska bus station (Dworzec Autobusowy Wilanowska; ul Puławska 145, Wilanowska; Ⓜ Wilanowska), south of the city centre as well as from Warszawa Zachodnia. Each station is next to the metro station of the same name. Book on its website for the lowest fares.

CAR

Poland's capital is well connected by roads with the rest of the country. Dual carriageway roads lead into the city where you are likely to encounter traffic, particularly during the week.

TRAIN

Warsaw has several train stations, but the one most travellers use is **Warszawa Centralna**

(Warsaw Central; www.pkp.pl; al Jerozolimskie 54, Śródmieście Północne; ☉24hr), with direct connections to every major Polish city, several international cities and many other places in between; check the online timetable in English at http://rozklad-pkp.pl for times and fares.

The modernised station has a shopping concourse with ticket counters, ticket machines, ATMs and several newsagents where you can buy public-transport tickets. There are also money-changing *kantors* (one of which is open 24 hours), a left-luggage office, self-service luggage lockers, cafes and mini-supermarkets.

You can buy tickets from ticket machines (instructions available in English), or one of the many ticket counters in both the main hall and the shopping concourse. Though, in theory, most ticket agents should be able to handle some English, not all can. It's best to write down your destination and travel dates and times to show the ticket seller.

ⓘ Getting Around

TO/FROM THE AIRPORT

Buy tickets for public transport from newsagents at the airports.

Warsaw Chopin Airport (p420) Both trains (4.40zł, every 30 minutes to every hour, 20 minutes) and buses (4.40zł, every 15 minutes, 30 minutes) run to the city centre. Taxis cost 35zł to 50zł and take 20 to 30 minutes.

Warsaw Modlin Airport (p420) Frequent buses (ticket on board bus/in advance 35/9zł) take around 55 minutes to central Warsaw. For the train, ride the shuttle bus to Modlin station (19zł, one hour, at least hourly). Taxis cost 159zł between 6am and 10pm, 199zł at other times and take 30 to 40 minutes.

BICYCLE

Warsaw is mostly flat and easy to navigate, and cycle paths are on the increase. However, Warsaw drivers are fast and aggressive so you may end up following the locals' lead and sharing the footpath with pedestrians.

It's worth registering online (10zł) for the public bike-rental system **Veturilo** (www.veturilo.waw.pl). Available from March to November, it's free to use a bicycle for up to 20 minutes; 1zł for up to one hour, 3zł for up to two hours, 5zł for up to three hours and 7zł for up to four hours. Each additional hour thereafter is 2zł. Use the website to find pickup and drop-off locations as well as where to find electric bikes.

CAR & MOTORCYCLE

Warsaw's street surfaces are not the most well maintained in Europe, so driving demands constant attention.

All the major international car-hire companies have offices in Warsaw, many based at the airport. Polish companies offer cheaper rates, but may have fewer English-speaking staff and rental options.

Most major hotels offer parking, although some charge handsomely for it – rates of 100zł are not uncommon.

On the streets the entire city centre is a paid parking zone from 8am to 6pm Monday to Friday. Evenings, weekends and public holidays are free. Look for ticket machines on the streets where you will pay 3zł for the first hour, 3.60zł for the second hour, 4.20zł for the third hour and 3zł for the fourth and subsequent hours. For full details see https://zdm.waw.pl.

PUBLIC TRANSPORT

Warsaw's extensive bus system is operated by ZTM (p412) and consists of buses, metro and tram lines, all using the same ticketing system.

A useful app and website for navigating the public transport system is **Jakdojade** (https://jakdojade.pl), which figures out the best route from A to B, directs you to the nearest stop and suggests the best ticket to buy.

Operating Hours

Main routes operate from about 5am to midnight, and services are frequent and punctual, though often crowded during rush hours (7am to 9am and 3.30pm to 6.30pm Monday to Friday).

After midnight several night bus routes link major suburbs to the city centre.

Ticketing

For single journeys buy a 20-minute ticket (3.40zł). There are also 75-/90-min tickets (4.40/7zł); all allow transfers.

If you will be using public transport a lot, consider a 24-hour ticket (zone one/one and two 15/26zł) or the three-day version (36/57zł).

A weekend ticket (24zł for all zones) is valid from 7pm Friday to 8am Monday.

Tickets valid for 30 and 90 days are also available but have to be bought from ZTM Passenger Service Points; see www.ztm.waw.pl for further details.

Tickets can also be bought at newsstands, post offices, metro stations and various general stores – look for a sign saying 'Sprzedaży Biletów ZTM'.

Foreign students under 26 years of age who have an International Student Identity Card (ISIC) get a discount on public transport tickets of 50%. Those aged six and under and over 70 years can ride for free, but you should have proof of age ID handy.

There are no conductors on public transport. Validate your ticket by feeding it (magnetic stripe facing down) into the yellow validator machine on the bus or tram or at the metro station gates the first time you board; this stamps it with the time and date.

As long as you stay within the zones covered by ZTM, you can also use the integrated bus/metro/tram tickets on suburban trains, including the service to Warsaw Chopin Airport.

Inspections are common and fines are high (up to 266zł!), so don't take the risk of riding without a ticket or with an unvalidated one.

Metro

The north–south M1 line runs from the southern suburb of Ursynów (Kabaty station) to Młociny in the north via the city centre.

The newer east–west M2 line runs from Rondo Daszyńskiego, west of the city centre, to Dworzec Wileński in Praga; there are plans to extend this line.

The lines intersect at Świętokrzyska station. Yellow signs with a big red letter 'M' indicate the entrances to metro stations.

Every metro station has a public toilet and there are lifts for passengers with disabilities.

TAXI

Taxis in Warsaw are easily available and not too expensive, costing 8zł flag fall and around 2/4zł per km during the day/night within the city centre. A 10-minute ride should cost around 20zł.

Beware of 'pirate' or 'mafia' taxis, which don't display a phone number or company logo – the drivers may try to overcharge you and appear rude and aggressive if you question the fare. They are becoming less common, but still haunt tourist spots occasionally looking for likely victims.

All official taxis in Warsaw have their meters adjusted to the appropriate tariff, so you just pay whatever the meter displays. When you board a taxi, make sure the meter is turned on in your presence, which ensures you don't have the previous passenger's fare added to yours.

Taxis can be waved down on the street, but it's preferable to order a taxi by phone or apps such as Taxify and Uber.

AROUND WARSAW

Kampinos National Park

Popularly known as the Puszcza Kampinoska, **Kampinos** (Kampinoski Park Narodowy; www.kampinoski-pn.gov.pl; ul Tetmajera 38, Izabelin) begins just outside Warsaw's northwestern administrative boundary and stretches west for about 40km. It's one of the largest national parks in Poland, with around three-quarters of its area covered by forest, mainly pine and oak. It's popular with Warsaw's hikers and cyclists, who use its 300km of marked walking and cycling trails. If you plan on exploring the park, buy a copy of the Compass *Kampinoski Park Narodowy* map (scale 1:30,000), available from bookshops in Warsaw or in app form at www.compass.krakow.pl.

The park includes Europe's largest area of inland sand dunes, mostly tree-covered and up to 30m high; it's a strange feeling to have sand between your toes so far from the sea.

Other parts of the park are barely accessible peat bogs that shelter much of its animal life.

The eastern part of the park, closer to the city, is favoured by walkers as it's accessible by public transport; the western part is less visited. As well as half- and one-day hikes, there are two long trails that traverse the entire length of the park, both starting from Dziekanów Leśny on the eastern edge of the park. The red trail (54km) ends in Brochów, and the green one (51km) in Żelazowa Wola.

Bivouac sites designated for camping are the only accommodation within the park boundaries, but hotels are close by in Czosnów, Laski, Leszno, Tułowice and Zaborów.

ⓘ Getting There & Away

The most popular jumping-off point for walks in the eastern part of the park is the village of Truskaw. To get there from central Warsaw, take the metro to its northern end at Młociny, then catch city bus 708 (two or three an hour on weekdays, hourly on Saturday).

Motobuss (www.motobuss.eu) runs buses between central Warsaw and Sochaczew that stop in Kampinos (9zł, two hours, 12 daily). Buses depart from near Centrum metro station in Warsaw.

Żelazowa Wola

The tiny village of Żelazowa Wola (zheh-lah-zo-vah vo-lah), 53km west of Warsaw, is the birthplace of Fryderyk Chopin. The house where he was born on 1 March 1810 has been reconstructed and furnished in period style to create a **museum** (Dom Urodzenia Fryderyka Chopina; 46 863 3300; www.chopin.museum; Żelazowa Wola 15; adult/child museum & park 23/14zł, park only 7/4zł, Wed free; museum 9am-7pm Tue-Sun Apr-Sep, to 5pm Oct-Mar, park daily). It's a lovely little country house with extensive, beautiful gardens. Exhibits examine the story of the Chopin family's time here. The tranquillity and charm of the place make it a lovely stop.

Piano recitals are normally held here each Sunday from May to September. There are usually two concerts, up to an hour long, at noon and 3pm; there's no fee other than the park entry ticket. Other seasonal recitals can be heard from Thursday to Saturday. The museum is a branch of the Fryderyk Chopin Museum in Warsaw. The modern visitor centre has lockers and a cafe.

ⓘ Getting There & Away

Motobuss (www.motobuss.eu) runs buses between central Warsaw and Sochaczew that stop in Żelazowa Wola (11zł, two hours, 12 daily). Buses depart from near Centrum metro station.

Communist Architecture

Much of Poland was reconstructed after WWII, according to plans drawn up in Moscow and in keeping with the then communist and socialist-realist aesthetic. The result was some fantastic follies, including Warsaw's Palace of Culture & Science, and more serious efforts that reflect the very different reality of only a few decades ago.

1. Palace of Culture & Science (p52)
This socialist palace in Warsaw was a gift of friendship from the Soviet Union.

2. Hotel Forum (p149)
The Brutalist Hotel Forum in Kraków has been repurposed as a bar, the Forum Przestrzenie.

3. Kielce Bus Station (p169)
The coolest bus station in the country dates from the 1970s and is shaped like a UFO.

4. Monument to the Victims of June 1956 (p286)
Huge monument in Poznan commemorating workers who died during industrial strikes.

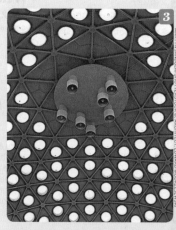

Mazovia & Podlasie

POP 6.5 MILLION

Best Places to Eat

➡ Quale Restaurant (p92)

➡ Tawerna Fisza (p111)

➡ Restauracja Rozmarino (p112)

➡ Sztuka Mięsa (p100)

➡ OFF Piotrkowska Center (p91)

Best Places to Stay

➡ Hotel Tumski (p97)

➡ Vienna House Andel's Łódź (p91)

➡ Kiermusy Dworek Nad Łąkami (p102)

➡ Hotel Branicki (p100)

➡ Wejmutka (p108)

Why Go?

The rolling landscape of Mazovia (Mazowsze in Polish) has had an eventful history. Once a duchy, this central region is dotted with castles, cathedrals and palaces, the biggest of which reside in the riverside towns of Płock and Pułtusk. Łódź, the provincial capital, is Poland's third-largest metropolis and the region's cultural and nightlife centre. The ups and downs of the city's industrial past are reflected in its mix of gritty and restored architecture and the ever-growing list of attractions that play off its complex history.

To the east, Podlasie is rural and remote. Aside from a few urban centres, this province abutting the Lithuanian and Belarusian borders is a verdant expanse of farmland, forest and lakes. Its four national parks are splendid: Narew and Biebrza for their marshlands; Wigry for its lakes; and Białowieża for its primeval forest and wild European bison, the kings of Polish fauna.

When to Go
Łódź

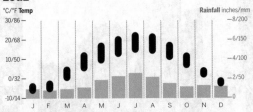

May & Jun Celebrate spring amid the lush primeval greenery of Białowieża National Park.

Jun Visit Łódź as life moves outdoors across the city and cafes and bars are jammed under the stars.

Sep Enjoy the last of the warm weather while kayaking the Augustów Canal.

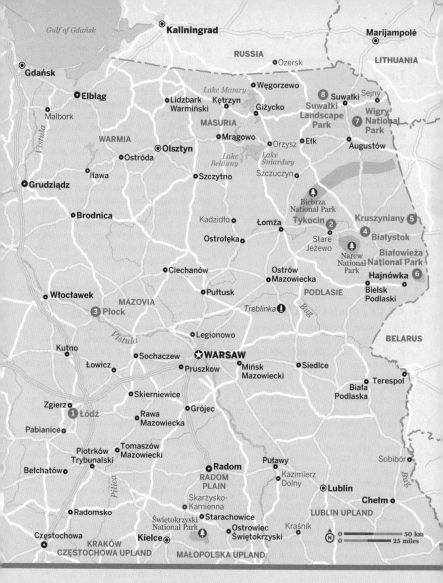

Mazovia & Podlasie Highlights

1 Łódź (p86) Experiencing the city's repurposed industrial heritage and nightlife.

2 Tykocin (p102) Learning from tangible links to Poland's lost Jewish heritage.

3 Płock (p95) Marvelling at the art nouveau treasures in the Mazovian Museum.

4 Białystok (p98) Strolling the elaborate formal gardens at Branicki Palace.

5 Kruszyniany (p105) Exploring the last remnants of Poland's Tatar culture.

6 Białowieża National Park (p106) Searching primeval forest for a glimpse of the rare European bison.

7 Wigry National Park (p113) Hiking in the untrammelled northeast Polish countryside.

8 Suwałki Landscape Park (p112) Catching your breath as sunshine reveals the stunning scenery.

MAZOVIA

Łódź

POP 690,000

Łódź (pronounced *woodge*) is a red-brick city that grew fabulously wealthy in the 19th century on the back of its massive textile industry, then went into decline after WWII. Since 2000 it has been gradually reinventing itself as a modern metropolis (it is Poland's third-largest city) and rebuilding its once-crumbling city centre.

Today the city is famous for its architecture (both historic and modern), colourful street art, Jewish heritage, many fine museums and art galleries and its swinging, affordable nightlife. It is also the centre of Poland's film industry.

◉ Sights

◉ City Centre & EC1

Łódź' revamped city centre is focused around Łódź Fabryczna train station near where you'll find **EC1** (Map p88; ☑ 42 600 6100; www.ec1lodz.pl; ul Targowa 1/3; ☒ Kilińskiego-Tuwima) FREE, which takes its name from its original incarnation as the city's first heating and power plant (Elektro-Ciepłownia 1). Opened in 1906 and closed down in 2000, the coal-fired power station, cooling tower and ancillary buildings have been beautifully renovated and adapted to house a planetarium, the National Centre for Film Culture (slated to open in 2020) and **Centre for Science & Technology** (Centrum Nauki i Techniki; Map p88; www.centrumnaukiec1.pl; EC1, ul Targowa 1/3; adult/child 23/17zł Mon-Fri, 31/22zł Sat & Sun; ☉ 9am-7pm Tue-Fri, 10am-8pm Sat & Sun; ☜). Here you can explore the dissected heart of the giant furnaces and boilers, and interact with hands-on exhibits that explain fundamental scientific principles ranging from atomic physics to electromagnetism to optics.

Herbst Palace Museum   MUSEUM

(Muzeum Pałac Herbsta; ☑ 42 674 9698; www.msl.org.pl; ul Przędzalniana 72; adult/child 15/8zł, free Fri; ☉ 11am-5pm Tue-Sun; ☒ 55) Now a branch of the Museum of Art, this building started life in 1875 as a grand villa of the Herbst family. Although the owners fled before WWII, taking all the furnishings and art with them, the interior has been restored and furnished like the original, giving an insight into how barons of industry once lived. There's also a separate exhibition of Polish and European art from the 15th to early 20th centuries (adult/child 10/5zł).

Film Museum   MUSEUM

(Muzeum Kinematografii; Map p88; www.kinomuzeum.pl; Plac Zwycięstwa 1; adult/child 10/7zł, free Tue; ☉ 10am-5pm Tue, 9am-4pm Wed & Fri, 11am-6pm Thu, Sat & Sun; ☒ Piłsudskiego-Kilińskiego) Housed in the palatial home of 'Cotton King' Karol Scheibler, this attraction is actually two museums in one. The basement and 1st floor are devoted to the history of Polish cinema and contain props, film posters and archaic camera equipment connected to the city's cinematic past. Everything changes, however, once you reach the ground floor, where Scheibler's luxurious apartments – frequently used as film and TV sets – reveal the great wealth of 19th-century Łódź.

MS1 Museum of Art   MUSEUM

(MS1 Muzeum Sztuki; Map p88; ☑ 42 639 9878; www.msl.org.pl; ul Więckowskiego 36; adult/child 10/5zł, free Fri; ☉ 10am-6pm Tue, 11am-7pm Wed-Sun; ☒ Gdańska-1 Maja) The original branch of the city's art museum is three blocks west of ul Piotrkowska, housed in the impressive palace that was once home to Maurycy Poznański (son of Izrael, of Manufaktura fame). It houses changing exhibitions of contemporary art, and is a venue for concerts and film screenings. A combined ticket for MS1, MS2 and Herbst Palace costs adult/child 30/20zł.

Central Museum of Textiles   MUSEUM

(Centralne Muzeum Włókiennictwa; ☑ 42 683 2684; https://cmwl.pl; ul Piotrkowska 282; adult/child 10/6zł, free Thu; ☉ 10am-5pm Tue, 9am-4pm Wed & Fri, 11am-6pm Thu, Sat & Sun; ☒ Piotrkowska-pl Katedralny) Dig deeper into Łódź' industrial past at this museum located in Ludwig Geyer's gorgeous White Factory (Biała Fabryka), the city's oldest textile mill, dating from 1839. The collection consists of textile machinery, early looms and fabrics, clothing and other objects related to the industry.

◉ Manufaktura

The huge – and hugely impressive – **Manufaktura** (Map p88; www.manufaktura.com; ul Karskiego 5; ☉ 9am-10pm; ☒ Zachodnia-Manufaktura) shopping mall deserves to be listed as a tourist attraction in its own right. It's within a massive complex of red-brick buildings that was once a 19th-century textile mill belonging to Izrael Poznański, Łódź' wealthiest citizen. In addition to nearly every chain

ŁÓDŹ' GRAND BOULEVARD

Ul Piotrkowska began life in the early 19th century as the road from Łódź to the town of Piotrków Trybunalski (hence its name). By the beginning of the 20th century Piotrkowska had grown into an elegant boulevard, lined with art nouveau buildings and expensive restaurants, but in the wake of WWII it became a gloomy, grey street of soot-blackened facades and half-empty shops.

Its revival began in the 1990s, when the Piotrkowska Street Foundation was created by a group of local artists and architects with the aim of turning the derelict thoroughfare into a lively European avenue. It has also become a sort of homage to successful locals, hosting monuments dedicated to the city's most famous sons and daughters.

From north to south, here are some highlights of buildings and public art for a stroll:

Plac Wolności The 20th century in Łódź is embodied in this one square. Monuments honour those who died for the country's 1918 independence, the grungy Soviet-style buildings replaced grander buildings owned by Jews and destroyed in the war, while ornate survivors recall the city's lost wealth.

Nos 11 and 12 At the cross-street with ul Rewolucji 1905 roku, note these two lavishly detailed and now-restored apartment buildings. Both were built by Jewish industrialists in the 19th century and are typical of buildings that once filled Łódź' streets.

No 72 The front of the Grand Hotel (p91) features the Avenue of the Stars (*Aleja Gwiazd*), a series of bronze stars set in the pavement in imitation of Los Angeles' Hollywood Boulevard. Each is dedicated to a well-known name in Polish film.

No 78 The eminent Polish pianist Artur Rubinstein once lived here. *Rubinstein's Piano*, in front, is a bronze sculpture much loved by Instagram-happy tourists.

No 86 Stop for a moment to take in the over-the-top ornamentation, griffins and all.

No 104 The bronze sculpture is **Tuwim's Bench**, created in memory of local poet Julian Tuwim. Touch his nose – it's supposed to bring good luck. It sits in front of the 1880 Italian renaissance City Hall.

No 135 The 1924 Nobel Prize winner for literature, Władysław Reymont, sits on a large travel trunk in **Reymont's Chest**.

Although much of ul Piotrkowska is pedestrianised, you can go for a ride on a *riksza* (bicycle rickshaw); expect to pay around 6zł per person for a ride from one end to the other (agree on the price beforehand).

store familiar to EU residents, there are cafes, restaurants, a multiplex cinema, an Imax theatre, and several worthwhile museums. It gets thronged with weekend mall rats. Be sure to seek out the beautiful brick **Factory Gate** on the south side. It dates to 1880.

★ **City Museum of Łódź** MUSEUM
(Muzeum Miasta Łodzi; Map p88; ☑ 42 254 9000; www.muzeum-lodz.pl; ul Ogrodowa 15; adult/child 12/8zł, free Wed; ⊙ 10am-4pm Tue-Thu, noon-6pm Fri-Sun; ⛕ Zachodnia-Manufaktura) Adjacent to the Manufaktura mall, this museum is housed in the impressive palace of 19th-century textile baron Izrael Kalmanowicz Poznański. The opulent apartments are a clear indication of the Poznańskis' wealth, bedecked with elaborate dark-wood wall panelling, delicate stained-glass windows

and a grand ballroom. Despite taking a back seat to the building itself, the 1st-floor exhibitions are interesting, covering famous Łódź citizens such as pianist Artur Rubinstein and writer Jerzy Kosiński, while those in the basement cover the city's history.

MS2 Museum of Art MUSEUM
(MS2 Muzeum Sztuki; Map p88; www.msl.org.pl; ul Ogrodowa 19; adult/child 15/8zł, free Fri; ⊙ 10am-6pm Tue, 11am-7pm Wed-Sun; ⛕ Zachodnia-Manufaktura) This gallery in the Manufaktura complex houses the city's impressive collection of experimental and avant-garde works from the 20th and 21st centuries. The setting, a former textile mill on the edge of the Manufaktura mall, is a treat. There's a good in-house cafe. A combined ticket for MS1, MS2 and Herbst Palace costs adult/child 30/20zł.

Łódź

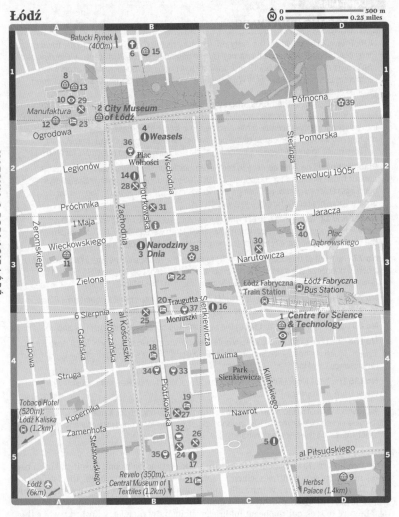

Experymentarium MUSEUM

(Map p88; ☎42 633 5262; www.experymentarium.pl; ul Drewnowska 58; adult/child 17/14zł; ⊘10am-10pm Mon-Fri, to 10.30pm Sat, to 9pm Sun; 🖪; 🚊Zachodnia-Manufaktura) Seemingly designed for kids and high-school science nerds, this interactive science museum in Manufaktura is a blast at any age. The exhibits are built around staid subjects such as chemistry and astronomy, but the displays encourage visitors to touch, play and learn. Explore the cosmic tunnel, laser games and optical illusions.

Museum of the Factory MUSEUM

(Muzeum Fabryki; Map p88; ☎42 664 9293; www.muzeumfabryki.pl; ul Drewnowska 58; adult/child 9/6zł; ⊘9am-5pm Tue-Fri, 11am-5pm Sat & Sun; 🖪; 🚊Zachodnia-Manufaktura) This industrial museum within the Manufaktura complex shows Łódź factories at their productive best, when they made goods to be sold rather than served as venues for goods for sale. There are old textile machines, fascinating maps and a short video of the textile king himself, Izrael Kalmanowicz Poznański. An observation deck allows you to survey Manufaktura, his factory empire.

Łódź

Jewish Łódź

In 1940 the Germans sealed off the northern part of Łódź to create the Litzmannstadt Ghetto (after the German name for the city) – the second-biggest Jewish ghetto in Poland, after Warsaw. It was the first of the big urban Jewish ghettos to be set up by the Germans and the last to be liquidated, in 1944. At its height, the ghetto held around 200,000 people – mostly local Jews but also sizeable groups from across Europe.

When the Red Army liberated Łódź in 1945, only 880 Jews remained. After the war, few of the survivors elected to return to Łódź. Today you can still get a sense of the ghetto. Important buildings survive and much of the area still feels blighted, some eight decades on. Some places worth visiting include:

➡ **Plac Kościelny**

(Church Sq) The start of the ghetto. Incongruously, it is dominated by the red brick steeples of **Church of the Assumption of Our Blessed Mary** (Kościół pw. Wniebowzięcia Najświętszej Maryi Panny; Map p88; plac Kościelny; 🚊 Zachodnia-Lutomierska), which could be seen from all points in the ghetto. It was used to store the possessions of Jews killed in the death camps during the war. Most notorious was the **Red House** (Czerwony Dom; Map p88; ul Kościelna 8/10; 🚊 Zachodnia-Lutomierska), where the German police tortured Jews to find out where they had hid their valuables.

➡ **Bałucki Rynek**

(🚊 Zgierska-Bałucki Rynek) The administrative heart of the ghetto, where the Gestapo and Rumkowski had their offices. In the market here, starving ghetto residents bartered their valuables for scraps of food.

➡ **Radegast Station**

(Stacja Radegast; www.lodz-ghetto.com; al Pamięci Ofiar; ⊙10am-4pm; 🚊 Doly) A memorial to the 145,000 people sent from here to their deaths.

➡ **Jewish Cemetery**

(Cmentarz Żydowski; ☎42 639 7233; www.jewish-lodzcemetery.org; ul Zmienna; adult/child 10/8zł; ⊙9am-5pm Sun-Thu, to 3pm Fri; 🚊 Doly) A moody and evocative place that recalls Łódź' once thriving Jewish community, which numbered 230,000 in 1939. The ride on tram 6 to these two sights passes through a large swathe of the former ghetto. Look for the many murals showing the images of children killed by the Nazis.

The following are good resources for information on the Jewish Łódź:

LOCAL KNOWLEDGE

ŁÓDŹ STREET ART

Łódź is famous for its abundant street art, which grew out of the Urban Forms Festival in 2009; today more than 100 murals and installations add colour and life to the city's rapidly rejuvenating centre. The tourist office will point you to the best-known examples, and many are documented on the Urban Forms (www.urbanforms.org) website. Here are our top six, all within easy reach of Piotrkowska street:

Apus Apus (Map p88; ul Kilińskiego 127; 🚌 Piłsudskiego-Kilińskiego) Created by the Portuguese artist Artur Bordalo, this giant image of a common swift (Latin name *Apus apus*) has been constructed from discarded plastic and metal rubbish.

Narodziny Dnia (The Birth of Day; Map p88; ul Wieckowskiego 4; 🚌 Zachodnia-Więckowskiego) A courtyard covered in the fantastical imaginings of Polish artist Wojciech Siudmak – imps, harlequins and brightly coloured birds.

Pasaż Róży (Rose's Passage; Map p88; ul Piotrkowska 3; 🚌 Legionów-Zachodnia) The work of designer Joanna Rajkowska, a typical Łódź courtyard passage has been completely lined with mirror fragments arranged in swirling floral patterns; truly spectacular.

Rubinstein Mural (Map p88; cnr Sienkiewicza & Traugutta; 🚌 Narutowicza-Kilińskiego) This colourful 2014 mural captures the impish sense of humour of Łódź' most famous son, the classical pianist Artur Rubinstein (1887–1982).

Untitled (Map p88; ul Roosevelta 5; 🚌 Piotrkowska Centrum) A collaboration between Brazilian muralists Osgemeos and Spanish street artist Aryz, this weird and wonderful artwork displays a mating of styles.

Weasels (Map p88; ul Nowomiejska 5; 🚌 Północna-Nowomiejska) A crowd-pleasing gaggle of weasels cavort on the side of a building in this mural by ROA.

➡ **Łódź In Your Pocket** The free city guide has an excellent ghetto walking tour.

➡ **www.lodz-ghetto.com** A comprehensive historical website.

➡ **Field Guide to Łódź** (www.taube philanthropies.org/files/assets/pdf/2017/FieldGuide-Lodz-FINAL.pdf) A superb downloadable guide with walking tours.

🎇 Festivals & Events

⭐ **Łódź Design Festival**   CULTURAL
(www.lodzdesign.com; ☉ May) Major international design fair celebrates myriad forms of design such as graphic, industrial, architecture, fashion, art and more. There are competitions and shows across the city for a week. At night there are concerts and performances.

Fotofestiwal   PHOTOGRAPHY
(www.fotofestiwal.com) Held annually from May to June, this is one of Poland's most prominent festivals of photography and visual arts.

Łódź Four Cultures Festival   PERFORMING ARTS
(www.4kultury.pl; Wojska Polskiego 83, Park Ocalałych; ☉ Sep; 🚌 Wojska Polskiego-Głowackiego) Theatre, music, film and visual arts festival held each year celebrating the city's historic role as a meeting place of four cultures: Polish, Jewish, Russian and German.

🛏 Sleeping

Music Hostel   HOSTEL €
(Map p88; ☎ 53 353 3263; www.music-hostel.pl; ul Piotrkowska 60; dm 35-55zł; r 100-130zł; 🅿 🛜; 🚌 Kościuszki-Zielona) Enter through the passageway at ul Piotrkowska 60 and walk to the back of the courtyard to find this small and hip hostel. The theme here is music, with albums and posters of Hendrix, the Beatles and others on the walls. There are 30 beds across six light, airy rooms that feature wooden bunks and big windows.

Tobaco Hotel   BOUTIQUE HOTEL €€
(☎ 42 207 0707; www.hoteltobaco.pl; ul Kopernika 64; r 165-350zł; 🅿 ✳ 🛜; 🚌 Kopernika-Tobaco Park) Channeling Łódź' industrial heritage, this former two-storey cigarette factory juxtaposes bare red brick and patches of concrete with bold modern lines and designer colour schemes. Rooms are neat and functional rather than luxurious, and guests have use of a fitness room and terrace. Piotrkowska is a mere 10 minutes away by tram.

Hotel ibis Łódź Centrum   HOTEL €€
(Map p88; ☎ 42 638 6700; www.accorhotels.com; Piłsudskiego 11; r from 200zł; 🅿 ✳ 🛜; 🚌 Piotrkowska Centrum) This modern, six-storey chain hotel has a soaring atrium lobby and perfectly

functional rooms. Its advantages are availability of rooms when other places are booked and an ideal location. Ask for a corner room (they end in 01 and 15) on a high floor for great views of the city. Excellent service for travellers on business.

Good Time Aparthotel
APARTMENT €€

(Map p88; ☑ 42 207 3232; http://good-time. com.pl; ul Piotrkowska 120; apt 150-400zł; P🗗; 🗗 Kościuszki-Zamenhofa) Spacious studios and one-bedroom apartments, all with kitchen facilities. The bare wood floors are restored as is the rest of this vaguely elegant 19th-century heritage building in a fine location. The decor is all primary colors, slightly muted to provide a sense of peace. No elevator; the entrance is off a courtyard.

City Center Rooms
HOTEL €€

(Map p88; ☑ 78 608 0808; www.citycenterrooms. pl; ul Piotrkowska 91; s/d from 200/250zł; P🗗; 🗗 Kościuszki-Struga) Reasonably priced accommodation in an excellent location just off the main drag, with entry via a pleasant courtyard. Rooms are clean and bright, with modern furnishings, and come with extras such as electric kettles. Some rooms have kitchenettes for self-catering; ask for these when booking.

Grand Hotel
HOTEL €€

(Map p88; ☑ 42 633 9920; www.grand.hotel.com. pl; ul Piotrkowska 72; s/d from 180/200zł; P🗗; 🗗 Kościuszki-Zielona) If you enjoyed *The Grand Budapest Hotel* movie, this local landmark is the place for you. Established in 1888, this once-opulent hotel has been undergoing a (very) gradual renovation since 2010. The lobby and corridors exude a faded grandeur, and the extravagant former ballroom is a wonder to behold. Bedrooms, while comfortable, are undistinguished. Some lifts may not work.

Revelo
HOTEL €€

(☑ 42 636 8686; www.revelo.pl; ul Wigury 4/6; r from 250zł; P🗗; 🗗 Piotrkowska-Żwirki) A restaurant with rooms mixing old and new in a beautiful villa dating from 1925. Staff greet you dressed in 1920s outfits and lead you up dark-wood stairs (no lift) to immaculate rooms with period furniture, brass bedsteads and thoroughly modern bathrooms. Downstairs is a good restaurant and attached garden. With only six rooms, it's best to book ahead.

★ Vienna House Andel's Łódź
HOTEL €€€

(Map p88; ☑ 42 279 1000; www.viennahouse. com; ul Ogrodowa 17; r 400-600zł; P✳🗗🗗; 🗗 Zachodnia-Manufaktura) Part of the red-brick 19th-century Manufaktura factory complex, this postmodern palace easily qualifies as Łódź' poshest hotel. The sleek lobby wows on entry, as do the curvy designer chairs. Rooms are contemporary, with stylish bathrooms containing big tubs. There are on-site restaurants and a pool. Many Łódź highlights are just a short walk away.

🍴 Eating

Pączkarnia Nadziany Pączek
BAKERY €

(Map p88; ☑ 66 447 7277; Piotrkowska 7; doughnut from 3zł; ⊙ 9am-6pm; 🗗 Pomorska-pl Wolność) Throw open a window, let the smell of freshly fried dough out and you can bet a line of smiling Poles will quickly form hoping for a *nadziany pączek* (filled doughnut). This small shop is a couple of cuts above the norm; yes, the doughnuts are still hot, but the fillings are high quality and everything is made with care. Don't delay, join the queue.

★ OFF Piotrkowska Center
FOOD HALL €€

(Map p88; ☑ 42 272 3072; www.offpiotrkowska. com; ul Piotrkowska 138/140; 🗗 Piotrkowska Centrum) Created on the site of a former cotton mill, these old brick factory buildings bring together artists, designers, architects, boutiques, bars, clubs, cafes and restaurants. Stroll, browse, grab a drink or a meal. There's a great stall with ramen on the Piotrkowska side, but explore your options as there are many and they're both varied and good.

Mitmi Restobar
BISTRO €€

(Map p88; ☑ 50 852 3566; www.facebook.com/ MITMIrestobar; Off Piotrkowska, ul Piotrkowska 138/140; mains 25-50zł; ⊙ noon-10pm Sun-Thu, to 11pm Fri & Sat; 🗗 Piotrkowska Centrum) Modern Polish cuisine at its best. This wildly popular bistro is always packed with diners enjoying the seasonal menu of dishes sourced locally. Choices range from casual to elaborate, from burgers to duck. The phrase sous vide appears. It's got an energetic casual vibe: the space is all bare wood and exposed brick. Good wine list; book ahead.

Anatewka
JEWISH €€

(Map p88; ☑ 42 630 3635; www.anatewka.com; ul 6 Sierpnia 2; mains 29-69zł; ⊙ 11am-11pm; 🗗 Kościuszki-Zielona) This old-style, woodsy restaurant is often packed with diners eager to sample excellent roast duck and goose dishes. The atmosphere is warm and convivial, and the dining experience is rounded off with live music some nights. Don't miss anything with mushrooms, especially the soups. Big outside terrace in summer.

Zakład Gastronomiczny POLISH €€

(Map p88; ☑ 51 192 0018; http://zakladgastrono miczny.com.pl; Piotrkowska 22; mains 15-48zł; ⊙ 9am-8pm; 🖬 Zachodnia-Próchnika) The food is nominally Polish but it's influenced by many of its EU cousins – not a bad thing. The simple breakfast plate of scrambled eggs with bacon is typical of the fare at this simple bistro: perfectly prepared with lovely little touches. Croissants come with organic honey. Lunch and dinner feature creative fare such as roast duck with beets *and* gnocchi.

Otwarte Drzwi ITALIAN €€

(Map p88; ☑ 50 285 5779; www.otwarte-drzwi.com; ul Piotrkowska 120; mains 19-38zł; ⊙ noon-10pm Mon-Thu, to 11pm Fri & Sat, to 9pm Sun; 🖫 🖬; 🖬 Kościuszki-Zamenhofa) Head through the passage at Piotrkowska 120 and on the left you'll find the outdoor seating area belonging to this cosy Italian restaurant. The wood-fired pizzas are thin and crisp, pasta dishes span the gamut of faves, and service is swift and smiling. Gets crowded at weekends.

★ **Quale Restaurant** INTERNATIONAL €€€

(Map p88; ☑ 72 312 3130; https://quale restaurant.pl; Narutowicza 48; set menu 180zł, mains 40-82zł; 🖬 Narutowicza-pl Dąbrowskiego) Fine dining in Łódź: this elegant restaurant sets a gracious tone from the moment you set foot on the marble floor. The menu changes regularly, but always features classic Polish foods such as goose, duck, pork and trout, prepared in exquisite ways. The tasting menu is never the same twice and is great value for its quality and presentation.

Polka POLISH €€€

(Map p88; ☑ 42 630 3530; http://lodz.restauracja polka.pl; Manufaktura, Ogrodowa 19a; mains 40-70zł; ⊙ 11am-10pm; 🖬; 🖬 Zachodnia-Manufaktura) The over-the-top twee decor here is what might result if your spinster aunt took acid. But it shouldn't be a surprise given that Polka is the brainchild of flamboyant Polish TV personality and chef Magda Gessler. The menu is a greatest hits of local foods – expect potatoes, cabbage, pork and more in myriad forms. Everything is well prepared and service is polished.

Affogato FUSION €€€

(Map p88; ☑ 42 630 0300; www.affogato.pl; ul Piotrkowska 144; mains 36-78zł; ⊙ 1-10pm Tue-Thu, to midnight Fri & Sat, to 7pm Sun; 🖫; 🖬 Piotrkowska Centrum) Towards the southern end of ul Piotrkowska, this place combines slick decor with a creative menu that takes the best of Polish produce – mushrooms, pork, trout, game, beetroot – and gives it the fusion treatment, adding French, Italian and Mediterranean flavours. Drink your way through the creative cocktail menu in the well-lit bar.

🍷 Drinking & Nightlife

★ **Z Innej Beczki** CRAFT BEER

(Map p88; ☑ 72 013 1313; www.facebook.com/wielo kran.z.innej.beczki; ul Moniuszki 6; ⊙ 5pm-midnight Sun-Thu, 3pm-2am Fri & Sat; 🖫; 🖬 Kilińskego-Przystanek mBank) Tucked away unexpectedly to the side of the crumbling concrete facade of the YMCA, this mellow bar and tree-shaded beer garden feels like a secret hideaway, concealed in the basement of a 19th-century villa. It's one of the city's best pubs, with over a dozen taps dispensing a range of Polish and international craft beers.

★ **Łódź Kaliska** CLUB

(Map p88; ☑ 42 630 6955; ul Piotrkowska 102; ⊙ 5pm-2am Mon-Thu, to 6am Fri & Sat; 🖫; 🖬 Kościuszki-Struga) With its open-door policy, this renowned pub/club attracts a broad cross-section of Łódź society. The unusual decor – stripped-back walls covered in cheeky suggestive photos from the bar's namesake group of conceptual artists – fits well with the dim red lighting and boho atmosphere. In summer the crowds spill onto an outdoor terrace above the alley, under a web of lightbulbs above.

Brick Coffee Factory COFFEE

(Map p88; ☑ 57 063 0136; www.facebook.com/ thebrickcoffeefactory; ul Piotrkowska 136; ⊙ 8am-8pm Sun-Thu, to 9pm Fri & Sat; 🖫; 🖬 Kościuszki-Zielona) This small but stylish cafe, with massive timber slabs for tables and counters, serves the best coffee on Piotrkowska. There's nitro cold brew on the menu as well as the usual suspects. It's so polished you might think this is a chain, but it's not.

Pop'n'Art PUB

(Map p88; ☑ 78 608 4343; www.facebook.com/pop artodz; plac Wolności 6; ⊙ 2pm-1am; 🖬 Pomorska-pl Wolności) An edgy yet relaxed bar popular with mural painters. It's small but has a devoted following who come for the craft cocktails and the live music that ranges from electro to jazz. The snack menu includes the house speciality beloved by one and all: cheese toast.

PiwPaw CRAFT BEER

(Map p88; ☑ 53 473 4117; www.piwpaw.pl; Piotrkowska 147; ⊙ 11am-midnight Sun-Thu, to 2am Fri & Sat; 🖬 Piotrkowska Centrum) Dozens of craft beers and microbrews on tap lure in discerning quaffers. Tall windows allow plenty of good people-watching of the passing Piotrkowska parade. Inside it's exposed Łódź red brick, outside there's a thicket of seasonal pavement tables.

Piotrkowska Klub   BAR
(Map p88; ☑ 42 630 6573; www.97.com.pl; ul Piotrkowska 97; ⊙ noon-10pm Mon-Thu, to 2am Fri & Sat, 1-10pm Sun; ⊞ Kościuszki-Struga) Easily recognisable by the two-storey, wrought-iron-and-glass drinking area that stands outside the front door, this bar has great views up and down its namesake street. Inside it's more sedate, with wood panelling and cosy booths tucked into quiet corners.

☆ Entertainment

**Filharmonia Łódzka
im Artura Rubinsteina**   CLASSICAL MUSIC
(Artur Rubinstein Philharmonic Orchestra of Łódz; Map p88; ☑ 42 664 7979; www.filharmonia.lodz. pl; ul Narutowicza 20/22; ⊙ box office 10am-6pm Mon-Fri; ⊞) Can you go wrong when the orchestra is named for native son Artur Rubinstein? Performances range from chamber music to the full orchestra.

Teatr Muzyczny   THEATRE
(Musical Theatre; Map p88; ☑ 50 724 8564; www. teatr-muzyczny.lodz.pl; ul Północna 47/51; ⊙ box office 11am-6.30pm Tue-Fri, noon-6.30pm Sat, 3-6.30pm Sun; ⊞ Pomorska-Kamińskiego) Stages mostly operettas and musicals; the venue for blockbuster theatrical roadshows.

Teatr Wielki   OPERA
(Grand Theatre; Map p88; ☑ 42 633 3186; www.opera lodz.com; Plac Dąbrowskiego; ⊙ box office noon-7pm Mon-Sat; ⊞ Narutowicza-pl Dąbrowskiego) The city's main venue for opera and ballet also stages festival events and touring shows.

❶ Information

Fabricum (☑ 50 809 2086; www.fabricum.pl; ul Drewnowska 58; ⊙ 9am-5pm Mon-Fri; ⊞ Zachodnia-Manufaktura) Offers guided tours of Łódź and the surrounding region.

Tourist Information Centre (Centrum Informacji Turystycznej; Map p88; ☑ 42 208 8181; www. lodz.travel; ul Piotrkowska 28; ⊙ 9am-7pm Mon-Fri, 10am-6pm Sat, 10am-4pm Sun May-Sep, 9am-6pm Mon-Fri, 10am-6pm Sat, 10am-4pm Sun Oct-Apr; ☎; ⊞ Zachodnia-Więckowskiego) Provides general tourist information; has a number of worthwhile free booklets in English, including several themed walking tours. Staff can help you navigate through Łódź' busy calendar.

❶ Getting There & Away

AIR

Łódź' airport (p420) is 6km southwest of the city centre. It's serviced by Lufthansa (Munich) and Ryanair (London Stansted, East Midlands and Dublin and Athens).

BUS

Łódź Fabryczna bus station (Dworzec autobusowy Fabryczna; Map p88; Aleja Rodziny Poznańskich; ⊞ Dw Łódź Fabryczna) is located next to Łódź Fabryczna train station, but not all bus operators use it; some intercity services depart from the bus terminal outside **Łódź Kaliska train station** (off ul Karolewska; ⊞ Dw Łódź Kaliska) to the west of the city centre.

FlixBus (www.flixbus.com) operates services from Łódź Fabryczna to Warsaw (24zł, two hours, several daily), Poznań (30zł, three hours, several daily), Wrocław (30zł, 3¼ hours, several daily) and Kraków (45zł, 4½ hours, several daily). Book early for lower fares.

Deutsche Bahn (www.bahn.com) operates an overnight bus service between Berlin and Łódź Kaliska (from 15zł to 65zł, 6½ hours).

TRAIN

The city's most central train station, **Łódź Fabryczna** (Dworzec Łódź Fabryczna; Plac Bronisława Sałacińskiego 1; ⊞ Dw Łódź Fabryczna), is architecturally stunning after a massive reconstruction project. There are fast and frequent services to Warsaw (31zł, 1½ hours).

Łódź Kaliska (p93) serves trains to Łowicz (25zł, one hour, hourly), Kraków (80zł, four to five hours, five daily; via Warsaw), Wrocław (from 33zł, five hours, one daily) and Poznań (from 33zł, 4¼ hours, four daily).

❶ Getting Around

For airport transfers, city buses 65A and 65B run from the airport to Łódź Kaliska train station, from where you'll have to transfer to a tram to reach the city centre (4.40zł, 20 minutes, twice hourly). A taxi to the centre will cost about 30zł to 40zł.

Łódź' public transport system includes trams and buses. Buy tickets on board. A ticket becomes valid for a set length of time after you validate it in a device on board, and remains valid for unlimited transfers. Tickets valid for 20/40/60 minutes cost 2.80/3.60/4.40zł; a one-day ticket costs 11zł. One of Europe's best transit deals is the unlimited ride weekend ticket for a mere 10zł. It's good from 6pm Friday to 3am Monday.

Order a taxi through MPT (42 19191) or Merc Radio (42 650 5050); daytime fares start at 6zł plus 2.20zł per kilometre. Uber is active in Łódź. *Riksza* (bicycle rickshaws) ply ul Piotrkowska and cost about 6zł per person per trip (agree to a price in advance).

WORTH A TRIP

ARKADIA & NIEBORÓW

Hiding among the trees in the countryside around 4km southeast of Łowicz are two slices of gentile 17th century Poland.

With its overgrown ruins, peeling pavilions, temples and follies, the landscaped garden at **Arkadia Park** (📷 46 838 5635; www.nieborow.art.pl; off Hwy 70, Arkadia; adult/child 12/8zł; ⊙ park 10am-dusk, Temple of Diana Apr-Oct) is a romantic pagan enclave in a sea of Catholicism. The park was laid out by Princess Helena Radziwiłł in the 1770s as an 'idyllic land of peace and happiness', but after the death of the princess, the park fell into decay. Most of the works of art were taken to nearby **Nieborów Palace** (📷 46 838 5635; www. nieborow.art.pl; ul Aleja Lipowa 35, Nieborów; adult/child 22/13zł, park only 12/8zł, free Mon; ⊙ 10am-4pm Mar, Nov & Dec, 10am-6pm Apr-Oct, park open year-round), now a museum, and the abandoned buildings fell gradually into ruin.

Nowadays, an air of decay only adds to the charm of the place. Tree-shrouded ruins are dotted throughout the park, including a red-brick Gothic House (Domek Gotycki) perched above Sybil's Grotto, a 'Roman' aqueduct, and the impressive Archpriest's Sanctuary (Przybytek Arcykapłana), a fanciful mock ruin dominated by a classical bas-relief of Hope feeding a chimera. The focus of Arkadia is the Temple of Diana (Świątynia Diany), which overlooks a large lake and houses a display of Roman sculpture and funerary monuments.

The stunning Nieborów Palace, a classic example of baroque architecture, was designed by Tylman van Gameren for Cardinal Radziejowski, the archbishop of Gniezno and primate of Poland. In 1774 Prince Michał Hieronim Radziwiłł bought the palace, and he and his wife Helena set about cramming it with as much furniture and works of art as they possibly could. More than half of the palace rooms are devoted to the museum.

Part of the ground floor features 1st-century Roman sculpture and bas-reliefs collected by Helena, and highly unusual black-oak panelling from the late 19th century. The stairwell leading to the 1st floor, with its ornamental Dutch tiles dating from around 1700, is worth the entry fee alone. The grounds around the palace, which thankfully has not been over restored, are serene and worth a wander.

Arkadia and Nieborów are on the Łowicz–Skierniewice road (Hwy 70) and reachable by bus from Łowicz. You can also hike or bike along a specially marked cycling path, known as the 'Prince Bike Trail' (Szlak Książęcy). The blue-marked path runs about 14km and starts at the Stary Rynek in Łowicz, near the entrance to the museum.

Rent bikes from **Cykel** (📷 79 023 3675; https:// rowerycykel.pl; Stary Rynek 1A; bicycle rental per day from 20zł; ⊙ 10am-6pm Mon-Fri, 10am-2pm Sat; 🚇 Zgierska-pl Kościelny), which has a wide range of bikes and offers good weekend deals. Or pick up one of the public bikes (www.lodzkirower publiczny.pl) parked at stations dotted around the city. Register in advance.

Łowicz

POP 28,900

For much of the year Łowicz (*wo*-veech) is close to slipping into a permanent coma, but when **Corpus Christi** (Boże Ciało; ⊙ May or Jun) comes around, it's *the* place to be. The flamboyant procession through town is one of Poland's grandest and oldest celebrations.

For over 600 years **Łowicz Cathedral** (Katedra w Łowiczu; 📷 46 837 3173; www.katedra. lowicz.pl; Stary Rynek 24/30; ⊙ 10am-4pm May-Sep, other times for Mass) was the seat of the archbishops of Gniezno, the supreme Church authority in Poland. A stroll around the centre can take a pleasant hour, more if the cathedral, which has an interior embellished with glittering gold, is open. You can also check out the **museum** (Muzeum w Łowiczu; 📷 46 837 3928; www.muzeumlowicz.pl; Stary Rynek 5/7; adult/child 12/7zł; ⊙ 10am-4pm Tue-Sun) housed in a 17th-century missionary college designed by Dutch architect Tylman van Gameren; its highlight is the former priests' chapel, with its fading baroque frescoes (1695) by Italian artist Michelangelo Palloni.

The town's **Tourist Information Centre** (Centrum Informacji Turystycznej; 📷 46 837 3433; www.lowicz.eu; Stary Rynek 17; ⊙ 9am-5pm) offers rooms for rent above the office and has bike rentals (per hourr/day 6/25zł).

A couple of good places to eat are **Polonia** (📷 46 838 3018; https://lowicz-polonia.pl; Stary Rynek 4; mains 20-40zł, s/d from 140/190zł; ⊙ 10am-11pm; 🛜) with a fine, tree-shaded location overlooking the Stary Rynek (Old Market); and elegant **Powroty** (☑66 200 5658; www.facebook.com/pg/Powroty.Lowicz; Stary Rynek 24/30c; mains 19-32zł; ☺11am-10pm) in the shadow of the cathedral.

❶ Getting There & Away

The **bus station** (ul 3 Maja 1) and **train station** (ul Drorcowa) are near each other, about a five-minute walk east from the Stary Rynek. There are trains to Łódź (20zł, two hours, six daily) and Warsaw (23zł, one hour, hourly).

There are regular bus services to many outlying towns and villages, including hourly buses running to Skierniewice that pass through Nieborów (7zł, 15 minutes). To reach Arkadia, board a bus for Nieborów and ask the driver to stop at Arkadia Park (6zł, 10 minutes).

Płock

POP 120,300

Płock (pwotsk), dramatically perched on a cliff high above the Vistula, has a long history and a pleasing old centre. It also has the remnants of a Gothic castle, a glorious cathedral and the finest collection of art nouveau art and architecture in the country.

Płock was a royal residence between 1079 and 1138 and received its municipal charter in 1237. The city walls were built in the 14th century and the town developed as a wealthy trading centre until the 16th century. The flooding of the Vistula in 1532, when half the castle and part of the defensive walls slid into the river, was merely a portent of further disasters to come, and the wars, fires, plagues and pogroms that struck the town in the following centuries ended its importance. Still frayed at the edges, Płock rewards anyone willing to follow the twists and turns of its long history.

◉ Sights

Most of the main attractions are grouped to the southeast of the Stary Rynek along a picturesque ridge overlooking the Vistula. Plaques in English offer historic details.

To the northwest of the castle stretches the Old Town. At the northern end of ul Grodzka is the Stary Rynek, formerly the heart of 14th-century Płock. Restoration of the city's old treasures is ongoing. Down at the river, much effort is going into creating vast new parks and attractions, including the river pier.

Don't miss the promenade that follows the bluff and the various new walkways linking the Old Town to the riverfront.

★**Cathedral** CHURCH

(Katedra w Płocku; Map p96; ☑24 262 3435; www.katedraplock.pl; ul Tumska; ☺10am-5.30pm Mon-Sat, 2-5.30pm Sun) This 12th-century cathedral is topped with a 16th-century Renaissance dome. Its interior has a number of tombstones and altarpieces, and polychromatic art nouveau frescoes. The royal chapel holds the sarcophagi of two Polish kings, Władysław Herman and his son Bolesław Krzywousty, who lived in Płock during their reigns. Both are in immaculate condition (the tombs, not the kings).

★**Mazovian Museum** MUSEUM

(Muzeum Mazowieckie; Map p96; ☑24 262 4491; www.muzeumplock.art.pl; ul Tumska 8; adult/child 10/5zł, free Thu; ☺10am-5pm Tue-Sun May–mid-Oct, to 4pm mid-Oct–Apr) Two excellent collections in one large museum: on one side there's a stunning array of art-nouveau furniture, decorative items, paintings and glassware that attest to Płock's prewar wealth. Exhibits show the influence of both the florid Parisian style of art nouveau as well as its sterner, more geometric Viennese cousin, Secession. On the other side is a comprehensive history of the region, from an enormous model of 18th-century Płock to the struggles of the communist era.

Museum of Mazovian Jews MUSEUM

(Muzeum Żydów Mazowieckich; Map p96; ☑24 364 8696; http://synagogaplocka.pl; ul Kwiatka 7; ☺10am-5pm Tue-Sun May–mid-Oct, to 4pm mid-Oct–Apr) [FREE] Prior to WWII there were 9000 Jews living in and around Płock. Most were killed by the Nazi Germans. Among their legacies is this small synagogue building that is now a museum tracing the history of this once vibrant community. This part of town was the heart of the Jewish ghetto before it was liquidated in 1941.

River Pier PIER

(Rzeka Molo; Map p96; ul Rybaki) Watch the Vistula laze by from one of Europe's longest river piers (358m). Part of the vast post industrial rehabilitation of the riverfront, this glassy construct is the dock for cruise boats in summer. Have a drink at the seasonal cafe at the tip.

Castle CASTLE

(Map p96; ul Tumska) The picturesque remnants of this 13th-century Gothic castle are courtesy of a major flood of the Vistula in

Płock

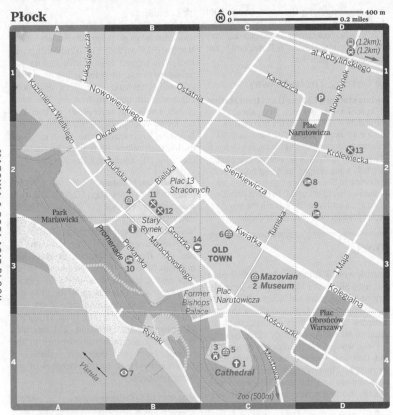

N 0 —— 400 m
0 —— 0.2 miles

Płock

1532, when half the castle and part of the walls slid into the river.

The iconic features of Płock are the last vestiges of the castle, two red-brick towers: the **Clock Tower** (Wieża Zegarowa) and the **Noblemen's Tower** (Wieża Szlachecka). You'll have to gaze at them from the promenade and park, as they are not open to the public.

City Hall　　　　　HISTORIC BUILDING
(Ratusz; Map p96; Stary Rynek 1) The old market square is dominated by this attractive building at its northwest end. From atop the town hall, a trumpeter plays at noon and 6pm each day. As an added spectacle for the noon event, a mechanical King Władysław Herman knights his son Bolesław Krzywousty.

Diocesan Museum
MUSEUM

(Muzeum Diecezjalne; Map p96; ☑ 24 262 2623; www.mdplock.pl; ul Tumska 3a; adult/child 16/8zł; ⊙ 10.30am-2pm Tue-Fri, 10am-4pm Sat) The main collection is in the 16th-century Benedictine abbey building that links the two castle towers. Exhibits include a large collection of manuscripts, paintings, sculpture, vestments and tapestries. Most of the exhibits are religious in nature, such as the 12th-century Płock Bible, but there are a few secular items, including the Charter of Płock from 1237 and some medieval weaponry. There's an annex in the brick building near the cathedral entrance.

🛏 Sleeping

Hostel Kamienica
HOSTEL €

(Map p96; ☑ 24 268 8977; www.hostel-kamienica. pl; ul Tumska 16; dm 90zł, s/d from 170/270zł; P 🕏) Decent budget lodgings in a 19th-century building, a short walk from the Rynek, with colourful dorms and decent private rooms. There's a kitchen, laundry, lockers on the premises, and nearby grocery stores and markets. There are one-, two-, three- and four-bed rooms.

★ Hotel Tumski
HOTEL €€

(Map p96; ☑ 24 262 9060; www.hoteltumski.pl; ul Piekarska 9; r 250-400zł; P ✳ 🕏) Rooms at the city's nicest hotel enjoy sweeping river views. There's much attention to detail here, from the crisp period styling of the rooms to the elegant public spaces. There is a sunny terrace for balmy days. Parking costs 25zł per day.

Hotel Herman
HOTEL €€

(Map p96; ☑ 24 367 0000; https://hotelherman. pl; ul Sienkiewicza 30; r 200-400zł; P 🕏) Small four-star hotel with a garden courtyard with parking. Rooms have a 19th-century motif and all modern accoutrements. Service is good and the location is handy.

🍴 Eating & Drinking

Rynek Market
MARKET €

(Map p96; Królewiecka 19; ⊙ 7am-5pm Mon-Sat) Ages-old tumbledown covered market with dozens of stalls selling produce of the region. Locals prize the honey, strawberries, plums and apples, depending on the season. Also flower stalls and variety shops. Just across the street, the permanent long lines are for the doughnut shop, Stara Pączkarnia. Get 'em while they're hot.

Browar Tumski
POLISH €€

(Map p96; ☑ 24 268 6939; www.browartumski.pl; Stary Rynek 13; mains 18-60zł; ⊙ noon-10pm Sun-Thu, to midnight Fri & Sat; 🕏 ♪) Tasty food served on the main square, with the added benefit of craft beer brewed on the premises. Styles range from light to dark. The menu holds few surprises, with the usual items like pork cutlets, duck and fish, but the list of vegetarian meals is good. Lots of outdoor tables.

Restauracja Art Deco
POLISH €€

(Map p96; ☑ 60 131 1153; http://artdecoplock.pl; Stary Rynek 17; mains 15-45zł; ⊙ 11am-9.30pm) Set in the middle of the sunny side of the Stary Rynek in an ornate 18th-century baroque

MAZOVIA & PODLASIE PŁOCK

WORTH A TRIP

TREBLINKA

In a remote clearing, hidden in a Mazovian pine forest, stands a granite monolith; around it is a small field of 17,000 jagged, upright stones, many engraved with the name of a town or village. Beneath the grass, mingled with the sand, lie the ashes of some 800,000 people. Treblinka, the site of the Nazi Germany's second-largest extermination camp after Auschwitz-Birkenau, is an indelible part of the Holocaust. The **memorial** (Muzeum Walki i Męczeństwa; https://muzeumtreblinka.eu; off Hwy 627; ⊙ site 24hr, museum 9am-6.30pm) includes a small museum; the entire site is rarely crowded.

Between July 1942 and August 1943, on average more than 2000 people a day, mostly Jews, were brought to Treblinka II, as the extermination camp was known, in trains of boxcars. Most lived less than an hour after they arrived. Following an insurrection by inmates working as slaves in August 1943, the extermination camp was demolished. The area was ploughed over and the trees you see today were planted. Realisation of Treblinka's significance happened slowly after WWII, and the current memorial dates to the 1960s.

Treblinka is an easy day trip from Warsaw, but you'll need your own wheels to visit. It's not on any obvious tourist route but can be reached off the S8 motorway between Warsaw and Białystok. Head south on Hwy 627 for 25km from Ostrów Mazowiecka. From Warsaw the drive will take about 1½ hours.

building, this place has the comfiest outdoor tables on the square, and a menu of Polish favourites, including *czernina staropolska* (duck-blood soup), roast pork, and potato dumplings with pork crackling.

Sempre CAFE
(Map p96; ul Grodzka 9; snacks 10-15zł; ⊙10am-8pm) Colourful cafe on the nightlife strip, serving a range of good cakes and beverages in an interior filled with comfy couches. Good people-watching outside.

❶ Information

Tourist Information Centre (Centrum Informacji Turystycznej; Map p96; ☑24 367 1944; www.turystykaplock.eu; Stary Rynek 8; ⊙9am-5pm Mon-Fri, 10am-4pm Sat & Sun May-Sep, 8am-2pm Mon-Fri Oct-Apr; ☎) Provides a wealth of information on the town and the region.

❶ Getting There & Away

The combined **train and bus station** (ul Chopina) is nearly 2km northeast of the Old Town, in a colourful modern building that looks as though it was built from Lego bricks. Though buses are the speedier option, there are 10 trains each day to the busy rail hub Kutno (16zł, one hour), from where you can catch onward trains to much of Poland, including Warsaw and Łódź.

There are frequent buses to Warsaw (25zł, two hours) and Łódź (30zł, 2¼ hours).

To get to the centre from the train and bus station, take bus 20 or 26 (2.80zł).

SOUTHERN PODLASIE

Southern Podlasie (pod-*lah*-sheh) fills a large swathe of northeastern Poland, hogging much of the country's border with Belarus. More than any other region in this vast country, it is here that the influence of foreign cultures can be felt the strongest. Onion-shaped Orthodox domes and Belarusian words hint at the next country east. You'll also be witness to remnants of 17th-century Tatar settlements. And echoes of the Jews, who before WWII were up to half of the local population, are still heard.

Despite its varied cultural make-up, the main attraction here is nature. Podlasie literally means 'the land close to the forest', a moniker it has for good reason. A rich pocket of the forest that once covered the region remains within the Białowieża National Park. Southern Podlasie is also home to vast and bird-filled lowland marshes, which fall under the protection of the Biebrza and Narew National Parks.

Białystok

POP 293,400

Białystok (byah-*wi*-stok) is Podlasie's metropolis and a large, busy city. Attractions are limited, but its proximity to the region's national parks makes it a good base, and the historic mix of Polish, Jewish and Belarusian cultures gives it a special atmosphere found in no other Polish city.

During WWII the Germans destroyed the city, murdering more than half its residents, including the once-thriving Jewish community, which had been more than half of the population. Most of the industrial base and central district were obliterated. Postwar reconstruction concentrated on tangible issues such as the recovery of industry, infrastructure and state administration. As you can still see today, historic and aesthetic values receded into the background.

Today Białystok has a fine range of restaurants, cultural institutions and places to stay. On a sunny day the Rynek and Park Pałacowy offer atmospheric interludes amid urban energy fuelled by 50,000 university students.

◉ Sights

The centre of the city and the locus of evening activity is the triangular Rynek Kościuszki, the former market square, with its 18th-century town hall in the middle. The tourist office offers maps with several interesting themed walks around the centre.

★**Branicki Palace** HISTORIC BUILDING
(Pałac Branickich; ☑85 748 5467; www.umb.edu.pl; ul Kilińskiego 1; park free, palace & museums combined ticket adult/child 20/10zł; ⊙park dawn-dusk, palace & museums 10am-5pm Tue-Fri, 9am Sat & Sun) This grand former residence of Jan Klemens Branicki is surrounded by Park Pałacowy. Though he lost to his brother-in-law Stanisław August Poniatowski in the 1764 royal elections, he built a luxurious palace on a scale to rival the king's. Burned down in 1944 by the retreating Germans, the exterior was restored to its 18th-century form, although the interior was largely modernised. The palace now houses a medical university, but you can learn more at two museums.

The manicured gardens are getting more elegant each year courtesy of EU development funds. They are free to enjoy and give Białystok a whiff of Versailles. New exhibits in the palace museum in the basement outline the tortured history of the complex.

Białystok

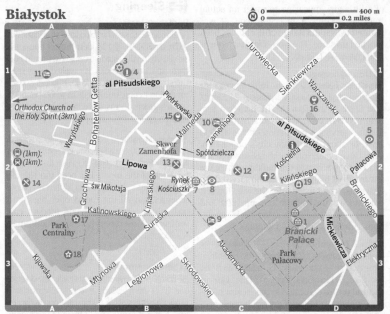

Białystok

◎ Top Sights

◎ Sights

◎ Sleeping

◎ Eating

◎ Drinking & Nightlife

◎ Entertainment

◎ Shopping

Nearby, the **Museum of the History of Medicine & Pharmacy** (Muzeum Historii Medycyny i Farmacji; ☑ 85 748 5467; www.umb.edu.pl; ul Kilińskiego 1; adult/child 12/6zł; ☉ 10am-5pm Tue-Fri, 9am-5pm Sat & Sun) has medical oddities on display and has a couple of rooms meant to evoke the lost beauty of the old palace.

Rynek Kościuszki   SQUARE
Białystok's focal point, the much-rebuilt Rynek is an odd trapezoidal shape. Important buildings from the city's past have been reconstructed here, including the central town hall, home to the **Podlasie Museum** (Muzeum Podlaskie; ☑ 85 740 7731; www.muzeum.bialystok.pl; Rynek Kościuszki 10; adult/child 10/5zł, free Sun; ☉ 10am-5pm Tue-Sun). On the west side of the building, note the plaque with the poignant 1930s photo of the vibrant and largely Jewish market that was once here. It and the people would be gone in a decade.

Girl With a Water Can Mural   PUBLIC ART
(Mural 'Dziewczyna z konewką'; www.behance.net/gallery/11332311/The-legend-of-giants; al Józefa Piłsudskiego 11/4) This four-storey high mural

of a little girl appearing to water an actual tree has become a Białystok icon. It was painted by Natalia Rak in 2013 and has been touched up since. The work's formal name is *The Legend of Giants.*

Cytron Synagogue SYNAGOGUE
(Sleńdziński Gallery; ☎85 651 7670; http://galeria slendzinskich.pl; Ludwika Waryńskiego 24; adult/child 6/3zł; ⊙9am-5pm Mon-Fri, 11am-5pm Sun) Before WWII, central Białystok had 60 synagogues serving a population of over 40,000 Jews, or about half of the city's population. Only three synagogue buildings survived the war, one of which was this building where the few hundred Białystok Jews who survived the Holocaust worshipped after the war. Today it is a branch of the Podlasie Museum (p99) and is used as an art gallery and for special exhibitions. Admission is free on Sundays.

Ludwik Zamenhof Centre CULTURAL CENTRE
(Centrum Ludwika Zamenhofa; www.centrum zamenhofa.pl; ul Warszawska 19; adult/child 8/4zł, free Sun; ⊙10am-5pm Tue-Sun) This vibrant cultural centre dedicated to the creator of Esperanto hosts a range of art exhibitions, concerts, lectures, and performing arts events. Its interesting permanent exhibition, 'The Bialystok of Young Zamenhof', brings to life the multicultural city of the 19th century via sound, light and photography of the era.

Białystok Cathedral CATHEDRAL
(Cathedral Basilica of the Assumption of the Blessed Virgin Mary; ☎85 741 5890; www.katedra bialostocka.pl; Kościelna 2; ⊙6am-7pm) This grand neo-Gothic brick cathedral dates from 1905. It's attached to a late-Renaissance parish church (1627) with a fascinating interior and an 18th-century baroque presbytery. The story goes that the large church was attached to the older church to get around a Russian ban on building new Catholic churches.

Orthodox Church of the Holy Spirit CHURCH
(Cerkiew Św Ducha; ☎72 830 8558; http://swiete goducha.cerkiew.pl; ul Antoniuk Fabryczny 13; ⊙office 8-11am & 3-5pm Mon-Fri, 8-11am Sat) Begun in the early 1980s, this monumental building is Poland's largest Orthodox church, 3km northwest of the centre. The central onion-shaped dome is topped with a large cross (weighing 1500kg) symbolising Christ, while 12 smaller crosses around it represent the apostles. The spacious interior has a spectacular main iconostasis and a fantastic chandelier. Bus 5 from ul Sienkiewicza stops nearby. Stop into the office or call the church to get access.

Sleeping

Podlasie Hostel HOSTEL €
(☎85 652 4250; www.hostelpodlasie.pl; al Piłsudskiego 7b; dm 28-34zł; 📶) Modern hostel housed in an old-style villa, incongruously set amid concrete apartment blocks (it's tucked away from the street behind block No 7). It offers accommodation in pine bunk beds in wood-panelled, seasick-green dorms of six to 16 beds, with a kitchen and 24-hour reception.

★**Hotel Branicki** HOTEL €€
(☎85 665 2500; www.hotelbranicki.com; ul Zamenhofa 25; r from 270zł; P❄📶) Posh and romantic. Each of the rooms has been individually designed and decorated in different colour schemes, but all the rooms offer big comfy beds, thick cotton sheets and modern conveniences. Most rooms have air-conditioning. It's located near the Rynek. Guests love the sprawling breakfast buffet.

Esperanto Hotel HOTEL €€
(☎85 740 9900; www.hotelesperanto.net; ul Legionowa 10; r from 250zł; P❄📶) Comfortable modern hotel with a restaurant on the premises, located a quick walk from the Rynek on the edge of the Branicki Palace grounds. Superior rooms are worth the upgrade: they're large and have sofas. Some rooms have balconies with airy views. There's underground parking.

Eating

Astoria POLISH €
(☎85 665 2150; http://astoriacentrum.pl; ul. Sienkiewicza 4; mains 8-15zł; ⊙9am-8pm) Adjoining posher options under the same name, this is a milk bar for the modern age. The decor is chipper, the servers engaging, kind and helpful. The food is pure Polish 101, with all the classics prepared well and priced cheap. Grab a tray, point at what you want and enjoy local comfort food at its best.

★**Sztuka Mięsa** POLISH €€
(☎85 742 0740; http://sztukamiesa.com.pl; ul Krakowska 11; mains: 21-48zł; ⊙9am-10pm Mon-Fri, noon-11pm Sat, noon-8pm Sun) Leading Polish cuisine to the next level, this excellent restaurant works with a range of local providers to serve superb dishes featuring local meats. The owners worked in top restaurants in the most Polish of American cities, Chicago. Their signature pork chop is among the best anywhere, their burger possibly Poland's best. Service is sharp and unfussy. Booking is essential.

Babka
EASTERN EUROPEAN €€

(☑ 69 027 3707; ul Lipowa 2; mains 20-45zł; ⊙ 11am-10pm) Brightly lit, with sprightly service and decorated with colourful regional motifs, Babka has a good 'greatest hits' menu of eastern European fare. A little Jewish here, a little Polish there amid a sprinkling of Belarusian. Servers are charming; great location on the Rynek.

🍷 Drinking & Nightlife

Gram Off On
PUB

(☑ 78 293 2228; www.facebook.com/kawiarnia.gram offon; ul Icchoka Malmeda 17; ⊙ noon-midnight) Everything you want in a cheery local pub: great regional microbrews, savvy bartenders, lots of comfy seating inside and out, games to play and decent snacks. Don't miss the local spruce beer from Browar Markowy. Despite the address, the pub faces ul Piotrkowska.

Zmiana Klimatu
CLUB

(☑ 576 907 106; www.zmianaklimatu.eu; ul Warszawska 6; cover 10-20zł; ⊙ 8pm-4am Fri & Sat) Very democratic! That's how locals describe this dance club popular with Białystok's masses of students (although the demo is all ages). Wear your hoodie or your best frock. The sound ranges from rock to rap to R&B to techno and beyond. Many nights there's live music and dance troupes.

☆ Entertainment

Opera i Filharmonia
Podlaska
OPERA, CLASSICAL MUSIC

(Podlasie Opera and Philharmonic; ☑ 85 732 2331; www.oifp.eu; ul Podleśna 2; tickets 20-60zł; ⊙ box office 9am-6pm Mon-Fri) From a distance, this huge venue looks either like a prison or something left behind by the Soviet military, despite its pretty park-like setting. But the performances within are top-notch, with good music and opera on offer throughout the year. It's home to the Białystok Symphony Orchestra.

Białostocki Teatr Lalek
THEATRE

(Białystok Puppet Theatre; ☑ 85 742 5033; www. btl.bialystok.pl; ul Kalinowskiego 1; tickets 15-40zł; ⊙ box office 8am-noon Tue & Wed, to noon & 3.30-7pm Thu & Fri, 3.30-7pm Sat; performances Sep-Jun) One of Poland's best puppet theatres (among just a few!), this venue stages children's shows, such as *Pinocchio* or *Punch & Judy*, as well as traditional Polish stories. It also stages some wildly inventive works aimed at adults – although everything is usually in Polish.

LGBTQ ISSUES

In July 2019 Białystok's first LGBTQ pride parade turned violent when thousands of protestors first tried to break up the parade and then assaulted some of those marching. Since then, local people report that they do not feel safe exhibiting any behavior or clothing that would identify them as a part of the LGBTQ community or as a supporter. Visitors should know that even rainbow imagery can cause a hostile reaction from some people.

🛍 Shopping

Sljedzik
GIFTS & SOUVENIRS

(☑ 739 001 001; http://sljedzik.pl; ul Kilińskiego 13; ⊙ 10am-6pm Mon-Sat, 10am-4pm, Sun, Apr-Sep) Several cuts above the typical souvenir joint, this fascinating shop is filled with artful handicrafts, foodstuffs unique to the region, local microbrews, items bearing the delightful image of the 'girl with watering can' mural, maps, guidebooks and much more. Ask about the herring paraphernalia. Note: despite the address, the entrance is on the building's backside off Plac Jana Pawłall.

ℹ Information

Tourist Office (☑ 85 879 7149; www.odkryj. bialystok.pl; Kościelna 1a; ⊙ 8am-4pm Mon-Fri) The city tourist office has a huge amount of information in English, including some excellent themed walking tours. However, the office is not really set up to help beyond giving out materials. In years past, there was a summer-only office in the gatehouse at Branicki Palace, but its future is not assured.

ℹ Getting There & Away

The modern **bus station** (www.pks.bialystok.pl; ul Bohaterów Monte Cassino 10) is surrounded by a bevy of shacks selling snacks. In contrast, the elegant and historical **train station** (Kolejowa 9) dates to 1862 when it was built for the Warsaw to St Petersburg line. Both are near each other about 1.5km west of the city centre and are connected by a pedestrian overpass.

BUS

There are frequent buses to Warsaw (28zł, 2½ hours) and Augustów (14zł, 1½ hours). Other long-haul destinations include Lublin (40zł, 4½ hours, two daily) and Gdańsk (74zł, nine hours, two daily). Buses to Grodno, in Belarus, depart several times a day (40zł, three hours).

TRAIN

The main intercity trains serve Warsaw (30zł, 2½ hours, several daily). There are six trains daily to Suwałki (15zł, two hours) via Augustów (14zł, 1½ hours).

Trains cross the border to Grodno in Belarus (28zł, 2½ hours, one daily). Book this journey online via the Belarusian Railway site (www.rw.by) or buy the ticket at the station. From Friday to Monday, there are trains to Kaunas in Lithuania (48zł, five hours), where you can easily connect to Vilnius.

🛈 Getting Around

From the stations you can walk to the centre in 25 minutes, but the route will only appeal to fans of Soviet-era architecture. Take bus 1, 2 or 4 from the train station or bus 100 from the bus station to reach the centre. The fare is 3.50zł payable to the driver.

Tykocin

POP 2000

Jews arrived in Tykocin (ti-ko-cheen) in the 16th century, and their community grew to define the town's character for the next four centuries. But the slaughter of the town's Jewish residents in the summer of 1941 has defined the town ever since.

On 25 August, shortly after Nazi Germany declared war on the Soviet Union, the Germans called the town's nearly 2000 Jewish residents to the Rynek, from where they were taken to the Łopuchowo Forest, about 8km west of Tykocin, and shot. They were buried in mass graves.

Today, it's fair to say that Tykocin has never recovered from the massacre. In 1950, owing to the loss of half of its population, it was deprived of its town charter, to become an ordinary village. It recovered its charter in 1994, but remains a sleepy backwater. An unmissable site, Poland's grandest surviving synagogue, recalls all that was lost.

◉ Sights

Tykocin is relatively compact. The eastern section of town was the traditional Catholic part, centred on Plac Czarnieckiego and the 1750 Church of the Holy Trinity.

The Jewish section is 500m to the west, beyond the Rynek. Here you'll find the former synagogue. About 500m further west is the old Jewish cemetery (Cmentarz Żydowski), though today it's nothing more than an abandoned field with a few headstones popping up through the weeds.

★ **Tykocin Museum** MUSEUM
(Muzeum w Tykocinie; 🕿 85 718 1613; www. muzeum.bialystok.pl; Sokołowska 5; adult/child 16/8zł; ⊗ 10am-6pm Tue-Sun May-Sep, 10am-5pm Tue-Sat Oct-Apr) Tykocin's former synagogue, erected in 1642, is considered to be the best-preserved Jewish house of worship in Poland and is an extraordinary window into a lost culture. Much of the original interior has been preserved and reconstructed. Adjacent to the former prayer room is a small exhibition containing photos and documents of Tykocin's Jewish community and objects related to religious ritual, such as elaborate brass and silver *hanukiahs* (candelabras), Talmudic books and liturgical equipment.

In 2018, a comprehensive restoration of the exterior was completed. The synagogue's original 17th-century colours of deep pink and turquoise were restored.

Standing opposite the synagogue, the small **Talmudic House** (ul Kozia 2) dates to 1772. It houses an annex of the museum and is where you buy tickets. The permanent exhibition recreates the life and work of Zygmunt Bujnowski, a local painter who achieved some fame before his death in 1927. There is also a reconstructed one-room pharmacy and various special exhibitions. The audio guide is essential for bringing these exhibits to life.

🛏 Sleeping & Eating

Villa Regent HOTEL €
(🕿 85 718 7476; www.villaregent.eu; ul Sokołowksa 3; s/d from 120/140zł; P 🕏) Standing just east of the old synagogue, this good-value hotel offers the best accommodation in town. The rooms are old fashioned in a cozy way and are well appointed. The restaurant is good, serving a mix of traditional Jewish and Polish cooking.

★ **Kiermusy Dworek Nad Łąkami** RESORT €€
(🕿 85 718 7444; www.kiermusy.com.pl; Kiermusy 12, Kiermusy; s/d from 150/180zł; P 🕏) This relatively isolated resort, about 4km west of Tykocin in Kiermusy village, defies easy description. It's part traditional inn and part bungalow accommodation, though the bungalows border on luxurious. The inn is decorated in traditional style, while the houses have a distinctive rustic look. The on-site tavern, **Karczma Rzym** (mains 16-35zł; ⊗ noon-10pm), is worth seeking out even if you're not staying here.

WORTH A TRIP

JEDWABNE

Those prone to mystical thoughts could be forgiven if they claim to hear cries of anguish from the ground in this part of Poland. Virtually every village was the scene of unimaginable horror as whole communities were rounded up and murdered during WWII. Jedwabne, 40km west of Tykocin, is no exception.

On July 10, 1941, over 300 local Jews were rounded up and marched into a barn near the Rynek. The doors were locked and the barn was set on fire, incinerating the people inside. In the years since, a small **memorial** (Pomnik Pogromu w Jedwabnem; ul Krasickiego) was built on the spot. It includes charred wood from the barn and is within sight of the steeples of the town's Catholic church.

For years the memorial sat in obscurity. Historians were in wide agreement that the Jews' Catholic neighbours had organised the killings. However, the ruling Polish Law and Justice Party has made it a crime to suggest any Polish complicity in the Holocaust and there have been efforts to rewrite history to say that Germans forced the Poles to do the killings. It was even suggested that the memorial be dug up to somehow find evidence exonerating the Poles (a suggestion that brought a strong rebuke from Israel).

Meanwhile, nearly eight decades on, the memorial remains, at least for now. It abuts an open field just 650m from the Rynek.

★ **Restauracja Tejsza** JEWISH €
(☑ 85 718 7750; http://tejsza.eu; ul Kozia 2; mains 9-20zł; ⊙10am-6pm Mon-Fri) In the basement of the Talmudic House (enter from the back), this basic eatery serves excellent and inexpensive home-cooked kosher meals, including some fine pierogi and homemade *kuglem* and *kreplech,* a tasty beef and dumplings dish. There's an outdoor seating area. Save room for dessert.

❶ Getting There & Away

Tykocin is served by regular buses from Białystok (48zł, 35 minutes); buses stop at the Rynek, 100m from the old synagogue.

Biebrza National Park

Biebrza National Park (Biebrzański Park Narodowy; ☑ 85 738 0620; www.biebrza.org.pl; Osowiec-Twierdza 8, Goniądz; adult/child 8/4zł) is Poland's largest, stretching more than 100km from the Belarus border to the Narew River near Tykocin. Established in 1993, Biebrza (*byehb-zhah*) is an important preserve, protecting the Biebrza Valley, Central Europe's largest wetlands and natural bog.

The varied landscape has a serenity across its open and untouched swathes of nature. River sprawls, peat bogs, marshes and swampy forests are home to seas of reeds, moss and medicinal herbs. Inhabitants include wolves, wild boar, foxes, roe deer, otters and beavers. About half of the country's elk population, around 600

animals, live here. Birdwatchers can spot the 270 or so bird species (over half of those in Poland) that call the park home.

You can appreciate the park on a quick outing centred on the village of Osowiec-Twierdza. There are excellent short walks here. More adventurous visitors can enjoy hiking, kayaking and cycling across the park.

◎ Sights & Activities

The park can be divided into three areas: the **Northern Basin** (Basen Północny), the smallest and least-visited area of the park; the **Middle Basin** (Basen Środkowy), stretching along the Biebrza River's broad middle course and featuring a combination of wet forests and boglands; and the equally extensive **Southern Basin** (Basen Południowy), where most of the terrain is taken up by marshes and peat bogs.

Dikes, boulders and dunes among the bogs provide access to some splendid birdwatching sites. The visitor centre in Osowiec-Twierdza can provide maps and information.

The principal water route for kayaking flows from the town of Lipsk downstream along the Biebrza to the village of Wizna. This 140km stretch can be paddled in seven to nine days. Campsites along the river allow for overnight stops, and food is available in towns on the way. You can also paddle along for a few hours or a day and cover part of the route; a handy two-hour stretch runs from Goniądz to Osowiec-Twierdza.

Access to kayak trails costs 8zł for adults and 4zł for students and children per day.

NAREW NATIONAL PARK

This 73 sq km **park** (Narwiański Park Narodowy; ☑85 718 1417; www.npn.pl; Kurowo; adult/child 5/2.50zł) protects an unusual stretch of the Narew River. Nicknamed the 'Polish Amazon' it is where the river splits into dozens of channels that spread out across a 2km-wide valley, forming a constellation of swampy islets in between. Much of it is inaccessible to visitors, though you can kayak on stretches of the river and some of its tributaries.

There's also a network of paths and gravel roads that encircle the park, which can be hiked or biked. There's a good nature hike starting from the **Narew National Park Headquarters** (☑85 718 1417; www.npn.pl; Kurowo; kayak per hour/day 10/35zł, camping per person 10zł; ⊙10am-6pm May-Sep, 7.30am-3.30pm Mon-Fri Oct-Apr) where the helpful staff can provide maps, advise on walks and rent out kayaks and space to pitch a tent.

Kurowo lies 5km south of the town of Stare Jeżewo, which is 30km west of Białystok along the S8 motorway to Warsaw. Stare Jeżewo is serviced by frequent buses from Białystok (12zł, 30 minutes, hourly), but from there you'll have to walk along a 5km dirt track to Kurowo.

You can hire a kayak or canoe at the visitor centre or try **Biebrza Adventure** (☑69 154 0162; www.splywytratwami.pl; Wroceń 44, Goniądz; kayaks/bikes per day from 25/30zł) which also rents bikes for cycling in the park.

★ **Osowiec-Twierdza Boardwalk**   NATURAL FEATURE
(Osowiec-Twierdza) Part of the 9km of walking paths near the visitor centre, this 1km-long boardwalk has sweeping views of the sea of reeds across the marshes and the Biebrza River, especially from the wooden observation tower. It's about 2km northwest of the visitor centre; the path linking the two crosses the river, where there are more good views. Don't miss the moody ruins of the sprawling 19th-century concrete fortifications built by Tsar Alexander III to protect this strategic narrow river crossing.

Red Marsh   NATURAL FEATURE
(Czerwone Bagno; Grzędy) One of Biebrza's most important areas, the Red Marsh (Czerwone Bagno) in the Middle Basin is a strictly protected area of bog forest. A 1km educational trail ends overlooking the marsh, from where you can fully appreciate the natural beauty and if you have great luck, spot one of 400 resident elk. The trail begins near Grzędy; ask at the visitor centre for directions.

🛏 Sleeping & Eating

The area is sprinkled with hotels, hostels and campgrounds. Outside the park, Goniądz is a good place to stay. The park visitor centre has details of the many agritourism options.

Park Campsite   CAMPGROUND €
(☑85 738 3035; www.biebrza.org.pl; Osowiec-Twierdza; adult/child per night 12/6zł; ⊙May-Sep) Just 1.5km northwest of the visitor centre, this campsite is set on a quiet, grassy expanse next to the water. Facilities are limited. Other good park campgrounds with car access are in Grzędy (a gateway to the Red Marsh) and Barwik.

Bartlowizna   HOTEL €€
(☑85 738 0630; http://biebrza.com.pl; ul Nadbiebrzańska 32, Goniądz; s/d from 140/210zł; 🅿🛜) This 55-room complex has a bucolic spot right on the river. Rooms have a woodsy charm. There is a decent restaurant and a deck where you can spot fowl while quaffing a brew.

ℹ Information

Park admission can be paid at the **visitor centre** (☑85 738 0620; www.biebrza.org.pl; Osowiec-Twierdza 8, Goniądz; ⊙7.30am-5pm Mon-Fri, 8am-5pm Sat & Sun May-Sep, 7.30am-3.30pm Mon-Fri Oct-Apr), just 150m from Osowiec-Twierdza train station. The helpful English-speaking staff provide information about the park and its facilities. The centre can hook you up with an English-speaking guide (per hour from 25zł). The office is stocked with excellent maps and brochures on the park. The 1:100,000-scale *Biebrzański Park Tourist Map* (10zł) is among the best, with descriptions of half- and full-day hiking and kayaking trips in English.

ℹ Getting There & Away

Osowiec-Twierdza is 50km northwest of Białystok, and sits on a railway line from Białystok (14zł, 50 minutes, four daily). The park visitor centre is just 150m from the **train station** (Osowiec-Twierdza). Having your own transport is a huge advantage, as you can easily access most of the park's major attractions.

Kruszyniany

POP 200

Close to the Belarusian border to the east and northeast of Białystok, Kruszyniany (kroo-shi-nya-ni) is noted for its timber mosque, which, coupled with the one in **Bohoniki** (Meczet w Bohonikach; ☑ 66 703 7691; www.bohoniki.eu; Bohoniki; adult/child 6/3zł; ⊗8am-7pm May-Sep), are the only surviving historic mosques in Poland. Both were built by the Muslim Tatars who settled here at the end of the 17th century.

The village is an atmospheric setting for the mosque and nearby cemetery. The few streets are quiet, which lets you hear the rustling of the leaves in the birch trees. A good restaurant rewards those who linger. Nearby roads offer beautiful driving through the pastoral countryside.

⊙ Sights

★ Kruszyniany Mosque   MOSQUE
(Meczet w Kruszynianach; ☑ 50 254 3871; www.kruszyniany.com.pl; Kruszyniany; adult/child 5/3zł; ⊗9am-7pm May-Sep, by appointment Oct-Apr) This beautiful green mosque was built by the Muslim Tatars who settled here at the end of the 17th century. It's a rustic wooden construction, in many ways similar to old timber Christian churches. You'll find it hidden in a cluster of trees, set back from the main road. The mosque's modest interior, made entirely from pine, is divided into two rooms; the smaller one is designated for women, who (other than tourists) are not allowed into the main prayer hall.

Mizar   CEMETERY
(Muslim Cemetery) The Muslim cemetery is located in a patch of thick woodland 100m east of the mosque. The recent gravestones are Christian in style, showing the extent of cultural assimilation that has taken place. Go deeper into the wood, where you'll find old tombstones hidden in the undergrowth. Some of them are inscribed in Russian, a legacy of tsarist times.

⌴ Sleeping & Eating

Dworek Pod Lipami   HOTEL €
(☑ 85 722 7554; www.dworekpodlipami.pl; ul Kruszyniany 51, Kruszyniany; s/d from 70/130zł; P ⊙) Lovely manor house with comfortable rooms and friendly staff. Traditional Tatar

MAZOVIA & PODLASIE KRUSZYNIANY

THE TATARS OF POLAND

In the 13th century, large parts of Eastern and Central Europe were ravaged by hordes of fierce Mongol horsemen from Central Asia. These savage nomadic warriors (commonly, though confusingly, referred to as the Tatars) came from the great Mongol empire of Genghis Khan, which at its peak stretched from the Black Sea to the Pacific Ocean.

They first invaded Poland in 1241 and repeatedly overran and destroyed much of Silesia and Małopolska, including the royal city of Kraków. They withdrew from Europe as fast as they came, leaving few traces other than some folk stories. Not long after, the Mongol empire broke up into various independent khanates.

By the end of the 14th century, Poland and Lithuania were facing a different threat, from the Teutonic Knights, who were swiftly expanding southward and eastward. As a measure of protection, Lithuania (which was soon to enter into a political alliance with Poland) began looking for migrants to settle its scarcely inhabited borderlands. To that end, it welcomed refugees and prisoners of war from the Crimean and Volgan khanates, offspring of the once-powerful Golden Horde state ruled by the heirs of Genghis Khan. These new settlers were Muslim Tatars.

The Tatars' military involvement in Polish affairs began in 1410 at the Battle of Grunwald, where King Władysław II Jagiełło defeated the Teutonic Knights; in this battle, a small unit of Tatar horsemen fought alongside Polish-Lithuanian forces. From that time on, the numbers of Tatar settlers grew, and so did their participation in battles to defend their adopted homeland. By the 17th century, they had several cavalry formations to reinforce Polish troops in the many wars of that time.

In 1683, after the victory over the Turks at the Battle of Vienna, Jan III Sobieski granted land in the eastern strip of Poland to those Tatars who had fought under the Polish flag. The Tatars founded new settlements and built their mosques. Of all these villages, only Kruszyniany and Bohoniki have preserved some of their Tatar inheritance, though apart from their mosques and cemeteries not much else remains.

LOGGING BIAŁOWIEŻA?

In recent years Białowieża has been the scene of protests. The Polish government has been attempting to allow logging in and around the reserve. Before the European Court of Justice ordered a halt, large tracts of centuries-old trees were cut down for lumber.

The government argues that infestations of the spruce beetle are killing trees and that the only way to save the forest, essentially, is to cut it down and replant it with oak and ash trees. Conservationists are outraged and there have been mass protests. In 2019 Unesco noted that the forest had been 'disrupted' but that it could return to its wild state if simply left alone.

food and drink from the region are served in its restaurant, such as *babka ziemniaczana* (potato cakes) and *barszcz* (hot beetroot soup).

Tatarska Jurta TATAR €€
(☑ 85 749 4052; www.kruszyniany.pl; Kruszyniany 58, Kruszyniany; mains 15-25zł; ⊙ 11am-6pm) A welcoming Tatar restaurant that serves traditional dishes and wonderful homemade cakes. It's a short walk from the mosque. It was lavishly rebuilt in 2019 after a fire.

❶ Getting There & Away

Kruszyniany is about 50km from Białystok and makes for a good half-day excursion. Take Hwy 65 east almost to Belarus, then turn north. Your own vehicle is best to explore the area but there are buses from Białystok (18zł, 1½ hours, four daily).

Białowieża National Park

Green, lush and mysterious, **Białowieża National Park** (☑ 85 682 9702; www.pttk. bialowieza.pl; adult/child 12/8zł; 🚍 from Hajnówka or Białystok) covers an area of about 105 sq km and is part of a bigger forest known as the Białowieża Forest (Puszcza Białowieska), which straddles the border between Poland and Belarus. Białowieża (byah-wo-*vyeh*-zhah) park is famous for two reasons. First, it's home to the European bison, the continent's largest land mammal.

Second, the park shelters what's considered to be Europe's largest swathe of original lowland forest, known in Polish as *puszcza* (primeval forest). Much of the park has been undisturbed for centuries, leaving a fascinating mix of old- and new-growth forest. It's been designated both a Unesco World Heritage Site and a Biosphere Reserve.

These days, the village of Białowieża is a popular summer weekend destination. People come mainly for the chance to hike, bike

and, possibly, spot a bison (aside from the one on the label of a bottle of Żubr beer).

The park owes its existence largely to royalty. It was a private hunting ground for the Polish monarchs and later for Russian tsars, and as such was protected for centuries by royal patronage. Although much of its royal heritage has been lost, you can still get a whiff of the former grandeur in the rectangular Palace Park (Park Pałacowy).

The current national park dates to 1921. It's divided into three zones: the Strict Nature Preserve (Obręb Ochronny Orłówka), which has old growth that's accessible only under the supervision of a guide; an area of secondary protection (Obręb Ochronny Hwoźna) that does not require a guide and has abundant hiking and biking paths; and several small bison reserves (Ośrodek Hodowli Żubrów).

◉ Sights

★ **Strict Nature Preserve** FOREST
(Obręb Ochronny Orłówka; www.bpn.com.pl; adult/child 6/3zł) This is the oldest section of the Białowieża National Park and covers an area of around 47.5 sq km, bordered to the north and west by the marshy Hwoźna and Narewka Rivers, and to the east by the Belovezhskaya Pushcha National Park in Belarus.

This part of the park can only be entered in the company of an official guide.

Palace Park PARK
(Park Pałacowy; www.bpn.com.pl) Palace Park was laid out in the 19th century around a splendid residence built for the Russian tsar, on the site of an ancient royal hunting lodge once used by Polish kings. The southern entrance to the park, beside the PTTK office, leads across a pond past a stone obelisk, which commemorates a bison hunt led by King August III Saxon in 1752. The royal bag that day was 42 bison, 13 elk and two roe deer.

European Bison
Show Reserve   WILDLIFE RESERVE
(Rezerwat Pokazowy Żubra; ☑ 85 682 9700; www.
bpn.com.pl; off Hwy 689; adult/child 10/5zł;
⊙ 9am-5pm May-Sep, 8am-4pm Tue-Sun Oct-Apr;
🅿) This modern and large enclosed animal
park around 4km west of Palace Park is your
best chance to see an actual bison. Though
the bison died out in the wild in 1919, it's
been successfully reintroduced here and
elsewhere in the park. The reserve holds
several other species in large cages or pens
that are typical of the *puszcza*, including
elk, wild boar, wolves and roe deer.

Nature and Forest Museum   MUSEUM
(Muzeum Przyrodniczo-Leśne; ☑ 85 681 2275;
www.bpn.com.pl; Park Pałacowy; adult/child
15/11zł; ⊙ 9am-4.30pm Mon-Fri, to 5pm Sat & Sun
mid-Apr–mid-Oct, 9am-4pm Tue-Sun mid-Oct–mid-
Apr) Located in the modern visitors centre
and hotel, this museum features exhibitions
relating to the park's flora and fauna (mostly
forest scenes with stuffed animals and a collection of plants), the park's history, and the
archaeology and ethnography of the region.
The viewing tower provides terrific views,
and just north of the museum you will find
a grove of 250-year-old oaks.

🏃 Activities

The starting point for excursions into the
national park is Białowieża village. This is
where you organise visits to the Strict Nature Preserve. Most hotels and pensions in
Białowieża have bikes available for guests.

Maps are available for sale at both the
PTTK office (p108) and the Białowieża National Park Information Centre (p108), as
well as at hotels and shops around Białowieża. The 1:50,000 *Puszcza Białowieska*
map (16zł) has a street plan of Białowieża, and marked cycle and walking paths
through the forest.

If you'd like to explore the park on your
own, the secondary protected zone that
lies largely to the north of the Strict Nature
Preserve, and the vast puszcza, to the west
and north of the park proper, do not require
a guide to enter and are criss-crossed by
hundreds of kilometres of wonderful, well-
marked hiking and cycling paths.

Numerous agencies offer guides into the
Strict Nature Preserve but only a few have
English-speaking guides. Rates are very
similar between the outfits. Guides typically
offer two types of tours. A shorter tour takes
about three hours and covers about 4.5km. A
longer tour lasts about six hours and covers
around 20km.

Most of the guide agencies can also arrange
other tours in the park. On busy weekends,
there are regular group tours with English-
speaking guides, which can be joined easily. Guides usually charge a flat fee, whether
they are leading one or 12 people, so travellers can join up to cut expenses. There are
also per-person entrance fees that can range
from 6zł to 35zł depending on the route.

PTTK   HIKING
(☑ 85 681 2295; www.pttk.bialowieza.pl; ul Kolejowa 17; guided hikes from 260zł; ⊙ 8am-6pm)
Provides guides for a variety of visits to the
Strict Nature Preserve and other parts of the
park. Tours run for up to three hours, with
one to 12 people. Also runs bike trips, which
include time across the Belarusian border,
and organises trips by britzka (horse-drawn
cart) or sledge in winter (from 310zł for four
people) into the preserve and the bison park.

Wild Forest   HIKING
(☑ 60 129 1355; www.wildlifephotography.pl; prices
vary) Run by professional wildlife photographer and biologist Marek Kosinski, this
company specialises in photography hikes
and has its own blinds set up in the park.

MAZOVIA & PODLASIE BIAŁOWIEŻA NATIONAL PARK

ℹ️ HIKING INTO BELARUS

Belarus offers limited visa-free entry to the Belovezhskaya Pushcha National Park on
its side of the border, when crossing by foot or bicycle at the border crossing point 4km
south of Białowieża. Individual visitors must apply ahead of time by following the 'Visa
Free' link at the National Park's website (https://npbp.by/eng).

The special-entry permit lasts for up to three days, and visitors using it are not allowed
to travel further into Belarus without an appropriate visa. Using the website, visitors
agree to a lengthy list of restrictions and rules, then indicate when they will arrive at the
border crossing. Eventually a form is generated, which you print out and present with your
passport at the border. Given that nature doesn't recognise borders, this is an excellent
way to fully explore the forest.

Rent a Bike
CYCLING

(☑66 045 1540; ul Olgi Gabiec 11; bicycle hire per hour/day from 5/35zł) Across the street from Hotel Żubrówka, this agency rents a wide variety of bikes for exploring the national park. It also sells maps.

Biuro Turystyki Ryś
HIKING

(☑85 681 2249; www.turystyka-rys.pl; ul Krzyże 22; English-language guided walks from 220zł) Besides guided hikes, this agent organises winter activities, bonfires and other services, including accordion players.

🛏 Sleeping

In warmer months, the road approaching Białowieża is lined with dozens of signs advertising *pokoje gościnne* (guest rooms) in private homes (per person 40zł to 50zł). There are many guesthouses and hotels. Some are rather luxe, which appeals to the huge numbers of weekenders from Warsaw. Book in advance in summer.

Dworek Gawra
GUESTHOUSE €

(☑85 681 2804; https://gawra.bialowieza.pl; ul Polecha 2; r 100-190zł; P☎) Quiet, cozy place in a woodsy compound just behind the Hotel Żubrówka. It has large rooms lined with timber in a hunting-lodge style, overlooking a pretty garden. Rooms are spread across three different sections, so sizes and facilities vary; some even have their own fireplaces. A large buffet breakfast is 24zł.

★ Wejmutka
GUESTHOUSE €€

(☑85 681 2117; www.wejmutka.pl; ul Kolejowa 1a; s/d from 150/180zł; P☎) Rambling hunting lodge that features a beautiful dining and sitting area, plus cosy rooms. The location is ideal, within easy walking distance of the Palace Park. The guesthouse caters to birdwatchers. It also organises special-interest nature tours as well as seminars and multiday biodiversity events.

BNP Guesthouse
HOTEL €€

(Pokoje Gościnne BPN; ☑85 682 9729; www.noclegi.bpn.com.pl; Palace Park; r 130-200zł; P✳☎) Stay right in the heart of Palace Park in this modern hotel located in the visitor centre. Rooms are contemporary hotel style and are comfortable. There is a shared kitchen area for guest use.

Pensjonat Unikat
GUESTHOUSE €€

(☑85 681 2109; www.unikat.bialowieza.pl; ul Waszkiewicza 39; s/d from 130/150zł; P☎) This timber guesthouse has functional, large rooms, and a good restaurant serving a rural Polish menu of pierogi (dumplings) and venison. It's a comfortable option, about 400m east of the eastern gate of Palace Park. Look for the bison statue out front.

Hotel Żubrówka
HOTEL €€€

(☑85 682 9400; www.hotel-zubrowka.pl; ul Olgi Gabiec 6; r from 360zł; P✳☎☎☎) Białowieża's most central hotel has a big lobby leading to a bar, and a restaurant serving regional dishes. Rooms have luxe touches, and suites have open fireplaces. There's also a spa centre and sauna on-site, accompanied by an indoor swimming pool.

🍴 Eating

Pokusa
POLISH €€

(www.restauracja-pokusa.pl; ul Olgi Gabiec 15; mains 22-40zł; ⊙11am-10pm May-Sep, to 8pm Oct-Apr) Centrally located in a country-style house, this eatery offers creative regional cooking, including good fried fish and many game dishes. Much is sourced locally, including the many varieties of farmhouse cheeses. It's across from the Hotel Żubrówka. There's a small garden at the back.

Carska
POLISH €€€

(☑85 681 2119; www.carska.pl; ul Stacja Towarowa 4; mains 30-90zł; ⊙10am-11pm) Set in a woodsy grove in what was once the tsar's private railway station, 2km southeast of the village centre, this restaurant offers elegant meals amid period antiques. It specialises in game, such as *polędwiczka z dzika* (tenderloin of wild boar). A string of old railroad cars altered to evoke memories of tsarist times has been converted into holiday apartments.

ℹ Information

ATM (ul Stoczek) Near the eastern entrance to Palace Park.

National Park Information Centre (Punkt Informacji Turystycznej BPN; ☑85 681 2901; www.bpn.com.pl; Park Pałacowy; ⊙8.30am-4.30pm) A small office located near the Nature and Forest Museum. Has brochures and maps in English, although for detailed assistance you are better off at one of the agencies.

PTTK Tourist Office (☑85 681 2295; www.pttk.bialowieza.pl; ul Kolejowa 17; ⊙8am-6pm) At the southern entrance to Palace Park; can help arrange guides and accommodation. Sells maps and answers questions in multiple languages from a tiny office.

ℹ Getting There & Away

Transport to this World Heritage site by public transport is complicated. Frequent buses and minibuses (6zł, 30 minutes, half-hourly) connect Białowieża to the larger regional city of Hajnówka, from where you can make onward connections. Buses run hourly from Hajnówka to Białystok (10zł, 1½ hours). Direct Białowieża to Białystok minibuses are operated by Voyager-Trans (14zł, two hours, five daily).

To travel by rail from Hajnówka to Warsaw, there is one daily connection: catch a train to Siedlce (22zł, 2¼ hours) then change to a Warsaw train (23zł, one hour).

There are three bus stops in Białowieża: one at the entrance to the village, one just after Hotel Żubrówka (closest to the PTTK office), and one just past the post office (near the eastern gate of Palace Park).

AUGUSTÓW-SUWAŁKI REGION

Outstanding natural beauty is the hallmark of northern Podlasie, otherwise known as Suwalszczyzna. Large swathes of pristine forest and rugged hills with deep valleys in the north are highlights, but its defining feature is water. Over 200 lakes are laced together with rivers and canals. From spring to autumn, the waters are alive with boats and kayaks.

Like the rest of Poland, the modern population here consists predominantly of Poles, but it was for centuries an ethnic and religious mosaic comprising Poles, Lithuanians, Belarusians, Tatars, Germans, Jews and Russians. Traces of this complex cultural mix can still be found, especially on menus.

Despite its natural beauty and historical ethnic make-up, the region attracts few visitors from outside Poland's borders. It is therefore the perfect place to avoid the summer crowds that swamp the Great Masurian Lakes to the west; find your own peaceful pocket and revel in the watery beauty.

Augustów

POP 30,400

Augustów (aw-*goos*-toof) is a small town straddling the Netta River as it enters Lake Necko. It's the gateway to the Suwałki region and is close to a number of natural wonders.

The town itself has retained little historical character due to WWII – during a two-month battle in 1944, the town switched hands several times and much of it was destroyed. Its history, however, dates back to the time of King Zygmunt II August, who in 1557 founded the town and modestly named it after himself. Despite the strategic location, its development only really began in the 19th century after the construction of the canal bearing the town's name.

AUGUSTÓW CANAL

Built in the 1820s, the Augustów Canal (Kanał Augustowski) is a 104km-long waterway connecting the Biebrza and Niemen Rivers. Linking lakes and stretches of river, it's a picturesque route marked by old locks and floodgates. No longer used commercially, it's now a popular tourist attraction and kayak route.

The canal was built by the short-lived Congress Kingdom of Poland. It was intended to provide the country with an alternative outlet to the Baltic Sea, since the lower Vistula was in the hands of a hostile Prussia. The project aimed to connect the tributaries of the Vistula with the Niemen River and to reach the Baltic at the port of Ventspils in Latvia.

The Polish part of the waterway was designed by an army engineer, General Ignacy Prądzyński, and built in just seven years (1824–30), though final works continued until 1839. The Russians were meant to build their part from the town of Kaunas up to Ventspils around the same time, but the work was never completed.

The Augustów Canal ended up as a regional waterway, and though it contributed to local development, it never became an international trade route. Its route includes 28km of lakes, 34km of canalised rivers and 40km of canal proper. There are 18 locks along the way (14 in Poland), whose purpose is to bridge the 55m change in water level. The lock in Augustów itself has an extra twist to its history: badly damaged in WWII, it was rebuilt in 1947 in a different place.

The whole Polish stretch of the canal is navigable, but tourist boats from Augustów go only as far east as Lake Studzieniczne – the locks beyond this point are inoperative. By kayak, you can continue to the border with Belarus.

Augustów-Suwałki Region

Today, Augustów has the aspirations of a posh resort town that are tempered by a somewhat shabby reality. It shakes off its winter torpor during the busy summer season, when it's a popular weekend escape from Warsaw.

🏃 Activities

Augustów is all about being outside. The city's perch on Lake Necko and its flat terrain make it ideal for biking (there are 281km of bike routes). One of the most enjoyable, family-friendly pedals is to head out along the shoreline of the lake, where a bike trail follows the edge for a few kilometres. Most places to stay have bikes for guests. There are also rental agencies.

There's also swimming – though water temps in summer rarely rise above a bracing 20°C – at the City Beach (Plaża Miejska), north of the centre along the southern shore of Lake Necko.

Kayaking

Kayaking is one of the most popular pursuits in Augustów, whether it be a couple of hours of paddling in Lake Necko or a multiday kayaking expedition along the region's lakes and rivers. Numerous local operators, including many hotels and hostels, offer package tours that run anywhere from a day to two weeks, depending on the river and the operator. Alternatively, kayaks can be hired to head out on your own.

The Czarna Hańcza River is the most popular kayaking destination in the region. The traditional route normally starts at Lake Wigry and follows the river downstream through the Augustów Forest to the Augustów Canal. The trip takes six to eight days, depending on how fast you paddle. Various shorter trips are also available. There are over 340km of mapped kayak routes in the area.

Other rivers used for kayaking trips include the Rospuda (four to six days) and the Biebrza (seven to 10 days); some companies also offer trips to rivers in neighbouring Lithuania (seven days).

Sailboats can be rented from 120zł per day. Proof of skills will be required. The lakes offer ideal conditions.

Szot
KAYAKING

(☎ 87 644 6758; www.szot.pl; ul Konwaliowa 2; kayak rental per day from 26zł, one-day tour from 60zł; ⊙ 9am-5pm Mon-Fri Oct-Apr, 8am-7pm daily May-Sep) Has an excellent selection of guided short and long trips by kayak with English-friendly guides. Also rents kayaks, bikes and gear. Offers lessons. Meeting spots for gear rental and tours at various locations on the waterfront.

Boat Excursions

Large tour boats ply the waters on various itineraries from late spring through early autumn. For a more intimate journey, walk along ul Rybacka on the southern shore of the Netta River (which links the lake to the Augustów Canal) to find various private operators offering custom trips for up to eight people at prices starting at about 25zł per person.

Żegluga Augustowska
BOATING

(☎ 87 643 2881; www.zeglugaaugustowska.pl; ul 29 Listopada 7; boat tours from 30zł; ⊙ 10am-4pm Jul & Aug, to 3pm Apr-Jun, Sep & Oct) Large tour boats ply the surrounding lakes and a part of the Augustów Canal. Boats depart around once an hour. In spring and autumn, the cruises don't run daily. The shortest trips ply Lake Necko and Lake Białe.

Jan Wojtuszko
KAYAKING

(☎ 60 495 8673; www.kajaki.augustow.pl; ul Nadrzeczna 62; kayak rental per hour/day 10/30zł; ⊙ 8am-6pm May-Sep) Family-run enterprise with kayaks, paddleboats and bikes for hire.

🛏 Sleeping & Eating

Hotel Szuflada
HOTEL €€

(☎ 87 644 6315; www.szuflada.augustow.pl; ul Skorupki 2c; r 120-280zł; 🛜) Quality offering just a couple of steps away from the Rynek, but within easy walking distance of the lake. Rooms are above the Szuflada Bistro one of Augustów's better restaurants. The decor is simple but some rooms have small balconies. Very good value.

★ Hotel Warszawa
HOTEL €€€

(☎ 87 643 8500; www.hotelwarszawa.pl; ul Zdrojowa 1; r 270-550zł; 🅿🔄🛜♨) A resort hotel with plenty of trimmings such as a restaurant, a bar, a sauna, bikes and boats. Rooms are suitably comfortable and colourfully decorated. The four-storey complex is discreetly hidden among trees near the lake. The city centre is about 2km away, either by foot along a busy road or following a more looping – and picturesque – path along the lake's perimeter.

★ Tawerna Fisza
POLISH €€

(☎ 73 002 3730; www.facebook.com/Tawerna Fisza; ul Rybacka 19; mains 27-43zł; ⊙ noon-10pm Mon-Sat, to 8pm Sun; 🍴) The most creative restaurant in town has a fine waterfront location next to a park. Tables and wicker seats sprawl all over outside in summer and there's a small playground. The menu features regional ingredients that vary by the season. Expect meaty mains and many seafood choices.

Szuflada Bistro
POLISH €€

(☎ 87 644 6315; www.szuflada.augustow.pl; ul Skorupki 2c; mains 13-45zł; ⊙ 11am-11pm; 🛜) One of Augustów's best year-round restaurants. Basement and ground-floor tables attract a smart crowd of locals for drinks and upscale snacks at night. Meals are inventive and creative, with interesting takes on local cuisine. Many preparations enjoy artful presentation. Good beer and wine list.

🛈 Information

Tourist Information Centre (Centrum Informacji Turystycznej; ☎ 87 643 2883; www.augustow.eu; Rynek Zygmunta Augusta 19; ⊙ 8am-8pm Mon-Fri, 9am-8pm Sat & Sun Jul & Aug, 8am-5pm Mon-Fri, 10am-3pm Sat & Sun May & Jun, Sep, 8am-4pm Mon-Fri Oct-Apr; 🛜) Directly next to the bus station.

🛈 Getting There & Away

The **bus station** (Rynek Zygmunta Augusta 19) is on the southern side of the Rynek and handles frequent services to Białystok (14zł, 1½ hours) and Suwałki (9zł, 30 minutes). There are several buses direct to Warsaw (37zł, 4¾ hours); all come from Suwałki and can be full.

Augustów's **train station** (Dworcowa 1) is a long way from the town centre; a taxi from here to the Rynek will cost about 30zł. There are two trains daily to Warsaw (38zł, 4¼ hours). There are six direct trains to Białystok (14zł, 1½ hours), and Suwałki (10zł, 30 minutes).

Suwałki

POP 69,600

Suwałki (soo-*vahw*-kee) is the largest town in the region, but lacks Augustów's watery charm and immediate proximity to lakes and rivers. There's little inherently alluring about the town, but it does make a good gateway to the surrounding countryside, particularly the nearby Wigry National Park.

The town first appeared on the map at the end of the 17th century as one of the villages established by the Camaldolese monks from Wigry. The small multinational community grew slowly; at different times it included Jews, Lithuanians, Tatars, Russians, Germans and Old Believers, a religious group that split off from the Russian Orthodox Church in the 17th century. Very few members of any of these groups are still present in the town today. The centre still exudes a faded 19th century neoclassical order and charm.

☉ Sights

★**Suwałki Landscape Park**   NATURE RESERVE
(Suwalski Park Krajobrazowy; ☑ 87 569 1801; www.spk.org.pl; Suwałki Landscape Park Office, Malesowizna-Turtul; ☺ park office 8am-6pm Mon-Fri, 10am-5pm Sat Jul & Aug, 8am-3.30pm Mon-Fri Sep-Jun) The Suwałki Landscape Park is a cluster of pristine lakes and rugged hills that's worth a detour. Covering some 63 sq km, the park encompasses land that was formed in the late Ice Age. The result are dozens of startlingly clear Nordic lakes amid rolling hills and valleys. It's a perfect escape for walking or cycling. The village of **Smolniki**, 20km north of Suwałki, is the most convenient base for the park, which is about halfway between Suwałki and the Lithuanian border.

There are three good viewpoints of the verdant splendour in the village. One of the numerous well-marked walking options is an hour's walk west to Lake Hańcza, the deepest lake in Poland. With its steep shores, stony bottom and amazing crystal-clear water, it's like being up in the mountains.

The 1:50,000 map *Suwalski Park Krajobrazowy* (10zł) is good for exploring the area. It has all the hiking trails marked on it, and sightseeing information in English. Three buses make the 35-minute trip (12zł) each day between Suwałki and Smolniki.

The park website lists many places to stay, including rooms at farms. One special sleeping option if you have your own wheels is the remote **Jaczno Guest Lodge** (Gościniec Jaczno; ☑ 87 568 3590; www.jaczno. com; Jaczne 3, Jeleniewo; s 245zł, d 300-365zł, apt 445-535zł; ⓟ🛜🏊). This natural hideaway is a series of timbered mountain chalets built around a beautifully restored stone farmhouse. Horses, rowboats and hikes through the woods are among the diversions. It's near the tiny village of Udziejek, about 6km from Smolniki. The restaurant serves dishes made with organic local and seasonal ingredients.

Cemetery   CEMETERY
(ul Zarzecze) One way to get a flavour of the town's former ethnic mix is to visit the sprawling cemetery about 1km west of the tourist office. It comprises several separate burial grounds for people of different creeds, including Catholic, Orthodox, Old Believers and Islamic areas. A separate gate leads to the old Jewish cemetery. Largely destroyed in WWII, it attests to Suwałki's once thriving Jewish community.

✵ Festivals & Events

Blues Festival   MUSIC
(http://suwalkiblues.com; ☺ mid-Jul) More than 300 international blues musicians perform during this big four-day festival. Much of the action at night centres on the Restauracja Rozmarino.

🛏 Sleeping & Eating

Velvet Hotel   HOTEL €€
(☑ 87 563 5252; www.hotelvelvet.pl; ul Kościuszki 128; r from 200zł; ⓟ🛜🛜) As smooth as the name suggests, this impressive hotel at the north end of ul Kościuszki contains contemporary, well-appointed rooms with bright decor. There's a spa on the premises, a sunny terrace and a decent restaurant.

Emmi Suwalska Manufaktura   CAFE €€
(☑ 60 149 2818; www.facebook.com/emmisuwalska manufakturalodowiczekolady; ul Kościuszki 82; snacks 4-12zł; ☺ 10am-8pm) Lively cafe serving a selection of sundaes, cakes and chocolates with tea or coffee. As the name implies, they make their own excellent ice cream here, which is reason enough to detour to Suwałki on a summer day.

★**Restauracja**
Rozmarino   INTERNATIONAL €€
(http://rozmarino.pl; ul Kościuszki 75; mains 12-45zł; ☺ 11am-11pm) Restaurant, bar, social centre,

THE DEEP, DARK AUGUSTÓW FOREST

The Augustów Forest (Puszcza Augustowska) stretches east of Augustów as far as the Lithuania–Belarus border. At 1100 sq km, it's Poland's second largest continuous forest. It's a remnant of the vast primeval forest that once covered much of eastern Poland and southern Lithuania.

The forest is mainly made up of pine and spruce, with colourful deciduous species such as birch, oak, elm, lime, maple and aspen. The wildlife is rich and diverse, and includes beavers, wild boar, wolves, deer and elk. Birds abound and the 55 lakes are well stocked with fish. It was virtually unexplored until the 17th century, but today is crisscrossed by paved roads, dirt tracks, and walking and cycling paths. Despite this, there are large stretches that are almost untouched, and if you want to get far off the beaten track in Poland then this is a great swathe of nature in which to do it. (In fact it was a hiding place for underground fighters during WWII.)

You can explore part of the forest using private transport; roads will take you along the Augustów Canal to the Belarus border. Many of the rough tracks are perfectly OK for bikes; on foot you can get almost everywhere except the swamps.

music venue, art gallery, this lively joint is the best thing going in the heart of Suwałki. Enjoy good pizza under the atrium, then pop back out to the beer garden for a drink or have a coffee at a pavement table out front. Watch for live rock, jazz, poetry reading and more.

U Alika EASTERN EUROPEAN €€
(☑88 538 5723; http://kuchniaualika.pl; ul Kościuszki 98; mains 12-30zł; ☺11am-7pm) Enjoy the foods of the region at this humble house on the main drag. Dine amid antiques and sample Tatar staples such as hearty soups with dumplings and meaty stews and casseroles. Other dishes are drawn from Poland and Belarus – cabbage never tasted so good.

ℹ Information

Tourist Office (☑87 566 2079; www.um. suwalki.pl; ul Hamerszmita 16; ☺8am-6pm Mon-Fri, 9am-3pm Sat & Sun May-Sep, 8am-4pm Mon-Fri Oct-Apr) An excellent tourist office with loads of info on the region in English, plus refreshments, gifts and more. It's one block west of ul Kościuszki, on the western edge of Park Konstytucji 3 Maja. Rents bikes for 4/25zł per hour/day.

ℹ Getting There & Away

The decrepit **train station** (off ul Kolejowa) is 1.5km northeast of the centre; the **bus station** (ul Utrata) is closer to the central area. Trains are useful mostly for longer journeys, with six daily departures to Białystok (15zł, two hours) via Augustów (10zł, 30 minutes), and two to Warsaw (40zł, five hours).

Hourly buses run to Augustów (9zł, 45 minutes) and Białystok (19zł, 2¼ hours).

Wigry National Park

On the north side of Augustów Forest is a sparkling inkblot of a lake and one of the highlights of Podlasie: Lake Wigry. At 21 sq km, the lake is the largest in the region and one of the deepest, reaching 73m at its greatest depth. Its notched and twisting shoreline forms numerous bays and peninsulas; and there are more than a dozen islands on the lake, which is the namesake feature of Wigry National Park (Wigierski Park Narodowy; ☑87 566 2079; www.wigry.org.pl). Just east of Suwałki, the dense forest and plethora of smaller lakes make it a popular destination for kayakers, cyclists and hikers. The Czarna Hańcza River flows through the park, linking up with the Augustów Canal further downstream.

The village of Stary Folwark, 11km east of Suwałki, is the park hub, with a museum, beach and services. The tiny village of Wigry is atmospherically located on a small peninsula in the lake.

◉ Sights

Camaldolese Monastery MONASTERY
(Pokamedulski Klasztor; www.wigry.pro; Wigry 11, Wigry) Spectacularly located on a peninsula of the lake is this former Camaldolese monastery, built by the death-obsessed Camaldolese monks soon after they were brought to Wigry by King Jan II Kazimierz Waza in 1667. The whole complex, complete with a church and 17 hermitages, was originally on an island, which was later connected to the shore. It has now been turned into a **guesthouse**

(☑87 566 2499; s/d from 121/205zł, apt 300-400zł; [P]📶) and cafe, providing an atmospheric base for exploring the park.

Wigry Museum
MUSEUM

(Muzeum Wigier; www.wigry.org.pl; Stary Folwark 48, Stary Folwark; adult/child 10/5zł; ⊙10am-3pm) This large museum has exhibitions on the flora and fauna to be found in the park and lake. It's near a public beach and pier with fine views of the monastery.

🏃 Activities

★ Nature Path
WALKING

(Ścieżka Natury; Wigry National Park Headquarters, Krzywe;) Two looping nature trails at the park headquarters offer a combined 4km of walks through a cross-section of the local flora and fauna. Look for beaver dens, shimmering lakes, red squirrels, myriad birds and stands of oak, maple and elm. Amid air scented with wild ginger, there are plaques explaining the region's natural wonders. Get a small highlights map in English from the office.

PTTK Office
KAYAKING

(☑51 503 6082; www.suwalki.pttk.pl; Wigry Lake, Stary Folwark 55; kayak/bike per day 26/25zł; ⊙8am-5pm May-Sep) Operates kayak trips down the Czarna Hańcza and Rospuda Rivers (from 20zł); also hires out kayaks and bikes. Rental office is located 13km east of Suwałki on its own beach at Wigry Lake in the heart of the national park.

Wigry Narrow-Gauge Railway
RAIL

(Wigierska Kolej Wąskotorowa; www.augustowska.pl; Płociczno Tartak 40, Płociczno; adult/child 32/22zł; ⊙1pm May & Sep, 10am & 1pm Jun, 10am, 1pm & 4pm Jul & Aug) Train lovers can get their fix riding this narrow-gauge train that skirts the southern fringes of Wigry National Park from Płociczno-Tartak to Krusznik. The trip takes about 2½ hours, passing through lush forest and providing views of Lake Wigry. There are also kayak and canoe tours on offer.

🛏 Sleeping

U Haliny
GUESTHOUSE €

(☑87 563 7042; https://suwalszczyzna.com.pl/oferta/on/Pensjonat-u-Haliny/132; Wigry 12, Wigry; r per person 60zł; [P]📶) Friendly holiday complex with rooms and a campground on a great lakeside location near the monastery. Hearty meals are served and you can rent kayaks, canoes and bikes.

ⓘ Information

The **park headquarters** (☑87 563 2540; www.wigry.win.pl; Krzywe 82, Krzywe; ⊙7am-4pm Mon-Fri, 9am-4pm Sat & Sun) are 6km east of Suwałki on the road to Sejny. It's an easy ride along a good bike path beside the Suwałki–Sejny road. The enthusiastic staff can recommend hikes of various lengths, kayaking routes and more. There is a good selection of info on the park in English. An excellent looping nature trail starts right outside the office.

ⓘ Getting There & Away

Access is easiest from the Suwałki–Sejny road, which crosses the northern part of the park near the museum. The road is serviced by regular buses. If you want to go directly to the monastery, there is only one daily bus to Wigry from Suwałki (45 minutes, 12zł).

Bikes are an excellent way to explore the park. Rent them at the Tourist Office (p113) in Suwałki or at the PTTK Office on the lake.

Sejny

Sejny, 30km east of Suwałki, is the last Polish town before the Ogrodniki border crossing to Lithuania, 12km beyond. It's a quiet backwater that feels like it's on the edge of the (Polish) world.

The town grew up around the Dominican monastery, which was founded in 1602 by monks from Vilnius. The order was expelled by the Prussian authorities in 1804 and never returned, but the proud two-towered silhouette of its **Church of St Mary** (Bazylika Mniejsza Nawiedzenia NMP; www.sejny.diecezja.elk.pl; Plac Św Agaty 1; ⊙hours vary) still dominates the town from its northern end. It dates from the 1610s, but the facade was thoroughly remodelled 150 years later in the so-called Vilnius baroque style. Its pastel interior has harmonious rococo decoration.

Although there's a parking lot attendant who will ask for money, the church is often locked. Weekday masses are held in the morning and evening.

Hourly buses run from Sejny to Suwałki (14zł, 40 minutes) but the best way to visit is to stop off as part of a circular tour of Wigry National Park between Augustów and Suwałki.

Kraków

POP 765,320

Best Places to Eat

➡ Sąsiedzi (p144)

➡ Ed Red (p142)

➡ Art Restaurant (p142)

➡ Youmiko Sushi (p144)

➡ ZaKładka Food & Wine (p144)

Best Places to Stay

➡ U Pana Cogito (p140)

➡ INX Design Hotel (p139)

➡ Hotel Stary (p139)

➡ Balthazar Design Hotel (p138)

➡ Goodbye Lenin Revolution Hostel (p137)

Why Go?

If you believe the legends, Kraków was founded on the defeat of a dragon and, it's true, a mythical atmosphere permeates its medieval streets and squares. Wawel Royal Castle is a major drawcard, while the Old Town contains soaring churches, impressive museums and the vast Rynek Główny, Europe's largest market square. In the former Jewish quarter, Kazimierz, remnant synagogues reflect the tragedy of the 20th century, just as its lively squares and backstreets symbolise the renewal of the 21st. Here and throughout the Old Town are hundreds of restaurants, bars and clubs. However, there's more to the former royal capital than history and nightlife. As you walk through the Old Town, you'll find yourself overwhelmed by the harmony of a quiet back street, the 'just so' nature of the architecture and light. It's at times like these that Kraków reveals its harmonious blend of past and present.

When to Go

Kraków

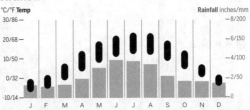

May & Jun As spring ends, the Lajkonik Pageant features a grand parade.

Jun & Jul The Jewish Culture Festival marks the highlight of Kazimierz's cultural calendar.

Dec Christmas sees the world-famous *szopki* (Nativity scenes) competition.

Kraków Highlights

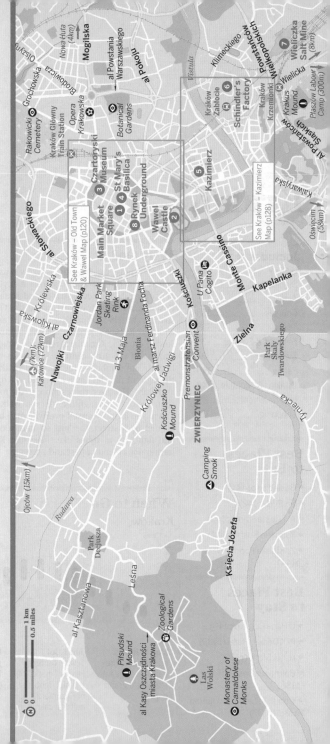

1 Main Market Square
(p119) Admiring the size of Europe's biggest market square.

2 Wawel Royal Castle
(p117) Immersing yourself in centuries of Polish history.

3 Czartoryski Museum
(p124) Discovering what an 'ermine' is.

4 St Mary's Basilica
(p119) Hearing the call of the trumpeter.

5 Kazimierz (p148)
Carousing in the city's liveliest clubs.

6 Schindler's Factory (p131)
Learning WWII history in a place where it was made.

7 Wieliczka Salt Mine
(p134) Marvelling at underground salt sculptures.

8 Rynek Underground
(p119) Heading down under for a multimedia extravaganza.

History

The history of Poland's former royal capital reads like an epic novel. Kraków became the capital of Poland in 1038, but was burned to the ground in 1241 by marauding Tatars. Under the enlightened leadership of Kazimierz III Wielki (Casimir III the Great; 1333–70), the city thrived in the 14th century, symbolised by the founding in 1364 of Jagiellonian University. The city's status slipped in 1596 when Zygmunt III Waza (Sigismund III Vasa, 1587-1632) moved Poland's capital to Warsaw, though Kraków remained the site of coronations and burials. In the 19th century the occupying Austrian Empire relegated the city to the peripheral province of Galicia.

After independent Poland was restored following WWI, Kraków thrived until WWII. The German occupation during the war led to the murder of the city's academic elite and the slaughter of tens of thousands of its Jewish citizens in the Holocaust. The communist government that came after the war heaped on more misery by building a heavily polluting steelworks at Nowa Huta, just a few kilometres east of the Old Town.

Kraków, particularly its most famous resident Karol Wojtyła (Pope John Paul II, 1920–2005), played an important role in the anticommunist movement of the 1970s and '80s. The former pope remains a source of pride for city residents. Today, Kraków is again on the upswing. It's Poland's leading tourist destination and second-biggest city.

◉ Sights

Most of Kraków's big-ticket sights – including Wawel Royal Castle, the Old Town Square and historic Kazimierz – are concentrated in the city centre, within a 15-minute walk of each other. But you really need two days to take in the highlights – one for Wawel and the Market Square, and one for Schindler's Factory and Kazimierz. Be aware that Wawel Royal Castle and Schindler's Factory operate a timed-entry system, which will need advance planning to ensure admission at busy times.

◉ Wawel Hill & Around

The symbol of a nation, Wawel Hill, just south of the Old Town and connected to it by ul Grodzka, is the silent guardian of a millennium of Polish history. The hilltop castle was the seat of kings and queens from the earliest days of the Polish state and the site of the most solemn ceremonies and most celebrated moments. Many Polish monarchs found their final resting place below Wawel Cathedral.

★ Wawel Royal Castle   CASTLE
(Zamek Królewski na Wawelu; Map p120; ◨ Wawel Visitor Centre 12 422 5155; www.wawel.krakow.pl; Wawel Hill; ⬓ 6, 8, 10, 13, 18) As the political and cultural heart of Poland through the 16th century, Wawel Royal Castle is a potent symbol of national identity. It's now a museum containing five separate sections: Crown Treasury and Armoury (p118), State Rooms, Royal Private Apartments (p118), Lost Wawel (p118) and the Exhibition of Oriental Art (p118). Each requires a separate ticket. Of the five, the State Rooms and Royal Private Apartments are the most impressive, but to be honest, the best part is just wandering around the castle grounds – open 6am to dusk.

The Renaissance palace you see today dates from the 16th century. An original, smaller residence was built in the early 11th century by King Bolesław I Chrobry. Kazimierz III Wielki (Casimir III the Great) turned it into a formidable Gothic castle, but when it burned down in 1499, Zygmunt I Stary (Sigismund I the Old; 1506–48) commissioned a new residence. Within 30 years, the current Italian-inspired palace was in place. Despite further extensions and alterations, the three-storey structure, complete with a courtyard arcaded on three sides, has been preserved to this day.

Repeatedly sacked and vandalised by the Swedish and Prussian armies, the castle was occupied in the 19th century by the Austrians, who intended to make Wawel a barracks, while moving the royal tombs elsewhere. They never got that far, but they did turn the royal kitchen and coach house into a military hospital and raze two churches. They also built a new ring of massive brick walls, largely ruining the original Gothic fortifications.

After Kraków was incorporated into re-established Poland after WWI, restoration work began and continued until the outbreak of WWII. The work was resumed after the war and has been able to recover a good deal of the castle's earlier external form and interior decoration.

➡ State Rooms
(Map p120; ◨ Wawel Visitor Centre 12 422 5155; www.wawel.krakow.pl; Wawel Hill; adult/concession 20/12zł; ◷ 9.30am-1pm Mon, to 5pm Tue-Fri, 10am-5pm Sat & Sun, shorter hours Nov-Mar; ⬓ 6, 8, 10, 13, 18) The State Rooms constitute the largest

and most impressive exhibition in the castle; the entrance is in the southeastern corner of the courtyard, from where you'll ascend to the 2nd floor. Proceed through a chain of two-dozen rooms and chambers of the castle, restored in their original Renaissance and early-baroque style and crammed with period furnishings, tapestries and works of art.

The two most memorable interiors are on the 2nd floor. The **Hall of Senators**, originally used for senate sessions, court ceremonies, balls and theatre performances, houses a magnificent series of six 16th-century Arras tapestries following the story of Adam and Eve, Cain and Abel, or Noah (they are rotated periodically).

The **Hall of Deputies** has a fantastic coffered ceiling with 30 individually carved and painted wooden heads staring back at you. Meant to illustrate the life cycle of man from birth to death, they are all that have survived from a total of 194 heads that were carved around 1535 by Sebastian Tauerbach. There's also a tapestry with the Polish insignia dating from 1560.

➡️ **Royal Private Apartments**

(Map p120; ✏️ Wawel Visitor Centre 12 422 5155; www.wawel.krakow.pl; Wawel Hill; adult/concession 27/21zł; ⊙9.30am-5pm Tue-Fri, from 10am Sat & Sun, shorter hours Nov-Mar; 🚌6, 8, 10, 13, 18) This tour lends insight into how the monarchs and their families once lived. You'll see plenty of magnificent old tapestries, mostly northern French and Flemish, hanging on the walls. The collection was largely assembled by Zygmunt II August (Sigismund II Augustus; 1548–72). Other highlights include the so-called Hen's Foot, Jadwiga's gemlike chapel in the northeast tower, and the sumptuous Gdańsk-made furniture in the Alchemy Room and annex.

➡️ **Crown Treasury & Armoury**

(Map p120; ✏️ Wawel Visitor Centre 12 422 5155; www.wawel.krakow.pl; Wawel Hill; adult/concession 18/10zł; ⊙9.30am-5pm Tue-Fri, from 10am Sat & Sun, shorter hours Nov-Mar; 🚌6, 8, 10, 13, 18) Housed in vaulted Gothic rooms surviving from the 14th-century castle, the most famous object in the treasury is the *Szczerbiec* (Jagged Sword), dating from the mid-13th century, which was used at all Polish coronations from 1320 onward. The armoury features a collection of old weapons from various epochs – from crossbows, swords, lances and halberds from the 15th to 17th centuries to muskets, rifles, pistols and cannon from later years.

➡️ **Lost Wawel**

(Map p120; ✏️ Wawel Visitor Centre 12 422 5155; www.wawel.krakow.pl; Wawel Hill; adult/concession 10/7zł; ⊙9.30am-1pm Mon, to 5pm Tue-Fri, 10am-5pm Sat & Sun, shorter hours Nov-Mar; 🚌6, 8, 10, 13, 18) Accommodated in the old royal kitchen, this exhibition features remnants of the late-10th-century Rotunda of SS Felix and Adauctus, reputedly the first church in Poland, as well as various archaeological finds (including colourful ceramic tiles from the castle stoves) and models of previous Wawel churches.

➡️ **Exhibition of Oriental Art**

(Map p120; ✏️ Wawel Visitor Centre 12 422 5155; www.wawel.krakow.pl; Wawel Hill; adult/concession 8/5zł; ⊙9.30am-5pm Tue-Fri, from 10am Sat & Sun, shorter hours Nov-Mar; 🚌6, 8, 10, 13, 18) A collection of 17th-century Turkish banners and weaponry, captured after the Battle of Vienna and displayed along with a variety of old Persian carpets, Chinese and Japanese ceramics, and other Asian antiques.

★ **Wawel Cathedral** CHURCH

(Map p120; ✏️ 12 429 9515; www.katedra-wawelska.pl; Wawel Hill; ⊙9am-5pm Mon-Sat, from 12.30pm Sun Apr-Oct, to 4pm Nov-Mar; 🚌6, 8, 10, 13, 18) FREE Wawel Cathedral has witnessed many coronations, funerals and burials of Poland's monarchs and nobles. The present cathedral is basically a Gothic, but chapels in different styles were built around it later. The showpiece is the **Sigismund Chapel** (Kaplica Zygmuntowska) on the southern wall. It's often referred to as the most beautiful Renaissance chapel north of the Alps, recognisable from the outside by its gilded dome. An audio guide (8zł) helps to put it all in context.

This is the third church on this site, consecrated in 1364. The original was founded in the 11th century by King Bolesław I Chrobry and replaced with a Romanesque construction around 1140. When that burned down in 1305, only the Crypt of St Leonard survived. Highlights include the Holy Cross Chapel, Sigismund Chapel, Sigismund Bell, and the Crypt of St Leonard and Royal Crypts.

Before you enter, note the massive iron door and, hanging on a chain to the left, the supposed bones of the Wawel dragon. They are believed to have magical powers; as long as they remain, the cathedral will survive. (They are actually fossilised whale and mammoth bones.)

Once inside, you'll get lost in a maze of sarcophagi, tombstones and altarpieces scattered throughout the nave, chancel and ambulatory. Highlights include the Holy Cross Chapel (Kaplica Świętokrzyska), distinguished by its 15th-century Byzantine frescoes and the red marble sarcophagus (1492), and the Tomb of St Queen Hedwig (Sarkofag Św Królowej Jadwigi), a much beloved and humble 14th-century monarch whose unpretentious wooden coronation regalia is on display nearby.

In the centre of the cathedral stands the flamboyant baroque Shrine of St Stanislaus (Konfesja Św Stanisława), dedicated to the bishop of Kraków, canonised in 1253 and now the patron saint of Poland. The silver sarcophagus, adorned with 12 relief scenes from the saint's life, was made in Gdańsk between 1663 and 1691; note the engravings on the inside of the ornamented canopy erected about 40 years later.

From the nave, descend from the left-hand aisle to the Crypt of St Leonard, the only remnant of the 12th-century Romanesque cathedral extant. Follow through to get to the Royal Crypts (Groby Królewskie) where, along with kings such as Jan III Sobieski, many national heroes and leaders, including Tadeusz Kościuszko, Józef Piłsudski and WWII General Władysław Sikorski, are buried.

You can climb the tower via 70 steps to see the Sigismund Bell (Dzwon Zygmunta). Cast in 1520, it's 2m high and 2.5m wide, and weighs 11 tonnes, making it the largest historic bell in Poland. Its clapper weighs 350kg, and eight strong men are needed to ring the bell, which happens only on the most important church holidays and for significant state events. The views from here are worth the climb.

Entry to the cathedral itself is free. A combined ticket (adult/concession 12/7zł) provides entry to the Royal Crypts and Sigismund Bell, as well as the Wawel Cathedral Museum, diagonally opposite the cathedral itself.

Wawel Cathedral Museum　　MUSEUM
(Map p120; ☑12 429 9515; www.katedra-wawelska. pl; Wawel Hill; adult/concession 12/7zł; ⊙9am-5pm Mon-Sat; ⊞6, 8, 10, 13, 18) Diagonally opposite the cathedral is this treasury of historical and religious objects from the cathedral. There are plenty of exhibits, including church plate and royal funerary regalia, but not a single crown. They were all stolen from the treasury by the Prussians in 1795 and reputedly melted down.

◉ Old Town

The centre of Kraków life since the Tatar invasions of the 13th century, and the most important area for visitors, the Old Town, with its graceful Main Market Square (Rynek Główny) at the heart, is filled with historic buildings and monuments. It's also packed with restaurants, galleries and allegedly more bars per square metre than anywhere else in Europe. It has featured on Unesco's World Heritage List since 1978, and is largely car-free.

Main Market Square　　SQUARE
The vast Main Market Square (Rynek Główny; Map p120; ⊞1, 6, 8, 13, 18) is the focus of the Old Town, and is Europe's largest medieval town square (200m by 200m). Its most prominent features are the 16th-century Cloth Hall (p123) at the centre, a 15th-century Town Hall Tower (p124) and a striking bronze statue of 19th-century romantic poet Adam Mickiewicz on the square's eastern side.

★**Rynek Underground**　　MUSEUM
(Map p120; ☑12 426 5060; www.podziemiarynku. com; Rynek Główny 1; adult/concession 21/18zł, free Tue; ⊙10am-8pm Wed-Mon, to 4pm Tue; ⊞; ⊞1, 6, 8, 13, 18) This fascinating attraction beneath the market square consists of an underground route through medieval market stalls and other long-forgotten chambers. The 'Middle Ages meets 21st century' experience is enhanced by holograms and audiovisual wizardry. Buy tickets at an office on the western side of the Cloth Hall (Sukiennice 21), where an electronic board shows tour times and tickets available. The entrance to the tunnels is on the northeastern end of the Cloth Hall.

★**St Mary's Basilica**　　CHURCH
(Basilica of the Assumption of Our Lady; Map p120; ☑12 422 0521; www.mariacki.com; Plac Mariacki 5, Rynek Główny; adult/concession 10/5zł; ⊙11.30am-6pm Mon-Sat, from 2pm Sun; ⊞1, 6, 8, 13, 18) This striking brick church, best known simply as St Mary's, is dominated by two towers of different heights. The first church here was built in the 1220s and following its destruction during a Tatar raid, construction of the basilica began. Tour the exquisite interior, with its remarkable carved wooden altarpiece, and in summer climb the tower (adult/ concession 15/10zł) for excellent views. Don't miss the hourly *hejnał* (bugle call) from the taller tower.

The main church entrance, through a baroque portal added to the southwestern

Old Town & Wawel

al Mickiewicza

Karmelicka

Michałowskiego

Dolnych Młynów

Karmelicka

KLEPARZ

Batorego

Łobzowska

Biskupia

Asnyka

Garbarska

Rajska

Czysta

Szujskiego

Krupnicza

Studencka

Loretańska

Kapucyńska

Jabłonowskich

marsz Piłsudskiego

Reformacka

sw Tomasza

Plac
Szczepański

Szczepańska

Szewska

Podwale

sw Anny

Collegium
Maius

Gołębia

Olszewskiego

Straszewskiego

Rynek
Główny

Jagiellońska

Wiślna

Bracka

Al marsz
Ferdinanda Focha

Krasińskiego

Smoleńsk

Retoryka

Smoleńsk

Dunin-Wąsowicza

Syrokomli

Morawskiego

Włóczków

Kościuszki

Most Dębnicki

Felicjanek

Mała

Zwierzyniecka

Plac Na
Groblach

Plac Na Groblach

Powiśle

Vistula

DĘBNIKI

Straszewskiego

Franciszkańska

Basilica of
St Francis

Poselska

Trałowska

Podzamcze

Wawel
Cathedral

Wawel
Royal Castle

Wawel
Hill

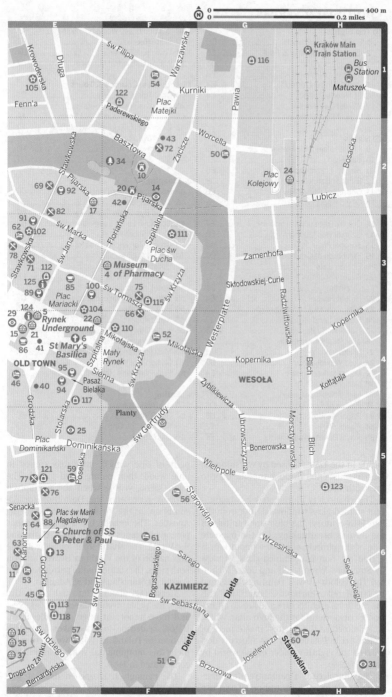

Old Town & Wawel

facade in the 1750s, is used by worshippers; tourists must enter through the side door to the southeast.

The chancel is illuminated by magnificent stained-glass windows dating from the late 14th century; the blue star vaulting of the nave is breathtaking. On the opposite side of the church, above the organ loft, is a fine art nouveau stained-glass window by Stanisław Wyspiański and Józef Mehoffer. The colourful wall paintings, designed by Jan Matejko, harmonise beautifully with the medieval architecture and are an appropriate background for the high altar, which is acclaimed as the greatest masterpiece of Gothic art in Poland and was allegedly designated the eighth wonder of the world by Pablo Picasso.

The altarpiece is a pentaptych (an altarpiece consisting of a central panel and two pairs of side wings), intricately carved in lime wood, then painted and gilded. The main scene, visible when the pentaptych is open, represents the Dormition (or Assumption) of the Virgin surrounded by the Apostles. The outside has a dozen sections portraying scenes from the life of Christ and the Virgin. The altarpiece is topped with the Coronation of the Virgin in Heaven and, on both sides, the statues of the patron saints of Poland, St Stanislaus and St Adalbert.

Measuring about 13m high and 11m wide, the pentaptych is the country's largest and most important piece of medieval art. It took a decade for its maker, Veit Stoss (known in Poland as Wit Stwosz), to complete this monumental work before it was consecrated in 1489.

The pentaptych is opened daily at precisely 11.50am and closed at 5.30pm, except

KRAKÓW SIGHTS

for Saturday when it's left open for the Sunday-morning mass. The altarpiece apart, don't miss the delicate crucifix on the baroque altar in the head of the right-hand aisle, another work by Veit Stoss, and the still larger crucifix placed on the rood screen, attributed to pupils of the master.

Cloth Hall
HISTORIC BUILDING

(Sukiennice; Map p120; Rynek Główny 1/3; 🚌 1, 6, 8, 13, 18) **FREE** Dominating the centre of the Main Market Square, this building was once the heart of Kraków's medieval clothing trade. Created in the early 14th century when a roof was put over two rows of stalls, it was extended into a 108m-long Gothic structure, then rebuilt in Renaissance style after a 1555 fire; the arcades were a late-19th-century addition. The ground floor is now a busy trading centre for crafts and souvenirs; the upper floor houses the **Gallery of 19th-Century Polish Painting** (Map p120; ☑ 12 433 5400; www.mnk.pl; adult/concession 20/15zł, free Sun; ⊙ 9am-5pm Tue-Fri, 10am-6pm Sat, 10am-4pm Sun).

Historical Museum of Kraków
MUSEUM

(Krzysztofory Palace; Map p120; ☑ 12 619 2335; www.mhk.pl; Rynek Główny 35; adult/concession 12/8zł, free Sat; ⊙ 10am-5.30pm Tue-Sun; 🚌 2, 4, 14, 18, 20, 24, 44) At the northern corner of the square, the collection within the 17th-century Krzysztofory Palace is home to Cyberteka, an interactive exhibition which charts the city from the earliest days to WWI. The museum features a bit of everything related to the city's past, including old clocks, armour, paintings, Kraków's celebrated *szopki* (Nativity scenes), and the costume of the Lajkonik.

Town Hall Tower TOWER

(Wieża Ratuszowa; Map p120; ☑12 426 4334; www.muzeumkrakowa.pl; Rynek Główny 1; adult/concession 10/8zł; ⊙10.30am-6pm Apr-Oct; 🚋1, 6, 8, 13, 18) Southwest of the Cloth Hall, this soaring tower is all that is left of the 15th-century town hall which was dismantled in the 1820s. The 70m-tall tower can be climbed in the warmer months.

North of the Market Square

⭐**Museum of Pharmacy** MUSEUM

(Muzeum Farmacj; Map p120; ☑12 421 9279; www.muzeum.farmacja.uj.edu.pl; ul Floriańska 25; adult/concession 14/8zł; ⊙noon-6.30pm Tue, 9.30am-3pm Wed-Sun; 🚋2, 4, 14, 18, 20, 24, 44) The name of this museum doesn't sound that exciting, but the Jagiellonian University Medical School's Museum of Pharmacy is one of the largest museums of its kind in Europe and arguably the best. Accommodated in a beautiful historic townhouse worth the visit alone, it features a 22,000-piece collection, which includes old laboratory equipment, rare pharmaceutical instruments, heaps of glassware, stoneware, mortars, jars, barrels, medical books and documents.

⭐**Czartoryski Museum** MUSEUM

(Map p120; ☑12 370 5460; www.mnk.pl; ul Św Jana 19; 🚋2, 4, 14, 18, 20, 24, 44) The Czartoryski boasts the city's richest art collection, including Leonardo Da Vinci's 15th-century masterpiece, *Lady with an Ermine* (1489–90). Other exhibitions include Greek, Roman, Egyptian and Etruscan art as well as Turkish weaponry. The museum closed in 2010 for renovation and was set to reopen as a branch of the National Museum at the end of 2019. Until then, *Lady with an Ermine* is on display at the National Museum (p126) main branch.

DON'T MISS

STROLLING THE PLANTY

Tracing the path of the medieval city's moat, wrapping around the Old Town from Wawel Royal Castle, the **Planty Park** (Map p120; 🚋2, 4, 6, 8, 13, 14, 18, 19, 20, 24, 44) is an everyday piece of people's lives in Kraków. The wide paths are filled with walkers, cyclists, prams, rollerbladers and everything in between. You'll find public art, cafes, ponds, statues, magnificent floral displays, and lots and lots of benches, dedicated to Polish authors past and present.

City Defence Walls HISTORIC SITE

(Mury Obronne; Map p120; ☑12 421 1361; www.muzeumkrakowa.pl; ul Pijarska; adult/concession 9/7zł; ⊙10.30am-6pm May-Oct; 🚋2, 4, 14, 18, 20, 24, 44) This small museum includes entry to both the **Florian Gate** (ul Floriańska; adult/concession 9/7zł; ⊙10.30am-6pm Apr-Oct) and **Barbican** (Barbakan; Barbakan; adult/concession 9/7zł; ⊙10.30am-6pm Apr-Oct), among the few surviving remnants of the city's medieval defence walls. The Florian Gate was once the city's main entrance and dates from the 14th century. The Barbican, a circular bastion adorned with seven turrets, was built at the end of the 15th century to lend additional protection. It was once connected to the gate by a narrow passage running over a moat.

History Land MUSEUM

(Map p120; ☑530 903 053; www.historyland.pl; Plac Jana Nowaka Jeziorańskiego 3; adult/concession 27/24zł; ⊙9am-5pm Mon-Fri, 10am-6pm Sat & Sun; ⊕; 🚋2, 3, 4, 5, 10, 14, 17, 19, 20, 44, 50, 52) Modern, kids-oriented historical exhibition that uses both LEGO building blocks and virtual-reality technology to tell key stories of Poland's national history in a way that engages the senses. The exhibition is located in the former main train station building.

South of the Market Square

There are several key sights south of the Main Market Square and along ul Grodzka heading south toward Wawel Hill.

⭐**Basilica of St Francis** CHURCH

(Bazylika Św Franciszka; Map p120; ☑12 422 5376; www.franciszkanska.pl; Plac Wszystkich Świętych 5; ⊙10am-4pm Mon-Sat, from 1pm Sun; 🚋1, 6, 8, 13, 18) Duck into the dark basilica on a sunny day to admire the artistry of Stanisław Wyspiański, who designed the fantastic art nouveau stained-glass windows. The multicoloured deity in the chancel above the organ loft is a masterpiece. From the transept, you can also enter the Gothic cloister of the Franciscan Monastery to admire the fragments of 15th-century frescoes. Closed to tourists during mass.

Papal Window MEMORIAL

(Map p120; ul Franciszkańska 3; 🚋1, 6, 8, 13, 18) When visiting Kraków, Pope John Paul II used to address his followers from this window of the Bishop's Palace, overlooking ul Franciszkańska. The area is filled with candles on important anniversaries, such as the former pope's birthday and anniversary of his death. These days, there's a photo of John Paul II in the window to keep his memory alive.

FIRE COMPANY BUGLE BOYS

Every hour the *hejnał* (bugle call) is sounded four times on a trumpet from the higher tower of St Mary's Basilica. Now a musical symbol of the city, this simple melody was played in medieval times as a warning call. Intriguingly, it breaks off abruptly in midbar. Legend links it to the Tatar invasions – when the watchman on duty spotted the enemy and sounded the alarm, a Tatar arrow pierced his throat midphrase.

Holy Trinity Basilica MONASTERY
(Dominican Church; Map p120; ☑12 423 1613; www.krakow.dominikanie.pl; ul Stolarska 12; ☉9.30am-11.30am & 1.30pm-4.30pm; ☐1, 6, 8, 13, 18) **FREE** Originally built in the 13th century, this massive church was badly damaged by fire in 1850. Note the original 14th-century doorway at the main (western) entrance to the church. The monastery, just behind the northern wall of the church, is accessible from the street (enter an unmarked door at Stolarska 12). Closed to tourists during Sunday mass.

★**Church of SS Peter & Paul** CHURCH
(Map p120; ☑12 350 6365; www.apostolowie.pl; ul Grodzka 52a; ☉9am-5pm Tue-Sat, 1.30-5pm Sun; ☐6, 8, 10, 13, 18) The Jesuits erected this church, the first baroque building in Kraków, after they had been brought to the city in 1583 to do battle with supporters of the Reformation. Designed on the Latin cross layout and topped with a large skylit dome, the church has a refreshingly sober interior, apart from some fine stucco decoration on the vault.

The exterior is marked by a row of striking statues of the apostles that date from the early 18th century. The interior holds the longest Foucault's pendulum in Poland (46.5m), used to determine the rotation of the earth. Regular demonstrations of the pendulum, with an explanation in Polish, are normally held on Thursday mornings (10am, 11am and noon). The church is used in the evenings for classical music concerts.

Bishop Erazm Ciołek Palace MUSEUM
(Map p120; ☑12 433 5920; www.mnk.pl; ul Kanonicza 17; adult/concession 10/5zł; ☉9am-4pm Tue-Fri, 10am-6pm Sat, 10am-4pm Sun; ☐6, 8, 10, 13, 18) Quaint Kanonicza is the perfect street to put a palace and fill it with age-old paintings and sculpture. This newish branch of the National Museum contains two exhibits of religious artwork. The Art of Old Poland (12th to 18th centuries) includes loads of Gothic paintings, altar pieces and a room devoted to Veit Stoss. A second exhibit focuses on Orthodox art.

Archaeological Museum MUSEUM
(Map p120; ☑12 422 7560; www.ma.krakow.pl; ul Poselska 3; adult/concession 12/7zł, free Sun; ☉9am-3pm Mon, Wed & Fri, to 6pm Tue & Thu, 11am-4pm Sun; ☐1, 6, 8, 13, 18) You can learn about the Małopolska region's history from the Palaeolithic period up until the early Middle Ages here, but you'll be most enthralled by the collection of ancient Egyptian artefacts, including both human and animal mummies. There are also more than 4000 iron coins from the 9th century. The gardens are a lovely place for a stroll.

Church of St Andrew CHURCH
(Map p120; ☑12 422 1612; ul Grodzka 54; ☉8am-6pm Mon-Fri; ☐6, 8, 10, 13, 18) This church is almost a thousand years old. Built towards the end of the 11th century, much of its austere Romanesque stone exterior has been preserved. As soon as you enter, though, you're in a totally different world; its small interior was subjected to a radical baroque overhaul in the 18th century.

West of the Market Square

There are several important sights to the west of the Main Market Square and across the Planty in the bustling neighbourhood west of the Old Town.

★**Collegium Maius** MUSEUM
(Map p120; ☑12 663 1488; www.maius.uj.edu.pl; ul Jagiellońska 15; adult/concession tour 16/12zł, exhibition 7/5zł; ☉9am-2.20pm Mon-Fri, to 1.30pm Sat; ☐2, 8, 13, 18, 20) The Collegium Maius, part of Jagiellonian University, is the oldest surviving university building in Poland, and one of the finest examples of 15th-century Gothic architecture in the city. It's best known for its star pupil, Polish astronomer and mathematician Nicolaus Copernicus. Guided tours (from 10am) show off some of his manuscripts as well as scientific books and instruments from those times. Check out the magnificent arcaded courtyard and clock (7am to dusk) and a small temporary exhibition on science.

KRAKÓW SIGHTS

National Museum
MUSEUM

(Muzeum Narodowe w Krakowie; Map p120; ☑ 12 433 5744; www.mnk.pl; al 3 Maja 1; adult/concession 28/19zł, free Sun; ⊙ 9am-5pm Tue-Fri, 10am-6pm Sat, 10am-4pm Sun; ☑ 20) Three permanent exhibitions – the Gallery of 20th-Century Polish Painting, the Gallery of Decorative Art, and Polish Arms and National Colours – are housed in this main branch of the National Museum in Kraków, 500m west of the Old Town down ul Piłsudskiego. The most notable collection is the painting gallery, which houses an extensive collection of Polish painting (and some sculpture) covering the period from 1890 until the present day.

There are several stained-glass designs (including the ones for Wawel Cathedral) by Stanisław Wyspiański, and an impressive selection of paintings by Witkacy (Stanisław Ignacy Witkiewicz). Jacek Malczewski and Olga Boznańska are also well represented. Of the postwar artists, take particular note of the works by Tadeusz Kantor, Jerzy Nowosielski and Władysław Hasior. Through most of 2019, the museum is also home to Leonardo Da Vinci's masterpiece, *Woman with an Ermine*.

Stained Glass
Workshop & Museum
MUSEUM

(Map p120; ☑ 512 937 979; www.muzeumwitrazu.pl; al Krasińskiego 23; tours adult/concession 35/29zł; ⊙ 11.30am-6pm Tue-Fri; ☑ 20) This combination museum and workshop highlights the beauty of stained glass and the considerable skill (and artistic talent) it takes to produce it. Visits are by guided tour and tours in English are offered on the hour from noon until 5pm.

Jordan Park
PARK

(Park Jordana; al 3 Maja 11; ☑; ☑ 20) Named after its founder Henryk Jordan, this park is a favourite for many. You'll find dog walkers enjoying open fields, kids on climbing frames, outdoor yoga classes, and much more. Stretch out on the grass in summer, or try ice skating (adult/concession 12/10zł; ⊙ 9am-9pm, to 10pm Fri & Sat Dec-Mar) at the rink in winter.

Krakowski Park
PARK

(Park Krakowski; Map p120; ☑; ☑ 4, 8, 13, 14, 24, 44) Renovated in spring 2018, this park is a lovely place to spend an hour with children, walking a dog or on your own. Added plants bring colour and attract bees to the area and you'll find ducks swimming in the central pond beneath a large overhanging willow tree. There's also a nook for borrowing and reading magazines and a fantastic play area for kids.

Palace of Fine Arts
GALLERY

(Pałac Sztuki; Map p120; ☑ 12 422 6616; www.palac-sztuki.krakow.pl; Plac Szczepański 4; adult/concession 15/10zł; ⊙ 8.15am-6pm Mon-Fri, from 10am Sat & Sun; ☑ 2, 4, 14, 18, 20, 24, 44) The centrepiece of the art nouveau Plac Szczepański is this elaborate edifice on its western side. An incredible frieze circles the building (product of Jacek Malczewski), while the busts on the facade honour Polish artists. The building is used for temporary art exhibits.

Europeum
MUSEUM

(Centre for European Culture; Map p120; ☑ 12 433 5760; www.mnk.pl; Plac Sikorskiego 6; adult/concession 10/5zł, free Sun; ⊙ 9am-4pm Tue-Fri, 10am-6pm Sat, 10am-4pm Sun; ☑ 4, 8, 13, 14, 24, 44) This oft-overlooked museum, housed in an old granary, holds the National Museum's most important collection of European paintings. Around 100 works are on display, covering seven centuries of European art. Important paintings include Lorenzo Lotto's *Adoration of the Infant Jesus* (early 16th century) and a work by Pieter Brueghel the Younger.

Józef Mehoffer House
MUSEUM

(Dom Józefa Mehoffera; Map p120; ☑ 12 433 5889; www.mnk.pl; ul Krupnicza 26; adult/concession 10/5zł, free Sun; ⊙ 10am-4pm Tue & Sun, to 6pm Sat; ☑ 2, 4, 8, 13, 14, 18, 20, 24) The 'Young Poland' artist lived in this stately home from 1932 until his death in 1946. The museum preserves the elegant interiors, with many original furnishings and artwork. Look out for work by the artist, including stained-glass windows and portraits of his wife. Be sure not to miss the lovely garden.

⊙ Kazimierz

For much of its 700-year history, Kazimierz, southeast of the Old Town, was an independent town with its own municipal charter and laws. Its mixed Jewish and Christian populations over the centuries created a pair of distinctive communities side by side. These days, Kazimierz does double-duty. It's home to many of the most important tourist attractions, including evocative Jewish-heritage sites, as well as some of the city's most-popular cafes, clubs and restaurants.

Jewish Quarter

The eastern part of Kazimierz became, over the centuries, a centre of Jewish culture equal to no other in the country. However, with the mass deportation and extermination of the Jewish people of Kraków by the German occupiers during WWII, the folklore, life and atmosphere of the quarter was tragically extinguished. Kazimierz became a run-down area after WWII, but in recent years this area has regained some of its Jewish character via the establishment of kosher restaurants complete with live klezmer music, along with museums devoted to Jewish culture. Miraculously, several synagogues survived the war, and most are available to visit.

★ **Galicia Jewish Museum** MUSEUM
(Map p128; ☏ 12 421 6842; www.galiciajewishmuseum.org; ul Dajwór 18; adult/concession 16/11zł; ⊙ 10am-6pm; 🚊 3, 19, 24) This museum both commemorates Jewish victims of the Holocaust and celebrates the Jewish culture and history of the former Austro-Hungarian region of Galicia. It features an impressive photographic exhibition depicting modern-day remnants of southeastern Poland's once-thriving Jewish community, called 'Traces of Memory', along with video testimony of survivors and regular temporary exhibits. The museum also leads guided tours of the Jewish sites of Kazimierz.

Old Synagogue MUSEUM
(Stara Synagoga; Map p128; ☏ 12 422 0962; www.muzeumkrakowa.pl; ul Szeroka 24; adult/concession 11/9zł; free Mon; ⊙ 10am-2pm Mon, 9am-5pm Tue-Sun; 🚊 3, 19, 24) This synagogue, dating from the 15th century, is the oldest surviving Jewish house of worship in Poland. During WWII, it was plundered and partly destroyed by the Germans, but later restored. The prayer hall, complete with a reconstructed *bimah* (raised platform at the centre where the Torah is read) and the original *aron kodesh* (the niche in the eastern wall where Torah scrolls are kept), houses an exhibition of important liturgical objects.

New Jewish Cemetery CEMETERY
(Nowy Cmentarz Żidowsky; Map p120; ul Miodowa 55; ⊙ 9am-6pm Sun-Thu; 🚊 3, 19, 24) This enormous cemetery dates from 1800 and was the

KRAKÓW SIGHTS

THE RISE & FALL (& RISE) OF KAZIMIERZ

Kazimierz was founded in 1335 by Kazimierz III Wielki on the southern fringe of Kraków. Thanks to privileges granted by the king, the town developed swiftly and soon had its own town hall, a market square almost as large as Kraków's, and two huge churches. The town was encircled with defensive walls and by the end of the 14th century was Małopolska's most important and wealthiest city after Kraków.

The first Jews settled in Kazimierz soon after its foundation, but it wasn't until 1494, when they were expelled from within the walls of Kraków by King Jan Olbracht, that their numbers rapidly rose. They settled in a prescribed area of Kazimierz, northeast of the Christian quarter, with the two sectors separated by a wall.

The subsequent history of Kazimierz was punctuated by fires, floods and plagues, with both Christian and Jewish communities living side by side, though confined to their own sectors. The Jewish quarter became home to Jews fleeing persecution from all corners of Europe, and it grew particularly quickly, gradually determining the character of the whole town. It became the most important Jewish centre of all Poland.

At the end of the 18th century Kazimierz was administratively incorporated into Kraków, and in the 1820s the walls were pulled down. At the outbreak of WWII Kazimierz was a predominantly Jewish suburb, with a distinctive culture and atmosphere. During the war, the Germans forcibly moved Jewish residents across the river to a purpose-built restricted ghetto in Podgórze. From there, the Jews were eventually dispersed to labour and concentration camps. Of the 65,000 Jews living in Kraków (most of whom lived in Kazimierz) in 1939, only a few thousand survived the war.

During communist rule, Kazimierz was largely a forgotten district of Kraków, and descended into something of a slum. Then in the early 1990s along came Steven Spielberg to shoot *Schindler's List* and everything changed overnight. Kazimierz was actually not the setting of the movie's plot – most of the events portrayed in the film took place in or near the Podgórze ghetto, Oskar Schindler's factory and the Płaszów extermination camp, all of which were further southeast beyond the Vistula.

Kazimierz

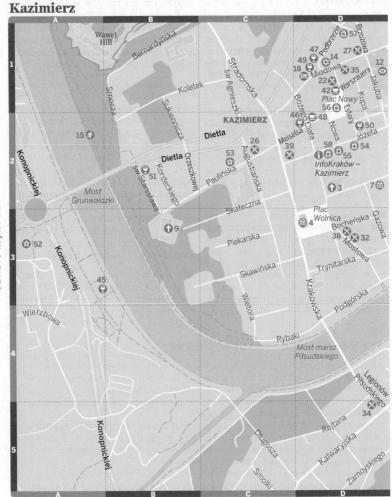

main burial ground for Kazimierz's Jewish population up until WWII. Many of the grave markers were destroyed during the German occupation and some of the recovered tombstones are visible on the cemetery walls. Around 9000 tombstones are still visible, though many remain untended as whole families perished in the Holocaust. Follow ul Miodowa below a railway bridge and find the small gate to the cemetery.

Remuh Synagogue   SYNAGOGUE
(Map p128; ☎ 12 429 5735; www.krakow.jewish.org.pl; ul Szeroka 40; adult/concession 10/5zł; ◷ 9am-6pm Sun-Thu; ◻ 3, 19, 24) Near the northern

end of ul Szeroka is the district's smallest synagogue and one of only two in the area still used regularly for religious services. The Remuh Synagogue was established in 1558 by a rich merchant, Israel Isserles, and is associated with his son Rabbi Moses Isserles, a philosopher and scholar.

The admission fee covers access to the adjacent Remuh Cemetery. This evocative cemetery dates from the Renaissance period of the 16th century. It was the quarter's main burial ground before it was closed for hygienic reasons in the late-18th century, when the larger New Jewish Cemetery (p127) was established. During WWII, the

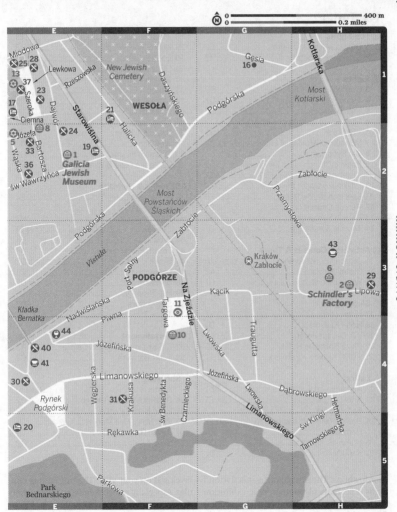

Germans vandalised the tombstones, but some 700 grave markers, including some outstanding Renaissance examples, have been recovered. The admission includes entry to the synagogue.

Temple Synagogue SYNAGOGUE
(Synagoga Tempel; Map p128; ☎12 430 5411; www.krakow.jewish.org.pl; ul Miodowa 24; adult/student 10/5zł; ☺9am-3pm Mon-Fri; ☒3, 17, 19, 22, 24, 52) One of the quarter's most visually arresting synagogues, the Temple dates from the mid-19th century. It was built in Moorish style and then given a lavish makeover in the past 20 years after being partially

destroyed by the occupying Germany army in WWII. It's inactive these days, but still holds occasional concerts and special events.

High Synagogue SYNAGOGUE
(Synagoga Wysoka; Map p128; ☎12 430 6889; www.krakow.jewish.org.pl; ul Józefa 38; adult/concession 12/9zł; ☺9.30am-7pm; ☒3, 19, 24) This former place of worship was built around 1560, in Renaissance style, and is the third-oldest synagogue after the Old (p127) and Remuh synagogues. The High Synagogue takes its name from the fact that the prayer hall was situated on the 1st (upper) floor, while the ground floor was given

Kazimierz

over to shops. The synagogue is inactive and holds a permanent photographic exhibition on the families of Kazimierz. The ground floor holds a branch of the Jewish bookshop chain, Austeria (p153).

Museum of Municipal Engineering
MUSEUM

(Muzeum Inżynierii Miejskiej; Map p128; ☑12 428 6600; www.mimk.com.pl; ul Św Wawrzyńca 15; adult/child 15/10zł, free Tue; ☺9am-4pm Tue-Thu, to 6pm Fri, 10am-6pm Sat & Sun; ☻; ☒3, 19, 24) Trams and trucks fill the yard of this former tram depot, while inside there's a fun collection of cars and motorbikes. A room of hands-on magnetic and water experiments and some interactive science quizzes are sure to keep kids occupied, too. The museum is planning an extensive renovation, meaning that some rooms and exhibits may

be closed on your visit. The museum is popular, especially on weekends, so book tickets in advance over the website.

Western Kazimierz

Corpus Christi Church
CHURCH

(Parafia Bożego Ciała w Krakowie; Map p128; ☑12 430 5995; www.bozecialo.net; ul Bożego Ciała 26; ☺7am-7pm; ☒6, 8, 10, 13) In the northeastern corner of Plac Wolnica and founded in 1340, this was the first church in Kazimierz and for a long time the town's parish church. Its interior has been almost totally fitted out with baroque furnishings, including the huge high altar, extraordinary massive carved stalls in the chancel and a boat-shaped pulpit. Note the surviving early-15th-century stained-glass window in the sanctuary and the crucifix hanging above the chancel.

Ethnographic Museum
MUSEUM

(Muzeum Etnograficzne; Map p128; ☑12 430 5575; www.etnomuzeum.eu; Plac Wolnica 1; adult/concession 13/7zł, free Sun; ⊙11am-7pm Tue-Sun; ☐6, 8, 10, 13) The permanent exhibition here features the reconstructed interiors of traditional Polish peasant cottages and workshops, folk costumes, craft and trade exhibits, extraordinary nativity scenes, and folk and religious painting and wood-carving. The museum is housed within the former town hall of Kazimierz. It was built in the late 14th century and then significantly extended in the 16th century, during which it acquired its Renaissance appearance.

Pauline Church of
SS Michael & Stanislaus
CHURCH

(Skałka; Map p128; ☑12 619 0900; www.skalka.paulini.pl; ul Skałeczna 15; ⊙9am-7pm; ☐6, 8, 10, 13) Skałka, as this functioning monastery and religious shrine is called locally, dates to the early days of the Polish kingdom. In 1079, Bishop Stanisław Szczepanowski, later declared a Polish patron saint, was beheaded here by King Bolesław Śmiały (Boleslaus the Bold): the tree trunk where the deed was done is next to the altar. The church's baroque look comes from a mid-18th-century redesign. The crypt (closed December to February) shelters several eminent cultural figures, including Nobel-winning poet Czesław Miłosz (1911–2004).

⊙ Podgórze

This rapidly gentrifying, though still largely working-class suburb across the river from Kazimierz would receive few visitors if it weren't for the notorious role the area played during WWII. It was here the Germans herded some 16,000 Jews into a ghetto before sending them off to concentration camps. The most important sights recall these events, including the famed factory of Oskar Schindler, where many lives were saved. Otherwise it's mostly residential, with pockets of life but nothing to compare to Kazimierz or the Old Town.

★ Schindler's Factory
MUSEUM

(Fabryka Schindlera; Map p128; ☑12 257 1017; www.muzeumkrakowa.pl; ul Lipowa 4; adult/concession 24/18zł, free Mon; ⊙10am-4pm Mon, 9am-8pm Tue-Sun; ☐3, 19, 24) Despite the name, this museum covers more than the story of Oskar Schindler, the Nazi German industrialist who famously saved the lives of members of his Jewish labour force during the Holocaust. It also expands to include all aspects of the German occupation of Kraków from 1939 to 1945 through a series of well-organised, interactive exhibits. Take a tram to Plac Bohaterów Getta, then follow ul Kącik east under the railway line to find the museum.

Given the museum's popularity, it's highly advisable to book tickets in advance over a special ticketing website: www.bilety.mhk.pl.

Plac Bohaterów Getta
SQUARE

(Heroes of the Ghetto Square; Map p128; Plac Bohaterów Getta; ☐3, 19, 24) Known as Plac Zgody during the German occupation of WWII, this public square marks the beginning of the purpose-built Jewish wartime ghetto that stretched for several blocks in this part of Podgórze (there is a map showing the extent of the ghetto on the northern edge near a former German command post). During the

---

PODGÓRZE'S HEROES

Podgórze was home to at least two prominent Gentiles who risked their own lives to save Jewish people during the Holocaust.

The best known of course is Oskar Schindler, the heavy-drinking profiteer and antihero, whose story was told to millions through Thomas Keneally's book *Schindler's Ark* (1982) and Steven Spielberg's mega-hit film *Schindler's List* (1993).

Schindler originally saved the lives of Jews because he needed their cheap labour at his enamelware factory, though he went on to use his connections and pay bribes to keep his employees from being shipped off to concentration camps.

The other was pharmacist Tadeusz Pankiewicz, who was allowed to operate the Pharmacy Under the Eagle (p132) in the ghetto until the final deportation. Pankiewicz dispensed medicines (often without charge), carried news from the outside world and even allowed use of the establishment as a safe house on occasion.

As is movingly quoted at the end of Spielberg's film, in reference to a passage in the Talmud, 'Whoever saves one life, saves the world entire.'

war, the space served as a meeting ground for ghetto residents. It was also a deportation site as the ghetto was liquidated in 1942–43.

The 70 oversized metal chairs that stand on the square are part of a permanent street-art exhibit and are meant to stand in for the victims of German oppression who are no longer here.

Pharmacy Under the Eagle   MUSEUM
(Apteka Pod Orłem; Map p128; ☑12 656 5625; www.muzeumkrakowa.pl; Plac Bohaterów Getta 18; adult/concession 11/9zł, free Mon; ☺10am-2pm Mon, 9am-5pm Tue-Sun; ⌂3, 19, 24) This former pharmacy, on the south side of Plac Bohaterów Getta, tells the story of owner Tadeusz Pankiewicz, who risked life and limb trying to help the Jewish residents of the Podgórze ghetto during WWII. Pankiewicz, a Polish Gentile, was later honoured by Israel as being 'Righteous Among the Nations' for his efforts. The pharmacy's interior has been restored to its wartime appearance and tells the story of the ghetto and the role of the pharmacy in daily life.

Museum of Contemporary Art in Kraków   MUSEUM
(Map p128; ☑12 263 4000; www.mocak.pl; ul Lipowa 4; adult/concession 14/7zł, free Tue; ☺11am-7pm Tue-Sun; ⌂3, 19, 24) MOCAK is one of the city's most important venues for displaying contemporary art. The main draws here are high-quality rotating exhibitions, rather than an impressive permanent collection. As it's right next to Schindler's Factory, the two attractions can be combined for an absorbing day out.

Płaszów Labour Camp   HISTORIC SITE
(ul Jerozolimska, Płaszów; ☺dawn-dusk; ⌂3, 6, 11, 13, 24) FREE The former Płaszów forced-labour and concentration camp was built by occupying Germans during WWII to facilitate liquidation of the nearby Podgórze Jewish ghetto. At its height in 1943–44, the camp held some 25,000 people. These days, almost nothing of the camp survives with the exception of a few plaques. It's not easy to find. Enter via ul Jerozolimska (off ul Wielicka) or follow a path leading south from the Krakus Mound along the edge of the Liban Quarry.

Krakus Mound   MONUMENT
(Kopiec Krakusa; ul Maryewskiego, Podgórze; ☺dawn-dusk; ⌂3, 6, 11, 13, 24) FREE Nobody knows the exact origins of the 16m-high mound that towers over Podgórze. According to legend, it was the burial site of the city's founder, Krakus. Excavations in the 1930s could not confirm the story, but they did discover artefacts dating to the 8th century. The mysterious mound offers 360-degree panoramic views, including to the Old Town, Kazimierz, Nowa Huta and Płaszów.

◉ Western Kraków

★Kościuszko Mound   MONUMENT
(Kopiec Kościuszki; ☑12 425 1111; www.kopiec kosciuszki.pl; al Waszyngtona 1, Zwierzyniec; adult/concession 14/10zł; ☺9.30am-dusk; ⬆; ⌂100, 101) This mound, dedicated to Polish (and American) military hero Tadeusz Kościuszko (1746–1817), was erected between 1820 and 1823. It stands 34m high and includes soil from both the Polish and American battlefields where Kościuszko fought. The views over the city are spectacular. Admission includes the hike up the mound as well as a tour of the adjacent 19th-century fort, with exhibitions on Kościuszko's life. The memorial is located in Zwierzyniec, 3km west of the Old Town.

Piłsudski Mound   MONUMENT
(Kopiec Piłsudskiego w Krakowie; Zwierzyniec; ⌂134) FREE This mound-based memorial was erected in honour of Marshal Józef Piłsudski after his death in 1935; it was formed from soil taken from WWI Polish battle sites. The views of the city are excellent. Bus 134, which terminates at the zoo, is the nearest public transport. You can also reach the mound from the Kościuszko Mound on foot via a well-marked trail, taking about 2½ hours.

Zoological Gardens   ZOO
(Ogród Zoologiczny; ☑12 425 3551; www.zoo-krakow.pl; al Kasy Oszczędności Miasta Krakowa 14, Zwierzyniec; adult/concession 18/10zł; ☺9am-5pm; ⬆; ⌂134) The 20-hectare zoological gardens are well-tended and home to about 1500 animals. Highlights include a pair of Indian elephants, pygmy hippopotamuses, and a herd of rare Asian horses (Przewalski) that once roamed the Mongolian steppes. Bus 134 heads to the zoo from its terminus near the National Museum.

Premonstratensian Convent   MONASTERY
(☑12 427 1318; www.norbertanki.w.krakow.pl; ul Kościuszki 88, Zwierzyniec; ⌂1, 2, 6) FREE This imposing, fortified monastery, on the banks of the Wisla, has been home to the Sisters of the Order of St Norbert for more than 800 years. It's also the starting point for the annual springtime Lajkonik Pageant (p136).

'REMEMBER YOU MUST DIE'

Memento Mori ('remember you must die') is the motto of the reclusive **Camaldolese monks** (Klasztor Kamedułów; www.kameduli.info; Srebrna Góra; ⏱ 10-11am & 3.30-4.30pm; 🚌 109, 229, 239, 269) FREE. Just to make sure they live by this motto, the monks keep the skulls of their predecessors in their hermitages. It's just one of many practices that have earned this ancient order a reputation for asceticism and austerity.

Part of the Benedictine family, the Camaldolese order came to Poland from Italy in 1603. Kraków was the first of the Camaldolese seats in Poland; a church and 20 hermitages were established here between 1603 and 1642, and the whole complex was walled in. Not much has changed since.

Opposite the entrance to the monastery is the massive white limestone facade of the church. Underneath the chancel of the church is the crypt of the hermits, where their bodies are sealed in niches. Latin inscriptions state the age of the deceased and period spent in the hermitage. After 80 years, the niches are opened and the remains removed to a place of permanent rest. It's then that the hermits take the skulls to keep them company in their shelters.

◉ Eastern Kraków & Nowa Huta

★ Museum of the People's Republic of Poland   MUSEUM

(Muzeum PRL; ☎ 12 446 7821; www.mprl.pl; Osiedle Centrum E1, Nowa Huta; adult/concession 10/8zł, free Tue; ⏱ 9am-4pm Mon-Fri; 🚌 4, 10, 21, 22, 44) This museum and exhibition space, located in the socialist-realist Światowid cinema, focuses on the communist history of Nowa Huta and of Poland in general. Rotating photographic exhibitions highlight various aspects of life under communism, with plenty of local tie-ins to life in Nowa Huta. There's an atomic fall-out shelter in the basement, with a small exhibition on Poland's emergency preparations in the event of nuclear war.

Stanisław Lem Science Garden   MUSEUM

(☎ 12 346 1285; www.ogroddoswiadczen.pl; al Pokoju 68, Czyżyny; adult/concession 12/10zł; ⏱ 8.30am-7pm Mon-Fri, from 10am Sat & Sun Apr-Sep, shorter hours Oct; 🚻; 🚌 1, 14, 22) Science nerds will enjoy a day out at this interactive science park, about 4km east of the Old Town, dedicated to the memory of Polish science fiction writer Stanisław Lem. The outdoor exhibits explore some of the bizarre consequences of the laws of science, mechanics, optics and acoustics, and invite visitors to get involved, peering through prisms and striking gongs. Explanations are in both Polish and English.

Nowa Huta Underground   MUSEUM

(☎ 12 426 5060; www.muzeumkrakowa.pl; Osiedle Szkolne 37, Nowa Huta; adult/concession 11/8zł; ⏱ tours 10am-5pm Tue-Sun; 🚻; 🚌 4, 21, 22, 44) Nowa Huta's newest attraction opened in 2019 and focuses on the quarter's extensive network of atomic fallout shelters, built up in the 1950s and '60s. The museum is located in the basement of a school and guided tours take visitors through an elaborate series of shelters, each holding an exhibition on various aspects of civil defence during Poland's communist regime.

Rakowicki Cemetery   CEMETERY

(Cmentarz Rakowicki; ☎ 12 619 9900; www.zck-krakow.pl; ul Rakowicka 26; ⏱ 7am-6pm; 🚌 2) Arguably the city's most prestigious burial ground and the final resting place of several notable Poles, including Wisława Szymborska (1923–2012), the 1996 Nobel prize winner for literature. Stroll through the grounds to admire the beautifully crafted tombstones, many of which are works of art in their own right.

Botanical Gardens   GARDENS

(Ogród Botaniczny; ☎ 12 663 3635; www.ogrod. uj.edu.pl; ul Kopernika 27; adult/concession 9zł/5zł; ⏱ 9am-7pm, greenhouses 10am-6pm Sat-Thu, museum 10am-2pm Thu & Fri, 11am-3pm Sun; 🚌 4, 10, 14, 20, 44, 52) The botanical gardens of Jagiellonian University comprise nearly ten hectares of green and flowery loveliness. Besides the fresh air and beautiful blooms, the gardens offer fascinating exhibits of medicinal plants, endangered species of Polish flora and plants described in the Bible. The amazing orchid collection dates to the 1860s.

THE WORKERS PARADISE OF NOWA HUTA

The youngest and largest of Kraków's suburbs, Nowa Huta (New Steelworks) is a result of the post-WWII rush toward industrialisation. In the early 1950s, the communist planners designed an enormous new residential district to house workers for a new steelworks to be built a few kilometres east of the centre of Kraków. The reigning style was socialist-realist and, to this day, the neighbourhood retains a hint of old communist feel.

The steelworks can't be visited, but you may want to have a peek at the suburb's austere socialist-realist lines (certainly a shock after the Old Town's medieval streets). In its day, Nowa Huta was held up as a model of communist-era town planning, and the architectural symmetry lends a funky retro feeling.

Trams from the main train station will drop you at **Plac Centralny** (⬛ 4, 10, 22, 44), the suburb's grand central square, which once had a statue of Lenin at its centre. From here, the best bet is to wander amid the stone-grey housing projects – still in remarkably good shape – where families continue to live and raise their children.

Outside of the planned community, the history of the Nowa Huta area stretches back centuries. About 1km east of Nowa Huta, you'll find the sprawling Cistercian Monastery and a remarkable wooden church dating from the 15th century.

⊙ Wieliczka

★ **Wieliczka Salt Mine**　　　　　MUSEUM
(📞 12 278 7302; www.kopalnia.pl; ul Daniłowicza 10, Wieliczka; adult/concession 94/74zł; ⏱ 7.30am-7.30pm Apr-Oct, 8am-5pm Nov-Mar; 🚼) Some 14km southeast of Kraków, the Wieliczka (vyeh-leech-kah) salt mine has been welcoming tourists since 1722 and today is one of Poland's most popular attractions. It's a subterranean labyrinth of tunnels and chambers – about 300km distributed over nine levels, the deepest being 327m underground – of which a small part is open to the public via two-hour guided tours. First-time visitors take a standard 'tourist' route of the main sights, while return visitors can opt for a more-immersive 'miners' route.

The salt-hewn formations include chapels with altarpieces and figures, while others are adorned with statues and monuments – and there are even underground lakes. The climax of the tour is the vast chamber (54m by 18m, and 12m high) housing the ornamented Chapel of St Kinga (Kaplica Św Kingi). Every single element here, from chandeliers to altarpieces, is made of salt. It took over 30 years (1895) for three men to complete this underground temple, and about 20,000 tonnes of rock salt had to be removed. Other highlights are the salt lake in the Erazm Barącz Chamber, whose water is denser than the Dead Sea, and the awe-inspiring 36m-high Stanisław Staszic Chamber.

Included in the entry price is a further one-hour tour of the Kraków Saltworks Museum, accommodated in 14 chambers on the third level of the mine, where the main tour ends, but most visitors appear to be 'salted out' by then. Here you can visit the underground restaurant, after which it's another 15-minute walk to the lift that takes you back up to the real world.

Visitors are guided in groups and the tour takes about two hours. You walk about 2km through the mine, so wear comfortable shoes. The temperature in the mine is 14°C. In July and August English-language tours depart every half-hour from 8.30am to 6pm. During the rest of the year there are between six and eight daily tours in English.

A second touring option is aimed at repeat visitors who have already seen the main sights. The 'miners' route bypasses the mine's highlights in favour of a more immersive experience – visitors wear standard mining clothes and gear (including respirators) and set off in groups of 20 to live the life of a salt-miner for the three-hour tour. It's great for older kids and more adventurous adults. The tour departs from the Regis Shaft, near the centre of Wieliczka.

To reach Wieliczka, both trains and buses depart regularly from the main train and bus stations. The trip costs around 4zł and takes around 30 minutes. Several tour operators, including Cracow City Tours (p136), run bus tours to the mine, starting at around 150zł, including admission.

🏃 Activities

Kraków's best activities are low key. A stroll along the Vistula or through one of the many parks, such as Planty (p124), Jordan (p126) or Krakowski (p126). Jordan Park offers the possibility of ice-skating in winter. There are plenty of guided tours to cater to everyone's tastes.

Ster   CRUISE
(Map p120; ☑ 601 560 250; www.rejsykrakow.com; cruise 1hr adult/concession 40/30zł, 5hr 85/70zł; ⊙ 10am-6pm May-Oct; ⊕; ☐ 1, 2, 6) One-hour river tours of Kraków landmarks and longer five-hour trips out to the Benedictine Abbey in Tyniec aboard the *Peter Pan* or *Sobieski* – the longer trip allows for a one-hour stop at the abbey before turning around. Reserve tickets online or by phone. The departure point is not far from the Dębnicki Bridge, below the Sheraton Kraków hotel, and accessed from ul Zwierzyniecka.

Statek Nimfa   CRUISE
(Map p128; ☑ 12 422 0855; www.statekkrakow.com; Wawel Pier; cruise 1hr adult/concession 40/30zł, 4hr 85/70zł; ⊙ 10am-6pm May-Oct; ⊕; ☐ 6, 8, 10, 13, 18) The pleasure boat *Nimfa* cruises along the Vistula River, departing from the pier below Wawel Royal Castle, and motoring past sights such as Kościuszko Mound, Skałka and Plac Bohaterów Getta, with up-close views of all six bridges. The four-hour tour goes all the way to Tyniec. Reserve tickets online or by phone.

🍲 Courses

A few companies offer food tours of the city. These usually entail visits to a handful of restaurants, with tastings paired with beer, wine or vodka. Cooking classes are also available.

Delicious Poland   COOKING
(www.deliciouspoland.com) Offers two food tours daily and tastings of a dozen traditional Polish specialities. They also have vodka- and craft-beer-sampling crawls and courses for cooking pierogi. Check the website for a full menu and to register. Tours normally meet in Eastern Kraków, though they occasionally start in front of the Old Synagogue (p127) in Kazimierz – check when you book.

Eat Polska   COOKING
(https://eatpolska.com/foodtour) Offers a fun menu of guided food-tastings, beer- and vodka-quaffing, and classes on making pierogi and other traditional foods. Choose a tour and register over the website.

☞ Tours

Many companies offer guided tours of the city or of particular neighbourhoods. These usually involve walking, but tours on bus, bike and golf cart are common. A guided tour also makes good sense for day-trip destinations like the Wieliczka Salt Mine because the tour company can sort out travel and ticketing logistics.

★ Free Walking Tour   WALKING
(Map p120; ☑ 513 875 815; www.freewalkingtour.com; ☐ 2, 4, 14, 18, 20, 24, 44) **FREE** These walking tours of the Old Town and Kazimierz are provided by licensed tour guides who make their money from tips. The Old Town tours depart four times daily from March to October (shorter hours November to February) from near the Florian Gate (p124). Look for a guide holding a yellow umbrella. Check the website for other tours.

WowKrakow!   BUS
(Jordan Group; Map p128; ☑ 601 502 129; www.wowkrakow.pl; ul Gęsia 8; per 24/48hr 60/90zł; ⊙ 8am-6pm Mon-Fri; ☐ 3, 19, 24) Popular 'Hop-On Hop-Off' bus tour that allows passengers to stop at their leisure at some 15 different areas of interest around town. Buses depart hourly from near the Galeria Kazimierz. See the website for an up-to-date timetable and route. The parent company, Jordan Group (p154), also sells international bus tickets and airport transfers.

Cool Tour Company   CYCLING
(Map p120; ☑ 12 430 2034; www.krakowbiketour.com; ul Grodzka 2; ☐ 1, 6, 8, 13, 18) Cool Tour Company offers a four-hour spin on wheels around town (90zł) that departs twice daily from May to September at 10am and 3pm. The tour takes in everything from the Old Town walls and Wawel Hill to Oskar Schindler's factory in Podgórze. Check the website for other cycling and walking tours.

> **ⓘ TOURING NOWA HUTA**
>
> A guided tour can be an enjoyable way of exploring Nowa Huta, the socialist-realist workers' suburb. Companies such as **Crazy Guides** (☑ 500 091 200; www.crazyguides.com) offer rides in old-school, communist-era Trabant cars and explore the area's old nuclear-fallout shelters.

KRAKÓW TOURS

Kraków Pub Crawl WALKING
(Map p120; ☑500 575 221; www.krawlthrough
krakow.com; Rynek Główny; tours 60zł; ⊙9pm Mon-
Sun; ☑1, 6, 8, 13, 18) This tour, which visits four
venues and includes unlimited drinks for an
hour at the first bar, starts out from the Main
Market Square in front of the Adam Mickiewicz statue. Book in advance over the website or simply show up for the tour.

Krk Bike Rental BICYCLE HIRE
(☑509 267 733; www.krkbikerental.pl; ul Św Anny
4; per hr/day 12/60zł; ☑1, 6, 8, 13, 18) This outfit
runs 3½-hour city tours (per person 90zł,
minimum three people), which must be
booked in advance. It also rents city bikes
and mountain bikes, as well as electric bikes
(per hour/day 20/100zł).

Krak Tourist TOURS
(☑501 050 939; www.kraktourist.pl) Offers guided tours of the city, based on themes such as
'Christian and Jewish Kazimierz', the 'Kings
Road', 'Kraków Legends' and 'Styles in Art'.

Cracovia Walking Tours WALKING
(Map p120; ☑537 226 125; www.cracoviawalking
tours.com; Rynek Główny 1/3; ⊙tours 10.15pm;
☑1, 6, 8, 13, 18) FREE Two-hour walking tours,
conducted by licensed guides, through the
Old Town. Also does tours to Kazimierz and
Podgórze. All tours depart from the Main Market Square (in front of the Adam Mickiewicz
Statue). Consult the website for a full list of
tours and times. Register online or by phone,
or simply turn up for the tour in person.

Jarden Tourist Agency CULTURAL
(Map p128; ☑12 421 7166; www.jarden.pl; ul Szeroka
2; ⊙9am-6pm Mon-Fri, from 10am Sat & Sun; ☑3,
19, 24) Mainly Jewish-themed tours, including two- and three-hour walking tours of
Kraków's Kazimierz and Podgórze, as well as a
popular two-hour driving tour of places made
famous by the film *Schindler's List*. Tours are
priced per person, ranging from 50zł to 100zł,
depending on the number participating.

Cracow City Tours – Old Town TOURS
(Map p120; ☑12 421 1327; www.cracowcitytours.pl; ul
Floriańska 44; city tour adult/concession 120/100zł;
⊙10am-8pm; ☑2, 4, 14, 18, 20, 24, 44) A decent
range of city walking and bus tours, including
a popular four-hour bus tour (120zł), as well
as longer day excursions to the Wieliczka Salt
Mine (180zł) and the Auschwitz-Birkenau Memorial and Museum (155zł). Bus tours depart
from a branch office on **Plac Matejki** (Map
p120; ☑12 421 1333; Plac Matejki 2; ⊙8am-6pm),
just north of Florian Gate.

🎊 Festivals & Events

Kraków has one of the richest cycles of annual events in Poland. The first port of call
for information is the nearest branch of the
InfoKraków tourist office. The Kraków Festival Guide website (www.krakowfestival.
com) maintains a handy list in English.

Shanties MUSIC
(International Festival of Sailors' Songs; www.
shanties.pl; ⊙Feb) Going strong since 1981,
despite Kraków's inland location. Held at the

ICONIC LAJKONIK: KRAKÓW'S COLOURFUL HORSEMAN

A curious symbol of Kraków is the Lajkonik, a bearded man dressed in richly embroidered
garments and a tall pointed hat, riding a hobbyhorse. He comes to life on the Thursday
after Corpus Christi (late May or June) and heads a joyful **pageant** (www.mhk.pl; ⊙May or
Jun) from the Premonstratensian Convent (p132) in Zwierzyniec to the Old Town's Main
Market Square.

Exact details of the Lajkonik's origins are hard to pin down, but one story involves
a Tatar assault on Kraków in 1287. A group of raftsmen discovered the tent of the
commanding khan on a foray outside the city walls and dispatched the unsuspecting
Tatar leader and his generals in a lightning raid. The raftsmen's leader then wore the
khan's richly decorated outfit back to the city.

The pageant, accompanied by a musical band, lasts about six hours, during which
the Lajkonik takes to dancing, jumping, greeting passersby, popping into cafes en route,
collecting donations and striking people with his mace, which is said to bring them good
luck. Once the pageant reaches the main square, the Lajkonik is greeted by the mayor
and presented with a symbolic ransom and a goblet of wine.

The Lajkonik's garb and his hobbyhorse were designed by Stanisław Wyspiański; the
original design is kept in the Historical Museum of Kraków (p123). It consists of a wooden
frame covered with leather and embroidered with nearly a thousand pearls and coral
beads. The whole outfit weighs about 40kg.

Stary Port (Map p120; ☑ 508 227 752; www.stary port.com.pl; ul Straszewskiego 27; ⊘ noon-midnight, to 3am Fri & Sat; ☎; ☐ 1, 6, 8, 13, 18) and other venues across the city.

Juvenalia CULTURAL
(www.juwenalia.krakow.pl; ⊘ May) During this carnival, students receive symbolic keys to the town's gates and take over the city for four days and three nights. There's live music, street dancing, fancy-dress parades, masquerades and lots of fun.

Kraków Film Festival FILM
(www.kff.com.pl; ⊘ late May–early Jun) Film festival that's been going strong for more than half a century and screens hundreds of movies from various countries.

Miłosz Festival LITERATURE
(www.miloszfestival.pl; ⊘ Jun) Dedicated to the late Polish poet and Nobel laureate Czesław Miłosz, this festival celebrates Polish and Central European poetry through readings, discussion groups and music. Held at various venues.

Wianki Festival MUSIC
(www.wianki.krakow.pl; ⊘ Jun) Boisterous, outdoor midsummer-night concert held along the Vistula River, just below Wawel Royal Castle, accompanied by lots of dancing and fireworks.

★ Jewish Culture Festival CULTURAL
(www.jewishfestival.pl; ⊘ late Jun–early Jul) A 10-day celebration of Jewish arts and culture, with theatre, film, music and art exhibitions. Concludes with a grand open-air klezmer concert on ul Szeroka.

International Festival of Street Theatre THEATRE
(www.teatrkto.pl) Takes place on the Main Market Square across four days in early July.

Pierogi Festival FOOD & DRINK
(www.biurofestiwalowe.pl; Mały Rynek; ⊘ Aug) Three-day celebration of the mighty dumpling.

Divine Comedy International Theatre Festival THEATRE
(Boska Komedia; www.boskakomedia.pl) The best of Polish dramatic comedy as well as presentations by visiting foreign theatre troupes. Held at various venues in December.

Kraków Christmas Crib Competition CHRISTMAS
(www.szopki.eu) Held on the main square beside the statue of Adam Mickiewicz on the first Thursday of December. The 'cribs' are nativity scenes, but different from those found elsewhere in the world. Kraków's *szopki* are elaborate compositions built in an architectural, usually church-like, form and made in astonishing detail from cardboard, wood, tinfoil and the like.

🛏 Sleeping

As Poland's premier tourist destination, Kraków has plenty of accommodation options. However, advance booking is recommended for anywhere central. The Old Town has a selection of accommodation across all budget ranges. Kazimierz also has a number of hostels and atmospheric hotels in a relatively quiet location. Note that the more expensive hotels sometimes quote prices in euros.

🛏 Old Town & Around

The Old Town and adjoining neighbourhoods offer a plentiful supply of budget places, typically bright, clean, modern hostels with multilingual staff and extras such as washing machines and dryers. There are a decent number of midrange hotels within walking distance of the Main Market Square and other major sights, and no shortage of places for a top-end splurge.

★ Goodbye Lenin Revolution Hostel HOSTEL €
(Map p120; ☑ 12 341 4666; www.goodbyelenin.pl; ul Dolnych Młynów 9; dm 55-65zł, d 160zł; ☎; ☐ 2, 4, 14, 18, 20, 24, 44) The folks at Kazimierz's 'Goodbye Lenin' have opened up a second location here, just across the street from the bars and nights spots of the Tytano tobacco factory complex. Expect the same clean, well-run standards of the original hostel, and the jaunty (but toned-down here) communist-design kitsch. Dorm rooms have four to eight beds, including an all-female dorm.

Pink Panther's Hostel HOSTEL €
(Map p120; ☑ 12 422 0935; www.pinkpanthers hostel.com; ul Św Tomasza 8/10; dm 50-72zł, d 230zł; @ ☎; ☐ 2, 4, 14, 18, 20, 24, 44) A self-described party hostel, this is a good choice for budget travellers in town to enjoy the nightlife. Simple dorm accommodation in four- to 14-bed dorms, with some private doubles. The staff put on organised pub crawls, as well as themed nights, in the public area and small terrace. Note it's two floors up, and there's no lift.

Cracow Hostel
HOSTEL €

(Map p120; ☑ 12 429 1106; www.cracowhostel.com; Rynek Główny 18; dm 46-70zł, r 270zł; 🛜; 🏠1, 6, 8, 13, 18) Location, location, location. This standard hostel on three floors may not be the best in town, with somewhat cramped rooms of between four and 18 beds. But it's perched high above the Main Market Square, with an amazing view from the comfortable lounge. There's also a pretty apartment on offer with big windows that's very attractively priced for the locale.

Greg & Tom Home Hostel
HOSTEL €

(Map p120; ☑ 12 422 4100; www.gregtomhostel.com; ul Pawia 12/7; dm 65-70zł, d150zł; @🛜; 🏠3, 5, 17, 19, 50) This well-run hostel is spread over three locations, though check-in is handled at this branch, close to the main train and bus stations. The staff are friendly, the rooms are clean and laundry facilities are included. Accommodation is in four- and six-bed mixed dorms, as well as some private doubles. Book in advance as this place is popular.

★ Balthazar Design Hotel
BOUTIQUE HOTEL €€

(Map p120; ☑ 12 446 6000; www.balthazarhotel.com; ul Grodzka 63; s/d 310/430zł; ✳@🛜; 🏠6, 8, 10, 13, 18) The Balthazar opened to strong reviews in early 2019 for its bold design, cleanliness, location close to Wawel Royal Castle and very good food, including at the in-house Restaurant Fiorentina. The rooms and lobby areas are a riot of colours and patterns, with each space uniquely designed to highlight period details.

★ Hotel Indigo
BOUTIQUE HOTEL €€

(Map p120; ☑ 12 300 3030; www.hotelindigo.com; ul Św Filipa 18; r from 500zł; P✳🛜; 🏠2, 4, 14, 18, 20, 24, 44) Part of the InterContinental chain, the Indigo occupies a 19th-century townhouse once lived in by Polish painter Jan Matejko. The eye-popping room design features lots of art, set off by exposed brick and beautifully beamed ceilings in some rooms. There's a highly rated in-house restaurant and the sites of the Old Town are about 10 minutes' walk away.

Hotel Pod Wawelem
HOTEL €€

(Map p120; ☑ 12 426 2626; www.hotelpodwawelem.pl; Plac Na Groblach 22; s 300zł, d 380-410zł, ste 460zł; ✳@🛜; 🏠1, 2, 6) At the foot of Wawel and overlooking the river, this hotel gets high marks for crisp, up-to-date design and an excellent breakfast buffet. The rooms are generously proportioned and look either onto the river or the castle. The view from the rooftop cafe is stunning. Not suited for drivers, as parking in this part of town is difficult.

Hotel Wawel
HOTEL €€

(Map p120; ☑ 12 424 1300; www.hotelwawel.pl; ul Poselska 22; s/d 380/540zł; ✳🛜🏊; 🏠1, 2, 6) Ideally located off central ul Grodzka, this hotel contains large, comfortable and stylish rooms. It's set far back from the main drag, but the pealing of church bells in the morning is still audible. Nevertheless, it's a romantic place, made nicer by a beautiful garden as well as a spa and steam room.

Hotel Amadeus
HOTEL €€

(Map p120; ☑ 12 429 6070; www.hotel-amadeus.pl; ul Mikołajska 20; s/d 500/600zł; ✳@🛜; 🏠3, 10, 24, 52) Amadeus, with its Mozart-inspired flair, is one of Kraków's most refined hotels. Its rooms are tastefully furnished (if somewhat small) and service is of a high standard. There's a sauna and a small fitness centre, and a well-regarded gourmet restaurant. Check out the photos of famous guests in the lobby.

Hotel Royal
HOTEL €€

(Map p120; ☑ 12 421 3500; www.amwhotele.pl; ul Św Gertrudy 26-29; s/d from 270/370zł; P@🛜; 🏠6, 8, 10, 13, 18) The rooms within this large and impressive art nouveau edifice could use an update but will appeal to travellers who love period details like high ceilings and spiral staircases. The location is excellent, just a few minutes walk to Wawel Hill. The in-house restaurant (featuring traditional Polish cooking) and garden get high marks.

Grand Ascot Hotel
BOUTIQUE HOTEL €€

(Map p120; ☑ 12 446 7602; www.grandascot.pl; ul Józefa Szujskiego 4; s/d 550/650zł; P✳🛜; 🏠2, 4, 8, 13, 14, 18, 20, 24) Gleaming, white-clad modern hotel within easy walking distance of the attractions, restaurants and bars of this very trendy part of town. The rooms and public areas embrace a stylish, minimalist aesthetic, with tastefully chosen wood grains, retro lighting and neutral fabrics. There's an on-site bar, though there are many alternatives on its doorstep. Rates drop outside of the summer season.

★ Metropolitan Boutique Hotel
BOUTIQUE HOTEL €€€

(Map p120; ☑ 12 442 7500; www.hotelmetropolitan.pl; ul Joselewicza 19; s/d 600/650zł; P✳@🛜; 🏠3, 19, 24) An excellent choice for travellers who prefer a Kazimierz location but who want more comfort than hotels in that part of town usually offer. This luxury boutique fuses modern design within the confines of a 19th-century townhouse. The rooms are done out in chocolate browns, enlivened by bold stripes and patterns. Service is excellent, as is the in-house 'FAB Fusion' restaurant.

★**Hotel Stary** HOTEL €€€

(Map p120; ☑ 12 384 0808; www.stary.hotel.com. pl; ul Szczepańska 5; s/d 850/950zł; ❄@🛜🏊; 🚋2, 4, 14, 18, 20, 24, 44) Each of the 78 rooms at this four-storey hotel in an 18th-century aristocratic residence is individually designed and exudes charm. Period details, like exposed-beam ceilings and shiny parquet flooring, have been retained or given a modern gloss, such as the marble in the baths. Some rooms have balconies. Enjoy drinks on the rooftop terrace or soak in the pool.

Hotel Copernicus HOTEL €€€

(Map p120; ☑ 12 424 3400; https://copernicus. hotel.com.pl; ul Kanonicza 16; s 800zł, d 900-1000zł; ❄🛜🏊; 🚋6, 8, 10, 13, 18) Nestled in two beautifully restored buildings in one of Kraków's most picturesque and atmospheric streets, the Copernicus is one of the city's finest and most luxurious hotels. The rooftop terrace with spectacular views over Wawel and the swimming pool in a medieval vaulted brick cellar add to the hotel's allure.

🛏 **Kazimierz & Podgórze**

In addition to some hostels in the vicinity of busy ul Dietla, Kazimierz has a small selection of interesting midrange hotels, some with a distinctive Jewish flavour. In the past couple of years, as the neighbourhood has become more popular, new, trendy boutiques have moved in. It's a pleasant and peaceful area in which to stay. Podgórze, just across the river from Kazimierz, is a little quieter and out of the action, but everything is just a short walk away. On the downside, there are not many hotels here.

Good Bye Lenin Pub & Garden HOSTEL €

(Map p120; ☑ 506 270 541; www.goodbyelenin.pl; ul Joselewicza 23; dm 55-65zł, d 160zł; 🛜; 🚋3, 19, 24) This cheerful place has a cheeky communist theme with absurd paintings and statues mocking the imagery of the era. Most dorm rooms have four to 10 beds, including an all-female dorm. The small garden out front is popular for lounging and barbecue. The hostel can be tricky to find. It's located in an alley to the right as you approach from ul Starowiślna.

Hostel Atlantis HOSTEL €

(Map p120; ☑ 12 421 0861; www.atlantishostel. pl; ul Dietla 58; dm from 45zł, d/tr 190/220zł; 🛜; 🚋3, 9, 11, 19, 22, 24, 50, 52) Colourful, well-maintained hostel situated near the southern end of the Old Town, within easy walking distance of Kazimierz's Plac Nowy and Wawel Hill. The prices for a bunk in a four-, six- or eight-bed dorm room are some of the cheapest in the city and a great choice for travellers on a tight budget.

Mundo Hostel HOSTEL €

(Map p120; ☑ 12 422 6113; www.mundohostel.eu; ul Sarego 10; dm 60-65zł, d 170-190zł; @🛜; 🚋1, 6, 8, 10, 13, 18) Attractive, well-maintained hostel in a quiet courtyard location neatly placed between the Old Town and Kazimierz. Each room is decorated for a different country; for example the Tibet room is decked out with colourful prayer flags. Barbecues take place in summer. There's a bright, fully equipped kitchen for do-it-yourself meals.

★**PURO Kraków Kazimierz** HOTEL €€

(Map p128; ☑ 12 889 9000; www.purohotel.pl; ul Halicka 14a; s/d 350/450zł; P❄🛜; 🚋3, 19, 24) Everything you want in a hotel and nothing you don't need might be a suitable motto for this clean, modern, minimalist boutique chain. The bedrooms are all white linens and light woods. There's a bar on-site and, though the location lies just outside Kazimierz, all of that district's attractions, restaurants and bars are within an easy five- to 10-minute walk.

★**INX Design Hotel** BOUTIQUE HOTEL €€

(Map p128; ☑ 12 354 4590; www.inxdesignhotel.pl; ul Starowiślna 91; s/d 380/450zł; P❄@🛜; 🚋3, 19, 24) The owners of this trendy Kazimierz boutique have thought hard about design, drawing on Polish modernist painter Zofia Stryjeńska for inspiration. The result is a clean, modern hotel, with funky art deco inspired details. The location is five minutes' walk from central Plac Nowy and right on a tram line for exploring further afield.

★**Plaza Boutique Hotel** BOUTIQUE HOTEL €€

(Map p128; ☑ 690 624 251; www.plazahotelkrakow. pl; ul Legionów Józefa Piłsudskiego 17; s/d 250/300zł; P❄🛜; 🚋6, 8, 10, 13) Just a tad shy of its advertised four stars, though an excellent choice. The rooms are spotless and sport a crisp, contemporary look, with a splash of colour. The Plaza has a small but well-equipped fitness centre and a good in-house restaurant. The English-speaking reception is helpful. The location, near the center of Podgórze, is well-served by trams to the centre.

Hotel Eden
HOTEL €€

(Map p128; ☑12 430 6565; www.hoteleden.pl; ul Ciemna 15; s/d from 220/330zł; ❄ 🖥; 🖥3, 19, 24) Located within three meticulously restored 15th-century townhouses (which can be spotted in some of the street scenes in the film *Schindler's List*), the Eden has comfortable rooms and comes complete with a sauna and the only *mikvah* (traditional Jewish bath) in Kraków. Kosher meals are available on request.

Hotel Kazimierz
HOTEL €€

(Map p128; ☑12 421 6629; www.hk.com.pl; ul Miodowa 16; s/d 420/520zł; P ❄ @ 🖥; 🖥6, 8, 10, 13) Prices have risen dramatically at this popular hotel near the centre of Kazimierz, putting it right on the border of good value/ overpriced. The room furnishings are on the plain side, but clean and cosy. The breakfast buffet, included in most room packages, is excellent. The central location puts you right on the doorstep of the neighbourhood's attractions and restaurants.

Hotel Pugetów
HISTORIC HOTEL €€€

(Map p120; ☑12 432 4950; www.donimirski.com/ hotel-pugetow; ul Starowiślna 15a; s/d 550/700zł; P ❄ 🖥; 🖥1, 3, 17, 19, 22, 24, 52) This charming historic hotel stands proudly next to the 19th-century neo-Renaissance palace of the same name. It offers just seven rooms with distinctive names and identities (eg the 'Joseph Conrad' and the 'Bonaparte'). Think embroidered bathrobes, black-marble baths and a fabulous breakfast room in the basement.

🛏 Outside the Centre

Camping Smok
CAMPGROUND €

(☑12 429 8300; www.smok.krakow.pl; ul Kamedulska 18, Zwierzyniec; site per person/tent 30/20zł, d/tr 180/240zł; P 🖥; 🖥1, 2, 6) This quiet camping ground is around 4km west of the Old Town in leafy Zwierzyniec. Also on offer are good-value double and triple rooms. To get here from the train station, take tram 1, 2 or 6 to the end of the line at Salwator and change for any westbound bus, asking the driver to stop at the campground.

★ U Pana Cogito
HOTEL €€

(☑12 269 7200; www.pcogito.pl; ul Bałuckiego 6, Dębniki; s/d/q 280/330/400zł; P ❄ @ 🖥; 🖥17, 18, 22, 52) White and cream seem to be the colours of choice at this friendly 14-room hotel in a lovely mansion across the river and southwest of the centre. All rooms have big bathrooms and refrigerators; for extra privacy, there's an apartment with a separate entrance. The hotel also has its own restaurant, also done out in fresh, minimalist white.

🍴 Eating

Kraków has a rapidly evolving food scene that just gets better and better. Both the Old Town and Kazimierz are packed with restaurants serving a wide range of international cuisines and catering to every pocket. Kazimierz has several restaurants offering Jewish-style cuisine. You'll find quick bites and street eats everywhere.

🍴 Old Town & Around

When it comes to eating out, the Old Town and immediate surroundings are home to the best of the best, and there's lots of variety for every budget. The top end includes very fancy Polish or French restaurants, where food is served on white linens, often in a regally appointed Gothic cellar. Moving down the price chain, you'll find Indian, Italian and Asian restaurants, all the way to vegan bakeries and delicious cafe meals. There's plenty of street and fast-food options as well.

★ Glonojad
VEGETARIAN €

(Map p120; ☑12 346 1677; www.glonojad.com; Plac Matejki 2; mains 15-22zł; ⊙8am-10pm Mon-Fri, from 9am Sat & Sun; 🖥 🖥; 🖥2, 4, 14, 18, 20, 24, 44) This appealing and popular self-service cafeteria has a great view on to Plac Matejki, just north of the Barbican. The diverse menu has a variety of tempting vegetarian dishes including samosas, curries, potato pancakes, falafel, veggie lasagne and soups. The breakfast menu is served till noon.

Cakester
BAKERY €

(Map p120; ☑12 307 0503; www.facebook.com/ cakestercafekrakow; ul Św Tomasza 25; mains 15-30zł; ⊙9am-8pm; 🖥 🖥; 🖥3, 10, 24, 52) Cheery throwback bakery with plenty of breakfasts, toasted sandwiches, pancakes and waffles on the menu, as well as excellent coffees and shakes. The big draw is the attention to dietary preferences. Whether you're vegan, vegetarian or gluten-free, there's plenty of choice.

Chimera Salad Bar
VEGETARIAN €

(Map p120; ☑12 292 1212; www.chimera.com.pl; ul Św Anny 3; mains 15-30zł; ⊙9am-10pm; 🖥 🖥; 🖥2, 8, 13, 18, 20) The ideal quick and simple Old Town lunch: grab a plate (big or small) and fill it with all those veggie items that look so good. The covered courtyard provides a delightful setting. Be careful not to wander into the restaurant of the same name downstairs, which is good but significantly more expensive.

Charlotte Chleb i Wino
BAKERY €

(Map p120; ☑ 600 807 880; www.bistrocharlotte.pl; Plac Szczepański 2; salads & sandwiches 15-30zł; ⊙7am-midnight Mon-Fri, to 1am Fri, 8am-1pm Sat, 8am-10pm Sun; 🛜; 🚊2, 4, 14, 18, 20, 24, 44) This is the Kraków branch of a popular Warsaw restaurant serving croissants, French breads, salads and sandwiches. The crowds on artsy Plac Szczepański are suitably stylish as they tuck into their croque monsieurs and sip from excellent but affordable French wines. The perfect stop for morning coffee.

U Babci Maliny
POLISH €

(Map p120; ☑ 12 422 7601; www.kuchniaubabci maliny.pl; ul Sławkowska 17; mains 12-25zł; ⊙11am-11pm Mon-Fri, from noon Sat & Sun; 🛜; 🚊2, 4, 14, 18, 20, 24, 44) This rustic basement is hidden within the courtyard of the Polish Academy of Learning. Simply descend the stairs like you know where you're going and follow your nose to the dumplings, meat dishes and salads. One of the specialities worth a try is the house *żurek* (a sour rye soup flavoured with sausage), served here in a bread bowl.

Bar Grodzki
POLISH €

(Map p120; ☑ 12 422 6807; www.grodzkibar. zaprasza.net; ul Grodzka 47/4; mains 10-20zł; ⊙9am-7pm Mon-Sat, from 10am Sun; ☑; 🚊1, 6, 8, 13, 18) Delightful, family-run *bar mleczny* (milk bar), but a slight step up from the typical cafeteria setting. Line up at the steam table and choose your food. Highlights include a range of coleslaws, classic Polish mains like stuffed cabbage rolls and delicious *kompot* (juice of stewed fruit).

Milkbar Tomasza
POLISH €

(Map p120; ☑ 12 422 1706; ul Św Tomasza 24; mains 12-20zł; ⊙8am-8pm Tue-Sat, from 9am Sun; 🛜; 🚊3, 10, 24, 52) A modern take on a traditional Polish *bar mleczny*, where the panini sit proudly beside the pierogi. It's a clean casual space, with lots of light, bright colours and exposed brick walls.

Polskie Smaki
POLISH €

(Map p120; ☑ 12 429 3869; www.polskie-smaki. pl; ul Św Tomasza 5; mains 12-22zł; ⊙9am-10pm; ☑; 🚊2, 4, 14, 18, 20, 24, 44) This place has more atmosphere than your typical milk bar, thanks to the Gothic vaulted ceiling, but the food is still straightforward and simple. Look for things like stuffed peppers, pork cutlets and fried liver with mushrooms.

Hawełka
POLISH €€

(Map p120; ☑ 12 422 0631; www.hawelka.pl; Rynek Główny 34; mains 48-64zł; ⊙noon-11pm; 🛜; 🚊2, 4, 14, 18, 20, 24, 44) Anyone who values art nouveau or the paintings of Gustav Klimt should be prepared to be dazzled. Step inside and travel back 100 years. The traditional Polish food, like Kraków-style duck, is nothing to sneeze at either and the daily lunch specials (32zł) are excellent value. Eat out on the main square in nice weather.

Chimera
POLISH €€

(Map p120; ☑ 12 292 1212; www.chimera.com.pl; ul Św Anny 3; mains 40-65zł; ⊙noon-10pm; 🛜; 🚊2, 8, 13, 18, 20) Not to be confused with the salad bar of the same name, this is a Kraków classic. The vaulted 14th century cellar is the perfect setting to sample their speciality roasted lamb, goose or game meats.

STREET FOOD: POLISH PIZZA & BELGIAN FRIES

Kraków has loads of restaurants, but come 11pm most serious food options close down. Thankfully, street-food vendors keep going, giving you ample opportunity to quash the late-night munchies. Kazimierz, specifically **Plac Nowy** (Map p128; ⊙from 7am; 🚊6, 8, 10, 13), is ground zero for Polish pizza – otherwise known as *zapiekanka*. It's essentially half of a baguette, topped with cheese, ham and mushrooms. It's a cheap, filling snack that tastes especially delicious after midnight. Indeed, there may be no reason to eat it before midnight.

Not your cup of tea? No worries. Try out the various **food trucks** (Map p128; www. facebook.com/skwerjudah; ul Św Wawrzyńca 16; mains 8-20zł; ⊙noon-11pm, to 1am Fri & Sat, to 10pm Sun; 🚊3, 19, 24) that have set up shop on an isolated square a couple blocks southeast of Plac Nowy. There you'll find burgers, ice cream, stuffed baked potatoes and a local favourite: Belgian fries. A more traditional option is to have a grilled sausage, served nightly (except Sunday) till 3am from a sidewalk vendor at **Hala Targowa** (Map p120; ul Grzegórzecka 3; ⊙7am-3pm, to noon Sun; 🚊1, 17, 19, 22).

KRAKÓW EATING

⭐**Art Restaurant** POLISH €€€
(Art Restauracja; Map p120; ☑537 872 193; www.
artrestauracja.com; ul Kanonicza 15; mains 60-90zł;
seven-/nine-course tasting menu 239/289zł; ☺1-
10pm; ⭐; ◻6, 8, 10, 13, 18) Easily the most ambitious restaurant in this part of town, the
Art is all white linens and swish service, but
forget any notion of fusty food. The menu
highlights farm-fresh ingredients and local
sourcing, with plenty of unusual touches
like red-pepper jam served with lamb saddle. Book on the terrace in nice weather. The
lunch menu is great value (69zł).

⭐**Ed Red** STEAK €€€
(Map p120; ☑690 900 555; www.edred.pl; ul
Sławkowska 3; mains 40-70zł; ☺1pm-11pm Sun-
Thu, to midnight Fri & Sat; ⭐; ◻2, 4, 14, 18, 20,
24, 44) This is a solid splurge option for the
steaks – cuts include New York strip, ribeye
and T-bone – made from dry-aged beef and
using only local producers. Other mains
include beef cheeks served on buckwheat,
wild boar and free-range chicken. The interior, with walls painted in muted blues and
browns, is straight out of a magazine.

Wentzl POLISH €€€
(Map p120; ☑12 429 5299; www.restauracjawentzl.
com.pl; Rynek Główny 19; mains 45-90zł; ☺1-11pm;
⭐; ◻1, 6, 8, 13, 18) This historic place, dating
back to 1792, is perched above the Main Market Square, with timbered ceilings, oriental
carpets and fine oil paintings all around.
The food is sublime – cognac-flavoured foie
gras, duck fillet glazed with honey, Baltic
cod served with lentils and spinach – and
the service is of a high standard.

Cyrano de Bergerac FRENCH €€€
(Map p120; ☑12 411 7288; www.cyranodebergerac.
pl; ul Sławkowska 26; mains 62-92zł; ☺noon-11pm;
⭐☑; ◻2, 4, 14, 18, 20, 24, 44) One of Kraków's
top spots for fine dining, this restaurant
serves authentic French cuisine in one of the
most beautiful cellars in the city. Artwork
and tapestries add to the romance and in
warmer months there's seating in a covered
courtyard.

The Black Duck POLISH €€€
(Czarna Kaczka; Map p120; ☑12 426 5440; www.
facebook.com/CzarnaKaczka; ul Poselska 22; mains
45-90zł; ☺noon-11pm; ⭐; ◻1, 6, 8, 13, 18) The
duck meat at this restaurant arrives specially from Poznań, and good use is made of it.
From duck pierogi to duck soup with meat-
balls, as well as a whole roasted duck for
two, this twist on Polish cuisine offers fine

dining and an amazing array of dishes. Try
the three-course vodka tasting (from 14zł) to
get things moving.

Pod Aniołami POLISH €€€
(Map p120; ☑12 421 3999; www.podaniolami.pl;
ul Grodzka 35; mains 45-80zł; ☺1pm-midnight;
⭐; ◻1, 6, 8, 13, 18) This is the quintessential
old Kraków restaurant; its main dining
room occupies a Gothic cellar from the
13th century. Heavy wood furniture, stone
walls and fraying tapestries evoke the Middle Ages, as do the grilled meats cooked
over a beech-wood fire.The wild boar steak
marinated in juniper berry comes highly
recommended.

Miód Malina POLISH €€€
(Map p120; ☑12 430 0411; www.miodmalina.
pl; ul Grodzka 40; mains 40-80zł; ☺noon-11pm;
⭐; ◻1, 6, 8, 13, 18) The charmingly named
Honey Raspberry serves high-quality Polish cooking in colourful surrounds. Grab
a window seat and order the wild mushrooms in cream, and any of the duck or
veal dishes. There's a variety of beef steaks
on the menu as well. The grilled sheep's-
cheese appetiser, served with cranberry
jelly, is a regional speciality. Reservations
essential.

✖ West of the Old Town

Smakołyki POLISH €
(Map p120; ☑12 430 3099; www.smakolyki.eu; ul
Straszewskiego 28; mains 12-30zł; ☺8am-10pm
Mon-Sat, from 9am Sun; ☑; ◻4, 8, 13, 14, 24, 44)
If you like big portions and low prices, this
restaurant just outside the Planty by Jagiellonian University is the place to go. Meaning
'treats' in Polish, Smakołyki is full of them. If
not strictly traditional Polish food, it's nevertheless wholesome and delicious, and the
view from the large window makes for great
people-watching.

Veganic VEGETARIAN €
(Map p120; ☑668 468 469; www.veganic.
restaurant; ul Dolnych Młynów 10; mains 24-28zł;
☺9am-10pm Tue-Sun, from noon Mon; ⭐☑; ◻2,
4, 14, 18, 20, 24, 44) Veganic's cosy armchairs
and outdoor courtyard make for a welcoming setting for very good vegan and vegetarian food, like tofu burgers, pastas and
stuffed cabbage leaves. There's also lots of
gluten-free items to try, and the staff goes
out of its way to help you choose. Find it
within the up-and-coming Tytano tobacco
factory complex.

THE KING OF PRETZELS

One of the unmistakable signs you've arrived in Kraków are the stalls placed seemingly at every street corner selling the *obwarzanek* (ob-va-*zhan*-ek), a hefty pretzel. This street snack resembles its German cousins, though it is somewhat larger and denser than the average Germanic bread-based snack and is created by entwining two strands of dough before baking.

This popular ring of baked bread, traditionally encrusted with poppy seeds, sesame seeds or salt, gives daily employment to myriad men and women while ensuring them a dose of fresh outdoor air (though selling it in winter must, admittedly, be less fun).

It's also a historic curiosity that has outlived numerous kings, republics and military occupiers. There's evidence of *obwarzanki* (pretzels) being baked as far back as the 14th century, and Cracovians still happily purchase them in large numbers as a quick bite on the way to work or study – in fact 150,000 are baked every day. Feel free to join in the pretzel celebration, though note that they're definitely much better in the morning than the afternoon, a promising sign perhaps that they contain little in the way of artificial preservatives.

Bar Mleczny Górnik

POLISH €

(Map p120; ☑ 12 632 6899; www.facebook.com/barmleczny.gornik; ul Czysta 1; mains 7-11zł; ☉8am-6pm Mon-Fri, to 4pm Sat; 🚋2, 4, 14, 18, 20, 24, 44) Typical Polish milk bar, serving cheap, edible renditions of Polish classics. Turn up at the counter with a plastic tray, point to what you want and then try to find a free seat somewhere. The daily lunch specials (10zł) include a soup and main course and are excellent value.

Międzymiastowa

INTERNATIONAL €€

(Map p120; ☑ 577 304 450; www.facebook.com/miedzymiastowakrakow; ul Dolnych Młynów 10; mains 35-50zł; ☉9am-midnight Mon-Fri, from 10am Sat & Sun; 🍴; 🚋2, 4, 14, 18, 20, 24, 44) It's hard to classify this stylish, urban space deep within the Tytano tobacco factory complex. It's an excellent choice for a burger or casual bite, but many come simply to sip from some legendary gin-based cocktails, including those flavoured with rhubarb, peach, cucumber and thyme.

Restauracja Pod Norenami

VEGETARIAN €€

(Map p120; ☑ 661 219 289; www.podnorenami.pl; ul Krupnicza 6; mains 25-40zł; ☉noon-10pm; 🛜🍴👶; 🚋2, 4, 8, 13, 14, 18, 20, 24) A warm and inviting Asian-fusion restaurant that's ideal for vegans and vegetarians. The menu runs from Japanese to Thai to Vietnamese, with lots of spicy noodle and rice dishes as well as vegetarian sushi. There's an inventive menu for kids as well, with items like dumplings with banana and chocolate. Book in advance.

Dynia

INTERNATIONAL €€

(Map p120; ☑ 12 430 0838; www.dynia.krakow.pl; ul Krupnicza 20; mains 26-40zł; ☉9am-11pm; 🛜; 🚋2, 4, 8, 13, 14, 18, 20, 24) While Dynia's interior is chic – with leather furniture and avant-garde floral arrangements – it is the courtyard that is the most enticing. Crumbling brick walls surround the fern-filled space, evoking an atmosphere of elegance amid decay. The name means pumpkin and there are plenty of pumpkin-based soups and mains plus other low-cal and vegetarian options – and a great selection of breakfasts (16zł to 25zł).

✗ Kazimierz & Podgórze

Taking a meal in one of Kazimierz's Jewish-themed restaurants is one of the highlights of a visit here. Away from the Jewish quarter, Kazimierz is awash in restaurants to suit all appetites and budgets. Podgórze is something of a disappointment for eating. The area around Plac Bohaterów Getta and Schindler's Factory is a culinary desert, saved by a handful of decent options.

Hummus Amamamusi

MIDDLE EASTERN €

(Map p128; ☑ 533 306 288; www.hummus-amamamusi.pl; ul Meiselsa 4; mains 20-35zł; ☉9am-8pm Mon-Fri, from 10am Sat & Sun; 🛜🍴; 🚋6, 8, 10, 13, 18) Hummus is undergoing a renaissance in Kraków and this tiny place on the western side of busy ul Krakowska has transformed the humble chickpea spread into an art form. Choose from various flavours, either 'classic' or seasoned with chilli, horseradish or garlic, and served in edible cornflour bowls.

Lody Si Gela
ICE CREAM €

(Map p128; ☑ 609 475 537; www.sigela.pl; ul Staro-
mostowa 1; per scoop 4zł; ⏱ 11am-8pm; 🖉 🖩;
🖩 6, 8, 10, 11, 13, 19) Hugely popular ice-cream
parlor, featuring all the usual hits plus lots
of offbeat flavours like fiery wasabi. Vegans
will find lots of options here as well. Line up
at the counter and take away, though there's
also a small eating area inside with children's
books and toys.

Alchemia od Kuchni
BURGERS €

(Map p128; ☑ 882 044 299; www.odkuchni.com;
ul Estery 5; mains 25-30zł; ⏱ noon-11pm; 🖥 🖉;
🖩 3, 17, 19, 22, 24, 52) Craft beers, burgers
and hummus 'bowls' – a scoop of hummus topped with fish or beef sauce – all
served up in a minimalist urban setting of
exposed brick and concrete flooring. The
vibe is just right for a casual meal and
meet-up.

Massolit Cooks
VEGAN €

(Map p128; ☑ 12 422 1982; www.facebook.com/
massolitcooks; ul Józefa 25; breakfasts 16-20zł,
mains 18zł; ⏱ 10am-5pm Tue-Fri, to 8pm Sat &
Sun; 🖥 🖉; 🖩 3, 19, 24) Vegans and vegetarians will love this addition to the Jewish
quarter. American-style bagels and desserts
like pumpkin pie from the satellite bakery,
as well as delicious veggie and vegan mains
are on offer in this shabby-chic restaurant,
part of a small local chain. Fans of Russian
literature will also appreciate the origin of
the name.

Mazaya Falafel
MIDDLE EASTERN €

(Map p128; www.mazaya-falafel.pl; ul Legionów
Józefa Piłsudskiego 2; set menus 14-20zł; ⏱ 10am-
10pm; 🖩 6, 8, 10, 13) The Podgórze branch of
a local chain of Middle Eastern fast-food
outlets serves up excellent, life-affirming set
menus of falafel and hummus. Most people
order to take away, though there are a few
tables for dining in.

Marchewka z Groszkiem
POLISH €

(Map p128; ☑ 12 430 0795; www.marchewka
zgroszkiem.pl; ul Mostowa 2; mains 15-35zł;
⏱ 9am-10pm; 🖥 🖉; 🖩 6, 8, 10, 13) Traditional Polish cooking, with hints of influence
from neighbouring countries such as
Ukraine, Hungary and Lithuania. Excellent potato pancakes and a delicious boiled
beef with horseradish sauce are highlights
of the menu. There are a few outside tables
from which to admire the parade of people on one of Kazimierz's up-and-coming
streets.

Bagelmama
BAGELS €

(Map p128; ☑ 12 346 1646; www.bagelmama.com;
ul Dajwór 10b; bagels 15-20zł; ⏱ 9am-5pm; 🖥 🖉;
🖩 3, 19, 24) How clever of someone to think of
selling bagels in the Jewish quarter. Whether you are a bagel traditionalist (lox and
cream cheese) or a bagel innovator (warm
brie and tomato), you'll find something you
like. There are also soups, salads and wraps
for a perfect easy lunch.

★ Youmiko Sushi
JAPANESE €€

(Map p128; ☑ 666 471 176; www.facebook.com/
YoumikoSushi; ul Józefa 2; sushi sets 25-40zł;
⏱ 1.30-9pm Mon-Thu, to 10pm Fri & Sat, to 8pm
Sun; 🖥 🖉; 🖩 6, 8, 10, 13) Tiny bar and table
joint serving some of Kazimerz's best sushi
in a casual, hipster-friendly setting. Lots of
vegan items on the menu, and on Sundays
it's vegan-only.

★ ZaKładka Food & Wine
BISTRO €€

(Map p128; ☑ 12 442 7442; www.zakladkabistro.pl;
ul Józefińska 2; mains 35-45zł; ⏱ 1-9.45pm Mon-
Thu, to 10.30pm Fri & Sat, noon-9pm Sun; 🖥 🖉;
🖩 6, 8, 10, 11, 13, 19) This bistro specialises in
simple French-inspired cooking centred on
veal, rabbit, fresh fish and mussels, as well
as several vegetarian items, and is one of the
best places in the neighbourhood. Expect
courteous but formal service and an excellent wine list. The simplicity of the presentation extends to the decor: beige walls, black
tables and wooden floors.

★ Sąsiedzi
POLISH €€

(Map p128; ☑ 12 654 8353; www.sasiedzi.oberza.pl;
ul Miodowa 25; mains 40-80zł; ⏱ noon-10pm Mon-
Thu, to 11pm Fri-Sun; 🖥; 🖩 3, 19, 24) A perfect
combination of excellent Polish and international mains and unfussy, relaxed service.
Dine downstairs in an evocative cellar, or
in the secluded garden. The quality of the
cooking rivals the best in this part of the city.
If you've been hankering to try wild boar,
goose leg confit or even horsemeat tenderloin, this is the place to give it a go. Reservations are recommended.

Krako Slow Wines
INTERNATIONAL €€

(Map p128; ☑ 669 225 222; www.krakoslowwines.
pl; ul Lipowa 6f; mains 20-40zł; ⏱ 10am-10pm
Sun-Thu, to midnight Fri & Sat; 🖥 🖉; 🖩 3, 19, 24)
It's hard to accurately characterise this little
wine bar and restaurant, which serves the
best-value lunches within 100m of Schindler's Factory. The emphasis is on the wine,
but it also serves excellent beer, coffee, salads, snacks and hummus sandwiches, and

its Caucasian barbecue (Tuesday to Saturday) turns out mouthwatering Georgian-and Armenian-style shashlik and kebab.

Karakter
POLISH €€

(Map p128; ☑795 818 123; www.facebook.com/karakter.restauracja; ul Brzozowa 17; mains 40-50zł; ⊙noon-11pm Tue-Sun, from 5pm Mon; 🖘; 🚌3, 19, 24) Karakter feels unique in Kazimierz in that there's no theme or shtick, only a menu that promises a modern whole-animal, farm-to-table approach and unusual mains like horse sweetbread schnitzel and bull testicles. The sleek, understated interior puts the focus squarely on the plate. Service is excellent and the lunch menu (35zł) is a low-risk way of sampling the spoils.

Restauracja Pod Baranem
POLISH €€

(Map p120; ☑12 429 4022; www.podbaranem.com; ul Św Gertrudy 21; mains 40-70zł; ⊙noon-10pm; 🖘☑; 🚌1, 6, 8, 10, 13, 18) Just what Kraków needed: a beautiful sit-down restaurant, complete with white linens and candles on the table and original art on the walls, that also just happens to serve gluten-free well-done Polish mains like pierogi, potato pancakes and pork chops.

Hamsa
JEWISH €€

(Map p128; ☑515 150 145; www.hamsa.pl; ul Szeroka 2; mains 40-65zł; ⊙10am-10.30pm Mon-Fri, 9am-11pm Sat & Sun; 🖘☑; 🚌3, 19, 24) How can a place miss when it calls itself a 'hummus and happiness' restaurant? The light, uncluttered interior is a welcome tonic to the kitschy Jewish-themed restaurants in the area. The menu features a full range of Middle Eastern salads, plus spicy grilled chicken and fish. Good selection of vegetarian and gluten-free options.

Dawno Temu Na Kazimierzu
JEWISH €€

(Once upon a Time in Kazimierz; Map p128; ☑12 421 2117; www.dawnotemu.nakazimierzu.pl; ul Szeroka 1; mains 20-50zł; ⊙10am-10.30pm Mon-Sat, to 11pm Sun; 🚌3, 19, 24) Arguably the smallest and most atmospheric of several restaurants in Kazimierz playing on the old-time Jewish theme. The traditional Polish-Jewish cooking (think hearty variations of lamb and duck) is very good, and the warm, candle-lit space, with klezmer music playing in the background, make this the perfect spot to enjoy this part of Kraków.

Manzana
MEXICAN €€

(Map p128; ☑514 786 813; www.manzanarestaurant.com; ul Krakusa 11; mains 28-36zł; ⊙9am-10pm

Mon-Sat, to 9pm Sun; 🖘☑; 🚌6, 8, 10, 13) Manzana is slightly more upscale than is usual for a Mexican restaurant in this part of the world, with a sleek interior and enormous bar. That said, the menu features the same mix of tacos, burritos and quesadillas you're used to, at reasonable prices for the quality. Creative mains like fiesta chicken pasta use tequila as a cooking ingredient. Reservations recommended.

Well Done
BARBECUE €€

(Map p128; ☑607 132 001; www.welldonego.pl; ul Mostowa 2; mains 25-40zł; ⊙noon-11pm Mon-Fri, from 9am Sat & Sun; 🖘; 🚌6, 8, 10, 13) Very likable barbecue and burger joint poised along shady ul Mostowa, with its string of trendy restaurants and cafes. The grill-masters know how to impart that smoky flavour to burgers, steaks and chicken breasts. The interior is kind of retro-diner, while there are a few picnic tables out front.

Ariel
JEWISH €€

(Map p128; ☑12 421 7920; www.ariel-krakow.pl; ul Szeroka 17/18; mains 30-60zł; ⊙10am-midnight; 🖘; 🚌3, 19, 24) One of several Jewish restaurants in and around ul Szeroka, this atmospheric joint is packed with old-fashioned timber furniture and portraits, and serves a range of traditional dishes such as goose neck stuffed with chicken livers. Try the Berdytchov soup (beef, honey and cinnamon) for a tasty starter. There's often live klezmer music here at night.

Klezmer-Hois
JEWISH €€

(Map p128; ☑12 411 1245; www.klezmer.pl; ul Szeroka 6; mains 35-60zł; ⊙7am-9.30pm; 🖘; 🚌3,19, 24) Perhaps better than any other restaurant in the area, Klezmer-Hois evokes pre-war Kazimierz, with its tables covered in lace and artwork inspired by the *shtetl* (Jewish town). Warm up with a bowl of delicious soup invented by Yankiel the Innkeeper of Berdytchov. In the evenings, folks gather for concerts of traditional Jewish music (8pm).

Szara Kazimierz
POLISH €€€

(Map p128; ☑12 429 1219; www.szarakazimierz.pl; ul Szeroka 39; mains 60-80zł; ⊙11am-11pm; 🖘☑; 🚌3, 19, 24) A step up in both price and quality from the several nearby restaurants on ul Szeroka. Szara is the go-to if you're looking for dishes that are inspired by Kazimierz's Jewish heritage, like goose and rabbit, without being surrounded by klezmer music or Jewish-themed kitsch. Reserve on weekend evenings.

KRAKÓW EATING

Drinking & Nightlife

The Main Market Square is ringed with bars and cafes whose outdoor tables offer great people-watching spots. Kazimierz also has a lively bar scene centred on Plac Nowy and surrounding streets. The area around Plac Wolnica in the western part of Kazimierz has blossomed in recent years into another cafe/bar cluster.

 Old Town

★**Bunkier Cafe**　　　　　　　　CAFE

(Map p120; ☑️12 431 0585; www.bunkiercafe.pl; Plac Szczepański 3a; ⊙9am-1am; 🛜; 🚋2, 4, 14, 18, 20, 24, 44) The Bunkier is a wonderful cafe with an enormous glassed-in terrace tacked on to the **Bunkier Sztuki** (Gallery of Contemporary Art; Map p120; www.bunkier.art.pl; adult/concession 12/6zł, free Tue; ⊙11am-7pm Tue-Sat; 🚋2, 8, 13, 18, 20), a cutting-edge gallery northwest of the Main Market Square. The garden space is heated in winter and always has a buzz. There is excellent coffee, unfiltered beers and homemade lemonades, plus light bites such as burgers and salads. Enter from the Planty.

★**Café Camelot**　　　　　　　　CAFE

(Map p120; ☑️12 421 0123; www.lochcamelot.art.pl; ul Św Tomasza 17; ⊙9am-midnight; 🛜; 🚋2, 4, 14, 18, 20, 24) For coffee and cake, try this genteel haven attached to a theatre of the same name and hidden around an obscure street corner in the Old Town. Its cosy rooms are cluttered with lace-covered candlelit tables and a quirky collection of wooden figurines featuring spiritual or folkloric scenes. A great choice for breakfasts and brunches.

★**Dziórawy Kocioł**　　　　　　CAFE

(Leaky Cauldron; Map p120; ☑️12 422 5884; www.facebook.com/dziorawykociol; ul Grodzka 50/1; ⊙9am-10pm; 🛜🐾; 🚋1, 6, 8, 13, 18) Harry Potter fans should head to this quaint basement cafe hidden away on ul Grodzka. It's aptly decorated from tip to toe with magical memorabilia, Hogwarts House flags and hand-drawn character sketches. There is some deliciously sweet Butterbeer on the menu, as well as lots of appropriately named cakes.

Lindo　　　　　　　　　　GAY & LESBIAN

(Map p120; ☑️798 648 143; www.facebook.com/LindoKrakow; ul Sławkowska 23; ⊙4pm-midnight Sun & Mon, to 2am Tue-Sat; 🛜; 🚋2, 4, 14, 18, 20, 24, 44) A relative rarity for Kraków's Old Town: a gay-friendly bar and cafe within easy walking distance of the Main Market Square. The

bar's located on two levels, with a big cellar that gets lively on weekend nights. The staff is friendly and welcoming.

Spokój　　　　　　　　　　　BAR

(Map p120; ☑️501 652 478; www.facebook.com/spokojcisza; ul Bracka 3-5; ⊙10am-3am, noon-3am Sat & Sun; 🛜; 🚋1, 6, 8, 13, 18) Trendy young Kraków residents populate this hidden retro bar. Surrounded by colourful '70s-style decor, mismatched furniture and a permeating orange hue, you'll soon find yourself settling into the low sofas and being transported back through the decades. To find Spokój, go through the archway at Bracka 3 until you reach the end and walk up some steps.

Café Noworolski　　　　　　　CAFE

(Map p120; ☑️515 100 998; www.noworolski.com.pl; Rynek Główny 1/3; ⊙8.30am-midnight; 🚋1, 6, 8, 13, 18) Even if you don't stop for a coffee or small bite, pause to admire the stunning art nouveau interiors by Polish artist Józef Mehoffer. As the sign says, the Noworolski has been here since 1910, serving the likes of Lenin in the early years, and later becoming a favourite haunt of occupying German officers during WWII.

Pauza　　　　　　　　　　　BAR

(Map p120; ☑️608 601 522; www.facebook.com/KlubPauza; ul Stolarska 5; ⊙10-4am, to 2am Sun; 🛜; 🚋1, 6, 8, 13, 18) Walk up a flight stairs from within the Pasaż Bielaka (p147) to find this beloved street-smart bar, known for its arty and alternative atmosphere.

Viva la Pinta　　　　　　　BEER GARDEN

(Map p120; ☑️12 378 97 22; ul Floriańska 13; ⊙4pm-midnight Mon-Sat, from 2pm Sun; 🛜; 🚋2, 4, 14, 18, 20, 24, 44) You'll find beers from main provider Browar Pinta as well as local craft beers at this quaint beer garden, hidden in a courtyard off ul Floriańska. It's particularly popular in summer, when people are clamouring for a few hours in the sun. Grab your seat before it starts to fill up from late-afternoon onward.

Krakowskie Zakąski　　　　BEER GARDEN

(Map p120; ☑️575 300 347; www.facebook.com/Krakowskiezakaski; ul Sławkowska 16; ⊙4pm-1am Mon-Wed, to 2am Thu-Sun; 🛜; 🚋2, 4, 14, 18, 20, 24, 44) With few seats inside, the main draw here is the cosy courtyard beer garden. Zakąski is often overlooked compared to the neighbouring establishments, though it's admittedly great for stretching out on a deck chair on a warm summer evening.

Klub Społem CLUB

(Map p120; ☑12 421 7979; www.pubspolem.pl; ul Św Tomasza 4; ⊙7pm-3am Sun-Tue, to 4am Wed & Thu, to 5am Fri & Sat; ☐2, 4, 14, 18, 20, 24, 44) Just off Plac Szczepańska is this deceptively large underground bar and club. With communist throwback memorabilia covering the walls, and tunes of the '60s through to the '90s, Społem is a cosy and fun find for a night of cheap beer and dancing.

Feniks CLUB

(Map p120; ☑604 234 288; www.feniksklub.com; ul Św Jana 2; ⊙4pm-2am Tue & Wed, to 4am Thu, to 5am Fri & Sat; ☎; ☐1, 6, 8, 13, 18) Clubs in Kraków come and go with the season, but Feniks, hiding in plain sight on the main square, is still largely unchanged from communist days. The red-velvet curtains and white tablecloths lend a throwback feel to a time when couples still put on their best to rock around the clock.

Pasaż Bielaka BAR

(Map p120; ☑535 519 602; www.facebook.com/PasazBielaka; Pasaż Bielaka, ul Stolarska 5; ⊙4pm-2am Sun-Thu, to 5am Fri & Sat; ☎; ☐1, 6, 8, 13, 18) A few metres off the Main Market Square, the old Kino Pasaż passageway has been transformed into this hideaway for students to lounge on beanbag chairs and chill out over coffee and beer. In warm weather everyone huddles around white wooden tables made from old construction pallets. Weekend evenings get packed and the crowd spills out onto ul Stolarska.

Nowa Prowincja CAFE

(Map p120; ☑12 430 5959; www.facebook.com/pg/nowaprowincja; ul Bracka 3-5; ⊙8am-midnight Mon-Thu, to 1am Fri & Sat, 9am-midnight Sun; ☐1, 6, 8, 13, 18) You'll love this bi-level bohemian cafe, where Kraków's coolest cats come to drink strong coffee and think deep thoughts.

🍸 West of the Old Town

Much of the carousing these days west of the Old Town takes place in a former tobacco factory just off ul Dolnych Młynów. The 'Tytano' works lay abandoned for more than a decade before enterprising developers recognised the potential for an authentic hipster hang-out. These days, the six decrepit buildings of the old factory hold all manner of restaurants, bars and dance clubs (https://tytano.org).

BAR OR CAFE?

In Kraków, it's not often easy to tell the difference. The drinking scene is dominated by two types of venues: creative cafes that also serve alcohol; and bohemian bars that also serve coffee. In both, you can also normally grab a bite to eat. Indeed, whatever the primary purpose, Kraków specialises in places with an artsy atmosphere, usually furnished with mismatched chairs and tables, eclectic artwork and casually cool-looking patrons. Not too posh, but not too pleb either.

★ **Mercy Brown** COCKTAIL BAR

(Map p120; ☑531 706 692; ul Straszewskiego 28; ⊙7pm-1.30am Wed & Thu, to 2.30am Fri & Sat; ☎; ☐4, 8, 13, 14, 24, 44) This hidden bar shows just how far word-of-mouth goes. It's not easy to find – nevertheless, it's so popular you need a reservation to get in. The allure is obvious: a taste of the 1920s, with low-lit chandeliers, plush armchairs and a long bar stacked with liquor. Monthly burlesque shows, jazz concerts and artistically made cocktails make this a unique experience.

Scena54 CLUB

(Map p120; ☑12 378 3778; www.scena54.pl; ul Dolnych Młynów 10; ⊙7pm-1am Wed & Thu, to 4am Fri & Sat; ☎; ☐2, 4, 14, 18, 20, 24, 44) The name harkens back to bawdy New York of the 1980s, and the Scena54 dance club is aimed at older guests (here meaning 30s to 50s), who might still have hazy memories of those days. Check the website for special throwback, DJ and ladies' nights that are sure to bring out the crowds. The club is located in the Tytano complex.

Weźże Krafta CRAFT BEER

(Map p120; ☑12 307 4050; www.wezze-krafta.ontap.pl; ul Dolnych Młynów 10; ⊙4pm-2am Mon-Fri, from 2pm Sat & Sun; ☎; ☐2, 4, 14, 18, 20, 24, 44) Just what Kraków needed: a warehouse-sized craft beer emporium with something like 25 craft beers on tap and enough space to handle loud, rowdy groups. It's situated toward the middle of the popular Tytano complex. It's understandably popular, meaning your best plan is to arrive early to grab a table.

Meho Cafe
CAFE

(Map p120; ☑ 600 480 049; www.facebook.com/
MehoCafe; ul Krupnicza 26; ⊙ 10am-10pm; ☎;
☐ 2, 4, 8, 13, 14, 18, 20, 24) A handful of tables
are carefully arranged around a leafy oak
tree in the Mehoffer House (p126) garden.
In case of rain, you can sit inside the cosy
cafe. Service is leisurely, so sit back and
enjoy the delightful setting. In addition to
coffee and tea, they also have a light lunch
menu of salads, tortillas and risottos.

Piwiarnia Warka
PUB

(Map p120; ☑ 508 318 115; www.facebook.com/
PiwiarniaKrakow; ul Karmelicka 43a; ⊙ noon-
midnight; ☎; ☐ 4, 8, 13, 14, 24, 44) This informal
pub/restaurant perches on one of the busiest
streets in Kraków, but its outdoor annex is
sheltered enough to provide an ideal combination of privacy and people-watching. It's
an especially popular place during football
(soccer). The beer bites, pizzas and burgers
(23zł to 28zł) are decent too and reasonably
priced.

Café Szafe
CAFE

(Map p120; ☑ 663 905 652; www.cafeszafe.com; ul
Felicjanek 10; ⊙ 9am-2am Mon-Fri, from 10am Sat
& Sun; ☎; ☐ 1, 2, 6) The colourful cafe on the
corner is a cupboard full of surprises, from
the whimsical sculptured creatures lurking
in the corners to the intriguing artwork that
hangs on the walls. The place hosts concerts,
films and other arty events.

📍 Kazimierz

As Kazimierz developed into a popular
locale for nightspots in the 1990s and early
2000s, the area's cafes and bars adopted
a kind of eclectic, junk-shop-chic decor,
and that casual aesthetic still sets the tone
today. The best places tend to be dark (often candle-lit), threadbare and chill. Of
course, there's no shortage of rowdy beer
joints, modern coffee shops and cocktail
bars too.

★ Hevre
CLUB

(Map p128; ☑ 509 413 626; www.facebook.com/
hevrekazimierz; ul Meiselsa 18; ⊙ 9am-midnight;
☎; ☐ 6, 8, 10, 13) After all of those tiny,
cramped Kazimierz bars, spacious Hevre, occupying an enormous former Jewish prayer
house, is a breath of fresh air. By day, Hevre
serves as a civilised combo cafe/restaurant
(mains from 25zł) and a superb place to chill
over a good book or laptop. After dark, the

crowds pile in for DJs and dancing upstairs
and downstairs.

★ Cheder
CAFE

(Map p128; ☑ 515 732 226; www.cheder.pl; ul
Józefa 36; ⊙ 10am-10pm; ☎; ☐ 3, 19, 24) Unlike
most of the other Jewish-themed places in
Kazimierz, this one aims to entertain *and*
educate. Named after a traditional Hebrew
school, the cafe offers access to a decent library in Polish and English, regular readings
and films, real Israeli coffee, brewed in a traditional Turkish copper pot with cinnamon
and cardamom, and snacks such as homemade hummus.

Singer Café
BAR

(Map p128; ☑ 12 292 0622; ul Estery 20; ⊙ 9am-
4am; ☎; ☐ 3, 19, 24) A laidback hang-out of the
Kazimierz cognoscenti, this relaxed cafe-bar's
moody candlelit interior is full of character.
Alternatively, sit outside and converse over a
sewing machine affixed to the table.

Mleczarnia
CAFE

(Map p128; ☑ 12 421 8532; www.mle.pl; ul Meiselsa 20; ⊙ 10am-1am; ☎; ☐ 6, 8, 10, 13) Wins the
prize for best little beer garden – located
across the street from the cafe. Shady trees
and blooming roses make this place tops for
a sunny-afternoon drink. If it's raining, the
cafe itself is warm and cosy, with crowded
bookshelves and portrait-covered walls. Interesting beverages available include mead
and cocoa with cherry vodka. Self service.

Alchemia
CAFE

(Map p128; ☑ 12 421 2200; www.alchemia.com.pl;
ul Estery 5; ⊙ 9am-2am Tue-Sun, from 10am Mon;
☎; ☐ 3, 19, 24) This landmark Kazimierz
cafe set the district's shabby-cool aesthetic of candlelit tables and a companionable
gloom years ago and is still going strong
today. Alchemia hosts occasional live-
music gigs and theatrical events through
the week.

La Habana
BAR

(Pub La Habana; Map p128; ☑ 881 403 026; www.
facebook.com/publahabana; ul Miodowa 22;
⊙ 10am-midnight Sun-Thu, to 2am Fri & Sat; ☎;
☐ 3, 19, 24) Find a corner at this Cuban-
themed bar known for its great cocktails
and cosy atmosphere. Smokers can purchase cigars at the bar and enjoy them
upstairs in the closed-off smoking area.
Otherwise, grab a Cuba libre, chat to the
friendly bar staff and settle into a low sofa
to soak up the vibe.

T.E.A. Time Brew Pub MICROBREWERY
(Map p128; ☑ 517 601 503; www.teatimebrewery. com; ul Dietla 1; ☺ 4pm-1am Sun-Thu, to 2am Fri, noon-2am Sat; ☎; ☒ Stradom) The first and only real-ale pub in Kraków was started by an Englishman with a taste for the proper stuff. Brewed on-site, the beer goes from cask to hand pump, producing favourites such as Black Prince and Misty Mountain Hop; the menu changes every week. Catch the weekly pub quiz on Mondays and settle in with some snacks. Pints 9zł to 12zł.

Pub Propaganda BAR
(Map p128; ☑ 600 331 922; www.pubpropaganda. pl; ul Miodowa 20; ☺ 4pm-2am Sun-Thu, to 5am Fri & Sat; ☎; ☒ 3, 19, 24) This is another one of those places full of communist nostalgia, but so real are the banners and mementos here that we almost started singing *The Internationale*. Killer cocktails.

🍷 Podgórze

Podgórze scores marginally better for drinking and nightlife than it does for eating. There's an attractive row of cafes and bars just at the nub of the Bernatek Footbridge. The area around Schindler's Factory and Plac Bohaterów Getta, though, can get very quiet at night.

★ Forum Przestrzenie BAR
(Hotel Forum; Map p128; ☑ 515 424 724; www.forum przestrzenie.com; ul Maria Konopnickiej 28; ☺ 10am-midnight Sun-Thu, to 2am Fri & Sat; ☎; ☒ 8, 10, 11, 19) In a highly creative re-use of an old communist-era eyesore, the Hotel Forum has been repurposed as a trendy, retro coffee and cocktail bar – and occasional venue for DJs, live music, film screenings and happenings. In warm weather, lounge chairs are spread out on a patio overlooking the river.

Absurdalia Cafe CAFE
(Map p128; www.facebook.com/absurdaliacafe; ul Brodzińskiego 6; ☺ 10am-10pm; ☎; ☒ 6, 8, 10, 11, 13, 19) Arguably the most-welcoming of a string of similar cafes that runs along the first block you encounter just off the Bernatek Footbridge. Relax in an easy chair and enjoy the coffee and cakes.

BAL CAFE
(Map p128; ☑ 734 411 733; www.facebook.com/ balnazablociu; ul Ślusarska 9; ☺ 8am-9pm; ☎; ☒ 3, 19, 24) Trendy industrial-style cafe and breakfast bar tucked into a repurposed warehouse in Podgórze's Zabłocie district. Great for

> ### CLUBBING IN KRAKÓW
>
> With tens of thousands of university students, it's a safe assumption that nightlife, particularly from Thursday to Sunday morning, revolves around clubbing. The scene, truth be told, is not that much different from any other similarly sized European city, but the venues, often Old Town cellars, lend a local flavour. Most places on most nights will have DJs or recorded music, but there's a decent live-music scene as well.

coffee as well as light eats, sandwiches, vegetarian entrees and salads throughout the day.

Drukarnia CLUB
(Map p128; ☑ 12 656 6560; www.drukarniaclub.pl; ul Nadwiślańska 1; ☺ 9am-1am Sun-Thu, to 3am Fri & Sat; ☎; ☒ 6, 8, 10, 11, 13, 19) Not quite the legendary club it used to be, but nevertheless a reliable spot for a late-night drink and occasionally live music in the cavernous basement space. The ground-floor bar is divided into a scruffier half decorated to recall the bar's name (Drukarnia means Printing House), and a trendier but more sterile modern side.

☆ Entertainment

Kraków has a lively cultural life, particularly in theatre, music and visual arts, and there are numerous annual festivals. The city is also rich in jazz clubs and art-house cinema. The comprehensive Polish and English monthly magazine *Karnet* (www.karnet.krakow.pl), available at any branch of the tourist office, lists almost every event in the city.

Jazz & Live Music

Kraków's Old Town is home to several historic jazz haunts. In addition to hosting regular gigs, they're often venues for annual music festivals.

★ Harris Piano Jazz Bar JAZZ
(Map p120; ☑ 12 421 5741; www.harris.krakow.pl; Rynek Główny 28; tickets 20-80zł; ☺ 11am-2am; ☒ 1, 6, 8, 13, 18) Lively jazz haunt housed in an atmospheric, intimate cellar right on the Main Market Square. Harris hosts jazz and blues bands most nights from around 9.30pm, but try to arrive at least an hour earlier to get a seat (or book by phone). Wednesday nights see weekly jam sessions (admission free).

CHURCH & CHAMBER MUSIC

The baroque interior of a church can be an uplifting venue for classical music. From May to September, church and chamber concerts are staged around town. Buy tickets at the door before the concert or at any InfoKraków (p154) tourist office. The best venues include the **Church of SS Peter and Paul** (Map p120; ☑ 695 574 526; ul Grodzka 52a; tickets adult/concession 60/40zł; ⊙ 8pm; ☒ 1, 6, 8, 13, 18), south of the main square, which hosts evening concerts of Vivaldi, Bach, Chopin and Strauss performed by the Cracow Chamber Orchestra of St Maurice. For Fryderyk Chopin, Poland's best-known composer, head to the **Chopin Concert Hall** (Map p120; ☑ 604 093 570; www. cracowconcerts.com; ul Sławkowska 14; tickets 65zł; ⊙ 7.30pm; ☒ 2, 4, 14, 18, 20, 24, 44) in the Old Town.

Piwnica Pod Baranami
LIVE MUSIC

(Map p120; ☑ 12 421 2500; www.piwnicapod baranami.pl; Rynek Główny 27; tickets 20-30zł; ⊙ 11-2am; ☒ 1, 6, 8, 13, 18) Under the Rams has been a legendary place since it came into being in 1956 as a 'literary cabaret'. Nowadays, the program is a bit sporadic, but the space continues to host a summer jazz festival in July and several other concerts and cabaret shows throughout the year.

Klub Kwadrat
LIVE MUSIC

(☑ 12 647 5078; www.klubkwadrat.pl; ul Skarżyńskiego 1, Czyżyny; ⊙ 4pm-midnight; ☎; ☒ 125, 129, 138, 159, 172, 178, 502) This popular student club is a great place to catch up-and-coming Polish rock and indie groups, as well as visiting international acts. Check the website for what's on. Buy tickets at the door. The club is about 5km northeast of the Old Town and not easily accessible by tram. Best to reach by taxi or bus.

Jazz Club U Muniaka
JAZZ

(Map p120; ☑ 12 423 1205; www.jazzumuniaka. club; ul Floriańska 3; tickets 25-40zł; ⊙ 7pm-late; ☎; ☒ 2, 4, 14, 18, 20, 24, 44) Housed in a fine cellar, this is one of the best-known jazz outlets in Poland, the brainchild of saxophonist Janusz Muniak. There are concerts most nights from 9.30pm.

Szpitalna 1
LIVE MUSIC

(Map p120; ☑ 12 430 6661; www.facebook.com/ szpitalna1; ul Szpitalna 1; tickets 20-25zł; ⊙ 4pm-midnight Mon-Wed, to 3am Thu, to 7am Fri, 1pm-7am Sat, 1pm-1am Sun; ☒ 2, 4, 14, 18, 20, 24, 44) Awesome live music club and cocktail bar with an eclectic programme of electronica, rock and occasional stand-up comedy nights. The cocktail menu is equally eclectic, with lots of retro faves like Pina Coladas, Mai Tais, Brandy Alexanders and daiquiris. Check the club's Facebook page for a calendar and ticket prices.

Classical Music & Opera

Cracovians enjoy some world-class cultural institutions, including a strikingly modern opera house in the eastern part of the city and a philharmonic orchestra, which plays in its own space in the western part of town. The annual concert season runs from autumn to spring, and regular festivals and musical events pick up the slack in down times.

Kraków Philharmonic
CLASSICAL MUSIC

(Filharmonia im Karola Szymanowskiego w Krakowie; Map p120; ☑ 12 619 8733; www.filharmonia. krakow.pl; ul Zwierzyniecka 1; ☒ 1, 2, 6) Home to one of Poland's best orchestras. Check the website for a calendar of events. Buy tickets at the box office during working hours or an hour ahead of the performance.

Opera Krakowska
OPERA

(☑ 12 296 6262; www.opera.krakow.pl; ul Lubicz 48; tickets 28-200zł; ⊙ box office 10am-7pm Mon-Sat; ☒ 4, 5, 9, 10, 44, 52) The Kraków Opera performs in the strikingly modern building at the Mogilskie roundabout. The setting is decidedly 21st century, but the repertoire spans the ages, incorporating everything from Verdi to Bernstein.

Teatr im Słowackiego
OPERA, THEATRE

(Map p120; ☑ 12 424 4528; www.slowacki.krakow. pl; Plac Św Ducha 1; tickets 30-70zł; ⊙ box office 10am-7pm Mon-Sat; ☒ 2, 4, 14, 18, 20, 24, 44) This important theatre focuses on Polish classics and large-scale productions. It's in a large and opulent building (1893) that's patterned on the Paris Opera, and is northeast of the Main Market Square. Shows are often performed with English subtitles.

Cinema

Kraków is a great film city and has several cinemas around town devoted to independent and arthouse cinema. Check the website for screenings and note that foreign films are almost always shown in their original language with Polish subtitles. This may or may not be English, depending on the film's origin.

Kino Kijów Centrum   CINEMA

(Map p120; ☎12 433 0033; www.kijow.pl; al Krasińskiego 34; tickets 16-20zł; ⊚20) Loved by Cracovians for its retro '60s, communist-era design and architecture, Kijów is one of many independent cinemas in Kraków. It's also home to a film cafe (open 10am to 10pm) and club featuring live performances. There are several small and medium-sized cinemas, with 20 to 40 seats, and a larger hall that accommodates more than 800 – the largest screening room in Kraków.

Kino Pod Baranami   CINEMA

(Map p120; ☎12 423 0768; www.kinopodbaranami. pl; Rynek Główny 27; tickets 16-21zł; ☎; ⊚1, 6, 8, 13, 18) The Cinema Under the Rams is hidden inside a historic palace on a corner of the Main Market Square. There are three screening rooms given over to the best independent Polish and international cinema. Polish films are often screened with English subtitles.

Kino Agrafka   CINEMA

(Map p120; ☎12 430 0179; www.kinoagrafka.pl; ul Krowoderska 8; tickets 14-16zł; ⊙11am-10.30pm; ⊚18) This small but stylish cinema is housed inside a YMCA building not far from the Planty. It has just one screening room, but runs a regular repertoire of current, cult and foreign films. All are either shown or subtitled in English.

Theatre

Stary Theatre   THEATRE

(Teatr Stary; Map p120; ☎12 422 9080; www.stary. pl; ul Jagiellońska 1; adult/concession 70/40zł; ⊙box office 11am-7pm Mon-Sat, to 3.30pm Sun; ⊚2, 4, 14, 18, 20, 24) This is the city's best-known theatre company and it has attracted the cream of its actors. To overcome the language barrier, pick a Shakespeare play you know well from the repertoire, and take in the distinctive Polish interpretation. The box office is off Plac Szczepański.

Teatr Barakah   THEATRE

(Map p128; ☎12 397 8047; www.teatrbarakah. com; ul Paulińska 28; tickets 20-60zł; ⊚6, 8, 10, 13) Highly regarded local theatre. Most of the productions are in Polish though they also host occasional folk-music jam sessions and English-language lectures that are more accessible to visitors. Check the website for a current calendar. The attached cafe/bar (5pm to midnight, except Monday) draws a literate crowd for serious chats over alcoholic and non-alcoholic beverages.

🔒 Shopping

Kraków has a vast array of shops, selling everything from tacky T-shirts to exquisite crystal glassware. Most shops of interest are in the Old Town, Wawel Hill and Kazimierz. An obvious place to start (or perhaps end) your Kraków shopping is at the large souvenir market within the Cloth Hall (p123) in the centre of the Main Market Square.

🔒 Old Town & Around

The Old Town is home to an eclectic shopping scene. Many shops, selling items like fine art and antiques, are clearly aiming for high-end buyers. Visitors can choose from a good selection of amber and jewellery outfits, standard souvenir shops and a quirky poster gallery that's worth a visit even if you've got no intention of buying.

★ Galeria Plakatu   ART

(Map p120; ☎12 421 2640; www.cracowposter gallery.com; ul Stolarska 8-10; ⊙noon-5pm Mon-Fri, 11am-2pm Sat; ⊚1, 6, 8, 13, 18) Poland has always excelled in the underrated art of making film posters and this amazing shop has the city's largest and best choice of posters, created by many of Poland's most prominent graphic artists.

★ Galeria Dyląg   ART

(Map p120; ☎12 431 2521; www.dylag.pl; ul Św Tomasza 22; ⊙noon-6pm Mon-Fri; ⊚3, 10, 24, 52) Small exclusive art gallery features modern Polish artists from the 1940s to the 1970s. Look for the Polish drip paintings, reminiscent of Jackson Pollock, from the late '50s. Many of the pieces on sale here are from artists now displayed in museums.

KRAKÓW SHOPPING

AMBER, AMBER & AMBER

Amber, otherwise known as 'Baltic gold', is fossilised tree resin, usually found on the shores of the Baltic Sea. When it's cut and buffed it makes for a beautiful semi-precious 'stone' in a ring, necklace or brooch, and Kraków has plenty of galleries with beautiful and original designs and settings. Make sure to look around as prices can vary considerably.

★**Schubert**
World of Amber JEWELLERY
(Map p120; ☑ 12 430 2114; www.sukiennice.krakow.
pl; ul Grodzka 38; ⊗ 9am-8pm; 🚊 1, 6, 8, 13, 18) As
the name implies, this is more than a shop,
it's a celebration of all things amber. Even if
you're not in the market to buy, it's certainly
worth a peek in to see the amazing selection
of amber necklaces, earrings, brooches and
pendants.

Kacper Ryx GIFTS & SOUVENIRS
(Map p120; ☑ 12 426 4549; www.kacperryx.pl;
Plac Mariacki 3; ⊗ 11am-7pm Mon-Fri, to 6pm Sat,
noon-5pm Sun; 🚊 1, 6, 8, 13, 18) One-stop shopping for all your gift and souvenir needs.
High-quality carved woodworking, pottery,
traditional shirts and dresses – just about
anything you can think of to stick in the
suitcase to take home. Enter through the
Hipolit House (Kamienica Hipolitów; Map p120;
☑ 12 422 4219; www.muzeumkrakowa.pl; Plac Mariacki 3; adult/concession 10/8zł, free Wed; ⊗ 10am-
5.30pm Wed-Sun; 🚊 1, 6, 8, 13, 18), a branch of
the Kraków City History Museum that contains faithful recreations of townhouse interiors from the 17th to early 19th centuries,
which is situated next door.

Boruni JEWELLERY
(Map p120; ☑ 601 824 646; www.ambermuseum.
eu; ul Św Jana 4; ⊗ 9am-8pm; 🚊 1, 6, 8, 13, 18)
One-stop shopping for amberphiles at this
growing retail empire, with cases and cases of amber rings, necklaces, broaches and
earrings, plus a 'museum' (free admission),
where you can see how amber is cut, polished and set. Boruni includes a certificate
of quality with each purchase. There's another branch and **gallery** (Map p120; ☑ 12 428
5086; www.boruni.pl; ⊗ 9am-9pm; 🚊 6, 8, 10, 13,
18) at ul Grodzka 60.

POLISH SOUVENIRS

If you're in the market for the perfect
Polish souvenir, you'll have plenty of
choices in Kraków. You can't go wrong with
typical Polish food and drink. One staple is
Polish-made vodka, but the country also
turns out very good chocolates, honey and
jam. Poland is known for its glassware and
ceramics, particularly the colourful plates,
jugs and vases from the western Polish
town of Bolesławiec. There's also a wide
selection of handmade jewellery, including
exquisite original pieces.

Salon Antyków Pasja ANTIQUES
(Map p120; ☑ 12 429 1096; www.antykwariat-
pasja.pl; ul Jagiellońska 9; ⊗ 11am-7pm Mon-Fri,
11am-4pm Sat; 🚊 2, 4, 14, 18, 20, 24, 44) This
well-established antique salon is like a
small museum; its three rooms are stuffed
with clocks, maps, paintings, lamps, sculptures and furniture. Come to think of it,
it's better than a museum, because if you
see something you like, you can take it
home.

Kobalt Pottery & More CERAMICS
(Map p120; ☑ 798 380 431; www.facebook.com/
kobalt.pottery; ul Grodzka 62; ⊗ 10am-7pm; 🚊 6,
8, 10, 13, 18) Sells eye-poppingly beautiful ceramic designs from the western Polish city
of Bolesławiec. The dishes, plates and bowls
are all hand-painted with a unique stamping
and brush technique, and can be found in
kitchens around the country.

Stary Kleparz MARKET
(Map p120; ☑ 12 634 1532; www.starykleparz.com;
ul Paderewskiego, Rynek Kleparski; ⊗ 6am-6pm
Mon-Fri, to 4pm Sat, 8am-3pm Sun; 🚊 2, 4, 14, 18,
20, 24, 44) The city's most atmospheric and
historic place to shop for fresh fruits, vegetables and flowers is this sprawling covered
market, which dates back to the 12th century. You'll also find meats, cheeses, spices and bread, as well as clothes and other
necessities.

🏛 **Kazimierz**

Kazimierz might just be the city's best area
for shopping. Unlike Old Town, there are no
airs of exclusivity. Instead, the emphasis is
on small, privately owned shops and boutiques. There's a wide range of design shops,
jewellers, antique shops and art dealers. The
best stretch for shopping is the long row of
boutiques along ul Józefa.

★**Szpeje – Kazimierz** HOMEWARES
(Map p128; ☑ 798 504 458; www.szpeje.com; ul
Józefa 9; ⊗ noon-7pm Thu-Sun; 🚊 6, 8, 10, 13)
Eye-catching retro design shop, featuring
mainly reproductions of furnishings, lighting, ceramics and wall art from the 1960s
and '70s. There's also some excellent poster
and postcard art that's suitable for taking
home.

★**Błażko Jewellery Design** JEWELLERY
(Map p128; ☑ 579 056 456; www.blazko.pl; ul Józefa 11; ⊗ 11am-7pm Mon-Fri, to 3pm Sat; 🚊 6, 8, 10,
13) The eye-catching creations of designer

Grzegorz Błażko are on display in this small gallery and workshop, including his unique range of chequered enamel rings, pendants, bracelets, earrings and cufflinks. Most are silver.

Paon Nonchalant
CLOTHING

(Map p128; ☑ 534 484 399; www.facebook.com/paonnonchalant; ul Józefa 11; ☺ 11am-6pm Mon-Sat; ☒ 6, 8, 10, 13) Be sure to peek in here at Paon, one of only a handful of women's clothing shops in town to focus exclusively on garments and accessories made by independent Polish designers. Lots of stylish bags, laptop cases and scarves at prices that just about everyone can afford.

Raven Gallery
ART

(Map p128; ☑ 12 431 1129; www.raven.krakow.pl; ul Brzozowa 7; ☺ 11am-6pm Mon-Fri, to 3pm Sat; ☒ 17, 22, 52) This small private art gallery features the work of well-known Polish painters working from the 1930s to the present day. The gallery is particularly strong on cubist paintings from the 1920s and '30s, as well as abstract and socialist-realist painting from the 1950s and '60s.

Austeria
BOOKS

(Map p128; ☑ 12 430 6889; www.austeria.pl; ul Józefa 38; ☺ 9am-7pm; ☒ 3, 19, 24) Evocative bookstore located on the ground floor of the High Synagogue (p129) has arguably the best collection of Jewish-themed books and Judaica as well as themed-music CDs in Kraków.

🔒 Outside the Centre

★ Massolit Books & Cafe
BOOKS

(Map p120; ☑ 12 432 4150; www.massolit.com; ul Felicjanek 4; ☺ 10am-8pm Sun-Thu, to 9pm Fri & Sat; ☎; ☒ 1, 2, 6) Highly atmospheric book emporium selling English-language fiction and nonfiction, both new and secondhand. There's a cafe area with loads of character, starting among the bookshelves and extending into a moody back room. The collection is particularly strong on Polish and Central European authors in translation.

Dydo Poster Gallery
ART

(Dydo Galeria Plakatu; Map p120; ☑ 790 792 244; www.dydopostergallery.com; al Focha 1; ☺ 2.30-6.30pm; ☒ 20) Poles are respected around the world for the quality and artistry of their poster art. You'll find some of the best historic and retro posters as well as more modern designs here.

Szpeje - Nowa Huta
HOMEWARES

(☑ 798 504 458; Osiedle Centrum E1, Nowa Huta; ☺ 10am-4pm Tue-Sun; ☒ 4, 10, 21, 22, 44) Small vintage gift and design shop, located inside the Museum of the People's Republic of Poland (p133), featuring eye-catching retro ceramics and glassware of the 'Polish New Look' of the 1960s, as well as dinnerware, vases, lighting, small furniture items, posters and postcards. Pop in to take a look even if you're not in the market to buy.

ℹ️ Information

DANGERS & ANNOYANCES

Kraków is generally a safe city for travellers, although as a major tourist spot it has its fair share of pickpockets; be vigilant in crowded areas.

➡ If you're staying in the centre of the Old Town expect late-night noise from bars and clubs; ask for a room at the back.

➡ In summer, large numbers of tourists can mean long queues for top sights, such as the Wawel Royal Castle, and scarce seating in the more popular restaurants.

➡ Keep a wary eye out for horse-driven carriages around the Old Town, including along the pedestrianised streets.

INTERNET ACCESS

Many hotels, restaurants, cafes and clubs offer wi-fi free to customers. Simply ask the waiting staff or reception desk for the password to access. InfoKraków tourist offices offer free wi-fi and a computer terminal for a few minutes of free web surfing. Internet cafes are slowly disappearing, but at least two in the Old Town are still going strong.

Internet Café Hetmańska (☑ 12 430 0108; www.hetmanska24.com; ul Bracka 4; per hr 4zł; ☺ 24hr; ☒ 1, 6, 8, 13, 18) Well-placed Old Town internet cafe that's conveniently open day and night.

Klub Garinet (☑ 12 423 2233; www.garinet.pl; ul Floriańska 22; per hr 4zł; ☺ 10am-10pm; ☒ 2, 4, 14, 18, 20, 24, 44) Near the main square.

MEDICAL SERVICES

Apteka Całodobowa Dr. Max (☑ 12 631 1980; www.drmax.pl; ul Karmelicka 23; ☺ 24hr; ☒ 4, 8, 13, 14, 24, 44) This 24-hour pharmacy is west of the Old Town.

Medicina (☑ 600 062 337; www.medicina.pl; ul Barska 12, Dębniki; ☺ 7.30am-8pm Mon-Fri, to 2pm Sat; ☒ 17, 18, 22, 52) Private healthcare provider.

Medicover (☑ 500 900 500; www.medicover.pl; ul Podgórska 36; ☺ 7.30am-8pm Mon-Fri, 8am-4pm Sat; ☒ 3, 19, 24) Private clinic with English-speaking specialist doctors. Provides 24-hour emergency service.

Scandinavian Clinic (☑12 421 8948; www.
scandinavian-clinic.pl; Plac Szczepański 3;
☺8am-8pm Mon-Fri, to 2pm Sat; ☑2, 4, 14, 18,
20, 24, 44) Reliable dental clinic in the Old Town.

MONEY

ATMs, banks and *kantors* (exchange kiosks) are
spread out throughout the Old Town and Kazimierz. Credit cards are generally accepted and
often preferred to cash.

POST

Main Post Office (Poczta Polska; Map p120;
☑12 421 0348; www.poczta-polska.pl; ul
Westerplatte 20; ☺7.30am-8.30pm Mon-Fri,
8am-2pm Sat; ☑1, 3, 10, 24, 52) The main post
office is located east of the Old Town.

TELEPHONE

Galeria Krakowska (Map p120; ☑12 428
9902; www.galeriakrakowska.pl; ul Pawia 5;
☺9am-10pm, 10am-9pm Sun; ☎; ☑2, 3, 4,
10, 14, 20, 44, 52) Shopping centre, next to the
main train station, is a handy place to pick up a
Polish SIM card, as local telecoms companies
have outlets here.

TOURIST INFORMATION

InfoKraków (www.infokrakow.pl) The official
tourist information office has branches around
town. Cheerful service, free maps and help in
sorting out accommodation and transport.
Some branches also have free wi-fi.

Airport (☑12 285 5341; www.infokrakow.pl;
John Paul II International Airport, Balice;
☺9am-7pm; ☎)

Cloth Hall (Map p120; ☑12 354 2716; Rynek
Główny 1/3; ☺9am-7pm May-Oct, to 5pm Nov-
Apr; ☎; ☑1, 6, 8, 13, 18)

Congress Centre (Map p128; ☑12 354 2300;
ul Marii Konopnickiej 17, Ludwinów; ☎; ☑17,
18, 22, 52)

Kazimierz (Map p128; ☑12 354 2728; ul Józefa
7; ☺9am-5pm; ☎; ☑6, 8, 10, 13)

Nowa Huta (☑12 354 2714; Osiedle Zgody 7,
Now Huta; ☺10am-7pm; ☎; ☑4, 10, 22, 44)

Old Town (Map p120; ☑12 354 2725; ul Św
Jana 2; ☺9am-7pm; ☎; ☑1, 6, 8, 13, 18)

Wawel (Map p120; ☑12 354 2710; ul Powiśle
11; ☺9am-7pm, to 5pm Oct-Apr; ☎; ☑6, 8,
10, 13, 18)

TRAVEL AGENCIES

Jordan Group (☑12 422 60 91; www.jordan.pl;
ul Pawia 8; ☺8am-6pm Mon-Fri, 9am-2pm Sat;
☑3, 5, 17, 19, 50) Sells air tickets and intercity
train tickets.

WEBSITES

Magiczny Kraków (www.krakow.pl) Good
general information direct from city hall.
Kraków Info (www.krakow-info.com) Great
overview of practical tips.

Karnet Kraków (www.karnet.krakow.pl) Useful
schedule of cultural events.
In Your Pocket (www.inyourpocket.com/
poland/krakow) Irreverent reviews of accommodation, sights and entertainment.
Lonely Planet (www.lonelyplanet.com/krakow)
Destination information, hotel bookings, travellers' forums and more.

ⓘ Getting There & Away

AIR

Sleekly modern John Paul II International Airport
(p420) is located in Balice, 15km west of the centre. The airport handles all domestic and international flights and has car-hire desks, bank ATMs, a
tourist information office and currency exchanges.

The main Polish carrier **LOT** (☑12 422 8989;
www.lot.com; ul Stradomska 7; ☺9am-6pm
Mon-Fri; ☑6, 8, 10, 13, 18) flies to Warsaw and
major cities around Europe. A range of other
airlines, including several budget operators,
connect Kraków to cities in Europe.

BUS

Kraków's main **bus station** (Map p120; ☑703
403 340; www.mda.malopolska.pl; ul Bosacka
18; ☎; ☑2, 3, 4, 5, 10, 14, 17, 19, 20, 44, 50, 52)
is next to the main train station northeast of the
Old Town. Access is through the train station and
follow the signs. The station has ticket and information counters, storage lockers and vending
machines.

Nearly all intercity coaches, both domestic
and international, arrive at and depart from this
station. Handy bus services include **FlixBus**
(https://global.flixbus.com), **Leo Express**
(www.leoexpress.com), **Eurolines** (☑tickets
89 289 9091; www.eurolines.pl) and **Majer Bus**
(www.majerbus.pl). Consult the websites for
destinations, departure times and prices.

Below are approximate fares and travel times
for popular destinations:

CITY	PRICE (ZŁ)	TIME (HR)
Warsaw	from 36	5
Wrocław	from 36	3½
Zakopane	from 18	2¼
Berlin	from 100	7-8
Prague	from 90	5-6

TRAIN

The modern **Kraków Main Station** (Kraków
Główny; ☑22 391 9757; www.pkp.pl; ul Pawia
5a; ☎; ☑2, 3, 4, 5, 10, 14, 17, 19, 20, 44, 50, 52)
is on the northeastern edge of the Old Town,
entered via the Galeria Krakowska (p154) shopping centre. Mostly underground, the station is
beautifully laid out, with information booths and
ticket offices on several levels. Find the left-

luggage office (per day 6zł) and storage lockers (big/small locker per day 12/8zł) below platform 5. There are plenty of bank ATMs, restaurants and shops.

Find up-to-date timetables and ticketing options at www.intercity.pl. Below are approximate fares and travel times for popular destinations.

CITY	PRICE (ZŁ)	TIME (HR)
Budapest	350	10 (overnight)
Lviv	70	8
Prague	from 150	7¼ (overnight)
Vienna	from 200	8½ (overnight)
Warsaw	from 60	2½
Wrocław	45	3½

Getting Around

TO/FROM THE AIRPORT

Special airport trains connect the airport with Kraków's Main Station (9zł, 20 minutes, every 30 minutes). They run daily from about 4am to midnight.

City bus 208 runs from the airport to Kraków's main bus station (4.60zł, 45 minutes, hourly) between 4.30am and 10.30pm.

An official **Kraków Airport Taxi** (☎12 258 0258; www.krakowairport.pl; ☻call centre 6am-10pm) into the city centre should cost from 70zł to 90zł and take about 30 minutes.

Matuszek (Map p120; ☎32 236 1111; www.matuszek.com.pl; single/return 44/88zł) runs regular return shuttles from Kraków's bus station to Katowice's Pyrzowice Airport.

BICYCLE

Kraków is easy to negotiate by bike. Cycle paths follow both sides of the river and circumnavigate the Old Town in the Planty. Several tourist agencies around town offer cycling tours. InfoKraków tourist offices have free cycling maps.

Dwa Koła (☎12 421 5785; www.dwakola.internetdsl.pl; ul Józefa 5; per hr/day 7/50zł; ☻10am-6pm; ☒6, 8, 10, 13) Rents bikes, including with children's seats, by the hour or the day.

Krk Bike Rental (p136) Rents city bikes for puttering around town, as well as mountain bikes (per hour/day 12/60zł) and electric bikes (20/100zł). Also runs 3½-hour city cycling tours (per person 90zł, minimum three people).

Wavelo Kraków City Bike (☎12 290 3333; www.en.wavelo.pl) City-wide bike-share programme. Pay as you go from 0.19zł a minute, or rent for 12 hours at 29zł. For long-term visitors, there are monthly schemes too.

CAR & MOTORCYCLE

Kraków's cobblestoned roads are crowded with cars, and with trams and walking as two reasonable alternatives, there's little point in driving around the city. That said, a car can be useful for reaching outlying suburbs and nearby towns and cities.

Most of the big international car-rental firms have offices in Kraków and/or at Kraków's airport. Polish companies offer cheaper rates, but may have fewer English-speaking staff and rental options.

Mavo Rent a Car (☎792 044 444; www.mavorental.pl; ul Zwierzyniecka 24; ☻24hr; ☒1, 6, 8, 13, 18) Local in-town agency.

PUBLIC TRANSPORT

The city's extensive network of trams and buses is operated by the **Kraków Public Transport Authority** (Miejskie Przedsiębiorstwo Komunikacyjne/MPK; ☎12 19150; www.mpk.krakow.pl), abbreviated as MPK. The system runs daily from about 5am to 11pm.

Buses can be useful for reaching far-flung parts of the city, such as the Zoological Gardens or Kościuszko Mound, though not as practical for covering relatively small distances within the centre. In these cases, trams are preferable.

Rides require a valid ticket that can be bought from automated ticketing machines (automat biletów) onboard or at important stops. Some machines only take coins, while others also take bills and credit cards. You can also buy tickets from some news kiosks.

Tickets are valid for various time periods, from 20 minutes (3.40zł) and 50 minutes (4.60zł) to 24/48/72 hours (15/28/42zł). Remember to validate your ticket in stamping machines when you first board; spot checks are frequent.

TAXI

Taxis are relatively inexpensive and a viable option for moving from place to place. Most drivers are honest, though occasionally you'll run across a dishonest driver who'll jigger the meter or otherwise try to scam you. To minimise that likelihood, it's always best to order a taxi by phone rather than hail one in the street. Only use marked cabs and always ask for a receipt at the end of the ride.

The meter should start at 7zł and rises by 2.30zł per kilometre, increasing to 3.50zł per kilometre from 10pm to 6am and on Sundays.

App-based ride-share services like **Uber** and **Bolt** (Taxify) operate in Kraków and can be slightly cheaper than licensed taxis, though the quality and service vary greatly.

iTaxi (☎73 773 7737; www.itaxi.pl) From the website, download the app to your smartphone.

Radio Taxi Barbakan (☎609 400 400; www.barbakan.krakow.pl) Reliable radio-taxi service.

Historic Cities

Poland has been around for more than a millennium, and its cities reflect the architectural and economic changes over the centuries. Many important cities, including Warsaw, Gdańsk and Wrocław, were damaged in WWII and have been rebuilt. Others, such as Kraków and Toruń, emerged unscathed and look and feel much as they always have.

VELISHCHUK YEVHEN/SHUTTERSTOCK ©

NIGHTMAN1965/GETTY IMAGES ©

1. Kraków (p115)
Wawel Royal Castle (p117) incorporates 14th-century Gothic structures and 16th-century Renaissance and Baroque styles.

2. Wrocław (p238)
The town's market square is crammed with historic buildings and statues.

3. Warsaw (p46)
Castle Sq viewed from the doors of the Royal Castle (p50).

4. Gdańsk (p307)
The Żuraw (Crane; p315), built in the mid-15th century, was the largest medieval crane in Europe.

KONSTANTIN YOLSHIN/SHUTTERSTOCK ©

Małopolska

POP 5.2 MILLION

Why Go?

Małopolska, known in English as Lesser Poland, is the sprawling region that brushes up against Kraków. Covering much of the southeast, it's played an outsized role in Polish history. These days, it's mostly passed over by travellers who make a beeline for Kraków and then move on. That's a pity. The region is rich in natural beauty, with rolling hills and several national parks. Sandomierz, an ancient Gothic town on a bluff overlooking the Vistula River, is one of Poland's prettiest places. Zamość is a World Heritage site. The region is also rich in cultural diversity. Częstochowa is a pilgrimage site for Roman Catholics. To the east, cities and towns were once home to large, vibrant Jewish communities, and moving traces of their centuries-long existence and demise are important sights today.

Best Places to Eat

➡ Bajgiel (p187)
➡ Mandragora (p181)
➡ Solna 12 (p168)
➡ W Starej Piekarni (p173)
➡ Restauracja Muzealna (p192)

Best Places to Stay

➡ Hotel Pod Ciżemką (p173)
➡ Dom Architekta (p186)
➡ Hotel Senator (p191)
➡ Rezydencja Waksman (p181)
➡ Hotel Nihil Novi (p175)

When to Go
Lublin

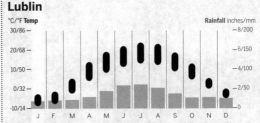

May & Jun The Corpus Christi holiday is marked by weekend festivals.

Aug Thousands of pilgrims gather at Częstochowa's Jasna Góra monastery.

Aug & Sep The International Meeting of Jazz Singers comes to Zamość.

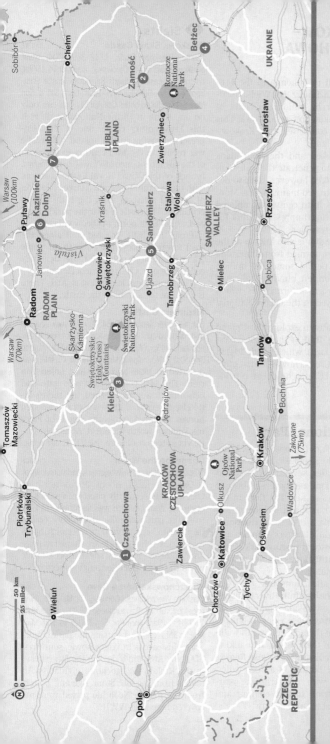

Małopolska Highlights

1 Częstochowa (p162)
Joining throngs of Catholic pilgrims visiting the Black Madonna.

2 Zamość (p188)
Roaming a jewel-like town

that's a monument to the Renaissance.

3 Kielce (p166) Having portraits peer down at you as you wander the Kraków Bishops' Palace.

4 Bełżec (p180) Finding new understanding of the Holocaust at the former camp's memorial.

5 Sandomierz (p170)
Absorbing the vibe sitting

on one of Poland's best town squares.

6 Kazimierz Dolny (p185) Taking a ferry trip to the ancient castle above Janowiec.

7 Lublin (p181) Following the legacy of the once-vital Jewish community.

THE KRAKÓW–CZĘSTOCHOWA UPLAND

When Silesia fell to Bohemia in the 14th century, King Kazimierz III Wielki fortified the frontier by building a chain of castles from Kraków to Częstochowa. This 100km stretch comprises the Kraków–Częstochowa Upland.

The plan worked and the Bohemians were never able to penetrate the wall. Centuries later, in 1655, however, the Swedes invaded and destroyed many castles. More turbulence in the 18th century completed the process, leaving impressive ruins for the 21st-century traveller.

The Upland region is also known as the Jura, having been formed from limestone in the Jurassic period some 150 million years ago. Erosion left hundreds of caves and oddly shaped rock formations, which can still be enjoyed in the Ojców National Park.

An excellent way to explore the Upland is by hiking the Trail of the Eagles' Nest (Szlak Orlich Gniazd), which winds 164km from Kraków to Częstochowa. Tourist offices in Kraków and Częstochowa can provide information.

Ojców National Park

Ojców National Park (Ojcowski Park Narodowy) may be the smallest in Poland, but it packs two castles, several caves, countless rock formations and oodles of bucolic hikes into its 21.5 sq km. The flora in the park is beech, fir, oak and hornbeam forest, and the fauna a diverse mix of small mammals, including badgers, ermines and beavers. This postcard-worthy park is one of the most beautiful areas of the Kraków–Częstochowa Upland.

Most tourist attractions line the road running along the Prądnik River between Ojców and Pieskowa Skała. There is no direct bus connecting these villages, but the flat 7km between them is well worth walking. A segment of the long-distance hiking route, Trail of the Eagles' Nest, also follows this road. At the bottom of a deep valley, Ojców swarms with day trippers year-round. Hit the trails to find comfort and solace in the local natural beauty.

👁 Sights

Pieskowa Skała Castle   CASTLE

(Zamek Pieskowa Skała; ☑ 12 389 6004; www.pieskowaskala.pl; ul Ojcowska; adult/child 11/9zł, Fri free; ⊙ castle grounds 8am-dusk, castle 9am-5pm Tue-Thu, 9am-1pm Fri, 10am-6pm Sat & Sun May-Sep, reduced hours Oct-Apr) If you can only do one thing in Ojców National Park, visit this 14th-century castle, one of the best-preserved castles in the upland. The castle was rebuilt in the 16th century in imitation of the royal residence of Wawel and is now a branch of the Wawel Royal Castle museum, with many exhibitions and a large collection of art and artefacts from the 15th to 19th centuries. The castle is near the park's north end, about 8km north of Ojców village.

From the castle, the red trail along the road towards Ojców takes you to an iconic 25m-tall limestone pillar; it's rather demurely called Hercules' Club (Maczuga Herkulesa).

The limited castle parking is 20zł. There is a decent restaurant in the castle.

Kazimierz Castle   RUINS

(Zamek Kazimierz; ☑ 12 648 9977; www.ojcowskiparknarodowy.pl; ul Ojcowska; adult/child 4/2zł; ⊙ 10am-4.45pm Apr & Sep, to 5.45pm May-Aug, to 3pm Oct & Nov, closed Mon) Ojców Castle was deserted in 1826, and has since fallen into ruin. The 14th-century entrance gate and octagonal tower are original, but there's little else to explore. The view of the wooden houses scattered across the slopes of Prądnik Valley is worth the effort. Access the castle via a steep trail from the PTTK car park.

Chapel on the Water   CHURCH

(Kaplica na Wodzie; www.ojcowskiparknarodowy.pl; ul Ojcowska) FREE About 300m north of Ojców is the frequently photographed Chapel on the Water, which was fashioned in 1901 from the bathhouse that originally stood in its place. In keeping with its exterior simplicity, the three altars inside are shaped as peasants' cottages. You may sneak a peek inside when the doors open for religious service.

Wierzchowska Górna Cave   CAVE

(Jaskinia Wierzchowska Górna; ☑ 12 411 0721; www.gacek.pl; ul Wł Bandurskiego 16/11; adult/child 15/13zł; ⊙ 9am-4pm Apr, Sep & Oct, to 5pm May-Aug, to 3pm Nov) Just outside the park boundaries, this cave is in Wierzchowie, southwest of Ojców. At 950m long, it is the largest cave in the Kraków–Częstochowa highlands. Artefacts from the late Stone Age and pottery from the middle Neolithic period were uncovered here after WWII.

🛏 Sleeping & Eating

Villa PTTK Zosia   HOSTEL €
(✏ 12 389 2008; www.dwzosia.pl; Złota Góra
4, Ojców; per person with/without bathroom
50/40zł; P 🗢) You can't beat the value or the
vibe at this historic wooden villa, just 1km
west up the hill from Ojców Castle. It offers
11 recently renovated rooms and facilities
such as a kitchen, and friendly common
areas. There are summer bonfires.

Zajazd Zazamcze   GUESTHOUSE €€
(✏ 12 389 2083; www.zajazdzazamcze.ojcow.
pl; Ojców 1b; s/d from 110/200zł; ⊘restaurant
9am-9pm; P 🗢) An easy walk from the
Ojców turnoff, Zajazd Zazamcze offers simple and airy rooms. The restaurant turns
out hearty and wholesome fare in its cosy
dining room and has a lovely garden.

★ Ojcowianin   POLISH €€
(✏ 12 389 2089; www.ojcowianin.pl; Ojców 15;
mains 15-30zł; ⊘9am-5pm) In a large rustic
country house in the heart of the village,
you can enjoy the rib-sticking fare of the
region (pork, trout, potatoes etc) in great
and tasty quantity. In summer there's a
great patio and frequent barbecues. It also
has an excellent office selling maps, guides,
gear and souvenirs and offering excellent
free advice. It can arrange tours.

ⓘ Information

The small **PTTK office** (✏ 12 389 2008;
www.ojcow.pttk.pl; Ojców 15; ⊘9am-5pm
Apr-Oct) is in the car park at the foot of Ojców
Castle.

The website www.ojcow.pl is an excellent
resource.

In Ojców village, Ojcowianin sells maps and
guides and offers advice and info.

ⓘ Getting There & Away

A minibus service links Kraków and Ojców
(8zł, 35 minutes, five daily). Buses depart
from the north side of Kraków at a small stop
near a taxi stand at the corner of ul Lubelska
and ul Prądnicka (tram stop: Przystanek
Tramwajowy Kraków) and arrive at the PTTK
office at the base of Ojców Castle. Consult
www.en.e-podroznik.pl for details.

The drive to the park passes through pretty
countryside amid rolling hills. Parking in
Ojców is a challenge on busy weekends. Lots
throughout the park charge from 5zł to 20zł,
which quickly adds up.

Częstochowa

POP 225,300

Every year, Częstochowa (chen-sto-*ho*-vah)
attracts four to five million visitors from
around the world who come to fall at the
feet of the *Black Madonna*. Some walk for
20 days over hundreds of kilometres with offerings for the Virgin. Others take a bus from
Kraków.

Poland's spiritual heartland is not just for
the faithful. The Monastery of Jasna Góra is
the country's national shrine and one of the
highlights of the region. Following an influx
of resources from the EU, renovations have
been working their way up the main thoroughfare towards the monastery, adding
new pride to ancient reverence.

During pilgrimage times – particularly
the day of Assumption on 15 August – hordes
of devotees become a main attraction for
people-watchers, and a deterrent for crowd-
weary wanderers.

History

The first known mention of Częstochowa
dates to 1220, with the monastery appearing about 150 years later. The name 'Jasna
Góra' means Bright Hill, and the fact that
the monastery was one of the few places in
the country to survive Swedish aggression
in the 17th century sealed it as a holy spot
in the minds of many.

The town's foundational charter was
granted in the 14th century under German
law by King Kazimierz III Wielki, placing
Częstochowa on an important trade route
from Russia. Agricultural and industrial development, aided by the Warsaw to
Vienna railway line, saw Częstochowa
evolve into an established industrial centre
by the end of the 19th century. By the outbreak of WWII, the city had some 140,000
inhabitants.

As with many Polish cities of its size,
Częstochowa had a sizeable Jewish community until the German occupation during
WWII. Most of the Jews were clustered in
the neighbourhood around the Stary Rynek
(the town's old market square) at the eastern
end of al Najświętszej Marii Panny (NMP),
which was also where Nazi Germany built
its wartime ghetto. At its peak, it held nearly 50,000 Jews. The ghetto was liquidated
in September and October of 1942, when
around 40,000 Jews were deported to the
extermination camp at Treblinka.

Częstochowa

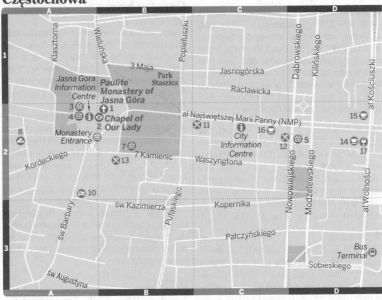

⊙ Sights

★ Paulite Monastery of Jasna Góra

MONASTERY

(Map p162; ☑ 34 365 3888; www.jci.jasnagora.pl; ul Kordeckiego 2; ⊙ 8am-5pm Mar-Oct, to 4pm Nov-Feb) FREE Poland's spiritual capital began with the arrival of the Paulite order from Hungary in 1382, who named the 293m hill in the western part of the city 'Jasna Góra' (Bright Hill) and erected this monastery. Believers are drawn to the site for miracles credited to the Black Madonna (p164) painting in the Chapel of Our Lady, though there are many other sights worth seeing, too. The information centre arranges guided tours in English. The monastery entrance is on the south side.

The oldest part of the monastery, the **Chapel of Our Lady** (Kaplica Cudownego Obrazu; Map p162; ⊙ 5am-9.45pm), contains the revered *Black Madonna*. The picture is unveiled to soaring music and prayer at 6am and 1.30pm (2pm Saturday and Sunday) and covered again at noon and 9.20pm (1pm and 9.20pm Saturday and Sunday). Be sure to note the walls displaying votive offerings brought by pilgrims. Adjoining the chapel is the impressive basilica (*bazylika*). Its present shape dates to the 17th century and the interior has opulent baroque furnishings.

On the northern side of the chapel, paintings in the Knights' Hall (Sala Rycerska) depict key events from the monastery's history; there's also an exact copy of the *Black Madonna*. Upstairs, the Golghota Gallery contains a series of unique paintings by celebrated local painter and cartoonist Jerzy Duda Gracz (1941–2004), whose evocative works are indicative of the monastery's ability to preserve its historical heritage while maintaining modern relevance. Note that many pilgrims traverse the circumference of the chapel on their knees.

The 106m **bell tower** (Map p162; admission by donation; ⊙ 9am-4pm Apr-Nov), the tallest historic church tower in Poland, offers views over the monastery complex and the expanse of al NMP. With many fallen predecessors, the current tower dates to 1906.

The small **600th Anniversary Museum** (Muzeum Sześćsetlecia; Map p162; ⊙ 9am-5pm Mar-Oct, to 4pm Nov-Feb) FREE contains fascinating artefacts, including the founding documents of Jasna Góra from 1382 and a cross made from steel from the rubble of the World Trade Center. Particularly moving are rosaries made from breadcrumbs by concentration camp prisoners. Lech Wałęsa's 1983 Nobel Peace Prize, donated by its recipient, can be found beyond the Father Kordecki Conference Room. Items related to Pope John Paul II abound.

Częstochowa

The **arsenal** (Map p162; ⊙ 9am-5pm Mar-Oct, to 4pm Nov-Feb) **FREE** contains various military mementos, including spoils of battle, offerings from soldiers and an impressive collection of Turkish weapons from the 1683 Battle of Vienna.

The 17th-century **treasury** (Skarbiec; Map p162; ⊙ 9am-5pm Mar-Oct, to 4pm Nov-Feb) **FREE** contains votive offerings dating to the 15th century. Since the 17th century, records have been kept of gifts given to the Madonna, including the many bejewelled shrouds.

Jewish Memorial   MONUMENT
(Umschlagplatz; Map p162; ul Strażacka 19) A small landmark near the Stary Rynek marks the deportation zone, the *Umschlagplatz*, from where tens of thousands of Jews were transported to their deaths at Treblinka in 1942. The memorial includes a copy of a hauntingly precise train timetable showing trains departing Częstochowa at 12.29pm and arriving at Treblinka at 5.25am the next morning.

**Museum of
Iron Ore Mining**   MUSEUM
(Map p162; ☎ 34 360 5631; www.muzeum czestochowa.pl; Park Staszica; adult/child 14/8zł, Wed free; ⊙ 11am-5pm Tue-Fri, to 6pm Sat & Sun Jun-Sep, 9am-3.30pm Tue-Fri, 11am-6pm Sat & Sun Oct-May; ♿) This early-20th-century park pavilion is part of the **Częstochowa Museum** (Muzeum Częstochowskie; Map p162; al NMP 45) and holds a permanent exhibition on iron-ore mining. Visitors descend underground and literally plunge into the world of mining. Exhibits include actual mine tunnels and a small train used to remove ore.

⛏ Festivals & Events

**Gaude Mater
Festival of Religious Music**   MUSIC
(☎ 34 324 3638; www.gaudemater.pl; ⊙ 1st week of May) Focuses on religious music from Christian, Jewish and Islamic traditions. Held throughout the city.

Marian Feast Days   RELIGIOUS
(www.jasnagora.pl; Paulite Monastery of Jasna Góra, ul Kordeckiego 2; ⊙ 3 May, 16 Jul, 15 Aug, 26 Aug, 12 Sep & 8 Dec) Draws believers in the tens of thousands, who camp out, sing songs and attend massive open-air masses.

Avenues–It's On   CULTURAL
(Aleje–tu się dzieje; www.czestochowa.pl; Jun-Aug) Over 120 free concerts and other cultural events are held around the city during the summer. Many take place along al NMP.

MAŁOPOLSKA CZĘSTOCHOWA

DON'T MISS

THE BLACK MADONNA OF CZĘSTOCHOWA

Unlike some other pilgrimage sites, Jasna Góra has never claimed the appearance of apparitions. Its fame is attributed to the presence of the *Black Madonna*, a 122cm by 82cm painting of the Virgin Mary with the Christ Child on a panel of cypress timber, which was crowned 'Queen of Poland' in 1717.

It is not known for sure when or where the *Black Madonna* was created, but some say she was painted by St Luke the Evangelist on a table in the house of the Holy Family and was brought to Częstochowa from Jerusalem via Constantinople. It arrived in Częstochowa in 1382.

In 1430, the face of the Madonna was slashed by Hussite warriors, battling against what they saw as papal abuses in Rome. The painting still bears the scars, either because they were left as a reminder of the sacrilegious attack or, as legend has it, because they continually reappeared despite attempts to repair them.

Legends about the *Black Madonna's* role in saving Jasna Góra from the Swedish Deluge in 1655, and in keeping the Russians at bay in 1920, are still extolled today. The widespread belief in the legends is evident from the votive offerings – from crutches and walking canes to jewellery and medals – that are presented to the Virgin by devoted pilgrims every day.

★ **Assumption** RELIGIOUS
(www.jasnagora.pl; Paulite Monastery of Jasna Góra, ul Kordeckiego 2; ◌ 15 Aug) Pilgrims have been travelling by foot to Jasna Góra for the Assumption since 1711.

📖 Sleeping

During pilgrimage periods, such as the Marian feast days, book well ahead, or stay elsewhere and make a day trip into Częstochowa. Otherwise, finding accommodation should not be a problem; options are many as most visitors to the *Black Madonna* do so on day trips from Kraków.

Pokoje Gościnne
Pod Klasztorem GUESTHOUSE €
(Map p162; ☑ 66 247 7832; www.podklasztorem. pl; ul Św Barbary 13; s/d from 80/140zł; 🅿 🕸) These plain, tidy rooms about 100m from the monastery complex are the best value in town. Don't expect much more than a pinewood bed and basic furnishings, but all 15 rooms have separate baths and everything is well tended. There's a garden at the back, and some units come with kitchens.

Camping Oleńka CAMPGROUND €
(Map p162; ☑ 34 360 6066; www.mosir.pl; ul Oleńki 22; per car/tent 15/20zł, 4-person bungalow with bath 140zł) This campground behind the monastery has space for around 400 people. There are also good-value self-contained bungalows. The campground is located about 100m southwest of the monastery complex.

Hotel Wenecki HOTEL €€
(Map p162; ☑ 34 324 3303; www.hotelwenecki.pl; ul Joselewicza 12; s/d from 150/180zł; 🅿 @ 🕸) The Wenecki is the nicest hotel at its price point in town, with the only drawback being its location about 20 minutes' walk from the monastery (though close to the train and bus stations). Rooms are slightly frayed, but clean. The beds are firm and the baths have handy extras, such as hair dryers. Breakfast costs an additional 20zł.

🍴 Eating

★ **PierożeQ** POLISH €
(Map p162; ☑ 51 515 6378; www.pierozeq.com; Feliksa Nowowiejskiego 4; mains 10zł; ◌ 10am-6pm Tue-Fri, 10.30am-3.30pm Sat) Follow your nose to this minimalist spot just inside a passage and you'll find what may be Poland's best pierogies – at least that's what locals in the know will tell you. The pierogies are very good and are made fresh all day long, which means they aren't those leaden lumps served elsewhere. There are usually seven varieties on offer.

Dobry Rok POLISH €€
(Map p162; ☑ 53 395 0533; www.dobry-rok.pl; al NMP 79; mains 25-75zł; ◌ 8am-10pm Mon-Fri, 9am-midnight Sat, 10am-10pm Sun; 🕸) Among the better of the string of restaurants that line the upper end of al NMP towards the monastery. There's a mix of Polish and international dishes, with local favourites including baked salmon and shrimp, and classic Polish sour soup. The service is formal.

U Braci
ITALIAN €€

(Map p162; ☑515 314 190; www.facebook.com/
ubraci1991; 7 Kamienic 17; mains 20-40zł; ⊙noon-
10pm Tue-Sun; 🕑) For pizza, pasta, burgers,
Polish dishes and gooey desserts near the
monastery, you could hardly do better than
this authentic Italian-accented restaurant,
just a few minutes walk from the main
monastery entrance. The decent wine and
drinks list includes top-notch coffee and
espresso.

 Drinking & Nightlife

★ Cafe Belg & Hostel
CAFE

(Map p162; ☑34 361 1324; www.facebook.com/
cafebelg; al NMP 32; ⊙10am-11.30pm Mon-Sat,
from 4pm Sun; 🕑) Inside a passage is Częstochowa's most interesting cafe. Choose from
a huge range of carefully curated teas or opt
for one of the excellent Polish microbrews.
Other libations include mulled wine and
fine coffees.

Breakfast is served and there are snacks
and desserts available all day (try the apple
pie). Cozy seating inside and sunny seating
outside.

Cafe Belg also operates a small hostel
(hostel per son 35zł, double 70zł) nearby.
There are eight beds in two rooms furnished
with comfortable modern furniture and antiques. There is a kitchen and it's possible to
rent the entire apartment.

Multitap
Piwiarnia Częstochowa
CRAFT BEER

(Map p162; ☑73 368 9943; www.facebook.com/
MultitapPiwiarniaCzestochowa; al NMP 31; ⊙4.30-
10pm Sun-Thu, to midnight Fri & Sat) At the back
of a courtyard off al NMP, you'll find this
welcoming pub with a dozen top Polish craft
brews on tap. Settle in at one of the seasonal
tables on the pavement.

Caffe del Corso
CAFE

(Map p162; ☑72 319 1974; al NMP 53; coffee 8 zł,
ice cream 20zł; ⊙8am-10pm Mon-Sat, 10am-10pm
Sun; 🕑) *The* place on al NMP for excellent
coffees and extravagant ice-cream concoctions and cakes, with a handsome two-
level terrace for people-watching. Also has
a range of salads, toasted sandwiches and
pancakes.

Café 29
CAFE

(Map p162; ☑34 361 2355; www.cafe29.pl;
al NMP 29; ⊙10am-10pm Mon-Thu, to 11pm
Fri & Sat, noon-10pm Sun; 🕑) Walk through
the passageway at al NMP 29 to find Café
29, a popular cafe with salads and light
bites, as well as coffee, beer and a full drinks
list.

Café 29 shares garden space with a few
other pubs, making this a one-stop warren
of nightlife. On summer nights the crowds
mill between them all.

ℹ Information

City Information Centre (Miejskie Centrum
Informacji; Map p162; ☑34 368 2250; www.
czestochowa.pl; al NMP 65; ⊙9am-5pm
Mon-Sat; 🕑) Enthusiastic and very helpful; has
maps and sights information, and a computer
for checking email.

Jasna Gora Information Centre (Jasnagór-
skie Centrum Informacji; Map p162; ☑34 377
7562; www.jasnagora.pl; ul Kordeckiego 2;
⊙9am-6pm May-Sep, to 5pm Mar, Apr & Oct,
to 4pm Nov-Feb) Information centre inside
the Jasna Góra monastery. Organises guided
tours of the major sites at the monastery
(100zł, minimum five people).

ℹ Getting There & Away

BUS

The **bus terminal** (Map p162; ☑information
34 379 1149; al Wolności 45; ⊙information
counter 9am-5pm) is close to the main train
station (about 2km east of the monastery).
For information on regional bus services, see
www.pks-czestochowa.pl.

FlixBus (www.flixbus.com) runs services
to a number of Polish towns; buy tickets
online. Services include:

Katowice 20zł, 1½ hours, five per day

Kraków 25zł, 2¼ hours, two per day

Łódź 25zł, 2½ hours, two per day

Warsaw 45zł, 3½ hours, four per day

TRAIN

The **train station** (off al Wolności) has a
modest amount of service. The station has
lockers. Note: on the north side of the plaza
in front of the train station is an extraordinary mural dedicated to its patron, a
local watchmaker.

There are eight daily fast trains to Warsaw
(40zł, 2½ hours). Kraków is more problem-
atic. There is one direct train a day (34zł,
two hours). Otherwise you have to make a
connection at Katowice. There are four trains
to Kielce (17zł, two hours).

THE MAŁOPOLSKA UPLAND

The Małopolska Upland is skirted by the Vistula and Pilica Rivers, but the centrepiece of this expanse is the Holy Cross Mountains (Góry Świętokrzyskie), a repository of natural beauty, witness to harrowing episodes in the country's history, and object of religious reverence. The main urban centre of Kielce, which sits at the foot of the mountains, is a convenient base from which to access this varied cultural landscape and the surrounding mountain ranges.

Kielce

POP 195,700

Kielce (*kyel*-tseh) is ringed by postwar housing projects that on a rainy day, or any day, can look downright dispiriting. But dig a little deeper and you'll find a lively city with an elegant core, centred on the Rynek (the main square), the cathedral, the remarkable Palace of the Kraków Bishops, and a pretty expanse of parkland surrounding both of them.

Kielce may be still in the throes of a multiyear renovation effort that has scrubbed the central areas and restored some lustre to the Rynek, but it's getting better. The long main thoroughfare, ul Sienkiewicza, has been spruced up and features cafes and shops. And the small Silnica River flowing through the middle of town is drawing modestly upscale new developments.

◉ Sights

★ **Kraków Bishops' Palace** MUSEUM
(Pałac Biskupów Krakówskich; Map p167; ☑ 41 344 4015; www.mnki.pl; Plac Zamkowy 1; adult/child 20/15zł, Sat free; ☺ 10am-6pm Tue-Sun May-Aug, 9am-5pm Sep-Apr) Kielce was the property of the Kraków Bishops from the 12th century through to 1789. This palace was built (from 1637 onwards) as one of their seats and remains a testament to the richness of that era. The highlight of a visit is the restored 17th- and 18th-century interiors, which still feel very lived in. Be sure to ask at the admission counter for a free (and excellent) English-language booklet on the sights. With the cathedral, this compound is reason enough to visit Kielce.

The centrepiece of the permanent exhibition is the former dining hall, where the whole brood of bishops stare down from their 56 portraits. The rest of this cavernous,

multilevel museum leads through collections of porcelain and historical armour, and various centuries and genres of Polish painting.

Kielce Cathedral BASILICA
(Map p167; ☑ 41 344 6307; www.kielcekatedra.pl; Plac NMP 3; ☺ dawn-dusk) FREE Kielce's cathedral looks nothing like the Romanesque church first erected here in 1171; it was rebuilt in the 17th century and dressed in baroque decorations. The cathedral's underground crypts are the final resting place for many bishops. It was given a massive overhaul in 2012 and has emerged gleaming. It overlooks Kraków Bishops' Palace.

Museum of Toys & Play MUSEUM
(Muzeum Zabawek i Zabawy; Map p167; ☑ 41 344 4078; www.muzeumzabawek.eu; Plac Wolności 2; adult/child 10/5zł; ☺ 9am-5pm Tue-Sun May-Oct, 8am-4pm Tue-Sun Nov-Apr; ☷) This fun-filled museum offers the chance to reminisce about all manner of toys. The room full of frogs somehow makes sense when you're there. Enter through the courtyard.

Museum for Intercultural Dialogue MUSEUM
(Muzeum Dialogu Kultur; Map p167; ☑ 41 344 4014; www.mnki.pl; Rynek 3/5; adult/child 13/8zł; ☺ 8am-4pm Mon-Fri, 10am-4pm Sun) This small, uplifting museum is dedicated to global efforts to promote peace and dialogue across cultural and ethnic groups. The museum also holds interesting temporary exhibitions.

Henryk Sienkiewicz Monument STATUE
(Map p167; ul Sienkiewicza) This monument to the Polish writer and Nobel Prize winner Henryk Sienkiewicz marks the eastern end of pedestrianised ul Sienkiewicza.

Jewish Pogrom Memorial MEMORIAL
(Map p167; ☑ 41 201 0238; Planty 7/9; 5zł; ☺ noon-4.30pm Mon-Fri) A plaque signed by former president Lech Wałęsa identifies the site of a post-WWII pogrom on 4 July 1946 committed by Poles against Jews who had survived the Holocaust. The origins of the pogrom are unclear – some believe it was instigated by communist authorities to discredit nationalist Poles – but the violence ended with 42 Jewish deaths. Inside there's a small but moving photo exhibition of Jewish life in Poland in the run-up to WWII.

Nine Poles were executed for taking part in the killings, although there's evidence that those killed may have been chosen at random for a show trial. The pogrom is often cited as one of the reasons so few

Kielce

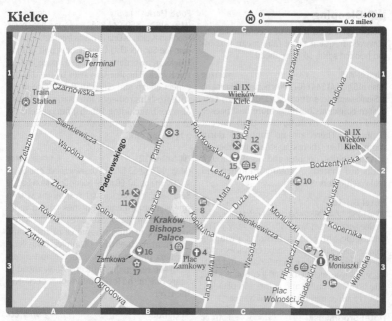

Kielce

◎ Top Sights
1 Kraków Bishops' Palace B3

◎ Sights
2 Henryk Sienkiewicz Monument D3
3 Jewish Pogrom Memorial B2
4 Kielce Cathedral C3
5 Museum for Intercultural Dialogue C2
6 Museum of Toys & Play D3

🛏 Sleeping
7 Hostel-Art D3
8 Hotel Bristol C2
9 Hotel Pod Złotą Różą D3
10 Hotel Śródmiejski D2

✕ Eating
11 Calimero Cafe B2
12 Food Park Orla Sq C2
13 Si Señor C2
14 Solna 12 .... B2

◎ Drinking & Nightlife
15 Craft Beer Pub C2
16 Zamkowe Tarasy B3

◎ Entertainment
17 Dom Środowisk Twórczych B3

surviving Jews decided to remain in Poland after the war. The names of the dead Jews are embedded in the sidewalk out front.

**Open-Air Museum
of the Kielce Village** MUSEUM
(Muzeum Wsi Kieleckiej; ☑ 41 315 4171; www.mwk. com.pl; Tokarnia 303, Chęciny; adult/child 14/8zł; ☺10am-6pm Tue-Sun Jul & Aug, 10am-5pm daily May, Jun, Sep & Oct, 9am-3pm Tue-Sun Nov-Mar, to 4pm Apr; 🚼) This 80-hectare open-air museum of traditional architecture is located in the village of Tokarnia, about 20km from Kielce. It's a pleasant half-day outing, particularly for kids. Several minibuses from

Kielce pass Tokarnia on their way to other destinations, as do five normal buses (6zł, 30 minutes) on their way to destinations such as Jędrzejów. Get off at the village of Tokarnia and continue in the same direction on foot for around 1km to the entrance.

🎊 Festivals & Events

Days of Kielce FAIR
(☺May/June) Kielce has an active social calendar, but the best fest by far is the Days of Kielce, which takes place over the weekend of the Corpus Christi holiday. The whole town shuts down for four days of street food, live music and general merriment.

🛏 Sleeping

Kielce has a good range of accommodation; however, frequent trade fairs mean it is often booked solid, so plan ahead.

Hostel-Art
HOSTEL €

(Map p167; ☑ 41 344 6617; www.hostel-art-kielce.pl; ul Sienkiewicza 4c; s/d from 100/130zł; @ 🛜) This design-conscious hostel is more flashpacker hotel (note the fresh flowers) than student flophouse. There are no multibed dorm rooms, rather there's a small number of private singles, doubles and quads (though baths are shared). A common kitchen will make self-caterers happy.

Hotel Bristol
HOTEL €€

(Map p167; ☑ 41 368 2460; www.bristol.kielce.pl; ul Sienkiewicza 21; s/d from 140/160zł; P 🛜) The turn-of-the-20th century Bristol is a winning choice. Inside the peaches and cream exterior, the compact rooms are comfortable and have big windows, and the central location is ideal. The breakfast buffet and coffee win plaudits. Reserve a free parking spot in advance.

Hotel Śródmiejski
HOTEL €€

(Map p167; ☑ 41 344 1507; www.hotelsrodmiejski.pl; ul Wesoła 5; s/d from 160/180zł; P @ 🛜) Every town should be so lucky as to have a small, family-run hotel so close to the action, yet still reasonably priced. The 21 rooms are large and tastefully furnished; some have balconies out over the street.

Hotel Pod Złotą Różą
HOTEL €€

(Map p167; ☑ 41 341 5002; www.zlotaroza.pl; Plac Moniuszki 7; s/d from 180/220zł; P ✳ @ 🛜) The small but meticulously refurbished rooms shine with a rich brown finish. There's no unnecessary ostentation here; it's just a compact, stylish place with an elegant restaurant and an ornate, celery-coloured facade.

🍴 Eating & Drinking

Kielce has plenty of good choices for eating. Look for new trendy cafes along the Silnica River.

Calimero Cafe
CAFE €

(Map p167; ☑ 73 051 6519; www.calimerocafe.pl; ul Solna 4; mains 10-20zł; ⊙ 10am-10pm; 🛜) Stylish cafe located along the Silnica River. The coffee is a local favourite as are the baked goods. Breakfast is served from late morning. Lunches include a big menu of fresh fare like salads and sandwiches. It serves homemade lemonade and smoothies.

Food Park Orla Sq
FOOD TRUCK €

(Map p167; ☑ 50 947 8653; www.facebook.com/FoodParkKielce; ul Orla 2; mains from 8zł; ⊙ 11am-3pm Tue-Sun Apr-Oct) Cheery new pod of food trucks in a verdant little open space just off the Rynek. The line-up varies by the day but expect cheap and cheerful Polish fare made with fresh ingredients. International hits are also sold, including kebabs, burgers etc. Sit at a picnic table, or grab a sun lounger and a beer and chill.

★ Solna 12
EUROPEAN €€€

(Map p167; ☑ 53 577 0370; www.solna12.pl; Solna 4a/12; mains 30-60zł; ⊙ noon-10pm Mon-Sat, to 8pm Sun) A large, casual restaurant with a fine seasonal menu of dishes with a modern take on European cuisine. The chefs are proud of the provenance of their fare, highlighting their use of apples from Sandomierz plus vegetables, cheese and meats from top regional producers. Book ahead to snare one of the lovely tables on a deck over the river.

Si Señor
SPANISH €€€

(Map p167; ☑ 41 341 1151; www.si-senor.pl; ul Kozia 3; mains 36-70zł; ⊙ noon-10pm Mon-Sat, to 7pm Sun; 🛜) Arguably Kielce's best restaurant, with an intimate, upscale dining room of brown leather chairs, subdued lighting and dark walls. The Spanish-influenced menu features steaks and seafood plus paella. The long wine list is heavy on Spanish labels. There's a small terrace out front. Note, this is not a Mexican joint with tequila shots.

★ Craft Beer Pub
CRAFT BEER

(Map p167; ☑ 72 454 5352; www.craft-beer-pub.ontap.pl; Piotrkowska 2; ⊙ 3-11pm Sun-Thu, to 1am Fri & Sat) An attractive and welcoming corner pub with exposed brick, black and white tile floors and big windows. The beer list is a treasure, as you'd expect from the name. The fine Polish craft brews on tap vary daily, and staff are skilled at offering suggestions.

Zamkowe Tarasy
BEER GARDEN

(Map p167; ☑ 41 344 7226; www.facebook.com/zamkowetarasy.kielce; ul Zamkowa 4; ⊙ 11am-late) On a warm summer evening, there's no better place in Kielce than this popular beer garden located at the leafy end of Zamkowa towards the park. Fetch a brew at the bar and then find a picnic table outside.

☆ Entertainment

Dom Środowisk Twórczych   LIVE MUSIC
(Map p167; ☑ 41 367 6770; www.palacykzielinski ego.pl; ul Zamkowa 5; ⊙ 11am-11pm) One of the best music venues in town, offering temporary exhibitions and live music (depending on the night, from classical to rock and jazz) in a resplendent but relaxed open-air space in a backyard garden. There's also a decent restaurant and cafe here. Buy tickets online.

ℹ Information

Tourist Office (ROT Świętokrzyskie; Map p167; ☑ 41 348 0060; www.swietokrzyskie.travel; ul Sienkiewicza 29; ⊙ 9am-5pm daily Jul & Aug, 9am-5pm Mon-Sat May, Jun & Sep, 9am-5pm Mon-Fri, 8am-4pm Sat Oct-Apr; ☎) Impressively helpful tourist office back off ul Sienkiewicza in the centre of town.

ℹ Getting There & Away

BUS

Kielce is home to what is arguably Poland's coolest **bus station** (Map p167; ul Czarnowska 12) – a renovated retro-futuristic, UFO-shaped building that dates from the 1970s.

There are buses to Święty Krzyż (5zł, one hour, four daily); Łódź (30zł, three hours, eight daily); Sandomierz (19zł, two to three hours, 10 daily); and Lublin (30zł, 3½ hours, eight daily).

Flixbus (www.flixbus.com) runs to Kraków (28zł, two hours, frequent), Radom (14zł, one hour, frequent) and Warsaw (28zł, three hours, eight daily).

TRAIN

The **train station** (plac Niepodległości 1, off ul Sienkiewicza), the key landmark at the western end of ul Sienkiewicza, services many destinations. There are trains to Radom (19zł, 1¼ hours, seven daily), Warsaw (44zł, 3¼ hours, four daily) and Kraków (30zł, 1¾ hours, four daily).

Świętokrzyski National Park

The 60 sq km **Świętokrzyski National Park** (Świętokrzyski Park Narodowy; ☑ 41 311 5106; www.swietokrzyskipn.org.pl; adult/child 7/3.50zł) covers a stretch of low-lying hills known as the Świętokrzyski Mountains. It offers a perfect full-day, back-to-nature respite from urban Poland and includes a particularly sacred site and some sweeping views. This is Poland's oldest mountainous geological formation and it shows its age.

Erosion has whittled down ancient peaks; look for unusual piles of broken *gołoborza* (quartzite rock) on the northern slopes that date far back into prehistory. The park draws hikers who usually follow the centuries-old pilgrimage route from the unappealing town of Nowa Słupia to the famous Benedictine monastery high in the hills at Święty Krzyż (Holy Cross).

◉ Sights & Activities

The full park-spanning hike from the Nowa Słupia park entrance to the Benedictine monastery at Święty Krzyż and onwards takes about six to seven hours and covers 18km. The end point is the hamlet of Święta Katarzyna. Alternatively, you can just hike up the somewhat steep segment from the Nowa Słupia park entrance to the monastery (around 2km). From Holy Cross, you can get a bus and connect back to Nowa Słupia.

Benedictine Monastery of Holy Cross   MONASTERY
(Święty Krzyż; ☑ 41 317 7021; www.swietykrzyz.pl; Święty Krzyż 1) FREE This hilltop monastery got its name from the segment of Jesus' cross that was supposedly kept here. The abbey is at the top of Łysa Góra (595m). It has a fascinating history going back nearly a millennium. Besides the 2km hike up from the Nowa Słupia entrance, there's access from the west via the village of Huta Szklana. While you can drive up, many prefer to park and hike up the moderately steep and bucolic 1.8km road to the monastery.

There are sweeping views of the region from the monastery grounds. Get a beer and a sausage from the snack stand and enjoy the view from a picnic table.

Most sources estimate the complex was built in the 11th century on an 8th- and 9th-century pagan worship site. In more recent times, with the abolition of the Benedictine Order by the Russians in 1819, the abbey was converted into a prison. After a brief period of restoration, under Nazi Germany the buildings were reconverted into prisons. The Gestapo tortured many monks here before transporting them to Auschwitz-Birkenau, and many Soviet prisoners of war were executed and buried in mass graves near the peak. Under communism, the abbey was transferred to the national park and renovations commenced.

MAŁOPOLSKA ŚWIĘTOKRZYSKI NATIONAL PARK

➡ Holy Cross Church

(Bazylika na Świętym Krzyżu; crypts adult/child 3/2zł; ⊙9am-5pm Mon-Sat, noon-5pm Sun & holidays) The Holy Cross Church in the Benedictine Monastery of Holy Cross was rebuilt several times over the years. The present-day church and its bright white mainly neoclassical interior date to the late 18th century. In addition to the church, you can also tour the crypts, where you'll see the mummified remains of nobleman Jeremi Michal Korybut.

🛏 Sleeping

Look for farmstays along the country roads circling the park. There's a hotel near the Benedictine Monastery of Holy Cross in Huta Szklana and a hostel in Nowa Słupia. Otherwise, the park is a good day trip from Kielce or Sandomierz.

Youth Hostel   HOSTEL €

(Schronisko Młodzieżowe; ☑413177016; www.ssm-checiny.pl; ul Świętokrzyska 61, Nowa Słupia; dm 24zł, d 47-51zł) This hostel in Nowa Słupia is well tended and has 56 beds in dorms and rooms for one to four people. The location is convenient for the entrance to the national park.

Jodłowy Dwór   HOTEL €€

(☑41 302 5028; www.jodlowydwor.com.pl; Huta Szklana 34; s/d from 120/160zł; Ⓟ🐾🛜) Though the exterior looks more like a modern housing estate, this lodge in the village at the base of the access road to the Benedictine Monastery of Holy Cross has decent digs for those who want to fully experience the holy site and Świętokrzyski National Park. It's a 2km walk uphill to the monastery through the park from the hotel.

ℹ Information

Nowa Słupia Park Entrance (www.swieto krzyskipn.org.pl; ul Świętokrzyska; adult/child 7/3.50zł; ⊙9am-5pm Apr-Oct) Park information and maps.

ℹ Getting There & Away

The park is 25km east of Kielce. Buses leave every hour or so from Kielce to Święta Katarzyna (8zł, 30 minutes), with some stopping at Święta Krzyż on the way. To get to Nowa Słupia (6zł, one hour), take a bus bound for either Jeziórko or Rudki.

THE SANDOMIERZ VALLEY

The Sandomierz Valley (Kotlina Sandomier-ska) covers an extensive area in and around the fork of the Vistula and San Rivers. In the heart of the valley is the hilltop town of Sandomierz – an underrated gem of Gothic splendour. Nearby are the fantastic fairy-tale ruins of Ujazd Castle.

Sandomierz

POP 24,600

The grandeur of Sandomierz's Old Town, with the impressive Gothic town hall sprouting from its Rynek (main square), remains relatively undiscovered. Immaculate buildings painted warming hues of brown, orange and yellow, many festooned with elegant wrought-iron balconies, line the lanes as locals nonchalantly wander by.

The town's position on a knoll above the Vistula River and wide plains beyond gives it commanding views and a certain regal air of being above it all. Yet the town remains relatively untouristy; while popular towns like Kazimierz Dolny groan under the weight of weekend mobs, Sandomierz serenely carries on. However, new restaurants and hotels hint that the secret's out: Sandomierz is one exquisite little highlight of eastern Poland.

History

No one is certain of precisely when Sandomierz came to life, but as far back as the 11th century the town was classified (by chronicler Gall Anonim) as a major settlement of the Polish kingdom, along with Kraków and Wrocław.

In the 13th century, repeated assaults by Tatar raiders meant that Sandomierz had to be resurrected several times, most significantly in 1260 when it was rebuilt uphill at the site it occupies today. During the reign of Kazimierz III Wielki (1333–70), Sandomierz became a significant trade hub and saw the construction of the Royal Castle, Opatów Gate and town hall. The town prospered until the mid-17th century, which saw both the arrival of the Jesuits and the invasion of the Swedes – an onslaught from which it never completely recovered.

After having survived WWII with its historic architecture relatively unscathed but its Jewish population of several thousand murdered, the next threat came in the 1960s

FINDING 365 WAYS TO DIE

The interiors of Sandomierz cathedral are suitably pious, but focus on the details beyond the initial ostentation and you'll discover a macabre side.

The paintings on the walls of the cathedral are by 18th-century artist Karol de Prevot (1708–37), who was apparently not a cheery guy. The four paintings on the back wall under the organ depict historic scenes such as the 1656 destruction of Sandomierz Castle by the Swedes. But it's the 12 paintings on the side walls that plunge into the dark side.

The series, *Martyrologium Romanum*, depicts the martyrdom of the Dominican Fathers and other people of Sandomierz at the hands of the Tatars between 1259 and 1260. The unfortunate subjects are being sawn, burned, hanged, whipped, quartered, sliced, diced and otherwise discourteously treated.

The 12 paintings are supposed to symbolise the 12 months of the year; next to each image of torture a number represents the day of the month. Legend has it that if you find the day and month on which you were born, you'll discover how you're going to die.

On a side note, Sandomierz cathedral is also notorious for other images within the *Martyrologium Romanum* series. There are portrayals that many ascribe to the 'blood libel' myth of Jews killing Catholic children for their blood. Covered by a red cloth since 2006, their location is currently obscured by a major structural refurbishment project.

when the town's most significant buildings started sliding into the river. The soft silt on which Sandomierz is built (and from which its underground cellars were carved) began to give way, necessitating a large-scale rescue operation. The injection of concrete and steel into the slippery soil stabilised the city and securely tethered – for now – its architectural assets.

◉ Sights

Sandomierz' market square (Rynek), distinctive for its trapezoidal shape and slope, is ringed with houses from different stylistic periods. Today, only Nos 10 and 27 have the arcades typical of 16th-century houses. The red rectangular **Town Hall**, erected in the 14th century, is the oldest building on the Rynek; the white **Clock Tower** was added in the 17th century, and the sundial on the southern wall (the work of Tadeusz Przypkowski) in 1958. There are plenty of cafes and public benches where you can laze away and soak up the scene.

Cathedral Basilica   CHURCH
(Bazylika Katedralna; ☑ 15 832 7343; www.katedra.sandomierz.org; ul Mariacka 10; ⊙ 11am-3pm Mon, 10am-3pm Tue-Sat, 1-4pm Sun) Built between 1360 and 1382, this massive church has retained much of its Gothic exterior, apart from the baroque facade added in the 17th century. The Russo-Byzantine frescoes in the chancel were painted in the 1420s.

Also note the impressive 17th-century baroque organ gallery, the marble altar dating to the 18th century, and the macabre and notorious paintings on the interior walls. The exterior red and black bricks recall the architecture of the Hanseatic League to the north.

Diocesan Museum   MUSEUM
(Muzeum Diecezjalne; ☑ 15 833 2670; www.domdlugosza.sandomierz.org; ul Długosza 9; adult/child 6/4zł; ⊙ 9am-4.30pm Tue-Sun May-Sep, 9am-3.30pm Tue-Sat, from 1.30pm Sun Oct-Apr) The quintessential example of Sandomierz' underrated assets, the medieval Długosz House (Dom Długosza) was built in 1476 for Poland's first historian, Jan Długosz. Today it houses the Diocesan Museum, with a treasure trove of medieval artwork, sculpture, tapestries, clothing, coins and ceramics.

Royal Castle &
Regional Museum   CASTLE
(Muzeum Okręgowe – Zamek; ☑ 15 832 2265; www.zamek-sandomierz.pl; ul Zamkowa 12; adult/child 15/10zł, Mon free; ⊙ 1-3pm Mon, 10am-6pm Tue-Sun May-Sep, 1-3pm Mon, 10am-4pm Tue-Sun Oct-Apr) The Royal Castle was built in the 14th century on the site of a previous wooden stronghold and was gradually extended during the next three centuries. It now accommodates the regional museum, which contains modest ethnographic, archaeological and art collections.

MAŁOPOLSKA SANDOMIERZ

CRAZY KRZYŻTOPÓR CASTLE

The minute village of Ujazd (oo-yahst), some 35km west of Sandomierz, is home to arguably Poland's most bizarre ruin. **Krzyżtopór Castle** (☑ 15 860 1133; www.krzyztopor.org.pl; off Hwy 758, Ujazd; adult/child 11/8zł; ☺ 8am-8pm Apr-Aug, to 6pm Mar, Sep & Oct, to 4pm Nov-Feb) was commissioned in the 1600s by eccentric governor Krzysztof Ossoliński and built according to his fantastic imagination, incorporating his love of magic and astrology, among other things. These days visitors are free to walk the grounds, climb the turrets, and marvel at what must have been one enormous manor.

The architect commissioned to create Ossoliński's dream was Italian Lorenzo Muretto (known in Poland as Wawrzyniec Senes), who worked on the mammoth project between 1631 and 1644.

History and legend offer zany accounts of the castle. It was designed to embody a calendar, with four towers representing the four seasons, 12 halls for the 12 months of the year, 52 rooms for the 52 weeks, and 365 windows for 365 days – plus one to be used only during leap years. Some cellars were used as stables for Ossoliński's 370 white stallions, and are adorned with mirrors and black marble. The crystal ceiling of the great dining hall is believed to have been the base of an enormous aquarium.

Perhaps the most enchanting – and far-fetched – tale is the claim that a tunnel ran under the manor, linking it to the castle of Ossoliński's brother. The 15km tunnel was believed to have been covered with sugar so the two brothers could visit each other on horse-drawn sledges, pretending they were travelling on snow.

Sadly, Ossoliński was barely able to enjoy his playground; he died in 1645, only a year after the castle was completed.

After damage done by the Swedes in the 1650s and the abandonment of the castle by its subsequent owners in 1770, this dreamland fell into ruin. Since WWII, talk of converting the castle into a hotel has petered out, leaving Krzyżtopór Castle as a landscape for the fantasies of its visitors.

To reach Ujazd by bus from Sandomierz, change at Opatów (8zł, 45 minutes, hourly, 30km) or Klimontów. Having your own wheels is preferable.

Underground Tourist Route TUNNEL
(Podziemna Trasa Turystyczna; ☑ 15 832 0843; www.sandomierskiepodziemia.eu; ul Rynek 10, entrance on ul Oleśnickiego; adult/child 13/9zł; ☺ 9am-7pm Apr-Sep, 10am-5pm Oct-Mar, last entry 1hr before closing) A 40-minute guided tour (in Polish) leads through a chain of 30-odd cellars tidily connected over 500m beneath the Old Town. The cellars – originally used for storage and sometimes for shelter during times of conflict – were built between the 13th and 17th centuries. The deepest point is about 12m below ground, but it feels like more, because of disorienting twists, turns and Escher-esque staircases.

Opatów Gate GATE
(Brama Opatowska; ☑ 66 871 3522; ul Opatowska; adult/child 6/4zł; ☺ 9am-7pm May-Sep, to 5pm Oct-Apr) The main entrance to the Old Town, and the only surviving gate of the four originally built, is 14th-century Opatów Gate. You can climb to the viewing platform at the top for a pleasant (though by no means bird's-eye) view of surrounding terrain and adjoining fragments of defensive walls.

🛏 Sleeping

In addition to Sandomierz's hotels, there are many private rooms and apartments available around the Old Town. Some of the best are on pretty ul Forteczna, a cobblestone lane just behind the Rynek.

Zielone Wzgórze GUESTHOUSE €
(☑ 70 847 7500; www.zielonewzgorze-sandomierz.e-meteor.pl; ul Forteczna 6; per person from 50zł; P ❄ 🛜) Comfortable guesthouse situated in the Old Town a couple of minutes' walk from the Rynek, with ordinary rooms and a beautiful back terrace with views out over the Sandomierz Valley. The air-con in rooms is uncommon and very welcome on a hot summer night.

Willa na Skarpie GUESTHOUSE €
(☑ 66 544 5180; www.naskarpie.nocowanie.pl; ul Forteczna 8; per person 50-60zł; P 🛜) Comfy guesthouse two minutes' walk from the main square, with two rooms, and a handsome covered terrace with views out over the valley. There's a barbecue for guest use.

★**Hotel Pod Ciżemką** HOTEL €€
(☑15 832 0550; www.hotelcizemka.pl; Rynek 27; s/d from 210/240zł; P 🛜) Pod Ciżemką is right on the Rynek and feels like an old-school hotel with centuries of history. Set in a 400-year-old house, the comfortable rooms are vaguely modern while the old-world elegance is reserved for the dining areas. Note there's no elevator, meaning you'll be climbing one or two flights.

Hotel Basztowy HOTEL €€
(☑15 833 3450; www.hotelbasztowy.pl; pl Ks J Poniatowskiego 2; s/d from 220/260zł; P @ 🛜) Among the regal pleasures at the refined Basztowy is a billiard room. Rooms, however, are simple, with a mix of period and 1990s furnishings. The breakfast buffet is big. It's a two-minute walk southwest of the Rynek.

✕ **Eating & Drinking**

★**W Starej Piekarni** POLISH €
(☑78 715 3350; ul Księdza Antoniego Rewery; mains from 10zł; ⊘11.30am-5pm Wed-Sun Apr-Oct) This bakery-cafe looks a bit tumbledown from the outside but inside you'll savour the kind of homestyle cooking people claim their grandmother perfected. Dine on long benches. There's usually a couple of soups on offer, along with staples like pierogi. But it's the traditional bread that stars; it comes by the loaf. Hours can be erratic; check the Facebook page.

★**Lapidarium pod Ratuszem** PUB FOOD €
(☑78 764 6484; www.lapidariumpodratuszem. pl; Rynek 1; mains 12-26zł; ⊘11.30am-11pm; 🛜) Simple food well prepared – big salad and cheese plates, craft beers and very good burgers – is the major drawcard at this cheery restaurant and cafe located in the town hall basement. Dine right on the Rynek during summer, though try to time your arrival outside popular times (or book in advance) as this place gets crowded.

Food Stands FOOD TRUCK €
(off ul Mały Rynek; mains from 5zł; ⊘10am-4pm Apr-Oct) Hidden away in an open space behind buildings is this pod of food trucks. The meals are simple and fresh; you'll have your choice of sausage and ice-cream vendors. Grab a seat at one of the picnic tables.

Restauracja Widnokrąg INTERNATIONAL €€
(☑66 006 5516; www.facebook.com/Restauracja Widnokrag; ul Opatowska 19; mains 20-50zł;

⊘8am-9pm Sun-Thu, to 11pm Fri & Sat) Right by the Opatów Gate, this vaguely Swedish-themed restaurant is a new and glitzy addition to town, aimed at visitors. Canned cool jazz plays from speakers above the large and sunny terrace. The food is fancified standards: steaks, roasts etc.

Café Mała CRÊPES €€
(☑60 210 2225; ul Sokolnickiego 3; mains 15-30zł; ⊘8.30am-9pm Mon-Thu, to 10pm Fri-Sun; 🛜✏) This cosy, French Provincial-style cafe just up from the Rynek is perfect for a coffee or meal, such as a savoury crêpe or something cheesy. People love the desserts and the fresh flowers on tables inside and out.

Iluzjon Art Cafe CAFE
(☑88 312 1416; www.iluzjoncafe.pl; Rynek 25/26; ⊘8am-11pm Mon-Thu, 10am-midnight Sat & Sun; 🛜) This stylish cafe on the Rynek serves excellent homemade lemonade, as well as coffees and teas, craft beers, frilly cocktails, and an enticing range of cakes and ice-cream sundaes. Breakfasts are popular and light meals are served throughout the day.

Café Bar Kordegarda CAFE
(☑60 210 2225; Rynek 12; ⊘noon-11pm; 🛜) One of several cafes with terraces above the Rynek's north side, Kordegarda offers drinks and light meals of pub standards. On summer evenings, the terrace with its enveloping wicker chairs is the place to be for imbibing and people-watching.

ℹ **Information**

Tourist Information Centre (Centrum Informacja Turystyczne; ☑15 644 6105; www.sandomierz.travel; Rynek 20; ⊘10am-5.30pm daily mid-Apr–Aug, 9am-5pm daily Sep, 8am-4pm Mon-Fri, 9am-5pm Sat & Sun Oct–mid-Apr; 🛜) Has basic information and offers a free simple map of the Old Town.

ℹ **Getting There & Away**

Train service is sparse and the station is inconvenient.

The small **bus terminal** (ul Listopada 11) is located 1.2km northwest of the Old Town. There's decent regional service, including buses to Kielce (17zł, two hours, several daily), Lublin (19zł, two hours, several daily) and Zamość (30zł, 3½ hours, one daily). There are several daily buses to Warsaw (44zł, four hours, several daily).

MAŁOPOLSKA SANDOMIERZ

THE RADOM PLAIN

The Radom Plain (Równina Radomska) extends between Małopolska to the south and Mazovia in the north. This gentle area is seldom visited by tourists, but Radom city is a pleasant enough place to decamp for the night, and one of the most expansive skansens (open-air museums of traditional architecture) in Małopolska is just outside the city.

Radom

POP 213,600

Radom is a large industrial city that offers few traditional attractions for visitors. That said, its main pedestrian thoroughfare, ul Żeromskiego, is diverting and dotted with historical sights. Radom's efforts to buff itself up lag behind other Polish cities (the Rynek is bedraggled), which is somehow fitting, given the city's gritty history.

Radom lies astride one of the country's most important rail connections, linking Kraków and Warsaw, and as such is a convenient stopover point. And, if you're coming from the south, Radom is only 90 minutes' drive from Warsaw's airport, making the city a more economical and more interesting place to stay the night before a flight.

Sights

Teasing out Radom's surviving historical buildings can be an adventure in sleuthing. Pick up the excellent – and invaluable – *A Walk Around Radom* guide and map at the tourist offices.

Museum Jacek Malczewski MUSEUM

(Muzeum im Jacka Malczewskiego; ☎48 362 4329; www.muzeum.edu.pl; Rynek 11; adult/child 9/7zł; ⏲10am-3pm Mon-Thu, to 5pm Fri, 11am-4pm Sat & Sun) Housed in a grand 18th-century collegiate building on the Rynek, this museum displays a collection of art by local painters, including its namesake Jacek Malczewski. Other exhibits cover local history, archaeology and, yes, even stamps. It's eclectic and oddly compelling. The facade features a mismatched jumble of plaques honoring local luminaries.

Radom Village Museum MUSEUM

(Muzeum Wsi Radomskiej; ☎48 332 9281; www.muzeum-radom.pl; ul Szydłowiecka 30; adult/child 10/6zł; ⏲9am-5pm Tue-Fri, 10am-6pm Sat & Sun May-Oct, 9am-3.30pm Mon-Fri, 10am-3pm Sat & Sun Nov-Apr) One of the most popular outings is the short hop to this outdoor folklore museum about 7km from the centre. Furnished interiors showcase styles from the whole region. Historic structures include thatched roof farmhouses, pottery kilns and forges. City bus 14 or 17 will get you within a few hundred metres of the entrance. Returning to Radom, turn left back onto the highway; the bus stop is in a small side street 20m or so past a turnoff.

Sleeping

There are several moderately priced hotels not far from the train and bus stations and near ul Żeromskiego.

Rynek 6 Hostel & Retro Pub GUESTHOUSE €

(☎69 360 2482; www.rynek6.radom.pl; Rynek 6; r from 120zł; P 📶) Not a hostel in a traditional sense – though one room has bunk beds – the Rynek 6 is more akin to a pension. Enjoy touches like the stylish room decor and the high-thread-count cottons on the beds. The property is located in one of the few renovated buildings on Radom's gritty Rynek.

Hotel Iskra HOTEL €

(☎48 363 8745; www.hoteliskra.radom.pl; ul Planty 4; s/d from 100/130zł; P 📶) Just a couple of minutes' walk from the train station, the Iskra is a revitalised former communist-era structure that offers bright, well-maintained rooms bigger than what's considered average today. The facade is painted in shades of fresh celery. On-site parking is a pricey 25zł.

★ **Hotel Nihil Novi** HOTEL €€

(☎48 332 9180; www.hotelnihilnovi.pl; Rynek 3; r from 300zł; ⏲restaurant 7am-10pm; P ❄ 📶) Easily Radom's best hotel, Nihil Novi combines colour and flair with a fine appreciation of heritage values. Rooms have bold style and all the expected comforts. The restaurant (mains 22zł to 60zł) serves a creative menu of Polish faves (goose, duck, pierogies) and crowd-pleasers like fine burgers. Enjoy the courtyard tables. Service is polished – now the Rynek out front needs to catch up.

Hotel Gromada HOTEL €€

(☎48 368 9100; www.gromada.pl; ul Narutowicza 9; s/d from 140/170zł, apt from 290zł; P @ 📶) This generic chain hotel has spacious rooms and an on-site restaurant. Apartments are reasonable value given their terrace and kitchen annex. It's a short walk from ul Żeromskiego.

✖ Eating & Drinking

Pleasant eateries can be found in and around ul Żeromskiego. Locals swear that **Zapiekanka** (Pizza Bar; ☑ 48 366 9517; ul Moniuszki 16; mains 7-12zł; ☺ 10am-7pm Mon-Fri, to 3pm Sat), a small window on ul Moniuszki, serves Poland's (well, at least Radom's) best *zapiekanki* (oven-baked, open-faced baguettes, slathered in cheese and sauce).

Piekarnia Pod Telegrafem BAKERY €
(☑ 72 889 2228; Żeromskiego 55; snacks from 3zł; ☺ 7am-6pm Mon-Fri, to 2pm Sat) Smart cafe on the main drag with a big case filled with baked goods, pastries and various gooey treats. Big windows and cosy booths make this a fine refuge on a rainy day.

Pivovaria PUB FOOD €€
(☑ 48 384 8878; www.pivovaria.pl; ul Moniuszki 26; mains 20-40zł; ☺ 11am-midnight Sun-Thu, to 2am Fri & Sat; ☎) This comfy pub brews its own excellent beer in many styles on the premises (try the pale ale). The menu tends towards simple grilled meats, pastas, salads and a few Polish treats. The cellar dining room is bright, and the main-floor cafe is a good place to relax with a coffee.

Piwiarnia PUB
(☑ 88 398 1713; ul Żeromskiego 15; ☺ 4-11.30pm Sun-Thu, to 1am Fri & Sat) A lively pub with good pizzas and burgers. It's located in a house dating back to 1857, but most patrons only take notice of the colourful cocktails and the wide range of beer. There's a lively vibe from the many students, especially on a warm evening when the big patio rocks.

ℹ Information

The excellent tourist office has two convenient locations: in the **train station** (☑ 48 360 0610; www.cit.radom.pl; Władysława Beliny-Prażmowskiego 2; ☺ 9am-5pm Mon-Sat) and the **Old Town** (☑ 48 360 0610; www.cit.radom.pl; Rwańska 16; ☺ 10am-5pm Mon-Fri year-round, 10am-5pm Sat May-Sep).

ℹ Getting There & Away

The **train station** (Władysława Beliny-Prażmowskiego 2) and **bus station** (Władysława Beliny-Prażmowskiego 8) are next to each other, 2km south of ul Żeromskiego.

JEWISH RADOM

Radom was a significant Jewish settlement, and the Jewish community here numbered around 30,000 just before WWII (about a quarter of the population). Unfortunately, few Jews survived the war and little of that heritage remains. Most Jews lived in the area around the (now very dilapidated) Rynek. Near here, you'll find four stones and a small memorial that mark where the **main synagogue** (cnr uls Bóżniczna & Podwalna) once stood.

About 4km east of the city centre is what remains of the former Jewish **cemetery** (ul Towarowa 5). The Germans destroyed the cemetery and used the grave markers as paving stones, but in the past decade some of the tombstones have been returned. The gate is usually locked and the entire area feels desolate and foreboding.

BUS

Regular buses serve Warsaw (20zł, 1¾ hours, frequent) and Kraków (30zł, 3½ hours, eight daily). Other services include Łódź (29zł, three hours, five daily), Kielce (14zł, one hour, frequent) and Lublin (17zł, two hours, hourly).

TRAIN

Radom lies on a major north–south train line. Trains run north to Warsaw (25zł, two hours, six daily) and south to Kielce (19zł, 1¼ hours, seven daily) and Kraków (52zł, 2¾ hours, four daily).

THE LUBLIN UPLAND

Stretching east of the Vistula and San Rivers up to the Ukrainian border is the Lublin Upland (Wyżyna Lubelska). Lublin, its biggest city, still bears the scars of WWII, but carries itself with dignity and has a thriving Old Town. The area also has Kazimierz Dolny, a quaint town on the banks of the Vistula that attracts weekenders looking to escape the city – and the 21st century. Also worth visiting is the extraordinary town of Zamość and the nearby village of Zwierzyniec, both built on the Renaissance dreams of nobleman Jan Zamoyski.

Lublin

MAŁOPOLSKA LUBLIN

0 200 m
0 0.2 miles

400 m

al Tysiąclecia

Minibus Station
Bus Station

Old Jewish Cemetery (600m);
New Jewish Cemetery (900m);
Jewish Orphans Memorial (3km)

Hotel Ilan (900m)

Zamkowa

Kowalska

Furmańska

Zamkowa

Lubartowska

Wodopojna

Plac
Podwale

Podwale

Plac po
Farze

Złota

Jezuicka

Podwale

Wyszyńskiego

(1.6km)

Grodzka

Plac
Zamkowy

Rynek

Rybna

Grodzka

Ku Farze

Szambelańska

Olejna

Bramowa

Plac
Katedralny

Łokietka

Królewska

Żmigród

Bernardyńska

Dolna Panny Marii

Plac Ofiar
Getta

Świętoduska

Przechodnia

Plac
Kozła

Zielona

Staszica

Plac
Wolności

Kapucyńska

Niecała

Radziwiłłowska

Plac
Litewski

Kościuszki

Peowiaków

Narutowicza

Górna

3 Maja

Kołłątaja

Peowiaków

Hempla

Chmielna

Ogrodowa

Krakowskie Przedmieście

Kartowicza

Okopowa

Spokojna

Ewangelicka

Chopina

Krótka

Lipowa

Wieniawska

Ogród
Saski

Lublin Village Museum (3.8km)

Aleje Racławickie

Grottgera

Cmentarz Rzymsko-Katolicki

Lublin

Lublin

POP 341,500

Lublin is the surprise of southeast Poland. The region's largest city, with a thriving cultural and academic scene, has a small but evocative Old Town and the surrounding historic precincts have a new sheen, giving new lustre to the Old Town's impressive stock of Renaissance and baroque townhouses.

That said, Lublin was ravaged during WWII and the forced industrialisation of the communist period added insult to injury. The city is also an important part of Poland's Jewish past. For centuries it was a leading centre of Jewish scholarship, giving rise to its nickname the 'Jewish Oxford'. That heritage came to a brutal end in WWII, especially at Majdanek, the concentration camp within Lublin's borders. Still, finding traces of the city's Jewish past can be a meaningful and moving part of a visit.

History

Though Lublin feels a little marginalised these days, located in the east of the country, for centuries it played a central role in Polish history. On three separate occasions it was Poland's de facto capital, at least temporarily.

In 1569 it was here in Lublin that the union between the Polish and Lithuanian kingdoms was signed, creating the largest state in Europe at the time. In 1918, at the end of WWI, Lublin was the site of the first government of newly independent Poland. In 1944, at the end of WWII, it was in Lublin that the first provisional communist government installed by the Soviets was housed.

On a more sombre note, in 1941, during WWII, Lublin was chosen by the Germans as the headquarters for Operation Reinhard, their secret plan to exterminate the Jewish population of German-occupied Poland. Two of the most infamous Operation Reinhard extermination camps, Sobibór and Bełżec, lie within a couple of hours' drive from Lublin.

◎ Sights

◎ Old Town

A good way to see Lublin is to start at the castle, walk up through the Old Town and then continue west along ul Krakowskie Przedmieście into Renaissance Lublin.

Lublin Castle   MUSEUM
(Map p176; ☑ 81 532 5001; www.muzeumlubelskie. pl; ul Zamkowa 9; adult/child 30/23zł; ☉ 10am-6pm Tue-Sun May-Sep, 9am-5pm Tue-Sun Oct-Apr) Lublin's royal castle dates to the 12th century, though it's been rebuilt many times since; the oldest surviving part is the impressive Romanesque **round tower** that dominates the courtyard. It was here in 1569 that Poland's union with Lithuania was signed. The castle is home to **Lublin Museum** and the 14th-century Gothic **Chapel of the Holy Trinity**, which contains Poland's finest examples of medieval frescoes; admission gives access to both and also to the tower.

The 14th-century chapel is considered a masterpiece of the Middle Ages, with Russian Byzantine–inspired frescoes painted

MAŁOPOLSKA LUBLIN

in 1418. They were later plastered over, but were rediscovered in 1897 and painstakingly restored over a 100-year period.

The museum's permanent collection features mainly art, folk art and weaponry. During WWII the occupying German army used the castle as a prison, holding as many as 40,000 inmates. The darkest day of the war here came in July 1944, just ahead of the prison's liberation by the Soviet Red Army, when the Germans executed 300 prisoners on the spot.

Kraków Gate   MUSEUM

(Brama Krakowska; Map p176; www.muzeum lubelskie.pl; Plac Łokietka 3; adult/child 5.50/4.50zł; ⊙10am-6pm Tue-Sun Jun-Aug, to 4pm Tue-Sun Sep-May) The only significant remnant of the fortified walls that once surrounded the Old Town is the 14th-century Gothic Kraków Gate, built during the reign of Kazimierz III Wielki following the Mongol attack in 1341. It received its octagonal Renaissance superstructure in the 16th century, and its baroque crown in 1782. These days it's home to the Historical Museum of Lublin and its small collection of documents and photographs of the town's history.

Trinitarian Tower   TOWER

(Map p176; ☑81 444 7450; ul Królewska 10, Plac Katedralny; adult/child 7/5zł; ⊙10am-5pm Tue-Sun) For an expansive view of the Old Town, climb to the top of Trinitarian Tower (1819), which houses the underrated Archdiocesan Museum. The chaotic layout of artworks in hidden nooks and crannies, combined with the lack of English explanations, means that you can discover ancient artefacts in the haphazard manner of Indiana Jones. Climb the 207 steps for views over old Lublin.

Dominican Priory   CHURCH

(Kościół Dominikanów; Map p176; ☑81 532 8990; www.lublin.dominikanie.pl; ul Złota 9; ⊙9am-4pm) FREE Originally a Gothic complex founded by King Kazimierz III Wielki in 1342, the Dominican Priory was rebuilt in Renaissance style after it was ravaged by fire in 1575. Two historic highlights inside the church are the Chapel of the Firlej Family (1615), containing family members' tombstones, and the Tyszkiewicz Chapel (1645–59), with impressive Renaissance stucco work. Outside of the south end of the complex is a small and pretty park with great views over the city.

For an insight into 18th-century Lublin, note the large historical painting *The Fire of Lublin*, which depicts a devastating fire of

1719 that destroyed much of the city. It's in the Szaniawski family chapel to your right as you enter the church.

Cathedral of
St John the Baptist   CHURCH

(Map p176; ☑69 532 2780; www.archikatedra. kuria.lublin.pl; Plac Katedralny; church free, treasury & crypt adult/child 4/3zł; ⊙treasury & crypt 10am-4pm Tue-Sat) This former Jesuit church dates from the 16th century and is the largest in Lublin; you can visit any time services are not taking place. The impressive interior is adorned with baroque trompe l'oeil frescoes by Moravian artist Józef Meyer. The **treasury** *(skarbiec)* houses precious gold and silverware, a 14th-century bronze baptismal font, and more Meyer frescoes. The vaulted roof of the so-called **acoustic vestry** *(zakrystia akustyczna)* echoes whispers from one corner across to the other.

◉ Outside the Centre

★ Majdanek   HISTORIC SITE

(Państwowe Muzeum na Majdanku; ☑81 710 2833; www.majdanek.eu; Droga Męczenników Majdanka 67; parking 5zł; ⊙9am-6pm Apr-Oct, to 4pm Nov-Mar, museum closed Mon; P) FREE Majdanek concentration camp, where tens of thousands of people, mainly Jews, were murdered by the Germans during WWII, lies on the outskirts of Lublin – guard towers and barbed-wire fences interrupting the suburban sprawl are a jarring juxtaposition. Allow half a day for the 5km walk around the 270-hectare camp; if pushed for time, visit the historical exhibition in barracks 62 and the photographic display in barracks 45. Majdanek is 4km southeast of the Kraków Gate: take bus 23.

Majdanek was Heinrich Himmler's idea. In 1941 he gave orders for a work camp to be built in Lublin that would use 25,000 to 50,000 people as slave labour for the German war effort. It was a prison for people not just from Poland but from almost 30 countries, plus Soviet prisoners of war. Of the 150,000 people who were imprisoned in Majdanek, 80,000 died, including 60,000 Jews. Many succumbed to disease, starvation and the forced labour. In the summer of 1942, the gas chambers were built as part of Operation Reinhard, the plan to exterminate Polish Jews. Majdanek then functioned more as a death camp as opposed to a labour camp. The surviving crematorium was built in 1943 to handle the ever-increasing number of bodies.

JEWISH LUBLIN

For centuries Lublin served as a centre of European Jewish culture, earning the nickname the 'Jerusalem' of the Polish kingdom. The first mention of Jews living here dates from the 14th century; around the same period they were granted rights by the king to settle in the area below the castle. Jewish historians look back on the 16th and 17th centuries as the high points for the community. The first census in 1550 shows 840 Jews lived in Lublin; 200 years later Lublin had the third-largest Jewish population in Poland. By the time WWII broke out, around a third of the city's 120,000 residents were Jewish.

For centuries, the city's Jews lived in the area surrounding Lublin Castle. These days, the area is mostly parking lots. It's hard to imagine that before the German occupation this was a densely populated community filled with streets, shops and houses. The **Grodzka Gate** (Brama Grodzka; Map p176; ☑ 81 534 6232; www.teatrnn.pl; ul Grodzka 21; adult/child 12/10zł; ⊙ tours 9.30am, 11am, 12.30pm & 2pm Mon-Fri) that links the Old Town and the castle area was once called the 'Jewish Gate', as it effectively marked the end of 'Christian' Lublin and the start of the Jewish quarter. Try to join a tour of the excellent exhibits on Lublin's Jewish history.

This centuries-old neighbourhood came to an end with the Nazi occupation of the city on 18 September 1939. The Germans initially moved the Jews into a restricted ghetto made up of part of the traditional Jewish quarter and a relatively small piece of territory marked by today's ul Kowalska and ul Lubartowska. The ghetto was liquidated in 1942, with most of the residents sent to their deaths at the extermination camps at Bełżec and Sobibór, and the Majdanek camp within Lublin. Of the approximately 40,000 Jewish Lubliners, only a few hundred survived the Holocaust.

Memories of the Holocaust languished during the communist period, but since 1989, the city has worked at recognising the contributions of the city's Jews. As a visitor, it's easy to visit many important sites.

To experience echoes of the lost Jewish community, take a walk to the area northeast of the bus station to see both the **Old Jewish Cemetery** (Cmentarz żydowski; ul Kalinowszczyzna) and the **New Jewish Cemetery** (ul Walecznych). The old cemetery dates to 1541. Once inside, it is a jumble of broken tombstone and old trees. There are views to the lost Jewish quarter around the castle. The new cemetery was established in 1829. Part was destroyed first by the Nazis and then by road-building projects. What survives today is a melancholy fragment of the past. Stop at the Hotel Ilan (p181) to get keys to both cemeteries. Starting at the bus station, a circular walk that includes the Hotel Ilan, the new cemetery and the old cemetery will cover about 3.4km.

Returning to the centre, the banality of evil is evident at the **former headquarters** (Map p176; ul Spokojna 1) of Operation Reinhard, which was the German name for the extermination of the Jews in occupied Poland. Today the building is a law school and the site is unmarked.

Finally, in the Old Town, the **former Jewish orphanage** (Map p176; ul Grodzka 11) is where on 24 March 1942 the Nazis seized over 100 children and three caregivers. They were taken to a sandlot in Lublin's east and killed. A new **memorial** (www.teatrnn. pl/pamiec/en/the-site-of-execution-of-the-children-from-orphanage; cnr ul Maszynowa & ul Łęczyńska) marks this site. In 1948, the bodies were reburied in the new cemetery where there is an older memorial.

A superb source of information on all things Jewish in Lublin is the group **Grodzka Gate-NN Theatre** (www.teatrnn.pl), which has an enormous amount of information on its website, including a detailed walking tour.

MAŁOPOLSKA LUBLIN

Visiting the camp involves navigating the vast site. The visitor service centre at the entrance is the place to get useful maps of the camp and view exhibitions. Two huge monuments date to 1969 and mark the camp entrance and the place where the ashes of the victims are buried. The historical exhibition in the reconstructed barracks also includes a very good exhibit about Lublin in WWII in barracks 44. Note that the gas chambers are closed for long-term stabilisation of the foundations.

FORGOTTEN HOLOCAUST: BEŁŻEC & SOBIBOR

When it comes to the Holocaust, much of the world's attention has gone to the atrocities of the Auschwitz–Birkenau extermination camp. In the far east of Poland are two camps – Sobibór and Bełżec – that are less well known, but that are important places to visit to understand the breadth of the Germans' extermination policy.

The **Bełżec memorial** (☎ 84 665 2510; www.belzec.eu; off Hwy 17, ul Ofiar Obozu Zagłady 4; parking 5zł; ⊘ memorial 9am-6pm daily Apr-Oct, to 4pm daily Nov-Mar, last entry 1hr before closing, museum 9am-5pm Tue-Sun May-Oct, to 4pm Tue-Sun Nov-Apr) FREE bears witness to the 600,000 Jews killed here in 1942 by the Nazi Germans as part of their 'Operation Reinhard', the German plan to eliminate the Jewish population of occupied Poland. There were only two known survivors from Bełżec. The memorial, moving in its simplicity, covers the surprisingly small site of the original camp. It includes some of the tracks used by the trains that brought people here (the same line can be seen outside the gates today). Visitors walk along a short path that is the same route that the Jews took to the gas chamber. The walls steadily grow taller – behind them are the ashes of the dead – until the sky itself is blotted out. Children under 14 are not permitted into the museum. Plan on spending one to two hours.

The site of the **Sobibór** (☎ arrange visits 82 571 9867; www.sobibor-memorial.eu) extermination camp is much more remote, buried in thick forest several kilometres from its namesake village. From April 1942 until the end of October 1943, more than 170,000 Jews died in the Sobibór gas chambers. This stark horror is omnipresent at the memorial where the disused railway tracks are little changed since 1943 when trains carrying thousands of doomed people arrived daily.

For several decades, the Sobibór memorial was a simple collection of monuments and a tiny museum. It was moving in its simplicity, the paucity of visitors adding to the contemplative atmosphere. The site is now being massively transformed. A new museum is set to open by 2021, with exhibits designed for visitors several generations removed from WWII. In the meantime, much of the memorial is technically closed, but you can arrange visits in advance and there is a public viewing area.

Bełżec lies about 130km south of Lublin and 45km south of Zamość and is reachable in summer by train and bus service from Lublin. Sobibór is as isolated today as it was almost 80 years ago. Although the train station is right across from the memorial, there aren't any trains. Even the village, some 8.5km from the memorial by road, lacks any useful bus service. You'll need your own vehicle here. Driving distances include: Lublin (90km), Chełm (45km) and Zamość (100km).

Lublin Village Museum MUSEUM
(Muzeum Wsi Lubelskiej; ☎ 81 533 8513; www.skansen.lublin.pl; ul Warszawska 96; adult/child 12/6zł; ⊘ 9am-6pm daily May-Sep, to 5pm daily Apr & Oct, to 3pm Tue-Sun Nov-Mar) This well-designed open-air museum, 5km west of the centre on the Warsaw road, covers an undulating terrain of 25 hectares.

Appearing as a traditional village of numerous buildings with fully equipped interiors, there is a fine manor house, a windmill, an Orthodox church and a carved timber gate (1903) designed by Stanisław Witkiewicz. Watch for special exhibits and cultural events. To get there from the centre, take bus 18 from the corner of ul 3 Maja and ul Żołnierzy Niepodległej (3.20zł).

🏃 Activities

One of the city's most popular activities is a stroll underground below the Rynek. If you'd rather walk above ground, check out the city's self-guided walking routes offered in audio-guide format and online from the tourist office.

Underground Route WALKING
(Trasa Podziemna; Map p176; ☎ tour bookings 81 534 6570; www.teatrnn.pl/podziemia; Rynek 1; adult/child 12/10zł; ⊘ 10am-4pm Tue-Fri, noon-5pm Sat & Sun) This 280m trail winds its way through interconnected cellars beneath the Old Town, with historical exhibitions along the way. Entry is by tour from the southwest side of the neoclassical Old Town Hall in the centre of the Rynek at approximately two-hourly intervals.

✿ Festivals & Events

As the largest city in eastern Poland, Lublin has an active cultural calendar, with something big (usually related to music or theatre) nearly every month of the year.

Codes Festival of Traditional
and Avant-Garde Music   MUSIC
(www.codes-festival.com; ⊙May) Dedicated to fusing archaic and new strains of music.

Festival of European Neighbours   THEATRE
(Festiwal Teatrów Europy Środkowej Sąsiedzi; www.festiwal-sasiedzi.pl; ⊙Jun) Popular theatre fest involving troupes from neighbouring countries. Held at venues across the city.

★ Magicians Carnival   PERFORMING ARTS
(Sztukmistrzów Carnaval; ☑81 533 0818; www.en.sztukmistrze.eu; ⊙Jul) More than 100 international magicians descend on Lublin for a festival of magic – but it's not all about rabbits getting pulled from hats, there are also acrobats, jugglers, mimes and other carnival performers. The action takes place on the streets and at venues around the city.

🛏 Sleeping

Lublin has a range of accommodation, from hostels and pensions to hotels. All are good value. There are many rooms and apartments for rent on the upper floors of buildings in the Old Town, many owned by the businesses below.

Folk Hostel   HOSTEL €
(Map p176; ☑88 722 3887; www.folkhostel.pl; ul Krakowskie Przedmieście 23; dm/s/d from 45/90/100zł; P🛜) This charming hostel ticks all the boxes, with friendly English-speaking staff, cheerfully decorated rooms and a fine central location. Although it overlooks the main street from the 2nd floor, the entrance is around the back, via a gate on Zielona. Limited on-site parking. Rooms sleep one to six people.

★ Rezydencja Waksman   HOTEL €€
(Map p176; ☑81 532 5454; www.waksman.pl; ul Grodzka 19; s/d from 180/200zł, apt from 250zł; P@🛜) Hotel Waksman deserves a blue ribbon for many reasons, not least of which is its ideal Old Town location. Each standard room has individual character, derived largely from the collection of antique furniture. The two apartments on the top floor are fine value: they offer ample space for lounging or working, and views over the Old Town and castle.

Vanilla Hotel   HOTEL €€
(Map p176; ☑81 536 6720; www.vanilla-hotel.pl; ul Krakowskie Przedmieście 12; s/d from 300/330zł; P✳@🛜) This sleekly gorgeous hotel on the main pedestrian plaza is anything but plain vanilla. The rooms are filled with inspired, even bold, styling: vibrant colours, big headboards, and retro lamps and furniture. There's lots of attention to detail here, which continues in the chic restaurant and coffee bar.

Hotel Ilan   HOTEL €€
(☑81 745 0347; www.hotelilan.pl; ul Lubartowska 85; s/d from 180/200zł; P✳🛜) In a grand prewar building that once housed a large rabbinical school, the Hotel Ilan is a centre for Jewish culture in Lublin. It even has an orthodox synagogue. The 38 rooms are very comfortable and the service is excellent. It's a short walk north of the centre. The hotel is also the official keeper of the keys for the new and old Jewish cemeteries.

IBB Grand Hotel   HOTEL €€
(Map p176; ☑81 446 6100; www.lublinianka.com; ul Krakowskie Przedmieście 56; s/d from 240/270zł; P✳@🛜🏊) What was the Commercial Chamber of Lublin 100 years ago is now a grand place to stay in Lublin. The classic foyer of this four-star hotel is relatively restrained and the same stylish minimalism translates to the calming pastel rooms. Some marble bathrooms include bathtubs. Enjoy the Turkish bath and sauna.

🍴 Eating

Lublin has a wide range of good places to eat in the centre.

Bosko   ICE CREAM €
(Map p176; ☑57 555 9771; www.facebook.com/LodyBosko; Krakowskie Przedmieście 4; treats from 5zł; ⊙10am-8.30pm) No need to check street numbers, just look for the permanent queue in front of this ice-cream shop that trumpets the provenance of its treats. Everything is made in-house and the flavours change with the seasons.

★ Mandragora   JEWISH €€
(Map p176; ☑81 536 2020; www.mandragora.lublin.pl; Rynek 9; mains 25-55zł; ⊙8.30am-10pm Sun-Thu, to midnight Fri & Sat; 🛜) There's good kitsch and there's bad kitsch, and at Mandragora, it's all good. Sure, 'Hava Nagila' is playing amid the lace tablecloths, knick-knacks and photos of old Lublin, but in the romantic Rynek setting it works wonderfully. The food is heartily Jewish, from roast duck with

tzimmes (stewed carrots and dried fruit) to salt beef. Service is engagingly delightful.

The restaurant also rents rooms at a renovated tenement house nearby. Stylishly white singles and doubles cost 200zł and 300zł.

Kardamon INTERNATIONAL €€€
(Map p176; ☑81 448 0257; www.kardamon.eu; ul Krakowskie Przedmieście 41; mains 38-69zł; ⊗noon-11pm Mon-Sat, to 10pm Sun; ☝) This fine restaurant is in a lush cellar on the main street. The menu is a mix of international staples along with Polish favourites such as *żurek* (sour rye soup), roast duck served with beetroot and a fine bevy of regional specialities like goose fillet. There's great attention to detail in the kitchen; save room for dessert.

🍷 Drinking & Entertainment

Pubs and bars are concentrated around the Rynek, along ul Krakowskie Przedmieście and in the nearby side streets. Look out for craft beers produced by the local Perla brewery.

★**Perłowa Pijalnia Piwa** CRAFT BEER
(Map p176; ☑81 710 1205; www.perla.pl/pijalnia-piwa; ul Bernardyńska 15a; ⊗2pm-midnight) The iconic Perla brewery runs this excellent brewpub. Count on at least a dozen of its beers on tap, including unfiltered, honey and several lagers. The porter is aged for nine months. The bar is stylish and there is a short menu of food that boasts its 'slow food' credentials, such as sausages made with organic meats, superb burgers, snacks and more.

U Szewca IRISH PUB
(Pub; Map p176; ☑81 532 8284; www.uszewca.pl; ul Grodzka 18; mains 18-35zł; ⊗9.30am-1am; ☝) Fun, faux-Irish pub that's right on the Rynek and popular with local Lubliners and visitors alike. Most people come for the good beer list, but there's also classic pub food (mains 18zł to 35zł) like pizzas, salads, snacks and the usual burgers. The name means 'shoemaker' and there's a historic display of an old shop inside.

Czarna Owca PUB
(Map p176; ☑81 532 4130; www.czarnaowcagastropub.pl; ul Narutowicza 9; ⊗1-11pm Sun-Thu, to 2am Fri & Sat) The 'Black Sheep' is a legendary Lublin watering hole (literally: it's in a basement), going strong into the small hours at weekends. In addition to Żywiec and Paulaner on draught and a selection of bottled Polish craft beers, it has a menu of gourmet burgers, pub grub and snacks (chicken nuggets!).

Centre for the Meeting of Cultures PERFORMING ARTS
(Centrum Spotkania Kultur, CSK; Map p176; ☑81 441 5670; www.spotkaniakultur.com; Plac Teatralny 1) A performing arts venue five decades in the making, the CSK has its roots in one of those ginormous communist-era projects that was meant to impress with its size. It finally opened after years of miscues in 2012 as a state-of-the-art arts venue. Theatre, opera and movies can be enjoyed here. Take in the vista from the observation deck.

Filharmonia Lubelska CLASSICAL MUSIC
(Filharmonia im H Wieniawskiego w Lublinie; Map p176; ☑81 531 5112; www.filharmonialubelska.pl; ul M Curie-Skłodowskiej 5; ⊗box office 11am-6pm Mon-Fri) This large auditorium stages classical and contemporary music concerts. It's located about 2km southwest of the Old Town. Buy tickets at the venue box office during the day or two hours before the show starts on the day of the performance. It's on the backside of the monumental Centre for the Meeting of Cultures.

Teatr Im H Ch Andersena PUPPET THEATRE
(Map p176; ☑81 532 3225; www.teatrandersena.pl; Plac Teatralny 1, Centre for the Meeting of Cultures; tickets from 30zł; ⊗box office 8am-noon Tue-Fri & 1hr before performances) Performances are in Polish, but the puppets of Hans Christian Andersen can be enjoyed in any language. Check the website for show times.

ℹ Information

Tourist Information Centre (LOITiK; Map p176; ☑81 532 4412; www.lublintravel.pl; ul Jezuicka 1/3; ⊗9am-7pm daily Apr-Oct, 9am-5pm Mon-Fri, 10am-5pm Sat & Sun Nov-Mar; ☝) Extremely helpful English-speaking staff. There are souvenirs for sale and lots of brochures, including handy maps. There's also a computer for internet access and lockers (per hour 2zł). Offers free audio guides.

ℹ Getting There & Away

BUS

FlixBus (www.flixbus.com) services connect the **bus station** (Map p176; ul Hutnicza 1) with major cities throughout Poland, including:
Kraków from 45zł, 5½ hours, four daily
Warsaw from 20zł, three hours, several daily.

Private minibuses run from the **minibus station** (Map p176; ul Nadstawna) adjoining the bus terminal to various destinations, including Zamość (15zł, 90 minutes, hourly) and Kazimierz Dolny (12zł, 1½ hours, roughly every hour).

TRAIN

The **train station** (plac Dworcowy) is 2km south of the Old Town. There are direct trains to Warsaw (from 31zł, three to 3½ hours, eight daily) and Zamość (16zł, 2¼ hours, three daily).

Kazimierz Dolny

POP 2600

For more than a century, the ancient river port of Kazimierz Dolny has been an artist colony and a haven for free thinkers. In more recent years, it's evolved into a hugely popular weekend getaway for Warsaw and Lublin residents.

Once you arrive, you'll see why. Kazimierz Dolny is picturesquely perched along the banks of the Vistula. Its main square, the Rynek, lined with historic buildings, is charming. The little lanes that radiate from the square are filled with quaint galleries, shops, and, naturally, myriad places to grab a beer or an ice cream cone.

One caveat: because of its popularity, avoid weekends April to October when traffic can stretch back kilometres and Kazimierz Dolny–bound buses are filled to bursting. This is doubly true on holiday weekends. Instead, aim for a weekday arrival. The serenity you'll enjoy will give you an idea why the town inspired artists like Władysław Słewiński.

History

Earliest accounts of settlement in the region refer to a wooden cloister along the Vistula in 1181. The town was formally founded in the 14th century by King Kazimierz III Wielki, who built a castle and gave the town its municipal charter. The town was called Dolny (lower), to distinguish it from the town of Kazimierz, upriver, which is today part of Kraków.

Kazimierz Dolny became a thriving trade centre, with grain, salt, wood and oxen being shipped to Gdańsk and further on for export. The 16th and early 17th centuries were particularly prosperous, and a number of splendid mansions and granaries were buily. By 1630, Kazimierz Dolny's population had risen above 2500 (about where it is now).

The high times came to an end with the Swedish wars of the mid-17th century, various epidemics, and the slow displacement of the Vistula bed toward the west, which allowed Puławy to overshadow it in the 19th century as the trade and cultural centre of the region.

At the end of the 19th century, attempts were made to revive Kazimierz Dolny as a tourist centre, but the two world wars caused serious damage to the town. WWII was particularly tragic. Before the war, Jews comprised around 50% of the population; by the end of 1942, the Germans had systematically rounded up and deported the entire community to the death camp at Bełżec.

Since the end of WWII, preservation efforts have gone a long way toward restoring the historical character of Kazimierz Dolny.

⊙ Sights

Most of the main sights, galleries and attractions are on or near the town's pretty Rynek. At the centre of the square is a wooden well, which still functions. Fine buildings line the square on all sides, a testament to the town's former prosperity.

From an architectural standpoint, the best Rynek buildings are probably the massively restored connecting **Houses of the Przybyła Brothers** (Kamienice Przybyłów; Map p184; Rynek 12), built in 1615 by brothers Mikołaj and Krzysztof, with rich Renaissance mannerist facades. Decorations depict the brothers' patron saints, St Nicholas (guardian of traders) and St Christopher (guardian of travellers). Also on the Rynek are the baroque-style **Gdańsk House** (Kamienica Gdańska; Map p184; Rynek 16) from 1795 and several characteristic arcaded houses with wooden-tiled roofs from the 18th and 19th centuries. Just south of the Rynek, the Mały Rynek was the heart of Jewish Kazimierz Dolny. Today there are still echoes of this lost community here.

In warm weather, the promenade along the Vistula River is justifiably popular. Some cafes set up tables with watery views along the banks. These can be a great relief if the paucity of local parking has caused you to abandon your car in a far off spot.

House of the Celej Family   MUSEUM
(Kamienica Celejowska; Map p184; ☑ 81 881 0288; www.mnkd.pl; ul Senatorska 11/13; adult/child 15/10zł; ⊙ 10am-5pm Apr-Oct, to 4pm Nov-Mar) This 1635 townhouse built for the Celej family is a branch of the Vistula River Museum. The focus is on art and several rooms on the upper floor are dedicated to the considerable output of artists who have called Kazimierz Dolny home. Some of the works are fantastic, some merely interesting, but the collection amply demonstrates the town's role in Poland's artistic history. The exterior is under massive renovation through 2020.

Kazimierz Dolny

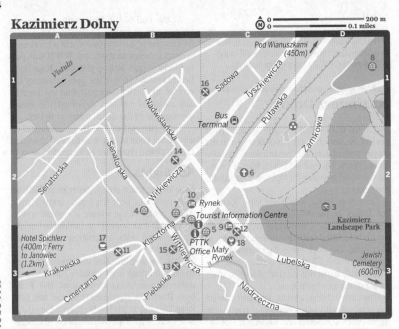

Kazimierz Dolny

Jewish Cemetery   CEMETERY
(Cmentarz Żydowski; ul Czerniawy; ⊙ 24hr) Over the centuries, Kazimierz Dolny had a significant Jewish population, and in the decades leading up to WWII as much as half the population was Jewish. While few traces of this community can be seen today, the Jewish Cemetery, outside of the centre, is moving and highly recommended. At the front of the cemetery is a monument to the community, assembled in 1984 from several hundred tombstone fragments. It's located 1.3km from the Rynek on the road to Opole Lubelskie.

Vistula River Museum   MUSEUM
(Muzeum Nadwiślańskie; Map p184; ☏ 81 881 0288; www.mnkd.pl; Rynek 19; adult/child 15/10zł; ⊙ 10am-5pm Apr-Oct, to 4pm Nov-Mar) The main branch of the museum has a great model showing how Kazimierz Dolny looked in 1910. There's a good bookstore with local history and art books. Temporary exhibitions are held here and there is an area devoted to the art of local goldsmiths through the ages.

Natural History Museum   MUSEUM
(Muzeum Przyrodnicze; ☏ 81 881 0326; www.mnkd.pl; ul Puławska 54; adult/child 15/10zł; ⊛) Another branch of the Vistula River Museum, the natural history museum is housed near the river in a massive 1591 granary. Due to reopen in 2019 after renovation, the displays look at local flora and fauna, including birds, animals, fish and insects.

THE CASTLE AT JANOWIEC

The village of Janowiec (yah-*no*-vyets) and its castle make for a delightful day trip from Kazimierz Dolny. You can get there by bus, but a much more scenic journey involves taking a ferry and combining that with either a bike ride or a short hike.

The castle was built in the first half of the 16th century by Italian architect Santi Gucci Fiorentino at the request of Mikołaj Firlej. Through many years and owners (including the Tarto, Lubomirski and Ostawski families), the castle grew to more than 100 rooms and became one of the most splendid in Poland. The Swedes began the process of ruination and two world wars completed the castle's demise.

The castle is still in ruins, but intense renovations have restored some rooms and revived external painted decorations. Upon entering the castle, note the red-and-white striped walls, the decor-of-the-day back in the 16th century.

The castle houses the **Janowiec Museum** (Oddział Zamek W Janowcu; ☑ 81 881 0288; www.mnkd.pl; ul Lubelska 20; adult/child 12/8zł; ⊗ castle & museum 10am-5pm daily Apr-Oct, 9am-3pm Thu-Tue Nov-Mar, castle only 5-8pm mid-Apr–mid-Sep), a branch of Kazimierz Dolny's Vistula River Museum. Inside the grounds, visitors can climb a few levels to viewing platforms offering a wide perspective of the castle and the surrounding countryside. Various rooms show exhibitions and contemporary art. The bluffs in the park beside the castle have sweeping views of the wide Vistula valley. Nearby is a **manor house** from the 1760s (another part of the museum), which offers insights into how Polish nobility lived.

Save time for cute little Janowiec village at the foot of the castle. Don't miss the 14th-century Gothic **parish church** (Rynek 6), extensively rebuilt in Renaissance style in the 1530s. Inside is the tomb of the Firlej family, carved in the workshop of Santi Gucci from 1586 to 1587.

Catch the car and passenger ferry (p188) on the Kazimierz Dolny side. After the five-minute crossing of the Vistula, there's a tranquil and flat 2km walk to Janowiec village, where you can climb the hill to the castle. Return the same way, following the signs to 'Prom'.

Parish Church   CHURCH

(Kościół Farny p w św Jana Chrzciciela i św Bartłomieja Apostoła; Map p184; ☑ 81 881 0870; www.kazimierz-fara.pl; ul Zamkowa 6; ⊗ 8am-6pm) The Gothic parish church presiding over the Rynek was built in the mid-14th century, and remodelled when Renaissance styles swept Poland in the 16th century.

The ornate wooden organ from 1620 sounds as lavish as it looks; organ recitals are often held here. Note the Renaissance choir stalls in the chancel and the stucco decoration of the nave's vault, a classic example of Lublin-Renaissance style and typical of the region. Be sure to look up at the stag-antler chandelier.

Castle   RUINS

(Zamek; Map p184; ul Zamkowa; 5zł; ⊗ 10am-6pm Apr-Oct, to 4pm Nov-Mar) Above the parish church along ul Zamkowa is what's left of Kazimierz Dolny's castle. Originally built in 1341 as a stronghold against the Tatar incursion, the castle was extended in the 16th century and embellished further during the Renaissance. The castle fell into ruin after its partial destruction by the Swedes; the remaining fragments offer a pleasant view over the town and the Vistula.

Hill of Three Crosses   VIEWPOINT

(Góra Trzech Krzyży; Map p184; ul Zamkowa) Uphill from the parish church, a path to the right leads to the Hill of Three Crosses, where the namesake crosses stand to commemorate victims of the plagues that swept through the town in the 18th century. There's some historical debate about the relationship between the crosses and the epidemics, as some historians believe the site was created to ward off the plague and cholera epidemics. Whatever the origin of the name, the hill affords sensational views.

Watchtower   HISTORIC BUILDING

(Map p184; ul Zamkowa; 5zł; ⊗ 10am-6pm Apr-Oct, to 4pm Nov-Mar) The watchtower, 100m uphill from the castle, dates from the end of the 13th century and is one of the oldest defensive structures of its kind in the country. The building's primary purpose was as a watchtower to protect an important river crossing in this area. These days, you can climb to the top to take in sweeping views of the river and valley.

Activities

In 1979, the area around Kazimierz was decreed the **Kazimierz Landscape Park** (Kazimierski Park Krajobrazowy). Many walking trails have been traced in its 150 sq km, winding through the distinct gorges of the region.

Hiking & Cycling

There are three easy short trails known as *szlaki spacerowe* (walking routes) signposted in yellow, green and red, and three significantly longer treks called *szlaki turystyczne* (tourist routes) marked in blue, green and red. Almost all these routes originate in the Rynek. The tourist information centre sells maps of the park and its trails.

Many of these same trails are also suited to cycling. Most area hiking maps also show bike trails. Bicycles can be hired at most places to stay, usually for around 10zł per hour.

Festivals & Events

Festival of Folk Bands & Singers
MUSIC

(Festiwal Kapel i Śpiewaków Ludowych; www.kazimierzdolny.pl) This highly acclaimed folk festival takes place in the last week of June. For more than three decades, performers from the region have gathered at Mały Rynek in traditional garb to perform folk music from eras (and tastes) gone by.

Two Riversides Festival
FILM

(Festiwal Dwa Brzegi; www.dwabrzegi.pl) Lasts around a week in early August and consists of musical concerts, art exhibitions, and indoor and outdoor screenings of foreign and national films. Events take place on both sides of the Vistula, in Kazimierz Dolny and Janowiec.

Sleeping

There are options aplenty in Kazimierz, but advanced bookings are essential on weekends from spring to fall. Rooms in private houses (50zł to 90zł) are easily found, as are holiday apartments, some of which are run like small hotels. If not booking online, look for *'pokoje'* (rooms) or *'noclegi'* (accommodation) signs. Two streets with many rooms are ul Krakowska and ul Sadowa.

Pod Wianuszkami
HOSTEL €

(☑81 881 0327; www.schroniskowianuszki.kazimierz-dolny.pl; ul Puławska 80; dm/s/d from 30/80/100zł; P) Another one of Kazimierz Dolny's old 17th-century limestone granaries has found a new life, this time as a hostel. The 20 rooms come in a variety of sizes and bed arrangements, all have private bathrooms. It's 1.5km northeast of town. Bikes are available for rent.

Dom Architekta
HOTEL €€

(Map p184; ☑81 883 5544; www.domarchitektasarp.pl; Rynek 20; s/d from 150/220zł; P🖥) This refurbished 17th-century townhouse occupies prime real estate on the Rynek, but despite the history and location – and the beautifully tiled and arcaded lobby, the hardwood floors, and the mock Renaissance garden out back – it remains relaxed and unstuffy. The rooms are furnished with an idiosyncratic collection of antiques that exude atmosphere.

Dawna Synagoga Beitenu
GUESTHOUSE €€

(Map p184; ☑692 578 677; www.beitenu.pl; ul Lubelska 4; r 110-200zł; 🖥) Kazimierz Dolny's former synagogue has a past as tortuous as the community it served. Parts trace back to the 16th century. After the destruction of WWII, it was reconstructed as a cinema. Now under the stewardship of a Jewish foundation, part has been transformed into a comfortable guesthouse in the heart of town. The rooms are stylish, with historical art.

Rezydencja Eger
BOUTIQUE HOTEL €€

(☑601 500 855; www.rezydencjaeger.pl; ul Czerniawy 53b; r 150-300zł) This elegant pension/boutique hotel is situated 2.5km from the centre on the road to Opole Lubelskie and offers sleek, stylish rooms in a palette of greys. Many rooms have balconies. The in-house restaurant serves excellent Polish-Hungarian food. Bathrooms are tricked out in marble. In summer there is often a two- or three-night minimum stay.

Hotel Spichlerz
HOTEL €€

(☑81 881 0036; www.spichlerzkazimierzdolny.pl; ul Krakowska 59/61; s/d from 180/200zł; P🖥) The hotel occupies a typically large, converted granary from 1636. The grounds in this rustic setting are lush. It's 1km west of the Rynek following ul Krakowska. The rooms are simple, but most come here to enjoy the setting, close to the river and ferry to Janowiec.

✖ Eating & Drinking

Bar Galeria
POLISH €

(Map p184; ul Plebanka 2; mains 15zł; ⊙11am-7pm) This little hole-in-the-wall promises *'pierogi domowe'* (homemade dumplings) and that's exactly what you get. They come seven pieces to an order in five varieties, including the usual meat and cabbage, all served by the same woman who cooked them. Tables are few, a couple are outside.

★ Bajgiel
JEWISH €€

(Map p184; ☑ 601 979 570; ul Lubelska 4a; mains 20-45zł; ⊙10am-9pm) One of the town's best restaurants recalls the Jewish community that was centred on the nearby Mały Rynek. Management is proud of its top-notch regional ingredients. Even a mundane beet salad is superlative. Extra touches abound, like mint and lemons in the carafes of water. The furnishings are an eclectic array of mismatched antiques.

Akuku
EASTERN EUROPEAN €€

(Map p184; ☑ 534 233 303; www.facebook.com/Akukukazimierzdolny; Krakowska 3; mains 25-45zł; ⊙noon-10pm; ☑) Artfully presented food is Akuku's hallmark. The name may mean 'peek-a-boo' but the delicious fare produced by the kitchen is right in plain sight. The menu changes regularly with the seasons but expect the flavours of eastern Europe in interesting creations. Less common fare like truffles and wild boar add interest. There's a big outside space with a rustic vibe.

Knajpa U Fryzjera
JEWISH €€

(Map p184; ☑81 888 5513; www.restauracja-ufryzjera.pl; ul Witkiewicza 2; mains 18-45zł; ⊙noon-9pm Mon-Fri, 9.30am-9pm Sat & Sun) Knajpa u Fryzjera is a kitschy restaurant that serves heaping plates of traditional Jewish–Central European mains – veal tongue, goose, beef brisket, stuffed peppers – in a welcoming, tourist-friendly environment. Weekend breakfast is served; there are outside tables aplenty.

Restauracja Kwadrans
POLISH €€

(Map p184; ☑81 882 1111; www.kwadrans.kazimierzdolny.pl; ul Sadowa 7a; mains 20-40zł; ⊙11am-10pm) Typical Polish fare served in an elegant space, with high ceilings, shiny parquet flooring, and antique clocks on the walls. Dine on the terrace in fine weather.

★ Przystanek Dobra
PUB

(Map p184; ☑502 722 432; www.facebook.com/korzeniowadobra; ul Lubelska 6; ⊙4-11pm Mon-Fri, from noon Sat & Sun Apr-Oct, shorter hours Nov-Mar) A fabulous, affable old-style bar on the Mały Rynek. The wood walls and floors are decades old but the vibe is fresh. There's good craft brews on tap and fine coffee. Enjoy excellent beet soup, goulash, salads and Jewish classics for weekend lunch and dinner. Gaze upon the weekend market from the large terrace furnished with charmingly mismatched furniture.

MAŁOPOLSKA KAZIMIERZ DOLNY

COCK-A-DOODLE-DOUGH

Spend any time in Kazimierz Dolny and you will soon wonder why its townspeople have such a proclivity for rooster-shaped bread. After seeing enough signs for *koguty* (roosters), you'll find yourself trying some. Then you'll discover that bread tastes like bread no matter how it's shaped, and promptly return to your initial question: Why?

Though its taste may be as bland, the rooster has an interesting history in Kazimierz. Many years ago, a rooster is believed to have averted certain disaster by warning the townsfolk of an approaching devil. This, combined with local bread-weaving traditions, resulted in the rooster's heroic portrayal in dough.

After a long golden era, when rooster-shaped bread was baked all over town, tensions suddenly surfaced. In 1996 **Piekarnia Sarzyński** (Map p184; ☑668 193 970; www.piekarnia.sarzynski.com.pl; ul Nadrzeczna 6; snacks from 3zł, restaurant mains 25-50zł; ⊙bakery 6am-7pm daily, restaurant noon-9pm Fri-Sun) bakery, convinced that its many years promoting the product and winning awards for its rooster renditions entitled it to exclusive rights, registered the rooster as a company trademark. The other bakers in town were outraged and demanded that the courts reinstate the rooster's status as the cultural (culinary?) property of the town.

Eight years later, the court released the rooster back into the public domain. But patent or not, the Sarzyński's version is tops.

Galeria Herbaciarnia U Dziwisza

TEAHOUSE

(Map p184; ☑ 502 628 220; www.herbaciarnia udziwisza.pl; ul Krakowska 6; teas from 6zł; ⊙ 11am-10pm; 🛜) A civilised taste of an era when tea was a pastime; it boasts more than 100 varieties of tea leaf and an appealing range of calorie-rich accompaniments. On sunny days enjoy a drink on the patio.

ℹ Information

PTTK Office (Map p184; ☑ 81 881 0046; Rynek 27; ⊙ 8am-5.30pm Mon-Fri, 10am-5.30pm Sat May-Sep, 8am-3.30pm Mon-Fri, 10am-2.30pm Sat Oct-Apr) The PTTK office is generally not much use, but it may be able to help find accommodation in private rooms (50zł to 90zł); it also sells hiking and cycling maps.

Tourist Information Centre (Map p184; ☑ 81 881 0709; www.kazimierz-dolny.pl; Rynek 15; ⊙ 9am-6pm Mon-Sat, to 5pm Sun Apr-Oct, 10am-5pm Tue-Sun Nov-Apr) The city's tiny tourist information centre is conveniently located on the main square, but aside from a free city map it has relatively little information in English. There are regional hiking and cycling maps for sale.

ℹ Getting There & Away

Kazimierz can be easily visited as a stop on a Lublin to Warsaw route, or as a day trip from Lublin. There's no train service in Kazimierz Dolny, although you can connect to trains to Warsaw by taking one of the frequent buses to Puławy.

Parking comes at a premium in both space and cost. Small private lots are scattered about, expect to pay 5/15zł per hour/day. On weekends many fill up.

BOAT

In summer, tour boats cruise the river (some in the style of Viking ships – remember the Swedish wars in the 1600s), stopping at Janowiec on the opposite side of the Vistula – check at the dock at the end of ul Nadwiślańska.

There's also a **car and passenger ferry** (PROM Linowy; ☑ 81 881 5815; www.prom-janowiec.pl; ul Krakowska; adult/child/car 6/4/9zł; ⊙ 8am-8pm Mon-Fri, to 9pm Sat & Sun Apr-Sep), which takes five minutes to sail over to the Janowiec landing. It departs from a small landing at the very end of ul Krakowska, 1km west of the Rynek. This saves a very long drive via Puławy.

BUS

The town's compact **bus terminal** (PKS; Map p184; ul Tyszkiewicza 10) is 100m north of the Rynek. Public bus 12 runs to Puławy (3zł, 45 minutes, every 30 to 60 minutes).

There are a dozen minibuses per day to Lublin (12zł, 1½ hours, roughly every hour).

HaloBus (☑ 602 664 419; www.halobus.com.pl; ul Tyszkiewicza 10) runs frequent daily fast buses to Warsaw (27zł, 2¾ hours).

Zamość

POP 65,200

The town of Zamość (*zah*-moshch) is unique in Poland as an almost perfectly preserved example of 16th-century Renaissance town planning. Zamość was made a Unesco World Heritage site in 1992, and an inflow of development funds since has rejuvenated the town's social media–perfect main square and the impressive fortifications that surround the Old Town.

The town owes its origins to a wealthy Polish nobleman, Jan Zamoyski (1542–1605), who came up with the idea to put a town here in the first place, and to the Paduan architect he hired to realise his dream, Bernando Morando. Zamość wears its Renaissance roots on its sleeve, embracing not one, but two grandiose nicknames: the 'Pearl of the Renaissance' and the 'Padua of the North'. Either way, Zamość is an under-appreciated Polish treasure and worth a trip.

History

Zamość began as something of a Renaissance-era housing estate. When Zamoyski, the country's chancellor and commander-in-chief at the time, decided to build his 'perfect' city, he looked to Italy rather than neighbouring Russia for artistic inspiration. Morando was hired to build Zamoyski's dream, and in doing so created a model city showcasing leading Italian theories of urban design. The project began in 1580, and within 11 years, some 217 houses had been built, with public buildings following soon afterwards.

By the end of the 16th century, the town's beauty – and its location on the crossroads of the Lublin–Lviv and Kraków–Kyiv trading routes – attracted international settlers, including Armenians, Jews, Hungarians, Greeks, Germans, Scots and Italians. Many of the original Jewish settlers here were descendants of Sephardic Jews, fleeing persecution in Spain at the end of the 15th century.

The fortifications, which are now partially restored, were built to protect the city and its inhabitants. They were tested many times but never fell to the enemy. The Cossack raid of 1648 proved little match for the strength of Zamość. Its impregnability was confirmed again in 1656, when Zamość, along with Częstochowa and Gdańsk, boldly withstood the Swedish siege.

Zamość was a key target of Hitler's plan for eastward expansion; German occupiers intended that some 60,000 ethnic Germans would be resettled here before the end of 1943 (former German president Horst Köhler was born near Zamość). Due to fierce resistance by the Polish Underground, the determination of the people of Zamość, and eventually the arrival of the Red Army, the number of Germans to relocate to the town barely reached 10,000. In the interim, however, the Jewish population was brutally expelled from the town and the surrounding areas.

⊙ Sights

⊙ Rynek Wielki & Around

The **Rynek Wielki** (Great Market Sq) is the heart of Zamość's attractive Old Town. This impressive Italianate Renaissance square (exactly 100m by 100m) is dominated by the lofty, mauve town hall and surrounded by colourful arcaded burghers' houses, many adorned with elegant designs (arcades were made compulsory by Jan Zamoyski).

Originally, all of the houses in the square were topped with decorative parapets, but these were removed in the 1820s; only some have been restored.

Each side of the Rynek (bar the northern side, which is dominated by the lofty mauve town hall) has eight houses bisected by two main axes of town; one runs west–east from the palace to the bastion, and the other joins the three market squares north to south.

Town Hall   HISTORIC BUILDING
(Map p190; Rynek Wielki) The town hall was built between 1639 and 1651, and features were added and extended over the years:

its curving stairway came in 1768. Zamoyski didn't want the town hall to overshadow the palace or interrupt the view, and so unusually placed it on the northern side of the square rather than in the centre. In summer, a bugler plays the town's traditional song at noon from the 52m-high clock tower.

Museum of Zamość   MUSEUM
(Muzeum Zamojskie; Map p190; ☑84 638 6494; www.muzeum-zamojskie.pl; ul Ormiańska 30; adult/child 12/6zł; ⊙9am-4pm Tue-Sun, to 5pm May-Sep) Two of the row of iconic and colourful Armenian houses on the northeast side of the Rynek shelter the Zamość museum, with intriguing displays such as a scale model of the 16th-century town and a letter to Jan Zamoyski from his architect, Bernardo Morando, with a hand-drawn plan of the square and names of the original occupants of each building. Also on display are archaeological finds, such as Gothic treasures from cemeteries in the Hrubieszów Valley.

★ Arsenal Museum   MUSEUM
(Muzeum Fortyfikacji i Broni Arsenał; Map p190; ☑84 638 4076; www.muzeum-zamojskie.pl; ul Zamkowa 2; combined admission adult/child 25/12zł; ⊙9am-5pm daily May-Sep, to 4pm Tue-Sun Oct-Apr) This museum of military hardware and the city's fortifications is housed in three separate areas along the city's western bastions. Start at the facility built into rebuilt Bastion III which has the ticket office. A model of the city comes to life with multimedia effects that dramatise the town's past. The second part is in the nearby 1820 Arsenal, which shows the life of the local defenders through the years, along with temporary exhibits.

Bastion VII   FORT
(Map p190; ☑84 639 3018; www.nadszaniec.zamosc.pl; ul Łukasińskiego 2; tour adult/child 10/7zł, viewing terrace only 2.50zł; ⊙9am-7pm May-Sep, to 6pm Apr & Oct, to 4pm Nov-Mar) On the eastern edge of the Old Town is the best surviving bastion from the original city walls. You can take a group walking tour (English text is available) that includes the renovated fortifications and casemates, the underground foundations, displays of military gear and history; it finishes with sweeping views over the city from a viewing terrace atop the bastion. Buy tickets inside the bastion, which has various market stalls.

Zamość

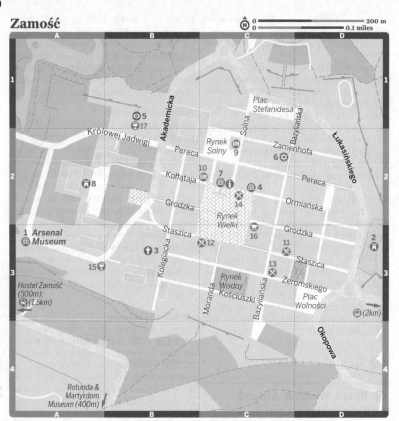

Zamość

◎ Top Sights

◎ Sights

◎ Sleeping

◎ Eating

◎ Drinking & Nightlife

Cathedral   CHURCH

(Map p190; ☎84 639 2614; www.katedra.zamo
jskolubaczowska.pl; ul Kolegiacka 1a; adult/child
3/1.50zł; ⊙dawn-dusk) The cathedral was built
by Morando between 1587 and 1598 as a votive offering and mausoleum for the Zamoys-
kis. The exterior changed dramatically in the
19th century, but the interior has maintained
many original features. Note the authentic
Lublin Renaissance–style vault, the stone
and stucco work, and the unusual arcaded
organ loft. In the high altar is a stunning
rococo silver tabernacle dating to 1745. Jan
Zamoyski's tomb is under the black marble
in the chapel, at the head of the right aisle.

Zamoyski Palace
PALACE

(Map p190; ul Akademicka 1) This former palace (closed to the public) was the main residence of Jan Zamoyski, and dates from 1586. It was built in accordance with Bernardo Morando's design concept for the town, but it lost much of its character when it was converted into a military hospital in the 1830s. These days it houses the municipal court. Most notable is a large statue of Zamoyski astride a horse on the building's east side.

Old Lublin Gate
HISTORIC SITE

(Stara Brama Lubelska; Map p190; Królowej Jadwigi 2) This former gate into the Old Town is a partly ruined brick structure. After its construction in 1588 it was walled up in 1604 to commemorate a victorious event. Austrian Archduke Maximilian (a claimant to the Polish throne) was taken prisoner by Jan Zamoyski in the battle of Byczyna and triumphantly 'escorted' into the town through the gate. He is said to have been the last person to have walked through it. Today it's the summer beer garden Wrota Kultury (p192).

◉ Jewish Quarter

The area around the Rynek Solny and ul Zamenhofa was once the heart of the Jewish quarter. Jews were granted permission to settle in Zamość in 1588, and by the mid-19th century they accounted for 60% of the town's 4000 people. By the eve of WWII their numbers had grown to 12,000 (45% of the total population). In 1941 they were forcibly removed by the occupying Germans to a ghetto formed to the west of the Old Town, and by the following year most had been killed at the Bełżec extermination camp.

Synagogue
SYNAGOGUE

(Map p190; www.zamosc.fodz.pl; ul Pereca 14; 7zł; ⊙10am-6pm Tue-Sun Mar-Oct, to 2pm Tue-Sun Nov-Feb) The city's fascinating synagogue was built around 1620 and served as the Jewish community's main house of worship until WWII, when it was shuttered by the Germans. The ceilings and design elements in the small main prayer room have been restored to their former opulence. A highlight of the exhibition is a gripping computer presentation on the history of the town's Jewish community and its eventual destruction by the Germans. Special exhibitions highlight Jewish life in Zamość.

◉ Beyond The Old Town

Rotunda & Martyrdom Museum
MUSEUM

(☑692 162 219; www.muzeum-zamojskie.pl; Droga Męczenników Rotundy; ⊙7am-8pm daily May-Oct, to 3pm Mon-Fri Nov-Apr) FREE About 500m southwest of the Old Town is the Rotunda – a ring-shaped fort 54m in diameter surrounding a circular yard. The rotunda was built in the 1820s as part of the defensive infrastructure of the town, but during WWII the German SS converted it into an interrogation centre. Some 8000 people from the Zamość area are believed to have been murdered here and their bodies burnt in the courtyard. The atmosphere is desolate.

The graveyard surrounding the rotunda is the resting place of many who were killed here, including Polish soldiers and members of the Polish underground. One of those killed was 16-year-old Grażyna Kierszniewska. Her father was in the underground and the Nazis captured her and held her hostage in order to capture her father. She was tortured and then shot but never revealed the location of her father.

🛏 Sleeping

Though accommodation in Zamość caters for most budgets, the selection is more limited than you'd expect from a town of this aesthetic fame. Be sure to book ahead in balmy months.

Hostel Zamość
HOSTEL €

(☑724 968 902; www.hostelzamosc.pl; ul Szczebrzeska 9; dm/s/d from 38/90/135zł; P@🛜) Family-friendly guesthouse is about 750m southwest of the Old Town and adjacent to the main train station. There are dorm beds as well as singles and doubles. It's nothing fancy, but everything is well-run and secure. There's a serene garden where kids can play, and anyone can relax. Breakfast costs 15zł.

Hotel Senator
HOTEL €€

(Map p190; ☑84 638 9990; www.senatorhotel.pl; ul Rynek Solny 4; s/d from 170/230zł; P❄@🛜) The Senator offers impressive value and more charm than its local competition. Rooms have a tasteful aesthetic, some have bold colours. The on-site restaurant, with its own fireplace, aims for medieval mellow (and looks like a medieval theatre set). Enjoy a coffee under the historic arcade.

MAŁOPOLSKA ZAMOŚĆ

Hotel Korunny
HOTEL €€

(📞 84 677 7100; www.hotelkoronny.pl; ul Koszary 7; r from 300zł; P🅿️❄️@🛜) The designers wanted to create a modern take on Renaissance Zamość, meaning overly plush carpets and curtains, chandeliers, and oversize rooms. It feels like an extravagance without the price. The breakfast buffet is bounteous and there's a terrace out back on which to take morning coffee. One downside is the remote location, 1.6km north of the Old Town.

Hotel Zamojski
HOTEL €€

(Map p190; 📞 84 639 2516; www.hotelzamojski. pl; ul Kołłątaja 2/4/6; s/d from 190/220zł; P🅿️❄️🛜) Occupying three interconnected, historic houses, this stolid hotel has an ideal location off the Rynek. Some rooms are bigger than others, some offer better views and all have a bland corporate decor that betrays the hotel's former affiliation with the Mercure chain. There's a small spa that gives the entry way the smell of old socks. The breakfast buffet is expansive.

✗ Eating & Drinking

Bar Asia
POLISH €

(Map p190; 📞 84 639 2304; ul Staszica 6; mains 8-11zł; ⊙ 8am-5pm Mon-Fri, to 4pm Sat) This old, cafeteria-style milk bar is a treasure. The name has obscure origins, but the food is fully grounded in Polish home-cooking. Everything is made just like mum made it and it's served fresh all day. The dining room is suitably bare bones but spotless. Staff are charming.

★ Restauracja Muzealna
ARMENIAN €€

(Map p190; 📞 84 638 7300; www.muzealna.com.pl; ul Ormiańska 30; mains 20-50zł; ⊙ 11am-11pm, reduced hours in winter) Occupying the basement of one of the iconic Armenian Houses on the Rynek, this restaurant offers up fare with a bit more zest than typical Polish cooking (although there's plenty of the latter). The spicy marinated kebabs are excellent, as is the house specialty, nettle soup. In summer, eat at tables out on the square.

Bohema
POLISH €€

(Map p190; 📞 84 627 1443; www.bohemazamosc. pl; ul Staszica 29; mains 18-50zł; ⊙ 10am-11pm; 🛜) Bohema is one of the better Rynek options, with good classic Polish food (try the 'mixed pierogi' set, with 12 dumplings or anything with the word 'pork' in the name) served in the vaulted basement dining rooms. Right off the square, the cafe has an appealing array of baked goods and cakes plus excellent coffee.

Corner Pub
POLISH €€

(Map p190; 📞 84 627 0694; www.cornerpub.pl; ul Żeromskiego 6; mains 22-50zł; ⊙ 11am-10pm Sun-Thu, to 11pm Fri & Sat; 🛜) This cosy pub (that thankfully is only vaguely faux Irish) is the place to head in the evening for fine regional Polish cooking, plus fish and chips, big burgers and pizza. There are a few garden tables in summer.

★ Kawa na Ławę
CAFE

(Map p190; 📞 507 673 351; www.kawanalawe.pl; ul Rynek Wielki 8; coffee from 7zł; ⊙ 9am-8pm) Zamość's best coffee is served in this cheery and cosy cafe on the Rynek. Pass the time playing a board game, or trying some of the exquisite homemade liquors. There are lavish desserts year-round; in summer, rich homemade ice cream is on offer to enjoy here or take away. The tables on the square are much sought after.

Jazz Club
BAR

(Klub Jazzowy; Map p190; 📞 502 578 442; www. facebook.com/pg/JazzKlubKosz; Szczebrzeska 3; ⊙ noon-midnight daily May-Sep, 5-11pm Thu-Sat Oct-Apr) This great bar with live jazz is located inside the city's Szczebrzeszka Gate in the defensive wall. In summer there are outside tables up high on the wall with great views.

Wrota Kultury
BEER GARDEN

(Cultural Gate; Map p190; 📞 502 659 248; www. facebook.com/wrotakultury; Królowej Jadwigi 2; ⊙ 5pm-midnight) While away the hours at this summertime beer garden at the 16th-century Old Lublin Gate. The vibe is funky and relaxed; well into the night, the happy crowds have been known to dance.

❶ Information

Tourist Office (Map p190; 📞 84 639 2292; www.travel.zamosc.pl; Rynek Wielki 13; bike rental per hour/day 5/25zł; ⊙ 8am-7pm daily May-Sep, 8am-5pm Mon-Fri, from 9am Sat & Sun Oct-Apr; 🛜) In the town hall, has maps, brochures and souvenirs. Staff can arrange walking tours of the town and rent bikes. There is also a computer for free internet use and a small gallery with rotating exhibits.

❶ Getting There & Away

BUS

The **bus station** (ul Hrubieszowska 9) is 2km east of the Old Town. Minibuses line up in front of the station.

Kraków 50zł, six hours, two daily
Lublin 15zł, 90 minutes, hourly
Warsaw 45zł, 4½ hours, six daily

TRAIN

Zamość has two renovated railway stations. The main **Zamość train station** (ul Szczebrzeska 11) is 800m from the west side of the Old Town while **Zamość Starówka train station** (ul Peowiaków 78) is 600m from the east side. Trains stop at both. There is service to Lublin (16zł, 2¼ hours, three daily).

Zwierzyniec & Roztocze National Park

POP 3200

The town of Zwierzyniec (zvyeh-*zhi*-nyets) is 32km southwest of Zamość; like Zamość, it was created by Jan Zamoyski, but on a more modest scale. In the 16th century the Polish nobleman built a summer palace and residential complex here, and tossed in an enormous game reserve for his recreational enjoyment. While the family's once-grand summer palace was pulled down in the 19th century (all that's left is a tiny chapel), the game reserve survives to this day and forms the core of the modern-day Roztocze National Park.

Zwierzyniec itself is best missed. It's little more than a sad-looking square surrounded by a few shops selling cheap clothing. Skip it for the enchanting park, with its hundreds of kilometres of unspoiled hiking and biking trails.

◎ Sights & Activities

Roztocze National Park   PARK
(Roztoczański Park Narodowy; ☑84 687 2286; www.roztoczanskipn.pl; ul Plażowa 2, Zwierzyniec) The park, which covers an area of 79 sq km, was a nature reserve for more than 350 years as part of the Zamoyski family estate. Today, it's home to a diverse range of flora and fauna, and is popular for its hiking and cycling opportunities. For a sampler of Roztocze's natural beauty, take the **Trail on Beech Mountain** (2.6km) south from the museum to the top of Bukowa Góra (Beech Mountain, 306m) along a former palace park lane.

The normal starting points for walks is the park visitor centre where you can buy park maps and get info. The symbol of the park is the Polish pony – a descendent of a wild horse known as the tarpan that died out in the 19th century. The horse was reintroduced to the park in 1982 and there's a small pony refuge near Echo Ponds. If you want to visit the pony reserve near Echo Ponds, there is a short route (1.2km) from the museum. Longer walks generally weave from Zwierzyniec through forest terrain to neighbouring villages (such as Florianka, known for its Polish pony breeding). Intersecting paths enable you to return by a different route or cut to another path.

Museum Educational Centre   MUSEUM
(Ośrodek Edukacyjno-Muzealny; ☑84 687 2286; www.roztoczanskipn.pl; ul Plażowa 3; adult/child 10/6zł; ☺9am-5pm Tue-Sun Apr-Oct, to 4pm Tue-Sun Nov-Mar) Located near the entrance to Roztocze National Park, this centre has interesting displays of local flora and fauna. It's close to the park visitor centre.

Chapel on the Water   CHAPEL
(Kościółek na wodzie; ☑84 687 2140; www.zwierzyniec.parafia.info.pl; ☺hours vary) Just near the Roztocze National Park Visitor Centre is this small chapel, St John of Nepomuk, the only significant structure remaining from the Zamoyski's residential complex. The small, heavily restored baroque church sits on one of four tiny islets on the small lake of Staw Kościelny (Church Pond), which was allegedly dug by Turkish and Tatar prisoners in the 1740s.

Zwierzyniec Brewery   BREWERY
(☑669 611 981; www.zwierzyniec.pl; Browarna 7; 10zł; ☺10am-4pm Fri-Sun May, Jun & Sep, 10am-4pm Wed-Sun Jul & Aug) The local brewery is owned by national giant Perła. It makes popular Czech-style Zwierzyniec lager. Tours of the brewery, which is right on the lake, trace its history going back to the 1600s. There is a summer beer garden outside that shows movies on balmy nights.

Letnisko   CYCLING
(Wypożyczalnia rowerów; ☑601 507 306; www.zwierzyniec-rowery.pl; ul 1 Maja 22; bike rental per hr/day from 15/30zł; ☺8am-8pm Apr-Oct) Good bike rental outfit, not far from the entrance to Roztocze National Park, where you can buy cycling and hiking maps. Has a wide range of bikes.

⊨ Sleeping & Eating

Zwierzyniec and the park are best visited on a day trip from Zamość. There are a couple local options should you linger. There are a few seasonal restaurants around Staw Kościelny (Church Pond).

Karczma Młyn
PENSION €

(☑ 84 687 2527; www.karczma-mlyn.pl; ul Wachniewskiej 1a; s/d from 90/120zł, mains 10-20zł; ☺ restaurant noon-9pm; ℗) This cheery inn with a postcard-perfect view of the baroque Chapel on the Water offers accommodation at reasonable prices, as well as the best meals in town. Eat in the back garden. The name means The Mill and it has a woodsy charm. The menu is hearty, country-style.

Relaks
PENSION €

(☑ 607 938 211; www.noclegizwierzyniec.pl; ul 2 Lutego 12a; s/d from 80/120zł; ℗☎) This well-mannered stucco chalet is on a small street behind the main square. Inside you'll find eight tidy and simple rooms done out in cheerful colours. Some have full baths, others only showers. One has a balcony, and several overlook a grilling gazebo in the back garden.

Camping Echo
CAMPGROUND €

(☑ 84 687 2314; www.echozwierzyniec.pl; ul Biłgorajska 5; campsites per adult/child 15/8zł, cottages from 85zł; ☺ mid-Apr–Sep; ℗) This pleasant family-oriented campground is close to the bus station and is right off a supermarket parking lot. It offers tent sites as well as comfy cottages for up to six people. Not all sites have shade.

ℹ Information

Roztocze National Park Visitor Centre
(☑ 84 687 2286; www.roztoczanskipn.pl; ul Plażowa 3; park admission adult/child 4/2zł; ☺ 8.30am-4.30 Apr-Oct, to 3pm Nov-Mar) The new park visitor centre sells maps and admission passes, plus it offers information. It's near the Museum Educational Centre; a snack stand is nearby. There's a small car park on-site, and many of the best hikes set out from here.

ℹ Getting There & Away

The **bus station** (ul Zamojska) is on ul Zamojska, just north of the lake. The park visitor centre is a 1km-walk south past the lake. Buses to Zamość (6zł, 45 minutes, hourly) are regular. The train station is poorly located and service is sparse.

Carpathian Mountains

Why Go?

When thinking about Poland, mountains are not the first thing to spring to mind, yet the country's southern border is defined by the beautiful and dramatic Carpathian (Karpaty) chain, the highest mountain range in Central Europe.

Its wooded hills and peaks are a beacon for hikers, cyclists and skiers, and because of the region's remoteness, this 'forgotten corner' has been able to preserve its traditional folkways better than most other parts of the country.

Perhaps best known is the resort of Zakopane in the heart of the Tatra Mountains (Tatry), but the prettiest hills are arguably in the Pieniny or Bieszczady ranges. Elsewhere, a mosaic of towns shelter Unesco-listed wooden churches and provide jumping-off points for a half-dozen national parks. Beyond those, historic regional centres such as Przemyśl, Tarnów and Sanok retell Poland's tumultuous history.

Best Places to Eat

→ Restauracja Buda (p225)
→ Cuda Wianki (p212)
→ Pół na Pół (p206)
→ U Becza (p226)
→ Stary Kredens (p216)

Best Places to Stay

→ Hotel Sabała (p200)
→ Małopolanka (p230)
→ Hotel GAL (p205)
→ Grand Hotel (p209)

When to Go
Zakopane

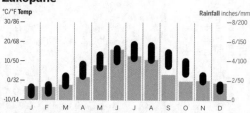

Jan–Mar
Zakopane is *the* place for winter sports in a season that lasts through March.

Apr–Jun
Welcome the arrival of spring in the remote Bieszczady range.

Jul–Aug
There's no better place in summer than on a raft on the Dunajec River.

Carpathian Mountains Highlights

1 Ustrzyki Górne (p219) Striking out for the blissfully wooded Bieszczady mountains.

2 Tarnów (p203) Tracing the 16th-century streets of this handsomely preserved town.

3 Zalipie (p205) Marvelling at the floral profusion of this hamlet's famed painted houses.

4 Icon Trail (p215) Heading out from Sanok to see the unique timber churches and icons they shelter.

5 Zakopane (p197) Using this much-loved resort as a base to hike or ski in the Tatras.

6 Dunajec Gorge (p233) Rafting past rock walls and abundant greenery.

7 Krynica (p229) Taking the waters or hiking the hills in this venerable spa town.

8 Rzeszów (p207) Exploring the medieval cellars and modern-day underground scene of a buzzing town.

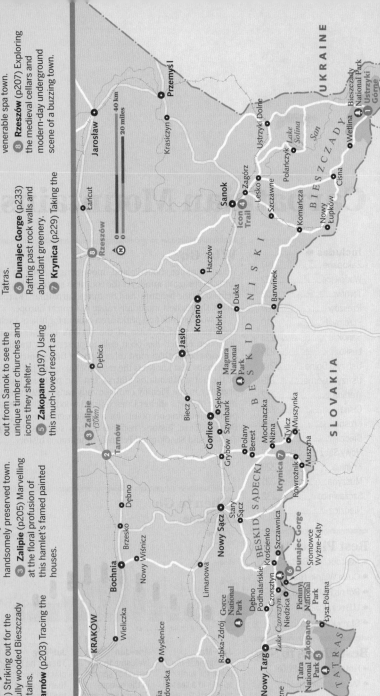

TATRA MOUNTAINS

Extending into Slovakia, the Tatras are the highest range of the Carpathians, with towering peaks and rocky defiles dropping hundreds of metres to icy lakes. There are no glaciers here, but patches of snow remain all year.

The range, roughly 900 sq km, stretches for 60km across the Polish–Slovakian border and is 15km at its widest point. About a quarter of it is Polish territory and forms the Tatra National Park (Tatrzański Park Narodowy), encompassing 211 sq km and headquartered in Zakopane. The Polish Tatras boast two dozen peaks exceeding 2000m, the highest of which is **Mt Rysy** (2499m).

At the northern foot of the Tatras lies the Podhale region, which extends from Zakopane to the city of Nowy Targ. Dotted with small villages populated by *górale* (highlanders), the Podhale is one of the few Polish regions where old folk traditions still form a part of everyday life.

Zakopane

POP 27,857

Nestled in the foothills of the Tatras, Zakopane is Poland's best-known mountain resort, famed for hiking in summer and skiing in winter, though at the height of the summer and winter seasons it can get positively overrun.

In addition to outdoor pursuits, Zakopane is known for its beautiful wooden villas, dating from the late 19th and early 20th centuries. Some of these now house museums, while others have been converted into hotels or pensions. The father of this craze for ornate timber houses was the architect Stanisław Witkiewicz (1851–1915), and his early 20th-century creations helped to establish Zakopane as a haven for painters, poets, writers and composers. Two of the town's most famous former residents include Witkiewicz's son, the writer and painter Stanisław Ignacy Witkiewicz (better known as 'Witkacy'), and the composer Karol Szymanowski.

◉ Sights

Most of Zakopane's cultural sights draw on the town's unique wooden architecture and its history as an artistic haven in the 19th and early 20th centuries.

◉ In The Centre

Tatra Park Nature Education Centre   MUSEUM
(Centrum Edukacji Przyrodniczej Tatrzańskiego Parku Narodowego; ☑ 18 202 3312; www.tpn.pl; ul Chałubińskiego 42a; ⊙ 9am-4.30pm May-Sep, 8am-3pm Mon-Sat Oct-Apr) FREE The national park's education centre walks visitors through the natural history of the mountains, including dioramas, interactive displays, kids' activities and a giant model of the Tatras. As numbers are limited to 40 people at a time, you may want to book through the website. Last entry is one hour before closing.

Museum of Zakopane Style   MUSEUM
(Willa Koliba; Map p198; ☑ 18 201 3602; www.muzeumtatrzanskie.pl; ul Kościeliska 18; adult/concession 7/5.50zł; ⊙ 10am-6pm Tue-Sat, 9am-3pm Sun Jul & Aug, 9am-5pm Wed-Sat, to 3pm Sep-Jun) Housed in the Willa Koliba, this was the first of several grand wooden villas designed by the noted Polish painter and architect Stanisław Witkiewicz in his 'Zakopane Style' (similar to the Arts and Crafts movement that swept the US and Britain at the turn of the 20th century). The museum is closed for renovation until 2020.

Old Church & Cemetery   CHURCH
(Stary Kościół i Cmentarz na Pęksowym Brzyzku; Map p198; ul Kościeliska 4; cemetery 2zł; ⊙ 8am-5pm) This small wooden church and atmospheric cemetery date from the mid-19th century. The Old Church has charming carved wooden decorations and pews, the Stations of the Cross painted on glass on the windows and an unusual open-fronted confessional. The adjoining cemetery is one of the country's most beautiful, featuring amazing wood-carved headstones, some resembling giant chess pieces. The noted Polish painter and creator of the Zakopane Style, Stanisław Witkiewicz, is buried here beneath a modest wooden grave marker.

Museum of Zakopane Style – Inspirations   MUSEUM
(Muzeum Stylu Zakopiańskiego – Inspiracje; ☑ 18 201 2294; www.muzeumtatrzanskie.pl; ul Droga do Rojów 6; adult/concession 6/4.50zł; ⊙ 10am-6pm Tue-Sat, 9am-3pm Sun Jul & Aug, 9am-5pm Wed-Sat, 9am-3pm Sun Sep-Jun) This companion museum to the main Zakopane Style museum is more of an ethnographic exhibition, highlighting the highlander folk roots and styles that inspired Witkiewicz in the first place.

Zakopane

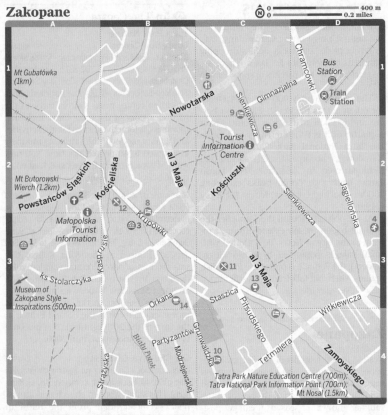

Zakopane

◎ Sights

1 Museum of Zakopane Style	A3
2 Old Church & Cemetery	A2
3 Tatra Museum	B3

☉ Activities, Courses & Tours

4 Aqua Park	D3
5 Sukces	C1

🛏 Sleeping

6 Grand Hotel Stamary	C2
7 Hotel Kasprowy Wierch	C4
8 Hotel Sabała	B2
9 Target Hostel	C1
10 Willa Carlton	C4

✖ Eating

11 Karczma Zapiecek	C3
12 Pstrąg Górski	B2

🍸 Drinking & Nightlife

13 Cafe Piano	C3
14 La Mano	B3

Tatra Museum   MUSEUM
(Map p198; ☎18 201 5205; www.muzeumtatr
zanskie.pl; ul Krupówki 10; adult/concession
7/5.50zł, free Sun; ⏰10am-6pm Tue-Sat, 9am-3pm
Sun Jul & Aug, 9am-5pm Wed-Sat, 9am-3pm Sun
Sep-Jun) This is the main branch of the Tatra
Museum, which occupies various branches
around Zakopane. Featuring old-fashioned
exhibits exploring the natural history, ethnography, geology and artistic traditions of
the Tatras, it's a good way to get a handle
on the region. Occupying a handsome early
20th-century brick building set back from
ul Krupówki, it also opens on Tuesdays between May and September.

◉ Outside The Centre

Morskie Oko   LAKE
(per person 5zł) Perched nearly 1400m above
sea level, the emerald-green 'Eye of the Sea'
is the largest lake in the Tatras and a popular
outing from Zakopane. Minibuses regularly

depart from ul Kościuszki, across from the main bus station, for Polana Palenica (10zł, 45 minutes), from where a 9km-long road continues uphill to the lake. Vehicles are not allowed, so you'll have to walk (about two hours each way) or take a horse-drawn carriage (50zł per person).

Travel agencies in town organise day trips.

 Activities

In addition to numerous hiking possibilities, there are lots of other things to do.

Skiing

Zakopane is Poland's capital of winter sports. The town's environs have a number of ski areas, ranging from flat surfaces for cross-country touring to steep slopes – suitable for everyone from beginners to advanced – served by 50 ski lifts and tows.

Mt Kasprowy Wierch (1985m) offers some of the most challenging ski slopes in the area, as well as the best conditions, with the spring skiing season sometimes extending as late as early May. You can get to the top in 20 minutes by **cable car** (Kolej Linowa Kasprowy Wierch; ☏22 444 6666; www.pkl.pl;

Kuźnice 14; adult/concession return 63/53zł; ⊙7am-9pm Jul-Sep, shorter hours rest of year) then stay in the mountains and use the two chairlifts, in the Goryczkowa and Gąsienicowa Valleys, on both sides of Mt Kasprowy. The view from the top is spectacular (clouds permitting) and you can stand with one foot in Poland and the other in Slovakia.

Mt Gubałówka is another popular ski area and it, too, offers some pistes and good conditions. It's easily accessible from central Zakopane by **funicular** (www.pkl.pl; adult/concession return 24/20zł, one way 18/16zł; ⊙9am-9.30pm Jul, Aug & Jan–mid-Feb, shorter hours rest of year), covering the 1298m-long route in 3½ minutes and climbing 300m from the lower station just north of ul Krupówki.

Some 2km to the west is **Mt Butorowski Wierch**, with its 1.6km-long chairlift. One more major ski area is at **Mt Nosal**, on the southeastern outskirts of Zakopane. Facilities include a chairlift and a dozen T-bars.

Ski-equipment hire is available from many outlets throughout Zakopane: try **Sukces.** (Map p198; ☏502 681 170; www.ski-sukces.zakopane.pl; ul Nowotarska 39; ⊙9am-7pm in season) Complete kits for skiing/snowboarding begin at 50zł a day.

HIKING IN THE TATRA MOUNTAINS

With a huge variety of trails covering nearly 300km, the Tatras are ideal for walking. No other area of Poland is so densely criss-crossed with hiking paths, and nowhere else will you find such a diversity of landscapes.

Although marked trails go all across the region, the most popular area for hiking is the **Tatra National Park**, which begins just south of Zakopane. Geographically the Tatras are divided into three parts: the West Tatras (Tatry Zachodnie), the High Tatras (Tatry Wysokie) to the east and the adjoining Belianske Tatras (Tatry Bielskie). All the areas are attractive, though they offer quite different scenery. In general the West Tatras are lower, gentler, easier to walk and safer. The High Tatras and Belianske Tatras are completely different: a land of bare granite peaks with alpine lakes at their bases. Hikers will face more challenges here, but also enjoy more dramatic scenery.

If you just want to go for a short walk, there are several picturesque and densely forested valleys south of Zakopane, of which **Dolina Strążyska** is the most attractive. It's long been a popular walking and picnic area for locals, and for reasonably fit walkers it should take no longer than 50 minutes to traverse its length via the red trail up to Polana Strążyska. From there you can come back the same way or transfer by the black trail to either of the neighbouring valleys, the **Dolina Białego** to the east being the usual way. It takes around an hour to get to this charming valley and another hour to go all the way down to Zakopane.

The most popular mountain climbed in the Tatras is **Mt Giewont** (1894m), the very symbol of Zakopane. You can reach it on the red trail in about 3½ hours from Zakopane. A reasonable level of fitness is required to attempt this climb.

Before you do any walking or climbing, you should get hold of the 1:25,000-scale *Tatrzański Park Narodowy* map (15zł), published by Sygnatura. It shows all the trails in the area, complete with walking times both uphill and downhill. Another option is the 1:30,000-scale *Tatry Polskie* (Polish Tatras) map (14zł), published by Compass.

Other Activities

An excellent place to cool off on a warm summer's day is **Aqua Park** (Map p198; ☑18 200 1122; www.aquapark.zakopane.pl; ul Jagiellońska 31; per 1hr/day adult 22/69zł, concession 17/56zł; ⊙9am-10pm; ⓓ), with indoor and outdoor pools, slides, various saunas and – incongruously – tenpin bowling.

In summer Mt Nosal is a popular spot for hang-gliding and paragliding. For information stop by one of the tourist offices or check out www.paraglidingmap.com, which has a good section on paragliding sites in Poland.

⚜ Festivals & Events

Throughout summer, the Villa Atma hosts a series of chamber music concerts (usually 40zł) to celebrate the music of Karol Szymanowski and other composers.

International Festival of Mountain Folklore
MUSIC

(Międzynarodowy Festiwal Folkloru Ziem Górskich; www.mffzg.pl; ⊙Aug) Starting out as a festival of Carpathian culture in 1965, Zakopane's late-summer festival now features folk music and dance groups from around the world, and is the town's biggest annual event.

⌕ Sleeping

Zakopane has no shortage of places to stay and, except for summer and winter holiday peaks, finding a bed is no problem. Even if the hotels and hostels are full, there will always be private rooms, which provide some of the best-value accommodation in town. Check at the tourist office for details (rooms should cost around 60zł per person) or look for signs reading *'pokoje'*, *'noclegi'* or *'zimmer frei'*.

Target Hostel
HOSTEL €

(Map p198; ☑730 955 730, 18 207 4596; www.targethostel.pl; ul Sienkiewicza 3b; dm/tw from 39/150zł; @ⓡ) This private, well-run hostel is within easy walking distance of the bus station – the entrance is downstairs from the street, beneath a clinic. Accommodation is in six- to 10-bed dorms, with classic pale-wood panelling and wooden floors. There's a common room and communal kitchen, and the staff are friendly and helpful.

Good Bye Lenin Hostel
HOSTEL €

(☑18 200 1330; ul Chłabówka 44; dm/d 40/120zł; ⓟ@ⓡ) This five-room place with 30 beds in a century-old farmhouse, at the end of a steep drive in the woods 5km southeast of central Zakopane, is as chill as you'll find. The management will pick you up from the bus or train station by prior arrangement.

Willa Carlton
HOTEL €€

(Map p198; ☑18 201 4415; www.carlton.pl; ul Grunwaldzka 11; s/d from160/279zł; ⓡ) This pretty pension occupies a grand old house away from the main drag that was built between the wars, but has been thoroughly modernised inside. Expect 21 light-filled rooms with modern furniture, an inviting shared balcony and a big comfy lounge lined with potted plants.

Hotel Kasprowy Wierch
HOTEL €€

(Map p198; ☑18 201 2738; www.hotelkasprowy.com; ul Krupówki 50b; d/tr 280/420zł; ⓡ) This late-19th-century Swiss-style villa has been a hotel since 1936, and sits pretty at the southern end of Zakopane's central promenade. The rooms don't quite match the historic exterior for charm, but are clean and comfortable enough. The in-house restaurant (mains 22zł to 30zł) offers the usual soups, grilled meats, dumplings and pancakes, and can be trusted to do them well.

★ Hotel Sabała
HOTEL €€€

(Map p198; ☑18 201 5092; www.sabala.zakopane.pl; ul Krupówki 11; s/d 350/490zł; ⓡⓢⓓ) Welcoming guests since 1898 but thoroughly up to date, this striking timber hotel has a superb location on Zakopane's picturesque pedestrian thoroughfare. Guests will find cosy, attic-style rooms, and a sauna, solarium and swimming pool to aid relaxation. The faux-rustic in-house restaurant is a great place to try finely cooked examples of the region's cuisine.

Grand Hotel Stamary
HISTORIC HOTEL €€€

(Map p198; ☑18 202 4510; www.stamary.pl; ul Kościuszki 19; s/d/ste 279/529/899zł; ⓟ✳@ⓡⓓ) Named for the opera singer who founded it, the 1905 Stamary is one of Zakopane's grand historic hotels, maintaining its eminence with thorough updates to its 54 stylish rooms. The on-site spa is delightful and inviting, with a swimming pool, jacuzzi, saunas and packages galore. The formal restaurant is a little stuffy, but does excellent steaks and regional dishes (31zł to 55zł).

✕ Eating & Drinking

Ul Krupówki is lined end to end with rustic *górale* (highlander-style) taverns featuring pretty much the same *jadło karpackie* (Carpathian cuisine), accompanied by hokey mountain music performed by a *kapela góralska* (folk-music ensemble). Look out for *oscypek*, traditional Tatra sheep's cheese, pressed into patterned, spindle-shaped moulds and then smoked. It's sold from kiosks in many central locations, starting at around 1.50zł per piece

Karczma Zapiecek   POLISH €€
(Map p198; ☑18 201 5699; www.karczma zapiecek.pl; ul Krupówki 43; mains 33-42zł; ⊘11am-11pm) One of the better choices among a group of similar highlander-style restaurants along ul Krupówki, Zapiecek offers great food, an old stove and a terrace. Traditional dishes include local *oscypek grillowany* (grilled smoked cheese) served with bacon or cranberries, *kaczka pieczona* (roast duck with pear, cranberry and potato dumplings) and *pstrąg z pieca* (baked trout).

Pstrąg Górski   SEAFOOD €€
(Map p198; ☑512 351 746; www.zakopane-restauracje.pl; ul Krupówki 6a; mains 22-45zł; ⊘10am-10pm; 🐾) The alpine-style 'Mountain Trout' serves some of the freshest trout, salmon and ocean fish in town. Decked out in abundant rustic timber and overlooking a narrow stream, it's an apt place to try local trout, priced at 6.50zł per 100g (whole fish) and served with horseradish, almonds and honey and many other accompaniments.

La Mano   COFFEE
(Map p198; www.facebook.com/lamanozakopane; ul Orkana 1f; ⊘9am-7pm Mon-Sat, 10am-6pm Sun; 🐾) This cafe, clearly a labour of love, serves the best coffee in town. The young owners' passion shows in the care taken over the beans and their extraction, and the selection of locally produced honey, fruit juices and compotes on sale. Sit out front overlooking the street, or head through the back for a view of the mountains.

Cafe Piano   BAR
(Map p198; ☑604 566 980; ul Krupówki 63; ⊘3pm-1am Sun-Thu, to 2am Fri & Sat; 🐾) This hideaway, situated down a back alley with a beautiful garden out back for the warmer months, is something of an insider's secret in Zakopane. Expect chess-playing locals, interesting beers, well-chosen music and even the occasional knees-up around the piano.

ℹ Information

Małopolska Tourist Information (Małopolski System Informacji Turystycznej; Map p198; ☑18 201 2004; www.visitmalopolska.pl; ul Kościeliska 7; ⊘9am-5pm Mon-Sat) The regional tourist information office has lots of info on the Tatras, as well as loads of brochures on neighbouring towns and cities, including Kraków.

Tatra National Park Information Point (Punkt Informacji Turystycznej; ☑18 202 3300; www.tpn.pl; ul Chałubińskiego 44; ⊘7am-3.30pm Mon-Sat) Located in a small building near the Rondo Jana Pawła II on the southern outskirts of the city. It's a good place for maps, guides and local weather and hiking information.

Tourist Information Centre (Centrum Informacji Turystycznej; Map p198; ☑18 201 2211; www.zakopane.pl; ul Kościuszki 17; ⊘9am-5pm Mon-Sat) Small but helpful municipal tourist office just south of the bus station on the walk towards the centre. It has free city maps and sells more detailed hiking maps.

ℹ Getting There & Away

Bus is far and away the best transport option for reaching Zakopane, though there are a few trains that still use the town's small train station.

Zakopane's **bus station** (PKS; Map p198; ul Kościuszki 25) is about 400m northeast of the centre along ul Kościuszki. Most buses and minibuses depart from here or the small minibus station across the street. Szwagropol operates bus services to Kraków (20zł, two hours, once or twice hourly). From mid-June to mid-October, Strama runs regular buses between Zakopane and Poprad, Slovakia (26zł, two hours, two to four daily).

ℹ Getting Around

Blue-and-white city buses (www.zakopane.eu/komunikacjamiejska) 11 and 14 link the extremities of the town; buy tickets (3zł flat fare) at the tourist office, or from machines on the bus.

Dozens of privately owned minibuses depart regularly (when full) from the bus station to hiking trailheads, including Kuznice (5zł, 15 minutes, for the Kasprowy Wierch cable car) and Morskie Oko (8zł, 30 minutes).

CARPATHIAN MOUNTAINS ZAKOPANE

CARPATHIAN FOOTHILLS

The Carpathian Foothills (Przedgórze Karpackie) form a green and hilly belt sloping from the Vistula and San River valleys in the north to the true mountains in the south. Except for Wadowice and Kalwaria Zebrzydowska, which are usually visited from Kraków, most sights in the region are located along the Kraków–Tarnów–Rzeszów–Przemyśl road. You'll find gentle forested hills, historic cities and plenty to see and do.

Wadowice

POP 19,386

The birthplace of one Karol Wojtyła – better known to the world as Pope John Paul II – Wadowice (vah-do-*vee*-tsah) has evolved into a popular pilgrimage destination in its own right. People come to walk the pretty cobblestones, pay their respects to the Wojtyła family home and, maybe most importantly, have a slice of the town's legendary cream cake, *kremówka*. The former pope himself was a big fan.

◉ Sights

Family Home of John Paul II   MUSEUM
(Dom Rodzinny Jana Pawła II; ☑ 33 823 2662, reservations (9am-1pm Mon-Fri) 33 823 3565; www.domjp2.pl; ul Kościelna 7; adult/concession 23/18zł incl Polish guide, 35/28zł incl English guide; ⊙ 9am-7pm May-Sep, to 4pm Nov-Mar, to 6pm Apr & Oct, last admission 80 minutes before closing)
The home where future pope Karol Wojtyła was born on 18 May 1920 is now a popular museum, restored to its historical appearance. The Wojtyła family lived in this small 1st-floor apartment, with just two rooms and a kitchen, from 1919 to 1938. Entry is by guided tour, with English-speaking guides available. Order tickets by phone or online, or buy them three doors down, at Plac Jana Pawła II 5. The museum closes on the last Tuesday of each month.

Minor Basilica   CHURCH
(Bazylika Mniejska; ☑ 33 873 2096; www.wadowicejp2.pl; Plac Jana Pawła II; ⊙ 8am-7pm)
In John Paul II Place stands the 18th-century Minor Basilica, dedicated to the Presentation of the Blessed Virgin Mary.

WORTH A TRIP

A PILGRIMAGE TO KALWARIA ZEBRZYDOWSKA

Fourteen kilometres east of Wadowice (35km southwest of Kraków), Kalwaria Zebrzydowska (kahl-*vah*-ryah zeb-zhi-*dof*-skah) is Poland's second-most important pilgrimage site after Jasna Góra in Częstochowa. The town owes its existence and fame to the squire of Kraków, Mikołaj Zebrzydowski, who commissioned the church and monastery for the Bernardine order in 1600. Having noticed a resemblance in the area to the topography of Jerusalem, he set about creating a place of worship similar to the Via Dolorosa in the Holy City. By 1617, 24 chapels were built over the surrounding hills, some of which looked as though they'd been brought directly from the mother city. As the place attracted growing numbers of pilgrims, more chapels were erected, eventually totalling 42. In 1999 Kalwaria Zebrzydowska (the name means 'Zebrydowski's Calvary') was added to Unesco's list of World Heritage sites.

The immense **Bernardine Monastery** (Klasztor Bernardynów; ☑ 33 876 6304; www.kalwaria.eu; ul Bernardyńska 46; ⊙ 8am-7pm) FREE, which contains impressive 16th- and 17th-century paintings in its cloister, serves as the spiritual centre of Kalwaria Zebrzydowska and flanks the area's most impressive church, the **Basilica of Our Lady of the Angels** (Bazylika Matki Bożej Anielskiej). The holiest image in the church is the icon of Mary in the Chapel of the Miraculous Image (Kaplica Cudownego Obrazu) to the left of the high altar. Tradition has it that the eyes shed tears of blood in 1641, and from that time miracles occurred.

Pilgrims come to Kalwaria year-round but especially on Marian feast days, when processions along the Calvary Trails (*Dróżki Kalwaryjskie*) linking the chapels take place. Kalwaria is also known for its **Passion plays**, a blend of religious ceremony and popular theatre re-enacting the final days of Christ's life and held here since the 17th century.

Trains from Kalwaria Zebrzydowska run regularly to Kraków (11zł, 1¼ hours) and Wadowice (6.50zł, 22 minutes). Buses also go to Kraków (6zł, 50 minutes) and Wadowice (4zł, 25 minutes).

An earlier brick church on the site was incorporated into the present church as its sanctuary, while outside is a monument to the pope, who lived next door and was baptised here in 1920. Pilgrims can see the font where he was baptised and, every Thursday at 6pm, pray before a reliquary containing a drop of his blood.

Town Museum MUSEUM
(Muzeum Miejskie; ☑ 33 873 8100; https://wck.wadowice.pl/muzeum; ul Kościelna 4; adult/concession 5/3zł; ⊘ 9am-5pm Mon-Fri, 10am-4pm Sat & Sun May-Sep, 9am-4pm Mon-Fri, 10am-4pm Sat Oct-Apr, last admission 30 minutes before closing) Located inside Wadowice's former town hall (which also houses the tourist office), the Town Museum comprises the five-room exhibit 'Wadowice: The City Where Everything Started' (words attributed to Pope John Paul II, the town's most famous son). Documents, maps and artefacts dating to the 16th century feature alongside tactile and multimedia exhibits on the city's development and the pope's pre-WWII life here.

🍷 Drinking

Kawiarna Mieszczańska CAFE
(☑ 500 363 842; ul Kościelna 6; ⊘ 9am-7pm Apr-Oct, to 5pm Nov-Mar; 🛜) Wadowice is famous in Poland for its *kremówka,* a calorific pastry of cream, eggs, sugar and a dash of vanilla that disappeared during WWII, but was resurrected in response to Pope John Paul II's fond reminiscences of it. Everyone claims to serve the real McCoy, but we think the best is here at Kawiarna Mieszczańska, next to the tourist office.

❶ Information

The **tourist office** (☑ 33 873 2365; www.it.wadowice.pl; ul Kościelna 4; ⊘ 9am-6pm Mon-Fri, 10am-4pm Sat & Sun May-Oct, 8am-4pm Mon-Fri, 10am-4pm Sat Nov-Apr) can provide a free booklet titled *Karol Wojtyła's Foot Trail,* which marks out the most important pope-related sights in town.

❶ Getting There & Away

Regular buses go to Kraków (11zł, 1¼ hours), Kalwaria Zebrzydowska (4zł, 25 minutes) and Katowice (19zł, 1¾ hours).

Trains also run regularly to Kraków (15zł, 1¾ hours) and Kalwaria Zebrzydowska (6.50zł, 22 minutes).

Tarnów

POP 114,053

Though you probably wouldn't guess it while strolling about its beautifully preserved Old Town, Tarnów (*tar*-noof) is an important regional industrial centre and transport hub. Of far more interest to travellers are its 16th-century streets, lined with tenements and radiating out from a handsome market square dominated by an impressive Gothic red-brick town hall dating to the 15th century. Add fine churches, a few museums, good food and the traces of a vibrant pre-WWII Jewish population, and you have a thoroughly appealing stopover.

History

The town layout – an oval centre with a large square in its middle – is unusual, suggesting the town was planned in medieval times. Tarnów is indeed an old city: it was already centuries old when its municipal privileges were granted in 1330. Developing as a trade centre on the busy Kraków–Kyiv route, the town enjoyed good times during the Polish Golden Age of the 15th and 16th centuries. But fires and other catastrophes then drove Tarnów into decline for almost 200 years.

Jewish life in Tarnów stretches back to the 15th century. By the 19th century, Jews accounted for half the city's population, but of the 25,000 living here in 1939, only a handful survived WWII. To remind itself and others of its past, Tarnów uses a stylised yellow Star of David in its tourist office logo.

The city is also one of the major centres for Poland's small Roma population and the museum here has one of Europe's few exhibitions of Roma history. The museum includes a small section on the Roma Holocaust, in which hundreds of Roma from around the Tarnów region were rounded up by the Germans and killed.

◎ Sights

Town Hall MUSEUM
(Muzeum Okręgowe w Tarnowie/Ratusz; Map p204; ☑ 14 621 2149; www.muzeum.tarnow.pl; Rynek 1; adult/concession 8/5zł, Sun free; ⊘ 9am-3pm Tue, Wed & Fri, to 5pm Thu, 10am-2pm Sun) Tarnów's arresting Gothic city hall, which draws all eyes in the Rynek, dates in its earliest parts to the 15th century. Given a later Renaissance makeover and renovated again in the 19th century, it retains its

CARPATHIAN MOUNTAINS TARNÓW

Tarnów

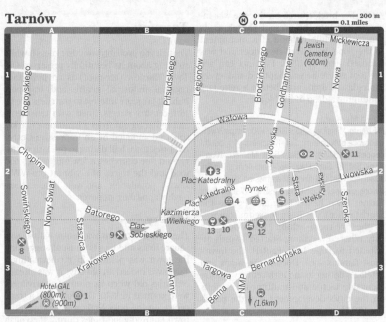

Tarnów

◉ Sights
1	Ethnographic Museum	A3
2	Former Synagogue	D2
3	Tarnów Cathedral	C2
4	Tarnów Regional Museum	C2
5	Town Hall	C2

⬢ Sleeping
6	Euro Hotel U Jana	C2
7	Tourist Information Centre	C3

⊗ Eating
8	Bar Mleczny Łasuch	A3
9	Kawiarnia Tatrzańska	B3
10	Pół na Pół	C3
11	The Nosh	D2

◯ Drinking & Nightlife
12	Alert Pub	C3
13	Pub Śródmieście	C3

ⓘ Information
	Tourist Information Centre	(see 7)

16th-century clock, one of Poland's oldest working examples. The hall holds a branch of the regional museum, where you can admire the grand interiors and extensive holdings of silver, art and glass once enjoyed by the town's ruling family.

Ethnographic Museum　　　MUSEUM
(Muzeum Etnograficzne; Map p204; ☏14 622 0625; www.muzeum.tarnow.pl; ul Krakowska 10; adult/concession 8/5zł, Sun free; ◔9am-5pm Tue, Wed & Fri, 10am-4pm Sun May-Sep, 9am-3pm Tue, Wed & Fri, 10am-2pm Sun Oct-Apr) This branch of the city's regional museum has Europe's only permanent collection relating to Roma culture. In the backyard there's an open-air exhibition of original Roma horse

carriages, and visitors to the museum can, on request, take part in a traditional fire ring with dancing. Exploring plenty of other regional cultures, the museum is housed in an 18th-century manor, featuring a double-floored granary and exterior walls with floral motifs from Zalipie.

Tarnów Cathedral　　　CATHEDRAL
(Bazylika katedralna pw Narodzenia Najświętszej Maryi Panny; Map p204; ☏14 621 4501; www.katedra.tarnow.opoka.org.pl; Plac Katedralny; ◔10am-noon & 5-6pm Mon-Fri, 10am-noon Sat) Tarnów's cathedral dates in part from the 14th century, but was remodelled at the end of the 19th century in neo-Gothic style. The interior shelters several Renaissance and

DON'T MISS

PAINTED HOUSES OF ZALIPIE

The village of Zalipie, 30km northwest of Tarnów, has been known as a centre for folk painting for more than a century, ever since its inhabitants started to decorate the inside and outside of their houses with wildly colourful floral designs. Today more than 20 such houses can be seen in Zalipie, with another dozen or so in the neighbouring villages of Kuzie, Niwka and Kłyż.

The best-known painter was Felicja Curyłowa (1904–74), and since her death her three-room farmhouse has been opened to the public as the **Felicja Curyłowa Farmstead Museum** (Muzeum Zagroda Felicji Curyłowej; %14 641 1912; www.muzeum. tarnow.pl; Zalipie 135, Olesno; adult/concession 8/5zł; h 8am-4pm Tue, Wed & Fri, 9am-5pm Sat & Sun). Every flat surface is painted with colourful flowers, and on display are painted dishes, icons and costumes. In order to help maintain the tradition, the **Painted Cottage** (Malowana Chata) contest for the best-decorated house has been held annually since 1948, during the weekend following Corpus Christi (late May or June). At the **House of Painters** (Dom Malarek; %14 641 1938; www.dommalarek.pl; Zalipie 12a; h 8am-6pm Mon-Fri, 11am-6pm Sat & Sun Jun-Aug, 8am-4pm Mon-Fri Sep-May; p), which serves as a centre for the village's artists, you can watch the painters at work.

You'll need your own wheels to get to Zalipie, a relaxed 40-minute drive from Tarnów.

---

baroque tombs, of which two in the chancel are among the largest in the country. Also of interest are the 15th-century oak stalls under the choir loft, a pair of ornately carved pulpits facing one another and two early 16th-century stone portals at the western and southern porches.

Tarnów Regional Museum   MUSEUM
(Muzeum Okręgowe w Tarnowie; Map p204; %14 621 2149; www.muzeum.tarnow.pl; Rynek 3; adult/concession 8/5zł, Sun free; h 9am-3pm Tue-Fri, 10am-2pm Sun) Two 16th-century townhouses on the central square comprise the main regional museum, largely used for rotating exhibitions. The main part of the small permanent exhibition is the ongoing restoration work of a giant panorama painting of the 1849 Battle of Sibiu in which local hero General Józef Bem (1791–1850) led a Hungarian insurrection against the combined forces of Austria and tsarist Russia. The museum is receiving renovations, which are due for completion at the end of 2019.

Former Synagogue   HISTORIC SITE
(Map p204; ul Żydowska 12) The Nazis' almost-complete destruction of Tarnów's synagogue, once the focus of spiritual life for the 25,000 Jews who lived here, is only more affecting for the incongruous survival of the four-columned brick *bimah* under which the Torah was read during services. It's now protected from further damage, and you can see the footings of the ill-fated building, alongside exhibitions celebrating Tarnów's Jewish community and lamenting its destruction.

Jewish Cemetery   CEMETERY
(Cmentarz Żydowski-Kirkut; ul Szpitalna) This former Jewish burial ground, the largest of its kind in southern Poland, lies 1km north of the centre. The cemetery dates from the 16th century and has about 4000 tombstones in various states of decay and disarray. It was ravaged by the Germans during WWII and the cemetery served as a place of mass slaughter in 1942 and 1943. The gates are often open; if not, ask for the key at the tourist information centre.

Sleeping

Tourist Information Centre   ACCOMMODATION SERVICES €
(Map p204; %14 688 9090; www.it.tarnow.pl; Rynek 7; s/d from 80/99zł; %) Tarnów's tourist information centre offers one of the best sleeping deals in town, letting out rooms above its office on the Rynek. Don't expect luxury: this is as basic as it gets – just a bed and bath. But you can't beat it for value. No breakfast, but several cafes are nearby. Call or email to reserve a room.

★ Hotel GAL   HOTEL €€
(%14 630 0350; www.hotel.tarnovia.pl; ul Dworcowa 5; s/d/tr 176/221/338zł; P @ %) Every Polish city should be so lucky to have a hotel this appealing so close to transport connections. The 1904 art nouveau building got a total makeover in 2014, leaving the large, light and airy rooms looking resplendent in contemporary style. There's free parking on site, the staff are friendly and the restaurant's good too (mains 28zł to 38zł).

CARPATHIAN MOUNTAINS TARNÓW

Euro Hotel U Jana
HOTEL €€

(Map p204; ☑14 626 0564; www.hotelujana.pl; Rynek 14; d/ste from 140/150zł; P❄🕸) This 13th-century hotel is not only classy, but is conveniently located right on the Rynek. The apartments have interesting artwork on the walls, the beds are huge and the bathrooms up to date. The very decent attached restaurant spills out onto the Rynek should the weather permit al fresco eating (or drinking). Nearby parking is 10zł per day.

✕ Eating & Drinking

The Nosh
JEWISH €

(Map p204; ☑600 590 714; http://thenosh koshercafe.com; Lwowska 2; mains 12-15zł; ☺8.30am-7pm Mon-Thu, to 5pm Fri, 10am-7pm Sun; 🕸) The Nosh is the first kosher cafe to open in Tarnów for 70 years, since the murder of the town's 25,000 Jewish citizens. Increasing interest in the homelands of European Jewry has seen more Jews return, some to stay. This wonderful little cafe, offering excellent coffee and cake, falafel, bagels with lox, salad and more is a landmark in this development.

Bar Mleczny Łasuch
POLISH €

(Map p204; ☑14 627 7123; ul Sowińskiego 4; mains 7-10zł; ☺8.30am-6.30pm Mon-Fri, 9am-3pm Sat) This place is a glorious throwback, with its orangey palette, well-preserved formica tables, spotless tile floor and general sense that nothing's changed since well before the fall of Communism. The food – Polish, with no frills and definitely no surprises – is really quite good, and is exceptional value.

★ Pół na Pół
POLISH €€

(Map p204; ☑14 627 8278; https://polnapol-tarnow.pl; Plac Wielkiego 2; mains 30-34zł; ☺noon-10pm Mon-Thu, to 11pm Fri-Sun; 🕸🅿) 'Half and Half' is something new in Tarnów: a modern, idiosyncratic, food-focused restaurant that takes forays into innovation without ever abandoning Polish roots or discarding deep cultural knowledge of how to treat the region's produce. Run by two sisters whose personalities are firmly implanted on the place, it's whimsical, sophisticated and even welcomes kids (with fairy floss!)

Kawiarnia Tatrzańska
POLISH €€

(Map p204; ☑14 622 4636; www.kudelski.pl; ul Krakowska 1; mains 27-35zł; ☺9am-10pm; 🕸) A stalwart of Tarnów's dining scene, this atmospherically old-school restaurant-cafe doesn't aim to pull any surprises, offering żurek (traditional sour rye soup), pierogi and the rest. There's a little novelty to be found however, such as the Zakopane-style pickled pork loin with grilled sheep's cheese. The attached 19th-century cafe makes a great stop for coffee, cake or ice cream.

Pub Śródmieście
PUB

(Map p204; ☑600 745 057; www.srodmiescie pub.pl; Plac Wielkiego 2; ☺11am-midnight; 🕸) The passage through the large building at the Rynek's west end leads to this colourful, cute and very welcoming tavern. Not quite sure if it's a cafe, pub or restaurant, it simply fulfils all three roles, with a mix of tables and chairs for different social configurations, a full bar and drinking food of the burger/wrap/quesadilla variety (15zł to 22zł).

Alert Pub
BAR

(Map p204; ☑14 676 0614; Rynek 9; ☺10am-midnight; 🕸) Set in beautifully decorated cellars, this studenty place offers plenty of drinks, a few budget dishes and dance music on some weekends. In summer it has tables on the Rynek.

ℹ Information

Tourist Information Centre (Map p204; ☑14 688 9090; www.it.tarnow.pl; Rynek 7; ☺8am-8pm Mon-Fri May-Oct, to 6pm Nov-Apr, 9am-5pm Sat & Sun year-round; 🕸) One of the best in the country, with super-friendly staff helping you to a wealth of useful brochures, and offering free internet access, wi-fi, bike rental (20zł per day) and low-cost accommodation above the office.

ℹ Getting There & Away

Unlike many train stations in Poland, Tarnów's **station** (Plac Dworcowy 1) is worth seeking out in its own right. The grand art nouveau structure was completed in 1910 and lovingly restored in 2010. It's located next to the bus terminal, 1.5km southwest of the Rynek. There are regular trains to Kraków (16zł, 1¼ hours), Rzeszów (17zł, 1¼ hours), Nowy Sącz (19zł, two hours) and Warsaw (67zł, four to five hours).

The **bus station** (PKS; ☑14 688 0755; www. pkstarnow.pl; ul Braci Saków 5; ☺info desk 8am-4pm Mon-Fri) offers regular connections to Kraków (12zł, 1½ hours), Rzeszów (16zł, 1¼ hours), Nowy Sącz (15zł, 1¼ hours) and Sanok (38zł, three hours).

Rzeszów

POP 179,952

The chief administrative and industrial centre of southeastern Poland, Rzeszów is a surprisingly elegant, medium-sized city boasting some fine museums and historic sights, and dining and drinking scenes enlivened by a large student population. Altogether it's a highly recommended sojourn if you're looking for some more urbanised fun to balance out your treks in the mountains. It's also a transport hub, meaning you're likely to pass through in any event.

Rzeszów started life in the 13th century as a remote Ruthenian settlement. Granted town rights by Casimir III in the mid-14th century, it grew rapidly in the 16th century when Mikołaj Spytek Ligęza, the local ruler, commissioned a church and a fortified castle. It later fell into the hands of the powerful Lubomirski clan, but this couldn't save the town from subsequent decline.

◉ Sights

Rzeszów's main square provides a grand and gregarious focal point to the town, and is lined with some lovely art nouveau townhouses. In the centre is a monument to Tadeusz Kościuszko, honoured by Poles and Americans alike. In the southwest corner, the 16th-century **town hall** (Map p208; Rynek 1) was wholly remodelled in neo-Gothic style in the 19th century.

★ **Underground Tourist Route**   TUNNEL
(Podziemna Trasa Turystyczna; Map p208; ☑ reservations 17 875 4774; www.trasa-podziemna.erzeszow. pl; Rynek 26; adult/concession 6.50/4.50zł; ⊙ 10am-7pm Tue-Fri, 11am-6pm Sat & Sat May-Sep, shorter hours rest of year; ⓘ) Rzeszów's prime attraction is this 396m-long route linking 25 old cellars beneath the central market square. The circuit took 17 years to complete and restore. The cellars date from the 14th to 18th centuries and reach depth of up to 10m. The 45-minute guided tours illuminate some of Rzeszów's history through the artefacts displayed, all found down here. Three English-language tours depart daily through the week (11.50am, 2.50pm and 4.50pm), with two on weekends (12.50pm and 2.50pm).

Rzeszów City Museum   MUSEUM
(Muzeum Historii Miasta Rzeszowa; Map p208; ☑ 17 875 4198; Rynek 12; adult/concession 5/4zł, permanent exhibits free Sun; ⊙ 8.3am-3.30pm Mon-Wed, to 5.30pm Fri, 10am-6pm first Sun of month) Six centuries of Rzeszów's life, triumphs and tribulations are revealed through the interesting exhibits of this worthwhile city museum, housed in a 17th-century tenement.

Rzeszów Regional Museum   MUSEUM
(Muzeum Okręgowe w Rzeszowie; Map p208; ☑ 17 853 6083; www.muzeum.rzeszow.pl; ul 3 Maja 19; adult/concession 10/8zł; ⊙ 8.30am-3.30pm Tue, Wed & Fri, to 5.30pm Thu, 10am-6pm Sun) Housed in a one-time Piarist monastery, complete with frescoed vaulting from the 17th century, the Rzeszów Regional Museum contains Polish paintings from the 18th to 20th centuries, wider European art from the 16th to 19th centuries, and displays on the archaeology underlying this time-worn city, from prehistoric times to today.

RZESZÓW'S JEWISH HERITAGE

As a regional hub, Rzeszów was for centuries home to a large number of Jews. At the outbreak of WWII, the Jewish population numbered around 18,000 – about one-third of the city's total. Following Rzeszów's 1939 seizure by the Nazis (who renamed it 'Reichshof'), persecution of the community began. Most were sent to the extermination camp at Bełżec in 1942, where they were murdered.

Not much trace of this once-vibrant community remains, with the exception of two impressive synagogues, northeast of the Rynek. The 18th-century **New Town Synagogue** (Synagoga Nowomiejska; Map p208; ul Sobieskiego 17) dates originally from the early 18th century and was built in a fusion of Renaissance and baroque styles. It was used by the Germans as a warehouse during WWII, fell into ruin after the war, and now houses a contemporary art gallery. Note the gate on the 1st floor – made of wrought iron and clay, it's the work of the contemporary sculptor Marian Kruczek.

The 17th-century **Old Town Synagogue** (Synagoga Staromiejska; Map p208; ul Bożnicza 4) is the smaller and older of the two. Built in Renaissance style, it was partly destroyed by the Nazis and now holds the city's archives. It's closed to the general public.

Rzeszów

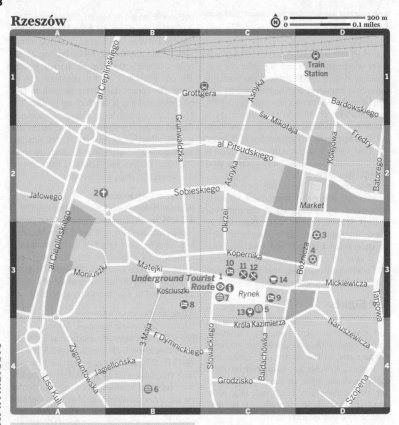

Rzeszów

Bernardine Church   CHURCH

(Kościół Bernardynów; Map p208; ul Sobieskiego)
Northwest of the Rynek is the Bernardine
Church, with its opulent furnishings and decoration. It was built for Ligęza as his mausoleum, and there are eight life-sized alabaster
effigies of his family in the side walls of the
chancel. In the gilded chapel to the right is an
early 16th-century statue of the Virgin Mary
to which numerous miracles have been attributed – wall paintings on both sides dating
from the 17th and 18th centuries show 100
people who were cured.

🛏 Sleeping

Rzeszów offers some quality budget hotels,
as befits a student town, with further options in higher brackets of luxury.

PTSM Alko Youth Hostel   HOSTEL €

(Schronisko Młodzieżowe PTSM Alko; Map p208;
☑ 17 853 4430; www.ptsm-alko.pl; Rynek 25; dm/
s/d/tr from 40/60/120/150zł; 🛜) Calling any

ŁAŃCUT: HOW THE OTHER HALF LIVED

Just 24km east of Rzeszów, Łańcut (wine-tsoot) has Poland's largest and richest aristocratic home. The building started life in the 15th century, and assumed its current magnificence in the 17th century. Just after WWII the 300-room castle was taken over by the state and opened as the **Castle Museum** (Muzeum Zamek; ☑17 225 2008; www.zamek-lancut.pl; ul Zamkowa 1; adult/concession incl entry to castle, stables & coach house with audio guide 35/27zł, castle only 28/23zł; ⊙11.45am-3pm Mon-Fri, 9.45am-5pm Sat & Sun Jun-Aug, shorter hours rest of year). The town also has a fine synagogue, and a few hotels and restaurants, if you want to linger.

In 1641 Prince Stanisław Lubomirski turned Łańcut's 15th-century fortified manor house into the grand fortress and residence that stands today. Now a museum, it's accessible by guided tour, or with personal audio guides. Among the highlights are the 17th-century Grand Hall, the Renaissance-style Eastern Corridor, the Great Vestibule, the Zodiac Room and the rococo Corner Room. The English-style park makes for delightful rambling, the restored Orchid House is blooming anew, and the stables house a collection of more than 1000 Orthodox icons.

Over the years, the residence has been reshaped and remodelled, gaining rococo and neoclassical elements. The final important alteration, at the end of the 19th century, gave the building its neo-baroque facades. The last private owner, Alfred Potocki, one of the richest men in pre-WWII Poland, accumulated a fabulous collection of art during his tenancy. Shortly before the arrival of the Red Army in July 1944, he loaded 11 railway carriages with the most valuable objects and fled with the collection to Liechtenstein. English-language guides for groups of up to 25 can be prearranged (160zł).

Just outside the park surrounding the castle is Łańcut's impressive **synagogue** (Plac Sobieskiego 16; admission 6zł; ⊙11am-4pm Mon-Fri, to 6pm Sat, 2-6pm Sun May-Aug, shorter hours rest of year), built in the 1760s to replace a 17th-century wooden original destroyed by fire. Saved from destruction during WWII by local grandees the Potocki family, who converted it into a granary, it's since been extensively restored and is one of the most beautiful and significant in the country. It has retained its splendid bimah and much of its original rococo decoration, and some liturgical items are on display.

hostel 'alko' seems to be inviting trouble, but this central, laid-back, 50-bed affair doesn't seem to attract undue merriment. There are no amenities to get excited about, aside from a communal kitchen, wardrobes, tables and basic beds in the rooms, but the Rynek location could hardly be better and the price is definitely right.

★ **Grand Hotel** BOUTIQUE HOTEL €€
(Map p208; ☑17 250 0000; www.grand-hotel.pl; ul Dymnickiego 1A; r standard/deluxe 230/325zł; P✳@🛜🏊) All we can say is 'wow'. This boutique hotel, a block from the Rynek, is one of the nicest we've seen in this part of Poland. Throw pillows in trendy earth tones adorn deep, comfortable beds and sofas, while the individually styled rooms could be straight out of an exuberant edition of *Wallpaper* magazine. Rates drop 10% on weekends.

Hotel Ambasadorski Rzeszów HOTEL €€
(Map p208; ☑17 250 2444; www.ambasadorski.com; Rynek 13/14; s/d 250/270zł; P✳🛜) This smart four-star hotel occupies a beautifully renovated 17th-century townhouse at the back of the Rynek. The modern rooms don't match the exterior's aesthetic appeal, but are plush, comfortable and acceptably quiet. There's a superior restaurant serving steaks, burgers and Polish favourites, and an adjoining coffee shop, Cukiernia Wiedeńska, that offers very good ice cream and cake confections.

✖ Eating & Drinking

Stary Browar Rzeszowski INTERNATIONAL €€
(Map p208; ☑17 250 0015; www.browar-rzeszow.pl; Rynek 23; mains 25-49zł; ⊙noon-11.30pm Sun-Thu, to 2am Fri & Sat; 🛜) This big, handsome brewpub on the main square serves oversized plates of steak, ribs and grilled meats, plus (as a nod to Poland) house-made pierogi and an enormous *golonka* (oven-baked pork knuckle) on a bed of coleslaw with a side of mashed potatoes. Dine on the Rynek when the weather permits, or find a warm niche inside.

★ **Kuchina Folk Lokalna** POLISH €€€
(Map p208; ☑ 17 250 0012; www.bristol-rzeszow.pl; Rynek 20-23; mains 52-59zł; ☺ 6.30am-11pm, with breaks between meals; ☏) The gorgeously designed, riotously colourful Folk is Rzeszów's destination diner. Taking Polish and European standards and top-notch ingredients, and allowing their imaginations just enough freedom to retain the origins of the dishes, the folks in the kitchen keep you on your toes. Expect oddities such as goose stomach with curry and broth, or venison saddle with peas, porcini and barley.

★ **Graciarnia u Plastików** BAR
(Map p208; ☑ 17 862 5647; www.graty.itl.pl; Rynek 10; ☺ 10am-2am Sun-Thu, to 4am Fri & Sat; ☏) It's not surprising this student bar just off the Rynek retains an arty vibe – sculptors, painters and other members of the Artistic Arts Workshop have been creating and kicking back here for 30 years, with their work augmenting the place's easy bohemian feel. Walk down a flight of steep stairs to find thrift-shop furnishings, sculptures, caricatures and a very laid-back vibe.

Bands, DJs, literary evenings and vernissage previews of exhibitions are commonly scheduled here.

Hola Lola CAFE
(Map p208; ☑ 730 119 180; ul Mickiewicza 3; ☺ 9am-11pm Mon-Thu, to 1am Fri, 10am-1am Sat, noon-11pm Sun; ☏) Industrial-yet-playful decor, big collaborative tables, expertly drawn coffees, strong wi-fi, plenty of laptop space and niches for getting deep and personal – no wonder Rzeszów's hipsters and students flock to this cafe/pub. In addition to very good coffee, there are lots of beers and lemonades to choose from, plus healthy-looking sandwiches, panini and salads.

ⓘ Information

Tourist Information Centre (Map p208; ☑ 17 875 4774; www.podkarpackie.travel; Rynek 26; ☺ 10am-7pm Tue-Fri, 11am-6pm Sat & Sun May-Sep, 10am-6pm Tue-Fri, 11am-5pm Sat & Sun Oct-Apr; ☏) Well resourced and located at the entrance to the Underground Tourist Route.

ⓘ Getting There & Away

Rzeszów International Airport is at Jasionka, 10km north of the city. Public buses ferry passengers from the terminal to the centre of town (3.60zł). Taxis cost about 60zł. Regular scheduled flights reach Tel Aviv, Warsaw, Newark and Munich.

The **bus station** (PKS; Map p208; ☑ information 17 852 3435; ul Grottgera) is about 500m north of the Rynek. Buses depart regularly for Tarnów (16zł, 1¼ hours), Sanok (15zł, two hours), Krosno (14zł, 1½ hours), Przemyśl (11zł, 1½ to two hours), Ustrzyki Dolne (21zł, three hours) and Ustrzyki Górne (31zł, 4¼ hours). Buses to Łańcut (3zł, 27 minutes) run frequently and are more convenient than trains, as they stop near the palace.

The **train station** (ul Grottgera) is north of the centre, about 100m east of the bus station. Trains depart regularly for Przemyśl (19zł, 1¼ to 1½ hours), Tarnów (17zł, 1¼ hours), Kraków (26zł, 1¾ to 2½ hours) and Warsaw (72zł, 5¼ hours).

Przemyśl

POP 65,000

Founded as far back as the 8th century, Przemyśl (*psheh*-mishl) has a long and varied history in which prosperity and peace has alternated with violence and decline. Thanks to its command of trade and strategic channels across Eastern Europe, it's been the prize of many a ruthless power. While not exactly on the tourist circuit, Przemyśl offers a grand market square, some beautiful churches and some worthwhile museums to explore.

History

Commanding terrain long fought over by Poland and Ruthenia (today's Ukraine) and entering the historical record in the 10th century, Przemyśl changed hands several times before being annexed by the Polish crown in 1340. It experienced its golden period as a centre of commerce and religion during the Renaissance, but afterwards fell into a decline cause by war and upheaval in the 17th century. During the Partitions of the late 18th century, it fell under Austrian administration.

Around 1850 the Austrians began to fortify Przemyśl. This work continued until the outbreak of WWI and resulted in one of the largest fortresses in Europe. It consisted of a double ring of earth ramparts, including a 15km-long inner circle and an outer girdle three times longer, with more than 60 forts placed at strategic points.

This formidable system played an important role in the early months of WWI and saw intense fighting between the Austro-Hungarian empire and tsarist Russia. The Austrian garrison eventually surrendered to

PRZEMYŚL'S JEWISH HERITAGE

Przemyśl was an important centre of Jewish life for centuries leading up to WWII. At the outbreak of the war, the Jewish community numbered around 24,000, or one-third of the city's population. The initial situation for Przemyśl's Jews during WWII was different from that in other Polish cities, owing to its easterly position. For the first two years of the war (when Germany and the Soviet Union were allies and had carved up Poland between them), the frontier (in this area, the San River) ran straight down the middle of Przemyśl. Most Jews found themselves in the Soviet occupation zone and were comparatively better off than their brethren in the Nazi-occupied areas (although some 7000 were deported to the Soviet Union). The situation deteriorated in 1941 after the Germans attacked the Soviet Union, occupied the entire town and began persecuting the Jews of Przemyśl and its surrounding areas in earnest. Most were eventually sent to their deaths at the German-run Bełżec extermination camp near Lublin in 1942.

The only significant remaining relics of the Jewish legacy are two synagogues (of four that existed before WWII), both dating from the end of the 19th century. The most important surviving synagogue is behind the building at ul Słowackiego 13, east of the Rynek. It functioned as a branch of the public library until 2015, but now stands vacant. The former Jewish cemetery (Cmentarz Żydowski; ⊙ 8am-6pm) FREE can also be visited – it's at the southern end of ul Słowackiego.

the Russians in 1915 due to a lack of provisions.

Przemyśl had the bad luck to end up in the crosshairs in WWII as well. The town marked the border between Nazi Germany and Stalin's Russia from 1939 to 1941, when the two countries were allied. The actual border followed the San River, meaning Przemyśl's southern half went to Russia and the northern half to Germany. After the Germans attacked the Russians in 1941, Przemyśl endured weeks of heavy shelling and fighting before eventually falling to the Germans.

⊙ Sights

Perched on a hillside and dominated by several mighty churches, Przemyśl's Old Town is a picturesque place. The sloping Rynek has preserved some of its old arcaded houses, mostly on its north and south sides. Many houses bear plaques in English giving the history of the place. Look especially at Nos 16 and 17. The former sports a beautifully restored Mannerist facade, while the latter boasts a surviving Renaissance portal from 1560.

Przemyśl Cathedral CATHEDRAL

(☑ 16 678 2766; www.katedra-przemysl.pl; ul Zamkowa 3; church & crypts by donation, tower free; ⊙ church 8am-6pm, crypts 9am-4pm Tue-Sun, tower 8.30am-4.30 Tue-Sat) Przemyśl's cathedral lords over the upper (southern) end of the Rynek. There's been a church

here since at least the 12th century, but the current manifestation began its life in 1495. The interior is impressive enough, but be sure to visit the crypts for a fascinating exhibit on burial customs, and the exposed wall of the original 12th-century rotunda. You can also climb the 71m-high freestanding bell tower, though the top windows are closed.

Franciscan Church
of St Mary Magdalene CHURCH

(Kościół Franciszkański Św Marii Magdaleny; ☑ 16 678 2460; www.przemysl.franciszkanie.pl; ul Franciszkańska 2a; ⊙ 8am-6pm) This beautifully evocative church, with its enormous pillars dwarfing the three baroque statues at the front, was built between 1754 and 1778 in late-baroque and classical style. The church has a beautiful rococo interior with a vaulted and frescoed nave.

Museum of the History
of the City of Przemyśl MUSEUM

(Muzeum Historii Miasta Przemyśla; ☑ 16 678 6501; http://mnzp.pl; Rynek 9; adult/child 10/5zł, free Wed; ⊙ 9am-4pm Tue-Sat, from noon Sun) Rynek 9, a dignified early 16th-century tenement house on Przemyśl's market square, is the venue for this intriguing and well-curated museum of the city's history. Exhibitions trace both the turbulent and settled periods of the city's past, extending into 16th-century cellars and rooms of the similarly venerable tenement behind, at Serbańska 7.

CARPATHIAN MOUNTAINS PRZEMYŚL

FAIRYTALE CASTLE OF KRASICZYN

The late-Renaissance **castle** (☑16 671 8312; www.krasiczyn.com.pl; Krasiczyn 179; adult/concession incl guided tour 12/8zł, park only 4/2zł; ⊙9am-5pm) in the village of Krasiczyn (krah-*shee*-chin), about 11km southwest of Przemyśl, seems right out of a fairy tale. Despite its heft, it's more of a stately home than a stronghold – ostentation trumped defensive strength when Italian architect Galeazzo Appiani built it between 1592 and 1618 for the wealthy Krasicki family. With its whitewashed walls, turreted towers and spacious, arcaded courtyard, it remains wonderfully photogenic. You can join Polish-language tours to see the interior (English-language tours cost 150zł for groups of at least five, and must be booked a day in advance), or just stroll the lovely English-style park outside.

The design of the towers was a conscious reflection of the social order at the time. The towers were named (clockwise from the southeastern corner) after God, the pope, the king and the nobility. The God Tower (Baszta Boska), topped with a dome, houses a chapel. The King Tower (Baszta Królewska), with its conical roof and little turrets, would make a lovely home for Rapunzel of long-haired fame. On the courtyard side of the castle walls are Renaissance graffiti decorations of Biblical scenes and Polish nobility.

There's a **hotel** (☑16 671 8321; www.krasiczyn.com.pl; Krasiczyn 179; s/d/tr/ste from 110/210/270/300zł; P 🛜) at the castle that offers several different types of rooms, ranging from relatively modest, good-value single and double rooms in the coach house to more opulent doubles and suites (250/500zł) in the castle itself. There's even a luxurious five-bed Hunter's Pavilion (600zł), which has its own kitchen and garden. Within the castle grounds is a decent **restaurant** (☑16 671 8321; www.krasiczyn.com.pl; Krasiczyn 179; mains 25-40zł; ⊙11am-10pm; P 🛜) that serves mostly Polish dishes in traditional surrounds.

The castle is an easy trip from Przemyśl (4.30zł, 25 minutes) on one of the frequent buses.

National Museum of Przemyśl
MUSEUM

(Muzeum Narodowe Ziemi Przemyskiej; ☑16 679 3000; http://mnzp.pl; Plac Joselewicza 1; adult/concession 10/5zł, free Thu; ⊙9am-4pm Tue-Sat, noon-4pm Sun) Przemyśl's impressive modern museum presents well-curated permanent exhibitions on the city's prehistoric and medieval times, its Jewish history and the story of Przemyśl Fortress in WWI (among other themes). Temporary exhibitions explore subjects such as the art of the Hutsul people of Ukraine and Poland, or the traumatic experience of the city during WWII.

🛏 Sleeping

Hotel Accademia
HOTEL €€

(☑412 654 222; www.hotelaccademia.pl; al 3 Maja 13; s/d/ste 150/190/290zł; P 🛜) The boxy, multi-storey Accademia is one of those modern hotels whose exterior suggests neglect, but which wins points for good value, a decent breakfast buffet and a good location by the San River, 10 minutes' walk from the Rynek. Many of the rooms have tranquil views over the river, but vary in states of presentation.

Hotel Europejski
HOTEL €€

(☑16 675 7100; www.hotel-europejski.pl; ul Sowiń skiego 4; s/d/tr 125/155/190zł; P 🛜) Housed in a renovated old building facing the attractive neoclassical train station (1895), this old-school but well-maintained place has 29 bright rooms with high ceilings and modern bathrooms. There's also a bar/restaurant.

🍴 Eating & Drinking

Bar Rubin
POLISH €

(☑16 678 2578; www.barrubin.pl; ul Kazimierza Wielkiego 19; mains 16-21zł; ⊙9am-8pm) This popular 1970s-style diner serves delicious traditional Polish food at reasonable prices. With its red laminate walls and chrome chairs, the interior has a pre-1989 milk-bar feel. One welcome touch, in summer, is air-conditioning. Walk east from the Rynek along pedestrianised ul Kazimierza Wielkiego and you'll find it.

★ Cuda Wianki
INTERNATIONAL €€

(☑533 090 999; Rynek 5; mains 31-38zł; ⊙11am-10pm Sun-Thu, to 11pm Fri & Sat; 🛜) Przemyśl's best restaurant aptly occupies a handsome, arched tenement on the main square. The warm interior of white brick walls, light woods and flowers on the table hint at a quality menu of inventive soups and salads, grilled seafood, creative meat courses and a liberal use of fresh herbs. Quality lunch specials, beers and teas also feature.

Dominikańska POLISH €€
(☑ 16 678 2075; www.dominikanska.com.pl; Plac Dominikańska 3; mains 28-40zł; ⊘ 10am-9pm; ⧉) You'll find excellent Polish cooking at this upscale restaurant on a small square on the western end of the Rynek. We're a big fan of the home-style *żurek* soup and the duck leg with cherries, dumplings and celery salad.

Rutyna BAR
(☑ 690 023 763; ul Serbańska 1; ⊘ 5pm-3am; ⧉) Well stocked with booze, bonhomie and boogying patrons, joyful little Rutyna is a great place for a cocktail, craft beer, or a dalliance with young locals. Themed parties and music are often part of the deal.

Kawiarnia Libera CAFE
(☑ 16 440 683; Rynek 26; ⊘ 10am-10m Mon-Thu, to 11pm Fri & Sat, 11am-9pm Sun; ⧉) This offbeat student cafe is connected to a bookstore of the same name on the northwestern side of the Rynek. Walk through a small metal gate to find what feels like a secret student meeting place inside, with eclectic furniture, lavish cakes and a stripped-back aesthetic.

🛍 Shopping

★ **Domowa**
Piekarnia & Spiżarnia FOOD
(Rynek 6; ⊘ 6am-8pm Mon-Fri, 9am-2pm Sat, 4-8pm Sun) Dedication to Polish bread-craft comes no more sincere than at this little wooden-shuttered bakery under an arcade on the Rynek. Antique equipment, wood-fired ovens, basic ingredients and awesome know-how produce breads, *rachuchy* (crisp yeast-battered apple pancakes), *babka,* biscuits and other sweetmeats possibly better than any you've ever tasted.

ℹ Information

Przemyśl's tiny **tourist information office** (☑ 16 675 2163; www.visit.przemysl.pl; ul Grodzka 1; ⊘ 9am-5pm Mon-Fri, 10am-6pm Sat & Sun Apr-Oct, 9am-5pm Mon-Fri, 10am-2pm Sat Nov-Mar; ⧉) is located just above the Rynek, on the southern side of the square. It has free maps, useful brochures in English and a computer on hand to check email.

ℹ Getting There & Away

The train and bus stations are next to each other on the northeastern edge of the town centre, about 600m from the Rynek.

Regular buses depart for Sanok (16zł, 1¾ hours), Ustrzyki Dolne (15zł, two hours), Rzeszów (11zł, 1½ to two hours) and Krasiczyn (4.30zł, 25 minutes).

Regular trains run to Rzeszów (22zł, 1¼ hours), Kraków (45zł, 3¼ hours) and Warsaw (73zł, 6½ to 7¼ hours).

BIESZCZADY

Part of the Outer Eastern Carpathians, the Bieszczady (byesh-*chah*-di) range in far southeastern Poland extends into Slovakia and Ukraine. Scantily populated and graced by thick woods and open meadows, it's one of the most attractive areas of the country. As tourist facilities are modest, roads sparse and public transport limited, the region has retained its relative isolation and is a wonderful off-the-beaten-track destination, popular with nature lovers and hikers.

The range's eastern end, the highest and most spectacular part, has been decreed the Bieszczady National Park (Bieszczadzki Park Narodowy), with its headquarters in Ustrzyki Górne. At 292 sq km, it's Poland's third-largest national park after Biebrza and Kampinos. Its highest peak is Mt Tarnica (1346m).

Sanok

POP 39,511
Sanok, nestled in a picturesque valley in the Bieszczady Foothills, is the largest city in the region and a logical base for starting your exploration of the Bieszczady. Settled since at least the 10th century, it has been subjected to Ruthenian, Hungarian, Austrian, Russian, German and Polish rule in its eventful history. Sitting on a prominence above the San River, it was here that the uneasy border between Nazi Germany and Soviet Russia ran, following their pre-WWII carve up of Poland and before they inevitably came to blows. Though it contains an important industrial zone, its elevated historical centre hasn't been spoiled, and offers an attractive town square and a clutch of worthy sights. Sanok is also the springboard for several fascinating thematic hiking trails, including the Icon Trail that takes in the surrounding countryside's wealth of wooden churches.

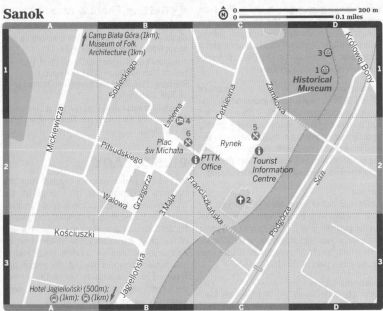

Sanok

⊙ Sights

★**Museum of Folk Architecture**   MUSEUM
(Muzeum Budownictwa Ludowego w Sanoku; ☎13 493 0177; www.skansen.mblsanok.pl; ul Rybickiego 3; adult/concession 17/12zł, free Tue; ⊗8am-6pm May-Sep, 8am-4pm Oct, 9am-2pm Nov-Mar, 9am-4pm Apr; 🚼) Sanok's Museum of Folk Architecture is Poland's largest skansen (open-air museum of traditional architecture). You'll find around 120 historic buildings here and gain insight into the cultures of the Boyks and Lemks (p217). Among the highlights are four timber churches (especially the 1667 St Nicholas's), an early 18th-century synagogue, an inn, a school and even a fire station. It's over the San River from the main town.

★**Historical Museum**   MUSEUM
(Muzeum Historyczne; Map p214; ☎13 463 0609; www.muzeum.sanok.pl; ul Zamkowa 2; adult/concession 17/13zł; ⊗8am-noon Mon, 9am-5pm Tue-Sun Apr-Oct, 8am-noon Mon, 9am-5pm Tue & Wed, 9am-3pm Thu-Sun Nov-Mar) Housed in the Renaissance-style castle, this museum is best known for its 700-piece collection of Ruthenian icons. The selection consists of about 260 large pieces dating from the 15th to the 18th centuries, most acquired after WWII from abandoned Uniat churches. The museum's other treasure is the collection of paintings by Zdzisław Beksiński (1929–2005) on the top floor. Beksiński, who was born in Sanok, was one of Poland's most remarkable contemporary painters, with a fantastical style all his own.

Sanok Castle   HISTORIC BUILDING
(Zamek; Map p214; ul Zamkowa 2) The 16th-century Renaissance-style fortress you see today is built over the foundations of a 14th-century Gothic castle that itself replaced the wooden original, destroyed by the Tatars in 1241. On a natural defensive strongpoint overlooking the San River, it's stout and handsome, and only partially spoiled

by the obviously new wing built to house the Historical Museum.

Franciscan Church of the Holy Cross CHURCH
(Kościół Franciszkanów Św Krzyża; Map p214; ☑13 463 2352; www.franciszkanie.esanok.pl; ul Franciszkanska 7; ☺8am-6pm) At the southeast corner of the Rynek is the Franciscan Church of the Holy Cross, the town's oldest. The interior and exterior are in baroque style and date to the mid-17th century, though recent archeological discoveries indicate 14th-century origins. The walls of the interior have a lacy, folksy feel, illuminated by the city's most famous piece of art: *The Miraculous Painting of the Virgin Mary in Consolation.*

Activities

Sanok is an excellent base for hiking and the starting point for several long-distance thematic hikes. The best known of these is the Icon Trail (Szlak Ikon), which takes you past tiny villages holding old Orthodox or Uniat churches. The most popular stretch is a 70km-long loop that begins and ends in Sanok and wends along the San River valley north of the city.

Another fascinating long-distance trail that passes through Sanok is sure to appeal to literature fans. The Švejk Trail, usually marked on maps in yellow, passes through town as it traces the comical journey across several countries of the 'Good Soldier Švejk'

in Czech writer Jaroslav Hašek's WWI novel of the same name.

Both trails, as well as several others, are designated on hiking maps of the Bieszczady available for purchase at the tourist information centre or the PTTK office. The tourist information centre also hands out a free photocopied, simplified trail map – not detailed enough to hike with, but showing the main villages and churches.

Sanok is also a good base for cycling – both mountain biking in the hills and less strenuous, though still rewarding rides along the San River. The better hiking maps usually also designate cycling trails, and the helpful staff at the tourist information centre can help plan out a ride. To get started buy a copy of the *Atlas Szlaków Rowerowych Podkarpackie* from the tourist office (50zł), which has all of the paths marked out.

Bicycles can be hired from **Camp Biała Góra** (☑13 463 2818; www.campsanok.pl; ul Rybickiego 1, Biała Góra; ℗) for 10/40zł per hour/day.

Sleeping & Eating

★**Hotel Sanvit** HOTEL €€
(Map p214; ☑13 465 5088; https://sanok.sanvit.pl; ul Łazienna 1; s/d/tr 140/195/240zł; ℗☎) Clean, reasonably priced and central, just west of the Rynek, the Sanvit is our top choice in Sanok. The 31 rooms are bright and modern, with shiny bathrooms. There's a restaurant and cafe, as well as a wellness centre with sauna, gym and a salt cave.

HIKING IN THE BIESZCZADY

The Bieszczady is one of the best places in Poland to go hiking. The region is beautiful and easy to walk around, and you don't need a tent or cooking equipment as mountain hostels are a day's walk apart and provide food. The main area for hiking is the national park, with Ustrzyki Górne and Wetlina being the most popular starting points, followed by Cisna.

Bieszczady National Park counts about a dozen well-marked hiking trails, with a total length of 130km. All three jumping-off points have PTTK hostels with helpful staff who can provide information, and all have boards outlining the trails, complete with walking times, both uphill and downhill. Ascending Mt Tarnica (the region's highest peak at 1346m) from Wołosate, southeast of Ustrzyki Górne, will take two to three hours. At least one of the trails reaches (but does not cross) the Ukrainian border at one point. Be sure to carry your passport when hiking in this area.

Mountain hostels will try their best to put you up for the night and feed you regardless of how crowded they get, but bear in mind that in July and August the floor will most likely be your bed, as these places are pretty small. Take a sleeping bag with you.

Get a copy of ExpressMap's laminated 1:65,000 *Bieszczady* map (20zł), which covers the entire region. You can buy it and similar maps at Hotel Górski in Ustrzyki Górne, or at tourist information offices in towns throughout the Bieszczady area.

Hotel Jagielloński
HOTEL €€

(☑ 13 463 1208; www.hoteljagiellonski.pl; ul Jagiellońska 49; s/d/tr 135/180/230zł; P 🛜) The 19-room Jagielloński, with distinctive wooden furniture, parquet floors, green-toned decor and a very good restaurant, represents decent value. Rooms are spacious, with full facilities, and the centre of town is less than 10 minutes' walk away.

Karczma Jadło Karpackie
POLISH €€

(Map p214; ☑ 13 464 6700; www.karczmasanok.pl; Rynek 12; mains 18-28zł; ⏱ 10am-10pm Apr-Oct, 11am-8pm Nov-Mar; 🛜) This amenable, folksy bar and restaurant on the main square serves up unusual Carpathian dishes, including *hreczanyki* (minced pork and buckwheat groats) and *ogórki małosolne* (lightly salted pickles). The interior is cluttered with threshes, harvest wreaths, cradles and other rural eclectica, or choose the terrace in nice weather.

★ Stary Kredens
POLISH €€€

(Map p214; ☑ 797 317 279; www.starykredens.com; Plac Świętego Michała 4; mains 34-47zł; ⏱ noon-10pm; 🛜) Sanok's best restaurant, the 'Old Sideboard' has high culinary ambitions, and it delivers. Imaginative starters such as turkey liver with caramelized onion, cherry liqueur and celery mousse, lead to more traditional treats. Wooden floors, lace tablecloths and antique furniture set the right tone.

❶ Getting There & Away

The train and bus stations are next to each other, connected by a pedestrian overpass, about 1.2km southeast of the Rynek.

There are regular buses to Rzeszów (15zł, two hours), Ustrzyki Dolne (8.50zł, one hour), Ustrzyki Górne (17zł, 2¼ hours), Cisna (13zł, 1½ hours), Wetlina (14zł, 1½ to two hours), Kraków (38zł, 4¼ hours) and Warsaw (64zł, seven to 7½ hours).

Trains are less frequent than buses, and run to Rzeszów (36zł, three hours) and Krosno (7.80zł, one hour).

Lesko

POP 5778

Founded in 1470 on the banks of the San River, Lesko had a mixed Polish-Ruthenian population for centuries, a reflection of the region's history. From the 16th century, many Jews arrived from Spain, fleeing the Inquisition. Their migration continued and by the 18th century Jews made up nearly two-thirds of the town's population.

WWII and the years that followed changed the ethnic picture altogether. The Jews were slaughtered by the Nazis, the Ukrainians were defeated by the Polish military and the Lemks were deported. The town was rebuilt and, without having developed any significant industry, is now a small tourist centre. While it may not be the 'Gateway to the Bieszczady' as it likes to call itself – that distinction really goes to Sanok – it is a pleasant stopover on the way south.

◉ Sights

Synagogue
SYNAGOGUE

(ul Joselewicza; adult/concession 4/2zł; ⏱ 10am-5pm May–mid-Oct) Lesko's impressive former synagogue is the only one of five to survive WWII. Built in the Mannerist style in the mid-17th century, it has an attached tower – evidence that it was once part of the town's fortifications. Little of the temple's original interior decoration has survived, and it now houses a seasonal art gallery, showcasing work from the Bieszczady.

Jewish Cemetery
CEMETERY

(Cmentarz Żydowski; ☑ 695 652 364; ul Moniuszki) Before WWII, Jews accounted for two-thirds of Lesko's population. This moving cemetery, dating back to the mid-16th century, has more than 2000 gravestones and gives a tiny hint of the size and importance of the community. To find the entrance, follow ul Moniuszki north (downhill) from the synagogue for 100m. The stairs on the right lead up to the cemetery. There are no set hours – call the telephone number listed and someone will come to let you in.

Parish Church of Our Lady
CHURCH

(Kościół Parafialny Najświętszej Marii Panny; ☑ 13 469 6533; www.lesko.przemyska.pl; ul Kościuszki 10; ⏱ 8am-6pm) Lesko's very pretty parish church, the oldest in Bieszczady, stands northwest of the centre of town. It was built in 1539 and its exterior still retains many Gothic features, including the eastern portal. The freestanding baroque bell tower was added in the mid-18th century.

🍴 Sleeping & Eating

There's nothing fancy, but you'll find a handful of options in central Lesko, most open throughout the year. As for eating, there's sadly not much choice.

BOYKS & LEMKS: A TALE OF TWO PEOPLES

The Bieszczady, along with the Beskid Niski and Beskid Sądecki further west, were settled from around the 13th century by various nomadic Slavic groups migrating northwards from the south and east. Most notable among them were the Wołosi from the Balkans and the Rusini from Ruthenia. Though they lived in the same areas and even intermarried for centuries, they maintained distinct ethnic identities, which came to be known as Bojkowie and Łemkowie.

The Bojkowie (Boyks) inhabited the eastern part of the Bieszczady, east of Cisna, while the Łemkowie (Lemks) populated the mountainous regions stretching from the western Bieszczady up to the Beskid Sądecki. The two groups had much in common culturally, including a shared Orthodox faith that was similar to that of their Ukrainian neighbours.

After the Union of Brest in 1596, in which some western Orthodox faiths broke with the Patriarch in Constantinople, most Lemks and Boyks turned to the Uniat Church, which accepted the supremacy of Rome but retained the old Eastern liturgy. This lasted until the end of the 19th century, when the Catholic Church began to impose the Latin rite. In response many Lemks and Boyks chose to revert to the more familiar traditions of the Orthodox Church. By WWII the total population of Lemks and Boyks was estimated at 200,000 to 300,000. Ethnic Poles were a minority.

The situation changed in the aftermath of WWII, when the borders of Poland and the Soviet Union were redrawn. Not everyone was satisfied with the new status quo, particularly a band of Ukrainian nationalists known as the Ukrainian Resistance Army, who were unhappy at finding themselves inside a newly reconstituted Poland. Civil war continued in the region for almost two years after Germany surrendered.

In a bid to rid the region of rebels, the postwar Polish government launched Operation Vistula (Akcja Wisła) in 1947 to expel the inhabitants of the region. Most residents were either deported to the Soviet Union or resettled in the western regions of Poland that had been recently regained from Germany. Ironically the largest groups to be deported were the Boyks and the Lemks, who had little to do with the conflict. Only 20,000 Lemks, and very few Boyks, were left in the region.

Today the most visible reminders of their legacy are the wooden Orthodox or Uniat churches dotting the countryside, many dilapidated but others still in decent condition. When hiking on remote trails, especially along the Ukrainian border in the Bieszczady, you'll find traces of destroyed villages, including ruined houses, orchards, churches and cemeteries.

Gościniec nad Sanem LODGE €
(☑ 604 790 070; https://gosciniecnadsanem.pl; ul Turystyczna 8; s/d 70/100zł; ⊘ May-Sep; 🅿 🛜) This woodsy, rustic lodge may be practically in central Lesko, but its river frontage, rough timber interior and 12 cosy en-suite rooms allow you to imagine yourself somewhere more remote. Hiking, fishing, sailing, horse riding and other lung-clearing pursuits are all on your doorstep.

Pensjonat Zamek HOTEL €
(☑ 13 469 6268; ul Piłsudskiego 7; s/d/apt from 80/130/220zł; 🅿 🛜) From the exterior, Lesko's ageing *zamek* (castle) looks none too inviting. Prospects change once you walk through the door to discover a well-run, atmospheric inn in which public areas retain some of the castle's 16th-century heritage.

The rooms themselves are unadorned, but comfortable.

ℹ Information

Tourist Office (☑ 13 469 6695; www.lesko.pl; Rynek 1; ⊘ 8am-4pm Mon-Fri) Helpful tourist office in a kiosk in the centre of the Rynek.

ℹ Getting There & Away

The bus station is on ul Piłsudskiego – the road to Sanok – about 1km northwest of the Rynek. There are regular buses to Sanok (5zł, 25 minutes), Krosno (14zł, 1¼ hours), Rzeszów (19zł, 2¼ to 2½ hours) and Kraków (50zł, 4½ hours).

For the Bieszczady, buses go to Cisna (9.50zł, one hour), Wetlina (12zł, 1½ hours), Ustrzyki Dolne (5.50zł, 40 minutes) and Ustrzyki Górne (15zł, two hours).

WHEN GOD WAS ON VACATION

Based on the number of day tours to Auschwitz-Birkenau on offer, especially out of Kraków, you would be forgiven for thinking the nightmare of the Holocaust, the time 'when God was on vacation' as some put it, was played out solely in the German-run extermination camps at Oświęcim in Silesia. But even a cursory trip around Galicia, the Austro-Hungarian province that was heavily Jewish and included many towns and cities in the south and east of modern-day Poland, will dispel that notion. As dozens of plaques, memorials and crude markers point out, hundreds of thousands of Polish Jews – in fact, a quarter of the three million annihilated – were murdered in their fields and forests at the hands of the Germans.

And the cemeteries... You may have wondered why they are so overgrown, their broken stones pitched this way and that. The answer is simple: there are no relatives left. Brothers, mothers, husbands, lovers, nephews and granddaughters – none survived the Holocaust.

When a Jew dies, a prayer, the Mourner's Kaddish, is recited for them. The kaddish is repeated at Yahrzeit, the first anniversary of the death, and annually after that. But virtually no Jews lying in cemeteries such as the one at Lesko have anyone to say this prayer for them.

Ustrzyki Dolne

POP 9635

While it has a museum and some nice trails and accommodation nearby, Ustrzyki Dolne (oost-*shi*-kee *dol*-neh) doesn't have much for travellers, and is only really worth a stop for those heading south into the Bieszczady. If you plan on hiking in the mountains independently, Ustrzyki Dolne is the last reliable place to exchange money and stock up on a decent range of provisions.

⊙ Sights & Activities

There are five colour-coded hiking trails that begin around the town centre, including the red-marked loop trail (4½ hours) that starts at the bus station and takes in some of the surrounding peaks. The trails, as well as some recommended cycling routes, can be found in the English-language *Town and Commune Guide*, available for 15zł at the tourist information office.

Natural History Museum MUSEUM
(Muzeum Przyrodnicze; ☑13 461 1091; www.bdpn.pl; ul Bełska 7; adult/concession 8/5zł; ⊙8am-4pm Tue-Sat mid-Nov–mid-Apr, 9am-5pm Tue-Sat mid-Apr–mid-Nov plus 9am-2pm Sun Jul & Aug) This modest museum, on a quiet street just a few metres north of the Rynek, is a good introduction to the geology, flora and fauna of the Bieszczady. The ground floor is given over to temporary exhibitions (such as photography in the Bieszczady) and staff can advise on what to see and do in the national park.

🛏 Sleeping & Eating

Gościniec

Dębowa Gazdówka GUESTHOUSE €€
(☑13 461 3081; www.debowagazdowka.pl; ul Łodyna 43, Łodyna; s/d/tr 120/160/195zł) This family-run wooden guesthouse in a village 5km north of Ustrzyki Dolne is better than anything in Ustrzyki Dolne itself. In addition to 22 comfy, basic rooms with exposed wooden walls and floors, you get a big sweeping view of the mountains and a good, country-style restaurant. Call or email ahead to get picked up from town.

Orlik PIZZA €
(☑13 471 1900; www.pizzeria-orlik.pl; Rynek 4a; pizza 19-21zł; ⊙10am-10pm) This modest pizzeria, on the southern side of the Rynek, is the best of a slim range of dining options in town. Expect big, satisfying pizzas plus surprisingly good espresso, served on the terrace in good weather (which may tempt you to finish with an ice cream from the external dessert bar).

ℹ Information

Tourist Information Office (Bieszczadzkie Centrum Informacji i Promocji; ☑13 471 1130; www.cit.ustrzyki-dolne.pl; Rynek 16; ⊙8am-5pm Mon-Fri, 9am-1pm Sat) Hands out a city map and the English-language Town and Commune Guide, both free. Also sells hiking and cycling maps of the Bieszczady area.

ℹ Getting There & Away

On ul Dworcowa, around 750m east of the Rynek, Ustrzyki Dolne's bus station has regular connections to Sanok (8.50zł, one hour), Lesko (5.50zł, 40 minutes), Ustrzyki Górne (12zł, 1¼ hours), Przemyśl (15zł, two hours), Rzeszów (21zł, three hours) and Kraków (50zł, five hours).

Ustrzyki Górne

POP 89

You mightn't deduce it from the sleepy string of buildings scattered along the main road, but Ustrzyki Górne ('Upper Ustrzyki') is the Bieszczady's premier hiking base. Since the Great Bieszczady Loop Road opened in 1962, the mountains have become more accessible, but this is still remote country and Ustrzyki Górne is a good example: it has a few mostly basic places to stay and eat, a little bit of life around the bus station and car park as you enter the village, and not much else. The village springs to life in summer then sinks into a deep sleep for most of the rest of the year, stirring only a little in winter when the cross-country skiers arrive.

Activities

The number-one activity here, at least in summer, is hiking. Ustrzyki Górne is the most popular base for hiking in Bieszczady National Park and several great walks along colour-coded trails start from here (most from near the camping ground or the bus station and car park).

You'll find several longer and shorter routes marked out on hiking maps, but one popular loop to get you started begins in the village of Wołosate (take the regular bus from Ustrzyki Górne – 4.50zł, seven minutes). From here follow the blue path (two hours) to the region's highest peak, Tarnica (1346m), and then head back to Ustrzyki Górne along the red path (two to three hours).

The park is full of fascinating sights and sounds: the remnants of villages abandoned or destroyed during Operation Vistula (p217), ancient cemeteries, peat reserves (complete with quicksand) and the cry of a lone wolf in the distance.

A decent hiking map, with information in English, is ExpressMap's widely available 1:65,000 *Bieszczady* (20zł). There's a store at the camping ground and a few small shops around the bus stop to buy provisions.

🛏 Sleeping

Ustrzyki Górne has some inviting seasonal camping, a hotel or two and a hostel.

Schronisko PTTK Kremenaros HOSTEL €
(☑ 13 461 0605; www.kremenaros.com.pl; Ustrzyki Górne 4; dm 30zł, d/tr 130/150zł; ☉ Apr-Oct; 🅿) This long-established hostel is the first building in the village when arriving from the west on the road from Wetlina. It's unfussy and basic, but staff are friendly and the atmosphere good. Rooms have between two and 10 beds (only the doubles have private bathrooms) and there's a rough-hewn bar/restaurant selling regional beers and simple mountain food.

Hotel Górski HOTEL €€
(☑ 13 461 0604; www.hotel-pttk.pl; Ustrzyki Górne 1A; s/d from 95/190zł; 🅿 🛜 🏊) At the northern end of the road to Ustrzyki Dolne and bedecked with flower baskets, this PTTK-run hotel is better than most options in Ustrzyki Górne. With 99 beds in clean and comfortable single to triple en-suite rooms, it's also the biggest place in town. There's a pool and sauna, a tiny gym and a reasonably priced bar/restaurant.

WORTH A TRIP

BEACH BREAK AT LAKE SOLINA

About 30km southwest of Ustrzyki Dolne and accessible by bus is **Solina Lake** (Jezioro Solińskie), a reservoir 27km long and 60m deep, created in 1968 when the San River was dammed. Today it is the Bieszczady region's most important centre for water sports and recreation.

Polańczyk, the attractive town on the irregularly shaped lake's western shore, offers visitors everything from sailing and windsurfing to fishing and beaches. The **tourist office** (☑ 13 469 2495; www.esolina.pl; Zdrojowa 1B; ☉ 9am-5pm Mon-Sat), just off Hwy 894 on the way to Lesko, can supply you with all the details.

Ul Zdrojowa is lined with hotels and sanatoriums, offering any number of treatments. Many are soulless blocks; instead head for **Pensjonat Korona** (☑ 13 469 2201; www. pensjonatkorona.pl; ul Zdrojowa 29; s/d 300/350zł; 🅿 🛜), a pleasant guesthouse with 35 beds at a lakeside locale on the peninsula. **Rzeczpospolita**, the colourful attached restaurant, serves very good Polish standards.

EWG3D/GETTY IMAGES ©

1. Zalipie (p205)
Folk-art designs adorn houses in Zalipie and surrounding vilages.

2. Dunajec Gorge (p233)
Rafting trips ferry vistors past stunning scenery along the Dunajec River.

3. Tarnów (p203)
A finely restored Old Town and some fascinating museums.

4. Mt Tarnica (p215)
Climbing Mt Tarnica (1346m) is one of the highlights of hiking in Bieszczady National Park.

FOTO MIGAWKI MD/SHUTTERSTOCK ©

✖ Eating & Drinking

Zajazd Pod Caryńską POLISH €€

(☏ 511 311 552; www.carynska.pl; Ustrzyki Górne 1A; mains 20-35zł; ◷ 11am-10pm; 🅿 🛜) This handsome traditional wooden lodge and restaurant in 'downtown' Ustrzyki Górne boasts the best kitchen in the immediate vicinity. Big plates of pork and potato pancakes, goulash, baked pork knuckle, mountain trout and lots of soups are on the menu. There are also 20 very pleasant rooms (double 170zł), most with balconies.

★ Bieszczadzka Legenda BAR

(☏ 698 013 469; http://bieszczadzka-legenda. pl; Ustrzyki Górne 2; ◷ 1pm-2am) Counterculture comes to the Bieszczady in the form of this welcoming, brightly painted clapboard cafe, bar and venue. Grab a coffee or beer, scout out a lounge chair and kick back to old-school reggae or off-beat Carpathian folk. There's food, including some lighter vegan and vegetarian options, and beer from Bieszczady craft brewer Ursa Maior.

❶ Getting There & Away

Buses connect Ustrzyki Górne fairly regularly with Ustrzyki Dolne (12zł, 1¼ hours), Krosno (25zł, 3½ hours), Rzeszów (31zł, 4¼ hours), Lesko (15zł, two hours) and Sanok (17zł, 2¼ hours). The frequency increases in July and August, when several services also go to Wetlina (7zł, 26 minutes) and Cisna (9zł, 50 minutes).

Wetlina

POP 301

Nestled in a valley coursed by the Wetlinka River, Wetlina is surrounded by forested uplands, and is a popular jumping-off spot for hiking in the Bieszczady. It stretches along one main road (Hwy 897) and has a limited choice of simple places to sleep and eat. Everything opens up in summer, but the town is pretty quiet at other times.

🛌 Sleeping & Eating

Wetlina sustains hotels, guesthouses, hostels and camping grounds. Much is seasonal, however, so be sure to arrange your accommodation in advance.

Dom Wycieczkowy PTTK HOSTEL €

(☏ 13 468 4615; www.wetlinapttk.pl; Wetlina 17; dm/d incl half-board 30/70zł; 🅿) This simple hostel offers beds year-round in doubles and five-bed dorms. In summer you can also stay

in cabins (27zł per person) or pitch your tent (13zł per person) on the 3.5-hectare grounds. The rustic restaurant has rough pine tables and is decorated with carved wooden figures.

★ W Starym Siole POLISH €€

(☏ 503 124 654; www.staresiolo.com; Wetlina 71; mains 25-40zł; ◷ 11am-11pm; 🅿 🛜) This repurposed peasant's hut from 1905 is the setting for possibly the best restaurant in this part of Poland. They pay keen attention to detail, from the custom woodworking in the dining room to the wine list and wonderful dishes such as ribs in cabbage leaves and fire-grilled mountain fish and meats.

❶ Getting There & Away

There are decent bus connections from Wetlina to Sanok (14zł, 1½ to two hours), Lesko (12zł, 1½ hours) and Cisna (6zł, 30 minutes). In summer there are also direct services to Ustrzyki Górne (7zł, 26 minutes).

Cisna

POP 457

Cisna sits on the borderland between territories once inhabited by the Boyks to the east and Lemks to the west. The region was densely populated before WWII; today Cisna counts fewer than 500 inhabitants, yet is still the largest village in the central part of the Bieszczady. Though not especially attractive in itself, Cisna has a decent choice of accommodation and is a good base for hiking. It is also the place to board the narrow-gauge tourist train.

🏃 Activities

Bieszczady Forest Railway RAIL

(Bieszczadzka Kolejka Leśna; ☏ 13 468 6335; www. kolejka.bieszczady.pl; Majdan 17; adult/child one way 21/16zł, return 25/20zł; ◷ late Apr-Oct; 🐾) The narrow-gauge Bieszczady Forest Railway was built at the end of the 19th century to transport timber. Some tracks were in use as recently as the 1990s, but the line has since been turned into a tourist attraction and is particularly popular with families. Based in Majdan, 2km west of Cisna, it has two runs on offer.

🛌 Sleeping & Eating

Cisna has plenty of places to stay, though most of these are tiny pensions or mountain hostels, and many close in quiet months. The tourist office is happy to help find rooms.

Bacówka Pod Honem
HOSTEL €

(☑660 116 025; http://bacowkapodhonem.pl; Cisna 82; dm with breakfast/full board 50/70zł, camping 15zł; P) This 47-bed mountain hostel is 668m above sea level on a slope 1km east of Cisna, at the end of a steep dirt track. It's simple and friendly, serves uncomplicated meals and is a good starting place for hikes to the peaks of Wołosań (1071m), Jaworne (992m) and Chryszczata (997m).

Cisna Peretka
LODGE €€

(☑13 468 6325; www.naturatour.pl; Cisna 105; s/d 95/190zł, cabin 215zł; P ≋) This comfortable holiday lodge has 34 beds in singles and doubles, plus another 10 seasonal A-frame cabins, open from May to September. Offers good proximity to the Połonina Wetlińska and Połonina Caryńska walking trails, plus bikes for rent.

Bar Siekierezada
POLISH €

(☑13 468 6466; www.siekierezada.pl; Cisna 92; mains 15-22zł; ⊗10am-11pm) This combination bar and art gallery also serves great, simple cooking such as sausages, pierogi, grilled meats and other local favourites. Even if you're not hungry, come to enjoy a beer under the antlers, axes and grinning pagan carvings that cover every surface, and check out the revolving exhibitions.

Pod Kudłatym Aniołem
POLISH €€

(☑664 390 898; www.kudlatyaniol.pl; Cisna 130; mains 29-37zł; ⊗11am-10pm; P 🐾) The place for hearty Carpathian dishes such as Boyko cabbage cakes with fried lamb and beetroot salad or Hutsul pierogi with *bryndza* (west Ukrainian dumplings with sheep's cheese), the 'Shaggy Angel' also offers interesting beers from small Polish, Ukrainian and Slovak brewers, and nine simple, comfortable rooms to sleep off any excesses (single/double 65/130zł).

❶ Information

The **Tourist Information Centre** (☑13 468 6465; www.cisna.pl; Cisna 23; ⊗8am-6pm Mon-Fri, to 4pm Sat; 🐾) is located in the county cultural centre in the middle of the village. The office offers wi-fi and stays open until 8pm weekdays in July and August.

❶ Getting There & Away

Cisna is connected by fairly regular buses to Sanok (13zł, 1½ hours) and Wetlina (6zł, 30 minutes). There are more seasonal buses in summer, including direct services to Ustrzyki Górne (9zł, 50 minutes).

BESKID NISKI

The Beskid Niski (Lower Beskid) is a gently sloping, forest-covered mountain range that runs for about 85km west to east along the Slovakian frontier, spilling into Poland's southern neighbour. Traditionally the home of Lemko people, it's bordered to the west by the Beskid Sądecki and to the east by the Bieszczady. As its name suggests, it is not a high outcrop: its tallest peak, Lackowa, doesn't quite hit 1000m, and much of it is made for easy walks. The Beskid Niski offers less spectacular vistas than the neighbouring Bieszczady (or the Tatras) but its dozens of small Orthodox and Uniat churches, especially in the western half of the region, are a strong draw.

Krosno
POP 47,471

Granted town rights by Casimir the Great in the 14th century and especially prosperous during the Renaissance – it was even nicknamed 'little Kraków' for a time – Krosno's fortunes dwindled from the 18th century onwards. It revived with the trade of linen and Hungarian wine and, in the mid-19th century, with the development of the oil industry. Today it is known throughout Poland for its ornamental and commercial glassworks.

Arranged mainly around the broad, cobbled market square, Krosno boasts enough attractions to occupy a pleasant half day, or there are enough good lodging and eating options to warrant an overnight stay.

◉ Sights

◉ Town Centre

The Old Town's spacious **Rynek** has retained some of its Renaissance appearance, notably in the houses fronted by wide arcaded passageways that line the southern and northeastern parts of the square. The best example is the 15th-century **Wójtowska Townhouse** (Kamienica Wójtowska; Rynek 7).

★ **Centre of Glass Heritage**
MUSEUM

(Centrum Dziedzictwa Szkła; ☑13 444 0031; www.miastoszkla.pl; ul Blich 2; adult/concession 18/14zł; ⊗9am-5pm Mon-Sat, from 11am Sun Sep-Jun, 10am-7pm Mon-Sat, from 11am Sun Jul & Aug; 🐾) Celebrating Krosno's five centuries as Poland's epicentre of glass production, this slick exhibition centre is the town's main attraction. The family-friendly museum, with three levels and English signage, tells the story of Krosno glassmaking, exhibits outstanding pieces in glass and allows visitors to work glass themselves. Sitting at the Rynek's northeastern corner, it extends underground, below the market square.

Franciscan Church of the Holy Cross CHURCH
(Kościół Franciszkanów Św Krzyża; ☑13 436 8088; www.krosno.franciszkanie.pl; ul Franciszkańska 5; ⊗8am-6pm) Southeast of the Rynek is this large Franciscan church, which grew from an early 15th century kernel (today the presbytery and sacristy) and is filled with neo-Gothic furnishings. The showpiece is the Oświęcim Family Chapel (Kaplica Oświęcimów), just to the left as you enter the church. Built in 1647 by Italian architect Vincenti Petroni and embellished with magnificent stucco work by another Italian master, Jan Falconi, this is considered one of the finest early baroque chapels in Poland.

Subcarpathian Museum MUSEUM
(Muzeum Podkarpackie; ☑13 432 1376; www.muzeum.krosno.pl; ul Piłsudskiego 16; adult/concession 10/5zł, Sun free; ⊗9am-4pm Tue-Fri, from 10am Sat & Sun May-Oct, 9am-3pm Tue-Fri, from 10am Sat & Sun Nov-Apr) Two hundred metres north of Krosno's Rynek is this diverting regional history museum, housed in the 15th-century Bishops' Palace. Expect interesting historical, archaeological and art exhibits illuminating the mountainous region. The highlight is an extensive collection of decorative old kerosene lamps, reputedly the largest in Europe.

Craft Museum MUSEUM
(Muzeum Rzemiosła; ☑13 474 8201; www.muzeumrzemiosla.pl; ul Piłsudskiego 19; adult/concession 5/3zł, Sat free; ⊗8am-6pm Mon-Fri, 10am-4pm Sat & Sun May-Sep, 8am-3.30pm Mon-Fri, 10am-2pm Sat Oct-Apr) Directly opposite the Subcarpathian Museum, about 200m north of the Rynek, the Craft Museum features ethnographic displays related to such local crafts and trades as clockmaking, weaving, saddlery and even hairdressing. The art nouveau building, dating from the turn of the 20th century, is interesting in its own right and served as the headquarters of a company that made tower clocks. Outside are several antique sleighs and carts.

⊙ Outside Krosno

★ Church of the Assumption of Mary CHURCH
(Kościół Wniebowzięcia Najświętszej Maryi Panny w Haczowie; ☑13 439 1012; www.parafiahaczow.pl; Haczów 605; ⊗8am-4pm) Located In the village of Haczów (hah-choof), 16km east of Krosno and accessible by bus, this is the largest timber Gothic church in Europe and is a Unesco World Heritage site. Built in the mid-15th century on the site of a predecessor founded by Władysław Jagiełło in 1388, its interior walls and coffered ceiling are covered in rare naive paintings dating from the late 15th century and restored in the 1990s.

Museum of the Oil & Gas Industry MUSEUM
(Muzeum Przemysłu Naftowego i Gazowniczego; ☑13 433 3478; www.bobrka.pl; ul Kopalniana 35, Bóbrka; adult/concession 12/7zł; ⊗9am-5pm Tue-Fri, 10am-6pm Sat & Sun May-Sep, 9am-5pm Tue-Sun Apr & Oct, 7am-3pm Tue-Sun Nov-Mar) Bóbrka,

HIKING IN THE BESKID NISKI

Two main trails cover the entire length of the Beskid Niski range. The Blue Tourist Trail (Niebieski Szlak Turystyczny) from Rzeszów passes through Grybów, goes southeast to the Slovakian border and then eastwards along the frontier to eventually bring you to Nowy Łupków near Komańcza. The Main Beskid Trail (Główny Szlak Beskidzki, marked in red) crosses the Blue Trail around Hańczowa, continues east along the northern slopes of the Beskid, and arrives at Komańcza. Both trails head further east into the Bieszczady.

You need four to six days to walk the whole of the Beskid Niski on either of these routes, but other trails, as well as a number of rough roads, link the two main trails. The major starting points for the Beskid Niski are Krynica, Grybów and Gorlice from the west; Komańcza and Sanok from the east; and Krosno and Dukla in the centre.

The 1:50,000 Beskid Niski map (19zł) from Compass will give you all the basic information you need for hiking. You can find this map, or similar versions from other companies, at tourist offices in Nowy Sącz, Krynica and Krosno.

17km southwest of Krosno, is the cradle of the Polish oil industry. It was here in 1854 that the world's first oil well was sunk by Ignacy Łukasiewicz, inventor of the paraffin lamp. Despite still producing oil, the site is now a curious open-air museum. From Krosno several buses go daily to Bóbrka (5zł, 30 minutes), though fewer depart at weekends. The site is at Chorkówa, about 2km north of the bus stop in central Bóbrka.

🛏️ Sleeping

Krosno is blessed with at least three quality choices to stay, depending on what you're looking for: atmosphere and charm or modern convenience.

Hotel Śnieżka   HOTEL €€
(☑13 432 3449; www.hotelsniezka.pl; ul Lewakowskiego 22; s/d 160/210zł; P❄@🕸) For atmosphere and charm, this attractive brick-red Victorian townhouse near the train and bus stations is hard to beat. You'll find 14 cosy rooms, all individually styled and sparklingly modern, with polished wood floors and big bathrooms. The in-house restaurant does a good line in traditional Polish cuisine, which may save you the 2km walk to the Rynek.

Hotel Krosno Nafta   HOTEL €€
(☑13 436 6212; www.hotel.nafta.pl; ul Lwowska 21; s/d 215/255zł; P@🕸) Occupying a five-storey, cream and lime-green box 1km southeast of the Rynek, this business-oriented hotel offers good rates, plus online and weekend discounts. There are 42 large, comfortable rooms, a bar and lounge area, a spa and sauna and a decent upmarket restaurant, the Naftaya.

Hotel Buda   HOTEL €€
(☑13 432 0053; ul Jagiellońska 4; d/tr/ste 150/200/250zł; P🕸) The location's not immediately appealing (next to the train tracks around 1km southwest of central Krosno, yet a little over 1km from the station), but this suburban hotel offers clean and comfortable rooms and the attached restaurant is the best in town.

🍴 Eating & Drinking

⭐ Restauracja Buda   POLISH €€
(☑13 432 0053; ul Jagiellońska 4; mains 28-40zł; ⊙10am-10pm; 🕸) This family-run restaurant, 1km southwest of the Rynek, is easily the best in Krosno. Expect excellent traditional Polish cooking such as duck fillet with potatoes and forest mushrooms alongside a smattering of international options such as spaghetti

carbonara and 'Mexican' chicken. The atmosphere is refined but not stuffy, and service matches the standards set by the kitchen.

Posmakuj   POLISH €€
(☑13 435 5650; www.posmakujkrosno.pl; Rynek 24; mains 28-38zł; ⊙noon-10pm Mon-Thu, to 11pm Fri & Sat, 11am-11pm Sun; 🕸) The best of the clutch of Polish and pizza joints lining Krosno's Rynek, Posmakuj shows the most ambition in the kitchen, sourcing regional ingredients such as sausage from Dobrucowa and lamb from Bieszczady. Dine on the terrace in warm weather or under the arches of the brick-lined cellar.

Klubokawiarnia Ferment   CAFE
(☑13 420 3242; ul Portiusa 4; ⊙4-11.30pm) This little hipster haunt on a small side street just off the northwestern corner of Krosno's Rynek does great coffee, Hungarian wines, cocktails and small snacks, all served up in a colourful, airy, modern space that doubles as a club and gallery.

🛍️ Shopping

Glass Studio Habrat   GLASS
(☑13 431 7239; www.studiohabrat.com; Rynek 28; ⊙10am-6pm Mon-Fri, to 2pm Sat) This sparsely furnished, stylish little retail gallery sells the work of Maciej Habrat, a second-generation Krosno glass-blower whose colourful plates, glasses, vases and decorative wares reflect the often playful, absurd and abstract styles pioneered at the Krosno glassworks.

ℹ️ Information

Tourist Information Centre (☑13 432 7707; www.krosno.pl; Rynek 5; ⊙9am-6pm Mon-Fri, 10am-4pm Sat & Sun May-Sep, 9am-4pm Mon-Fri, 10am-2pm Sat Oct-Apr; 🕸) At the southeast corner of the main square, the cheerful staff dispense maps and brochures. There's a small gift shop here as well as a free computer for surfing the web.

ℹ️ Getting There & Away

The train and bus stations sit eyeballing one another 1.5km west of the Rynek.

A dozen or so daily buses head eastwards for Sanok (14zł, 1½ hours), with connections to Ustrzyki Dolne (16zł, 2½ hours) and two to Ustrzyki Górne (25zł, 3½ hours). Frequent buses depart daily for Kraków (33zł, 3½ hours) and Rzeszów (14zł, 1½ hours). There are also frequent buses south to Dukla (6zł, 30 minutes) and Haczów (6zł, 30 minutes).

Rail connections are also quite good, with up to seven departures daily to Sanok (7.80zł, one hour) and three to Rzeszów via Jasło (13zł, two to three hours).

Biecz

POP 4697

One of the oldest settlements in Poland, Biecz (pronounced bee-ech) was a busy commercial centre with recognised civic rights by the 13th century. It benefited from the wine-trading route heading south over the Carpathians to Hungary, and some 30 crafts developed here. One 'craft' in particular is noteworthy: with the right to pass and carry out capital sentences, Biecz became a centre of public executions. In the 17th century the town's fortunes plunged, when the plague wiped out nearly all its inhabitants and new trade routes bypassed it. The sleepy atmosphere seems to have remained to this day, though some important historic monuments and a good museum make Biecz a highlight of the region.

Sights

Start your exploration at the spacious Rynek, which covers no less than an eighth of Biecz's entire area (making it Poland's largest market square relative to the size of the town). The main sights, including some impressive remnants of the old **town walls**, can be found west of the Rynek, along ul Węgierska.

Tower TOWER

(www.biecz.pl; Rynek 1; adult/concession 4/2zł; ⊙10am-9pm Tue-Sun, Jul & Aug, 9am-5pm May, Jun & Sep, 8am-4pm Oct-Apr) The tallest structure in town, Biecz's 58-metre-high town-hall tower offers commanding views of the Ropa Valley and Carpathian foothills. Built between 1569 and 1581 to replace a derelict predecessor, its bulbous cap is a 20th-century reconstruction. The original Renaissance decoration and an unusual 24-hour clock face on its eastern side have been restored, and beneath lies the 'Turma', a dungeon graffitied by forlorn occupants of bygone years.

Corpus Christi Parish Church CHURCH

(Kościół Parafialny Bożego Ciała; www.fara.biecz.pl; ul Kromera 16a; entry 5zł) Biecz's monumental Gothic parish church, rearing skywards in red brick, dates in its earliest parts to the 15th century and testifies to the Renaissance town's affluence. Inside, the chancel (the area surrounding the altar) holds most of its treasures, notably the late-Renaissance high altar and massive stalls, and an impressive crucifix from 1639. Group guided tours can be arranged through the Biecz Regional Museum (www.muzeum.biecz.pl) for 50zł; the church is 100m west of the Rynek.

House with a Tower MUSEUM

(Dom z Basztą; ☑13 447 1093; www.muzeum.biecz. pl; ul Węgierska 1; adult/concession 8/4zł; ⊙8am-4pm Tue-Sat Oct-Apr, 8am-5pm Tue-Fri, from 9am Sat & Sun May, Jun & Sep, 8am-7pm Tue-Fri, from 10am Sat & Sun Jul & Aug) This branch of the Biecz Regional Museum occupies what's called the 'House with a Tower', a 16th-century dwelling attached to a stout tower. Take a peek inside to see the contents of the Renaissance pharmacy that operated here until the 17th century, as well as musical instruments, Gothic, Renaissance and Baroque sculpture, traditional household utensils and artisans' tools and a cellar for storing Hungarian wine.

Sleeping & Eating

Hotel Restauracja Grodzka HOTEL €

(☑13 447 1121; www.restauracjagrodzka.pl; ul Wielkiego 35; s/d/apt 65/80/100zł; ⊙restaurant 8am-10pm Mon-Sat, from 10am Sun; P 🅿 🛜) The best of Biecz's slim range of acceptable lodging options is this 16-room budget hotel, located along the main road about 700m east of the Rynek. The rooms are plain but clean and the in-house restaurant is good value, with a big plate of potato pancakes covered in goulash costing just 16zł.

★U Becza POLISH €

(☑733 612 616; www.restauracjaubecza.pl; Rynek 2; mains 10-17zł; ⊙10am-10pm; 🛜) This handsome cafe and restaurant occupies the Doma Zbója Becza, a 15th-century townhouse on the main square. Step through the carriageway to the period interior, which is pleasantly low-key with heavy-beamed ceilings and wooden furnishings. You may not find better *gołąbki* (stuffed cabbage rolls) in all of Poland – order them with mushroom sauce.

Information

Tourist Information Office (☑13 440 6860; www.biecz.pl; Rynek 1; ⊙9am-5pm May, Jun, Sep & Oct, 10am-7pm Jul & Aug, 8am-4pm Mon-Fri Nov-Apr) A small, helpful office, located at the centre of the Rynek, below the tower.

Getting There & Away

All buses pass through and stop on the northeast and southwest sides of the Rynek. Buses to Jasło (6.50zł, 35 minutes) run regularly; from there you can get a train to Krosno (4.50zł, 30 minutes). There are a couple of daily departures to Nowy Sącz (14zł, 1½ hours).

BESKID SĄDECKI

Spreading out over 670 sq km on the Poland/Slovakia border, the Beskid Sądecki (*bes*-keed son-*dets*-kee) is an attractive mountain range of moderate height offering hiking, sightseeing and spa towns such as Krynica and Muszyna. The Beskid Sądecki comprises two subranges, the Pasmo Jaworzyny and the Pasmo Radziejowej, which are separated by the Poprad River valley. There are a number of peaks over 1000m, the highest being Mt Radziejowa (1261m).

The Beskid Sądecki was the westernmost territory populated by the Lemks, and a dozen of their charming rustic churches survive, particularly around Krynica and Muszyna. *Beskid Sądecki* maps (scale 1:50,000; 15zł) published by two different firms (WiT and Demart) are helpful for hikers and *cerkiew* (wooden church) peepers.

Nowy Sącz

POP 84,290

Nowy Sącz (*no*-vi sonch), the economic and cultural centre of the Sącz region, is a laid-back town with a large main square and a few decent attractions, most notably its large skansen (open-air museum of traditional architecture). It can also be a good base for further exploration of the surrounding countryside.

Founded in 1292 by Wenceslaus II of Bohemia and fortified in the middle of the following century, Nowy Sącz developed rapidly until the 16th century, thanks to its strategic position on trading crossroads. A period of decline in the 17th century gave way to a partial revival at the close of the 19th. It became a significant centre of Jewish life, with a Jewish population of 25,000 accounting for around a third of the town's total on the eve of WWII. Only around 10% survived the Holocaust. Nowy Sącz rebounded and expanded after WWII, and its historic district has been largely restored.

◎ Sights

Measuring 160m by 120m, Nowy Sącz's Rynek is the second largest in Poland (after Kraków's) and is lined with a harmonious collection of historic houses. The **town hall**, erected in the middle of 1897, incorporates a number of architectural styles, including art nouveau.

◎ City Centre

Gothic House   MUSEUM
(Dom Gotycki; ☑18 443 7708; www.muzeum.sacz.pl; ul Lwowska 3; adult/concession 8/5zł, free Sat; ⊙9.30am-3pm Tue-Thu, 9am-5pm Fri, 9am-4pm Sat) Built for canons of the nearby Collegiate Church in 1448, this broad-beamed brick townhouse now contains a branch of Nowy Sącz's regional museum. Dedicated to the religious and folk traditions of Sądecczyzna (the land surrounding Nowy Sącz), its permanent exhibitions include naive religious paintings and folkart woodcarvings collected from rural churches and roadside chapels throughout the region. The collection of 15th- to 19th-century Orthodox art, which includes a splendid iconostasis of the 17th century, is especially fine.

District Museum   MUSEUM
(Okręgowe muzeum w Nowym Sączu; ☑18 443 7708; www.muzeum.sacz.pl; ul Jagiellońska 56; adult/concession 8/5zł, Sat free; ⊙10am-5pm Tue-Sun) Occupying a stately pre-WWI bank, the main branch of Nowy Sącz's regional museum features permanent exhibitions exploring the city in the early days of Galician autonomy and during the two world wars. There are also temporary exhibitions and a collection of paintings by local boy Bolesław Barbacki (1891–1941).

Synagogue   SYNAGOGUE
(Galeria Dawna Synagoga w Nowym Sączu; ul Joselewicza 12) For centuries Jews lived in the area north of the Rynek. This is also the area where the Germans built their wartime Jewish ghetto, before shipping 25,000 residents to extermination camps in 1942. Not much of the community or the ghetto remains, with the exception of this beautiful 18th-century synagogue, which miraculously survived the war and has now been restored as a place of worship.

◎ Outside The Centre

★**Sącz Ethnographic Park**   MUSEUM
(Sądecki Park Etnograficzny; ☑18 444 3570; www.muzeum.sacz.pl; ul Wieniawy-Długoszowskiego 83B; adult/concession 14/8zł; ⊙10am-6pm Tue-Sun May–mid-Oct, 9am-3pm Tue-Sun mid-Oct–Apr; P⊞) About 3.5km southeast of central Nowy Sącz, this ethnographic park is one of the largest and best skansens in Poland. Houses and other buildings typical

COBBLESTONES IN STARY SĄCZ

Stary Sącz (*stah-ri* sonch) is the older and smaller sister of Nowy Sącz, with a pretty, cobblestoned main square and some fetching churches. There's also an excellent restaurant in the centre, making it an ideal day trip planned around lunch.

The town owes its existence to 13th-century Duchess Kinga, wife of King Bolesław Wstydliwy (Bolesław the Shy), who in the 1270s founded the convent of the Poor Clares here. After the king's death, Kinga entered the convent, where she lived for the last 13 years of her life, becoming its first abbess.

Though there's a small regional museum here, the main sights are two historic churches. The **Church of the Poor Clares** (Kościół SS Klarysek; www.klaryski.sacz.pl; Plac Św Kingi 1; ⊙8am-6pm) was where Stary Sącz was born. Commenced in Gothic style in 1285 and completed in 1332, it later gained opulent baroque fittings. The traces of its creator, Saint Kinga (1234–92), are clearly visible: the baroque frescoes in the nave depict scenes from her life, and her chapel on the south side boasts a 1470 statue of her on the altar. The pulpit (1671) on the opposite wall is an extraordinary piece of art.

The **Parish Church of St Elizabeth of Hungary** (Kościół Parafialny Św Elżbiety Węgierskiej; www.parafia.stary.sacz.pl; ul Kazimierza Wielkiego; ⊙8am-6pm) is two blocks south of the Rynek and dates from the town's 13th-century beginnings. It's been altered considerably over the years, particularly in the 17th and 18th centuries, and is now a textbook example of unbridled baroque.

For lunch or dinner in Stary Sącz, look no further than **Restauracja Marysieńka** (☑18 446 0072; Rynek 12; mains 18-22zł; ⊙10am-9pm; 🛜). Nothing fancy – just good Polish standards such as pierogi and crumbed pork chops served in a friendly, welcoming atmosphere.

of several ethnic cultures from the Carpathian Mountains and foothills are displayed. Guides conduct regular Polish-language tours inside the buildings; follow along with *The Sącz Ethnographic Park* guide, available in English from the skansen shop. There are around 70 buildings and other structures spread over 8 hectares, including a farmhouse, forge and windmill.

Jewish Cemetery CEMETERY

(Cmentarz Żydowski; ☑18 441 9381; ul Rybacka 4) Around 500m north of the Old Town, on the opposite side of the Kamienica River, is the former Jewish cemetery. It contains a couple of hundred headstones, including the *ohel* (monumental tomb) of Rebbe Chaim Halberstam, a place of Hasidic pilgrimage. During WWII it was the site of mass executions – there is a monument to the several hundred Jews taken from the Nowy Sącz wartime ghetto and shot here.

🛏 Sleeping & Eating

Accommodation options are adequate, rather than abundant, and include hostels, seasonal camping and the opportunity to stay in a reproduction of a 19th-century Galician town.

Dom Turysty PTTK HOSTEL €

(☑18 441 5012; http://majanowysacz.pl; ul Nadbrzeżna 40; s/d/tr 105/140/185zł; 🅿🛜) This year-round PTTK hostel has 21 spartan, spick-and-span rooms renovated in 2016. There's a restaurant, outdoor barbecue and a camping ground next door, open between May and September. The hostel is situated outside the centre, about 2km southeast of the Rynek, in the direction of the Sącz Ethnographic Park.

★ Miasteczko
Galicyjskie HISTORIC HOTEL €€

(☑18 441 6390; www.miasteczkogalicyjskie.pl; ul Lwowska 226; s/d/tr 145/230/305zł; 🅿🛜) 'Galician Town', a faithful reproduction of a township in the former Austro-Hungarian province of Galicia, gives overnighters the option to stay in a reproduced Galician house from the late 19th and early 20th centuries. The Austro-Hungarian provincial picturesque marries well with modern comforts such as excellent baths and beds, and the buffet breakfast is one of the best around.

Trattoria
ITALIAN €€

(☑ 18 307 0602; http://trattoriacaffe.pl; ul Wazów 8; mains 20-26zł; ⊙ 1-10pm Mon-Thu, 11am-11pm Fri & Sat, 11am-10pm Sun) A narrow alleyway south of the Rynek hides one of Nowy Sącz's best restaurants, a pleasant trattoria in a brightly lit cellar space. The pizzas are a sure bet, but the authentic pastas and *secondi* are definitely worth considering. You'll also find a great wine selection, good prices and an upstairs cafe for a lighter meal.

ⓘ Information

PTTK Office (☑ 18 443 7457; www.beskid. pttk.pl; Rynek 9; ⊙ 7am-3pm Mon, Wed & Thu, 11am-7pm Tue & Fri) Less helpful than the tourist information centre, the PTTK office is a good place to source hiking information and find out about possible overnight stays in PTTK-run mountain huts.

Tourist Information Centre (☑ 18 444 2422; www.ziemiasadecka.info; ul Szwedzka 2; ⊙ 9am-5pm Mon-Fri year round, 9am-1pm Sat Oct-May, 9am-5pm Sat Jun-Sep; ☎) Standard tourist office with limited information in English. There's a computer available for visitors to check email.

ⓘ Getting There & Away

The bus station is midway between the city centre and the train station, on Plac Dąbrowskiego. Buses run frequently to Kraków (18zł, 2¼ hours), Krynica (6.50zł, one to 1½ hours), Szczawnica (11zł, one hour) and Zakopane (20zł, 2¼ to 2½ hours).

The main train station is 2km south of the Old Town, with frequent city buses running between the two. Trains go regularly to Kraków (27zł, 2½ to 3½ hours), Krynica (16zł, 1½ hours), Stary Sącz (4.40zł, nine minutes) and Tarnów (19zł, two hours).

Krynica

POP 11,361

Set in attractive countryside amid the wooded hills of the Beskid Sądecki, Krynica (kri-*nee*-tsah), often known as Krynica-Zdrój (Krynica Spa), is Poland's largest spa and mountain health resort. Founded in the late 16th century, it's also one of its most venerable.

It's relaxed throughout much of the year, with visitors coming to take the restorative waters of around a dozen local mineral springs and to relax in the mountain air. In midsummer, though, you can banish any notion about quiet convalescence amid the pines. It morphs into a full-on holiday town, chock-a-block with families, long queues for ice cream and impromptu rock concerts on the promenade.

It wasn't always this way. In the early 20th century, Krynica was a fashionable hangout for the artistic and intellectual elite and continued to be so right up until WWII. Splendid villas and pensions from this period still blend into the wooded landscape.

⊙ Sights & Activities

As with many Polish towns, the main activity in Krynica is drinking. In this case it's not beer or vodka, but rather the bitter water that flows from one of around a dozen medicinal mineral springs.

Main Pump Room
SPRING

(Pijalnia Główna; ☑ 18 477 7432; http://pijalnia glowna.pl; ul Nowotorskiego 9/3; per glass/10 samples 1.70/13zł; ⊙ 10am-9pm) This modern structure on the main promenade looks more like a retro-futuristic airport terminal than a spa colonnade. But behind the plate-glass and

HIKING IN THE BESKID SĄDECKI

Krynica is an excellent springboard for hiking in the Beskid Sądecki. Two marked trails, green and red, head westwards from Krynica up to the top of **Mt Jaworzyna**, the highest peak around Krynica (1113m). It takes three hours to walk there by either trail (or you can get there faster on the Mt Jaworzyna cable car (p230)). At the top you'll have great views, and may even be able to spot the Tatras on a clear day.

Continue on the red trail northwest to **Hala Łabowska** (1038m), another three hours' walk from Mt Jaworzyna. The red trail carries on northwest to **Rytro** (four hours' walk). This route, leading mostly through the forest along the ridge of the main chain of the Beskid Sądecki, is spectacular and easy. From Rytro you can go back to Krynica by train or bus.

There are several PTTK mountain hostels along these trails, where you can usually find something to eat and bed down for the night. Before setting out, visit the PTTK office (p231) in Krynica to pick up maps and reserve space in the hostels.

WORTH A TRIP

WOODEN CHURCHES AROUND KRYNICA

The countryside surrounding Krynica, with its beautiful wooded valleys, hills and charming small villages, is worth exploring, particularly for the wealth of old wooden churches. An essential aid for exploring the region is one of the *Beskid Sądecki* maps, readily available in these parts. Most of the churches – all originally Uniat and Lemk – are accessible by bus, though it's better to travel with your own car or bicycle.

To the north of Krynica, 13km and 16km respectively on the road to Grybów, are good *cerkwie* (wooden churches) in **Berest** (1842) and **Polany** (1820). Both retain some of the old interior fittings, including iconostases and wall paintings. Buses ply this route regularly so you shouldn't have problems getting back to Krynica or continuing on to Grybów, from where there's frequent transport west to Nowy Sącz.

The 24km loop via Mochnaczka, Tylicz and Powroźnik to the east and south of Krynica is another interesting trip. Along the route, the village of **Tylicz** boasts two churches – a Catholic one and an Uniat *cerkiew* dating from 1743. The latter is used only for funerals. If you have your own transport, head due east for 3km to **Muszynka**, which is almost at the border with Slovakia. The striking *cerkiew* here dates from 1689.

From Tylicz a quiet backroad skirts the Muszyna River valley for 8km to **Powroźnik**, which features the oldest *cerkiew* in the region (1606) and the best known. The exterior is beautiful, and the church has an 18th-century iconostasis, several 17th-century icons on the side walls and a pulpit dating to 1700.

hothoused greenery you'll find the town's main dispensary of healing waters. Select from a menu of eight different mineral springs, each purporting to cure a different ailment. It also doubles as a cultural space, with a 350-seat concert hall.

Góra Parkowa Funicular CABLE CAR
(Kolej Linowa na Górę Parkową; ☎18 471 2262; www.pkl.pl; al Nowotarskiego 1; adult/concession, return 16/13zł, one way 11/8zł; ⏲10am-7pm May-Sep, to 6pm Oct-late Dec & late Feb-Apr, to 8pm late Dec-late Feb; 👪) The Góra Parkowa funicular railway is a fun family outing. The bottom station is near the northern end of the promenade in Park Zdrojowy, and cars depart every 15 minutes. The 142m ascent takes under three minutes. At the top you'll find pretty views in all directions, a giant slide and a tubing run for kids.

If it's a nice day, buy a one-way ticket and hike back down through the park to town.

Mt Jaworzyna Cable Car CABLE CAR
(Kolej Gondolowa na Jaworzynę; ☎18 471 5271; www.jaworzynakrynicka.pl; ul Czarny Potok 75; adult/concession return 28/23zł, one way 20/16zł; ⏲9am-6pm; 👪) More spectacular than the funicular in central Krynica, this cable-car ferries six-person bubbles from the Czarny Potok Valley, about a 6km drive west of town, to the top of Mt Jaworzyna (1113m). The 2220m journey takes around seven minutes and climbs 465m.

🛏 Sleeping & Eating

Krynica has a slew of hotels, pensions and holiday homes. Many places – particularly holiday homes – will offer half or full board, which can be convenient. There are also plenty of private rooms welcoming guests. The tourist office can arrange private accommodation for around 50/60zł per person without/with private bathroom. Remember that in high season (July and August, January and February) few owners will be interested in travellers staying just a night or two.

Pensjonat Witoldówka PENSION €
(☎18 471 5577; www.witoldowka-krynica.pl; ul Dietla 10; d/apt 140/200zł; Ⓟ@) Built in 1889 by Dr Bolesław Skórczewski to lodge patients taking Krynica's waters, this grand, Gothic, timber-built hotel is well located along the narrow Kryniczanka River, close to the main pump room. Its 40 upgraded rooms are comfortable and spacious, and there's a bar and restaurant on site.

★**Małopolanka** HOTEL €€
(☎18 471 5896; www.malopolanka.eu; ul Dietla 13; s/d/apt 140/220/320zł; Ⓟ@📶) This old-fashioned, 20-room pension and spa just off the promenade dates to 1924 and could still be a setting for an Agatha Christie whodunnit. There's a lively bar and restaurant (mains 34zł to 39zł) on the ground

floor, from where creaky wooden steps lead to eclectic rooms, well appointed in period style. There's also a spa with sauna, massage and various treatments.

Pod Zieloną Górką POLISH €€
(☑ 18 471 2177; www.zielonagorka.pl; al Nowotarskiego 5; mains 31-48zł; ⊙ 10am-11pm; 🔊) Dating to 1850, this atmospheric old-style pub comprises an informal family-friendly part with picnic tables, a slightly more upscale dining area with wood-beamed ceilings, lace tablecloths and beautiful porcelain chandeliers, and a park-side terrace for fine weather. The menu features Polish favourites, including pork knuckle cooked in beer, plus Guinness and Czech draughts on tap.

ℹ Information

PTTK Office (☑ 18 471 5576; www.krynica. pttk.pl; ul Zdrojowa 32; ⊙ 9am-4pm Mon-Fri, to 11am Sat) See this office for hiking and cycling maps of the surrounding area, as well as information on treks and overnighting in PTTK-maintained mountain cottages. It's on the main road, just above the southern end of al Nowotarskiego.

Tourist Information Point (☑ 18 472 5577; www.krynica-zdroj.pl; ul Zdrojowa 4/2; ⊙ 9am-5pm Mon-Fri, to 1pm Sat year-round, plus 10am-1pm Sun Jul & Aug; 🔊) Good English is spoken, there are heaps of maps and brochures, and you'll find a public-access computer. On the main drag just above the southern end of al Nowotarskiego.

ℹ Getting There & Away

The train and bus stations are next to one another on ul Ebersa in the southern part of town, about 1.2km from the centre.

Frequent buses run to Nowy Sącz (6.50zł, one to 1½ hours), Grybów (5.50zł, 50 minutes) and Muszyna (3.50zł, 15 minutes).

Regular trains serve Nowy Sącz (16zł, 1½ hours) via a roundabout but pleasant route, passing through Muszyna and Stary Sącz. Half a dozen daily trains go to Tarnów (26zł, 3½ hours).

Muszyna
POP 5123

Much smaller and quieter than Krynica, which is 11km to the southwest, Muszyna (moo-*shin*-na) is another spa town that exploits its mineral springs for tourism, with a sleepy centre and a number of old-fashioned sanatoria in the surrounding area.

◉ Sights & Activities

Most people come to Muszyna to relax and walk the hills and woods around town. Two popular hiking trails originate here and wend their way northwards up the mountains. The green trail takes you to Mt Jaworzyna (1113m), while the yellow one goes to the summit of Mt Pusta Wielka (1061m). You can get to either in around four hours, then continue on to Krynica. Any one of the *Beskid Sądecki* maps has all the details. For a shorter walk, clamber up to the ruins of the 14th-century Muszyna Castle, on a wooded prominence just over the Muszynka River from town. There's also a pretty promenade along the Poprad River, about 300m beyond the Rynek. To find it, follow ul Kity from the Rynek out of town about 200m and cross the rail tracks.

🛏 Sleeping

Sanatorium Uzdrowiskowe Korona SPA HOTEL €€
(☑ 18 477 7960; www.sanatoriumkorona.pl; ul Mściwujewskiego 2; s/d/apt 150/250/320zł; 🅿🔊⊠) Perched above the Poprad River 1km southwest of central Muszyna, this modern hotel-hydrotherapy centre has 120 beds in bright, well-maintained rooms and a good choice of spa treatments. The sanatorium also offers health packages including meals, accommodation and five daily treatments from 176zł per day (twin share, six-night minimum).

Hotel Klimek Spa SPA HOTEL €€€
(☑ 18 477 8222; www.hotel-klimek.com.pl; Złockie 107; s/d/tr 300/400/600zł; 🅿❄🔊⊠) In Złockie, about 2.5km northwest of the centre of Muszyna, this 53-room spa hotel is one of the best (and most expensive) places around, with a long list of hydrotherapy programmes and treatments on offer, plus a sauna, steam room and small water park. There's a good restaurant and bar on site, and packages can be found online.

✕ Eating & Drinking

Pizzera & Restauracja Rzym ITALIAN €€
(☑ 18 440 8370; www.restauracjarzym.pl; Rynek 25; mains 28-35zł; ⊙ 10am-10pm; 🔊) 'Rome', which looks like an unassuming pizzeria on the outside, is actually a pretty good all-around restaurant, with Polish dishes such as pierogi and potato pancakes sharing menu space with sous-vide chicken on polenta and pappardelle with demi-glace and forest mushrooms.

★ **Kawiarnia**
Artystyczna Szarotka CAFE
(☑ 18 471 4013; Rynek 14; ☺ 10am-6pm) This old-fashioned cafe and ice-cream parlour has been one of Muszyna's social hinges since 1963. It has fabulous ice-cream sundaes, homemade pies and cookies, as well as blocks of white and dark chocolate. The dining area is decorated with lace tablecloths, framed pictures, LPs and books, and there's a pretty flower-bedizened patio outside.

ⓘ Information

Vector Travel Agency (☑ 18 471 8003; www.btvector.com; ul Kościelna 1; ☺ 11am-5pm Mon-Fri, to 1pm Sat) In the absence of a public tourist information office, you can turn to this private travel agency on Muszyna's Rynek for local information, accommodation and activities.

ⓘ Getting There & Away

Buses to Krynica (3.50zł, 15 minutes) and Nowy Sącz (7zł, 1¼ hours) run frequently. Muszyna is also on the rail line linking Krynica (5.30zł, 17 minutes) with Nowy Sącz (14zł, 1¼ hours); trains run regularly to both destinations.

PIENINY

A startlingly beautiful, 35km-long mountain range between the Beskid Sądecki and the Tatras, the Pieniny consists of three separate ranges divided by the Dunajec River. The highest and most popular is the central range topped by Mt Trzy Korony (Three Crowns; 981m), overlooking the Dunajec Gorge. Almost all of this area is now the **Pieniny National Park** (Pieniński Park Narodowy), the headquarters of which is at Krościenko. To the east, behind the Dunajec River and south of Szczawnica, lies the Małe Pieniny (Small Pieniny), while to the west extends the Pieniny Spiskie. The latter outcrop, south of Czorsztyn Lake and including Niedzica, is the lowest and least spectacular, though the region around it, known as the Spisz, has an interesting blend of Polish and Slovakian cultures. Outdoor activities are a real draw throughout the region, while lovers of architecture will relish splendid castles and amazing old wooden churches.

Szczawnica

POP 5965

Picturesquely located along the Grajcarek River, Szczawnica (shchahv-*nee*-tsah) was a popular spa in the 19th century, and remains a favourite summer resort. Taking the waters and kicking back in sanatoria are only some of its attractions. It also has some modest ski slopes and is the disembarkation point for Dunajec Gorge raft trips.

The town spreads out for 4km along the main road, ul Główna, and is divided into two sections, Szczawnica Niżna (Szczawnica Lower) to the west and Szczawnica Wyżna (Szczawnica Upper) to the east, with the bus station more or less in between. Most of the tourist and spa facilities are in the upper section, which also boasts most of the fine old timber houses.

HIKING IN THE PIENINY

Almost all hiking concentrates on the central Pieniny range, a compact area of 40 sq km that now encompasses Pieniny National Park. Trails are well marked and short, and no trekking equipment is necessary. There are three starting points on the outskirts of the park, all providing accommodation and food. The most popular is Krościenko at the northern edge, then Szczawnica on the eastern rim and Sromowce Niżne to the south. Arm yourself with the 1:50,000 *Gorce i Pieniny, Pieniński Park Narodowy* map, which includes a 1:125,000 map of the park showing all hiking routes. It retails for around 21zł.

Many walkers start from the Rynek in Krościenko. Follow the yellow trail as far as the **Przełęcz Szopka** pass, then switch to the blue trail branching off to the left and head up to the top of **Mt Trzy Korony** (981m), the highest summit of the central range. If the weather is clear the reward for this two-hour walk is a breathtaking panorama that includes the Tatras, 35km to the southwest. You are now about 520m above the level of the Dunajec River.

WORTH A TRIP

RAFTING THE DUNAJEC GORGE

Dunajec Gorge (Przełom Dunajca) is a spectacular stretch of the Dunajec (doo-nah-yets) River that snakes from Czorsztyn Lake (Jezioro Czorsztyńskie) west for about 8km between steep cliffs, some of which are more than 300m high. The river is narrow, in one instance funnelling through a 12m-wide bottleneck, and changes incessantly from majestically quiet, deep stretches to shallow mountain rapids. Rafting the gorge is one of the most popular outdoor activities in the Carpathians; be advised, however, that this is not a white-water experience but a leisurely pleasure trip.

Operated by the Polish Association of Pieniny Rafters, which keeps things traditional, the raft trip begins in the small village of Sromowce Wyżne-Kąty, at the raft landing place. You'll take an 18km-long trip and disembark in Szczawnica. The journey takes about 2¼ hours, depending on the level of the river. Some rafts go further downstream to Krościenko (23km, 2¾ hours), but there's not much to see on that stretch of the river.

The raft itself is a set of five narrow, 6m-long, coffin-like canoes lashed together with rope. Holding 10 to 12 passengers, it is steered by two people, each decked out in embroidered folk costume and armed with a long navigating pole.

The trip to Szczawnica costs 57/34zł adult/concession, while the one to Krościenko is 71/41zł. Return bus tickets cost an additional 10/8zł.

All of the private travel agencies in Kraków, Zakopane and Nowy Targ offer rafting package tours, including transport, equipment and guides. Prices vary, but trips from Zakopane start at around 100zł and from Kraków at around 200zł. The tour sponsored by Szewczyk Travel (p234) in Szczawnica is around 65zł, including transport.

In summer Sromowce Wyżne-Kąty is serviced by regular buses from Szczawnica (8zł, 30 minutes). Another way of getting to Sromowce Wyżne-Kąty is to hike from Krościenko (8km, four hours) or Szczawnica (16km, four hours).

 Activities

Szczawnica is a good starting point for hiking in both the Pieniny and the Beskid Sądecki ranges. Three trails originate in town and two more begin at Jaworki, 7km to the southeast. Call in at the Pieniny Tourism Centre (p234) in the heart of town for maps and advice.

It's also an excellent centre for cycling, with some demanding mountain-bike trails in the hills, and a stunningly beautiful, family-friendly run that skirts the Dunajec Gorge for most of its length. The Dunajec Cycle Path starts at the base of the Palenica chairlift and runs 15km along the Dunajec River to the Slovak town of Červený Kláštor, then on to Niedzica. There are several rental outfits around town, including **Pod Kolejką** (✆604 897 778; www.podkolejka.com.pl; ul Głowna 7; 6/30zł per 1hr/day; ☉9am-7pm May-Sep) at the base of the chairlift.

Szczawnica Spa Pumproom SPA
(Pijalnia Uzdrowisko Szczawnica SA; ✆18 540 0422; www.uzdrowiskoszczawnica.pl; Plac Dietla 1; tastings 1.30zł; ☉7.30am-5.30pm Mon-Fri, 9am-5pm Sat & Sun) Walk 500m uphill from the centre of Szczawnica, along ul Zdrojowa, to take the waters at this handsome mineral-spring pump room, a re-creation of the 1863 *pijalnia* that burnt down in 2002. On tap are waters from six different springs (the local favourite and purported panacea is 'Helena'), with descriptions of their composition and benefits in English.

Water Park WATER PARK
(Park Wodny; ul Zdrojowa 4, Solar Spa Hotel; adult/concession 18/15zł; ☉10.30am-9pm Mon-Sat, from 10am Sun, last entry 7.45pm; ⊕) Located in the Solar Spa Hotel, this indoor 'water park' has a pool, waterslide, wave-maker and paddling pool, and is open to non-residents. Fees drop slightly on weekdays.

Palenica Chairlift SNOW SPORTS
(Kolej Krzesełkowa Palenica; www.pkl.pl; ul Głowna 7; adult/concession return 18/15zł, one way 13/10zł; ☉9am-7.30pm Jan–mid-Mar & Jul & Aug, shorter hours rest of year) The quad chairlift near the centre of Szczawnica heads up Palenica (720m), in around four minutes. In winter this is a popular snowboard run; in summer it's a great start to several mountain hikes.

📖 Sleeping & Eating

Most of the better places to stay are located in the upper part of the town, closer to the spa action; follow ul Zdrojowa uphill for 200m to 300m. Plenty of locals also rent out rooms, especially in summer. Look for signs along ul Główna and side streets and expect to pay from 60zł to 70zł per person for a room with a bathroom.

★ Hotel Batory   HOTEL €€
(📞 18 262 0207; www.batory-hotel.pl; ul Park Górny 13; s/d 230/280zł; 🅿 🛜) This folksy-looking, yet thoroughly renovated hotel offers 25 appealing rooms in a peaceful park location above Szczawnica. Wooden decorations, inviting balconies and a general air of competently managed peace are augmented by the in-house Salonik Spa and a restaurant (mains 27zł to 33zł) that ventures beyond the standard Polish playbook.

To find Batory follow ul Zdrojowa 500m uphill from the centre of town, then turn hard right at ul Park Górny.

Solar Spa Hotel   HOTEL €€€
(📞 18 262 0810; www.solarspa.pl; ul Zdrojowa 4; s/d 240/460zł; 🅿 @ 🛜 ⛱) This huge hotel and spa complex offers spacious, spotless and conservatively furnished rooms spread over four separate buildings. The list of spa treatments is extensive, there are two in-house restaurants and you'll find plenty of packages online. Included in the price is entry to the hotel's indoor water park (p233), with various pools, slides, jacuzzis, saunas and other diversions.

★ Café Helenka   INTERNATIONAL €€
(📞 18 540 0402; www.cafe-helenka.pl; Plac Dietla 1; mains 18-24zł; 🕙 10.30am-7pm Mon-Thu, 10am-8.30pm Fri-Sun; 🛜 🍴) Attached to Szczawnica's reconstructed Victorian pump room (p233), Café Helenka is a handsome, light-filled establishment with a broad terrace for warm-weather lingering. The menu offers pastas, salads and quiches alongside a smattering of Polish standards, and the cakes, coffee and ice cream are excellent. Vegetarian options are broader than elsewhere in town.

ℹ️ Information

Szewczyk Travel (📞 600 202 636; www.szewczyk travel.pl; ul Zdrojowa 2a; 🕙 9am-4pm Mon-Fri, to 2pm Sat) and the **Pieniny Tourism Centre** (Pienińskie Centrum Turystyki; 📞 18 262 2332; www.pieninskiecentrumturystyki.pl; ul Główna 1; 🕙 8am-4pm Mon-Sat) stand in for an official tourist office in Szczawnica, and can arrange rafting and other trips.

ℹ️ Getting There & Away

Regular buses run to Nowy Sącz (11zł, one hour), Stary Sącz (8zł, 50 minutes); and Kraków (22zł, 2¼ hours).

For the Dunajec Gorge take a bus (regular in high season) to Sromowce Wyżne-Kąty (8zł, 30 minutes) – the driver will set you down at the right place. There are also private minibuses that depart when full.

Niedzica

POP 2067

Five kilometres northwest of Sromowce Wyżne-Kąty, Niedzica (signposted as 'Niedzica Zamek') is known for its dramatically situated castle. Perched on a rocky hill above the southeastern end of Czorsztyn Lake, the castle was built in the early 14th century to protect the Hungarian frontier, as this region marked the northern border of that kingdom (and remained in Hungarian hands until the end of WWII). It was partially restored in the 1920s and again 50 years later, but it essentially looks the same as it did in the 17th century, managing to retain a graceful Renaissance shape.

👁 Sights & Activities

Niedzica Castle Museum   MUSEUM
(Muzeum Zamkowy w Niedzicy; 📞 18 262 9473; www.zamekwniedzicy.pl; ul Zamkowa 2; adult/concession 14/12zł; 🕙 9am-7pm daily May-Sep, 9am-4pm Tue-Sun Oct-Apr) Built in the 14th century and continually improved over the centuries in which it guarded Hungary's northern border, this superbly preserved lakeside castle now houses a regional history museum. There's not a tremendous amount to see – some period costumes, furnishings, hunting trophies, a chapel from the late 14th century and collections on the archaeology and history of the Spisz region – but there are fine views over the lake and surrounding area. Everything is signposted in English.

Harnaś   BOATING
(📞 18 275 0121; www.turystyka.wolski.pl; adult/concession 14/12zł; 🕙 May–mid-Oct) Equipped with a cafe and sun deck, the pleasure boat *Harnaś* plies the waters of Czorsztyn Lake every hour in the season (with a minimum of 20 passengers). Boats leave the pier beneath the castle to the northwest between 10am and 6pm for a 50-minute cruise. A simple ferry to Czorsztyn on the other lakeshore costs adult/concession 6/5zł each way.

ABANDONED BEAUTY OF CZORSZTYN

The village of Czorsztyn (chor-shtin), across the lake from Niedzica, boasts romantic **castle ruins** (Zamek w Czorsztynie; ☑18 262 5602; ul Zamkowa; adult/concession 6/3zł; ☺9am-6pm daily May-Sep, 10am-3pm Tue-Sun Oct-Apr; ℗) dating from the second half of the 13th century.

The fortress was built as the Polish counterpart to the Hungarian stronghold opposite at Niedzica (the customs frontier ran through the area). Extensively burned in 1790 it's now a picturesque ruin with a 15th-century gatehouse, courtyards, the remains of an old kitchen and a small exhibition on the Pieniny region. Best of all are the excellent views over the lake, the Dunajec River valley and the distant Tatras.

The village is just off the Krośnica–Sromowce Wyżne-Kąty road, accessible on the same bus you take for the Dunajec raft trip at Sromowce Wyżne-Kąty, or you can sail over in an hour from the Niedzica side.

🛏 Sleeping & Eating

Niedzica offers few sleeping options, but those it does are high quality.

Hotel Lokis HOTEL €€
(☑18 262 8540; www.lokis.com.pl; ul Cisowa 4; d/tr/apt 280/360/500zł; ℗☎) In a wonderful spot overlooking the lake, the Lokis is a modern hotel in a traditional-style gabled building. With 23 rooms, a gym and sauna, and a balcony with lake views (also available from the slightly more expensive rooms), it's one of the more inviting places to stay in the Spisz region.

Hotel Pieniny HOTEL €€
(☑18 262 9383; www.niedzica.pl; ul Kanada 38; s/d/tr 120/170/250zł; ℗☎) Halfway between the castle and Niedzica village to the south, this 52-room hotel is a reasonably priced option with plain but comfortable rooms. It's family friendly, with a tennis court, minigolf course and sauna, and bikes can be hired for 5/25zł per hour/day. Unusually for Poland, the hotel restaurant offers gluten-free options.

Karczma Hajduk POLISH €€
(☑18 262 9507; www.karczmahajduk.pl; Zamkowa 1; mains 15-25zł; ☺10am-6pm; ☎) This inn, the name of which recalls Niedzica Castle's Hungarian origins (*hajduks* were Hungarian mercenaries who fought against the Habsburgs in the 17th and 18th centuries), serves filling Polish dishes such as pierogi and grilled meats next door to the castle. There are outdoor seats overlooking the lake and castle, if weather permits.

ℹ Getting There & Away

You'll need your own wheels to visit Niedzica.

Silesia

Best Places to Eat

➡ Restauracja Jadka (p246)

➡ Tatiana (p274)

➡ Chata na Zaborskiej (p278)

➡ Chinkalnia Restauracja Gruzińska (p246)

➡ Rybex (p270)

Best Places to Stay

➡ Hotel Monopol (p245)

➡ Villa Navigator (p267)

➡ Hotel Fado (p253)

➡ Hotel Przy Oślej Bramie (p251)

Why Go?

Occupying the southwestern part of Poland, Silesia (Śląsk, pronounced *shlonsk* in Polish), is a diverse collection of historically powerful cities, industrial engine rooms and low-rising, farm-flanked mountains.

Wrocław, the region's historical capital and Poland's fourth-largest city, is the overwhelming draw here, yet smaller cities such as Nysa and Jelenia Góra also offer distinctive sights and activities. To the south, stretching over the Czech border, the Sudetes Mountains promise scenic beauty and idyllic resort towns, and are popular with hikers, bikers and spa fans.

The rich and turbulent history of this region is never far beneath its charm. Silesia boasts memorable architecture ranging from medieval fortresses to baroque cathedrals. Great tragedy is also remembered here: Silesia was where Nazi Germany set up the Auschwitz-Birkenau extermination camps, now preserved as an essential, unforgettable memorial.

When to Go
Wrocław

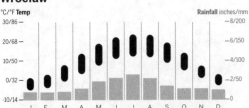

Apr Spring's vitality is a good match for the Jazz on the Odra festival in Wrocław.

Jun–Aug Summer is the season to enjoy hiking in the Sudetes Mountains.

Sep In autumn, celebrate Poland's little-known wine at Zielona Góra's Wine Festival.

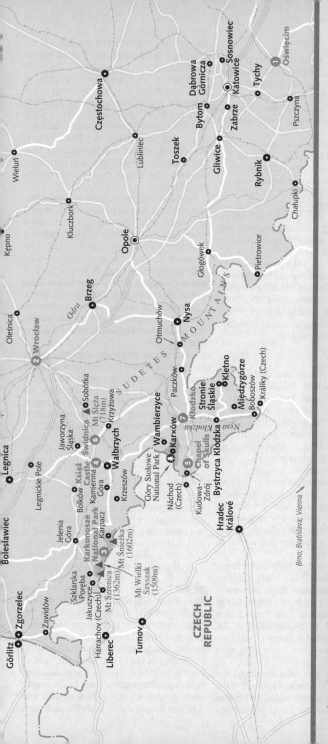

Silesia Highlights

1 **Auschwitz-Birkenau Memorial & Museum** (p277) Learning one of the world's most essential history lessons at this profoundly moving memorial in Oświęcim.

2 **Wrocław** (p238) Losing yourself in the medieval streets and rarefied atmosphere of Silesia's historical capital.

3 **Karkonosze National Park** (p255) Hiking between the wooded slopes of Mt Szrenica and Mt Śnieżka.

4 **Książ Castle** (p250) Rambling through this vast, historically layered fortress-palace.

5 **Chapel of Skulls** (p263) Eyeballing the certain end of all earthly things at this sacred ossuary near Kudowa-Zdrój.

6 **Church of Peace** (p252) Contemplating life in Świdnica's baroque timber church.

7 **Kłodzko Fortress** (p261) Scaling ramparts and scouring underground labyrinths at this 17th-century stronghold.

WROCŁAW

POP 630.131

Everyone loves Wrocław (*vrots*-wahf) and it's easy to see why. With an idyllic location on the Odra River, the venerable city comprises 12 islands, 130 bridges and verdant riverside parks. The beautifully preserved Cathedral Island is a treat for lovers of Gothic architecture.

Though in some ways it's a more manageable version of Kraków, with all the cultural attributes and entertainment offerings found in that popular destination, the capital of Lower Silesia has an appealing character all its own. Having absorbed Bohemian, Austrian and Prussian influences, the city has a unique architectural and cultural make-up, symbolised by its magnificent market square (Rynek).

But Wrocław is not just a pretty face – it's Poland's fourth-largest city and the major industrial, commercial and educational centre for the region. At the same time it's a lively cultural hub, with several theatres, major festivals, rampant nightlife and a population of more than 130,000 students.

History

Wrocław was originally founded on Cathedral Island (Ostrów Tumski). The first recorded Polish ruler, Duke Mieszko I, brought the town – together with most of Silesia – into the Polish state. It must have been a fair-sized settlement by the turn of the first millennium, as it was chosen, along with Kraków and Kołobrzeg, as one of Piast Poland's three bishoprics.

During the period of division in the 12th and 13th centuries, Wrocław was the capital of one of the principalities of the Silesian Piasts. Like most settlements in southern Poland, Wrocław was burned down by the Tatars. The town centre was then moved to the river's left bank.

Wrocław continued to grow under Bohemian administration (1335–1526), reaching the height of its prosperity in the 15th century and maintaining trade and cultural links with the Polish crown. New fortifications were constructed at the beginning of the 16th century, and the remains of the Fosa Miejska (City Moat) show where they were once positioned.

The Habsburgs, who ruled the city for the next two centuries, were less tolerant of the Polish and Czech communities, and things got even worse for the Slavic populations

after 1741, when Wrocław fell to Prussia. For the next two centuries the city was increasingly Germanised and became known as Breslau.

As one of the major eastern outposts of the Third Reich, Breslau was given a key defensive role in the last stages of WWII, with the whole city converted into a fortified compound, 'Fortress Breslau'. Besieged by the Red Army in February 1945, the Germans defended their last bastion until May, executing anyone who refused to fight. During the battle, 75% of the city was razed to the ground.

Of the prewar population of more than 600,000, an estimated 30% died, mostly as a result of the fighting and the botched evacuation that preceded it. The handful of Germans who remained were expelled to Germany, and the ruined city was resettled with people from Poland's prewar eastern regions, mostly from Lviv (Lwów in Polish), which had been ceded to the Soviet Union.

The difficult reconstruction of Wrocław continued well into the 1980s, when the city surpassed its prewar population level for the first time.

Since the fall of communism, the city has had some success in attracting new investment, including the presence of LG Electronics in nearby Kobierzyce. Wrocław has also established itself as a centre of finance and tourism, and was designated a 2016 European Capital of Culture by the EU.

◉ Sights

◉ Old Town

Wrocław's extensive Old Town is so full of historical buildings that you could wander around for weeks and still feel like you hadn't seen everything. It's the kind of area that well repays a wander through its backstreets after you've oriented yourself through a visit to the lively central square.

★ **Old Town Hall**　　HISTORIC BUILDING
(Stary Ratusz; Map p240; Rynek) This glorious Gothic edifice, Wrocław's quintessential photo opportunity, took shape over more than 200 years. The right-hand part of the eastern facade, with its austere early Gothic features, is the oldest, while the delicate carving to the left shows early Renaissance style. The astronomical clock in the centre, made of larch wood, was built in 1580. The southern facade, dating from the early 16th

century, is the most elaborate, with a pair of ornate bay windows and carved stone figures.

Step inside to peruse the **Museum of Bourgeois Art** (Muzeum Sztuki Mieszczańskiej; Map p240; www.muzeum.miejskie.wroclaw.pl; temporary exhibitions adult/concession 15/10zł; ⊙10am-5pm Wed-Sat, to 6pm Sun) FREE.

★**Wrocław Dwarves**   PUBLIC ART
(Wrocławskie Krasnale) See if you can spot the tiny bronze statue of a dwarf resting on the ground, just to the west of the Hansel & Gretel houses. A few metres away you'll spot firefighter dwarves, rushing to put out a blaze. These figures are part of a collection of over 300 scattered through the city. Though whimsical, they're also a reference to the symbol of the Orange Alternative (p244), a communist-era dissident group that used ridicule as a weapon.

★**Cathedral of
St Mary Magdalene**   CATHEDRAL
(Katedra św Marii Magdaleny; Map p240; ul Szewska 10; tower adult/concession 8/5zł; ⊙tower 10am-8pm Apr-Oct, to 7pm Nov-Mar) One block east of the Rynek is this mighty Gothic red-brick cathedral, dating to the 14th century. Its showpiece is a Romanesque portal from around 1280 on the exterior south wall, which originally adorned the Benedictine Abbey in Ołbin, but was moved here in 1546 after the abbey was demolished. You can climb the 72m-high tower and cross the Bridge of Penitents.

Hansel & Gretel   HISTORIC BUILDING
(Jaś i Małgosia; Map p240; ul Odrzańska 39/40) Set in the northwestern corner of the Rynek are two charming houses known locally as Jaś i Małgosia, better known to English and German speakers as Hansel and Gretel. They're linked by a baroque archway built in 1728, which once led to the church cemetery (the inscription in Latin reads 'Death is the gateway to life'). The 'Hansel' house is also known as the Copperplate Engraver's House, after local artist Eugeniusz Get-Stankiewicz, who had his studio here.

Church of St Elizabeth   BASILICA
(Kościół Św Elżbiety; Map p240; ul Św Elżbiety 1; tower admission 5zł; ⊙10am-7pm) This 14th-century Gothic basilica has a triple nave reaching to 30m and is lined by medieval chapels. It's one of Wrocław's most imposing churches, with a 90m-high tower looming over the Rynek's northwest corner. You can

climb the tower's 300-plus steps (the views are sublime) or admire ground-level treasures including a mid-15th-century sacramentary, or the carved medieval choir stalls.

⊙ **University Quarter**

★**Church of the
Holy Name of Jesus**   CHURCH
(Kościół Najświętszego Imienia Jezus; Map p240; www.uniwersytecki.archidiecezja.wroc.pl; Plac Uniwersytecki 1) Wrocław University's baroque-rococo church is arguably the most beautiful in the city. It was built by the Jesuits in the 1690s on the site of the former Piast castle. Its spectacular interior, painted to give the appearance of white marble, is crammed with ornate fittings and adorned with fine illusionist frescoes of the life of Jesus. See the website for the church's somewhat convoluted sightseeing hours.

★**University of Wrocław**   UNIVERSITY
(Uniwersytet Wrocławski; Map p240; www.uni.wroc.pl; Plac Uniwersytecki 1) Established by the Jesuits in the early 18th century, the University of Wrocław's main edifice was built between 1728 and 1742. While it's very much a functioning seat of scholarship, it is partly open to sightseers – enter through the grand blue-and-gold rococo gate at the western end to start exploring. The principal attraction is the baroque ceremonial hall known as the Aula Leopoldinum.

Aula Leopoldinum   ARCHITECTURE
(Map p240; Plac Uniwersytecki; adult/concession 12/8zł; ⊙10am-3.30pm Thu-Tue) On the first floor of the main building of the University of Wrocław, this ceremonial hall is Wrocław's most beautiful baroque interior, embellished with elaborate stuccoes, sculptures, paintings and a trompe l'oeil ceiling fresco. The more modest Oratorium Marianum, on the ground floor, is included in the admission fee, as is the Mathematical Tower, topped with a sphere and decorated with allegorical figures.

**Cathedral of SS
Vincent and James**   CATHEDRAL
(Kościół Św Wincentego i Św Jakuba; Map p240; Plac Nankiera 15a) The Gothic Cathedral of SS Vincent and James was originally a Romanesque basilica, founded in the early 13th century. The largest church in the city, it's now used by the Uniat (Eastern Rite Catholic) faithful.

Wrocław

Odra

31 Wyspa Słodowa

Piasek Island (Sand Island)

Church of the Holy Name of Jesus **1**

University of Wrocław Plac **5** Uniwersytecki

38

8

Plac Biskupa Nankiera

58

Grodzka

Garbary

Uniwersytecka

45

Odrzańska

Grodzka

Malarska św Elżbiety

Wężenna

49

Plac Nowy Targ

Nowy Świat

42 **57** **22**

Rzeźnicza

29

46

41

Kotlarska

Kuźnicza

Nożownicza

Krowia

Krańskiego

Piaskowa

12

Igielna

52

Podwale

Cieszyńskiego

6

św Mikołaja

50

14 św Mikołaja

48

Rynek

39

Szewska

Wita Stwosza

Ruska

53

44

40

Kiełbaśnicza

24

36

35 **43** **16**

37

33

2 Cathedral of St Mary Magdalene

Antoniego

55

Psie Budy

Plac Solny

32

3 Old Town Hall

Oławska

34 Plac Dominikański

Ruska

Szajnochy

Świdnicka

Szewska

Włodkowica

20

47

25

Krupnicza

27

Kazimierza Wielkiego

51

Sądowa

Fosa Miejska

Podwale

Modrzejewskiej Plac Wolności

11 **28**

56

Mennicza

Piotra Skargi

Nowa

Muzealna

Teatralna

Park Staromiejski

Podwale

18

Świdnicka

Fosa Miejska Podwale

Kościuszki

Łakowa

Kołłątaja

54

Piłsudskiego

Zapolskiej

Plac Kościuszki

Kolejowa

19

Piłsudskiego

Starowa

26

30

Gwarna

Dworcowa

Swobodna

Małachowskiego

Gwiaździsta

Wrocław Central **(300m)**

Old Jewish Cemetery (2km)

Wrocław Główny Train Station

⊙ East of the Old Town

★ Panorama of Racławice   MUSEUM

(Panorama Racławicka; Map p240; ☎71 344 2344; www.panoramaraclawicka.pl; ul Purkyniego 11; adult/concession 30/23zł; ⊙8am-7.30pm Apr-Oct, 9am-4.30pm Sun & Tue-Fri, to 5.30pm Sat Nov-Mar; ℗) Wrocław's pride and joy is this giant painting of the battle for Polish independence fought at Racławice on 4 April 1794, between the Polish army led by Tadeusz Kościuszko and Russian troops under General Alexander Tormasov. The Poles won but it was all for naught: months later the nationwide insurrection was crushed by the tsarist army. The canvas measures 15m by 114m, and is wrapped around the internal walls of a purpose-built rotunda.

Visits are by guided tour, departing every half hour. You move around the balcony, inspecting each scene in turn, while an audio guide provides recorded commentary. The small rotunda (free admission) behind the ticket office features a model of the battlefield and the uniforms of forces engaged in the battle.

The painting came into being when, a century after the battle, it was commissioned by a group of patriots in Lviv (then the Polish city of Lwów). The two main artists, Jan Styka and Wojciech Kossak, were helped by seven other painters who did the background scenes and details. They completed the monumental canvas in just over nine months, using 750kg of paint.

After WWII the painting was sent to Wrocław, but since it depicted a defeat of the Russians (then Poland's official friend and liberator), the communist authorities were reluctant to put it on display. The pavilion built for the panorama in 1967 sat empty until 1985, when the canvas was shown for the first time in more than four decades.

National Museum   MUSEUM

(Muzeum Narodowe; Map p240; www.mnwr.pl; Plac Powstańców Warszawy 5; adult/concession 20/15zł, free Sat; ⊙10am-5pm Tue-Fri, 10.30am-6pm Sat & Sun Apr-Oct, 10am-4pm Tue-Fri, to 5pm Sat & Sun Nov-Mar) Wrocław's National Museum is a treasure trove of fine art from across the ages. Medieval sculpture is displayed on the ground floor; exhibits include the Romanesque tympanum from the portal of the Church of St Mary Magdalene (p239, which depicts the Assumption of the Virgin Mary), and 14th-century sarcophagi from the Church of SS Vincent &

Wrocław

James (p239). There are also collections of Silesian paintings, ceramics, silverware and furnishings from the 16th to 19th centuries.

Museum of Architecture MUSEUM
(Muzeum Architektury; Map p240; www.ma.wroc.pl; ul Bernardyńska 5; adult/concession 10/7zł, Wed free; ⊙10am-6pm Tue-Sun) Taking over both artefacts and premises from the former Silesian Museum of Artistic Crafts and Antiquities, the Museum of Architecture is located in a 16th-century former Bernardine church and monastery. The collection features stone sculptures and stained-glass windows from historical buildings of the region, architectural designs and models and photographs. The oldest exhibit, a Romanesque tympanum, dates from 1165. The museum also has a 12th-century Jewish tombstone, a 1:500 scale model of Wrocław (1740), and a delightful cloister garden.

◎ Cathedral Island

The erstwhile Cathedral Island (Ostrów Tumski) – it became connected to the mainland in the 19th century – was the cradle of Wrocław. It was here that the Ślężanie, a tribe of West Slavs who gave their name to the region, constructed their stronghold in the 7th or 8th century. After the town was incorporated into the Polish state and a bishopric established in 1000, Wrocław's first church was built here. Over time a number of churches, monasteries and other religious buildings were constructed, giving a distinctive, markedly ecclesiastical character to the district.

Botanical Gardens
GARDENS

(Ogród Botaniczny; Map p240; ✆71 322 5957; www.ogrodbotaniczny.wroclaw.pl; ul Sienkiewicza 23; adult/concession 15/10zł; ⊙9am-6pm Apr & Sep, to 7pm May-Aug, to 5pm Oct) Cathedral Island contains the city's botanical gardens, a charming patch of greenery that's part of the University of Wrocław, serving educational and research purposes alongside recreational ones. Two-hour guided tours by expert staff can be arranged (250zł for groups of up to 30, in English).

Church of
Our Lady on the Sand
CHURCH

(Kościół Najświętszej Marii Panny na Piasku; Map p240; ul Św Jadwigi 1) This lofty 14th-century building dominates the tiny islet known as Sand Island (Wyspa Piasek). Almost all the fittings were destroyed during WWII and the half-dozen old triptychs you see inside were collected from other Silesian churches. The wonderful Romanesque tympanum in the south aisle is the only remnant of the original 12th-century church that once stood here. There's a mechanised *szopka* (nativity scene) in the first chapel to the right; make a small donation when an assistant turns it on.

Cathedral of
St John the Baptist
CHURCH

(Archikatedra Św Jana Chrzciciela; Map p240; www.katedra.archidiecezja.wroc.pl; Plac Katedralny 18; tower & chapels adult/concession 12/8zł; ⊙chapels noon-5pm Mon-Sat, 2-4pm Sun) The centrepiece of Cathedral Island, this three-aisled Gothic basilica was built between 1244 and 1590. Seriously damaged during WWII, it was later rebuilt in its original Gothic form. Entry to the church is free, but you need to buy a ticket to visit three beautiful baroque chapels, and to ascend to the viewpoint atop the 91m-high tower (there's a lift, but check the website to make sure it's open when you visit).

Church of St Giles
CHURCH

(Kościół Św Idziego; Map p240; Plac Św Idziego) In contrast to the enormous neighbouring Cathedral of St John the Baptist, the austere, brick-built Romanesque Church of St Giles seems barely a cupboard. But, built between 1218 and 1230, it is notable as the oldest surviving church in Wrocław, and sports an original Romanesque portal.

◉ West & South of the Old Town

The Anonymous Pedestrians
SCULPTURE

(Pomnik Anonimowego Przechodnia; Map p240; cnr uls Świdnicka & Piłsudskiego) Also known as *Passage*, this arresting sculpture depicts seven bronze pedestrians literally being swallowed by the pavement, only to re-emerge on the other side of the street. It was created by Jerzy Kalina and unveiled in 2005 to mark the 24th anniversary of the declaration of martial law. Look for it 500m west of the train station (p249).

White Stork Synagogue
SYNAGOGUE

(Synagoga Pod Białym Bocianem; Map p240; ✆71 787 3902; https://fbk.org.pl; ul Włodkowica 7; ⊙10am-5pm Mon-Thu, to 4pm Fri, 11am-4pm Sun) **FREE** This restored synagogue, built in exemplary classical style in 1829, is a reminder that this city was once home to more than 20,000 Jews. Restored by Wrocław's Jewish citizens from 1996, it now houses a permanent exhibition – *History Reclaimed* – on 800 years of Jewish life in Eastern Europe.

Church of SS Stanislaus,
Wenceslas and Dorothy
CHURCH

(Kościół Franciszkanów Św Stanisława, Wacława i Doroty; Map p240; Plac Franciszkańska) Founded in 1351, this massive Gothic assemblage just south of the Old Town commemorates the meeting between Polish King Kazimierz III Wielki (Casimir III the Great) and his Bohemian counterpart, Charles IV, at which they agreed to leave Silesia in Bohemia's hands. The church luckily escaped the devastation that most medieval buildings in Wrocław suffered in WWII. Note the sizeable rococo tomb at the start of the south aisle.

New Synagogue Memorial
MEMORIAL

(Pomnik Nowej Synagogi; Map p240; ul Łąkowa) This memorial marks the site of the New Synagogue, built in 1872. It was the country's second-largest synagogue, until it was torched on Kristallnacht (9 November 1938).

🏃 Tours & Activities

Gondola Bay
BOATING

(Zatoka Gondol; Map p240; ✆79 112 2858; www.visitwroclaw.eu/en/event/gondola-bay; Promenada Staromiejska; 2/3 person kayak per hour 15/19zł; ⊙10am-7pm Apr-Sep) You can get a different perspective of the city by viewing it from the water. Rent a kayak, rowing boat (per hour 25zł) or four-person motorboat (per hour 80zł) and paddle around Cathedral Island.

THE GNOMES ARE REVOLTING

How do unarmed civilians take on a totalitarian regime? For Wrocław University art history graduate Waldemar Fydrych, nicknamed 'Major', the answer was obvious – by ridiculing it.

In the early 1980s Fydrych set up the Orange Alternative (Pomarańczowa Alternatywa), a group that intended to place banana skins beneath the feet of Poland's humourless communist government. It initially painted pictures of dwarves on areas where the authorities had already painted over antigovernment graffiti – neatly drawing attention to the critical sentiments that had once been on display there.

In the second half of the decade the Alternative upped the ante by organising actions intended to both embarrass the regime and encourage independent thought. They handed out items in short supply such as toilet paper and feminine hygiene products; overdressed in red on the anniversary of Russia's communist revolution; and marched to demand the release of Father Christmas. The high point was a demonstration in 1988 in support of dwarves, in which thousands marched while wearing floppy orange hats.

Nowadays the communists are long gone and the dwarves have taken over the streets, in the form of small statues (p239) that are said to be a tribute to the icon of the Orange Alternative. 'Major' Fydrych has continued to campaign for change via silliness; in addition to continuing the Alternative's actions, he's twice run for election as Mayor of Warsaw under the slogan 'Merrier and more competent'. Though he didn't win the election, in 2012 Fydrych received his PhD from the capital's Academy of Fine Arts.

You can read more about the Orange Alternative's history and current activities at its 'virtual museum' (www.orangealternativemuseum.pl).

Wrocław Sightseeing Tours TOURS
(☑ 698 900 123, 604 063 949; www.wroclaw sightseeingtours.com) Operates guided walking tours (adult/concession 85/70zł) and bus tours (110/85zł) of the city, as well as day trips further afield in Lower Silesia and the Sudetes (from 260/190zł). Currently between offices, they're easily contacted by phone or email.

🎆 Festivals & Events

★ Wratislavia Cantans MUSIC
(www.wratislaviacantans.pl; ⊘ Sep) Starting out in 1966 as an international festival of accompanied choral music (oratorio and cantata), this festival has grown over the years to include other forms of classical and folk music. It's a highlight of Wrocław's cultural calendar.

Arsenal Nights MUSIC
(www.wieczorywarsenale.pl; ⊘ Jun-Jul) This festival of chamber music brings harmony to Wrocław's 15th-century **arsenal** (Map p240; ul Cieszyńskiego 9) for nine nights each summer.

Jazz on the Odra MUSIC
(Jazz nad Odrą; www.jazznadodra.pl) Running since 1964, this well-curated jazz festival consistently draws interesting acts to Wrocław

over five days in late April. Most shows take place at Impart, on ul Mazowiecka 17.

Musica Polonica Nova MUSIC
(www.musicapolonicanova.pl) This avant-garde contemporary music festival, held over a week in late April, includes installations, workshops and lectures, as well as performances.

🛌 Sleeping

Hostel Mleczarnia HOSTEL €
(Map p240; ☑ 71 787 7570; www.mleczarniahostel. pl; ul Włodkowica 5; dm/d 40/220zł; 🛜) Set in a quiet courtyard not far from the Rynek, this hostel has bags of charm, having been decorated in a deliberately old-fashioned style with antique furniture. There's a women-only dorm available, along with a kitchen and free laundry facilities. In the courtyard is the excellent Mleczarnia (p248) cafe-bar. The one double room is in a nearby flat.

Cinnamon Hostel HOSTEL €
(Map p240; ☑ 71 344 5858; www.facebook.com/ cinnamonhostel.wroclaw; ul Wielkiego 67; dm/s/d 50/120/160zł; 🛜) Right on the ring road and within spitting distance of pedestrianised ul Świdnicka, this charming and upbeat place has rooms (with two to 12

beds) named for spices and herbs, along with a kitchen, laundry and comfortable common room.

Hotel Patio
HOTEL €€

(Map p240; ☑71 375 0400; www.hotelpatio.pl; ul Kiełbaśnicza 24; s/d from 221/246zł; P ✳ 🕾)
Spread behind the Victorian facades of two adjoining tenements just off the Rynek, this pleasantly modernised little hotel offers 50 comfortable rooms in a variety of styles, including suites and apartments. A covered sunlit courtyard connects the two buildings. The buffet breakfast – with fish, fruit, pastries, eggs cooked various ways and plenty more – is one of the best in town.

Hotel Tumski
HOTEL €€

(Map p240; ☑71 322 6099; www.hotel-tumski.com.pl; Wyspa Słodowa 10; s/d 240/280zł; 🕾)
Located on an islet in the Odra, this neat 57-room hotel is surrounded by flowing water on three sides, yet is within easy walking distance of most of Wrocław's attractions. There's an in-house rustic-style restaurant serving both Polish and international cuisine, and another, on the Tumska-Słodowa 10 Barge, moored alongside.

Dwór Polski
HOTEL €€

(Map p240; ☑71 372 3415; www.dworpolski.wroclaw.pl; ul Kiełbaśnicza 2; s/d 260/360zł; P 🕾)
You couldn't ask for more character than this: a restored 16th-century house, complete with idiosyncratic rooms, some original dark-wood fittings and fixtures, and a popular restaurant (enter from Rynek 5). The atmospheric internal courtyard is a plus.

Hotel Piast
HOTEL €€

(Map p240; ☑71 769 6200; www.piastwroclaw.pl; ul Piłsudskiego 98; s/d from 224/259zł; ✳ 🕾)
Built in 1908 – then known as the Kronprinz (Crown Prince) – this was once one of the city's top hotels, its distinctive corner tower a landmark dominating the train station (p249) across the street. Completely renovated in 2014, its rooms are clean, spacious and good value, and the in-house restaurant is decent, with a breakfast buffet kicking off at 7am.

Hotel Europejski
HOTEL €€

(Map p240; ☑71 772 1000; www.silfor.pl; ul Piłsudskiego 88; s/d from 230/250zł; P ✳ 🕾)
Dating to 1876, when the erstwhile Hotel Hohenzollern-Hof was one of a clutch of large hotels near the train station (p249), the Europejski is now a smart business hotel offering professional service and clean, agreeable rooms. You can still see period fittings such as the imposing wooden reception desk, while the restaurant does its best to reimagine the belle époque.

Hotel Europeum
HOTEL €€

(Map p240; ☑71 371 4400; www.europeum.pl; ul Wielkiego 27a; s/d 315/355zł; P ✳ 🕾)
The business-oriented Hotel Europeum transcends its utilitarian niche with artistic flourishes in painted ceramic and glass, plus more attention to style in the thoroughly modern rooms. It's in a good location not far from the Rynek, and you can usually get weekend discounts. On-site restaurant Brasserie 27 looks more to Italy and France than Poland (mains 26zł to 47zł).

★ Hotel Monopol
LUXURY HOTEL €€€

(Map p240; ☑71 772 3777; www.monopolwroclaw.hotel.com.pl; ul Modrzejewskiej 2; d/ste from 577/833zł; ✳ 🕾 ⛲)
Built on the site of a ruined Franciscan priory in 1892, the Monopol is one of Wrocław's destination hotels, having housed such luminaries as Pablo Picasso and Marlene Dietrich (and the less-welcome Adolf Hitler). Behind its elaborate sculpted facade you'll find 135 rooms and apartments appointed to a fine degree of luxury.

Art Hotel
HOTEL €€€

(Map p240; ☑71 787 7400; www.arthotel.pl; ul Kiełbaśnicza 20; s/d/ste 410/525/820zł; P ✳ 🕾)
An elegant splurge in a renovated apartment building, with tasteful decor, decorative art, quality fittings and gleaming bathrooms. There's a top-notch Polish-French restaurant (mains 32zł to 54zł), a fitness room for working off any extra weight gained therein, and a massage studio on-site. Breakfast, while excellent, is a hefty 50zł per person (also what a night's underground parking will cost).

Grape Hotel
HOTEL €€€

(☑71 736 0400; www.grapehotel.pl; ul Parkowa 8; r/apt from 400/1000zł; P 🕾)
This up-market option, set between extensive parkland and the Stara Odra river about 3km from central Wrocław, offers 13 richly furnished wine-themed rooms and apartments in a whimsically turreted old house with its own lovely gardens. The viticultural theme is strong (they maintain a wine library), the breakfasts are excellent and there's a gym and sauna on-site.

✖ Eating

Pierogarnia Momos
DUMPLINGS €

(Map p240; ☑794 227 752; www.pierogarnia momos.pl; ul Więzienna 5; dumplings 13-20zł; ⊘11am-8pm Mon-Fri, noon-8.30pm Sat, to 8pm Sun; 🛜) Facing down a row of bland Italian restaurants across the street, this little dumpling specialist knows a higher standard of dough. Not content with the usual Polish repertoire, they've branched out into Chinese-style dim sum, South American empanadas, and even Georgian *chinkali* (pleated dumplings). There are also soups, sides and sweet dumplings to finish.

Lepione Kuźnicza
CAFETERIA €

(Map p240; ☑71 375 2065; http://lepione.pl; ul Kuźnicza 42; per 100g 3.59zł; ⊘8am-7pm Mon-Fri, from 7.30am Sat & Sun; 🛜🍴) This gleaming, white-tiled self-serve cafeteria with plate-glass windows is an update on the popular Polish *bar mleczny* (milk bar). It's aimed at students of the adjacent university (p239) but open to anyone. Fill up on salads, stews, grilled vegetables, pierogi and more, and walk away with change from 20zł. Hot food prices drop as much as 50% after 6pm each day.

★Chinkalnia
Restauracja Gruzińska
GEORGIAN €€

(Map p240; ☑71 330 7568; Sukiennice 3/4; mains 19-24zł; ⊘noon-10pm Mon-Wed, to 11pm Thu-Sat; 🛜) Georgian restaurants are popular in Poland, and this is one of the best. A tiny front dining room hung with Georgian artefacts encourages familiarity, as do the engaging waiters eager to share Georgian cuisine with you. Famous for their *chinkali* (pleated dumplings eaten upside down to avoid losing precious juice) they also do amazing stuffed breads, grills and salads.

★Panczo
TEX-MEX €€

(Map p240; ☑884 009 737; www.facebook.com/ panczobus; ul Antoniego 35/1a; mains 22-23zł; ⊘noon-11pm Sun-Thu, to midnight Fri & Sat; 🛜) Part of a Polish trend that has seen street-food businesses opening up in permanent premises, Panczo serves up huge portions of lip-smacking tacos, enchiladas and – the house speciality – burritos. The food is fresh, zingy and authentic, as are the margaritas (18zł to 22zł). Order food at the bar; ask for an English menu if there are none on the tables.

Masala
INDIAN €€

(Map p240; ☑71 302 6949; www.masala-grill.pl; ul Kuźnicza 3; mains 30-62zł; ⊘noon-10pm Sun-Tue, to 11pm Wed-Sat; 🍴) Masala produces well-cooked Indian dishes that will be familiar to any high-street curry aficionado. The room is cheerily decorated, staff members are friendly and competent, there are good-value set meals, and it's only a few steps from the Rynek. Plus, for each meal purchased, Masala pays for a student's meal at the Devamber Gurukul School in India.

Vega Bar Wegański
VEGAN €€

(Map p240; ☑713 443 934; www.facebook.com/ vega.bar.weganski.wroclaw; Rynek 1/2; mains 21-24zł; ⊘8am-8pm Mon-Thu, to 9pm Fri, 9am-9pm Sat, to 8pm Sun; 🛜🍴) This buzzing vegan restaurant and takeaway in the centre of the Rynek serves everything from breakfasts (until noon) of oatmeal and millet with vegan milk and seasonal fruits to hot, filling lunch dishes such as tempeh burgers, Thai curries, pizzas and meat-free pierogi. There are gluten-free options too, and even vegan ice cream. It also has a cafe upstairs.

★Restauracja Jadka
POLISH €€€

(Map p240; ☑71 343 6461; www.jadka.pl; ul Rzeźnicza 24/25; mains 67-87zł; ⊘5-11pm Mon-Sat, to 10pm Sun; 🛜) 🍴 Jadka takes creating fine Polish food very seriously – sourcing faultless local produce, working closely with the best suppliers, respecting the seasons and delving deeply into the history of Polish cooking yet accepting modern ways. Dishes such as smoked carp with cucumbers, nigella seeds and nasturtium, and venison with red cabbage and dumplings are an education and a delight.

Akropolis
GREEK €€€

(Map p240; ☑71 343 1413; http://akropolis.wroc. pl; Rynek 16/17; mains 32-49zł; ⊘noon-10pm Mon-Thu, to 11pm Fri-Sun; 🛜🍴) Easily confused with the Akropolis Taverna, a few doors along at Rynek 20/21, this restaurant serves excellent Greek food with great views of the market square, defying the law of inverse correlation between a restaurant's prospect and the quality of its kitchen. Expect loving renditions of Hellenic classics – the *arni sto fourno* (baked lamb in lemon sauce) is superb.

WORTH A TRIP

ŚLĘŻA LANDSCAPE PARK

Some 34km southwest of Wrocław, the solitary forested cone of Mt Ślęża rises to 718m above the surrounding open plain. It was one of the holy places of an ancient pagan tribe that set up cult sites in the area from at least the 5th century BC until the 11th century AD. The massif is surrounded by the 82-sq-km Ślęża Landscape Park; at its northern foot is the small town of Sobótka, the starting point for hikes to the top.

The summit of Ślęża – from which the name 'Silesia' may descend – was circled by a stone wall marking off the sanctuary where rituals were held; the remains of these ramparts survive to this day. Mysterious votive statues were crudely carved out of granite, and several of them are scattered over the mountain's slopes.

From Sobótka, follow the red route for a two-hour hike up the mountain. You'll find two statues called the Bear (Miś) and the Fish (Ryba) on the way, plus a tall television mast and a 19th-century church at the top.

Coming down, you can take the steeper but faster (1¼ hours) yellow route directly to the PTTK hostel, about 800m west of your starting point. On the road back into town you'll pass another stone statue, called the Monk (Mnich); it resembles an urn to untrained eyes.

Sobótka is easily reached by regular buses from Wrocław (7.50zł, 55 minutes) and Świdnica (6zł, 40 minutes).

Bernard CZECH €€€
(Map p240; ☑ 71 344 1054; www.bernard.wroclaw.pl; Rynek 35; mains 37-90zł; ⊙ 10.30am-11pm; 🛜)
This lively split-level bar-restaurant is inspired by the Czech beer of the same name, and the menu features plenty of Czech dishes such as *svíčková* (roast beef with cream sauce, cranberry jam and yeast dumplings) and roast pork knuckle, as well as burgers, steak and fish dishes, and plenty of beer. Breakfast is served from 10.30am to noon.

Karczma Lwowska POLISH €€€
(Map p240; ☑ 71 343 9887; www.lwowska.com.pl; Rynek 4; mains 33-49zł; ⊙ 11am-midnight; 🛜)
Karczma Lwowska serves up tasty Polish standards such as *gołąbki* (stuffed cabbage rolls) in the kind of rustic space where heavy ceramic mugs of beer are apropos. Dishes such as tripe with cream and cheese, and herrings on beetroot hail from the former eastern Poland (now western Ukraine), while photographs, artefacts and even music also invoke the bygone 'Polish Lviv'.

La Scala ITALIAN €€€
(Map p240; ☑ 71 372 5394; http://lascala.pl; Rynek 38; mains 49-66zł; ⊙ 11am-11pm; 🛜) La Scala pulls out most of the stops to produce authentic but relatively pricey Italian food. The cheaper trattoria at ground level serves good pizza and pasta in an atmospheric interior of checked tablecloths and timber tables.

🍷 Drinking & Nightlife

There are two areas to head for if you fancy a big night out: the outdoor tables around the Rynek or Pasaż Niepolda, off ul Ruska, west of the Old Town, which offers a bit more variety.

★**Vinyl Cafe** CAFE
(Map p240; ☑ 508 260 288; www.facebook.com/vinylcafe.wroclaw; ul Kotlarska 35/36; ⊙ 10am-midnight Mon-Thu, to 1am Fri & Sat, to 11pm Sun; 🛜)
This lovely, jumbled-together, bohemian-baiting little cafe sits on a nondescript side street north of the Rynek. Inside you'll find books, board games and vinyl galore (as decoration and musical medium) plus well-made coffee and a good range of teas, cakes and light meals. If you find yourself still here when the shadows lengthen, there's beer too.

Dojutra BAR
(Map p240; ul Antoniego 2/4; ⊙ 3pm-midnight Sun & Mon, to 2am Thu, to 4am Fri & Sat; 🛜)
This welcoming boho bar is good for meeting locals over an evening craft beer, or pushing on into the wee hours to the soundtrack of local DJs. If you're in need of ballast, a short menu of bar food featuring parmesan fries, fish burgers and tofu pad thai should be able to sort you out (mains 16zł to 18zł).

Klubokawiarnia Mleczarnia BAR

(Map p240; ☑71 788 2448; www.mle.pl; ul Włodkowica 5; ⊗8am-4am; 🛜) Hidden away in a courtyard in Wrocław's one-time Jewish neighbourhood, this riotously decorated bar is filled with salvaged bentwood chairs, scuffed tables bearing lace doilies and candlesticks, and framed vintage photographs. It turns out good coffee, interesting beers and light meals (19zł to 23zł). There's a nocturnal cellar for live performances, and in summer a beautiful courtyard garden opens. It's attached to the Hostel Mleczarnia (p244).

Literatka CAFE

(Map p240; ☑88 270 0304; Rynek 56/57; ⊗10am-midnight Sun-Wed, to 1am Thu, to 2am Fri & Sat; 🛜) Cafe by day, cocktail bar by night, this split-level book-lined hangout next to a library will attract the literary minded. The interior is a cosy blend of wood panelling, faded carpet and comfy chairs that invite lingering with something engrossing. Coffee and tea costs 9zł to 12zł.

Motyla Noga BAR

(Map p240; ☑71 319 4229; ul Więzienna 6; ⊗noon-1am Sun-Thu, to 3am Fri & Sat) Spread over three rooms and a courtyard in a superbly atmospheric medieval building that once served as the municipal prison, the 'Butterfly's Leg' evolves to meet different needs throughout the day: coffee and cake in the early afternoon; burgers, salads and dumplings for dinner (mains 20zł to 30zł); beers and bonhomie later on.

Wall St CLUB

(Map p240; ☑605 208 483; ul Ruska 51; varies; ⊗9pm-4am Tue-Thu, to 5am Fri-Sun) One of the big boys in Wrocław's modest clubland around Pasaż Niepolda, Wall St puts on EDM, trance, house and other nights, plus occasional comedy performances.

Szklarnia COCKTAIL BAR

(Map p240; ☑57 524 2456; https://szklarnia wroclaw.business.site; ul Ofiar Oświęcimskich 19; ⊗2pm-1am Mon-Thu, to 4am Fri & Sat, to midnight Sun) The 'Greenhouse', named for its verdure-filled atrium and shady outdoor terrace, happily balances stylishness with friendliness. Its tattooed young bartenders are happy to recommend a cocktail before vigorously shaking things up.

Set back from the street in a quadrangular cluster of like-minded bars and cafes, it's frequently enlivened by DJs and live music.

Papa Bar BAR

(Map p240; ☑71 341 0485; https://papabar.pl; ul Rzeźnicza 32/33; ⊗noon-1am Mon-Thu, to 2am Fri, 4pm-2am Sat, 4pm-1am Sun; 🛜) Centred around a huge wooden bar bristling with alcoholic ordinance, this cocktail bar and restaurant unashamedly proclaims itself 'the best bar in town'. Opinions vary, but there's no disputing the comfort and elegance of the space, or the deliciousness of well-shaken mixtures such as the Wrocław Sling, a refreshing vodka-and-citrus creation. Cocktails cost 24zł to 28zł.

Czekoladziarnia CAFE

(Map p240; ☑665 916 191; ul Więzienna 31; ⊗10am-10pm; 🛜) Push past the display counter of impeccably handcrafted chocolates (if you can), grab a bentwood chair or banquette in the sweet little cafe area, and prepare to enjoy wonderful hot chocolate (9zł to 12zł) and other sweet treats (desserts 16zł). Raid the display counter as you leave.

Cafe Artzat CAFE

(Map p240; ☑71 372 3766; www.artzatcafe.pl; ul Malarska 30; ⊗11am-11.30pm Mon-Wed, to midnight Thu, to 2am Fri & Sat, noon-11.30pm Sun; 🛜) Low-key Cafe Artzat is just north of the landmark Church of St Elizabeth (p239). With its bright vaulted ceilings, clusters of colourful but well-worn seating and walls plastered with mementoes, it's an inviting place to recharge over a drink and a good book.

Bezsenność Insomnia Club CLUB

(Map p240; ☑570 669 570; www.facebook.com/klubbezsennosc; ul Ruska 51; varies; ⊗7pm-3am Tue & Wed, to 5am Thu-Sat) With its alternative/rock/dance lineup and distressed decor, Insomnia attracts a high-end clientele and is one of the most popular clubs in town. It's located in the Pasaż Niepolda, home to a group of bars, clubs and restaurants, just off ul Ruska.

☆ Entertainment

The monthly freebie *Aktivist* (www.aktivist.pl/wroclaw) has listings in Polish; you can pick up a copy of the English-language *The Visitor* (www.thevisitor.pl) from the tourist office.

Kino Nowe Horyzonty CINEMA

(Map p240; ☑71 786 6566; www.kinonh.pl; ul Kazimierza Wielkiego 19a) Art-house cinema screening movies from around the world, including English-language films and others with English subtitles. There's a bistro/cafe open from 8am to 11pm.

Filharmonia CLASSICAL MUSIC
(Philharmonic Hall; Map p240; ☑ tickets 71 715 9700; www.nfm.wroclaw.pl; ul Piłsudskiego 19) The city's main concert hall stages performances of orchestral music, chamber music, jazz and popular artists.

Opera House OPERA
(Opera Wrocławska; Map p240; ☑ 71 370 8880; www.opera.wroclaw.pl; ul Świdnicka 35; ⏰ box office noon-7pm Mon-Sat, 11am-6pm Sun) Dating to 1841, when it was opened as the Breslau Opera, this venerable building is Wrocław's premiere venue for opera and ballet performances.

Wrocławski Teatr Współczesny THEATRE
(Wrocław Contemporary Theatre; Map p240; ☑ 71 358 8922; www.wteatrw.pl; ul Rzeźnicza 12; ⏰ box office noon-7pm Mon-Fri) Near the centre of town, this theatre stages productions from modern Polish and international playwrights.

🛍 Shopping

Hala Targowa FOOD
(Map p240; http://tradycjaijakosc.com.pl; ul Piaskowa 17; ⏰ 8am-6.30pm Mon-Sat) This early 20th-century covered market hall is a great place for fresh fruit and veg, Polish smallgoods, bread, cheeses and other treats. It also sells flowers, handicrafts, souvenirs and quite a lot of tat.

Galeria Dominikańska MALL
(Map p240; www.galeria-dominikanska.pl; Plac Dominikański 3; ⏰ 9.30am-9pm Mon-Sat, 10am-8pm Sun) Big shopping mall with a **supermarket** (www.carrefour.pl; ⏰ 8am-10pm Mon-Sat, 10am-9pm Sun; 🅿) and hundreds of shops selling everything under the sun.

ℹ Information

Post Office (Map p240; ☑ 71 347 1932; www. poczta-polska.pl; Rynek 28; ⏰ 24hr)
Tourist Office (Map p240; ☑ 71 344 3111; www.wroclaw-info.pl; Rynek 14; ⏰ 9am-7pm; 🛜) Open all week, and ever-ready with advice, brochures and maps (free and otherwise).

ℹ Getting There & Away

AIR

Wrocław Airport (p420) is in Strachowice, 13km west of the city centre. There are direct connections to many European cities through LOT, Lufthansa, Ryanair, Wizz Air and other carriers.

BUS

The **bus station** (Dworzec Centralny PKS; ☑ 703 400 444; ul Sucha 1/11) is 1.3km south of the Rynek, at the east end of the Wroclavia shopping mall, across the street from the main train station. Frequent services leave for:
Berlin (100zł, 4½ hours)
Kraków (30zł, 3½ hours)
Poznań (26zł, three hours)
Prague (75zł, 4½ hours)
Warsaw (36zł, 4½ to 5½ hours)

TRAIN

Trains depart from the impressive mock castle that is **Wrocław Główny** station (http://pkp. wroclaw.pl; ul Piłsudskiego 105), 1.2km south of the Rynek.

There are regular direct trains to the following places:
Katowice (33zł, 2¼ hours)
Kraków (45zł, 3½ hours)
Poznań (38zł, 2½ to 3¼ hours)
Warsaw (67zł, 3½ to six hours)

ℹ Getting Around

TO/FROM THE AIRPORT

The **WRO Airport Express** (www.polbus.pl/ wroclaw-airport-express) shuttle bus runs to the city centre (10zł, 30 minutes) every 50 minutes between 4am and midnight.

A taxi to the city centre costs 60zł to 80zł and takes around 20 minutes.

PUBLIC TRANSPORT

Wrocław has an efficient network of trams and buses covering the city centre and suburbs. Journeys within the centre cost 3zł; longer trips, fast buses and night buses (numbered over 200) are 3.20zł.

LOWER SILESIA

Detached from Germany after WWII and returned to Poland, Lower Silesia (Dolny Śląsk) is fertile lowland country extending along the upper and middle course of the Odra River. Settled since Neolithic times and passed throughout history between Habsburg Austria, Poland, Bohemia, Prussia and other central European powers, it remains full of interesting old towns and villages. Architecture buffs will have a field day with the region's wide assortment of castles and churches, and Lower Silesia's larger towns have more than enough attractions to tempt those with entertainment on their minds.

Książ

Located within a pretty forested area, Książ (pronounced *kshonzh*) is home to a magnificent castle), and makes for an easy day trip from Świdnica or even Wrocław.

◉ Sights

★ **Książ Castle**   CASTLE

(Zamek Książ; ☑74 664 3872; www.ksiaz. walbrzych.pl; ul Piastów Śląskich 1; adult/concession 35/25zł; ⊙9am-5pm Mon-Fri, to 6pm Sat & Sun Apr-Oct, 10am-3pm Mon-Fri, to 4pm Sat & Sun Nov-Mar; ℗) This impossibly photogenic castle, the largest in Silesia, commands a thickly wooded prominence in Książ. Following the destruction of an earlier stronghold in 1263, the Silesian Duke Bolko I built a castle here in the late 13th century. That fortress passed to the von Hobergs (later called the Hochbergs) in 1509, and was repeatedly assaulted and remodelled until well into the 20th century. Today you'll see a melange of styles from Romanesque onwards, with the oldest section at its heart.

The eastern part (to the right) is an 18th-century baroque addition, while the western segment was built between 1908 and 1923 in a neo-Renaissance style.

During WWII, under Hitler's direct orders, the German authorities confiscated the castle and began construction of a mysterious underground complex beneath the building and surrounding areas. Opened in 2018, the **Underground Tourist Route** now allows visitors to explore a 1.5km section of the works. An enhanced-entry ticket to the entire castle (adult/concession 47/37zł) entitles you to a 45-minute tour.

Following the war, the Soviet military used Książ as a barracks; from 1946 it was largely abandoned, and started falling into ruin. Luckily, restoration work began in 1974, and the lavish interiors can now be visited.

Thankfully, this is one Polish stately home that you can visit without having to accompany a Polish-language tour or wear shower caps over your shoes. As an individual visitor, you follow a prescribed (and rather convoluted) route through the castle, seeing a selection of rooms. The showpiece is Maximilian Hall, built in the first half of the 18th century. It's the largest room in the castle and completely restored to its original lavish form, including the ceiling (1733)

THE ENIGMATIC GIANT

In 1941 the Nazi government of Germany confiscated Schloss Fürstenstein (now Książ Castle) from the aristocratic Hochbergs, its owners for more than four centuries. The Nazis soon formed their own plan for the property, known as Project Riese (riese is the German word for 'giant'). As the name suggests, it was of mind-boggling proportions.

From 1943 construction began on a series of sprawling underground complexes beneath the castle and the Eulengebirge (now Góry Sowie) mountain range, part of the Sudetes. It was an enormous undertaking involving the creation of tunnels and chambers using explosives, concrete and steel. In addition to mining specialists, the project used forced labour from both prisoner-of-war and concentration camps.

The sheer scale of the work was a drain on the Nazi regime's resources. Hitler's armaments minister Albert Speer later admitted in his memoirs that the construction of the complex used more concrete than was available for building air-raid shelters across Germany in 1944.

What's most fascinating about Project Riese is that no one is quite sure what its vast subterranean chambers were for, as they were never completed and key witnesses and documents were lost in the postwar turmoil. Speer referred to a bunker complex, other references were made to bombproof underground factories, and many have assumed that Hitler intended to move his headquarters there. The wildest theories suggest that stolen treasures were hidden in the complex, or that the regime was undertaking an atomic-bomb program within its depths.

As you'll hear if you take the 45-minute tour of the complex, consensus remains elusive. For more details on the project and its aftermath, visit www.riese.krzyzowa.org.pl.

painted with mythological scenes. The identical fireplaces on either side of the room are sublime.

Along with the main rooms, including 'themed' salons (baroque, Chinese, white etc) on the 1st floor, you'll encounter various temporary exhibits and galleries en route, sometimes with objets d'art for sale. There's also an exhibition on the various dukes up to the castle's last owners, Prince Hans Heinrich XV and his wife Princess Daisy, who was born in Wales.

There are several restaurants and cafes dotted about the complex, including a grill and beer garden with leafy views on a terrace within the castle itself.

Approaching the castle from the car park, you'll pass through a large decorative free-standing gateway for your first view of the edifice, standing at end of a beautifully landscaped garden.

🛏 Sleeping

Hotel Przy Oślej Bramie
HOTEL €€

(☑74 664 9270; www.hotelzamekksiaz.pl; ul Piastów Śląskich 1; s/d 140/240zł; [P][奈]) This appealing little hotel offers rooms in four pretty stone buildings, set among delightful gardens just outside the gateway to mighty Książ Castle. Quiet and full of character, they're just the thing for dyed-in-the-wool romantics.

Hotel Książ
HOTEL €€

(☑74 664 3890; www.ksiaz.walbrzych.pl; ul Piastów Śląskich 1; s/d/tr 185/280/330zł; [P][奈]) Książ Castle, a vast ducal palace dating in parts to the 13th century, offers accommodation in three historical outbuildings. Rooms are comfortable and inoffensively decorated, with gleaming modern ensuites. The buffet breakfast should satisfy most appetites.

❶ Getting There & Away

The castle is 7.5km from Wałbrzych; you can reach it from a bus stop near Wałbrzych Miasto train station via city bus 8 (3zł, 30 minutes), which runs about every 45 minutes. From Świdnica, 14km to the east, catch a regular route 31 minibus in the direction of Wałbrzych (6zł, 30 minutes, every 20 minutes) and ask the driver to let you off on the main road turn-off to the castle (zamek). From here the castle is an easy 20-minute walk along a paved footpath.

Zielona Góra

POP 137,479

The pretty western town Zielona Góra (Green Mountain) lives up to at least half its name – there's little mountainous about it, but there's much leafy greenness shading its pedestrian streets.

The presence of nature is also a reminder that Zielona Góra (zhyeh-lo-na goo-rah) is one of only two Polish wine regions. It's a tradition running all the way back to the 14th century, though the climate is less than ideal and winemaking was never a very profitable endeavour here; the association with viticulture is today largely symbolic.

Like the majority of other towns in the region, Zielona Góra was founded by the Silesian Piasts. It was part of the Głogów Duchy, before passing to the Habsburgs in the 16th century and Prussia two centuries later. Unlike many other Silesian towns, however, Zielona Góra was relatively unscathed by WWII, meaning its prewar architecture has largely survived.

◉ Sights

Lubuski
Regional Museum
MUSEUM

(Muzeum Ziemi Lubuskiej; ☑68 327 2345; www.mzl.zgora.pl; al Niepodległości 15; adult/concession 10/5zł; ⊙11am-5pm Wed-Fri, 10am-3pm Sat, to 4pm Sun) The regional museum houses a collection of Silesian religious art from the 14th to 18th centuries, a fascinating clock gallery and a permanent exhibition of artwork by Marian Kruczek (1927–83). Kruczek used everyday objects – anything from buttons to spark plugs – to create striking assemblages, and this is the largest collection of his work in Poland. In the same building is the Wine Museum, illustrating the history of local winemaking, and the Museum of Torture.

Palm House
GARDENS

(Palmiarnia; ☑68 478 4550; www.palmiarnia.zgora.pl; ul Wrocławska 12a; ⊙noon-8pm Tue-Sun) **FREE** Located within the handsome Wine Park (Park Winny), this building is an extravagant home to various species of palms, plus cacti, and fish in aquariums. A restaurant and cafe threads through the building, allowing diners to enjoy the greenery from vantage points high and low.

Ethnographic Museum
MUSEUM

(Muzeum Etnograficzne; ☑ 68 321 1591; www.muzeumochla.pl; ul Muzealna 5, Ochla; adult/concession 10/6zł; ⊙ 10am-5pm May-Sep, to 3pm Oct-Apr; P) This skansen (outdoor ethnographic museum) brings together more than 60 traditional buildings from regions and cultures surrounding Zielona Góra. They've been resurrected on this 13-hectare site traversed by an educational trail. It's in Ochla, 7km south of Zielona Góra.

🛌 Sleeping

City Boutique Hotel
HOTEL €€

(☑ 68 415 2415; http://cityboutiquehotel.pl; ul Kupiecka 28; s/d 240/337zł; P 🛜) This slick 36-room hotel in the centre of Zielona Góra is unlike most of the town's traditional accommodation options, and is priced accordingly. It's definitely got eyes for the business trade, but there's no reason leisure travellers shouldn't take advantage of its spotless, comfortable rooms and excellent breakfasts.

Apartamenty Betti
HOTEL €€

(☑ 509 246 205; www.apartamentybetti.pl; ul Drzewna 1; s/d/tr 140/200/290zł; P 🛜) Betti has an attractive selection of rooms, which are spread through connected historical buildings near the **Rynek** (Old Market Square). The three apartments allow self-catering and more elbow room than the hotel accommodation. Parking is charged at 25zł per night, but you shouldn't have trouble finding somewhere on the street.

🍴 Eating

Leb Na Karku
FAST FOOD €

(☑ 538 426 583; http://lebnakarku.pl; Plac Pocztowy 5; sets 18-21zł; ⊙ noon-9pm Sun-Thu, to 10pm Fri & Sat; 🛜) Originally food-truck cuisine, the *bulas* (bao-like buns) at this unusual little shopfront-restaurant come stuffed with slow-cooked meat, salads, sauces and chips fried in dripping. Delicious, and definitely enhanced by beer.

★ OHY-AHY
BISTRO €€

(☑ 57 777 1200; http://ohyahy.pl; ul Kościelna 2; mains 22-29zł; ⊙ 11am-midnight Mon-Fri, noon-midnight Sat, to 11pm Sun; 🛜) Definitely something fresh for Zielona Góra, this chatty, informal eatery has proved a massive hit, offering wood-fired pizzas, burgers, pastas and a few Polish favourites in the kind of setting in which it's okay to have a beer at 11am, or breakfast at 3pm. A prime position on the Rynek, with space for tables in warm weather, doesn't hurt either.

Restauracja Winiarnia Bachus
POLISH €€€

(☑ 51 116 1212; http://winiarnia-bachus.pl; Stary Rynek 1; mains 38-54zł; ⊙ 1-10pm Tue-Thu, to 11.30pm Fri & Sat, to 8pm Sun; 🛜) Occupying the rough-brick cellars beneath the town hall, this restaurant makes good on its culinary ambitions, and is the best place in town to try local wine. It's pricey (roast wild boar or zander with crayfish and kohlrabi don't come cheaply) but it's good. If quiet jazz is your thing, you may also catch an occasional recital.

ℹ️ Information

Post Office (Plac Pocztowy 1; ⊙ 8am-8pm Mon, to 6pm Tue-Fri)

Tourist Office (☑ 68 323 2222; www.cit.zielona-gora.pl; Stary Rynek 1; ⊙ 9am-5pm Mon-Fri year-round, 10am-4pm Sat & Sun mid-Apr–mid-Oct, to 2pm Sat & Sun mid-Oct–mid-Apr; 🛜) Find advice, literature and wi-fi in this tourist office in the town hall.

ℹ️ Getting There & Away

The **bus station** (www.pks.zgora.pl; ul Dworcowa 27) is about 1.7km northeast of the city centre. Regular buses serve Poznań (35zł, three hours), Wrocław (13zł, 2¾ hours) and Jelenia Góra (40zł, 3¼ hours).

The **train station** (ul Dworcowa) is just east along ul Dworcowa from the bus station. There are regular trains to Wrocław (41zł, 2¼ to 2¾ hours), Poznań (24zł, two hours), Szczecin (51zł, 2½ hours) and Warsaw (65zł to 134zł, four to five hours).

Świdnica

POP 60,437

One of the wealthiest towns in Silesia during the Middle Ages, Świdnica (shfeed-*nee*-tsah) escaped major damage in WWII and has retained some important historical buildings, including its Unesco-protected Church of Peace. Though not a prime tourist destination, it's still an agreeable place for a stopover, and a convenient springboard for the impressive Książ Castle (p250), 15km southwest.

⊙ Sights

★ Church of Peace
CHURCH

(Kościół Pokoju; ☑ 74 852 2814; www.kosciolpokoju.pl; Plac Pokoju 6; adult/concession 10/5zł; ⊙ 9am-6pm Mon-Sat, from noon Sun Apr-Oct, 9am-3pm Mon-Sat, from noon Sun Nov-Mar) This magnificent building, the largest baroque timber church in Europe, was erected between 1656 and 1657 in just 10 months.

The builders were not trying to set any records; the Peace of Westphalia of 1648 allowed the Protestants of Silesia to build three churches as long as they took less than a year, had no belfry and used only clay, sand and wood for materials. The churches at Świdnica and Jawor remain; the one at Głogów burned down in 1758.

The Świdnica church is a shingled structure laid out in the form of a cross and contains not a single nail. The interior is a beautiful, peaceful place to sit in contemplation for a few minutes; the timber structure seems to possess an intimate inclusiveness that big stone churches sometimes lack. The baroque decoration, with paintings covering the walls and coffered ceiling, has been preserved intact. Along the walls, two storeys of galleries and several small balconies were installed, allowing some 3500 seated worshippers and 4000 standees. The church was added to Unesco's World Heritage List in 2001.

The church is 400m northeast of the Rynek; enter via the arched gateway off ul Kościelna.

Rynek

SQUARE

The Old Town's market square contains a bit of every architectural style – from baroque to postwar concrete structures – the cumulative effect of rebuilding after successive fires and the damage caused by Austrian, Prussian and Napoleonic sieges.

While exploring the Rynek, check out the bright yellow **town hall** and its **white tower** (Ratusz; www.wieza.swidnica.pl; tower entry adult/child 2/1zł; ⊙ tower 10am-6pm Tue-Sun); walk the 223 steps to the top (or take a lift) for free city views. The town hall also contains the Old Trades Museum (Muzeum Dawnego Kupiectwa; ☑ 74 852 1291; www.muzeum-kupiectwa.pl; Rynek 37; adult/concession 6/4zł, Fri free; ⊙ 10am-5pm Tue-Fri, from 11am Sat & Sun May-Sep, 10am-4pm Tue-Fri, 11am-5pm Sat & Sun Oct-Apr).

Church of SS Stanislaus and Wenceslas

CHURCH

(Kościół Św Stanisława i Wacława; www.katedra.swidnica.pl; Plac Jana Pawła II 1; ⊙ 10am-5.30pm Mon-Sat) East of the Rynek, this massive Gothic stone building has a facade adorned with four elegant 15th-century doorways and an 18m-high window (the stained glass is not original). The tower, completed in 1565, is 103m high, making it Poland's tallest historical church tower after that of the basilica in Częstochowa (106m). The spacious interior has a Gothic structure and ornate baroque decoration and furnishings.

🛌 Sleeping

Dom Rekolekcyjny

HOTEL €

(☑ 53 419 7230; ul Zamkowa 4; s/d/tr from 70/90/120zł; 🅿 🛜) Conveniently positioned just one block west of the Rynek (enter from ul Zamkowa), this pleasant accommodation run by the Pentecostal Church is excellent value and nowhere near as monastic as you might expect. Breakfast is not available, but there is a communal kitchen on the premises.

★ Hotel Fado

HOTEL €€

(☑ 74 666 6370; www.hotelfado.eu; ul Konopnickiej 6; s/d 205/275zł; 🅿 ❄ 🛜 🏊) Smart, central Hotel Fado has elegantly appointed rooms, illuminated by plenty of natural light. There's a bar and restaurant on the premises that try to fulfil the Portuguese theme that 'Fado' suggests, offering Portuguese (and Spanish) cheese, olives and meats, plus numerous Iberian wines. Not bad options to enjoy in the beer garden out front.

Esperanto

HOTEL €€

(☑ 74 632 2333; http://hotel-esperanto.pl; ul Stęczyńskiego 18; s/d/tr 200/240/290zł; 🅿 🛜) Not architecturally appealing, though modern and perfectly well set up, the Esperanto offers weary travellers a decent rest, a gym and sauna, and an indulgent breakfast buffet to set up the day.

🍴 Eating & Drinking

Kryształowa

POLISH €€

(☑ 74 663 3043; http://krysztalowa.com; ul Równa 3; mains 28-30zł; ⊙ noon-10pm Sun-Thu, to midnight Fri & Sat; 🛜) This appealing place – with its nooks, crannies, eclectica, mismatched furniture and general sense of putting guests at ease – does a fine line in the hearty fare Poland is known for. Huge butter-fried schnitzels, braised beef in creamy sauce with cranberries (that one's Czech), and potato pancakes are all plates to be approached with respect.

Rynek 43

POLISH €€

(☑ 74 850 1091; Rynek 43; mains 36-45zł; ⊙ noon-9pm Mon, Tue & Thu, to 10pm Fri & Sat, 1-9pm Sun; 🛜) The interior of this restaurant on the western side of the town hall complex is a little gloomy, but there's no criticising its beautiful courtyard hidden away beyond an arched passage. The friendly staff serve up a range of tasty Polish dishes, including regional specialities such as wild boar stew.

Baroccafé CAFE
(📱 534 065 609; Plac Pokoju 7; ⊘10am-10pm;
📶) This cafe occupying the gatehouse at
the entry to the Church of Peace (p252) is
a beautiful space with whitewashed brick
walls, old timberwork and inviting nooks
and tables. Aside from hot drinks, it also
offers light meals (10zł to 20zł) such as
charcuterie, salads and local cheese with
chokeberry jam.

ⓘ Information

Post Office (Plac Grunwaldzki 1; ⊘7am-
7.30pm Mon-Fri, 8am-2pm Sat) Opposite the
train station.

Tourist Office (📱 74 852 0290; www.um.
swidnica.pl; Town Hall, Rynek; ⊘10am-6pm)
On the north face of the town hall complex
(p253), this office has staff that are genuinely a
wealth of local information.

ⓘ Getting There & Away

Świdnica Miasto (Dworcowa) train station is
a convenient five-minute walk southwest from
the Rynek (p253), with the **bus station** (www.
pks.swidnica.pl; ul Kolejowa 1) behind it.

Regular buses run to Wrocław (15zł, 1¼ hours)
and Wałbrzych for Książ Castle (p250, 6zł, 20
minutes). Private minibuses to the same destinations also depart from here.

For decent rail connections, travel one
station to Jaworzyna Śląska, where you can
change for regular services to Wrocław (15zł,
45 minutes) and Jelenia Góra (20zł, 1½ hours).
The conductor on board the local trains can
sell you a through ticket from Świdnica to your
final stop.

SUDETES MOUNTAINS

The Sudetes Mountains run for more than
250km along the Czech–Polish border, extending into both Germany and the Czech
Republic. The highest part of this old and
eroded chain of mountains is the Karkonosze, reaching 1602m at Mt Śnieżka. Though
the Sudetes don't offer the most arresting
alpine scenery, they're amazingly varied
and heavily covered in forest, with spectacular geological formations such as those
at the Góry Stołowe National Park (p265).
Skiing, including Nordic skiing, is possible
at Karpacz and Szklarska Poręba.

To the north, the Sudetes gradually decline
into a belt of gently rolling foothills known
as the Przedgórze Sudeckie (Sudetes Foothills). This area is more densely populated,

and many towns and villages still boast some
of their centuries-old timber buildings. Combining visits to these historical settlements
with hikes into the mountains and relaxation in centuries-old spas is the best way to
explore the region.

Jelenia Góra
POP 83,860

Jelenia Góra (yeh-*len*-yah *goo*-rah) is set in
a beautiful valley surrounded by the Western Sudetes. The city has a relaxed feel and
an attractive appearance, with a scattering
of sights and some good restaurants. It's
the natural base for trips into the Karkonosze Mountains. Immediately to the south is
the adjoined spa town of Cieplice Śląskie-
Zdrój, with its pleasant spa park and relaxed air.

Jelenia Góra was founded in 1108 by King
Bolesław Krzywousty (Bolesław the Wry-
Mouthed), who was so taken by the beauty
of the place that he named it 'Deer Mountain'. Its role as a border stronghold came
later, under the rule of the powerful Duchy
of Świdnica-Jawor. Gold mining in the region gave way to glass production around
the 15th century, but weaving gave the town
a solid economic base, and its high-quality
linen was exported all over Europe.

ⓞ Sights

**Church of the
Exaltation of the Holy Cross** CHURCH
(Kościól Podwyższenia Krzyża Świętego; Map
p256; 📱 60 593 8513; www.kosciolgarnizonowy.
pl; ul 1 Maja 45; 4zł; ⊘10am-4pm Mon-Thu & Sat,
to 5pm Fri Apr-Oct, by appointment Nov-Mar) Jelenia Góra's main attraction is this massive
church. One of six new churches permitted
by the 1707 Treaty of Altranstädt, it was built
between 1709 and 1718 for a Lutheran con-
gregation, though it's been Catholic since
1947. The three-storey galleries plus the
dark, densely packed ground floor can accommodate 4000 people. The ceiling is embellished with illusionist baroque paintings
of scenes from the Old and New Testaments,
while the magnificent organ over the high
altar dates from 1729.

Rynek SQUARE
(Market Square; Map p256; Plac Ratuszowy) The
elongated market square, also called Plac
Ratuszowy, is lined with a harmonious
group of 17th- and 18th-century houses.

DON'T MISS

KARKONOSZE NATIONAL PARK

The **Karkonosze National Park** (Karkonoski Park Narodowy; ☑ park headquarters 75 755 3348; www.kpnmab.pl; ul Chałubińskiego 23, Jelenia Góra (park headquarters); park entry adult/concession 8/4zł; ⊙ park headquarters 7.30am-3.30pm Mon-Fri) is a 55.75-sq-km belt that runs along the Polish–Czech border for some 25km. The two main settlements here are the resort towns of Szklarska Poręba and Karpacz.

The range is divided by the Karkonosze Pass (Przełęcz Karkonoska; 1198m). The highest summit of the eastern section is Mt Śnieżka (1602m), while the western portion is topped by Mt Wielki Szyszak (1509m). The park is predominantly spruce forest up to an altitude of about 1250m.

The characteristic features of the Karkonosze landscape are kotły (cirques), huge hollows carved by glaciers during the Ice Age and bordered with steep cliffs. There are six cirques on the Polish side of the range, the most spectacular being Kocioł Małego Stawu and Kocioł Wielkiego Stawu near Mt Śnieżka, and Śnieżne Kotły at the foot of Mt Wielki Szyszak.

The Karkonosze range is known for its harsh climate, with heavy rainfall (snow in winter) and highly variable weather, including strong winds and mists at any time of year. Statistically, the best chances of good weather are in January, February, May and September.

The national park is the most popular hiking territory in the Sudetes and boasts 33 trails covering 100km. The two main gateways are Szklarska Poręba and Karpacz, from where most tourists ascend Mt Szrenica and Mt Śnieżka respectively. For longer walks, the red trail runs right along the ridge between the two peaks, with excellent views on both sides. The trail also passes along the upper edges of the kotły. You can walk the whole stretch in six to seven hours. If you start early enough, it's possible to do the Karpacz–Szklarska Poręba (or vice versa) trip within a day, preferably by using the chairlift to Mt Szrenica or Mt Kopa to speed up the initial ascent.

You can break the walk by taking any of the trails that branch off from the main route, or by stopping at one of the half-dozen mountain hostels.

The national park also has 19 mountain bike trails totalling some 450km; the tourist offices in Szklarska Poręba and Karpacz can supply you with an excellent free map of them.

The best map of the area is the 1:25,000 Karkonosze i Góry Izerskie (7zł), which also includes the Izera Mountains of the Western Sudetes, to the northeast of Szklarska Poręba.

Much of their charm is due to their porticoes and ground-floor arcades, which provide a covered passageway all around the square. The **town hall** (Ratusz; Map p256; Plac Ratuszowy 2) was built in 1749, after its predecessor collapsed.

Basilica of SS
Erasmus and Pancras BASILICA
(Bazylika świętego Erazma i świętego Pankracego; Map p256; http://bazylika.jgora.pl; Plac Kościelny) This basilica was erected in two stages in the late 14th and early 15th centuries; note the Gothic doorway in the southern entrance portraying Mary and St John at the foot of the cross. The interior, with its theatrical 22m-high rococo main altar crafted from brick-red marble, boasts mostly

baroque furnishings, including a richly decorated organ. These baroque features were added in the 18th century, following the basilica's reconstruction by the Jesuits after the ravages of the Thirty Years' War.

Karkonosze Museum MUSEUM
(Karkonoskie Muzeum Okręgowe; www.muzeum karkonoskie.pl; ul Matejki 28; adult/concession 10/5zł, Wed free; ⊙ 9am-5pm Tue-Sun) Karkonosze Museum, 650m south of the Rynek, is renowned for its extensive collection of glass dating from medieval times to the present – the art nouveau pieces are especially wonderful. On the museum grounds is a small *skansen* (open-air museum of traditional architecture) featuring traditional mountain huts typical of the Karkonosze Mountains.

Jelenia Góra

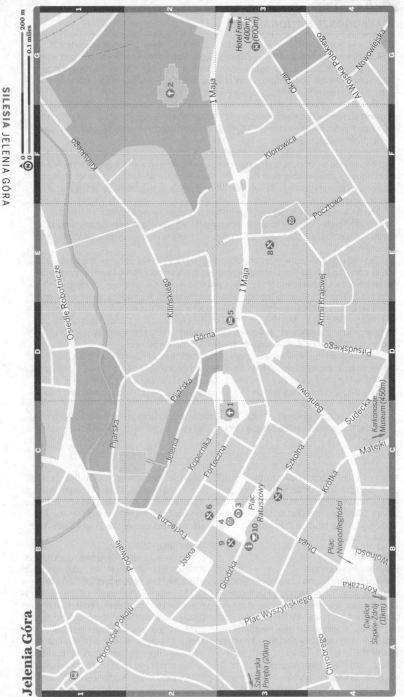

200 m
0.1 miles

Jelenia Góra

🛏 Sleeping

★ Hotel Fenix HOTEL €€
(☎75 641 6600; ul 1 Maja 88; s/d/apt
99/175/349zł; ℗🛜) More convenient for
the train station (p258) than the centre,
the Fenix dates to 1875, and is worth seeking out for its 36 modern, well-maintained
rooms, spa and wellness centre. Even if
you're not staying, consider dropping into
its excellent restaurant, which serves upmarket Polish dishes at very reasonable
prices (22zł to 25zł).

Merkury Centrum HOTEL €€
(Map p256; ☎71 875 5793; www.merkury
centrum.eu; ul 1 Maja 45; s/d/apt 170/245/310zł;
🛜) Occupying a handsome corner townhouse built in 1736, the Merkury is as appealing as it is well located, between the
Rynek (p254) and the Church of the Holy
Cross (p254). The buffet breakfast is more
than ample, and the smartly renovated
rooms make clever use of the building's
original geometry and timbering.

Hotel Bella HOTEL €€
(☎75 643 1250; https://hotelbella.pl; ul Zamoysk-
iego 3, Cieplice Śląskie-Zdrój; s/d from 130/185zł;
℗🛜) If you're in Jelenia Góra primarily
for the spa and would like to stay closer
to the action, the Bella in nearby Cieplice
is a very pleasant option adjacent to the
beautiful Spa Park (p258). The balconied,
three-storey building, picked out in cream
and mustard, offers comfortable, eccentri-
cally styled rooms.

🍴 Eating & Drinking

Pizzeria Tokaj PIZZA €
(Map p256; ☎75 752 4564; http://pizzeriatokaj.pl; ul
Pocztowa 8; small pizzas & mains 15-22zł; ⊙noon-
10pm Mon-Thu, 1pm-midnight Fri & Sat) A long-
term favourite in Jelenia Góra, Tokaj is a cafe-
bar serving a wide array of pizzas. There's a
good selection of pasta and salads as well.

Mała Arkadia POLISH €€
(Map p256; ☎60 691 9332; Plac Ratuszowy 25/26;
mains 24-27zł; ⊙9am-4pm Mon, to 5pm Tue, to
8pm Wed, to 9pm Thu, to 10pm Fri & Sat, 1-8pm Sun;
🛜) Within a cosy interior that resembles a
living room via its floral wallpaper and dark-
wood furnishings, this attractive restaurant
on the main square (p254) presents quality
Polish dishes such as *gołąbki*, potato pancakes and steak tartare.

Metafora POLISH €€
(Map p256; ☎75 752 2838; http://metaforapub.pl;
Plac Ratuszowy 49; mains 24-27zł; ⊙10am-11pm
Mon-Thu, to 1am Fri & Sat, 11am-11pm Sun; 🛜)
With framed photos dotting the walls, individual table lamps, a well-stocked bar and
a congenial atmosphere, Metafora is a good
bet on the central square (p254). It serves
mostly Polish favourites such as golden pork
schnitzels as big as your head, a variety of
salads and a few Italian options.

Restauracja Pokusa POLISH €€
(Map p256; ☎75 752 5347; Plac Ratuszowy 12;
mains 18-25zł; ⊙11am-11pm; 🛜) With outdoor
tables in the arcaded passageway encircling
the Rynek (p254), Pokusa is an agreeable option, with upbeat decor and a repertoire of
mostly Polish food. Beyond meat and game,
the list of salads is long, and there are a few
pasta options.

Pożegnanie z Afryką CAFE
(Map p256; ☎75 753 2100; www.pozegnanie.com;
Plac Ratuszowy 4; ⊙10am-6pm; 🛜) This inviting branch of the cafe chain 'Out of Africa'
peddles any number of imported beans
within its dim and character-packed premises and, of course, serves great coffee. Sip
and savour.

ℹ Information

Main Post Office (Map p256; ul Pocztowa
9/10; ⊙7am-9pm Mon-Fri, 9am-3pm Sat)
Tourist Office (Map p256; ☎51 950 9343;
https://turystyka.jeleniagora.pl; Plac
Ratuszowy 6/7; ⊙8am-4pm Mon-Fri, 10am-
2pm Sat & Sun; 🛜)

WORTH A TRIP

CIEPLICE ŚLĄSKIE-ZDRÓJ

Immediately to the south of Jelenia Góra, Cieplice (cheh-*plee*-tseh) is the oldest spa in the region, and a very restful place to squander an afternoon. Purportedly discovered by the same King Bolesław who named 'Deer Mountain' (Jelenia Góra), the sulphurous hot springs have been appreciated for a millennium, and the first spa house here was established as early as the late 13th century. The supposedly curative properties of the springs, which come out of the ground at a scalding 90°C, became truly popular in the late 18th century, paving the way for the building of the resort and spa town.

The lovely, wooded **Spa Park** (Park Zdrojowy; www.cieplice.pl; ul Cervi, Cieplice Śląskie-Zdrój) makes up much of Cieplice Śląskie-Zdrój's core. Founded in the 18th century and later re-landscaped in the English style, it holds an embarrassment of handsome fin-de-siècle pavilions and buildings, including the domed **Spa Theatre** (Teatr Zdrojowy) and the wooden open-air **Concert Shell** (Muszla Koncertowa).

Nearby, at the western end of pedestrian Plac Piastowski is the early 18th-century **Church of St John the Baptist** (Kościół Św Jana Chrzciciela; https://cieplice-pijarzy.pl; ul Cieplicka 9, Cieplice Śląskie-Zdrój), which contains an altarpiece painted by famed baroque artist Michael Willmann. Should you wish to sample the local waters, the statue-topped automatic pump in a small square near St John's dispenses free water from Cieplice's springs into whatever container you provide.

In the imposing red-brick monastic buildings adjoining the church, you'll find the diverting **Natural History Museum** (Muzeum Przyrodnicze; ☑ 75 755 1506; www.muzeum-cieplice.pl; ul Cieplicka 11a, Cieplice Śląskie-Zdrój; adult/concession 5/4zł, Sat free; ☉ 9am-6pm Wed-Fri, to 5pm Sat & Mon May-Sep, 9am-4pm Wed-Sat & Mon Oct-Apr; P ⊕). Its display of birds and butterflies from all over the world is built on the collection of the prominent Schaffgotsch family, local nobles who established the museum in 1876. Giant insects in the flowerbeds around the entrance provide great photo ops.

Cieplice Śląskie-Zdrój lies 11km south of Jelenia Góra's centre, and can be reached by suburban bus 17 (3zł, 15 minutes) from a stop near the bus station on ul Podwale. If you're staying closer to the train station, catch bus 9 from there instead. Buy your bus ticket from a street-side kiosk, then validate on board.

❶ Getting There & Away

The **train station** (ul 1 Maja) is about 1.5km east of the Rynek, while the **bus station** (Map p256; www.pks.jgora.pl; ul Obrońców Pokoju 1b) is on the opposite side of town, just northwest of the ring road.

BUS

Regular buses run to Karpacz (8zł, 50 minutes), including some minibuses which leave from the train station rather than the bus station. Regular services also head to Szklarska Poręba (7zł, 45 minutes), Świdnica (22zł, two hours) and Zielona Góra (40zł, 3¼ hours).

TRAIN

Regular trains service Szklarska Poręba (12zł, one hour), Wrocław (24zł, 2¼ hours) and Warsaw (69zł, 8½ hours). For Świdnica, buy a through ticket with a change at Jaworzyna Śląska.

Szklarska Poręba

POP 7002

At the foot of Mt Szrenica (1362m) at the western end of Karkonosze National Park, Szklarska Poręba (*shklahr*-skah po-*rem*-bah) is a lively little place in the right seasons, full of walkers, skiers and souvenir cudgels (mini-tomahawks). A major health resort and ski centre just 21km southwest of Jelenia Góra, it's the inevitable base for the region's many outdoor activities. Skirting the Kamienna River on its way down from the hills, the main street is ul Jedności Narodowej, which snakes up the slope to Nordic skiing hotspot Jakuszyce. Branching off it is ul 1 Maja. Both thoroughfares account for the bulk of the resort's accommodation, restaurants and outdoor-gear shops.

🏃 Activities

Ask at the tourist office (p260) for a list of businesses hiring out bikes and snow-sports gear, as these fluctuate from season to season.

Fischer Jakuszyce
SKIING

(📞 53 083 1254; https://biegowkijakuszyce.pl; Jakuszyce 8c, Jakuszyce; ⏱ 8.30am-6pm) This experienced, well-equipped rental shop can kit you out with cross-country gear to tackle the Jakuszyce trails. Prices per day start at 27zł for adults and 25zł for children, and get cheaper the longer you hire.

Rope Park Trollandia
ADVENTURE SPORTS

(Park Linowy Trollandia; 📞 66 122 0004; https://trollandia.pl; ul Jedności Narodowej; one course, adult/concession 29/24zł; ⏱ 10am-6pm May-Aug, 10am-6pm Sat & Sun Apr, Sep & Oct; 👶) This inventively designed high-ropes course in the centre of Szklarska Poręba is a great way to entertain kids in the warmer months without heading all the way into the hills. Hitched to a mobile safety harness, participants weave their way over one of four courses, ranging from one to six metres above the ground.

Mt Szrenica Chairlift
CABLE CAR

(📞 75 717 2118; www.sudetylift.com.pl; ul Turystyczna 25a; one way/return 39/42zł; ⏱ 9am-4.30pm) The Mt Szrenica chairlift rises 603m in two stages and deposits you at the top in about 25 minutes; it's used by skiers and snowboarders to reach five trails and two slopes in season, and by hikers the rest of the year. The lower station is 1km south of the centre, uphill along ul Turystyczna.

🛏 Sleeping

Hotel Jakuszyce
HOTEL €€

(📞 75 767 7693; www.hoteljakuszyce.pl; Jakuszyce 5a, Jakuszyce; s/d 140/250zł; 🅿 🕸 ♨) This well-established hotel in Jakuszyce – the cross-country skiing centre eight kilometres up the road from Szklarska Poręba – is a perfect base for hitting the 100-plus km of trails in the area. Rooms are warm, stylish and well maintained, and there's a spa and restaurant on-site, so you don't need to brave the cold again once you're done for the day.

Fantazja
HOTEL €€

(📞 75 717 2907; ul Jedności Narodowej 14; s/d 160/260zł; 🅿 🕸) Very central accommodation offering comfortable rooms, a solarium, massage services and a popular cafe/restaurant serving international dishes.

Mauritius
HOTEL €€

(📞 75 717 2083; www.mauritius.karkonosz.pl; ul Dworcowa 6; s/d/tr 95/170/255zł; 🅿 🕸) At the northern end of town next to the train station, this exotically named place is actually a basic holiday home run by the post office. A spacious terrace provides a great view of the mountains, and there's a dartboard and pool table for indoor amusement. Rooms with balconies and a cafe-bar add to the attraction.

Hotel Kryształ
HOTEL €€€

(📞 75 717 4930; www.hotelkrysztal.pl; ul 1 Maja 19; s/d 330/440zł; 🅿 🌸 🕸 ♨) The Kryształ offers resort-style accommodation in the heart of Szklarska Poręba. The decor in the public areas tends to the chintzy, but the expensively appointed rooms are decorated in earthy tones and are available in larger deluxe versions. On the premises you'll find a cafe, bar and restaurant, along with a swimming pool, spa, sauna and massage treatments.

🍴 Eating

Restauracja Młyn Łukasza
POLISH €€

(Lukasmühle; 📞 75 713 9334; www.mlynlukasza.pl; ul 1 Maja 16; mains 25-29zł; ⏱ 11am-10pm; 🕸) 'Luke's Mill' occupies an old watermill in central Szklarska Poręba. Built in 1870 and subsequently used for a variety of purposes, it's been given the rustic treatment inside and out. With waterside seating, regional beers and a reasonably priced menu featuring pierogi, soups and a range of meat dishes, it's one of the best bets in town.

Bistorante 654 m n.p.m
POLISH €€

(ul Jedności Narodowej 12; mains 29-39zł; ⏱ noon-late; 🕸) The in-house restaurant of the Willa Kaprys is a roomy, mellow place, with a polished central bar and dark bentwood chairs. The menu is evenly split between pizzas and pasta, and Polish dishes.

Metafora
POLISH €€€

(📞 75 717 3689; https://restauracjametafora.business.site; ul Objazdowa 1; mains 36-52zł; ⏱ 10am-10pm Mon-Fri, from 9am Sat & Sun; 🕸) Metafora serves pierogi and other Polish staples alongside a few regional specialities and more imaginative dishes. The dining room looks like the Disney interpretation of a Brothers Grimm cottage. With broad plank benches and outdoor seating in fine weather, it's also an inviting place to have a drink.

ℹ Information

Tourist Office (☑75 754 7740; www.szklarska poreba.pl; ul Jedności Narodowej 1a; ⊘8am-4pm Mon-Fri, 9am-5pm Sat)

ℹ Getting There & Away

Szklarska Poręba Górna train station is 350m north of the **post office** (ul Jedności Narodowej 8; ⊘8am-6pm Mon-Fri, to 2.30pm Sat), up a steep hill. The **bus station** (Plac PKS) is on the other side of the centre, about 450m southeast of the post office between ul Jedności Narodowej and the Kamienna River.

Regular buses head to Jelenia Góra (7zł, 45 minutes) and Wrocław (42zł, three to 3½ hours). In July and August there are also services to Karpacz (12zł, 45 minutes).

Regular trains go to Jelenia Góra (12zł, one hour), Wrocław (26zł, 3¾ hours) and Warsaw (74zł, 7½ to 10 hours).

Karpacz

POP 5026

Karpacz (*kar*-pach), 17km south of Jelenia Góra on the slopes of Mt Śnieżka, is one of the most popular mountain resorts in Poland, offering downhill and Nordic skiing in winter and hiking the rest of the year. Spread thinly over roads winding up the foothills, it's the natural base for many skiing and hiking trips, and has plenty of accommodation and a few attractions of its own.

Strung over 3km of the meandering ul Konstytucji 3 Maja, the resort doesn't have an obvious centre. The eastern part, known as Karpacz Dolny (Lower Karpacz), has most of the places to stay and eat, while the western part, Karpacz Górny (Upper Karpacz), is largely a collection of holiday homes. The Zbyszek chairlift to Mt Kopa (1377m), which opens up the skiable terrain above the town, is reached by a side road between the two.

◉ Sights

★**Wang Church**   CHURCH

(Kościół Wang; ☑75 752 8290; www.wang.com. pl; ul Na Śnieżkę 8; adult/concession 10/5zł; ⊘9am-6pm mid-Apr–Oct, to 5pm Nov–mid-Apr) Karpacz has a curious architectural gem – Wang Church, the only Nordic Romanesque building in Poland. Pronounced 'Vang', this remarkable wooden structure in Upper Karpacz was one of about 400 such chapels built in the early 12th century on the bank

of Lake Vang in southern Norway; only 28 of these 'stave churches' survive there today. King Friedrich Wilhelm IV of Prussia bought this one in 1841, had it dismantled piece by piece, and then transported to Karpacz via Berlin.

🏃 Activities

Zbyszek Chairlift   CABLE CAR

(☑50 618 9350; http://karpaczskiarena.pl; ul Turystyczna 4; one way/return 50/55zł; ⊘8.30am-5pm) If you prefer not to walk up Mt Kopa, this 2278m-long chairlift, which caters for skiers and snowboarders in winter, will take you up 528m in 17 minutes. From Mt Kopa, you can get to the top of Mt Śnieżka in less than an hour via the black trail.

🛏 Sleeping & Eating

★**Hotel Rezydencja**   HOTEL €€

(☑75 761 8020; www.hotelrezydencja.pl; ul Parkowa 6; r from 300zł; 🅿🛜) Housed in an 18th-century hilltop villa in terraced gardens overlooking the centre of Lower Karpacz, this is a stunner of a hotel. Its tastefully decorated rooms are among the most desirable in town. There's a spa, restaurant and cafe-bar on-site (mains 22zł to 25zł), and massage treatments can be arranged.

Hotel Biały Jar   HOTEL €€

(Rezydencja Biały Jar; ☑75 761 8951; www.bialy jar.pl; ul Konstytucji 3 Maja 79; s/d from 99/198zł; 🅿🛜) You can't miss this striking 1920s hotel as you climb Karpacz's main road: gabled, wood-trimmed and substantial, it's one of the town's most notable buildings. Aside from luxurious, individually styled rooms, the 'White Ravine' offers an on-site spa, a theatrically imagined 'highlander's' restaurant, and immediate access to five Karkonosze hiking trails.

Hotel Kolorowa   HOTEL €€

(☑75 761 9503; www.hotel-kolorowa.pl; ul Konstytucji 3 Maja 58; s/d from 80/160zł; 🅿🛜) This affordable hotel opposite the summer sleigh track in Lower Karpacz offers good standards, the all-important sweets on pillows, and some rooms with restful hillside views. The in-house restaurant, offering dishes such as venison tartare with smoked eggplant and dried egg-yolk, or duck with woodruff 'caviar' and chocolate sauce, is certainly something different (mains 33zł to 42zł).

Hotel Vivaldi
HOTEL €€

(☑75 761 9933; www.vivaldi.pl; ul Olimpijska 4; s/d/tr 225/290/400zł; ᴘ🛜🏊) A pale-yellow building in the midst of the spruce trees, the Vivaldi is a classy proposition on the winding road up to the chairlift and national park (p259) entrance. The rooms are modern and comfortable, if not overtly stylish, and there are saunas, a whirlpool spa and swimming pool to relax in.

Restauracja Aurora
RUSSIAN €€

(☑60 024 4281; www.aurora.karpacz.pl; ul Konstytucji 3 Maja 45; mains 27-30zł; ◷11am-10pm) This cosy Russian restaurant and bar bills itself as a 'minimuseum of Socialist Realism'. Decor features large portraits of communist bigwigs as well as red banners and posters from the era. The slightly mad menu includes such gems as 'Codename Stirlitz' (Czech dumplings with goulash) and 'Brezhnev Pork Knuckle'.

Central Bar
POLISH €€

(☑75 761 8592; ul Konstytucji 3 Maja 49; mains 20-24zł; ◷11am-10pm; 🛜) An atmospheric cross between a pub and a restaurant, the Central keeps locals happy with free-flowing draught beer, and simple but better-than-average Polish dishes such as beetroot soup with croquette and grilled *kiełbasa* (Polish sausage).

❶ Information

Biuro Turystyczne Karpacz (☑75 761 9547; www.btkarpacz.com.pl; ul Konstytucji 3 Maja 50; ◷9am-5pm Mon-Sat) is in the centre of Karpacz.

Tourist Office (☑75 761 8605; www.karpacz.pl; ul Konstytucji 3 Maja 25; ◷9am-5pm)

❶ Getting There & Away

Buses run regularly to Jelenia Góra (8zł, 50 minutes), as do minibuses; the latter terminate at the Jelenia Góra train station (p258) rather than its bus station. They go along Karpacz's main road, and you can pick them up from at least six points, though fewer go all the way to the Upper Karpacz stop. In summer there are also buses to Szklarska Poręba (12zł, 45 minutes).

Kłodzko

POP 28,750

Anecdotally present in historical records from the 10th century, Kłodzko occupies a strategic position that accounts for its enduring attraction: a monstrously powerful stone fortress, begun by the Austrians in 1662 and completed two centuries later by the Prussians. It's the dominant, even dominating, landmark of the town. It's also the best reason to pay a visit, although the winding streets of the Old Town, with interesting churches, museums and bridges, have a charm of their own.

One of the oldest settlements in Silesia, Kłodzko (*kwots*-koh) started out as a major trade centre thanks to its location on the Nysa Kłodzka River, a tributary of the Odra. Like most settlements in the region, it changed hands every century or so, with Bohemia, Austria and Prussia all having a crack; only after WWII did the town become uncontestedly Polish.

◉ Sights

★ Kłodzko Fortress
FORTRESS

(Twierdza Kłodzka; www.twierdza.klodzko.pl; ul Grodzisko 1; tunnels & fortress adult/concession 25/20zł; ◷9am-6pm May-Oct, to 3pm Nov-Apr) This mighty fortification, begun under Austrian rule in the mid-17th century on the site of former strongholds dating to the 10th century, was extended and modernised over the following 200 years. Today it covers 17 hectares, making it the largest and best-preserved fortification of its kind in Poland. The walls in the lower parts measure up to 11m thick, and taper to never less than 4m.

The entrance is up the hill north of the town's central **Rynek** (Market Square; Plac Bolesława Chrobrego).

On entering, you can wander around various pathways and chambers and go to the top of the fortress for a bird's-eye view of town. There are several exhibitions in the grounds, including a lapidarium containing old stone sculptures (mostly tombstones) collected from historical buildings around the region.

However, the real attraction here is the extensive network of defensive tunnels. Guided 40-minute tours of this so-called labyrinth begin on the hour, taking you on a 1km circuit including some passageways that are so low you have to bend over. The temperature ranges from 6°C to 8°C and the humidity is very high.

Altogether 40km of tunnels were drilled around the fortress; they served two purposes. Those under the fortifications were principally for communication, shelter and storage, while the others, running up to 500m away from the fortress, were designed to attack and destroy enemy artillery. The tunnels were divided into sectors and stuffed with gunpowder; when the enemy happened to move their guns into a particular sector, the relevant chamber could be blown up. This bizarre minefield was initiated in 1743 by a Dutch engineer, and by 1807 an immense labyrinth of tunnels had been built. The system was never actually used – at least not here.

★ Underground Tourist Route
TUNNEL

(Podziemna Trasa Turystyczna; www.podziemia. klodzko.pl; ul Zawiszy Czarnego 3; adult/concession 14/10zł; ⊙9am-6pm Apr-Oct, to 3pm Nov-Mar) This interesting set of tunnels dates in parts to the 13th century. The 600m route, enlivened by audiovisual exhibits, links cellars, warehouses for storing beer, and tunnels that were hollowed out under the Old Town over 400 years. You can walk the whole length in 15 minutes, exiting near the Kłodzko Fortress (p261).

The entrance is near the parish church.

Parish Church
CHURCH

(Kościół Parafialny; Plac Kościelny 9; ⊙noon-4pm Mon & Fri, from 10am Tue-Thu & Sat, 1-5pm Sun May-Sep, by appointment Oct-Apr) This church, southwest of the Rynek (p261) and dedicated to Our Lady of the Assumption, is the most imposing religious building in town.

It took almost 150 years before the massive Gothic structure was eventually completed in 1490. Inside, the altars, pulpit, pews, organ and carved confessionals all blaze with florid baroque ornamentation, and even the Gothic vaulting – usually left plain – has been sumptuously decorated with plasterwork.

Kłodzko Regional Museum
MUSEUM

(Muzeum Ziemi Kłodzkie; www.muzeum.klodzko.pl; ul Łukasiewicza 4; adult/concession 14/10zł, permanent exhibition free Sat; ⊙10am-4pm Tue-Sun Oct-Apr, 10am-5pm Tue-Fri, from 11am Sat & Sun May-Sep) Kłodzko's museum, 50m west of the parish church, has displays relating to the 1000-year history of the town and the region, plus a collection of contemporary glass by local artists (the area is noted for its glass production). The collection of antique clocks is also sure to delight horologists, while temporary exhibits explore themes such as Silesian ceramics.

St John's Bridge
BRIDGE

(Most Św Jana; ul Stwosza) Southeast of the Rynek (p261), this Gothic stone bridge, built somewhere between 1281 and 1390, spans the narrow Młynówka River. With half a dozen baroque statues flanking the sides, it's Kłodzko's scaled-down answer to the Charles Bridge in Prague.

🏃 Activities

The helpful and well-informed tourist office has information on activities as wideranging as rock climbing, hiking, cycling, horseback riding, skiing and taking to the waters.

If you're a snow-sports fan, the **Czarna Góra Ski Centre** (Czarna Góra Osrodek Narciarski; ☑74 884 3406; www.czarnagora.pl; ul Sienna 11, Stronie Śląskie) is easily accessible from Kłodzko, about 35km south by road.

🛏 Sleeping & Eating

Hotel Śnieżnik
HOTEL €

(☑74 865 9944; www.marhaba.ng.pl; ul Daszyńskiego 16; s/d 93/126zł; P🛜) Basic rooms with shower or full en suite are the choices at this budget establishment on the south side of town, backing onto the Młynówka River. Rooms without a bathroom are slightly cheaper, and foregoing breakfast can save you a further 13zł per person.

★ Casa D'Oro
HOTEL €€

(☑74 867 0216; ul Grottgera 7; s/d 130/190zł; 🛜) Located between the Rynek (p261) and the bus and train stations, this small attractive hotel is the handiest accommodation you'll find in Kłodzko. Its pleasantly appointed restaurant is worth dropping into for its menu of pierogi, *naleśniki* (crepes) and other Polish dishes (mains 20zł to 25zł).

Hotel Korona
HOTEL €€

(☑74 867 3737; www.hotel-korona.pl; ul Noworudzka 1; s/d 125/150zł; P🛜) Located in the far northwestern part of town, this modern establishment is a comfortable option with brick-and-timber interiors and a tangle of greenery out front. It has a colourful rustic-style restaurant doing mainly Polish favourites (mains 20zł to 30zł).

Bar Małgosia
CAFETERIA €

(ul Połabska 2; mains 8-10zł; ⊙7am-7pm Mon-Fri, 8am-6pm Sat, 9am-5pm Sun; 🍴) An old-fashioned self-service joint, Małgosia serves hearty Polish dishes such as *gołąbki* and *kotlet mielony* (minced pork chop) at crazily low prices in a soothing green interior. Just east of the train and bus stations.

Nota Bene POLISH €€

(☑60 139 2077; ul Grottgera 8a; mains 25-32zł; ☺11am-9pm Sun, Tue & Wed, to 10pm Thu, to 11pm Fri & Sat; ☎) Note well: this place isn't Italian, despite the name, but Polish. Sitting in a long, light-filled dining room with polished tile floors and river views, it seems right to choose fish dishes such as Polish herring or whole trout from the Kłodzko valley, baked with tomatoes, olives, capers and potatoes.

Restauracja w Ratuszu POLISH €€

(www.wratuszu.pl; Plac Bolesława Chrobrego 3; mains 20-65zł; ☺10am-9pm; ☎) Housed within the town hall (as the name indicates) this pleasantly old-fashioned restaurant serves a good range of regional dishes and Polish favourites (tripe soup, zander with chanterelles, roast pork knuckle with Silesian dumplings), and has a tree-shaded terrace for the warmer months.

❶ Information

Main Post Office (Plac Jagiełły 2; ☺8am-8pm Mon-Fri, to 3pm Sat)

PTTK Office (www.klodzko.pttk.pl; ul Wita Stwosza 1; ☺9am-5pm Tue, noon-6pm Thu & Fri)

Tourist Office (☑74 865 4689; www.klodzko. pl; ul Czeska, below Kłodzko Fortress; ☺9am-5pm)

❶ Getting There & Away

BUS

Kłodzko's **bus station** (www.pks-klodzko.pl; Plac Jedności 1) is the transport hub of the region. Buses run regularly to Kudowa-Zdrój (11zł, one to 1¼ hours), Bystrzyca Kłodzka (8zł, 35 minutes), Wrocław (15zł, 1¾ hours) and Nysa (13zł, one hour).

TRAIN

Kłodzko's centrally located **Kłodzko Miasto** (Plac Jedności) station, next to the bus station, has trains to Bystrzyca Kłodzka (6.50zł, 17 minutes), Kudowa-Zdrój (9zł, one hour) and Wrocław (20zł, 1¾ hours). There are more long-distance trains from the main station, Kłodzko Główne, 2km north.

Kudowa-Zdrój

POP 10,429

Kudowa-Zdrój (koo-*do*-va zdruy) is an appealing spa town 37km west of Kłodzko, favoured by a mild climate and mineral springs, the benefits of which have been sought for centuries. Renowned since the 18th century, it's one of the oldest spas in Europe, with well-preserved architecture and an appealingly landscaped spa park tucked under wooded hills.

It's a wonderful place for recharging before or after enjoying the more strenuous activities the region has to offer, and is the ideal jumping-off point for the marvellous Góry Stołowe National Park (p265).

◉ Sights

★**Chapel of Skulls** CHAPEL

(Kaplica Czaszek; ☑60 554 0927; www.czermna.pl; ul Moniuszki 8, Czermna; adult/concession 6/3zł; ☺9am-5.30pm May & Jun, 9.30am-5pm Jul-Sep, 10am-4.30pm Oct, to 3.30pm Nov-Apr; ℗) You can't miss this macabre chapel in the Church of St Bartholomew's grounds at Czermna, 2km north of Kudowa's town centre. The length of its walls and ceiling are covered with human skulls and bones – about 3000 of them, with another 20,000 to 30,000 filling the crypt below (p266). One of only three such chapels in Europe, it was inspired by Rome's Capuchin Crypt. The overall effect is stunning; sadly, photography isn't permitted

Table Mountains National Park Ecocentre NATURE CENTER

(Ekocentrum Parku Narodowego Gór Stołowych; ☑74 865 4929; https://ekocentrum.pngs.com.pl; ul Słoneczna 31a; ☺9am-4pm Jan-Apr & Oct-Nov, to 5pm May-Sep, to 3pm Dec) This enthusiastically run centre brings the ecology of the Góry Stołowe National Park (p265) to life through a variety of interesting displays and a film that can be followed in English using free headsets.

🏃 Activities

Spa Park HEALTH & FITNESS

(Park Zdrojowy) Kudowa has an attractive 17-hectare spa park, but most treatments on offer involve room and board at one of the sanatoriums.

However, anyone can try two of the local mineral waters at the Pump Room in the southeastern corner.

The Galos Salt Caves (Jaskinie Solno Galos; www.galos.pl; normal/reduced entry 12/10zł; ⊙9am-6pm) establishment to the west claims to relieve all your ills via remarkable artificial sea-salt chambers, as does its rival Solana Salt Grotto (Grota Solna Solana; www.solana.pl; ul Zdrojowa 41/12; normal/reduced entry 12/9zł; ⊙10am-noon & 2-8pm Mon-Sat, 11am-8pm Sun), near the tourist office. The prices of their treatments vary with the different packages available, so enquire at each venue.

The Water World Aqua Park (Aqua Park Wodny Świat; www.basenkudowa.pl; ul Moniuszki 2a; first hour adult/concession 14/11zł; ⊙9am-9pm Mon-Fri, from 10am Sat & Sun), on the southern edge of the park opposite where the buses stop, offers more active watery fun.

➧ Pump Room

(Pijalnia; adult/concession 1.50/0.80zł; ⊙7am-7pm Mon-Fri, from 9am Sat & Sun) If you want (literally) a taste of what the spa park has to offer, this Pump Room in the southeastern corner serves up two of the local mineral waters. Outside is a larch-lined well dating to 1587, indicating the centuries over which people have come to Kudowa to take the waters.

🛌 Sleeping

⭐ Willa Sanssouci-Dauc   HOTEL €€

(☏74 866 1350; https://sanssouci-dauc.pl; ul Pogodna 3; s/d/tr 150/200/270zł; P🖥) Located in a lovely buttercup-coloured villa built in 1894, the Sanssouci-Dauc has comfortable, ample rooms and good service. If you're feeling lucky, give the wishing well in the garden a go.

Willa Sudety   HOTEL €€

(☏74 866 1223; www.willa-sudety.pl; ul Zdrojowa 32; s/d 120/204zł; P🖥) This well-placed hotel and recreation centre offers affordable accommodation in an attractive custard-yellow building. There's table tennis on the premises, and the management can arrange activities and excursions including hiking and cycling. Three-night minimums apply in peak periods.

Pensjonat Akacja   HOTEL €€

(☏74 866 2712; http://akacja.eu; ul Kombatantów 5; s/d/tr 125/165/215zł; P🖥) This modernised villa is a family-run business providing excellent accommodation in a quiet spot with plenty of space. Interiors are spic and span with folksy decoration, and some upper-floor rooms have balconies.

Uzdrowiska Kłodzkie   VILLA €€

(☏74 868 0400; www.zuk-sa.pl; ul Moniuszki 2; s/d 219/358zł; P🖥) The Kłodzko Spa Company administers two fine old villa sanatoriums in the centre of town, providing an unparalleled variety of rooms. The emphasis is on medical treatment, but they will accept casual guests. Reception is housed within the elegant Polonia sanatorium; nearby is Zameczek, the sister sanatorium.

🍴 Eating

Cudova Bistro   BISTRO €€

(☏88 770 8007; www.cudovabistro.pl; ul Zdrojowa 44; mains 27-30zł; ⊙10am-10pm; 🖥) Overlooking the spa park (p263), this bright contemporary eatery serves a tasty selection of Polish dishes and pizzas. There's a cosy back room for more intimacy, and also serves breakfast.

Czeska Restauracja Zdrojowa   CZECH €€

(☏74 866 2133; https://czech-restaurant.eu; ul Słoneczna 1; mains 34-39zł; ⊙noon-10pm Sun-Thu, to 11pm Fri & Sat) With leather-backed chairs, a polished wood bar, and street-side tables for warm weather, this Czech restaurant is one of the more inviting options in Kudowa. Expect the rib-sticking cuisine Poland's southern neighbour is known for: meat, dumplings, sauerkraut and beer (both in the food and in half-litre glasses).

Café Domek   PIZZA €€

(☏74 866 1575; http://villavenus.nazwa.pl/cafedomek; ul Zdrojowa 36; mains 26-30zł; ⊙noon-11pm; 🖥) This all-rounder does pizza and more substantial mains, and serves draught beer. There's a broad tiled terrace out front, ideal for relaxing and refuelling after a day of hiking in the Góry Stołowe National Park.

ℹ Information

Post Office (ul 1 Maja 12; ⊙8am-7pm Mon-Fri, to 2pm Sat)

Tourist Office (☏74 866 1387; www.kudowa.pl; ul Zdrojowa 44; ⊙8am-4pm Mon-Sat)

ℹ Getting There & Away

Buses depart from a stand in the town centre, on ul 1 Maja between the intersections of ul Poznańska and ul Lubelska. There are frequent departures for Kłodzko (11zł, one to 1¼ hours) and Wrocław (25zł, 2¾ hours).

There are also 11 buses each day to Náchod in the Czech Republic (5zł, 20 minutes).

It's possible to arrive and depart from Kudowa-Zdrój by rail, though the train station is 1.7km south of the spa park (p263) along ul Zdrojowa and ul Główna. There are daily services to Kłodzko (9zł, one hour).

Bystrzyca Kłodzka

POP 10,652

Established as Habelschwerdt by German colonists in the 13th century, Bystrzyca Kłodzka (bist-*shi*-tsah *kwots*-kah) is a sleepy, atmospheric old town that has retained much of its medieval architecture and layout. Perched on a natural defensive prominence, the town was repeatedly sacked, flooded, burned, and depopulated by plague across an eventful Middle Ages, but always managed to rise again. Ironically, it survived WWII virtually unmolested.

Though there aren't that many specific attractions, its city walls and gates are some of the most complete in Poland, and the squares and narrow streets of the Old Town have an appealing character.

◉ Sights

In the 14th century the town was granted municipal status and surrounded by fortified city walls, some elements of which are still in place. The most substantial structures include the **Water Gate** (Brama Wodna; ul Podmiejska), just south of the **Rynek** (Market Square; Plac Wolności), and the **Kłodzko Tower** (Baszta Kłodzka; ul Okrzei 13/15; ☉10am-4.30pm May-Sep, to 3.30pm Oct-Apr) FREE, which you can climb, on the north side of the Old Town.

Phillumenistic Museum   MUSEUM
(Muzeum Filumenistyczne; ☑74 811 0637; www. muzeum-filumenistyczne.pl; Mały Rynek 1; adult/concession 9/7zł; ☉9am-5pm Tue-Sat, 10am-4pm Sun Jul & Aug, 8am-4pm Mon-Sat, 10am-3pm Sun Sep-Jun) East of the Rynek, the Knights' Tower (Baszta Rycerska) was reshaped in the 19th century and turned into the belfry of the Protestant church that had been built alongside it. After WWII the church was occupied by this rather esoteric museum, which displays lighters, matchbox labels and other paraphernalia related to fire-lighting and -breathing. On the small square outside the museum stands the old whipping post from 1566; the Latin inscription on its top reads 'God punishes the impious'.

**Parish Church of
St Michael the Archangel**   CHURCH
(Kościół Parafialny Św Michała Archanioła; www.parafiabystrzyca.dbv.pl; Plac Skłodowskiej 3) This Gothic place of worship sits at the highest point of the Old Town, as befits a building that's been here in various manifestations since the 13th century. It has a nave and just one aisle with a row of six Gothic columns running right across the middle, plus a 16th-century font, baroque sculptures and a 15th-century Madonna with Child.

SILESIA BYSTRZYCA KŁODZKA

WORTH A TRIP

GÓRY STOŁOWE NATIONAL PARK

The **Góry Stołowe** (goo-ri sto-wo-veh; Table Mountains; Park Narodowy Gór Stołowych; www.pngs.com.pl; car/adult/concession 20/10/3zł) are among the most spectacular ranges of the Sudetes, as they're topped by a plateau punctuated by fantastic rock formations.

One of the highlights of the 63-sq-km park is Szczeliniec Wielki, its highest outcrop. Both German poet Goethe and the USA's sixth president, John Quincy Adams, walked here and admired the dramatic scenery. From a distance, the plateau looks like a high ridge adorned with pinnacles, rising abruptly from the surrounding fields.

From just beyond Karłów, a small village about 1km south of the plateau, you ascend 682 stone steps, which takes about 40 minutes. From there, the one-hour trail around the summit gives excellent views of both the mountain scenery and the rock formations, before arriving back at its starting point.

About 4km to the west, the Błędne Skały are another impressive feature, comprising hundreds of 'Errant Rocks', some up to 11m in diameter. They were deposited by glaciers in vaguely geometric shapes, forming a vast stone labyrinth. A sometimes very narrow trail runs between the rocks.

To get to Karłów, catch a privately run minibus from Kudowa-Zdrój (8zł, 20 minutes). Alternatively, take one of the frequent buses from Kudowa-Zdrój to Polanica-Zdrój (9zł, 35 minutes, half-hourly), from where there are three daily buses to Karłów (10zł, 50 minutes).

HEAD CASES

The Chapel of Skulls (p263), in Czermna immediately north of Kudowa-Zdrój, was built in 1776 and looks pretty modest from the outside. Inside, however, it's a different story: thousands of neatly arranged skulls and bones decorate the walls, with more suspended from the ceiling. It's the only chapel of its kind in Poland and one of just three in Europe.

The creator of this unusual 'Sanctuary of Silence' was one Václav Tomášek, a Czech parish priest (Czermna belonged to the Prague Archdiocese at that time). Inspired by Rome's Capuchin Crypt, he and the local gravedigger spent two decades collecting human skeletons, which they then cleaned and conserved. The 'decoration' of the chapel wasn't completed until 1804. Skulls and bones that didn't fit on the walls and the ceiling were deposited in a 4m-deep crypt.

Since the region was the borderland of the Polish, Czech and German cultures, and of Catholic, Hussite and Protestant traditions, many of the bones belonged to victims of nationalist and religious conflicts. The skeletons came mostly from numerous mass graves, the result of two Silesian wars (1740–42 and 1744–45) and the Seven Years' War (1756–63). The cholera epidemic that plagued the region also contributed to such an impressive quantity of raw material.

Several anatomically interesting skulls are displayed on the main altar, including those of a Tatar warrior, a giant and a victim of syphilis. Alongside them are the skulls of the mastermind of the enterprise – the priest and the gravedigger – at one with their work for all eternity.

🛏 Sleeping & Eating

Hotel Abis HOTEL €€
(☑ 74 811 0645; www.hotelabis.pl; ul Strażacka 28; s/d/tr 125/190/240zł; 🅿🛜) Set on spacious grounds on the western edge of Bystrzyca Kłodzka, the 85-bed Abis is an unpretentious, good-value hotel that you shouldn't regret choosing. Kids are well looked after with indoor and outdoor play areas, and there's a bar, restaurant (Polish mains 32zł), volleyball court and barbecue for everyone's enjoyment.

Hotel Castle HOTEL €€
(☑ 74 812 0560; www.hotelcastle.pl; ul Okrzei 26; s/d 140/220zł; 🅿🛜) Oddly (or logically?) for a town that has so much genuine medieval architecture, the builders of this hotel imagined it as a twee ahistorical 'castle', and called it just that. Appearances aside, it has the best lodgings in a town where rooms of any quality are scarce. Naturally, the in-house restaurant has been decked out in baronial splendour.

Kawiarnia Kulturalna CAFE
(☑ 73 331 0596; www.kawiarniakulturalna.com; ul Polskiego 26/15; ⊙ 2-10pm; 🛜🎮) Brick-solid yet imaginative, the 'Cultural Cafe' is a lovely find in Bystrzyca Kłodzka. Strewn with art (some for sale) and frequented by artists, it's the kind of place where you can disappear into a nook to read for hours, have a few beers with the regulars, or enjoy a delicious meal while taking in the creativity that surrounds you.

ℹ Information

Tourist Office (☑ 74 811 3731; www.bystrzyca klodzka.pl; Mały Rynek 2/1; ⊙ 8am-5pm Mon-Fri, 10am-4pm Sat)

ℹ Getting There & Away

The **bus station** (www.pks-klodzko.pl; ul Sienkiewicza 5), on ul Sienkiewicza 400m north of the parish church (p265), has regular services to Kłodzko (8zł, 35 minutes) and Boboszów (11zł, one hour) near the Czech border.

The train station is just east of the tourist office. From here regular trains connect with Kłodzko Miasto (p263) (6.50zł, 17 minutes) and Wrocław (22zł, two hours).

UPPER SILESIA

Heavily developed and industrialised, Upper Silesia (Górny Śląsk) occupies just 2% of Poland's territory, yet is home to a full 9% of the population. Thanks to large deposits of coal, it's long been the nation's centre of heavy industry, and sustains the most densely urbanised area in Central Europe. Under socialism this region was the 'reddest' in Poland and relatively well treated as a result.

Katowice, the region's largest city, offers cultural highlights that outstrip its utilitarian appearance. Beyond this urban web, the region has its share of attractive cities and towns.

Upper Silesia is where the German Nazis built the Auschwitz-Birkenau extermination camp complex. Preserved as though frozen in 1945, this essential site is now a profoundly moving and important memorial (p277).

Nysa

POP 45,681

It has to be admitted that Nysa (*ni*-sah) doesn't boast the harmonious architecture of many other Silesian towns. Around 80% of its buildings were destroyed during fierce battles between German and Soviet forces in 1945, and some of the postwar reconstruction leaves a lot to be desired aesthetically. Still, the mishmash of old and new is intriguing in its own way, especially the juxtaposition of Nysa's principal attraction – its dramatic cathedral – and other historical remnants with communist-era and more recent erections.

For centuries Nysa was one of the most important religious centres in Silesia. In the 17th century it became a seat of the Catholic bishops, who were in flight from newly 'Reformed' Wrocław. The bishops soon made Nysa a bastion of the Counter-Reformation – so strong was their hold that the town came to be known as the 'Silesian Rome'.

◉ Sights

There are several interesting remains of fortifications around Nysa. The restored 17th-century **St Hedwig's Bastion** (Bastion Św Jadwigi; ul Piastowska 19), two blocks northwest of the Rynek, was once home to a Prussian garrison.

The only significant traces of the town's medieval defences are two 14th-century brick towers: the **Ziębice Tower** (Wieża Ziębicka; ul Krzywoustego), west of the Rynek, with unusual turrets and dragon guttering; and the white-plastered **Wrocław Tower** (Wieża Bramy Wrocławskiej; ul Wrocławska), 200m northeast towards the train station.

★ Cathedral of
SS James and Agnes CATHEDRAL
(Katedra Św Jakuba i Agnieszki; www.bazylika-nysa.pl; Plac Katedralny 7) Nysa's mighty cathedral dominates the northern end of the Rynek with its imposing walls of time-soiled brick and a vast gabled roof – one of the steepest in Europe. Built in two stages, its current Gothic exterior dates to 1430 – aside from remodelling after a fire in 1542, little has

changed. Of note are the fine stone double portal and the 18 brick columns striding across an austere, echoing interior last updated in the late 19th century.

Nysa Museum MUSEUM
(Muzeum w Nysie; www.muzeum.nysa.pl; ul Jarosława 11; adult/concession 12/8zł, Wed free; ⊙9am-3.45pm Tue-Fri, 10am-3pm Sat & Sun) Established in Nysa's grand 17th-century Bishops' Palace in 1897, this museum exhibits local archaeology from prehistory up to early modern times; photos documenting war damage; and a model of the town in its heyday. Another section deals with witches of the region; it's not recommended for children under 12. You'll also find Dutch and Flemish paintings from the 16th to the 19th centuries, including works by Albrecht Dürer and Lucas Cranach the Elder.

Rynek SQUARE
(Market Square) Diverse architecture within Nysa's vast market square suggests the extent of damage done in WWII. Only the southern side retains anything akin to its historical appearance, with restored houses dating from the 16th century. The detached building facing them, the 1604 **Town Weighing House** (Dom Wagi Miejskiej; Rynek 38), retains fragments of 19th-century painting on a side wall. Just around the corner, on ul Bracka, are more historical houses and a 1701 copy of Rome's baroque Triton Fountain.

Just past the fountain is the twin-towered **Church of SS Peter and Paul** (Kościół Św Piotra i Pawła; www.piotripawel.nysa.pl; ul Bracka 18), built in 1727 for the Order of the Holy Sepulchre. It has one of Silesia's best baroque interiors, complete with an opulent high altar, organ and trompe l'oeil wall paintings.

⌹ Sleeping & Eating

★ Villa Navigator HOTEL €€
(📞77 433 4170; www.villanavigator.pl; ul Wyspiańskiego 11; s/d 120/160zł; P🛜) This charming family-run hotel in a pre-WWI house close to the Nysa Kłodzka River is a delight, from the antique furniture to the oil paintings, potted plants and sociable breakfasts in the parlour. For a visual treat, ask for the Danzig room (number 4) or the Secessionist room (number 3).

Hotel Fryderyk HOTEL €€
(📞77 421 0426; www.hotel.nysa.pl; ul Szopena 12; r from 190zł; P✳🛜) Making contemporary

use of an antique building in the centre of Nysa, the Fryderyk offers comfortable rooms decorated in a palette of dark brown, bronze and cream. There's an accomplished Polish restaurant on the premises (mains 28zł to 45zł).

Hotel Piast HOTEL €€
(☑77 433 4084; www.hotel-piast.com.pl; ul Krzywoustego 14; s/d 171/213zł; 🛜) A central location, well-appointed rooms and an on-site cafe/restaurant are the ongoing selling points of this established hotel, which has been welcoming guests since 1975. It's across the road from the 14th-century Ziębice Tower (p267).

Bar Popularny CAFETERIA €
(Rynek 23; mains 8-9zł; ☺8am-6pm Mon-Fri, to 4pm Sat) Cheap as chips and enduringly popular with the locals, this unreformed *bar mleczny* (milk bar) on the main square (p267) looks drab and basic, but the food is tasty. The set meals are real bargains.

★ Bistro Madame POLISH €€
(☑77 433 4880; http://bistromadame.pl; Rynek 26; mains 25-35zł; ☺9am-10pm; 🛜) Celebrity chef Magda Gessler is the drawcard behind this upscale restaurant on the Rynek (p267). The interior is a bit to swallow – tricked out in plum, custard and green tones with the odd chandelier thrown in – but the Frenchified Polish food is very good. Expect creamy sauces, rich meat dishes and unapologetic desserts.

ℹ Information

Post Office (ul Krzywoustego 21; ☺8am-7pm Mon-Fri, 9am-2pm Sat)
PTTK Office (☑88 368 0078; https://pttk.nysa.pl; ul Poznańska 1; ☺4-5.30pm Tue & Thu)
Tourist Office (☑77 433 4971; ul Piastowska 19; ☺8am-4pm)

ℹ Getting There & Away

Nysa's bus and train stations face one another on ul Racławicka, about 800m northeast of the Rynek (p267).

Regular buses run to Kłodzko (13zł, one hour), Opole (11zł, 1½ hours) and Wrocław (15zł, 1½ hours).

Trains also run reasonably frequently to Opole (14zł, 1½ hours) and Wrocław (19zł, 1¾ hours).

Opole
POP 131,867

Best known within Poland for the National Festival of Polish Song (p270), Opole is a medium-sized industrial centre with an attractive Old Town flanking the Młynówka Canal, once the bed of the Odra River.

Positioned on the border of Upper and Lower Silesia, the city is the capital of its own voivodeship (province) called Opolskie. The region is known for its prominent German minority, which survived the repatriations that followed WWII. It numbers about 100,000 and is represented in local government.

The first Slav stronghold here was built in the 9th century. In the 13th century Opole became the capital of its principality and was ruled by a line of Silesian Piasts until 1532, even though it was part of Bohemia from 1327. Later, Opole fell to Austria, then to Prussia. After significant destruction in WWII, the city became Polish in 1945.

◉ Sights

★ Franciscan Church of the Holy Trinity CHURCH
(Kościół Franciszkanów Św Trójcy; Map p269; Plac Wolności 2; ☺10am-6.30pm Mon-Sat, noon-6pm Sun) This church off the southern corner of the **Rynek** (Market Square; Map p269) was built of brick around 1330. It boasts an ornate high altar, an 18th-century organ and a domed Renaissance chapel in the left-hand aisle, separated by a fine late-16th-century wrought-iron grille. A highlight is the Chapel of St Anne, accessible from the right-hand aisle through a doorway with a tympanum. The Gothic-vaulted chapel houses a pair of massive sandstone double tombs (where local dukes were interred) dating to the 1380s.

Opole Silesian Museum MUSEUM
(Muzeum Śląska Opolskiego; Map p269; www.muzeum.opole.pl; Mały Rynek 7; adult/concession 10/6zł; ☺9am-4pm Tue-Thu, noon-8pm Fri, noon-6pm Sat & Sun) Two blocks east of the market square, this museum is housed in a former Jesuit college dating to 1698, with the more recent addition of a glass-and-concrete annexe. The permanent display features the prehistory and history of the city and the surrounding area (as far back as 300,000 years), and there are always worthwhile temporary exhibitions. Enter from ul Muzealna.

Opole

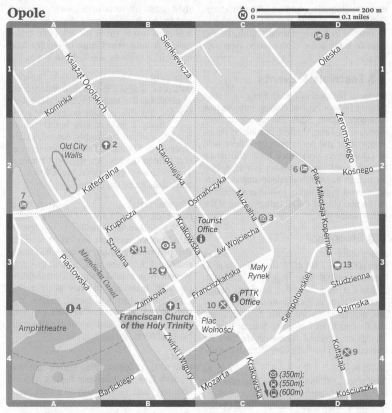

N 0 ——————— 200 m
   0 ——————— 0.1 miles

Opole

◉ Top Sights

◉ Sights

🛏 Sleeping

✗ Eating

🍷 Drinking & Nightlife

Holy Cross Cathedral   CHURCH
(Katedra Św Krzyża; Map p269; ul Katedralna 2)
Dating to the late 13th century, this Gothic
cathedral just north of the Rynek features
73m-high towers and mostly baroque interior furnishing. The lovely bronze gate at
the western entrance was erected in 1995 to
mark the church's 700th year.

Piast Tower   TOWER
(Wieża Piastowska; Map p269; www.wieza
piastowska.pl; ul Piastowska 14; adult/concession
10/6zł; ☉ 9am-5pm Mon-Fri, 11am-4pm Sat & Sun)
The only vestige of the doughty castle that
once housed Opole's dukes is this tilting
33m-high watchtower, with walls 3m thick
and foundations 6m deep. Built in the early
13th century, the castle was pulled down in

the 1920s to make room for office buildings. Entry is by 30-minute guided tours for up to 10 people, in which you can climb the 163 steps to the top for a panoramic view over the city.

Festivals & Events

National Festival of Polish Song   MUSIC

(Krajowy Festiwal Piosenki Polskiej; http://festiwal opole.com; tickets 80zł) Occupying a long weekend in June, this celebration of Polish songwriting and performance has been held in Opole every year since 1963, and is the biggest event on the town's calendar. Performances at Opole's outdoor amphitheatre are a great opportunity to immerse yourself in the pop side of Polish culture, even if the lyrics escape you.

🛏 Sleeping

Szara Willa   HOTEL €€

(Map p269; ☏77 441 4577; www.szarawilla.pl; ul Oleska 11; s/d 269/319zł; P 🕿) The 'Grey Villa' has a crisp modern feel, featuring design elements with an Asian influence. All rooms are generously sized with high ceilings; the four in front look onto a large terrace. There's an attached fitness centre (free for guests), plus a bowling alley (10% discount).

Hotel Piast   HOTEL €€

(Map p269; ☏77 454 9710; www.hotel-piast.com; ul Piastowska 1; s/d/tr 190/210/260zł; P ❄🕿) Commanding the best location of all Opole's accommodation, the Piast sits next to lock gates on the northern tip of Pasieka Island, where the Odra River parts from its historical channel, the Młynówka. Its 25 comfortable rooms are classy with a conservative style. There's a bar on the premises.

Hotel Kamienica   HOTEL €€

(Map p269; ☏77 546 6196; www.hotelkamienica. com.pl; Plac Kopernika 14; s/d/tr 175/240/335zł; P 🕿) This neat and tidy three-star hotel offers 23 rooms behind the Old Town. Rooms are simple but comfortable, and there's an on-site restaurant serving Thai cuisine (mains 28zł to 33zł). Parking at the Solaris Centre (the shopping centre across the road) is 15zł for 24 hours.

🍴 Eating & Drinking

★Rybex   SEAFOOD €

(Map p269; ☏77 454 3330; ul Krakowska 10; mains 15-25zł; ☉9am-6pm Mon-Fri, to 2pm Sat) Part deli, part quick-and-satisfying fish bar, Rybex sells all sorts of smoked, preserved and fresh fish to take away, or can fry you up a fillet or two to eat at the few plain tables inside. A long-term fixture of Opole's food scene, it's a must for smoked-fish lovers.

Hamburg   BURGERS €

(Map p269; ☏57 028 1570; http://hamburg.opole. pl; ul Kołłątaja 16a; burgers 19-20zł; ☉11am-10pm Mon-Sat; 🕿) This popular burger bar could be in many a modern city, but there's no need to disdain its freshly cooked, generously stuffed burgers. The Blu (blue cheese) and Gringo (cactus) are the most unusual. There's also a veggie option, and a few soups and salads grace the menu.

Wegeneracja   VEGETARIAN €€

(Map p269; ☏72 423 4244; ul Młyńska 1; mains 18-28zł; ☉11am-9pm Mon-Thu, to midnight Fri, noon-10pm Sat, noon-7pm Sun; 🕿🍴) With its stripped-wood counter, whitewashed walls, reclaimed furniture and potted greenery, Wegeneracja exudes calm, an atmosphere the staff maintains as they bring coffee, cake, soups, tortillas, falafel, salads, casseroles and other meat-free treats to your table. Gluten-free and vegan options, plus regional beers, ice the cake.

Pauza   CAFE

(Map p269; ul Ozimska 19b; ☉10am-8pm Mon-Fri, from 11am Sat, from noon Sun) A relaxed split-level cafe tucked away in a backstreet, this is the perfect place for coffee and cake after a hard day's sightseeing. There's a smattering of outdoor seating too. Enter from ul Podgórna.

Maska   PUB

(Map p269; ☏50 849 1760; www.pubmaska.pl; Rynek 4-6; ☉10am-1am Mon-Thu, to 2am Fri & Sat, 11am-midnight Sun; 🕿) A place of wine, song and gathering since the 19th century and throughout the years of the PRL, this atmospheric pub on the main square (p268) is ideal for a recuperative drink, and perhaps some filling Polish food.

ℹ Information

Main Post Office (ul Krakowska 46; ☉6am-10pm)

PTTK Office (Map p269; ☏77 454 5113; www. opole.pttk.pl; ul Krakowska 15; ☉10am-4.30pm Mon-Fri)

Tourist Office (Map p269; ☏77 451 1987; www.opole.pl; Rynek 23; ☉10am-6pm Mon-Fri, to 3pm Sat & Sun Apr-Oct, 9am-5pm Mon-Fri, 10am-3pm Sat Nov-Mar; 🕿)

ℹ Getting There & Away

The train station and **bus station** (www.pks. opole.pl; ul 1 Maja 4) face each other at the end of ul Krakowska, south of the Old Town.

Regular buses head to Nysa (11zł, 1½ hours), Wrocław (10zł, 1½ hours) and Katowice (15zł, 1¾ hours).

Opole is on the main rail line between Katowice (24zł, 1½ hours) and Wrocław (19zł, one hour), with regular services in both directions. There are also regular trains to Kraków (40zł, 2½ hours), Częstochowa (24zł, one hour) and Warsaw (123zł, three hours).

Katowice

POP 310,764

Katowice (kah-to-*vee*-tseh) is the largest constituent of the so-called Upper Silesian Urban Area, a vast conurbation with a population approaching three million. Built on coal wealth, the rural village that once snoozed here exploded into a modern industrial city in the 19th century.

While Katowice today is a product of that 19th-century industrial boom, it only became a city in the interwar period. After WWII, at the height of the Stalinist cult craze, it was renamed Stalinogród, but reverted to its old name soon after Old Whiskers died, in 1953. A major commercial and cultural centre, Katowice isn't pretty, but its museums, restaurants and urban buzz are easily enough to justify a stopover.

◉ Sights

★ Museum of Katowice History at Nikiszowiec MUSEUM

(Muzeum Historii Katowic w Nikiszowcu; ✐ 32 353 9559; www.mhk.katowice.pl; ul Rymarska 4, Nikiszowiec; adult/concession 10/5zł; ⊙ 10am-6pm Tue-Fri, 11am-5pm Sat & Sun; P) This branch of Katowice's museum, an ethnographic exploration of working-class and industrial life in Upper Silesia, lies in the distinctive suburb of Nikiszowiec, 6km southeast of the city centre. The entire district is a unique estate created for the families of the miners who worked a nearby shaft between 1908 and 1924. Comprising nine red-brick blocks interconnected by gateways, the complex was designed to be self-sufficient, with shops, restaurants, a swimming pool, a hospital, a school and a detention centre.

Take bus 30 and alight at the Nikiszowiec Szpital stop.

★ Silesian Museum MUSEUM

(Muzeum Śląskie; Map p272; ✐ 32 213 0870; www.muzeumslaskie.pl; ul Dobrowolskiego 1; full-access tickets adult/concession 24/16zł, Tue free; ⊙ 10am-8pm Tue-Sun; P) A symbol of Katowice's transition from a centre of heavy industry to one of culture, the Silesian Museum sits in an ingeniously repurposed coal mine in the city's 'Cultural Zone', north of the Rynek (Market Square; Map p272). Spread over four levels sinking to 13m below ground, landmarked by the mine's decommissioned hoist tower, it features permanent exhibits such as *Silesian Religious Art*, *Upper Silesia Over the Ages* and *Polish Art after 1945*, plus temporary shows on artistic, political and social themes.

Upper Silesian Ethnographic Park MUSEUM

(Górnośląski Park Etnograficzny; ✐ 32 241 0718; www.muzeumgpe-chorzow.pl; ul Parkowa 25, Chorzów; adult/concession 10/7zł, free Mon; ⊙ 9am-7pm Mon-Fri, 10am-9pm Sat & Sun May-Aug, shorter hours rest of year; P; ᆱ 0, 6, 11, 19 or 23) This sprawling open-air museum contains scores of traditional wooden buildings spread over 20 hectares, representing architectural styles from Upper Silesia, Zagłębie Dąbrowskie and other regions. It's situated within Chorzów's even bigger Provincial Park of Culture and Recreation, which also houses a stadium, a zoo, amusement grounds and a planetarium, about 3km northwest of the centre. Mondays are free, but without admission to the interior of the buildings.

Get off the tram at the Chorzów Stadion Śląski stop.

Cathedral of Christ the King CATHEDRAL

(Katedra Chrystusa Króla; Map p272; https://katedra.archidiecezjakatowicka.pl; ul Plebiscytowa 49a; ⊙ 6am-6.30pm) With a base measuring 89m by 53m, this is Poland's largest cathedral. Erected between 1927 and 1955, the neoclassical sandstone basilica's progress was understandably delayed by the tumultuous 1940s. Its vast interior is topped with a large dome that rises 59m from the floor, but apart from colourful stained-glass windows and an unusual 'wheel' crucifix, it's a model of austerity.

SILESIA KATOWICE

Katowice

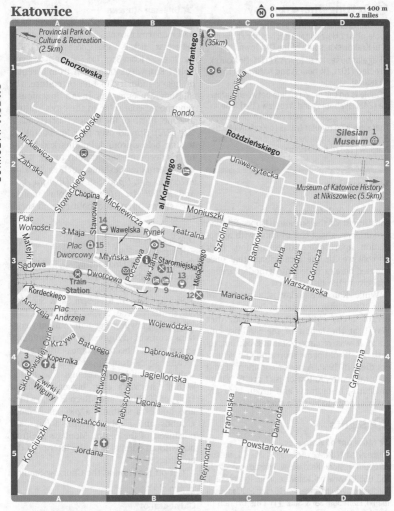

Katowice

⊚ Top Sights
1 Silesian Museum D2

⊚ Sights
2 Cathedral of Christ the King A5
3 Cloud Scraper A4
4 Garrison Church of St Casimir
   the Prince A4
5 Rynek B3
6 Spodek C1

⊟ Sleeping
7 Hotel Diament B3
8 Hotel Katowice B2

9 Hotel Monopol B3
10 Jopi Hostel B4

⊗ Eating
11 Tatiana B3
12 Złoty Osioł B3

⊖ Drinking & Nightlife
13 Absurdalna B3
14 Kofeina Bistro A3

⊟ Shopping
15 Galeria Katowicka A3

WORTH A TRIP

TOSZEK

The small town of Toszek is worth a detour on your way from Katowice to Wrocław simply to look around its impressive gothic **castle** (Zamek w Toszku; www.zamektoszek.eu; ul Zamkowa; entry 4zł; ⊘11am-6pm Sat & Sun mid-Apr–Jun & Sep–mid-Oct, Tue-Fri Jul & Aug). First mentioned in surviving records in 1222, some experts believe it's originally from the 12th century. Reaching its apogee in the 15th century, it housed successive Silesian dukes, Habsburg nobles and commercial magnates, before burning down in 1811. Today it houses a culture centre and stages various events and festivals.

On the other side of town, there's an unusual sight awaiting book lovers – the **psychiatric hospital** (Szpital Psychiatryczny; ul Gliwicka 5, Toszek) where British novelist PG Wodehouse (p274) was interned by the Germans in WWII. After the war it operated as a political prison of the Soviet Union's feared NKVD secret police. Within the complex are grounds that were used as an exercise yard for the prisoners, beyond which was their dining hall and hospital.

Though you can't enter, you can get a good view of its grim red-brick exterior from the dishevelled park across the road.

Frequent trains call at Toszek from Opole (14zł, 50 minutes). From the train station (p275), turn left and take a 20-minute walk along ul Dworcowa to the town centre.

Spodek STADIUM
(Map p272; ☑32 438 4030; www.spodekkatowice. pl; al Korfantego 35) Built of reinforced concrete between 1964 and 1971, Spodek – which means 'saucer' – really does look like a UFO has landed just north of central Katowice. Aside from being a venue for indoor sports such as basketball, handball and volleyball, it's played host to rock acts, including Deep Purple and Pearl Jam.

Cloud Scraper NOTABLE BUILDING
(Drapacz Chmur; Map p272; ul Żwirki i Wigury 15-17) This blocky, 14-storey, 60m-high apartment building was Poland's tallest building from 1934 until 1955. Considered the purest example of functionalism in the country, its preeminent height made it the ideal perch for snipers resisting the Nazi invasion of 1939. Today, the venerable edifice is coated in a patina of grime.

Garrison Church of St Casimir the Prince CHURCH
(Parafia Wojskowa Św Kazimierza; Map p272; ☑32 251 3511; www.garnizonowa.wiara.org.pl; ul Skłodowskiej-Curie 20) The Garrison Church of St Casimir, a functionalist concrete-and-brick affair with lovely art deco interiors, was built between 1930 and 1933 (the year before the skyscraper opposite, also a functionalist landmark, was completed). Outside masses, the church isn't always open without prior arrangement.

🛏 Sleeping

Jopi Hostel HOSTEL €
(Map p272; ☑32 204 3432; www.jopihostel.pl; ul Plebiscytowa 23; dm 41-51zł, s/d 101/107zł; 🛜) Set back from the street on a concrete courtyard, Jopi offers modern rooms just south of the train station (p275). There's a well-equipped kitchen, a comfortable lounge/ dining area and cheery yellow-and-lime decor in the rooms.

★**Hotel Diament** HOTEL €€
(Map p272; ☑32 253 9041; www.hotelediament.pl/ hotele/hotel-diament-plaza-katowice; ul Dworcowa 9; s/d from 224/249zł; P☀🛜) Business-friendly Diament is a member of a Silesian hotel chain with two other hotels in town, including one at Katowice's iconic Spodek (Flying Saucer) stadium. Comfortable, convenient and reliably friendly, it's great value for the comfort level. Booking online usually secures a lower rate.

Hotel Katowice HOTEL €€
(Map p272; ☑32 258 8281; www.hotel-katowice. com.pl; al Korfantego 9; s/d 155/200zł; P🛜) Only a Soviet central planner could admire the quadrilinear exterior of this functionalist communist-era relic, but the rooms have been renovated to a comfortable and aesthetically pleasing standard, and the city centre's just outside your door. Amenities include a bar and restaurant.

WHAT HO! PG WODEHOUSE BEHIND BARS

In May 1940, British novelist PG Wodehouse – creator of the masterful valet Jeeves and his hapless employer Bertie Wooster – was captured by the German army at his home in France. In September he was moved to a civilian internment camp within the grounds of a psychiatric hospital (p273) in German Tost, now Toszek (p273).

Wodehouse, then 58, coped well with the privations of camp life, but was unimpressed with what he could see of Toszek through the barred windows, writing: 'If this is Upper Silesia, what must Lower Silesia be like?'

The internationally famous author was treated well by his captors, being allowed to work on a rented typewriter. In 1941, he was invited by the German authorities to make a series of radio broadcasts to reassure his readers in still-neutral America of his good health. Naively, Wodehouse agreed, unaware of the defiant mood in the UK after the Blitz and the Battle of Britain. The broadcasts caused an outpouring of indignation and accusations of collaboration.

Although after the war British intelligence secretly cleared Wodehouse of any wrongdoing, the incident left its mark. The author never returned to Britain, living out his days on Long Island, New York.

★ Hotel Monopol
HOTEL €€€

(Map p272; ☑ 32 782 8282; www.monopolkatowice. hotel.com.pl; ul Dworcowa 5; s/d 595/780zł; P❋@🛜🏊) This tasteful reincarnation of Katowice's most celebrated prewar hotel offers high levels of comfort and friendly, helpful staff. Rooms are full of stylish walnut and chrome surfaces, and bathrooms feature huge shower heads. There are also two restaurants, a fitness centre with two saunas, and a swimming pool. Check out the handsome 19th-century mosaic under glass in the foyer.

🍴 Eating & Drinking

Katowice has a very credible dining scene, including good Asian options and haute Polish. The densest dining zone lies between uls Wojewódzka and Warszawska, from Galeria Katowicka (Map p272; www. galeriakatowicka.eu; ul 3 Maja 30; ⊗9am-9pm Mon-Sat, 10am-8pm Sun) shopping centre in the west to ul Francuska in the east.

Złoty Osioł
VEGETARIAN €

(Map p272; ☑ 32 253 0113; http://wegebar.com; ul Mariacka 1; mains 15-18zł; ⊗10am-10pm Mon-Sat, noon-10pm Sun; 🛜🍴) A cheerful, popular vegetarian cafe just off one of Katowice's main nightlife strips, the 'Golden Donkey' offers vegetarian and vegan fare in a charming interior of mismatched tablecloths and vaguely hippy art. The millet with spicy vegetables, baked pear and cashews is a good bet, or choose from various lasagnas, pancakes and casseroles.

★ Tatiana
POLISH €€€

(Map p272; ☑ 32 203 7413; www.restauracja tatiana.pl; ul Staromiejska 5; mains 55-79zł; ⊗1-11pm Mon-Sat, to 10pm Sun) Perhaps Katowice's best restaurant, Tatiana takes Polish food, particularly that of Silesia, and elevates it without uprooting it. Expect mains such as saddle of venison in burnt hay with barley-and-mushroom stuffed cabbage rolls and smoked plum mousse, and top-notch levels of food and wine service. Book ahead to be sure of a dinner-time table.

Absurdalna
MICROBREWERY

(Map p272; ☑ 537 670 270; www.absurdalna.pl; ul Dworcowa 3; ⊗3pm-12.30am Sun-Thu, to 2.30am Fri & Sat; 🛜) Decked out in surreal art, lit by a galaxy of candy-coloured globes dangling from the ceiling and boasting 15-plus intriguing draught beers alongside a fine selection of craft meads, Absurdalna is a very Polish hipster hangout. Moreish drinking food such as pulled-pork quesadillas and burgers topped with local grilled sheep's cheese round off one of central Katowice's best drinking options.

Kofeina Bistro
CAFE

(Map p272; ul 3 Maja 13; ⊗8am-6pm Mon-Fri, 9am-6pm Sat, 9am-2pm Sun; 🛜) This bright modern cafe serves some of Katowice's best coffee, along with a selection of cakes and light meals.

ℹ Information

Post Office (Map p272; www.poczta-polska.pl; ul Pocztowa 9; ⊘24hr)

Tourist Office (Map p272; 📞 32 259 3808; www.katowice.eu; Rynek 13; ⊘9am-7pm Mon-Fri, to 5pm Sat & Sun Apr-Oct, 9am-5pm Mon-Sat, to 1pm Sun Nov-Mar)

ℹ Getting There & Away

AIR

Katowice Airport (p420) is in Pyrzowice, 35km north of the city. There are domestic flights to Warsaw (three daily), and international services to numerous European cities.

Public buses AP1 and AP2 run to Katowice's central **train station** (Plac Kaczyńskich 1) (14zł, 40 minutes). You can also transfer between the airport and Katowice train station via shuttle services run by **Matuszek** (📞 32 236 1111; www.matuszek.com.pl; single/return to Katowice 20/40zł, to Kraków 44/88zł). Buying tickets on the bus rather than booking online incurs an extra 5zł fee each way. The company also runs services from Katowice Airport to Kraków.

BUS

The main **bus station** (Map p272; www.katowicedworzec.pl; ul Piotra Skargi 1), some 600m north of the train station, handles most regional, long-distance and international services. Other short-haul regional buses depart from the underground bus station integrated with the train station in the city centre.

For most long-distance journeys the train will be a better option, though private firm **Polski Bus** (www.polskibus.com) operates a number of useful bus services.

DESTINATION	TIME (HRS)	FREQUENCY
Berlin	7¼-9¼	4 daily
Bratislava	4¾	1 daily
Częstochowa	1½	7 daily
Vienna	5¾	4 daily
Warsaw	4½-5½	1 daily
Wrocław	2½	every 2hrs
Zakopane	3¾	5 daily

The frequent PKS buses to Oświęcim (10zł, one hour) may also be useful.

TRAIN

Trains are the main means of transport in Upper Silesia and beyond. Katowice's busy modern train station is in the city centre.

DESTINATION	FARE (ZŁ)	TIME & FREQUENCY
Częstochowa	26	1½hr; at least hourly
Kraków	17	2hr; every 1-2hrs
Opole	29	1¼hr; every 1-2hrs
Oświęcim	13	1hr; 9 daily
Poznań	63	4-5½hr; 7 daily
Pszczyna	13	40min; at least hourly
Warsaw	62-150	2½-3½hr; at least hourly
Wrocław	33	2½hr; 10 daily

Pszczyna

POP 26,066

One of the oldest towns in Silesia (its origins go back to the 11th century), Pszczyna (*pshchi-nah*, the 'pearl of Silesia') is an attractive burg with a handsome market square (p276) presided over by a grand ducal castle.

The town was home to the Piast dynasty for hundreds of years. In 1847, after centuries of changing ownership, it became the property of the powerful Hochberg family of Prussia.

In the last months of WWI Pszczyna was the flashpoint of the first of three consecutive Silesian uprisings in which Polish peasants took up arms and demanded that the region be incorporated into Poland. Their wishes were granted in 1921, following a plebiscite held by the League of Nations.

◉ Sights

Castle Museum   MUSEUM

(Muzeum Zamkowe; 📞 32 210 3037; www.zamek-pszczyna.pl; ul Brama Wybrańców 1; museum adult/concession 20/11zł, armoury adult/concession 6/3.50zł, exhibition pass adult/concession 11/7zł; ⊘9am-5pm Tue-Fri, 10am-5pm Sat, 10am-6pm Sun, 11am-3pm Mon Jul & Aug, shorter hours rest of year) This grandiose ducal residence dates back to the 12th century, when the Opole dukes built a hunting lodge here. Rebuilt as a Renaissance palace in the 17th century, it has been enlarged several times, most recently in the 1870s. Today it houses the Castle Museum, comprising about a dozen rooms over three floors. The castle's interiors feature bedchambers, drawing rooms and salons filled with tapestries, ceramics, paintings and hunting trophies.

Unforgettable are the library – panelled entirely in walnut – and the stunning Mirror Chamber, which hosts occasional chamber music concerts. Some of the palace's rooms also contain themed exhibitions, including a collection of 16th- to 20th-century weapons and armour in the basement, and more than 200 diminutive portraits in the third-floor Cabinet of Miniatures. Behind the castle is the extensive English-style Castle Park along the Pszczynka River.

The Hochbergs, who owned Pszczyna Castle (Zamek w Pszczynie) until 1945, furnished their home according to their status – they were among the richest families in Europe, ruling vast swathes of land from their Silesian family seat, the castle (p250) at Książ. Priceless works of art completed the scene, but most were lost during WWII.

Those wanting more detailed information should pick up a copy of the English-language guidebook *The Castle Museum in Pszczyna* (16zł) from the ticket office or tourist office.

Rynek SQUARE

(Market Square) Pszczyna's elongated, leafy market square is lined with old burghers' houses dating mostly from the 18th and 19th centuries. On its northern side is the Protestant church and, next to it at No 2, the town hall, both remodelled last century. Behind the town hall is the 14th-century parish church, extensively rebuilt over the years, with a typically lavish interior featuring a ceiling painting of the Ascension. To the west of the square sits Pszczyna Castle, now a museum (p275).

Bison Show Farm ZOO

(Pokazowa Zagroda Żubrów; ☎32 447 0503; www.zubry.pszczyna.pl; ul Żorska 5; adultchild 16/12zł; ⏲9am-4pm; P 🚸) The European bison, the continent's largest mammal, grazes contentedly on this 10-hectare 'farm' on the western edge of Pszczyna's great belt of parkland. Watch the burly beasts from the safety of the observation deck, learn about them in the educational centre, or stroll along a forest path with displays on the local ecosystem. Other southern Polish natives, including moufflon, deer and geese are also kept here. Check the website for bison feeding times, which occur at two-hourly intervals.

Sleeping & Eating

Hotel PTTK HOTEL €

(☎32 210 3233; www.pttk-pszczyna.slask.pl/hotel; ul Bogedaina 16; s/d with bathroom from 75/99zł; P 📶) Close to the station some 500m south of central Pszczyna, this budget hotel occupies a former red-brick prison that housed its last inmate in 1975. There's nothing cell-like about the rooms now, though nine of the cheaper ones share facilities. Breakfast is not included, but there's a kitchen for guest use.

Pensonjat Piano Nobile HOTEL €€

(☎32 447 7881; www.pianonobile.com.pl; Rynek 16; s/d from 140/190zł; 📶) This darkly stylish hotel is within an impressively renovated early 18th-century residence conveniently located on the market square. Its seven rooms are immaculate and comfortably appointed, and there's a cafe-restaurant, Dolce Vita, on-site.

Café U Telemanna CAFE €

(☎32 449 1520; http://utelemanna.pl; ul Brama Wybrańców 1; snacks 16-18zł; ⏲9am-5pm Mon-Thu, to 8pm Fri & Sat, 10am-7pm Sun) Located in the courtyard of Pszczyna Castle (p275), this is a good pit stop for a drink or a snack – such as cake, salad or pancakes – after sightseeing in the castle/museum. The cafe is named after composer Georg Philipp Telemann (1681–1767), who lived here for four years in the early 18th century.

★**Frykówka** POLISH €€

(☎32 449 0020; www.frykowka.pl; Rynek 3; mains 32-38zł; ⏲noon-10pm Mon-Thu, 10am-midnight Fri & Sat, 11am-10pm Sun; 📶) This elegant, well-regarded restaurant on the Rynek offers classic Polish cooking, finessed to a higher standard than most. Their *gołąbki* are stuffed with goose, while rabbit is stewed in rosemary and served with herb-roasted dumplings. The setting is a handsome tenement dating to the early 19th century.

Information

Tourist Office (☎32 212 9999; ul Brama Wybrańców 1; ⏲8am-4pm) Just inside Pszczyna Castle (p275) gate.

Getting There & Away

The attractively restored train station is to the east of the centre, with buses leaving from stands next to the station along ul Sokoła. Trains are the best option; services to Katowice (12zł, 40 minutes) run at least hourly, and the train to Vienna (4½ hours) stops here twice a day.

Oświęcim

POP 40,342

One of Upper Silesia's oldest towns, Oświęcim (osh-*fyen*-cheem) is today a quiet, medium-sized industrial city on the border with Małopolska. The Polish place name may be unfamiliar to most foreigners, but the German equivalent, Auschwitz, is not. The name is immediately synonymous with the largest attempt at genocide in human history. Though visiting the eerily preserved camps is a disturbing experience, it's an essential element in understanding the full evil of the Holocaust.

◉ Sights

★ Auschwitz-Birkenau Memorial & Museum   HISTORIC SITE

(Auschwitz-Birkenau Miejsce Pamięci i Muzeum; ☑ guides 33 844 8100; www.auschwitz.org; ul Stanisławy Leszczyńskiej; tour adult/concession 60/55zł; ⊙ 7.30am-7pm Jun-Aug, to 6pm Apr-May & Sep, to 5pm Mar & Oct, to 4pm Feb, to 3pm Jan & Nov, to 2pm Dec; 🅿) **FREE** Auschwitz-Birkenau is synonymous with the Holocaust. More than a million Jews, and many Poles and Roma, were murdered here by German Nazis during WWII. Both sections of the camp – Auschwitz I and the much larger outlying Birkenau (Auschwitz II) – have been preserved and are open to visitors. It's essential to visit both to appreciate the extent and horror of the place.

From April to October it's compulsory to join a tour if you arrive between 10am and 3pm.

Book well ahead either online or by phone, or turn up early (before 9.30am). English-language tours leave at numerous times throughout the day, generally most frequently between 10am and 1.30pm, when they operate half-hourly. Most tours include a short documentary film about the liberation of the camp by Soviet troops in January 1945 (not recommended for children under 14).

The museum's visitor centre is at the entrance to the Auschwitz I site. Photography and filming are permitted throughout the camp without the use of a flash or tripod. There's a self-service snack bar by the entrance as well as a *kantor* (private currency-exchange office), free left-luggage room and bookshops with publications about the site.

If not on a tour, get a copy of the museum-produced *Auschwitz Birkenau Guidebook* (5zł). It includes plans of both camps.

The Auschwitz extermination camp was established in prewar Polish army barracks on the outskirts of Oświęcim by German occupiers in April 1940. Auschwitz was originally intended for Polish political prisoners, but the camp was then adapted for the wholesale extermination of the Jews of Europe in fulfilment of German Nazi ideology. For this purpose, the much larger camp at Birkenau (Brzezinka) was built 2km west of the original site in 1941 and 1942, followed by another one in Monowitz (Monowice), several kilometres to the west.

➡ Auschwitz I   HISTORIC SITE

Auschwitz I was only partially destroyed by the fleeing Germans, and many of the original brick buildings stand to this day as a bleak testament to the camp's history. Some 13 of the 30 surviving prison blocks now house museum exhibitions – either general, or dedicated to victims from particular countries or ethnic groups that lost people at Auschwitz. Presented without unnecessary comment, the collections of suitcases, pots, artificial limbs, gas canisters and human hair speak for themselves.

From the visitors centre in the entrance building, you enter the barbed-wire encampment through the infamous gate, displaying the grimly cynical message in German: 'Arbeit Macht Frei' ('Work Sets You Free'). The sign is in fact a replica, which replaced the original when it was stolen in late 2009. Though it was recovered within a few days, it had been cut into pieces by the thieves and took 17 months to restore. The replica has remained in place, with the original sign now on display within the museum.

The closing times quoted above are times of last entry: it's possible to spend another 90 minutes here, once in.

➡ Birkenau (Auschwitz II)   HISTORIC SITE

Though much of Birkenau was destroyed by the retreating Germans, the size of the place, fenced off with long lines of barbed wire and watchtowers stretching almost as far as your eye can see, will give you some idea of the scale of the crime; climb the tower at the entrance gate to get the full effect. If you're not part of a tour, make sure to leave enough time (at least an hour) to walk around the camp.

It was actually at Birkenau, not Auschwitz, that most of the killing took place. Massive (175 hectares) and purpose-built for efficiency, the camp had more than 300 prison barracks – they were actually stables built for horses, but housed 300 people each. Birkenau had four huge gas chambers, complete with crematoria. Each could asphyxiate 2000 people at one time, and were fitted with electric lifts to raise the bodies to the ovens more quickly and conveniently.

Auschwitz Jewish Center   MUSEUM

(Centrum Żydowskie w Oświęcimiu; www.ajcf.pl; Plac Skarbka 5; adult/concession 10/6zł; ⊙ 10am-6pm Sun-Fri Apr-Sep, to 5pm Sun-Fri Oct-Mar) In the centre of Oświęcim, this museum commemorates the Jewish community that flourished here from the 16th century until WWII. On one side is the restored Chevra Lomdei Mishnayot synagogue, built in 1913 to add to nearly 30 that served the town before the Holocaust. Adjoining that is the former home of the Kornreich family, now filled with photographs and artefacts documenting Jewish Oświęcim and the terrible process of its extermination.

🛏 Sleeping & Eating

Centre for
Dialogue and Prayer   GUESTHOUSE €€

(Centrum Dialogu i Modlitwy; ☑ 33 843 1000; www.cdim.pl; ul Kolbego 1; sites per person 43zł, s/d 138/276zł; P ☎) This Catholic facility, which promotes reflecting on and learning from the Holocaust, is located 800m southwest of the Auschwitz I (p277) site. It also provides comfortable and quiet accommodation in rooms of two to six beds (most with en suite), plus a campsite and a restaurant. Full board is available.

Hotel Olecki   HOTEL €€

(☑ 33 847 5000; www.hotelolecki.pl; ul Leszczyńskiej 16; s/d 180/210zł; P ☎) This hotel near the entrance to Auschwitz-Birkenau (p277) is the most comfortable and conveniently located accommodation in Oświęcim. Its restaurant serves both Polish and international cuisine, and has a beer garden.

Chata na Zaborskiej   POLISH €€

(☑ 33 400 0182; www.chatanazaborskiej.pl; ul Zaborska 40; mains 27-32zł; ⊙ 11am-10pm Mon-Sat, noon-8pm Sun; P) The 'Cottage on Zaborska' is an unlikely discovery on this busy stretch of road, albeit one set back from the traffic at the end of a long drive. Woodsy, folksy and boasting a mean Polish kitchen, it's the best place in Oświęcim for *barszcz* (beetroot soup), *piecuchy* (yeast-dough pastries) and hearty Polish mains.

ℹ Information

Tourist Office (☑ 33 843 0091; www.it. oswiecim.pl; ul Leszczyńskiej 12; ⊙ 8am-6pm May-Sep, to 5pm Apr & Oct, to 4pm Nov-Mar; ☎) In the complex across the road from the entrance to the Auschwitz I site, this office has literature and advice about Oświęcim and the surrounding area.

ℹ Getting There & Away

Oświęcim is about 30km southeast of Katowice and 50km west of Kraków

FROM KRAKÓW

For most visitors, the jump-off point for Oświęcim is Kraków.

Buses (12zł, 1¾ hours) are more convenient than trains, as they drop you off near the entrance to Auschwitz (the train station is 1.6km away). There are also numerous minibuses to Oświęcim from the minibus stands off ul Pawia, next to Galeria Krakowska.

Road signs to Oświęcim will point you along the two-lane N44, but it's faster going via the A4 toll motorway (exit at Chrzanów and take road 933). Turn up early (before 9.30am) if you want to bag a spot at the site's own car park (13zł for the whole day). Alternatively, there are several private parking lots within walking distance, or use the less busy car park at Birkenau (10zł) and take the shuttle bus to Auschwitz I.

FROM KATOWICE

Buses from Katowice to Oświęcim (10zł, 55 minutes), drop you off outside the train station, where frequent local buses (2.70zł, five minutes) connect to the main Auschwitz I site. The first bus departs Katowice at 8am; the last return from Oświęcim train station is around 4.30pm.

There are frequent daily trains (8zł, 50 minutes) from Katowice to Oświęcim.

ℹ Getting Around

A free shuttle bus links Auschwitz I with Birkenau, departing at 10- to 20-minute intervals (between 10.30am and 7pm) from April to October, then half-hourly from November to March. Alternatively, it's an easy 2km walk between the two sites.

Wielkopolska

POP 3.5 MILLION

Best Places to Eat

➡ Drukarnia (p291)

➡ Momo (p290)

➡ Thai Wok (p291)

➡ Pierożak (p290)

➡ Loft 46 (p294)

Best Places to Stay

➡ Blow Up Hall 5050 (p290)

➡ Poco Loco Hostel (p289)

➡ Hotel Palazzo Rosso (p287)

➡ Rezydencja Solei (p288)

Why Go?

If you want to experience the essence of Poland's eventful history, head for Wielkopolska. The region's name means Greater Poland, and this is where the Polish state was founded in the Middle Ages. Centuries later, the local population has an understandable pride in its long history.

Poznań is a lively and attractive city with plenty of interesting sights and good restaurants. Beyond, the Wielkopolska countryside offers a selection of charming towns and rural scenery. Among the region's attractions are castles, steam trains, palaces, churches, nature reserves and a memorable Iron Age settlement in Biskupin. And at the heart of it all is the great cathedral of Gniezno, the birthplace of Catholic Poland.

It's an impressive menu, but Wielkopolska is also a great place to strike out on your own. Wherever you end up, you'll be sure to find something of historic interest; it's that kind of place.

When to Go
Poznań

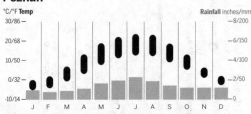

Mar–May Welcome spring by hiking through Wielkopolska National Park near Poznań.

Jun Summer is the time for alternative theatre and other arts at Poznań's Malta Festival.

Sep Iron Age culture is commemorated in autumn at the archaeological festival in Biskupin.

Wielkopolska Highlights

1 Poznań (p281) Exploring the culture, restaurants and nightlife in Wielkopolska's lively and attractive capital.

2 Biskupin Archaeological Reserve (p298) Travelling back to the Iron Age at this fortified village.

3 Gniezno Cathedral (p296) Exploring the chapels and crypt of this monumental double-towered cathedral.

4 Kórnik (p294) Visiting the small, distinctive castle in this sleepy, lakeside town.

5 Rogalin Palace Museum (p295) Exploring the opulence and habits of noble life at this fascinating palace.

6 Żnin District Railway (p301) Chugging through the bucolic landscape on a steam train outside Żnin.

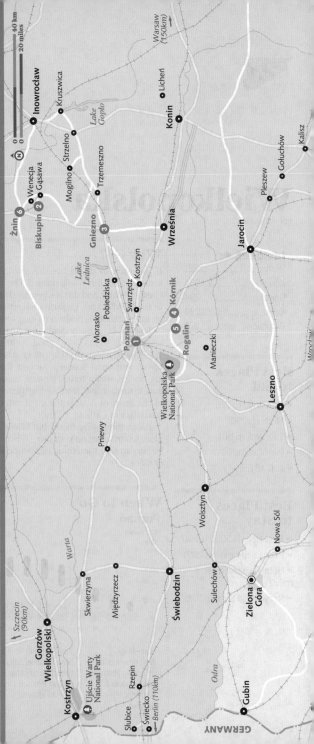

POZNAŃ

POP 554,700

Stroll into Poznań's Old Town square on any evening and you'll receive an instant introduction to the characteristic energy of Wielkopolska's capital. The city centre is buzzing at any time of the day, and positively jumping by night, full of people heading to its many restaurants, pubs and clubs. The combination of international business travellers attending its numerous trade fairs and the city's huge student population has created a distinctive vibe quite independent of tourism.

In addition to its energetic personality, Poznań offers many historical attractions – this is, after all, the 1000-year-old birthplace of the Polish nation – and its plentiful transport links make it a great base from which to explore the quieter surrounding countryside.

History

The history of Poznań and the history of Poland were much the same thing in the nation's earliest days. The city was founded as a 9th-century settlement on the easily defensible island of Ostrów Tumski, during the reign of Poland's first ruler, Duke Mieszko I. Some historians even claim that it was here, not in Gniezno, that the duke's baptism took place in 966.

Mieszko's son, the first Polish king, Bolesław Chrobry, further strengthened the island, and the troops of the Holy Roman Empire that conquered the region in 1005 didn't even bother to lay siege to it. The Bohemian Prince Bratislav (Brzetysław), however, liked a challenge and damaged the town considerably in 1038. This marked the end for Poznań as the royal seat (though kings were buried here until 1296), as subsequent rulers chose Kraków as their capital.

Poznań continued to develop as a commercial centre – in 1253 a new town centre was laid out on the left bank of the Warta River. Soon afterwards a castle was built and the town was encircled with defensive walls. Poznań's trade flourished during the Renaissance period, and by the end of the 16th century the population had passed the 20,000 mark.

But into every city's life a little rain must fall. From the mid-17th century on, Swedish, Prussian and Russian invasions, together with a series of natural disasters, battered the city. In the Second Partition of 1793, Poznań fell under Prussian occupation and was renamed Posen, later becoming part of Germany and experiencing steady industrial growth up to the outbreak of WWI.

The Wielkopolska Uprising, which broke out against Germany in Poznań in December 1918, led to the city's addition to the newly recreated Polish state. Poznań's long trading traditions were then revived with the establishment of regular trade fairs in 1921.

The city fell into German hands once more during WWII, and was incorporated into Hitler's Third Reich. In 1945 the battle for its liberation took a month and did a huge amount of damage.

In the postwar era, Poznań was one of the first cities to feel the forceful hand of the communist regime, during a massive workers' strike in June 1956. The spontaneous demonstration, cruelly crushed by tanks, turned out to be the first of a wave of popular protests on the long and painful road to overcoming communist rule.

Since the return of democracy, Poznań has taken advantage of its business traditions and favourable location near Germany to develop its role as an important educational and industrial centre.

◎ Sights

The historic heart of the city is centred on the lively and attractive Stary Rynek (Old Market Square). It was laid out in 1253 and contains a vibrant mix of sights, restaurants and entertainment outlets.

◎ Old Town

★ Parish Church   CHURCH

(Kościół Farny; Map p284; ul Gołębia; ⊙7am-dusk; ⊟Wrocławska) Two blocks south of the Rynek, this church was originally built for the Jesuits by architects from Italy, and completed only after more than 80 years of work (1651–1732). The impressive baroque structure has an ornamented facade, and a lofty interior supported on massive columns which is crammed with monumental altars.

Town Hall   HISTORIC BUILDING

(Ratusz; Map p284; Stary Rynek 1; ⊟Plac Wielkopolski, ⊟Wrocławska) Poznań's Renaissance town hall, topped with a 61m-high tower, instantly attracts attention. Its graceful form replaced a 13th-century Gothic structure, which burned down in the early 16th century. Every day at noon two metal goats appear through a pair of small doors

Greater Poznań

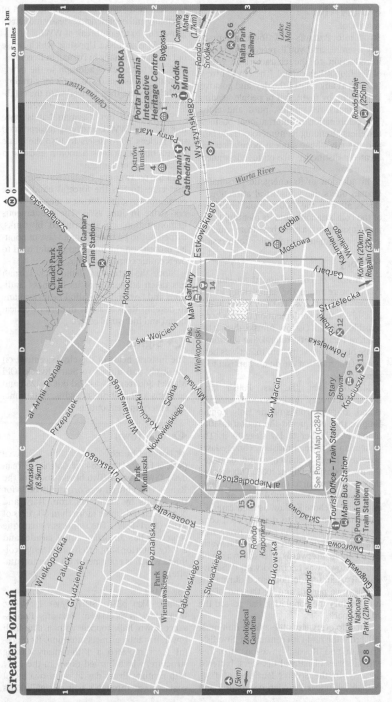

ŚRÓDKA

Porta Posnania Interactive Heritage Centre 1

3 Śródka Mural

Byogoska

Camping Malta (1.7km)

6

Rondo Śródka

Malta Park Railway

Lake Malta

Warta River

Panny Marii

Ostrów Tumski 4

Poznań Cathedral 2

Wyszyńskiego

7

Rondo Rataje (250m)

Cybina River

Szelągowska

Estkowskiego

Poznań Garbary Train Station

5 Grobla

Mostowa

Kazimierza Wielkiego

Kórnik (20km); Rogalin (32km)

Citadel Park (Park Cytadela)

Północna

Garbary

Strzelecka

Małe Garbary

14

al Armii Poznań

św Wojciech

Plac Wielkopolski

Rybaki 12

Połwiejska

13

Przepadek

Pułaskiego

Wieniawskiego

Kościuszki

Solna

Nowowiejskiego

Młyńska

Wielkopolski

Stary Browar

9

Kościuszki

Morasko (8.5km)

Park Moniuszki

św Marcin

See Poznań Map (p284)

Wielkopolska

Pałucka

Grudzienic

Poznańska

Park Wieniawskiego

Roosevelta

Słowackiego

Dąbrowskiego

al Niepodległości

15

Rondo Kaponiera

10

Składowa

Tourist Office – Train Station

Main Bus Station

Poznań Główny Train Station

Bukowska

Dworcowa

Głogowska

Zoological Gardens

Fairgrounds

Wielkopolska National Park (21km)

(5km)

8

1 km

0.5 miles

N

Greater Poznań

WIELKOPOLSKA POZNAŃ

above the clock and butt their horns together 12 times, in deference to an old legend. These days, the town hall is home to the city's Historical Museum.

Historical Museum of Poznań
MUSEUM
(Muzeum Historii Miasta Poznania; Map p284; ✆61 856 8000; www.mnp.art.pl; Stary Rynek 1; adult/concession 7/5zł, Sat free; ◉11am-5pm Tue-Thu, noon-9pm Fri, 11am-6pm Sat & Sun; ◉Plac Wielkopolski, ◉Wrocławska) This museum in Poznań's town hall displays an interesting exhibition on the city's history in splendid interiors. The richly ornamented Renaissance Hall on the 1st floor is a real gem, with its original stucco work and paintings from 1555. The 2nd floor contains artefacts from the Prussian/German period, documents illustrating city life in the 1920s and '30s, and a collection of interesting memorabilia from the past two centuries.

Museum of Applied Arts
MUSEUM
(Muzeum Sztuk Użytkowych; Map p284; www.mnp.art.pl; Góra Przemysława 1; adult/concession 12/8zł, Tue Free; ◉11am-5pm Tue-Thu, noon-9pm Fri, 11am-6pm Sat & Sun; ◉Plac Wielkopolski) Housed within Poznań's **castle** (Zamek) (which looks more like a palace), this museum's collection includes furniture, gold and silverware, glass, ceramics, weapons, clocks, watches and sundials from Europe and the Far East, dating from the Middle Ages to modern times.

Fish Sellers' Houses
HISTORIC BUILDING
(Domki Budnicze; Map p284; ◉Plac Wielkopolski, ◉Wrocławska) South of the town hall is this endearing row of small arcaded buildings. They were built in the 16th century on the site of fish stalls and later reconstructed after major WWII damage.

Museum of Musical Instruments
MUSEUM
(Muzeum Instrumentów Muzycznych; Map p284; ✆61 856 8000; www.mnp.art.pl; Stary Rynek 45; ◉Plac Wielkopolski, ◉Wrocławska) The museum prides itself on stringed insturments, but there are any others, from whistles to concert pianos, including intriguing musical devices such as a typewriter for musician notation and a polyphon, the precursor of the record player. There is also an exhibit of Chopin memorabilia from the composer's visit to Wielkopolski.

Ethnographic Museum
MUSEUM
(Muzeum Etnograficzne; Map p282; ✆61 856 8000; www.mnp.art.pl; ul Grobla 25; adult/concession 7/5zł, Sat free; ◉11am-5pm Tue-Thu, noon-9pm Fri, 11am-6pm Sat & Sun; ◉Most Świętego Rocha) Southeast of the Rynek is this good collection of folk woodcarving and traditional costumes of the region. Of particular note are the large roadside posts and crosses on display.

Archaeological Museum
MUSEUM
(Muzeum Archeologiczne; Map p284; ✆61 852 8251; www.muzarp.poznan.pl; ul Wodna 27; adult/concession 8/4zł, Sat free; ◉9am-4pm Tue-Fri, 10am-5pm Sat, noon-4pm Sun; ◉Wrocławska) Located off the southeastern corner of the Rynek, inside the 16th-century **Górka Palace**. Before going in, stop and have a look at the fine Renaissance doorway on the building's eastern facade. The museum presents the prehistory of the region, from the Stone Age to the early medieval period, as well as housing an extensive Egyptian collection.

Croissant Museum
MUSEUM
(Rogalowe Muzeum; Map p284; ✆69 007 7800; www.rogalowemuzeum.pl; Stary Rynek 41; adult/

Poznań

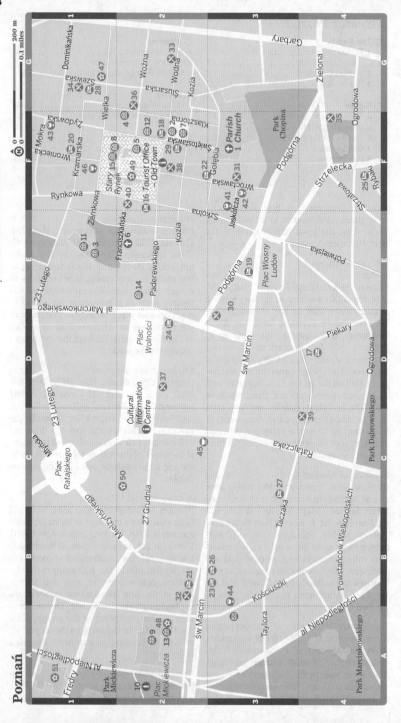

N 0 — 200 m
0 — 0.1 miles

Poznań

concession 18/16zł; ⊙ 11.10am-3pm; 🚊 Wrocławska) Located in a historic townhouse on the main square, this institution is devoted to the sweet St Martin's croissants peculiar to Poznań. In four sessions each day (at 11.10am, 12.30pm, 1.45pm and 3pm) visitors are told about the croissant's history, and can take part in making a batch. Note the 1.45pm session is the only one usually translated into English, so bookings are advisable. Enter from ul Klasztorna 23, one block east of the Rynek.

Franciscan Church   CHURCH
(Kościół Franciszkanów; Map p284; ul Franciszkańska 2; ⊙ 7am-dusk; 🚊 Plac Wielkopolski) Construction of this richly decorated baroque church was begun in 1674 and completed only in 1757. Highlights are its magnificent frescoes, including those in the chancel and in the main nave, which portray scenes from the life of St Francis. Stalls in the presbytery bear sculptures of dragons. The Chapel of the Virgin Mary in the left transept has a carved oak altar and a diminutive but beautiful picture of the Virgin Mary, framed by silver.

◎ West of the Old Town

National Museum   MUSEUM
(Muzeum Narodowe; Map p284; www.mnp.art.pl; al Marcinkowskiego 9; adult/concession 12/8zł, Sat free; ⊙ 11am-5pm Tue-Thu, noon-9pm Fri, 11am-6pm Sat & Sun; 🚊 Marcinkowskiego) This museum houses an extensive collection of Polish and European art displayed across numerous rooms. Polish painting of the last two centuries is represented by almost all the big names, including Jan Matejko, Stanisław Wyspiański and Jacek Malczewski. Look out for the distinctive work of Tadeusz Makowski, a 20th-century artist who created curious human figures from basic geometric shapes. An older, noteworthy curiosity is the museum's collection of coffin portraits.

Monument to the
Victims of June 1956 MONUMENT
(Pomnik Ofiar Czerwca 1956; Map p284; Plac Mickiewicza; 🚊 Zamek, 🚊 Gwarna) On Plac Mickiewicza you'll find one of Poznań's most significant memorials, which commemorates the ill-fated workers' protest of 1956 (p293). The monument, consisting of two 20m-tall crosses bound together, was unveiled on 28 June 1981, the 25th anniversary of the strike, at a ceremony attended by more than 100,000 people. It's a huge, evocative landmark, similar to Gdańsk's Monument to the Fallen Shipyard Workers (p317).

Palm House GARDENS
(Palmiarnia; Map p282; www.palmiarnia.poznan.pl; ul Matejki 18; adult/concession 10/7zł; ⊙9am-5pm Tue-Sat, to 6pm Sun; 🚊 Park Wilsona) A short walk from the main train station along ul Głogowska, Park Wilsona contains one of the biggest greenhouses in Europe. Constructed in 1910, it houses thousands of species of tropical and subtropical plants, including the continent's largest cactus collection and its tallest bamboo trees.

Museum of
Poznań June 1956 MUSEUM
(Muzeum Poznańskiego Czerwca 1956; Map p284; 📱61 852 9464; www.muzeumniepodleglosci. poznan.pl; ul Św Marcin 80/82; adult/concession 8/5zł, Tue free; ⊙10am-5pm Tue-Sat, to 4pm Sun; 🚊 Zamek, 🚊 Gwarna) Within the grand neo-Romanesque Kaiserhaus built from 1904 to 1910 for German Emperor Wilhelm II, this museum offers details of the massive 1956 workers' strike in Poznań. Entering this is like stepping back into 1956, but descriptions are only in Polish.

◉ Ostrów Tumski

To the east of the Old Town, over the Warta River, is the island of Ostrów Tumski (Cathedral Island). You're walking through deep history here, the place where Poznań was founded, and with it the Polish state. The original 9th-century settlement was gradually transformed into an oval stronghold surrounded by wood-and-earth ramparts, with an early stone palace. Mieszko I added a cathedral and further fortifications, and by the end of the 10th century Poznań was the most powerful stronghold in the country.

★ Poznań Cathedral CHURCH
(Katedra Poznańska; Map p282; www.katedra.arch poznan.pl; ul Ostrów Tumski 17; church free, crypt adult/concession 3.50/2.50zł; ⊙9am-5pm Mon-Sat mid-Mar–mid-Nov, 9.30am-4pm mid-Nov–mid-Mar; 🚊 Katedra) Ostrów Tumski is dominated by this monumental double-towered cathedral. Essentially Gothic with additions from later periods, notably the baroque upper towers, the cathedral was damaged in 1945 and took 11 years to rebuild. Early Polish kings were buried in the crypt – apart from fragments of their tombs, you can see the relics of the original church dating from 968, and of the Romanesque building from the second half of the 11th century.

The aisles and the ambulatory are ringed by a dozen chapels containing numerous tombstones. The most famous is the Golden Chapel behind the high altar, which houses the remains of the first two kings of Poland: Mieszko I and Bolesław Chrobry.

★ Porta Posnania
Interactive Heritage Centre MUSEUM
(Brama Poznania ICHOT; Map p282; 📱61 647 7634; www.bramapoznania.pl; ul Gdańska 2; adult/concession 18/12zł incl audio guide; ⊙9am-6pm Tue-Fri, 10am-7pm Sat & Sun; 🚊 Katedra) This cutting-edge multimedia museum provides an entertaining and insightful history of the birth of the Polish nation. It tells the tale through Ostrów Tumski's (Cathedral Island's) eventful history using imaginatively arranged interactive displays, as well as maps, movies and models. It's located opposite the island's eastern shore and is linked to the cathedral area by footbridge. The multilingual audio guide brings it all together from the time of first settlement on the island to the present day.

★ Śródka Mural PUBLIC ART
(Map p282; ul Śródka 3; 🚊 Rondo Śródka, 🚊 Katedra) FREE Just east of Ostrów Tumski (Cathedral Island) in the centre of the Śródka district you will find a sensational trompe-l'œil mural by artist Arleta Kolasińska. It covers the entire side of a building to make the wall appear three-dimensional and depicts Śródka in the 1920s, with amusing details like the trumpeter on the roof, the cat even higher up, a woman at the window, and a fat-bellied butcher posing at the doorway. Its true beauty though is its overall visual effect.

Archdiocesan Museum
MUSEUM

(Muzeum Archidiecezjalne; Map p282; ☑61 852 6195; www.muzeum.poznan.pl; ul Lubrańskiego 1; adult/concession 10/7zł; ☉10am-5pm Tue-Fri, 9am-3pm Sat; 🚊Rondo Śródka) North of the cathedral on Ostrów Tumski (Cathedral Island), this museum is located within the former Lubrański Academy, the first high school in Poznań (1518). Within its walls you'll find a collection of sacred art from the 12th century onwards.

◉ Lake Malta

Malta Park Railway
TOURIST RAILWAY

(Kolejka Parkowa Maltanka; Map p282; www.mpk. poznan.pl/maltanka; ul Jana Pawła II; adult/concession 6/4zł; ☉10am-6.30pm Apr-Sep; 🚊Rondo Śródka) East of Ostrów Tumski on the far bank of the river, beyond the Rondo Śródka intersection, you'll find the western terminus of this tourist railway. It runs miniature trains along the shoreline of the 70-hectare artificial Lake Malta (Jezioro Maltańskie), a favourite summer spot for families, picnickers and boating enthusiasts. The railway terminates at the New Zoo.

New Zoo
ZOO

(Nowe Zoo; ☑61 877 3517; www.zoo.poznan.pl; ul Krańcowa 81; adult/concession 20/10zł; ☉9am-7pm Apr-Sep, to 4pm Oct-Mar; 🚻; 🚊Nowe Zoo, 🚊Krańcowa) This sprawling institution covers 116 hectares at the eastern end of Lake Malta. It houses diverse species, including Baltic grey seals, in a leafy pine forest environment. Trams 6 and 8 drop you nearby. Or take the tram to Baraniaka stop and change to bus 184.

☆☆ Festivals & Events

Poznań's trade fairs are its pride and joy, though few are of interest to casual visitors. The main ones take place in January, June, September and October, with dozens of other trade shows of varying size throughout the year. July, August and December are almost free of fairs. The town also has some high-profile cultural events.

Blues Express
MUSIC

(www.bluesexpress.pl; 100zł; ☉Jul) The ingredients are as heady as a sweltering day in the Mississippi Delta: a steam train, blues concerts at station stops along the way, and carriages full of revellers and travellers. This has been going on for over 25 years, with a steam train doing a return trip from Poznań to Zakrzewo on a musical odyssey through the countryside.

St Martin's Day
PARADE

(☉11 Nov) Parades and festivities descend on the town, but the highlight is the baking and eating of St Martin's sweet croissants.

Old Jazz Festival
MUSIC

(www.oldjazzfestival.pl; ☉mid-Sep) A range of local and international jazz performers strut their stuff at various venues, mostly on and off Rynek, and mostly Dixie jazz.

St John's Fair
CULTURAL

(Jarmark Świętojański; www.targowiska.com.pl/ jarmarki; ☉mid- to late-Jun) Take in street-artist performances and buy craft items and local foods from the stalls on the Stary Rynek.

🛌 Sleeping

As a commercial hub, Poznań is big on business-oriented hotels, but there's a good range of more characterful accommodation in and around the Old Town, and rates are often lower at weekends.

Try not to arrive in the city during one of its numerous trade fairs – accommodation rates double and beds become scarce. Check the events calendar at www.mtp.pl/en.

🛌 Old Town

Tey Hostel
HOSTEL €

(Map p284; ☑61 639 3497; www.tey-hostel.pl; ul Świętosławska 12; dm 25-40zł, s 58-150zł, d 70-200zł; ☎; 🚊Wrocławska) This centrally located hostel offers comfortable accommodation with modern furniture and smart, contemporary decor in pastel shades. There's a spacious kitchen and lounge, and all beds have reading lamps and lockers. The cheaper private rooms have shared bathrooms.

★Puro Poznań Stare Miasto
BOUTIQUE HOTEL €€

(Map p282; ☑61 333 1000; www.purohotel.pl/en/ poznan; Stawna 12; r from 250zł; P❄☎; 🚊Plac Wielkopolski) The homegrown Puro hotel chain's Poznań outpost ticks all the boxes – central location, underground car park, designer decor, comfortable lobby with free coffee machine, fast reliable wi-fi, helpful staff, and sharply styled bedrooms flooded with light. The buffet breakfast costs 65zł and is well worth the expense.

★Hotel Palazzo Rosso
HOTEL €€

(Map p284; ☑61 227 5447; www.hotelpalazzo rosso.pl; ul Gołębia 6; s 180-250zł, d 220-280zł; P☎; 🚊Wrocławska) Inside this remarkable

STRIKING OUT

The June 1956 industrial strike in Poznań was the first mass protest in the Soviet bloc, breaking out just three years after Stalin's death.

It originated in the city's largest industrial plant, the Cegielski metalworks (then named after Stalin), which produced railway stock. When the workers demanded the refund of an unfairly charged tax, the factory management refused and simply threw the workers' delegates out of the meeting room. This sparked a spontaneous strike the next day, in which the metalworkers, joined by workers from other local industrial plants, headed for Plac Mickiewicza (then named Plac Stalina).

The 100,000-strong crowd that gathered (a quarter of the city's total population) demanded 'bread and freedom', insisting that changes had to be introduced to improve working conditions, and requested that authorities come and discuss the issue. The demonstration was disregarded by city officials.

Matters soon got out of hand. The angry crowd stormed police headquarters and the Communist Party building, releasing 257 prisoners from jail after disarming the guards. Shortly afterwards, a battle for the secret-police headquarters broke out; it was there that the bloodshed began when police started firing at people surrounding the building. Tanks were introduced to the action while troops were hastily brought from Wrocław and told they were there to pacify a German riot.

Fierce street battles continued for the whole night and part of the next day, resulting in a total of at least 76 dead and 900 wounded. More than 300 people were arrested, 58 of whom were indicted.

These figures make the protest the most tragic in communist Poland, yet it was underreported and for a long time overlooked. The historic importance of the revolt has only recently been recognised and given the status it deserves, an event on par with the internationally famous shipyard strikes in Gdańsk.

The Museum of Poznań June 1956 (p286) is dedicated to the uprising. Entering this is like stepping back into 1956, but descriptions are only in Polish.

17th-century house you will find 46 rooms in tasteful dark hues complementing the wooden ceilings on some floors. These are offset by the modern glass lift rising above the adjoining restaurant courtyard (rooms away from the courtyard are quieter). Two family rooms for 340zł have twin beds and sofa beds, sleeping up to five people.

Garden Boutique Residence HOTEL €€
(Map p284; ☑ 61 222 2999; www.gardenhotel.pl; ul Wroniecka 24; s 235zł, d 295zł, breakfast 35zł; ☎; 🚇 Plac Wielkopolski) Some of the rooms are on the small side and you may find yourself negotiating a lot of stairs, but there is genuine historic charm to 'the Garden', and it's all very well-kept and well-run. It also has the advantage of a central location and proximity to restaurants, cafes and bars.

Rosemary's Hostel HOSTEL €€
(Map p284; ☑ 61 855 2761; wroclawska13@gmail.com; ul Wrocławska 13; r 150-300zł; ☎; 🚇 Wrocławska) You don't need to be a fan of Polish director Roman Polanski to stay here, but it certainly helps. Rooms are named after his films, including the late-1960s

horror classic *Rosemary's Baby*. Nothing spine-chilling here though, just tasteful rooms, the cheapest with showers and toilets off the corridor. It has a guest kitchen and free coffee and tea. Breakfast costs 15zł, and there's complimentary use of bikes.

Rezydencja Solei HOTEL €€
(Map p284; ☑ 510 110 130; www.hotel-solei.pl; ul Szewska 2; s/d from 139/239zł, ste 319zł; ☎; 🚇 Plac Wielkopolski) Temptingly close to the Rynek, this tiny hotel offers small but cosy rooms in an old-fashioned residential style, with wallpaper and timber furniture striking a homey note. The attic suite is amazingly large and can accommodate up to four people.

Brovaria HOTEL €€
(Map p284; ☑ 61 858 6868; www.brovaria.pl; Stary Rynek 73/74; s 250-290zł, d 290-340zł; @ ☎; 🚇 Plac Wielkopolski, 🚇 Wrocławska) This multi-faceted hotel also operates as a restaurant and bar. Most impressive of all is its in-house boutique brewery (p291), whose operations you can view within the building. The elegant rooms have tasteful dark

timber tones, and some have views onto the Rynek.

Dom Polonii
PENSION €€

(Map p284; ☑ 61 852 7121; poznan@swp.org.pl; Stary Rynek 51; tw 160zł; ☐ Wrocławska) Dating from 1488, this accommodation belonging to a community association is tucked into a corner of the market square, offering just two double rooms to anyone who's organised enough to book sufficiently in advance. The only way you could get more central would be by tunnelling under the town hall. No breakfast, and only in summer.

🛏 West of the Old Town

★ Poco Loco Hostel
HOSTEL €

(Map p284; ☑ 796 230 555; www.hostel.poco-loco. pl; ul Taczaka 23; dm 39-55zł, r 120-200zł; @☎; ☐ Marcinskowskiego) Clean, well-run and central, this is one of the city's most popular hostels and for a good reason. There's dorm accommodation in four- to 10-bunk rooms plus private rooms for two to four people. There's a shared kitchen plus laundry facilities and computers. The managers are adventure travellers and pride themselves on offering good-value lodging.

★ NH Poznań
HOTEL €€

(Map p284; ☑ 61 624 8800; www.nh-hotels.com; ul Św Marcin 67; r 260-460zł; P ❋ @ ☎; ☐ Gwarna) Rooms are large and very stylishly decorated in subdued tones in this excellent choice in the centre, about a 15-minute walk from Stary Rynek. Twin beds can also be pushed together to form doubles if you want and use of the sauna and small fitness room are included in the stay. Some rooms also have bath tubs.

Hotel Royal
HOTEL €€

(Map p284; ☑ 61 858 2300; www.hotel-royal.com. pl; ul Św Marcin 71; s 220-285zł, d 260-320zł, ste 400-500zł; ❋ ☎; ☐ Gwarna) Tasteful terracotta tones predominate in this smart, refined hotel, situated on the main road leading into the city centre. Opt for a spacious suite for extra elbow room, or just hang around the lobby perusing the photos of famous Polish TV stars who've laid their heads here.

Hotel Rzymski
HOTEL €€

(Map p284; ☑ 61 852 8121; www.hotelrzymski.pl; al Marcinkowskiego 22; s 290zł, d 330-395zł; @ ☎; ☐ Marcinkowskiego) If walls could talk, this hotel would have a story worth listening to. It began life as the German-owned Hotel de

Rome, changed to Polish ownership, was used in WWII as a hotel for the German military, then became Polish owned once more, still with the same name (Rzym is Rome in Polish). The rooms are comfortable and the multilingual staff helpful.

Hotel Lech
HOTEL €€

(Map p284; ☑ 61 853 0151; www.hotel-lech.poznan. pl; ul Św Marcin 74; s/d 140/210zł; ☎; ☐ Gwarna) A comfortable choice, with very basic fittings and high ceilings. It's located midway between the train station and the Old Town. Flash your ISIC student card for a substantial discount. Some staff speak English.

Hotel Mercure Poznań
HOTEL €€

(Map p282; ☑ 61 855 8000; https://mercure. accorhotels.com; ul Roosevelta 20; r from 260zł; P ❋ ☎; ☐ Bałtyk, ☐ Rondo Kaponiera) In a gigantic modern building off a busy main road 500m west of the Kaiserhaus, this hotel offers all the expected facilities for business travellers, including a gym, a restaurant and a bar. The location is handy for the train station, and the airport bus drops off at the nearby Bałtyk stop. But it's a bit of a walk to the Old Town.

Breakfast is usually not included.

🛏 South of the Old Town

Hotel Stare Miasto
HOTEL €€

(Map p284; ☑ 61 663 6242; www.hotelstaremiasto. pl; ul Rybaki 36; s/d from 275/340zł; P ❋ ☎; ☐ Wrocławska) This stylish value-for-money hotel has a tastefully chandeliered foyer and spacious breakfast room. Rooms can be small but are clean and bright with lovely starched white sheets. Some upper rooms have skylights in place of windows.

Don Prestige Residence
HOTEL €€

(Map p284; ☑ 61 859 0590; www.donprestige.com; ul Św Marcin 2; s/d 300/360zł; P ❋ @ ☎; ☐ Wrocławska) While some hotels try to make you feel like you're at home, the Don Prestige makes you wish your home was a bit more like this. Its rooms are outfitted with stylish contemporary furniture and fittings, including parquet floors and air-conditioning. There's a classy cocktail bar on the premises.

Capital Apartments
APARTMENT €€

(Map p284; ☑ 61 852 5300; www.capitalapart.pl; ul Piekary 16; apt 150-360zł; ☎; ☐ Wrocławska) This company maintains a number of modern apartments dotted around the city centre, all within walking distance of the

Stary Rynek. They're a good-value option if you're tired of hotel breakfasts and want to prepare your own food, or if the lack of laundrettes in Poland has you desperate for a washing machine.

★ **Blow Up Hall 5050** BOUTIQUE HOTEL €€€
(Map p282; ☑ 61 657 9980; www.blowuphall5050.
com; ul Kościuszki 42; s 450zł, d 450-1100zł;
P❋♠; ☐ Półwiejska) Housed within the solid ex-brewery walls of the Stary Browar shopping mall, this unusual hotel offers an experience that feels a bit like sleeping in an art gallery. The soaring lobby is an extravaganza of red brick, steel and glass, while the cutting-edge designer bedrooms sport a decor of dazzling white and gleaming black, with shiny angular furniture and fittings.

🛌 Lake Malta

Camping Malta CAMPGROUND €
(☑ 61 876 6203; www.campingmalta.poznan.pl;
ul Krańcowa 98; camping per person 20zł, per tent 10zł; s 195zł, d 260-300zł; P@; ☐ Krańcowa)
Malta is the best of Poznań's camping grounds and the closest to the centre – it's on the northeastern shore of Lake Malta, 3km east of the Old Town. Heated bungalows provide good all-year shelter.

✖ Eating

Poznań's sophisticated dining scene centres on the Old Town, whose narrow streets contain eateries offering every cuisine imaginable.

The local culinary speciality is *rogale marcińskie* (St Martin's croissant), a sweet pastry that contains white poppy seeds, dried fruit, orange peel and walnuts. You can find it in cafes and patisseries *(cukierna)* all over town.

✖ Old Town

★ **Pierożak** POLISH €
(Map p284; ☑ 504 007 200; www.pierozak.eu;
Wrocławska 23; pierogi 1.20-1.60zł; ⊙ 11am-9pm Mon-Fri, noon-9pm Sat & Sun; ✔; ☐ Wrocławska)
Walking into this small pierogi eatery is like stepping into a Polish home kitchen, with a few tables out the back and several women up front preparing the pierogi fresh before your eyes. These Polish dumplings are sold eat-in and take-away in traditional, deluxe and sweet versions, with numerous vegetarian options such as cottage cheese and berry.

Wiejskie Jadło POLISH €€
(Map p284; ☑ 61 853 6600; www.wiejskie-jadlo.pl;
Stary Rynek 77; mains 22-55zł; ⊙ noon-11pm;
☐ Marcinkowskiego) This compact Polish restaurant, hidden a short distance back from the Rynek, serves what it says on the sign – *wiejskie jadło* (country food). It offers a range of filling dishes including several kinds of pierogi, *żurek* (sour rye soup) served in a hollow loaf, roast pork knuckle and beef with beetroot, all dished up in a rustic farmhouse setting.

Kuro by Panamo JAPANESE €€
(Map p284; ☑ 61 887 0430; www.kurosushi.pl; ul Wodna 8/9; 20-60 piece sushi sets 70-210zł, ramen 21-28zł; ⊙ 1-10pm Mon-Wed, noon-11pm Thu-Sun;
✔; ☐ Wrocławska) The ramen and udon dishes might not be the most authentic of Japanese flavours but the food is well-prepared and tastefully presented, staff are friendly and the atmosphere is low-key and elegant. Lone diners will feel comfortable at one of the smaller tables at the back. The lunch sets are also good value.

Tapas Bar SPANISH €€
(Map p284; ☑ 61 852 8532; www.tapas.pl; Stary Rynek 60; mains 25-90zł; ⊙ noon-midnight;
☐ Wrocławska) This atmospheric place dishes up authentic tapas and Spanish wine in a room lined with intriguing bric-a-brac, including jars of stuffed olives, Mediterranean-themed artwork and bright red candles. Tapas dishes cost about 30zł, so forget the mains and share with friends. There's a breakfast menu too.

Pizzeria da Luigi ITALIAN €€
(Map p284; ☑ 61 851 7311; ul Woźna 1; pizza 17-28zł, pasta 15-35zł; ⊙ noon-6pm Mon, to 9pm Tue-Thu, to 10pm Fri & Sat, to 8pm Sun;
☐ Wrocławska) The smell of delicious pizza dominates this small and unpretentious pizza and pasta place with upstairs and downstairs sections.

★ **Momo** MEDITERRANEAN €€€
(Map p284; ☑ 501 415 136; www.momolovebite.pl;
ul Szewska 2; mains 45-95 zł; ⊙ 1-9pm Mon & Sun, to 11pm Tue-Sat; ♠; ☐ Plac Wielkopolski) This hip restaurant serves pasta, steaks and seafood at communal wooden tables in a stylish atmosphere. Its seafood dishes are popular, as are its wines from a very decent sized wine list. It's also a place where you can inexpensively wash a starter or soup down with a drink.

Eatalia MEDITERRANEAN €€€
(Map p284; ☑61 278 7186; www.eatalia.pl; ul Wrocławska 15; mains 40-80zł; ⊘noon-10pm Mon & Tue, to 11pm Wed-Sat, to 8pm Sun; 🚊Wrocławska) The cuisine in this upmarket restaurant is very much Italian influenced, but the really interesting stuff begins with the meats, which are mostly slow-cooked *sous vide* (under vacuum). Despite the formal atmosphere, Eatalia still manages to provide a relaxed dining experience, and tables along the side and out the back will allow those eating alone to feel comfortable.

✖ West of the Old Town

★Thai Wok ASIAN €€
(Map p284; ☑508 528 989; www.fastwok.pl; ul Ratajczaka 18, in Apollo Passage; mains 19-28zł; ⊘11am-8pm Mon-Thu, to 9pm Fri, noon-9pm Sat, to 7pm Sun; 🕾🖉🖬; 🚊Marcinskowskiego) Located just off ul Ratajczaka in the attractive Apollo passage, Thai Wok goes beyond its name to delve into a couple of Indonesian and Chinese dishes as well as its Thai mainstays. The atmosphere is low-key, the curries excellent and there's summer outdoor seating. Kids are welcome here, and it does take-away.

Kuchnia Wandy POLISH €€
(Map p284; ☑884 850 500; ul Św Marcin 76; mains 29-49zł; ⊘8am-9pm Mon-Thu, to 10pm Fri, 9am-10pm Sat, to 9pm Sun; 🕾; 🚊Gwarna) Especially if you're based in one of the nearby hotels on Św Marcin, then you'll gravitate towards Kuchnia Wandy for its range of poultry, red meats and pierogi at the wooden tables in a stylish, minimalist atmosphere.

Restauracja Delicja FRENCH, ITALIAN €€€
(Map p284; ☑61 852 1128; www.delicja.eu; Plac Wolności 5; mains 65-100zł; ⊘2-10pm; 🚊Plac Wolności) One of Poznań's top restaurants, Delicja is tucked away off Plac Wolności, with its own miniature courtyard and an illustrious reputation for top-notch French and Italian cuisine.

✖ South of the Old Town

Stary Browar Food Court INTERNATIONAL €
(Map p282; ul Półwiejska 42, Stary Browar Shopping Mall; mains 10-20zł; ⊘9am-9pm; 🕾🖉; 🚊Półwiejska) The dining section on the second level of this gigantic Stary Browar shopping mall 750m south of the Rynek offers decent food in chic surrounds, including

Chinese, Italian and seafood dishes. There are also cafes scattered through the complex, and the building's spectacular old-meets-new architecture is worth a visit in its own right. The information desk has a helpful gastronomic guide.

Bar Wegetariański VEGETARIAN €
(Map p282; ul Rybaki 10; mains 14-20zł; ⊘11am-7pm Mon-Fri; 🖉; 🚊Półwiejska) This cheap eatery 500m south of the Rynek offers tasty meat-free dishes, including its signature wholemeal crêpes stuffed with mushrooms and cabbage. It's in a homely little space, with dishes prepared in a domestic-style open kitchen behind the counter.

★Drukarnia INTERNATIONAL €€
(Map p284; ☑61 850 1420; www.facebook.com/poznandrukarnia; ul Podgórna 6; mains 26-78zł; ⊘7am-10pm Mon-Wed, to midnight Thu & Fri, 10am-midnight Sat, to 10pm Sun; 🕾; 🚊Marcinskowskiego) This sleek eatery with exposed girders above concrete floors is a top spot for breakfast (served to noon weekdays, 1pm weekends). Choices include a full English (sausage, bacon, eggs and beans) and trad Polish (fried eggs with tomato, cucumber and chives). Later on there's a menu featuring steaks and burgers, as well as a decent wine list.

Papierówka POLISH €€€
(Map p284; ☑797 471 388; ul Zielona 8; mains 35-80zł; ⊘1-10pm Mon-Sat, to 8pm Sun; 🖉; 🚊Plac Bernardyński) Set alongside pleasant parkland, Papierówka has reinvented itself out of a long family tradition, serving seasonal dishes from a small menu. The little touches make the experience here; even the sparkling water is served with fresh mint and fruits. The speciality is duck, though expect a couple of red-meat and fish choices, as well as a vegetarian dish.

🍺 Drinking & Nightlife

★Brovaria BREWERY
(Map p284; ☑61 858 6868; www.brovaria.pl; Stary Rynek 73-74; ⊘10am-midnight; 🚊Plac Wielkopolski, 🚊Wrocławska) Brovaria has a lot of different acts up its sleeve. As well as being a hotel (p288) and restaurant, it is a microbrewery serving pilsner, honey, dark, wheat and seasonal beers. You can choose between the front bar, the beer hall, or downstairs in a pleasant cellar section. Should you feel peckish, the menu is served across all areas (mains 26zł to 39zł).

Chmielnik
BAR

(Map p282; ☑790 333 946; www.facebook.com/chmielnikpub; ul Żydowska 27; ⊙4pm-midnight Mon-Wed, to 1am Thu, to 2am Fri, 2pm-2am Sat, 1-11pm Sun; ☎; 🚊Plac Wielkopolski) This is the ideal place to sample the output of the booming Polish craft-beer scene, with over 150 brews in stock. Lounge and sip in the pleasant wood-lined interior or in the garden terrace out the back – yes, those are hops and grapevines growing amid the greenery.

Stragan
CAFE

(Map p284; ☑789 233 965; www.facebook.com/stragankawiarnia; ul Ratajczaka 31; ⊙8am-9pm Mon-Fri, 9am-8pm Sat & Sun; ☎; 🚊Gwarna) A cool, contemporary cafe in which even the most bearded hipster would feel at home. Coffee ranges from the 500ml black Chemex brew to flat whites, complemented by excellent cakes and light meals. Also serves breakfast (to noon) and bagels (all day); order at the counter.

Czekolada
CLUB

(Map p284; ☑665 550 891; www.klubczekolada.pl/poznan; ul Wrocławska 18; ⊙9pm-late; ☎; 🚊Wrocławska) If you feel like dressing up and dancing, this super-smooth venue is what you're looking for. Chandeliers and good cocktails add touches of class.

PRL
BAR

(Map p284; www.facebook.com/prlpubpoznan; ul Żydowska 11; ⊙4pm-late; 🚊Plac Wielkopolski) Not easy to find even with a map and compass, this tiny subterranean bar is decorated with communist-era memorabilia, from uniforms to chunky appliances. It's grungy but fun. Enter through the narrow door on ul Mokra.

Van Diesel Music Club
CLUB

(Map p284; ☑515 065 459; www.vandiesel.pl; Stary Rynek 88; ⊙9pm-5am Fri & Sat; 🚊Plac Wielkopolski, 🚊Wrocławska) Happening venue on the main square, with DJs varying their offerings between pop, house, R&B, soul and dance. Given the variety, you're sure to find a night that will get you on the dance floor.

Ptasie Radio
BAR

(Map p284; ☑61 853 6451; www.ptasieradio.pl; ul Kościuszki 74; ⊙8am-midnight Mon-Fri, 10am-midnight Sat, 9am-11pm Sun; ☎; 🚊Gwarna) A funky drinking hole, 'Bird Radio' is a retro riot of chipped wooden tables, potted plants and bird images everywhere (the name comes from a famous Polish poem). It's a mellow place for a coffee or something stronger. There's also a breakfast menu.

Czarna Owca
BAR, CLUB

(Map p284; ☑537 674 757; www.facebook.com/pg/czarnaowcaclub; ul Jaskółcza 13; ⊙9pm-late Thu-Sat; ☎; 🚊Wrocławska) Calling your bar the 'Black Sheep' hardly encourages good behaviour, so sipping a quiet pint is seldom on the agenda here. When you've finished boozing in the dark, intimate bar, join the herd on the downstairs dance floor for DJs playing house, pop, rock, Latin or retro sounds, depending on the night.

Proletaryat
BAR

(Map p284; ☑508 173 608; www.facebook.com/Proletaryat; ul Wrocławska 9; ⊙3pm-late; ☎; 🚊Plac Wielkopolski) This bright-red communist-nostalgia bar sports an array of socialist-era gear on the walls, including military insignia, portraits of Brezhnev and Marx, and the obligatory bust of Lenin in the window. Play 'spot the communist leader' while sipping a boutique beer from the Czarnków Brewery.

☆ Entertainment

Poznań's comprehensive monthly *iks* (4.90zł) contains listings of everything from museums to outdoor activities. The free *afisz* pamphlet lists key events. Both are available from the tourist offices. The Cultural Information Centre sells tickets at no mark up mainly for concerts and theatre.

Centrum Kultury Zamek
CONCERT VENUE

(Castle Cultural Centre; Map p284; ☑61 646 5260; www.ckzamek.pl; ul Św Marcin 80/82; ☎; 🚊Gwarna, 🚊Zamek) Within the grand neo-Romanesque Kaiserhaus (p286), built from 1904 to 1910 for German emperor Wilhelm II, this active cultural hub hosts cinema, art and music events.

Meskalina
LIVE MUSIC

(Map p284; ☑508 171 749; www.meskalina.com; Stary Rynek 6; ⊙6pm-1.30am Tue-Thu & Sun, to 3.30am Fri & Sat; ☎; 🚊Plac Wielkopolski, 🚊Wrocławska) A bar, club and live music haunt, Meskalina crosses a lot of different venue types and music genres, with everything from live pop acts, dance and electronic in a relaxed atmosphere right on the Rynek.

Filharmonia
CLASSICAL MUSIC

(Philharmonic Hall; Map p282; ☑61 853 6935; www.filharmoniapoznanska.pl; ul Św Marcin 81; ⊙box office 1-6pm; 🚊Zamek, 🚊Gwarna) This musical institution holds concerts at least weekly by the house symphony orchestra. Poznań also has Poland's best boys' choir, the Poznańskie Słowiki (Poznań Nightingales), who can be heard here. Buy tickets at the box office or one hour before performances.

Blue Note Jazz Club JAZZ
(Map p284; ☑ 61 851 0408; www.bluenote.poznan.pl; ul Kościuszki 79; ⛎ Zamek, ⛎ Gwarna) Blue Note, a major live jazz spot and occasional dance club within the Kaiserhaus (p286), hosts regular concerts and jam sessions by local groups, as well as the occasional big name. It's only open for gigs, so check the online program first.

BaRock LIVE MUSIC
(Map p284; ☑ 502 287 755; www.facebook.com/BaRockClubPoznan; ul Wielka 9; ⊙ 7pm-late Thu-Sat; ⛎ Plac Wielkopolski) Super-smooth basement venue that hosts regular live music gigs and stand-up comedy acts.

Teatr Wielki OPERA, BALLET
(Map p284; ☑ 61 659 0231; www.opera.poznan.pl; ul Fredry 9; ⛎ Gwarna) Usual stage for opera, ballet and various visiting performances.

Teatr Polski THEATRE
(Map p284; ☑ 61 852 5628; www.teatr-polski.pl; ul 27 Grudnia 8/10; ⛎ Plac Wolności) The Polish Theatre is Poznań's main repertory stage.

❶ Information

The Poznań City Card (one day, 49zł) is available at all city information centres. It provides free entry to major museums, sizeable discounts at restaurants and recreational activities, and unlimited public transport use.

Airport Information (☑ 61 849 2140; www.poznan.travel; Poznań Airport, ul Bukowska 285; ⊙ 24hr; ⛁ 159) Tourist and airport information desk at Poznań Airport.

City Post Office (Map p284; ul Kościuszki 77; ⊙ 7am-8pm Mon-Fri, 8am-3pm Sat; ⛎ Zamek)

Cultural Information Centre (Centrum Informacji Kulturalnej (CIK); Map p284; ☑ 61 851 9645; www.poznan.pl/mim/cim/en; ul Ratajczaka 44; ⊙ 10am-7pm Mon-Fri, to 5pm Sat; ⛎ Plac Wolności) Specialises in cultural events and cultural tourism. It sells tickets to major cultural venues, primarily the performing arts.

Tourist Office – Old Town (Informacja Turystyczna Stary Rynek; Map p284; ☑ 61 852 6156; www.poznan.travel; Stary Rynek 59/60; ⊙ 9.30am-6pm Mon-Sat, to 5pm Sun; ⛎ Plac Wielkopolski, ⛎ Wrocławska, ⛎ Marcinkowskiego) Located conveniently on the main square.

Tourist Office – Train Station (Informacja Turystyczna Dworzec Główny PKP; Map p282; ☑ 61 633 1016; www.poznan.travel; ul Dworcowa 2; ⊙ 9am-5pm; ⛎ Poznań Główny, ⛎ Most Dworcowy) At Poznań Główny train station.

❶ Getting There & Away

AIR

Poznań's **airport** (☑ 61 849 2343; www.airport-poznan.com.pl; ul Bukowska 285) is in the suburb of Ławica, 7km west of the centre.

There are flights from Poznań to Warsaw with LOT, and to UK, Irish and European cities with Ryanair and Wizz Air. Lufthansa has flights to Germany.

BUS

The **main bus station** (Dworzec autobusowy w Poznaniu; Map p282; ☑ 703 303 330; www.pks.poznan.pl; ul Stanisława Matyi 2; ⛎ Poznań Główny, ⛎ Most Dworcowy) is at the north end of the Avenida shopping mall, downstairs from the main train station. A second **Rondo Rataje bus station** (Rondo Rataje; ⛎ Rondo Rataje) has mainly short-distance services. Destinations from the main bus station include the following.

Berlin from 49zł, three to four hours, six daily

Gdańsk 26zł, five hours, three daily

Prague 79zł, eight hours, twice daily

Warsaw 39zł, four to five hours, seven daily

Wrocław 15zł, 3½ hours, twice daily

TRAIN

Poznań Główny train station is 15km southwest of the Old Town square, entered via Level 1 of the Avenida shopping mall. Destinations:

Gdańsk 56zł, 3½ hours, eight daily

Kraków 66zł, five to six hours, eight daily

Toruń 35zł, 1½ hours, 12 daily

Warsaw from 55zł, four hours, 12 daily

Wrocław 38zł, 2½ hours, hourly

❶ Getting Around

TO/FROM THE AIRPORT

From 5.30am to 11pm, city bus 159 runs from the airport to the main bus station beside Poznań Główny train station (4.60zł, 20 minutes, three per hour).

Night bus 242 runs to the Rondo Kaponiera stop just north of Poznań Główny (4.60zł, 20 minutes, hourly).

A taxi should cost around 30zł to 40zł (20 minutes).

PUBLIC TRANSPORT

Tickets for the city's trams and buses cost 3zł for a 10-minute ride, and 4.60zł for a ride of up to 40 minutes. Approximate journey times are posted at stops. A 24-hour ticket costs 13.60zł, 48-hour ticket 21zł and a seven-day ticket 47zł.

Trams going close to Stary Rynek leave from Most Dworcowy, near the main train station. After exiting the shopping centre at Poznań Główny, turn left, and then turn right at the main intersection. Take tram 5 to the stops Marcinkowskiego or Wrocławska, or tram 8 to Plac Wielkopolski.

Kórnik

POP 7250

The town of Kórnik, 20km southeast of Poznań, is proof that mad German kings didn't have a monopoly on eccentric castle design. The highlight of the town is its unconventional castle, originally built by the powerful Górka family in the 15th century. Odd castles aside, the town is a pleasant place to visit, not least because it backs onto a chain of small lakes with promenades and trails, lending a spacious and breezy feel. The provincial atmosphere combined with the lakes and frequent transport connections with Poznań makes it a popular day trip from Wielkopolska's capital.

◉ Sights

Castle Museum
MUSEUM

(☑61 817 0081; www.bkpan.poznan.pl; ul Zamkowa 5; adult/concession 16/8zł; ◷10am-4pm Tue-Sun Mar-mid-Dec) Kórnik Castle's present-day appearance dates from the mid-19th century, when its owner, Tytus Działyński, gave the castle an outlandish mock-Gothic character, partly based on a design by German architect Karl Friedrich Schinkel. The building now looks as though two halves of completely different castles were spliced together, perhaps by force, and provides interesting photos from varying angles.

Part of the castle is open as a museum. You can wander through its 19th-century interiors, dotted with items collected by the family.

The collection was expanded by Działyński's son Jan and his nephew Władysław Zamoyski; the latter donated the castle and its contents to the state in 1924.

Its treasures are well presented in a surprisingly light-filled space, and include some intriguing pieces like elaborately designed furniture, medieval weaponry and crockery from past centuries. Its spectacular Moorish hall (clearly influenced by the Alhambra in Granada) on the 1st floor was created as a memorable setting for the display of armour and military accessories.

Sometimes in the high season special exhibits are set up in the museum, including copies made of valuable books, such as Copernicus' masterwork, *De Revolutionibus Orbium Coelestium* (On the Revolutions of the Heavenly Spheres). The original is safely stored here in Kórnik Library, part of the Polish National Academy of Sciences.

A coach house on the opposite side of the road holds three London coaches, brought from Paris by Jan Działyński in 1856, whereas the Galeria Klaudynówka, a servants' house from 1791, sometimes has exhibitions on special topics.

Kórnik Arboretum
GARDENS

(Arboretum Kórnickie; ☑61 817 0033; www.idpan. poznan.pl; ul Parkowa 5; adult/concession 7/5zł; ◷10am-6pm, to 4pm Oct-Mar) Behind Kórnik's castle is this large, English-style park known as the Arboretum, which was laid out during the castle's reconstruction and stocked with exotic species of trees and shrubs from Europe's leading nurseries. Today the Arboretum is run by a scientific research institute and has some 3000 plant species and varieties; the best times to visit are May to June and September to October, when the greatest number of specimens come into flower.

✖ Eating

★ Loft 46
INTERNATIONAL €€

(☑692 384 501; www.facebook.com/loft46 restauracja; Plac Niepodległości 46; mains 32-69zł; ◷9am-10pm; ☑) This cafe and restaurant directly across the road from the church serves a small but delicious range of soups, salads, pasta, poultry and red-meat dishes in a stylishly contemporary setting. It has a small but very decent wine list of mainly Italian and French wines, served by the glass or bottle

ℹ Getting There & Away

There are frequent buses from Poznań bus station (6.50zł, 25 minutes), stopping at the Rynek in Kórnik, a three-minute walk from the castle. Follow the road as it veers to the right past the town hall and becomes ul Zamkowa. Some buses run from the Rondo Rataje bus station (p293) in Poznań.

Gniezno

POP 70,300

Appearances can be deceptive: at first glance, you'd never guess that relaxed Gniezno (*gnyez*-no) played a huge part in the founding of Poland. Its Old Town is a charming collection of winding streets and colourful, slope-roofed buildings centred on a pleasant cobblestone square and the city's famous cathedral.

ROGALIN PALACE MUSEUM

Rogalin, situated some 30km south of Poznań, has an impressive, two-storey **baroque palace** (Muzeum Pałac w Rogalinie; ☎ 61 813 8800; https://rogalin.mnp.art.pl; ul Arciszewskiego 2; adult/concession palace 15/10zł, combined tour 35/25zł, free one day of the week; ◷ 9.30am-4pm Tue-Sat, 10am-5pm Sun) that was home to Polish aristocratic clan, the Raczyński family. The central structure and two modest symmetrical wings are linked to the main body by curving galleries, forming a giant horseshoe around a vast forecourt. Tours are with multilingual audio guides. Combined tickets also give admission to the London Study, Portrait Gallery, Coach House and Painting Gallery.

The 45-minute palace tour with audio guide focuses entirely on the history of the palace and the Raczyński family.

If you have bought a combined ticket, make your way across the grounds afterwards to the Painting Gallery (Galeria Obrazów), an adapted greenhouse with an impressive display of Polish and European canvases from the 19th and early 20th centuries. The Polish collection includes some first-class work, with Jacek Malczewski best represented. The dominant work, though, is Jan Matejko's massive Joan of Arc.

The London Study and Portrait Gallery are located on the opposite side of the courtyard. The London Study is a recreation of that used by Edward B Raczynski, who stayed in London after Poland was invaded by Germany in 1939. He lived in the UK until he died at the ripe old age of 101. The Coach House is small but interesting, housing a dozen old coaches in different designs.

Opposite the main house is a small French garden, which leads into the larger English landscaped park, originally laid out in primeval oak forest. Not much of the park's design can be deciphered today, but the ancient oak trees are still here, some of them centuries old. The three most imposing specimens have been fenced off and baptised with the names Lech, Czech and Rus, after the legendary founders of the Polish, Czech and Russian nations. If you have the time, stroll through the landscape in and around the palace and make a picnic of the day in warm weather.

Entrance to the palace is free one weekday each week (the actual day generally changes each year).

One more place to see is the chapel, built in the 1820s to serve as a mausoleum for the Raczyński family. It's a replica of the Roman temple known as the Maison Carrée in Nîmes, southern France. It lies 300m east of the entrance to the palace grounds. If you'd like to visit outside of regular opening hours, book ahead.

Depending on whether you visit on a weekday or Saturday (it's barely possible by public transport on a Sunday), there are two ways to reach Rogalin from Poznań. A direct PKS bus leaves the bus station in Poznań on Saturday at 10.30am (11.30zł, 45 minutes). One returns to Poznań just before 4pm. Check these times with the bus information office at the bus station before setting out.

To get to Rogalin from Poznań on a weekday, take a train to the Poznań satellite town of Mosina (6.50zł, 25 minutes, hourly) and change there to bus 699 to Rogalin (3.20zł, 25 minutes). A 9.40am train to Mosina connects with a 10:30am bus to Rogalin. Bus 699 leaves Rogalin in the late afternoon at 4.27pm. The tourist information office at Poznań Główny train station can help with planning.

Gniezno served as both a royal and a religious seat, and is considered to be the cradle of the Polish state, as it was here that the various tribes of the region were first united as Poles in the 10th century. In a key development, Duke Mieszko I is thought to have been baptised here in 966, thus raising the autonomous region of Wielkopolska from obscurity to the rank of Christianised nations. Later, in 1025, Bolesław Chrobry was crowned in the local cathedral as the first Polish king. The town is still the formal ecclesiastical capital of the Church of Poland.

Gniezno

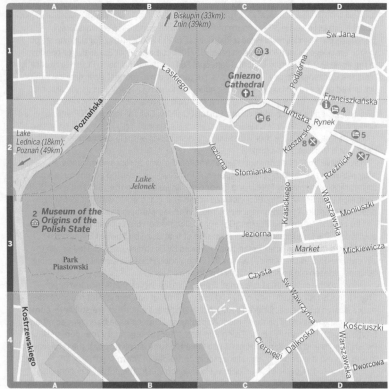

◉ Sights

★ Gniezno Cathedral   CHURCH

(Katedra Gnieźnieńska; Map p296; ☎61 426
3778; www.wzgorzelecha.pl; ul Łaskiego 9; tower
adult/concession 4/2zł, doors 6/4zł, underground
5/3zł, audio guide 21/11zł; ☺9am-5pm Mon-Sat,
tower 9am-5pm Mon-Sat, 1-3pm & 4-5.30pm Sun,
tower closed Nov-Apr) Gniezno's history and
character are inextricably intertwined with
its cathedral, an imposing, double-towered
brick Gothic structure. The present church
was constructed after the Teutonic Knights
destroyed the previous Romanesque cathedral in 1331. Chapels sprouted up around
it, and the interior was redecorated in successive styles.

After considerable damage in WWII, it
was rebuilt according to the original Gothic
structure. You can climb the tower for city
views. The audio guide takes in the cathedral, tower, crypt and Romanesque bronze
doors.

Its focal point is the elaborate silver sarcophagus of St Adalbert, which is in the
chancel. The baroque coffin was the work of
Peter van den Rennen and was made in 1662
in Gdańsk. It's topped with a semi-reclining
figure of the saint, who looks remarkably
lively considering his unfortunate demise.

Adalbert was a Bohemian bishop who
passed through Gniezno in 997, on a missionary trip to convert the Prussians, a
heathen Baltic tribe inhabiting what is now
Masuria in northeastern Poland. The pagans
were less than enthusiastic about accepting
the new faith and terminated the bishop's efforts by cutting off his head. Bolesław Chrobry recovered the bishop's body, paying its
weight in gold, then buried it in Gniezno's
cathedral in 999. In the same year, Pope
Sylvester canonised the martyr. This contributed to Gniezno's elevation to an archbishopric a year later, and also led to the
placing of several important memorials to
the saint in the church.

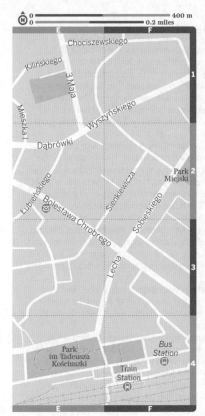

Gniezno

the late-15th-century bronze tomb of Archbishop Jakub from Sienna. Also note an expressive wooden crucifix from around 1440, placed high on the rood beam at the entrance to the chancel.

All along the aisles and the ambulatory are chapels, built from the 15th to 18th centuries, and separated from the aisles by decorative wrought-iron screens. There are 17 screens in all, ranging in style from Gothic and Renaissance to baroque, and constituting one of the most beautiful collections of its kind to be gathered in a single church in Poland. Inside the chapels are some fine tombstones, altarpieces, paintings and wall decorations – well worth a closer look.

One interesting modern artwork sits in the body of the church: a statue of Cardinal Stefan Wyszyński, the Polish primate credited with persuading the Soviets to relax their anti-religious stance during the communist era. The panelled piece shows various scenes from the cardinal's eventful life and career.

Unless you attend holy mass, visiting the cathedral itself on Sunday is very limited. Admission for the doors and to the basement are with a Polish speaking guide.

One example is the pair of Romanesque bronze doors from around 1175, in the back of the right-hand (southern) aisle, at the entrance from the porch. Undeniably one of the best examples of Romanesque art in Europe, the doors depict, in bas-relief, 18 scenes from the life of St Adalbert.

Framing the doors is the exquisite 15th-century Gothic portal with the scene of the Last Judgement in its tympanum. In the opposite porch, right across the nave, is another elaborate Gothic portal, dating from the same period, this one with the scene of the Crucifixion in its tympanum.

The nearby entrance in the back wall of the church leads downstairs to the basement, where the relics of the previous Romanesque cathedral can be seen, along with the Gothic tombstones of the bishops.

Also on this back wall are two carved tombstones. To the left is the red-marble tomb of Primate Zbigniew Oleśnicki, attributed to Veit Stoss, and to the right is

⭐**Museum of the
Origins of the Polish State** MUSEUM
(Muzeum Początków Państwa Polskiego; Map p296; ☏ 61 426 4641; www.mppp.pl; ul Kostrzewskiego 1; adult/concession 14/10zł; ⊙ 9am-6pm Tue-Sun) On the western side of Lake Jelonek, this museum illustrates Gniezno's pivotal role in Polish history. The permanent collection contains archaeological finds and works of art related

WORTH A TRIP

BISKUPIN ARCHAEOLOGICAL RESERVE

Biskupin Archaeological Reserve (Rezerwat Archeologiczny w Biskupinie; ☑52 302 5055; www.biskupin.pl; Biskupin; adult/concession 12/8zł; ☉9am-6pm) Biskupin's re-created Iron Age town site, with its wooden palisades, thatched roofs and costumed historical re-enactors, is a stimulating way to learn about the distant past. The fortified lake town was built about 2700 years ago by a tribe of the Lusatian culture, then rediscovered in 1933 by a school teacher who noticed wooden stakes poking out of the lake. You can either wander through the grounds on your own or organise an English-speaking guide in advance for 150zł.

Once past the gate, follow the path to the museum, which presents finds excavated on and around the island, together with background information. There's also a model of the town as it once looked. The interiors of a few houses have been fitted out as they may have been 2700 years ago. Within the thatched structures you'll find various stalls selling handcrafted arrows, jewellery and replica coins, and a man in period garb giving hatchet-throwing demonstrations out front. The ticket office sells publications about the site in English.

Biskupin's **Archaeological Festival** (Festyn Archeologiczny; www.biskupin.pl; Biskupin Archaeological Reserve, Biskupin; adult/concession 15/12zł; ☉Sep) is a highlight of the region, with demonstrations of ancient cultures including dance, handcrafts and food. You'll also witness rousing re-enactments of battles between Germanic and Slavic tribes, providing a colourful (and photogenic) spectacle.

The pleasure boat **Diabeł Wenecki** (Venetian Devil; Biskupin; trips 10zł; ☉9am-6pm May-Sep) departs several times a day for a short trip around the lake from the wharf near the Archaeological Reserve gateway. Leaves every 30 minutes, or when it has 10 passengers.

There are five to six weekday bus connections with the archaeological reserve at Biskupin to/from Żnin (6.50zł, 20 minutes) and to/from Gąsawa (4.10zł, three minutes) but none on weekends. The last bus leaves the museum for Żnin just after 3pm. Buses also run between Żnin and Gąsawa every one or two hours weekdays, and several times on Saturday and Sunday (5zł, 15 minutes). If you get stuck at the reserve in Biskupin, walk 2km to Gąsawa and take an evening bus back. Five weekday buses run from Żnin to Gniezno (14zł, one hour, last one at 12.15pm), but fewer on weekends. Most continue on to Poznań (21zł, 1½ hours).

A narrow-gauge tourist train operates from May to September, from Żnin to Gąsawa, passing Biskupin on the way (7zł to 10zł, 40 minutes). The Biskupin station is right by the entrance to the reserve. In Żnin, the station is 150m east of the bus station; in Gąsawa it's 700m southwest of the Rynek on the Gniezno road.

to the development of the Polish nation, from pre-Slavic times to the end of the Piast dynasty. Admission includes a multilingual 3D film about Poland under the Piasts. An interesting feature of the museum is how it tells a narrative over time through clever use of its exhibits.

Archdiocesan Museum　　　　MUSEUM
(Muzeum Archidiecezji Gnieźnieńskiej; Map p296; ☑61 426 3778; www.muzeumag.com; ul Kolegiaty 2; adult/concession 10/6zł; ☉9am-5pm Mon-Sat, to 4pm Sun) North of the cathedral, behind St George's Church, this museum holds a collection of sacred sculptures and paintings, liturgical fabrics, coffin portraits and votive offerings.

🛏 Sleeping & Eating

Hotel Pietrak

Adalbertus & Dom Pielgrzyma　　HOTEL €
(Map p296; ☑61 426 1360; www.pietrak.pl; ul Tumska 7a; s 133zł, d 142zł; 🅿🛜) One of two hotels in the Pietrak (p299) family of hotels in Gniezno, the Adalbertus has more the character of a 'pilgrim hotel', with comfortable but rather old-fashioned rooms in a superb location set back in a garden alongside the cathedral. It also has an Italian restaurant.

City Hotel　　　　　　　　　HOTEL €
(Map p296; ☑61 425 3535; www.hotelgniezno.com; Rynek 15; s 90-120zł, d 110-150zł; 🛜) This hotel doesn't make much effort to live up to its prestigious position on the Rynek – rooms contain

fairly basic furnishings. But the price is right, and the rooms and the cafe look out onto the square. Enter via the kebab shop downstairs.

★ **Hotel Pietrak** HOTEL €€
(Map p296; ☑ 61 426 1497; www.pietrak.pl; ul Bolesława Chrobrego 3; s 180zł, d 210-250zł; ℗ 🌐) Located in two 18th-century burghers' houses just shy of the Rynek, the Pietrak has modern rooms but the rich colours and select furnishings lend an historical touch. This is complemented by facilities that include a fitness centre with a spa. The restaurant serves up quality food and operates a colourful beer garden in summer.

Żuraw i Czapla INTERNATIONAL €€
(Map p296; ☑ 61 428 2614; www.facebook.com/zurawiczaplagniezno; Rynek 6; burgers 25-30zł, pizza & pasta 20-25zł; ⊙ noon-11pm; 🌐 ☑) Located right on Rynek, Żuraw i Czapla (Crane & Heron) serves burgers, pizza, pasta and a range of salads in a modern and comfortable atmosphere. If you only drop in for coffee or a drink, you can relax in their pink lounge chairs.

Restauracja Ratuszowa POLISH €€
(Map p296; ☑ 61 424 3223; www.ratuszowa.gniezno.pl; ul Bolesława Chrobrego 41; mains 18-65zł; ⊙ noon-10pm Mon-Fri, to 8pm Sat & Sun) This restaurant has an elegantly old-fashioned interior within the town hall building and a spacious deck on the street in the warmer months. There are plenty of meaty options on the menu, along with fish and pasta dishes.

ⓘ **Information**

Post Office (Map p296; ul Bolesława Chrobrego 36; ⊙ 8am-8pm Mon-Fri, to 2pm Sat)
Tourist Office (Map p296; ☑ 61 428 4100; www.szlakpiastowski.com.pl; Rynek 14; ⊙ 9am-5pm Mon-Fri, 10am-6pm Sat & Sun, closed Sat & Sun Oct-Apr) Also provides free internet access.

ⓘ **Getting There & Away**

The **bus station** (Map p296; www.pks.gniezno.pl; ul Pocztowa) and train station are next to each other, about 800m south of the Rynek.

Three to five buses run each day to Żnin (14zł, one hour), where you can change for the narrow-gauge train or bus to Biskupin. The 9.40am bus to Żnin allows time to visit the archaeological reserve in Biskupin on weekdays but you will probably need to stay overnight there (a weekday service goes back to Żnin at 3pm).

Trains run regularly to Poznań (14zł, 45 minutes, hourly). There are also departures to Toruń (26zł, 1½ hours, nine daily), Gdańsk (57zł, three hours, eight daily) and Wrocław (52zł, three hours, five daily).

Kalisz
POP 105,400

Given how little the average traveller knows about Kalisz (*kah*-leesh), its centre comes as a pleasant surprise, revealing a charming collection of city parks, gently curving streets and simple but harmonious architecture.

Kalisz has the longest documented history of any town in Poland: it was mentioned by Claudius Ptolemy in his renowned *Geography* of the 2nd century AD as Calisia, a trading settlement on the Amber Route between the Roman Empire and the Baltic Sea.

In more modern times, Kalisz was razed to the ground by the invading Germans in the first days of WWI. Within a month, the population dropped from 70,000 to 5000 and most buildings were reduced to ruins. The town was rebuilt on the old street plan, but in a new architectural style. Today it has something of a sprawling, provincial character and lends itself to short stopovers.

◉ **Sights**

The Old Town sits in the angle between the Prosna and Bernardynka Rivers, with a dozen small bridges and the City Park (Park Miejski) stretching to the southeast.

Zawodzie
Archaeological Reserve MUSEUM
(Rezerwat Archeologiczny Zawodzie; ☑ 62 757 1608; ul Pobożnego 87; adult/concession 5/3zł; ⊙ 10am-3pm Tue-Fri, to 6pm Sat & Sun May-Sep; 🚌 Częstochowska Rypinek) Located upon the site of a 10,000-year-old village, this reserve includes full-sized facsimiles of timber structures of the era, along with authentic archaeological remains. To take a pleasant 30-minute walk there from the vicinity of the Prosna River (near Hotel Europa), head east along al Wolności, following it to the right past the theatre as it becomes ul Częstochowska. Once across the canal, turn left and follow the Prosna River as far as ul Zawodzie. This street takes you to the reserve.

Główny Rynek SQUARE
(Main Market Square; 🚌 Plac Jana Pawła II) This low-key but attractive market square, host to several cafes and restaurants, is the heart of Kalisz' historical centre. The site has been a town square since the 13th century and is dominated by the **Town Hall** (Wieża Ratuszowa; ⊙ tower closed for renovation), its most important historic building.

Kalisz Regional Museum
MUSEUM

(Muzeum Okręgowe Ziemi Kaliskiej; ul Kościuszki 12; ☐ Chopina) This regional museum was being restored and revamped when we last visited. When it reopens (anticipated for 2020), visitors can expect exhibits telling the story of Kalisz, as well as archaeological exhibits from the city and surrounding regions. The building itself is an interesting combination of the historic and a zig-zag-like modern attachment, and a walk through the streets around it offers insight into the 1920s architectural character of the Kalisz, including a school next door dating from 1918.

St Nicholas' Church
CHURCH

(Kościół Św Mikołaja; ul Kanonicka 5; ☐ Plac Jana Pawła II) Dating from the 13th century, this church was originally Gothic but has been modernised several times. The painting *Descent from the Cross* over the high altar is a copy. The original, painted in Rubens' workshop around 1617 and donated to the church, was burnt or stolen during a mysterious fire in 1973.

Collegiate Church
CHURCH

(Bazylika Kolegiacka Wniebowzięcia; Plac Jana Pawła II 3; ☉ 7am-dusk; ☐ Plac Jana Pawła II) Typical example of a lavish Catholic church, first constructed in 1353 and rebuilt in the 18th century. It boasts a baroque interior flooded with gilt and glitter and is a popular pilgrimage site thanks to an allegedly miraculous picture of the Holy Family, dating from the 17th century.

Bernardine Church
CHURCH

(Kościół Pobernardyński; ul Stawiszyńska 2; ☉ 7am-dusk; ☐ Plac Jana Pawła II) The 1607 former Bernardine Church, now owned by the Jesuits, has a spectacular interior. It is unprepossessing from the outside, but its wide nave glows with sumptuous baroque decoration. The altars and the wall paintings on the vault date from around the mid-18th century.

Centre of Drawing & Graphic Arts
GALLERY

(Centrum Rysunki i Grafiki; ☑ 62 757 2999; ul Kolegialna 4; adult/concession 5/3zł, Sun free; ☉ 10am-3.30pm Tue-Fri, to 3pm Sat & Sun; ☐ Plac Jana Pawła II) Displays temporary exhibits of drawings and graphic arts, including works by Tadeusz Kulisiewicz (1899–1988), a Kalisz-born artist known mainly for his drawings. Enter from ul Łazienna.

🛏️ Sleeping & Eating

★ Baba Hostel
HOSTEL €

(☑ 887 081 887; www.babahostel.pl; ul Babina 19; dm 40zł, s 79-99zł, d 89-119zł; ☎; ☐ Nowy Rynek Babina) Bright hostel not far from the centre of town, with comfortable contemporary-styled rooms. Bathrooms are shared in the cheaper rooms, and there's a washing machine and kitchen for guest use. Breakfast costs an extra 9zł.

★ Hotel Europa
HOTEL €€

(☑ 62 767 2032; www.hotel-europa.pl; al Wolności 5; s 185zł, d 230zł, tr 275zł, ste 425-590zł; P ❄ ☎; ☐ Śródmiejska Złoty Róg) If you've schlepped through numerous three-star hotels in a hot Polish summer, you'll weep with joy on encountering this excellent hotel's deluxe doubles with air-conditioning, kettles and gleaming bathrooms. Go crazy and shell out for the Egyptian-themed suite. You'll find it just south of the Old Town across the Prosna River.

Hotel Roma
HOTEL €€

(☑ 62 501 7555; www.roma.kalisz.pl; ul Chopina 9; s 230-300zł, d 310zł, apt 380zł; P ☎; ☐ Nowy Rynek Babina) A nice surprise in a shabbier part of town, this white villa-style accommodation 500m northwest of the Rynek offers just seven spacious rooms with skylights, above the in-house Italian restaurant with a garden courtyard.

★ Bajeczny
CAFETERIA €

(ul Złota 8; mains 5-12zł; ☉ 8am-6pm Mon-Fri, noon-4pm Sat & Sun; ☑; ☐ Plac Jana Pawła II) This renovated *bar mleczny* sweeps aside the communist-era reputation of milk bars as drab and functional. Sit within its fresh, bright interior decked out with white furniture, potted plants and zany lightshades, and enjoy all the Polish classics from pierogi to *naleśniki* (crêpes).

Antonio
ITALIAN €€

(ul Śródmiejska 21; mains 18-45zł; ☉ 11am-11pm; ☐ Plac Jana Pawła II) If you're not hungry after smelling the garlic aroma drifting up to the street from this cellar restaurant just southwest of the Rynek, you must have just eaten. The dining area features red-checked tablecloths, candlelight, roses, Renaissance-inspired artwork and quality Italian food.

> **WORTH A TRIP**
>
> ## ŻNIN DISTRICT RAILWAY
>
> For an entertaining day trip on narrow rails, step aboard a train running along this heritage **railway** (Żnińska Kolej Powiatowa; ul Potockiego 4; one way/return 12/20zł). This narrow-gauge line was opened in 1894 to carry sugar beets to the local sugar factory, and also functioned as public transport. The passenger service was cancelled in 1962, but the line lives on as a tourist attraction.
>
> Once the train leaves the dinky narrow-gauge station at Żnin (east of the town's bus station), it trundles very slowly through a succession of low green hills covered with crops, pausing briefly at a stop serving the village of Wenecja before reaching the Wenecja Narrow Gauge Railway Museum, a showcase of narrow little engines, carriages and their associated memorabilia. Across the rails from the museum are the ruins of a 14th-century castle.
>
> The next stop on the line is the Archaeological Reserve at Biskupin, a major attraction; then the train finally reaches the village of Gąsawa. The main sight of interest here is St Nicholas' Church, a 17th-century wooden structure with an unusual mix of architectural styles: Gothic, baroque, neoclassical and more modern additions. When the church was renovated in 1999, the workers discovered original frescoes that had been covered up by a mixture of reeds and plaster. The paintings depict saints and other Biblical figures, and have been revealed by careful 'excavation'.
>
> If you take an early train from Żnin, it's possible to stop off at the railway museum, Biskupin and Gąsawa, then return to Żnin on the last train of the day. Four trains depart from Żnin daily from May to August between 9am and 1.50pm. An extra train departs Żnin at 3.35pm during Biskupin's archaeological festival, and Saturday and Sunday in July and August, making the return journey from Gąsawa at 5.10pm. The tourist office in Żnin can help with times.
>
> Unless you have your own transport, you will probably need to stay overnight at Hotel Martina in Żnin.

ℹ Information

Post Office (ul Zamkowa 18/20; ⊙ 8am-8pm Mon-Fri, to 3pm Sat; 🖳 Plac Jana Pawła II)

Tourist Office (📞 62 598 2731; www.cit.kalisz. pl; ul Chodyńskiego 3; ⊙ 9am-5pm Mon-Fri, 10am-2pm Sat & Sun; 🛜; 🖳 Plac Jana Pawła II) Helpful advice, internet access and an excellent free city map. Enter from ul Zamkowa.

ℹ Getting There & Around

The **bus station** (📞 62 768 0080; www.pks. kalisz.pl; ul Podmiejska 2a; 🖳 Górnośląska Dworzec PKS) and train station are close to each other, about 2km southwest of the Old Town. To get to the centre, take a city-bound local bus (2.70zł) from the stop on ul Górnośląska on the far side of the Galeria Amber mall next to the bus station.

There are 12 buses to Poznań daily (29zł, 2½ hours), many of which travel via Gołuchów (6zł, 20 minutes). There are also 10 buses daily to Wrocław (32zł, 2¾ hours) and four to Toruń (43zł, four hours). The half-hourly suburban bus A to Pleszew also passes through Gołuchów (5.50zł, 40 minutes); it picks up from Plac Jana Pawła II in central Kalisz.

There are also direct trains to Łódź (34zł, two hours, three daily), Warsaw (55zł, four hours, three daily), Wrocław (35zł, two hours, three daily) and Poznań (24zł to 37zł, 1½ to 2½ hours, seven daily). One direct train goes to Kraków (66zł, 4½ hours).

Gołuchów

POP 2200

This small village near Kalisz is unremarkable save for its attractive castle, which provides sufficient reason for a day trip.

◉ Sights

Castle Museum   MUSEUM
(Muzeum Zamek; www.mnp.art.pl; ul Działyńskich 2; adult/concession 10/7zł, Tue free; ⊙ 10am-4pm Tue-Sat, to 6pm Sun) Gołuchów's castle began life around 1560 as a small fortified mansion with octagonal towers at its corners, built by the Leszczyński family. Some 50 years later it was enlarged and reshaped into a palatial residence in the late Renaissance style. Abandoned at the end of the 17th century, it gradually fell into ruins until

the Działyński family, the owners of Kórnik castle, bought it in 1856. It was completely rebuilt between 1872 and 1885, when it acquired its French appearance.

The castle's stylistic mutation was essentially the brainchild of Izabela Czartoryska, daughter of Prince Adam Czartoryski and wife of Jan Działyński. She commissioned the French architect Eugène Viollet-le-Duc to reinvent the residence; under his supervision many architectural bits and pieces were brought from abroad, mainly from France and Italy, and incorporated into the building.

Having acquired large numbers of works of art, Izabela crammed them into her new palace, which became one of the largest private museums in Europe. During WWII the Nazis stole the art, but the building itself survived relatively undamaged. Part of the collection was recovered and is now once more on display in its rightful home.

On exhibition inside the building is a wealth of furniture, paintings, sculptures, weapons, tapestries, rugs and the like. One of the highlights is a collection of Greek vases from the 5th century BC. You enter the castle through a decorative 17th-century doorway, which leads into a graceful arcaded courtyard. Admission is strictly limited, with tours running for a set number of visitors every half-hour.

Museum of Forestry MUSEUM
(Muzeum Leśnictwa; ☑62 761 5045; www.okl. lasy.gov.pl; ul Działyńskich 2; adult/concession 7/4zł; ⊙10am-4pm Tue-Sun) To the south of Gołuchów's castle, this museum is housed in a former distillery which was considerably extended in 1874. It contains displays on the history of Polish forestry and the timber industry, along with a collection of contemporary art. Entry includes the museum's annexe, east of the castle, displaying ecological exhibits in an old coach house. The collection includes *księgi drzewne*, boxes shaped like books, which were used to collect seeds and other plant matter.

Another outpost you can visit as part of the same entry fee is a former farm which is now home to an exhibition of forestry techniques, 750m beyond the castle in the far north of the park. It contains tools and machinery used in forestry.

Several bison live relatively freely in a large, fenced-off **bison enclosure** (⊙7am-sunset) FREE, west of the park, 500m beyond the forestry techniques exhibition (follow the Żubry signs).

ℹ Getting There & Away

Suburban bus A goes roughly half-hourly to/from Kalisz (5.50zł, 40 minutes). Get off at the bus stand next to the cemetery, cross the main road and walk around the church to find the park entrance. About six PKS buses each day run both to Poznań (27zł, 2¼ hours) and Kalisz (6zł, 20 minutes).

Gdańsk & Pomerania

POP SIX MILLION

Best Places to Eat

➡ Gothic (p344)

➡ Atmosphere (p352)

➡ Bulaj (p328)

➡ Dym na Wodzie (p353)

➡ Bohema (p363)

➡ Tawerna Mestwin (p321)

Best Places to Stay

➡ Hotel Apollo (p355)

➡ Gotyk House (p319)

➡ Hotel Podewils (p320)

➡ Hotel Neptun (p349)

➡ Hotel Bayjonn (p328)

➡ Villa Red (p353)

Why Go?

Cream-hued beaches shelving smoothly into the nippy Baltic Sea, wind-crafted dunes vivid against leaden skies, stern red-brick churches and castles erected by a medieval order of pious knights, and silenced shipyards that once seethed with anti-communist tumult – this is Pomerania, Poland's north, a land with many faces.

The epicentre of Pomerania is Gdańsk, northern Poland's metropolis, a rapidly modernising city with a photogenic historic centre. Like most of the region, Gdańsk has changed hands many times over the centuries, each invader and overseer bequeathing a layer of architecture and culture for today's visitors to enjoy.

Away from the beaches and Gdańsk's miracles in red brick you'll discover Kashubia, a region that keeps the traditional fires burning, including its own language – the perfect place to slow down and escape Poland's beaten tracks.

When to Go
Gdańsk

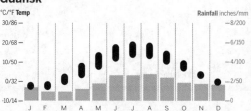

Apr
Go amber hunting after spring's high tides along Pomerania's white-sand beaches.

Aug
Enjoy local culture and bric-a-brac shopping during Gdańsk's Dominican Fair.

Dec
Explore the deserted dunes and lakes of Słowiński National Park.

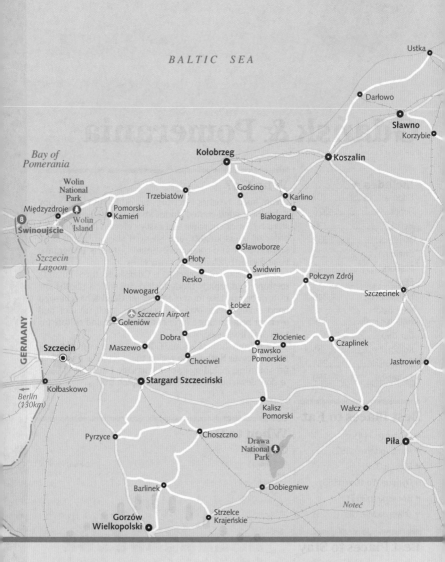

Gdańsk & Pomerania Highlights

1 **Długi Targ** (p311) Admiring the architecture of one of Poland's grandest thoroughfares in the centre of Gdańsk.

2 **Sopot** (p326) Boogying on the beach at one of Sopot's famous nightclubs.

3 **Museum of WWII** (p313) Taking an emotional journey through time at this amazing Gdańsk museum.

N
0 — 50 km
0 — 25 miles

Rozewie
Władysławowo
Chałupy
Jastarnia
Jurata
Puck
6 Hel

Słowiński
National Park
7
Rowy • Kluki
Smołdzino
• Łeba
Wejherowo
• Reda

RUSSIA

Gulf of Gdańsk

Słupsk
• Cewice
Lębork
Sierakowice
Czarna
Dąbrówka
Uniechowo •
KASHUBIA
• Bytów
Kościerzyna
Mt Wieżyca
(329m) ▲
• Kartuzy
*Gdańsk Lech
Wałęsa Airport*
2 **Sopot**
1
Gdańsk
3

Piaski
Krynica   *Mierzeja
Morska   Wiślana*
Sztutowo
Frombork

Elbląg

Vistula
Nogat
Tczew
4 **Malbork**
*Olsztyn
(75km)*

Miastko •
Wdzydze
Kiszewskie
**Starogard
Gdański**
• Pelplin
• Gniew

Bory Tucholskie
National Park
• Kwidzyn
*Olsztyn
(70km)*
• Iława

Człuchów •   Chojnice
• Tuchola

Sępolno
Krajeńskie
otów
• Więcbork
• Mąkowarsko
Koronowo
Grudziądz
• Świecie
Radzyń
Chełmiński
• Jabłonowo
Pomorskie
Che×mno
Wąbrzeźno
• Brodnica

obżenica •
Nakło nad
Notecią
Bydgoszcz
Chełmża
Golub-
Dobrzyń
• Rypin

Toruń
5
Kowalewo
Pomorskie

*Poznań
(50km)*
• Żnin
Inowrocław
Vistula
Lipno •
*Warsaw
(125km)*
Sierpc •

4 **Malbork Castle** (p343) Wandering the
halls, corridors and chapels of Europe's biggest
medieval fortress.

5 **Toruń** (p332) Marvelling at the Gothic
masterpieces that make Toruń one of Poland's
most intriguing destinations.

6 **Hel** (p330) Going to Hel and back to see
the seals and wander the dunes.

7 **Słowiński National Park** (p350) Doing a
spot of dune surfing in this intriguing park.

8 **Świnoujście Beach** (p358) Unfurling the
towel on one of Poland's best beaches.

GDAŃSK

POP 574,000

Like a ministate all to itself, Gdańsk has a unique feel that sets it apart from other cities in Poland. Centuries of maritime ebb and flow as a major Baltic port; streets of distinctively un-Polish architecture influenced by a united nations of wealthy merchants who shaped the city's past; the toing and froing of Danzig/Gdańsk between Teutonic Prussia and Slavic Poland; and the destruction wrought by WWII have all bequeathed a special atmosphere that makes Gdańsk an increasingly popular destination.

Visitors throng in ever greater numbers to wander historical thoroughfares lined with grand, elegantly proportioned buildings, and to enjoy a treasure trove of characterful bars and cafes, seafood restaurants, amber shops and intriguing museums, not to mention pleasure-boat cruises along the river and a wealth of maritime history to soak up in between brews at dockside beer gardens.

History

Describing Gdańsk's past as 'eventful' would be a major understatement. The official history of the much fought-over city is counted from the year 997, when the Bohemian Bishop Adalbert arrived here from Gniezno and baptised the inhabitants. The settlement developed as a port over the following centuries, expanding northwards into what is today the Old Town. The German community then arrived from Lübeck in the early 13th century, the first in a succession of migrants that crafted the town's cosmopolitan character.

In 1308 the Teutonic order seized Gdańsk and quickly turned it into a major trade centre, joining the Hanseatic League in 1361. In 1454 the locals decided on a spot of regime change, razing the Teutonic Knights' castle and pledging allegiance to the Polish monarch instead.

> ### ⓘ TRI-CITY AREA
>
> In and around Gdańsk, you're sure to come across the term Tri-City (Trójmiasto in Polish) on everything from tourist brochures to bus timetables. The three cities in question are tourist magnets Gdańsk and Sopot, along with the less-visited port of Gdynia.

From here, the only way was up: by the mid-16th century, the successful port of 40,000 was Poland's largest city and the most important centre of trade in Central Europe. Legions of international merchants joined the local German-Polish population, adding their own cultural influences to the city's unique blend.

Gdańsk was one of the very few Polish cities to withstand the Swedish Deluge of the 1650s, but the devastation of the surrounding area weakened its position, and in 1793 Prussia annexed the shrinking city. Just 14 years later, however, the Prussians were ousted by the Napoleonic army and its Polish allies.

It turned out to be a brief interlude – in 1815 the Congress of Vienna gave Gdańsk back to Prussia, which became part of Germany later in the century. In the years that followed, the Polish minority was systematically Germanised, the city's defences were reinforced and there was gradual but steady economic and industrial growth.

After Germany's defeat in WWI, the Treaty of Versailles granted the newly reformed Polish nation the so-called Polish Corridor, a strip of land stretching from Toruń to Gdańsk, providing the country with an outlet to the sea. Gdańsk itself was excluded and designated the Free City of Danzig, under the protection of the League of Nations. With the city having a German majority, however, the Polish population never had much political influence, and once Hitler came to power it was effectively a German port.

WWII started in Gdańsk when the German battleship *Schleswig-Holstein* fired the first shots at the Polish military post at Westerplatte. During the occupation of the city, Nazi Germany continued to use the local shipyards for building warships, with Poles used as forced labour. The Red Army pitched up in March 1945; during the fierce battle that ensued the city centre virtually ceased to exist. The German residents either fled or died in the conflict. Their place was eventually taken by Polish newcomers, mainly from the territories lost to the Soviet Union in the east.

The complex reconstruction of the Main Town took over 20 years from 1949, though work on some interiors continued well into the 1990s. Nowhere else in Europe was such a large area of a historic city reconstructed from the ground up.

Tri-City Area

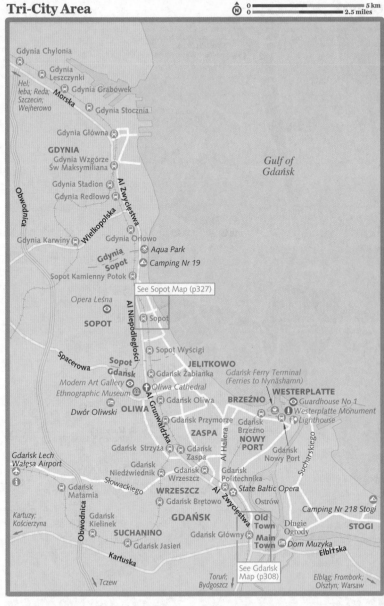

0 ——— 5 km
0 ——— 2.5 miles

Gdynia Chylonia
Gdynia Leszczynki
Hel; Łeba; Reda; Szczecin; Wejherowo
Gdynia Grabówek
Morska
Gdynia Stocznia
Gdynia Główna
GDYNIA
Gdynia Wzgórze Św Maksymiliana
Obwodnica
Al Zwycięstwa
Gdynia Stadion
Gdynia Redłowo
Wielkopolska
Gdynia Karwiny
Gdynia Orłowo
Gulf of Gdańsk
Gdynia Sopot
Aqua Park
Camping Nr 19
Sopot Kamienny Potok
See Sopot Map (p327)
Opera Leśna
Al Niepodległości
SOPOT
Sopot
Spacerowa
Sopot Wyścigi
Sopot Gdańsk
JELITKOWO
Gdańsk Żabianka
Gdańsk Ferry Terminal (Ferries to Nynäshamn)
Modern Art Gallery
Ethnographic Museum
Oliwa Cathedral
Al Grunwaldzka
Gdańsk Oliwa
BRZEŹNO
WESTERPLATTE
Guardhouse No 1
Westerplatte Monument
Lighthouse
Dwór Oliwski
OLIWA
Gdańsk Przymorze
Gdańsk Brzeźno
ZASPA
Al Hallera
NOWY PORT
Gdańsk Lech Wałęsa Airport
Gdańsk Strzyża
Gdańsk Zaspa
Gdańsk Nowy Port
Suchatskiego
Gdańsk Niedźwiednik
Gdańsk Wrzeszcz
Gdańsk Politechnika
Słowackiego
WRZESZCZ
Al Zwycięstwa
State Baltic Opera
Gdańsk Matarnia
Gdańsk Brętowo
Ostrów
Camping Nr 218 Stogi
Kartuzy; Kościerzyna
Obwodnica
Gdańsk Kielinek
GDAŃSK
SUCHANINO
Old Town
Długie Ogrody
STOGI
Gdańsk Jasień
Gdańsk Główny
Main Town
Dom Muzyka
Kartuska
Elbltska
Toruń; Bydgoszcz
See Gdańsk Map (p308)
Elbląg; Frombork; Olsztyn; Warsaw
Tczew

In December 1970 a huge workers' strike broke out in the shipyard and was 'pacified' by authorities as soon as the workers left the gates, leaving 44 dead. This was the second important challenge to the communist regime after that in Poznań in 1956. Gdańsk came to the fore again in 1980, when another popular protest paralysed the shipyard. This time it culminated in negotiations with the government and the foundation of Solidarity, a labour union fronted by Lech Wałęsa, the electrician who led the strike and subsequent talks. Wałęsa later became the first freely elected president in postwar Poland.

Gdańsk

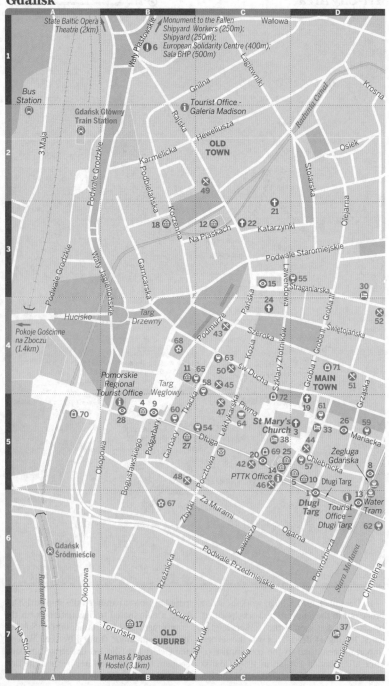

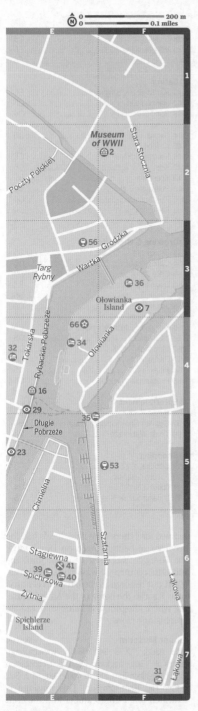

Postcommunist Gdańsk has consolidated its role as the region's leading administrative and industrial city, but tourism has been the big and rather unexpected success story. The city's optimistic, vibrant approach is reflected in the large new museum projects Gdańsk is funding and the new infrastructure being installed.

◉ Sights

◉ Main Town

Gdańsk's crown jewel is the Main Town (Główne Miasto), which looks much as it did some 300 to 400 years ago, during the height of its prosperity. As the largest of the city's historic quarters and the richest architecturally, it was the most carefully restored after WWII. Prussian additions from the Partition period were airbrushed out of this remarkably impressive re-creation, so the result is a snapshot of Gdańsk up to the end of the 18th century.

The town was originally laid out in the mid-14th century along a central axis consisting of ul Długa (Long St) and Długi Targ (Long Market). The latter was designed for trading, which would have taken place in the Rynek (Main Market Sq). This axis is also known as the Royal Way.

Royal Way　　　　　　　　　HISTORIC SITE
(Map p308) Lined by the city's grandest facades, the Royal Way was the route along which the Polish kings traditionally paraded during their periodic visits. Of the three Royal Ways in Poland (Warsaw, Kraków and Gdańsk), Gdańsk's is the shortest – it's only 500m long, but architecturally it is perhaps the most refined.

Upland Gate　　　　　　　　　GATE
(Brama Wyżynna; Map p308) This gate at the western end of Royal Way was the traditional entry point for kings. It was built in 1574 as part of the new fortifications, which were constructed outside the city's medieval walls to strengthen the system. Authorities weren't happy with the original structure, so in 1586 they commissioned Flemish artist, Willem van den Block, to embellish it, covering it with sandstone slabs and ornamenting it with three coats of arms: Prussia (unicorns), Poland (angels) and Gdańsk (lions).

GDAŃSK & POMERANIA GDAŃSK

Gdańsk

Foregate   GATE
(Przedbramie; Map p308; Targ Węglowy 26) The large 15th-century construction known as the Foregate consists of the Torture House (Katownia) to the west and a high Prison Tower (Wieża Więzienna) to the east, linked to one another by two walls. When the Upland Gate was built, the Foregate lost its defensive function and was turned into a jail. The Torture House then had an extra storey added as a court room and was topped with decorative Renaissance parapets.

A gallows was built on the square to the north, where public executions of condemned foreigners were held (locals had the 'privilege' of being hanged on Długi Targ). The Foregate was used as a jail until the mid-19th century. It was damaged during WWII but restored in the late 20th century; today it's also the home of the Amber Museum, where kilograms of 'Baltic gold' radiate a prehistoric glow.

Amber Museum   MUSEUM
(Map p308; ☎ 78 944 9649; www.muzeum gdansk.pl; Targ Węglowy 26; adult/concession 12/6zł; ⊙10am-1pm Tue, to 4pm Wed, Fri & Sat, to 6pm Thu, 11am-4pm Sun) This museum is dedicated to all things amber and the craft

of designing and creating amber jewellery. It's located in the Foregate, a former prison and torture chamber, so in addition to amber displays, there are also some startlingly realistic displays of torture chambers. Two for one!

Golden Gate   GATE
(Złota Brama; Map p308) Built in 1612, the Golden Gate was designed by Abraham van den Block, son of the man behind the decoration of the Upland Gate (p309). It's a sort of triumphal arch ornamented with a double-storey colonnade and topped with eight allegorical statues.

Uphagens' House   MUSEUM
(Dom Uphagena; Map p308; www.muzeum gdansk.pl; ul Długa 12; adult/concession 10/5zł, free Tue; ⊙10am-1pm Tue, to 4pm Wed, Fri & Sat, to 6pm Thu, 11am-4pm Sun) This historic 18th-century residence features ornate furniture. As you pass beyond the kitchen, take a minute to browse the family tree and history of the Uphagen family, outlined in English.

★ Długi Targ   SQUARE
(Long Market; Map p308) Długi Targ was once the main city market and is now the major focus for visitors. Things have gotten a bit touristy here over the last decade (dubious amber stalls, restaurant touts), but look up from the crowds to appreciate the period architecture, all of which is a very selective postwar rebuild, of course.

According to local legend, the **Neptune Fountain** (Fontana Neptuna; Map p308; Długi Targ) **FREE** next to the Town Hall once gushed forth with the trademark Gdańsk liqueur, Goldwasser. As the story goes, it spurted out of the trident one merry night and Neptune found himself endangered by crowds of drunken locals who couldn't believe their luck. Perhaps that's why, in 1634, the fountain was fenced off with a wrought-iron barrier. The bronze statue itself was the work of Flemish artist Peter Husen; made between 1606 and 1613, it is the oldest secular monument in Poland. A menagerie of stone sea creatures was added in the 1750s during the restoration of the fountain.

The nearby 1618 **Golden House** (Złota Kamienica; Map p308; Długi Targ), designed by Johan Voigt, has the richest facade in the city. In the friezes between storeys are 12 elaborately carved scenes interspersed with busts of famous historical figures, including two Polish kings.

The Long Market is flanked from the east by the **Green Gate** (Zielona Brama; Map p308), marking the river end of the Royal Way. It was built in the 1560s on the site of a medieval defensive gate and was supposed to be the residence of the kings. Today it houses an art gallery.

Historical Museum of Gdańsk   MUSEUM
(Ratusza Głównego Miasta; Map p308; www. muzeumgdansk.pl; Długa 46/47; adult/concession 12/6zł, tower 5zł; ⊙10am-1pm Tue, to 4pm Wed, Fri & Sat, to 6pm Thu, 11am-4pm Sun) This museum is located in the historic **town hall** (Map p308; Długi Targ), which claims Gdańsk's highest tower at 81.5m. The showpiece is the Red Room (Sala Czerwona), done up in Dutch Mannerist style from the end of the 16th century. The 2nd floor houses exhibitions related to Gdańsk's history, including imitations of old Gdańsk interiors. From here you can access the tower for great views across the city.

The Red Room's interior is not an imitation but the real deal; it was dismantled in 1942 and hidden outside the city until the end of the bombing. The richly carved fireplace (1593) and the marvellous portal (1596) all attract the eye, but the centre of attention is the ornamented ceiling – 25 paintings dominated by an oval centrepiece entitled *The Glorification of the Unity of Gdańsk with Poland*. Other striking rooms include the Winter Hall with its portraits of Gdańsk's mayors up to the 17th century and the Great Council Chamber with its huge oils of Polish kings.

★ St Mary's Church   CHURCH
(Map p308; www.bazylikamariacka.gdansk.pl; ul Podkramarska 5; tower adult/concession 10/5zł; ⊙church 8.30am-5.30pm Mon-Sat, 11am-noon & 1-5pm Sun year-round, longer hours Jul & Aug, tower 9am-6pm Apr & Sep-Nov, to 7pm May & Jun, to 9pm Jul & Aug, 10am-4pm Dec-Mar) Dominating the heart of the Old Town, St Mary's is often cited as the largest brick church in the world, its massive 78m-high tower dominating the Gdańsk cityscape. Begun in 1343, the building reached its present proportions in 1502. The high altar has a Gothic polyptych from the 1510s, with the Coronation of the Virgin depicted in its central panel. Don't miss the 15th-century astronomical clock in the northern transept, and the church tower (a climb of 405 steps).

The church's elephantine size is arresting and you feel even more antlike when you enter the building. Illuminated with natural light passing through 37 large windows, the three-naved interior, topped by an intricate Gothic vault, is bright and spacious. It was originally covered with frescoes, the remains of which are visible in the far right corner.

At first sight, the interior of the church looks almost empty, but walk around its 30-odd chapels to discover how many outstanding works of art have been accumulated. In the floor alone, there are about 300 grave slabs. In the chapel at the back of the northern aisle is a replica of Memling's *The Last Judgment* – the original is in the National Museum's Department of Early Art.

The most recent addition is the simple shrine to Paweł Adamowicz, the Gdańsk mayor who was stabbed to death at a charity event in 2019. The shrine contains his ashes.

Ulica Mariacka
STREET

(Map p308; ul Mariacka) The most atmospheric of all Gdańsk's streets and one of Poland's most photogenic lanes is this length of cobbles between the waterfront St Mary's Gate (p315) and the red-brick hulk of St Mary's Church (p311). Almost completely re-created after WWII, mostly on the basis of old documents, photographs and illustrations, every ornamental detail unearthed from the debris, including countless scary gargoyles, was incorporated.

It's the only street with a complete row of terraces, which lends the scene enormous charm. In recent years things have really come to life, with several artisan amber jewellery shops, some great cafes and bars, and one of northern Poland's most characterful hotels (Kamienica Gotyk). Some of the best stalls are set up here during the **Dominican Fair** (www.jarmarkdominika.pl; ⊙ Jul & Aug).

Artus Court Museum
MUSEUM

(Map p308; www.muzeumgdansk.pl; ul Długi Targ 43/44; adult/concession 10/5zł, free Tue; ⊙ 10am-1pm Tue, to 4pm Wed, Fri & Sat, to 6pm Thu, 11am-4pm Sun) Rising in all its embellished grandeur behind the Neptune Fountain (p311), the Artus Court is perhaps the single best-known house in Gdańsk. The court has been an essential stop for passing luminaries ever since its earliest days, and a photo display in the entrance shows an enviable selection of famous visitors, from King Henry IV of England to a host of contemporary presidents. It was comprehensively destroyed during WWII but was painstakingly restored from old photographs and historical records.

St Nicholas' Church
CHURCH

(Bazylika Św Mikołaja; Map p308; ul Świętojańska) Erected by the Dominican order on its arrival from Kraków in 1227, this is one of Gdańsk's oldest places of Christian worship and it feels that way inside. Amazingly, it was the only central church to escape damage in WWII – according to one story, the Soviet troops deliberately avoided shelling it, due to the high regard for St Nicholas in the Orthodox tradition. St Nick's closed in late 2018 when it was found the building was in danger of collapsing.

Great Arsenal
HISTORIC BUILDING

(Wielka Zbrojownia; Map p308; ul Tkacka) Ul Piwna terminates at the Great Arsenal, an architectural gem. The work of Antonius van Opbergen, it was built at the beginning of the 17th century and, like most of Gdańsk's architecture, clearly shows the influence of the Low Countries. The main eastern facade, framed within two side towers, is floridly decorated and guarded by figures of soldiers on the top. Military motifs predominate, and the city's coat of arms guards the doorways.

Royal Chapel
CHURCH

(Kaplica Królewska; Map p308; ul Świętego Ducha) Squeezed between two houses just to the north of St Mary's Church, and completely overshadowed by its massive neighbour, the small Royal Chapel is the only baroque church in old Gdańsk. It was built between

---

ℹ GDAŃSK TOURIST CARD

The **Gdańsk Tourist Card** (www.visitgdansk.com; adult/concession 50/30zł for 24 hours, 80/50zł for 72 hours – Sightseeing Package) provides discounts or free admission at almost all the city's museums, galleries, cultural institutions, hotels, restaurants and clubs. With so many service providers taking part, the ticket comes with a usefully thick booklet giving details on every location you can unsheathe it and what discounts to expect. There are two cheaper versions (Transportation Package and Wellness & SPA Package) but as these give virtually no free or discounted entry to sights, they are poor value for money. All three are available from the tourist offices and online.

1678 and 1681 to fulfil the last will of the primate of Poland at the time, Andrzej Olszowski. The chapel was designed by famous royal architect Tylman van Gameren, with the facade its most attractive feature.

National Museum's Department of Early Art   MUSEUM

(Muzeum Narodowe Oddział Sztuki Dawnej; Map p308; www.mng.gda.pl; ul Toruńska 1; adult/concession 10/6zł, free Fri; ⊙10am-5pm Tue-Sun May-Sep, 9am-4pm Oct-Apr) Located just outside the Main Town, the National Museum's Department of Early Art is housed in the vaulted interiors of a former Franciscan monastery. It covers the broad spectrum of Polish and international art and crafts, with extensive collections of paintings, woodcarvings, gold and silverware, embroidery, fabrics, porcelain, faience, wrought iron and furniture.

Market Hall   MARKET

(Hala Targowa; Map p308; Plac Dominikański; ⊙9am-6pm Mon-Fri, to 3pm Sat) Built on the site of a Dominican monastery, the late-19th-century Market Hall is more interesting for its wrought-iron railway-station architecture than for the procession of butchers, bakers and quick-buck makers inside. In the basement lurk the dusty remnants of the monastery.

◎ Gdańsk Waterfront

Lining the Motława River is Gdańsk's waterfront, once a busy quay crowded with hundreds of sailing ships loading and unloading their cargo, which was stored either in the cellars of the burghers' houses in town or in the granaries on the other side of the river, on Spichlerze Island. Today it's an enjoyable promenade lined with cafes, small art galleries and souvenir emporia that give way at the northern end to one of Poland's best museums, the new Museum of WWII, a highpoint of any visit to the city.

★ Museum of WWII   MUSEUM

(Muzeum II Wojny Światowej; Map p308; www. muzeum1939.pl; pl Władysława Bartoszewskiego 1; adult/concession 23/16zł, free Tue; ⊙10am-7pm Tue-Fri, to 8pm Sat & Sun; P) Opened in 2016, this striking piece of modern architecture is a bold addition to the northern end of Gdańsk's waterfront. It has rapidly become one of Gdańsk's must-visit attractions, tracing the fate of Poland during the world's greatest conflict and focusing on the human suffering it caused. Few leave unmoved.

> **ⓘ TICKETS FOR THE MUSEUM OF WWII**
>
> Only 200 visitors an hour are permitted to enter the Museum of WWII so to avoid the queues, make sure you buy your ticket in advance online. The museum is free on Tuesdays but the 200-visitors limit still applies and tickets are issued on a first-come-first-served basis. Get there early.

Covering 5000 sq metres, an absolute minimum of three hours is needed to do the main exhibition justice. Note that the museum is not suitable for children of any age.

The museum is divided into 18 sections, each one looking at an aspect of WWII and arranged (mercifully) in chronological order. Free maps are handed out with your ticket. Things kick off with the causes of the war – Nazi propaganda posters – and end with the Cold War – Communist propaganda posters. In between particularly striking exhibits include a huge mock-up of an interwar Warsaw street, the Holocaust section with its hundreds of Jewish faces rising 7m to the ceiling, a Sherman tank, an interesting section on meetings between the allies in Tehran, Casablanca, Moscow and Yalta and a massive, film-set-like bombed Warsaw courtyard complete with Russian tank. Room after room of uniforms, weapons, maps, documents and harrowing footage, all with brief explanations in English, will take up most of your time – you could literally spend an entire day here.

Little things to look out for along the way are the Nazi Christmas decorations bearing little swastikas, an Oscar-nominated film called *Siege,* shot by a US journalist in the first days of the Nazi invasion of Poland, personal objects belonging to both sides in the siege of Leningrad, artefacts from the Katyń massacre site and the radios sold in Czechoslovakia bearing little stickers promising the death penalty for listening to the BBC. There's also a section dedicated to Polish resistance, but surprisingly little about Gdańsk itself.

The building itself – all bare concrete painted black and grey – creates a heavy, sombre atmosphere. Many visitors leave visibly dazed, so powerful is the story this superb museum tells.

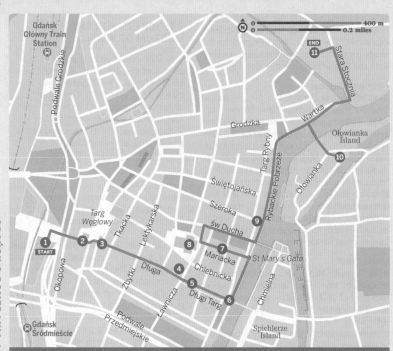

City Walk
Gdańsk: New & Old

START FORUM GDANSK
END MUSEUM OF WWII
LENGTH 2.7KM; TWO HOURS

Start your stroll through central Gdańsk at the ① **Forum Gdańsk** (p324), the city's confident new shopping mall, a bold statement of northern Poland's rejuvenation with its gleaming shops and impressive city vista.

Take the underpass beneath thundering Okopowa to reach Targ Węglowy where you'll find the ② **Upland Gate** (p309) and the ③ **Golden Gate** (p311), the latter housing the city's famous Amber Museum. Beyond the gates extends ul Długa, the main pedestrian route through the Main Town lined with high-gabled townhouses, shops and restaurants. Halfway along its length Długa widens to become Długi Targ dominated by the Town Hall housing the main branch of the ④ **Historical Museum of Gdańsk** (p311). Outside stands Gdańsk's most famous piece of sculpture, the ⑤ **Neptune Fountain** (p311), the God of the Sea brandishing his trident at the tourists.

Pass out of Długi Targ via the ⑥ **Green Gate** (p311) and take a left at the river. Across the water you'll see cranes bolting together new apartment blocks and hotels on Spichlerze Island. Head along the waterfront until you arrive at the St Mary's Gate. Pass through it to access ⑦ **ul Mariacka** (p312), one of Poland's most photogenic streets with cafes set on tiny terraces and subterranean amber shops. Blocking the end of Mariacka is one of the highlights of any visit to Gdańsk, ⑧ **St Mary's Church** (p311), the largest brick structure in the world, which towers over Gdańsk's skyline.

From the church take Św Ducha back to the waterfront and then go left. Almost immediately you'll reach the ⑨ **National Maritime Museum** (p315) and the Gdańsk Crane, a medieval marvel. Keep going along the Motława River past more medieval red-brick gates into the Old City and the 21st-century footbridge that links Ołowianka Island to the centre. If you've time, you can pop over to take a ride on the ⑩ **Big Wheel** (p315); otherwise continue until you see some odd red structures in front of you – this is the ⑪ **Museum of WWII** (p313), the city's top attraction. Make sure you've booked tickets beforehand and left enough time for a visit – or come back another day.

National Maritime Museum MUSEUM
(Narodowe Muzeum Morskie w Gdańsku; Map
p308; ☑ Maritime Cultural Centre 58 329 8700, information 58 301 8611; www.nmm.pl; ul Ołowianka
9-13; combined ticket for all sites adult/concession
23/13zł; ⊙ 10am-4pm Tue-Fri, to 6pm Sat & Sun)
This is a sprawling exhibition covering
Gdańsk's role as a Baltic seaport through
the centuries. The headquarters, the multi-
million-euro Maritime Cultural Centre, has
a permanent interactive exhibition 'People-
Ships-Ports'. Other exhibitions (which can
be visited individually with separate tickets) include the MS *Sołdek*, the first vessel
to be built at the Gdańsk shipyard in the
postwar years, and the Żuraw (Gdańsk Crane;
Map p308; www.nmm.pl; ul Szeroka 67/68; adult/
concession 10/6zł; ⊙ 10am-6pm daily Jul & Aug,
shorter hours & closed Mon Sep-Jun), a 15th-
century loading crane that was the biggest
in its day. The granaries across the river
house more displays.

The granary exhibits on Ołowianka Island
illustrate the history of Polish seafaring from
the earliest times to the present day. They
include models of old sailing warships and
ports, a 9th-century dugout, navigation instruments, ships' artillery, flags and the like.

Another interesting exhibit is a collection
of salvaged items from the *General Carle-
ton*, a British ship that mysteriously disappeared in the Baltic in 1785.

The museum's ferry service (per trip
1.50zł, free with the ticket for all sites), shuttles between the crane and the island every
15 minutes.

Big Wheel FERRIS WHEEL
(Koło Widokowe; Map p308; www.ambersky.pl;
Ołowianka 1; adult/concession 28/18zł; ⊙ 11am-
10pm Mon-Thu, to midnight Fri & Sat, from 10am
Sun; P ⊕) This London Eye–style big wheel
was installed as part of the clean up of
Ołowianka Island and is a welcome addi-
tion to this part of the city. The ride lasts 15

minutes and from the top of the rotation there
are fine views of the old centre and beyond.

Bread Gate GATE
(Brama Chlebnicka; Map p308; Chlebnicka) This
gate was built around 1450 while the city
was still under the Teutonic order, as shown
by the original city coat of arms consisting
of two crosses. The crown was added by
King Kazimierz Jagiellończyk in 1457, when
Gdańsk was incorporated into the kingdom.

St Mary's Gate GATE
(Brama Mariacka; Map p308) One of the grand-
est gates on the Gdańsk waterfront, the St
Mary's Gate dates to the 15th century.

⊙ Old Town

Despite its name, Gdańsk's Old Town (Stare
Miasto) was not the cradle of the city. The
earliest inhabited site, according to archaeologists, was in what is now the Main Town
area. Nonetheless, a settlement existed in
the Old Town from the late 10th century and
developed parallel to the Main Town.

Under the Teutonic order, the two parts
merged into a single urban entity, but the
Old Town was always poorer and had no
defensive system of its own. One other difference was that the Main Town was more
'German' while the Old Town had a larger
Polish population. During WWII it suffered
as much as its wealthier cousin but, apart
from a handful of buildings (mainly churches), it was not rebuilt.

St Bridget's Church CHURCH
(Kościół Św Brygidy; Map p308; ul Profesorska 17;
adult/concession 4/2zł; ⊙ 7am-7pm) Founded
over 700 years ago, St Bridget's was reduced
to medieval brick dust in 1945, and until 1970
only the outer walls were left standing. Very
little of the prewar furnishings survived, but
if you've taken a fancy to amber you're sure
to appreciate the spectacular 174cm-high

SPICHLERZE ISLAND

If you've been to Gdańsk before, you may get a shock as you arrive at the waterfront.
From WWII until recently, Spichlerze Island was an abandoned place of bombed-out
granaries, their red-brick skeletons visible reminders of the destruction that visited the
city in 1945. But today the island has been transformed Elbląg-style with modern offices,
chain hotels and snazzy apartment blocks crammed onto the waterfront with more set
to be added. The development has changed the character of Gdańsk's Motława riverfront
considerably though not all are happy with the scale of the buildings. The architects have
attempted to give the glass-and-steel structures a local feel but the blocks are too high
for historical purists. Expect more of this kind of development in coming years.

amber monstrance depicting the tree of life and the monumental high altar. This recent construction is the highlight of the interior and contains a record-breaking 6500kg of polished prehistoric tree resin.

Lech Wałęsa attended Mass here when he was an unknown electrician in the nearby shipyard. With the wave of strikes in 1980 the church became a strong supporter of the dockyard workers, and its priest, Henryk Jankowski, took every opportunity to express their views in his sermons. The church remains a record of the Solidarity period, with several contemporary works related to the trade union and to modern Polish history in general. You'll find the tombstone of murdered priest Jerzy Popiełuszko, the Katyń epitaph, a collection of crosses from the 1980 and '88 strikes, and a door covered with bas-reliefs of scenes from Solidarity's history – all in the right-hand (northern) aisle.

You can sneak in for free before 10am and after 6pm.

St Catherine's Church
CHURCH
(Kościół Św Katarzyny; Map p308; ul Profesorska 3) FREE The largest monument of the Old Town is St Catherine's Church, Gdańsk's oldest, which was begun in the 1220s. It was the parish church for the entire town until St Mary's was completed. As is common, the church evolved over centuries and only reached its final shape in the mid-15th century (save for the baroque top to the tower, added in 1634).

A major fire in May 2006 caused the roof to collapse and resulted in considerable damage to the interior. Much was restored, but the walls remain unrendered and work seems to have stalled for the time being – it will obviously be many years before this wonderful church is fully restored. There's a small exhibition on the fire, including dramatic TV news footage and photos.

Great Mill
HISTORIC BUILDING
(Wielki Młyn; Map p308; ul Na Piaskach) Standing conspicuously opposite St Catherine's Church, the Great Mill certainly lives up to its name. Created by the Teutonic Knights in northern Poland's typical red brick around 1350, it was medieval Europe's largest mill at over 40m long and 26m high. With a set of 18 monster millstones (now gone), each 5m in diameter, the mill produced 200 tonnes of flour per day right up until 1945.

Old Town Hall
HISTORIC BUILDING
(Ratusz Staromiejski; Map p308; www.nck.org.pl; ul Korzenna 33; ⊙8am-6pm Mon-Fri) The Old Town Hall was once the seat of the Old Town council. A well-proportioned Renaissance building crowned with a high central tower typical of its Flemish provenance, it was designed at the end of the 16th century by Antonius van Opbergen, the architect later responsible for the Great Arsenal. The brick structure is delicately ornamented in stone, including the central doorway and a frieze with the shields of Poland, Prussia and Gdańsk.

Berlin Wall
MONUMENT
(Map p308; Wały Piastowskie) Near the mammoth headquarters of Solidarność on Wały Piastowskie stands a lonely piece of the Berlin Wall. Next to it stands the wall Lech Wałęsa climbed over in 1980 to get into the shipyard.

◉ Shipyard Area

Gdańsk's former Lenin Shipyard is a key fragment of 20th-century European history. It was here that the first major cracks in Eastern Europe's communist wall appeared when discontent with the regime boiled over into strikes and dissent, brutally stamped out by armed force in 1970. A decade later an electrician named Lech Wałęsa emerged to rouse crowds of strikers here, leading to the formation of the Solidarity movement and ultimately to democracy for Poland and most of the Eastern bloc.

★European Solidarity Centre
MUSEUM
(Europejskie Centrum Solidarności; ☑58 772 4112; www.ecs.gda.pl; Plac Solidarności 1; bldg free, exhibition adult/concession 20/15zł; ⊙10am-6pm Mon-Fri, to 7pm Sat & Sun May-Sep, shorter hours Oct-Apr) Opened in 2014, and housed in a truly awful example of 21st-century architecture (its rusty steel plates were designed to evoke ships under construction), this exhibition has quickly become one of Gdańsk's unmissable museums. Audio guides clamped to ears, visitors wander through seven halls examining Poland's postwar fight for freedom, from the Gdańsk shipyard strikes of the 1970s to the round-table negotiations of the late 1980s and beyond. The displays blend state-of-the-art multimedia with real artefacts. Allow at least two hours.

IN A LEAGUE OF ITS OWN

It wasn't easy being a merchant in the Middle Ages. There were no chambers of commerce or Rotary Clubs, and traders received very little respect from the ruling classes. Local lords saw travelling salespeople as easy pickings, requiring them to pay heavy tolls as they moved from province to province in Central Europe. Taking to the sea wasn't much better, as pirates preyed upon merchants' slow-moving boats.

The answer to their problems was to band together in the Hanseatic League, a group of trading ports that formed in the late 13th century and wielded unprecedented economic power. The Hansa (from the German for 'association') was based in Germany, making good use of its central location, with members also scattered throughout Scandinavia, across the Baltic to Russia and west to the Netherlands. The League also had trading posts in cities like London and Venice. As a result, it could trade wax from Russia with items from English or Dutch manufacturers, or Swedish minerals with fruit from the Mediterranean.

The League took a far more muscular approach than that of today's business councils. It bribed rulers, built lighthouses and led expeditions against pirates, and on one memorable occasion raised an armed force that defeated the Danish military in 1368.

At its height the League had over 100 members, including major cities now within Poland such as Danzig (Gdańsk), Stettin (Szczecin), Thorn (Toruń) and Elbing (Elbląg).

But it was all downhill from there. With no standing army and no government beyond irregular assemblies of city representatives, the League was unable to withstand the rise of the new nation-states of the 15th century and the shift of trade to Atlantic ports after the discovery of the New World. The assembly met for the last time in 1669, and by the time of its eventual disintegration in 1863 its membership had been reduced to the core cities of Hamburg, Bremen and Lübeck.

Each hall is lettered and the exhibition runs chronologically from A to G. Hall A takes you to the 1970s shipyard, with yellow docker helmets lining the ceiling and a battered electric truck, the type Lech Wałęsa once worked on as an electrician. Film footage includes the negotiations between dockers and the communist regime and the signing of the 1980 agreements (the oversized comedy pen Wałęsa used to sign is sadly missing but you can buy a replica in the museum shop).

Hall B is all communist-era interiors, a fascinating retro experience that takes you to a prison cell, interrogation room and typical family living room. Solidarity and martial law are the themes of halls C and D, while hall E is a mock-up of the famous round table complete with TV cameras and name badges. An interesting section on the various revolutions across Eastern Europe follows in hall F, while hall G is a spartan affair dedicated to Pope John Paul II.

The special hall opposite the ticket desk hosts Polish-themed exhibitions, which are usually free.

Monument to the Fallen Shipyard Workers   MONUMENT

(Plac Solidarności) Just in front of the former shipyard gates, the striking Monument to the Fallen Shipyard Workers commemorates those killed in the riots of 1970. Unveiled on 16 December 1980, 10 years after the massacre, the monument is a set of three 42m-tall steel crosses, with a series of bronze bas-reliefs in their bases. The first monument in a communist country to commemorate the regime's victims, it became an instant symbol and remains so today.

Sala BHP   MUSEUM

(ul Doki 1; ⊙10am-6pm daily) FREE The Sala BHP is the former Health and Safety building where the 21 demands were signed off and where strikes were coordinated. The hall has been left exactly as it was then but now also hosts an exhibition on the shipyard, with models of ships it once built and a section on its fate today (it's now owned by a Ukrainian company and makes wind turbines). To reach it you pass through the original shipyard gate the workers once streamed through.

DOMINICAN FAIR

Gdańsk's biggest bash of the year is the Dominican Fair, held in the city since 1260. Launched by Dominican monks on Plac Dominikański as a feast day, the fun has spread to many streets in the Main Town and lasts for three weeks from the last Saturday of July.

Amid the stalls selling cheap Chinese charms, dubious antiques, general bric-a-brac and craft items, interesting events take place on four stages and various other venues around the city centre. It's a great time to be in Gdańsk, but accommodation can be madly expensive and unfilled beds are rare during the festivities.

◉ Westerplatte & Nowy Port

Westerplatte is a long peninsula at the entrance to the harbour, 7km north of the historical centre. When Gdańsk became a free city after WWI, Poland was permitted to maintain a post at this location, at the tip of the port zone. It served both trading and military purposes and had a garrison to protect it.

Bus 138 runs irregularly between Westerplatte and the main train station. It's also accessible via infrequent boat services from Gdańsk waterfront. The lighthouse in Nowy Port can be reached by tram 10 from outside Gdańsk Główny train station.

Lighthouse HISTORIC BUILDING
(Latarnia Morska; www.latarnia.gda.pl; ul Przemysłowa 6a; adult/concession 10/6zł; ⊙10am-7pm daily May-Aug, to 5pm Sat & Sun Sep) The first Polish bullets of WWII were fired from the windows of the Nowy Port Lighthouse. Today there are incredible views across the Bay of Gdańsk, including the Hel Peninsula, from the top.

Guardhouse No 1 HISTORIC BUILDING
(Wartownia Nr 1; www.muzeumgdansk.pl; ul Sucharskiego; adult/concession 5/3zł; ⊙9am-6pm mid-May–mid-Sep) The Westerplatte area is famous for one thing: it was here, at 4.45am on 1 September 1939, that the first shots of WWII were fired during the German invasion of Poland. The German battleship *Schleswig-Holstein* began shelling the Polish guard post. The garrison of just 182 men held out for seven days before surrendering.

◉ Oliwa a

A gentrified suburb about 9km from the historic centre, Oliwa has a fine cathedral set in a quiet park and provides an enjoyable half-day break from the dense attractions of the Main Town. To get here, take the commuter train from central Gdańsk and get off at Gdańsk Oliwa station, from where it's a 10-minute walk.

Oliwa Cathedral CHURCH
(www.archikatedraoliwa.pl; ul Nowickiego 5; ⊙9am-5pm) The first surprise as you approach the cathedral is the facade, a striking composition of two slim octagonal Gothic towers with a central baroque portion wedged between them. The interior looks extraordinarily long, mainly because of the unusual proportions of the building – the nave and chancel together are 90m long but only 8.3m wide. At the far end of this 'tunnel' is a baroque high altar (1688); the marble tombstone of the Pomeranian dukes (1613) is in the right transept.

The showpiece of the church is the organ. This glorious instrument, begun in 1763 and completed 30 years later, is renowned for its fine tone and the mechanised angels that blow trumpets and ring bells when the organ is in action. Recitals take place on some evenings and up to six times a day over the summer. Check the schedule on the website before setting off (click on 'Muzyka organowa').

Modern Art Gallery GALLERY
(www.mng.gda.pl; ul Cystersów 18; adult/concession 5/2.50zł, free Fri; ⊙10am-5pm Tue-Sun May-Aug, shorter hours Sep-Apr) Behind Oliwa Cathedral is an 18th-century abbots' palace, now home to the Polish modern-art branch of the National Museum of Gdańsk.

✦ Festivals & Events

International Organ
Music Festival MUSIC
(www.visitgdansk.com; ⊙mid-Jun–Aug) Organ recitals held in the Oliwa Cathedral throughout the summer.

Open'er Festival MUSIC
(www.opener.pl; ⊙Jul) One of Poland's biggest rock- and pop-music festivals featuring big international acts. Held at Gdynia-Kosakowo Airport.

International Festival of Open-Air & Street Theatre THEATRE
(FETA; www.feta.pl; ☉mid-Jul) Northern Poland's biggest street-theatre festival with performers converging on Gdańsk from all over Europe. Ul Długa is naturally the main stage.

International Shakespeare Festival THEATRE
(www.shakespearefestival.pl; ul Bogusławskiego 1; ☉late Jul) Performances of Eastern Europe's top Shakespeare festival take place at the Shakespeare Theatre (p323) on the southern flank of the Main Town. Performers come from all over the globe.

Sounds of the North Festival MUSIC
(www.nck.org.pl; ☉Aug) Held every two years in August (next in 2020 and 2022), featuring traditional folk music from the Baltic region.

🛏 Sleeping

Most of Gdańsk's accommodation is located in and around the Old Town, with new places spreading into rapidly developing Spichrzów Island and the east bank of the Motława River. At the bottom of the market, there's a good selection of hostels; at the top end look out for discounted rates at weekends and during low season (October to April).

★Mamas & Papas Hostel HOSTEL €
(☏79 257 8933; www.facebook.com/hostel mamaspapas; ul Nowiny 19; dm/tw from 50/130zł; 🅿@🛜) This family-run hostel set in a suburban home offers the best welcome in the Tri-City. It's a cosy affair with just 28 beds, a common room and kitchen, but it's the owners – experienced travellers who know what makes a good hostel experience – who make it special. The only drawback is the location, a 10-minute bus ride south of the centre.

Camping Nr 218 Stogi CAMPGROUND €
(☏58 307 3915; www.kemping-gdansk.pl; ul Wydmy 9; site per person/tent 17/12zł; ☉May-Sep) Located in a pine forest in the suburb of Stogi, about 5.5km northeast of the centre, this is the most convenient of Gdańsk's three camping grounds. Just 200m away is one of the city's best beaches, with the cleanest water you'll find for miles. Tram 8 from the main train station passes here (25 minutes).

★Gotyk House HOTEL €€
(Kamienica Gotyk; Map p308; ☏58 301 8567; www.gotykhouse.eu; ul Mariacka 1; r 339zł; 🛜) Wonderfully located near St Mary's Church (p311), this neat, Gothic-themed guesthouse is squeezed into Gdańsk's oldest building and the smallest townhouse in Mariacka. The seven compact rooms have Gothic touches such as pointy-arched doorways and hefty drapery, though most are thoroughly modern creations and bathrooms are definitely of the third millennium. Breakfast is served in your room.

Dom Muzyka HOTEL €€
(Map p308; ☏58 326 0600; www.dommuzyka.pl; ul Łąkowa 1/2; s/d from 140/165zł; ❄🛜) During the day, this understated hotel within a music college has a background soundtrack of random sounds and tuneful melodies. Its light-filled rooms hoist elegantly high ceilings and are discreetly decorated with old prints. Sparkling bathrooms complete the graceful look. There's a classy restaurant and bar off the foyer. It's about a 10-minute walk from the waterfront, across the river.

Staying Inn HOTEL €€
(Map p308; ☏58 354 1543; www.stayinngdansk. com; ul Piwna 28/31; s/d from 170/200zł; ❄🛜) If you don't plump for an apartment, this hotel may just be the city centre's best deal with up-to-the-second decor and gadgets, guest kitchen, common room, the city's fastest wi-fi, two rooms with disabled access and a heart-of-the-action location. Facilities, location and standards make this a good choice for businesspeople and backpackers, families and weekending couples.

Ołowianka B&B GUESTHOUSE €€
(Map p308; ☏53 440 7040; www.olowianka.eu; ul Ołowianka 3a; s/d from 150/200zł; 🅿🛜) Now slightly stranded amid the rapid gentrification of Ołowianka Island (but also right next to the new footbridge across the Motława), these cheap, basic but efficiently run digs are within ambling distance of all the sights and some rooms have pretty river views. There's a no-frills bar-restaurant downstairs. Breakfast is extra.

Willa Litarion HOTEL €€
(Map p308; ☏58 320 2553; www.litarion.pl; ul Spichrzowa 18; s/d from 170/250zł; 🛜) On Spichlerze Island, the 13 stylishly furnished, light-flooded rooms here are bedecked in well-tuned browns, creams and golds with the odd splash of other hues, and bathrooms are crisp. Due to the lowish prices, more often than not this place is booked up, so be sure to reserve ahead.

SONS OF DANZIG

As a lively cultural and intellectual centre, Gdańsk has spawned some famous personalities over the years. Here are the biggest names.

Johannes Hevelius (1611–87) Astronomer who produced one of the first detailed maps of the moon's surface.

Gabriel Daniel Fahrenheit (1686–1736) Inventor of the mercury thermometer.

Arthur Schopenhauer (1788–1860) Philosopher who felt that irrational human behaviour was driven by a force he called the 'will to live'.

Günter Grass (1927–2015) German author, Nobel laureate and perhaps Gdańsk's most famous son. Best known for his first novel *The Tin Drum*.

Lech Wałęsa (b 1943) Former Gdańsk dockyard electrician, Solidarity leader and Polish president.

Jacek Kaczmarski (1957–2004) Poet and singer-songwriter whose fierce opposition to the communist regime led to his exile in the 1980s.

Donald Tusk (b 1957) Poland's best-known politician, former prime minister and president of the European Council from 2014 until 2019.

Villa Pica Paca HOTEL €€
(Map p308; ☑ 58 320 2070; www.picapaca.com; ul Spichrzowa 20; s/d from 250/300zł; ☎) One of a cluster of small design hotels to have sprung up on Spichlerze Island's ul Spichrzowa, the Pica Paca won't quite do it for seasoned boutique-hotel dwellers, but it's an attention-grabbing place to tarry nonetheless. The eight cosy rooms and seven suites are all named after famous personalities, though some are better known than others (Nina Soentgerath room, anyone?).

The celebrity-obsessed theme continues in the Germanic minimalist breakfast room.

Dom Zachariasza Zappio HOSTEL €€
(Map p308; ☑ 58 322 0174; www.zappio.pl; ul Świętojańska 49; s/d 130/180zł; ☎) Occupying a labyrinthine, chunky-beamed former merchant's house, the Zappio is so big that families with kiddies and party animals won't get in each other's way. In addition to high-ceilinged rooms of various medieval shapes and sizes, this remarkable overnighter also has its own pub, bike rental, guest kitchen and 24-hour reception.

Dom Aktora HOTEL €€
(Map p308; ☑ 58 301 5901; www.domaktora.pl; ul Straganiarska 55/56; r/apt from 210/310zł; P ☎) The no-nonsense apartments at this former thespians' dorm are affordable and have simply equipped kitchens, making this a prime target for self-caterers. Bathrooms throughout are 21st-century conceptions, but otherwise not a huge amount has changed here decor-wise since the late-1990s. The breakfast is a buffet affair.

★ **Hotel Podewils** HOTEL €€€
(Map p308; ☑ 58 300 9560; www.podewils.pl; ul Szafarnia 2; s/d from 355/455zł; P ✻ ☎) The view from the Podewils across the river to the Main Town can't be beaten, though the owners probably wish they could take its cheery baroque facade and move it away from the flash riverside developments sprouting all around. Guest rooms are a vintage confection of elegant period furniture, classic prints and distinctive wallpaper.

Qubus Hotel HOTEL €€€
(Map p308; ☑ 58 752 2100; www.qubushotel.com; ul Chmielna 47/52; r from 450zł; P ✻ @ ☎) The only Pomeranian branch of the Polish Qubus chain, this 110-room mammoth in the city centre's southern reaches caters to both business clients and tourists. Inoffensively decorated rooms are generously proportioned and bathrooms pristine, but breakfast is extra. The hotel's boat takes guests to the city centre (from 10am to 4pm).

Hotel Królewski HOTEL €€€
(Map p308; ☑ 58 326 1111; www.hotelkrolewski.pl; ul Ołowianka 1; s/d from 280/340zł; P ☎) This sophisticated hotel marries its historical red-brick granary-building exterior with a 21st-century interior and top-notch service. The riverside location, just a hop across the Motława to the Main Town, makes this an outstanding base if you have the cash to splash, the new footbridge making the stroll to the other side much easier than before.

Eating

Restaurants of all kinds throng Old Town streets and the waterfront. Don't miss local specialities such as Baltic herring, served fried, pickled Scandinavian-style, or marinated in beetroot juice. Kashubian specialities such as duck and trout are also common.

Touts pester potential diners along ul Długa. While slightly irritating, a smile and a firm no usually get rid of them.

Bar Mleczny Stągiewna CAFETERIA €

(Map p308; ☑ 57 011 2222; ul Stągiewna 15; meals around 20zł; ☺ 9am-6pm; ☎ 🖟) The milk-bar 'concept' raised slightly upmarket, the food and ambience here are far from the workers' canteens of yore. Have your Polish staples heaped high downstairs then head for the light, wood-panelled dining spaces upstairs with prints of old Gdańsk on the walls and views onto busy Stągiewna. The staff and clientele are noticeably younger than in other milk bars.

Bar Neptun CAFETERIA €

(Map p308; ☑ 05 301 4988; www.barneptun.pl; ul Długa 33/34; meals 6-20zł; ☺ 7.30am-7pm Mon-Fri, 10am-6pm Sat & Sun, 1hr later Jun-Sep; ☎) It's surprising where some of Poland's communist-era milk bars have survived – this one is right on the main tourist drag. However, Neptun is a cut above your run-of-the-mill *bar mleczny*, with potted plants and decorative tiling. Popular with foreigners on a budget, it even has an English menu of Polish favourites such as *naleśniki* (crêpes) and *gołąbki* (cabbage rolls).

Bar Turysticzny CAFETERIA €

(Map p308; www.barturystyczny.pl; cnr uls Szeroka & Węglarska; mains 7-17zł; ☺ 8am-6pm) Gdańsk's most clean-cut milk bar may have 'since 1956' on the door, but inside it's received a postmillennium makeover. Though the interior may not be gritty enough for the average *bar mleczny* connoisseur, the exclusively Polish food is authentically basic, filling and tasty.

Pellowski Bakery CAFE €

(Map p308; www.pellowski.net; ul Rajska 5; cakes & snacks from 2zł; ☺ 6.30am-7.30pm Mon-Fri, to 7pm Sat, from 7am Sun) Pellowski's run over 20 cafe bakeries across the city centre and are Gdańsk's best-known bakers. This branch opens early enough throughout the week for a coffee-and-pastry breakfast.

★ **Tawerna Mestwin** POLISH €€

(Map p308; ☑ 58 301 7882; www.tawernamestwin. com; ul Straganiarska 20/23; mains 22-38zł; ☺ 11am-10pm Tue-Sun; ☎ 🖟) The speciality here is Kashubian regional cooking from the northwest of Poland, and dishes such as potato pancakes, stuffed cabbage rolls, fish soup and fried herring are as close to home cooking as you'll get in a restaurant. The interior is done out like a traditional farm cottage and the exposed beams and dark-green walls make for a cosy atmosphere.

Filharmonia FUSION €€

(Map p308; www.restauracjagdansk.pl; ul Ołwianka 1; mains 34-54zł; ☺ noon-10pm; ☎) Occupying a red-brick corner of the Philharmonia building facing the Targ Rybny (Fish Market) across the river, the cooks here dabble in fusion cuisine to admirable effect, successfully combining traditional with the exotic. If you came to Pomerania to gorge on braised flesh and ale, then these finicky creations will disappoint with their finesse, attention to detail and obsessive focus on taste.

Gvara POLISH €€

(Map p308; ☑ 79 588 9288; www.restauracja gvara.pl; Chlebnicka 48/51; mains 25-74zł; ☺ 9am-10pm Sun-Thu, to midnight Fri & Sat; ☎ 🖟) Take a retro-style seat under bare lightbulbs to enjoy some scrumptious Polish fare at this new bistro-restaurant. Your finger could do worse than land on the pierogi with duck, cranberries and walnuts in pear sauce or how about fried ice cream for dessert? There's a kids menu and the 19zł lunch is a steal.

Kafëbë BISTRO €€

(Map p308; ☑ 50 027 5286; ul Piwna 64; mains 22-39zł; ☺ 8am-9pm Sun-Thu, to 10pm Fri & Sat; ☎) Push open the heavy ornate door on ul Piwna to enter this folksy cafe with high-stacked gateaux, Kashubian burgers with curry sauce, fish pierogi and well-brewed coffee. Good for a lazy breakfast and an evening beer and all fuelling times in between.

Kresowa EASTERN EUROPEAN €€

(Map p308; www.kresowagdansk.com.pl; ul Ogarna 12; mains 19-45zł; ☺ noon-10pm) Take your taste buds to Poland's long-lost east and beyond at this two-level, 19th-century period restaurant with the mood of an Imperial-era Chekhovian parlour. Start with Ukrainian borscht, order a main of Lviv trout and finish with Polish cheesecake while sipping homemade *kvas* (partially fermented bread and water). There's even bison goulash for those who dare to ask.

Kos
INTERNATIONAL €€

(Map p308; www.restauracjakos.pl; ul Piwna 9/10; mains 18-37zł; ⏱9am-10pm Sun-Wed, to midnight Thu-Sat; 🛜🍴) If you're travelling with the family in tow, this internationally minded, kid-friendly place is an excellent choice. The crowd-pleasing menu is a pizza-pasta affair, plus Polish chops, sandwiches and hefty breakfasts. There's a playroom where the kids can rampage while parents monitor them upstairs via CCTV. Decor is all whites and greys, with splashes of strategic colour.

Kaszubska Marina
POLISH €€€

(Map p308; ☑73 412 6191; ul Długa 45; mains 36-59zł; ⏱noon-11pm daily) Go Kashubian at this delightful place opposite the Town Hall (p311), which manages to evoke a rural theme without a single ancient agricultural knick-knack or trussed waitress in sight. Admire the crisp interior of heavy wooden furniture decorated with stylised Kashubian motifs and soothing scenes of the countryside, while sampling finely prepared regional dishes.

The traditional duck with apple and *slivovitz* sauce (plum brandy) comes highly recommended.

Restauracja Pod Łososiem
POLISH €€€

(Map p308; ☑58 301 7652; www.podlososiem.com.pl; ul Szeroka 52/54; mains 40-110zł; ⏱noon-11pm) Founded in 1598 and famous for its fish dishes, this is one of Gdańsk's most highly regarded restaurants. Red leather seats, brass chandeliers and a gathering of gas lamps fill out the rather sober interior, illuminated by the speciality drink – Goldwasser. This gooey, sweet liqueur with flakes of gold was produced in its cellars from the 16th century until WWII.

Restauracja Gdańska
POLISH €€€

(Map p308; ☑58 305 7671; www.gdanska.pl; ul Św Ducha 16; mains 29-69zł; ⏱noon-midnight) Dining in any of the five over-the-top banqueting rooms and salons here is a bit like eating out in a well-stocked museum, with surroundings of antique furniture, oil paintings, model ships and random objets d'art. The upper-end traditional menu of herring, white Gdańsk-style *żurek* (traditional sour-rye soup), duck and slabs of cheesecake is as heavy as the sumptuous drapery.

Drinking & Nightlife

Getting a dose of Arabica, a jug of ale or something a lot, lot stronger is pretty easy in central Gdańsk, with cafes and bars scattered liberally. More characterful nooks can be found in ul Mariacka and ul Piwna. However, as anyone in town will concede, head to Sopot (p326) if you want a serious night out.

★ Józef K
BAR

(Map p308; ☑572 161 510; www.facebook.com/jozefk; ul Piwna 1/2; ⏱10am-2am Sun-Thu, to 4am Fri & Sat; 🛜) Is it a bar or a junk shop? You decide as you relax with a cocktail or a glass of excellent Polish perry on one of the battered sofas, illuminated by an old theatre spotlight. Downstairs is an open area where the party kicks off at weekends; upstairs is more intimate with lots of soft seating and well-stocked bookcases.

★ Flisak '76
COCKTAIL BAR

(Map p308; ul Chlebnicka 9; ⏱6pm-1am daily; 🛜) Around for over 40 years, this is Gdańsk's longest-established cocktail bar and still, according to many, the best. The funky retro interior complements the drinks that come in all kinds of containers and the crowd is a mix of local students and tourists. Located beneath the U Szkota pub.

Kozlovna Złota Brama
PUB

(Map p308; ☑51 971 6442; Długa 81/83; ⏱11am-11pm; 🛜) Typical Czech franchise pub belonging to the Pilsner Urquell brewery with a clean-cut, goat-themed interior ('kozel' means billy-goat in Czech), big jugs of Kozel, Urquell and nonalcoholic Birell beer and suitably salty mop-up material to induce your thirst for more. It's the first Kozlovna to hit Poland – more are sure to follow.

Probiernia Win
WINE BAR

(Map p308; ☑66 817 1778; Great Arsenal, Targ Weglowy 6; ⏱2-9pm Mon-Sat; 🛜) Finally someone has come up with a use for the huge space beneath the Great Arsenal, filling the mammoth building's cavernous underbelly with this superb wine bar. Not only can you take your taste buds for a treat – the selection of wines and tapas on offer is probably Gdańsk's best – there's also regular live music to enhance the laid-back ambience. Enter from ul Tkacka.

Brovarnia MICROBREWERY
(Map p308; www.brovarnia.pl; ul Szafarnia 9; ⊙1-11pm; 🛜) Pomerania's best microbrewery cooks up award-winning dark, wheat and lager beers in polished copper vats amid sepia photos of old Gdańsk. Tables are tightly packed but this place lacks a beer-hall feel, possibly as it's squeezed into vacant granary space in the posh Hotel Gdańsk.

Literacka WINE BAR
(Map p308; ☑50 043 1451; www.literacka.gda.pl; ul Mariacka 52; ⊙noon–last customer Fri-Mon, from 2pm Wed & Thu) This intimate, two-level wine bar stocks reds and whites from all over the world, including – wait for it – Poland! Staff know their Dornfelder from their Douce noir and there are inexpensive pasta dishes, sandwiches and soups to accompany your wine of choice.

Cafe Lamus BAR
(Map p308; ☑53 199 8832; www.facebook.com/cafelamus; Lawendowa 8, enter from Straganiarska; ⊙noon-1am; 🛜) This fun retro-style bar has a random scattering of 1970s sofas and armchairs (and deckchairs outside), big-print wallpaper, and a menu of Polish craft beers, cider and coffee. There's also a spillover bar for the Saturday-night crowd.

Cafe Ferber BAR
(Map p308; ☑79 101 0005; ul Długa 77/78; ⊙9am-late; 🛜) It's startling to step straight from Gdańsk's modern main street into this very modern cafe-bar, dominated by bright red panels, a suspended ceiling and boxy red lighting. The scarlet decor contrasts with its comfy armchairs, from which you can sip coffee and cocktail creations such as the *szary kot* (grey cat). On weekends, DJs spin tunes into the wee small hours.

Pikawa CAFE
(Map p308; ul Piwna 5/6; ⊙9am-10pm Sun-Thu, to 11pm Fri & Sat; 🛜) One of the early postcommunist originals, this well-worn, aromatic coffeehouse is still worth a shot for the expertly barristered brews and the huge blown-up images of Gdańsk on the walls.

Kamienica BAR
(Map p308; ul Mariacka 37/39; ⊙11am-10pm; 🛜) The pick of the bunch on ul Mariacka is this excellent two-level cafe with a calm, sophisticated atmosphere and the best patio on the block. As popular for a daytime caffeine-and-cake halt as it is for a sociable evening bevvy.

Miasto Aniołów CLUB
(Map p308; ☑58 768 5831; www.miastoaniolow.com.pl; ul Chmielna 26; ⊙9pm-4am Thu-Sat; 🛜) The 'City of Angels' covers all the bases – late-night revellers can hit the spacious dance floor, crash in the chill-out area or hang around the atmospheric deck overlooking the Motława River. Nightly DJs play disco and other dance-oriented sounds.

Parlament CLUB
(Map p308; www.parlament.com.pl; ul Św Ducha 2; ⊙9pm-late Thu-Sat; 🛜) Popular mainstream club with strutting nights devoted to the hits of yesteryear, pop, dance, R & B, electronic and hip-hop.

Degustatornia Dom Piwa PUB
(Map p308; ul Grodzka 16; ⊙1pm-midnight Mon-Thu & Sun, to 2am Fri & Sat) If beer brings you cheer, then the 180 types of ale, lager, porter and other hop-based concoctions will have you ecstatic. Tens of Polish bottled beers are poured alongside gems from the Czech Republic, England, Bavaria, Belgium and Ukraine. There are at least 15 beers on tap, often Polish craft affairs. The summer beer garden is one of Gdańsk's best.

☆ Entertainment

Gdańsk Shakespeare Theatre THEATRE
(Gdański Teatr Szekspirowski; Map p308; ☑58 351 0151; www.teatrszekspirowski.pl; Bogusławskiego 1; tours 18zł; ⊙tours 3.30pm, days vary) Built on the site of a 17th-century playhouse called the 'Fencing School' where English travelling troupes used to perform the Bard, this damn-ugly, black-brick 21st-century hulk of a theatre was purpose-built in 2014 to host the city's famous Shakespeare Festival (p319) as well as a year-round venue. The design combines old and new elements – the roof opens to create Globe-style authenticity.

English-language tours of the building run sporadically, usually on days when there's no performance – book online.

Baltic Philharmonic Hall CLASSICAL MUSIC
(Map p308; ☑58 320 6262; www.filharmonia.gda.pl; ul Ołowianka 1; ⊙box office 9.30am-4pm Tue, 10.30am-6pm Wed-Fri) The regular host of chamber-music concerts; also organises many of the major music festivals throughout the year.

State Baltic Opera Theatre OPERA
(☑58 763 4906; www.operabaltycka.pl; Al Zwycięstwa 15) Founded in 1950, Gdańsk's premier opera company resides in this opera

AMBER GAMBLER

One of the main reasons some come to Gdańsk is to source jewellery made of Baltic gold – fossilised tree resin found on the Baltic shores of Poland and Russia, commonly known as amber.

But beware: at some smaller, less-reputable stalls, you may not be getting the real deal, with some pieces containing well-crafted chunks of Russian or Chinese plastic.

Here are three ways locals recommend you can tell if the amber you are being offered is bona fide prehistoric sap. Not all shopkeepers will be happy to see you testing their wares in these ways, for obvious reasons.

➡ Take a lighter and put amber into the heat – it should give off a characteristic smell, like incense.

➡ Amber floats in 20% salt water, while plastic or synthetic amber won't.

➡ Rub amber against cloth and the static electricity produced attracts tiny pieces of paper.

house in the Wrzeszcz district, near the Politechnika train station. Alongside the usual operatic repertoire, it stages regular ballets. Symphonic concerts are also held here.

Teatr Wybrzeże   THEATRE
(Map p308; ☑58 301 1328; www.teatrwybrzeze.
pl; Targ Węglowy 1) Top productions of edgy
Polish and classic foreign plays next to the
Great Arsenal (p312) in the Main Town.

🔒 Shopping

Some visit Gdańsk to buy amber, which is found along the Baltic coast. The choice here is virtually unrivalled with plenty of city-centre shops, and the stones are more likely to be real than elsewhere in central and Eastern Europe. However, shopping isn't all about amber – Goldwasser makes an unusual take-home item and you can find pretty Kashubian handicrafts (p331).

Forum Gdańsk   MALL
(Map p308; ☑58 732 6120; www.forumgdansk.pl;
Targ Sienny 7; ⊙8am-10pm Mon-Sat, from 9am Sun;
🛜) This huge, decidedly upmarket shopping
centre was bolted together on wasteland
north of the Brama Wyżynna (Upland Gate)
in 2018 and is linked to Gdańsk Śródmie-
jśće SKM station. All the familiar names of
the international retail world display their
wares and there's a useful supermarket on
the lowest level. The open courtyard outside
provides a wonderful panorama of the old
centre's skyline.

Galeria Sztuki Kaszubskiej   ARTS & CRAFTS
(Map p308; ul Św Ducha; ⊙11am-6pm Mon-Sat
Jul & Aug, shorter hours Sep-Jun) For genuine
handmade Kashubian handicrafts, look no
further than this small shop near St Mary's
Church (p311). Porcelain and embroidery

dominate the range, much of which is designed and produced by the owner.

Galeria SAS   ART
(Map p308; www.galeriab.pl; ul Szeroka 18/19;
⊙10.30am-5pm Mon-Fri, to 4pm Sat) The quality oil paintings at this commercial gallery
make unique and interesting souvenirs. All
are by local artists and the owner is very
knowledgeable about her collection.

Cepelia   ARTS & CRAFTS
(Map p308; ul Długa 47; ⊙10am-6pm Mon-Fri, to
2pm Sat) A branch of the national Polish arts
and crafts chain and hence the most obvious
place to head for Kashubian trinkets.

ℹ Information

INTERNET RESOURCES
Trojmiasto.pl (www.guide.trojmiasto.pl)
Detailed Tri-City tourist guide.
Gdansk4U.pl (www.gdansk4u.pl) Gdańsk's
official tourist website.
Gdańsk City Portal (www.gdansk.pl) Excellent
city information site.

POST
Post Office (Map p308; ul Długa 23/28;
⊙24hr) The main post office with its old
interior under a glass roof is worth a look even
if you aren't sending anything. There's an ATM
and currency-exchange window.

TOURIST INFORMATION
Tourist Office – Długi Targ (Map p308; ☑58
301 4355; www.visitgdansk.com; Długi Targ
28/29; ⊙9am-7pm May-Aug, to 5pm Sep-Apr)
Tourist Office – Galeria Madison (Map p308;
www.visitgdansk.com; Galeria Madison, ul
Rajska 10; ⊙9am-7pm Mon-Sat, from 10am
Sun) Near the train station.

Tourist Office – Airport (☑ 58 348 1368; www.visitgdansk.com; ul Słowackiego 210, Gdańsk Lech Wałęsa Airport; ⊙ 24hr)

PTTK Office (Map p308; ☑ 58 301 6096; www.pttk-gdansk.pl; ul Długa 45; ⊙ 10am-6pm) Arranges foreign-language tours, excursions and central accommodation.

Pomorskie Regional Tourist Office (Map p308; ☑ 58 732 7041; www.pomorskie.travel; Brama Wyżynna, Wały Jagiellońskie 2a; ⊙ 9am-6pm daily year-round, to 8pm Mon-Fri Jun-Sep) Housed in the Upland Gate, this friendly regional tourist office has info on Gdańsk and the surrounding area.

ⓘ Getting There & Away

AIR

Gdańsk Lech Wałęsa Airport (p420) is 14km west of the city centre. There are direct flights to Warsaw with LOT, and to Kraków and Wrocław with Ryanair.

International flights to many European and UK cities are operated by budget airlines Ryanair and Wizz Air.

BOAT

Polferries (www.polferries.pl) runs car ferries from Gdańsk to Nynäshamn (near Stockholm) in Sweden (foot passenger from Skr620, car with driver from Skr1470, 19 hours, up to seven a week).

BUS

Gdańsk's crumbling **bus terminal** (PKS Gdańsk; Map p308; ul 3 Maja 12) is right behind the central train station, linked by an underground passageway.

Elbląg 18zł, 1½ hours, at least hourly

Kartuzy 9.50zł, one hour, hourly (Gryf bus)

Kościerzyna 16.50zł, 1½ hours, hourly

Lidzbark Warmiński 38zł, 2¾ hours, six daily

Olsztyn 70zł, 2¾ hours, hourly

Warsaw 20zł to 60zł, 4½ to six hours, at least hourly

There are plenty of connections from Gdańsk to Western European cities plus services east to Kaliningrad, Minsk and many places large and small in Ukraine.

TRAIN

The grand main train station, Gdańsk Główny, is on the western edge of the Old Town. SKM (www.skm.pkp.pl) operates regional rail services between Gdańsk and Gdynia, Lębork, Kościerzyna and Kartuzy.

Almost all long-distance trains to/from the south originate and terminate in Gdynia, while many trains running along the coast to western destinations start in Gdańsk and stop at Gdynia (and Sopot) en route.

Gdańsk has the following direct rail connections.

Lębork 13.50zł, 1¾ hours, eight daily

Malbork 13.50zł, 40 minutes, two or three an hour

Olsztyn 40zł, 2½ hours, six daily

Poznań 56zł, 3½ hours, eight daily

Szczecin 54zł, 5½ hours, four daily

Toruń 47zł, 2½ hours, nine daily

Warsaw 77zł, three to four hours, hourly

Wrocław 63zł, six to seven hours, six daily

ⓘ Getting Around

TO/FROM THE AIRPORT

Bus City bus 210 (www.ztm.gda.pl) runs from the airport to Gdańsk Główny train station and Brama Wyżynna (3.80zł, 35 minutes) in the city centre, every 30 minutes between 5.30am and 10.30pm, hourly on Saturday and Sunday.

Train SKM (www.skm.pkp.pl) trains run between Gdańsk Główny and the airport (3.80zł, 40 minutes) two or three times an hour; you normally need to change at Gdańsk Wrzeszcz.

BOAT

From May until September, Żegluga Gdańska (p331) runs pleasure boats and hydrofoils from Gdańsk's wharf, near the Green Gate, to Hel, Sopot and Westerplatte. ZTM operates the **Water Tram** (Tramwaj Wodny; Map p308; www.ztm.gda.pl) that runs to Westerplatte.

TRAIN

A commuter train, known as the SKM (Szybka Kolej Miejska; Fast City Train), runs constantly between Gdańsk Główny and Gdynia Główna (35 minutes), stopping at a dozen intermediate stations, including Sopot. The trains run every five to 10 minutes at peak times and every hour or so late at night. You buy tickets at the stations and validate them in the machines at the platform entrance (not on the train itself), or purchase them prevalidated from vending machines on the platform.

TRAM & BUS

These are a slower means of transport than the SKM train but cover more ground, running from 5am until around 11pm, when a handful of night lines takes over. Tickets cost 3.20zł for any one-way journey and 3.80zł for one hour's travel. A day ticket valid for a 24-hour period costs 13zł. Remember to validate your ticket in the vehicle, so it is stamped with the date and time.

SOPOT

POP 36,500

The junior partner in the Tri-City set-up, Sopot is a kind of Incongruity-on-Sea, a mix of elegant villas and marauding clubbers, an overdeveloped 21st-century seafront just streets away from typically Polish soot-cracked facades. Like the British seaside towns of Brighton and Eastbourne rolled into one, Sopot is about moneyed Poles flashing their cash in ritzy restaurants standing alongside old Polish literary-themed cafes, a strutting club scene illuminating pensioners taking to the waters while kids on the beach build sandcastles. Whatever Sopot has become, it certainly remains popular, with international visitors mingling with the Slavic waffle-and-ice-cream crowds on hot summer days then getting down at the beachside clubs on balmy Baltic eves.

Sights & Activities

Sopot's unavoidable spine is **Ulica Bohaterów Monte Cassino** (Heroes of Monte Cassino St), an attractive and invariably crowded mall stretching from the railway line to the pier. Many of Sopot's cafes and places of entertainment line its pedestrianised length, some of which can be found in the unmissable Crooked House.

Pier PIER
(Molo; Map p327; www.molo.sopot.pl; 5-8zł; ⊙4-8pm Mon-Fri, from 11.30am Sat & Sun May-Sep) At the end of Monte Cassino, beyond Plac Zdrojowy, is the famous Molo, Europe's longest wooden pier, built in 1928 and jutting 515m out into the Bay of Gdańsk. Various attractions along its length come and go with the seasons. The cheeky summer admission charge puts few off.

Sopot Museum MUSEUM
(Map p327; www.muzeumsopotu.pl; ul Poniatowskiego 8; adult/concession 10/5zł; ⊙10am-4pm Tue-Sun) At the southern end of the beachfront in a grand old villa, the Sopot Museum showcases 19th-century furniture and fittings, including some enormous, ornately carved wardrobes. Other displays include old sepia photos and maps of German Zoppot and other Baltic resorts. The building, an early-20th-century holiday home of a wealthy merchant, is worth a look in itself.

Opera Leśna THEATRE
(Forest Opera; ☑58 555 8400; www.operalesna. sopot.pl; ul Moniuszki 12) In a wooded hilly area of the town stands the Opera Leśna, an amphitheatre that seats 5000 people and is host to the prestigious August International Sopot Festival, a Eurovision-style song contest and festival famous across Central and Eastern Europe. Check the website for the summer program, which often includes big names from Eastern Europe and the odd illustrious name of yesteryear from the West.

Crooked House NOTABLE BUILDING
(Krzywy Domek; Map p327; www.krzywydomek. info; ul Bohaterów Monte Cassino 53) The warped, modern Crooked House is a typical piece of postcommunist architectural experimentation and well worth investigating. Concealed within its twin-level innards are some worthwhile clubs, bars and restaurants. Love it or hate it, most wander in to investigate at some point.

Tightrope Walker Statue STATUE
(Map p327; ul Bema) FREE While ambling your way along ul Bohaterów Monte Cassino towards the sea, take a right into ul Bema to see one of the most unusual statues in the Tri-City. An African fisherman carrying a net is suspended above the street on a tightrope, the piece of public art seeming to defy gravity. It's the work of Polish sculptor Jerzy Kedziora who specialises in these odd balancing spectacles.

Dom Zdrojowy SPRING
(Map p327; Plac Zdrojowy 2; ⊙10am-6pm) FREE Take the glazed lift to the 3rd floor of this spa house to enjoy a free sip of Sopot's natural, mineral-rich spring water that comes from a tap in the midst of a cafe.

Grand Hotel LANDMARK
(Map p327; Powstańców Warszawy 12/14) North of the pier is the landmark 1927 Grand Hotel, adjoining the long waterfront spa park that first popularised the town.

Aqua Park AMUSEMENT PARK
(www.aquaparksopot.pl; ul Zamkowa Góra 3/5; per hour/day 21/55zł Mon-Fri, 25/65zł Sat & Sun; ⊙8am-10pm; ▣) This large indoor aqua park has tubes, slides, spas and a wild river ride, the ideal place to take the kids if the Baltic weather is playing up.

Sleeping

Central Hostel Sopot HOSTEL €
(Map p327; ☑53 085 8717; www.centralsopot. com; ul Bohaterów Monte Cassino 15; dm/d from 85/200zł; ☞) Spacious both horizontally and

Sopot

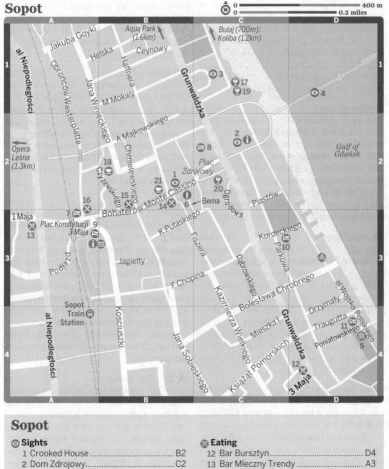

Sopot

⊙ Sights
1 Crooked House	B2
2 Dom Zdrojowy	C2
3 Grand Hotel	C1
4 Pier	D1
5 Sopot Museum	D4
6 Tightrope Walker Statue	B2

⊜ Sleeping
7 Central Hostel Sopot	A3
8 Hotel Bayjonn	C2
9 Hotel Rezydent	A3
10 Pensjonat Eden	C3
11 Pensjonat Wanda	D4

⊗ Eating
12 Bar Bursztyn	D4
13 Bar Mleczny Trendy	A3
14 Błękitny Pudel	B2
15 Browar Miejski	B2
16 Český Film	A2

⊜ Drinking & Nightlife
17 Klub Atelier	C1
18 Młody Byron	B2
19 Scena	C1
20 Spatif	C2
21 Zaścianek	B2

vertically, this three-storey former workers' hostel has dorms containing four to 10 beds plus myriad other stylish singles and doubles, all en suite. As there's no kitchen or common room, the place lacks atmosphere, but rooms are well-kept and the location-to-price ratio is a winner.

Campground Metropolis   CAMPGROUND €
(📱58 550 0445; www.domkisopot.pl; Al Niepodległości 899; per person/tent 17/15zł; 🛜) A large but often full camping ground located at the northern end of town near the beach (a five-minute walk from the Sopot Kamienny Potok train station).

Pensjonat Wanda
GUESTHOUSE €€

(Map p327; ☑58 551 5725; www.bws-hotele.pl; ul Poniatowskiego 7; s/d 200/260zł; [P][奈]) A traditional, 25-room guesthouse with en-suite rooms, some with balconies overlooking the sea and sand that makes them pretty good value for money. Decor is a mix of old and new, but bathrooms are all of recent vintage.

Pensjonat Eden
HOTEL €€

(Map p327; ☑58 551 1503; www.hotel-eden.pl; ul Kordeckiego 4/6; s/d from 200/300zł; [奈]) The crumbly facade of this early-20th-century villa doesn't promise much, but once inside this family-run guesthouse you'll receive a friendly welcome before being shown up to one of the 26 well-kept rooms, flaunting stylishly high ceilings and lots of fun-and-fusty furniture straight from granny's parlour.

★Hotel Bayjonn
HOTEL €€€

(Map p327; ☑730 717 171; www.bayjonnhotel.pl; ul Powstańców Warszawy 7; s 475-599zł, d 550-699zł; [P][奈]) Occupying an architecturally striking corner of the Haffner Centre, this award-winning design hotel is all retro stripes and faux '70s browns, but with stunningly contemporary bathrooms and little nods to the past in the shape of old German-era maps of Zoppot. Facilities are kept shiny, staff are friendly enough and the location is superb.

Hotel Rezydent
HOTEL €€€

(Map p327; ☑58 555 5800; www.hotelrezydent.pl; Plac Konstytucji 3 Maja 3; s/tw from 420/450zł; [P][✳][@][奈]) The Rezydent is the most elegant hotel in town, though you'll pay for the privilege of staying here. The tasteful tones of the rooms are set off by stylish carpets, timber furniture and lustrous bathrooms. When you're done luxuriating, there's a classy restaurant and pub downstairs, along with an art gallery, a sauna and massage services.

✗ Eating

Sopot's eating scene is one of the most sophisticated in Poland's north. Polish and Kashubian menus are common. From milk bars to luxury-hotel restaurants, all budgets are covered.

Bar Bursztyn
CAFETERIA €

(Map p327; www.barbursztyn.pl; ul Grunwaldzka 78-80, 8a; mains 9.50-20zł; ⊙8am-10pm; [奈]) A millennium away from the milk bars of yesteryear, this snazzy canteen with nightclub decor, polite English-speaking staff, free magazines, pagers that let you know when your order is ready, a toy corner and authentic pizzas blasts the worker's canteen concept into outer space. In fact, it has been described as *a bar mleczny* that's come back from the future.

Bar Mleczny Trendy
CAFETERIA €

(Map p327; Al Niepodległości 786; mains 13-18zł; ⊙11am-5.45pm Mon-Sat, noon-4.45pm Sun) Forget the awful name and the outward appearance, inside you'll find Sopot's best budget fare. No old-school *bar mleczny*, there's coffee, big monochrome prints of Sopot on the walls and the food is tasty and filling. Also, it's on the less glamorous side of the tracks so wholly tourist-free.

★Browar Miejski
POLISH €€

(Map p327; ☑58 342 0242; www.browarmiejski sopot.pl; ul Bohaterów Monte Cassino 35; mains 26-42zł; ⊙11am-11pm; [奈]) It's not just the beer that fills the 250 seats at Sopot's very own microbrewery with punters; the food here has also built up quite a reputation. Filling dishes such as wild boar, pork knuckle in beer sauce and goose complement the at-least-seven types of beer brewed in huge tanks in the 21st-century dining space.

Despite its seat-count, this place, inside and out on the terrace, fills quickly on summer evenings.

★Błękitny Pudel
CAFE €€

(Map p327; ul Bohaterów Monte Cassino 44; mains 23-60zł; ⊙9am–last customer; [奈]) This top pub-cafe, Sopot's longest survivor, is a real cosy knick-knack fest with the cobbled interior bedecked in wooden tennis rackets, balalaikas, richly upholstered divans and seemingly everything in between. Choose between the cosy interior and an outdoor pew for a bit of people watching.

Unusual menu items include black pudding in mushroom and cider sauce and Eton mess.

★Bulaj
SEAFOOD €€

(☑58 551 5129; www.bulaj.pl; al Franciszka Mamuszki 22; mains 21-57zł; ⊙11am-11pm; [♿]) One of northern Poland's best restaurants, foodies flock here to sample chef Artur Moroz' seafood dishes, served in a crisp but basic, pub-like environment. If you don't like fish, there's always local rabbit and duck on the menu, but it's the zander, cod and halibut most come for, prepared simply but deliciously. On the beach at entrance No 12.

Note that it isn't always open when it should be.

Český Film
CZECH €€
(Map p327; ☎ 58 716 1616; www.czeskasopot.pl; ul Bohaterów Monte Cassino 17; mains 23-49zł; ◷ 1-10pm Mon-Thu, to 11pm Fri, from noon Sat, to 9pm Sun; 🐾) The phrase Český Film (Czech film in Czech) in Polish means something surreal and incomprehensible, but there's no confusion about the quality of this typical Czech pub-restaurant at the top of BMC. Take a bench in the faux half-timbered dining room to wash down hearty Bohemian fare like beef goulash and roast duck with unsurpassed beers from Poland's southern neighbours.

 Drinking & Nightlife

Sopot has a vibrant club and live-music culture that's always changing; ask the locals about the current favourites or check www.sopot.klubowa.pl. Eastern Europe's best beach clubs line the dunes to the north of town. The scene here is also notably gay-friendly.

Koliba
CLUB
(☎ 50 135 9698; www.koliba.pl; ul Powstancow Warszawy 90, beach entrance 4; ◷ 24hr; 🐾) A beach hike or bike ride north along the Baltic, this totally incongruous, traditional Tatran mountain chalet is a restaurant by day, but at 9.30pm from Thursday to Saturday the tables and chairs are pushed back to create the Tri-City's most unlikely and unpretentious nightclub. Great beach access and Baltic-side terrace.

Młody Byron
CAFE
(Map p327; ul Czyżewskiego 12; ◷ noon-11pm) Far from the lubricated wannabes on ul BMC, this elegant minipalace houses a quaint little coffeehouse (the former U Hrabiego), where more bookish types take the cake and engage in highbrow banter.

Spatif
BAR
(Map p327; www.spatif.sopot.pl; ul Bohaterów Monte Cassino 54; ◷ 4pm-1am; 🐾) Head up the steps off ul BMC to find this unmissable, avant-garde place packed with charity-shop leftovers and backstage kitsch. The crowd ranges from wannabe novelists to Warsaw boob-job gals, the atmosphere more vodka-inspired the later things get. Not easy to get past face control at weekends.

Klub Atelier
CLUB
(Map p327; www.klubatelier.pl; al Franciszka Mamuszki 2) Classic Sopot club with beach access, a different big-name DJ every night and a cool, well-to-do Baltic feel attracting the Tri-City's beautiful people.

Scena
CLUB
(Map p327; www.scenaklub.pl; al Franciszka Mamuszki 2) Eclectic beach club with a calendar of jazz, DJs, live music and special events. One of Sopot's best.

Zaścianek
CAFE
(Map p327; ul Haffnera 3; ◷ 11am-10pm Sun-Thu, to 11pm Fri & Sat; 🐾) Delightful olde-worlde hideaway full of antique bric-a-brac, potted plants, oil paintings and intimate tables for two run by friendly owners. Popular with locals and well hidden from the holidaying mobs.

ℹ Information

Post Office (Map p327; ul Kościuszki 2; ◷ 8am-8pm Mon-Fri, to 2pm Sat)
Tourist Office (Map p327; ☎ 73 353 5205; www.visit.sopot.pl; Plac Zdrojowy 2; ◷ 10am-5pm; 🐾) One of northern Poland's best tourist offices with free wi-fi, a left-luggage facility, a cheap souvenir shop and lots of space to laze around. Also runs a **branch office** (Map p327; ☎ 73 353 5205; Dworcowa 4; ◷ 9am-5pm) in a hut opposite the train station.

ℹ Getting There & Away

All trains between Gdańsk and Gdynia stop in Sopot. SKM commuter trains to Gdańsk (3.80zł) run every five to 10 minutes at peak times. The train station is around 1km from the pier (p326).

HEL PENINSULA

Located north of the Tri-City, the Hel Peninsula (Półwysep Helski) is a 34km-long, crescent-shaped sandbank arcing out into the Baltic Sea. A mere 300m wide at the base, it's no wider than 500m for most of its length, though it does expand out to around 3km at the end to accommodate the 'capital' Hel. It reaches just 23m above sea level, and much of the landscape is covered with trees – picturesque, wind-deformed pines predominate.

The peninsula was formed over the course of about 8000 years by sea currents and winds, which gradually created an uninterrupted belt of sand. At the end of the 17th century, as old maps show, the sandbar was still cut by six inlets, making it a chain of islands. In the 19th century the peninsula was cut into separate pieces several times by storms. The edges have been strengthened and the movement of the sand has been reduced by vegetation, but the sandbar continues to grow.

Hel is a popular day trip from Gdańsk, though many Poles come here for beach holidays in summer. However, even at the height of the season (July to August) finding a secluded stretch of sand is not difficult.

Hel

POP 3900

Most English-speakers can't help cracking a smirk as they ask for their ticket to Hel. But this relaxed holiday town at the end of its long slender sandbar is far from purgatory. In fact, it's quite a pleasant getaway and feels a long way from Poland's 21st-century cares. The beach is the obvious main draw when it's hot; the rest of the year the town shows few vital signs.

Throughout history, Hel benefited from its strategic location at the maritime gateway to Gdańsk. By the 14th century Hel was a prosperous fishing port and trading centre. However, it was constantly threatened by storms and the shifting coastline, and declined in importance in the 18th century before reinventing itself as a popular seaside resort.

◉ Sights

Fokarium AQUARIUM
(☑58 675 0836; www.fokarium.com; ul Morska 2; 5zł; ⊙9.30am-8pm) Just off the beach in the centre of town is the Fokarium, where Baltic grey seals can be seen in captivity. The three large pools are home to half a dozen of the creatures, and feeding takes place at 11am and 2pm when keepers put these incredibly obedient animals through their paces for fishy rewards. You'll need a 5zł piece to unlock the main turnstile – the small museum inside is free.

Note that many animal welfare groups make compelling arguments against keeping marine mammals in captivity.

Lighthouse LIGHTHOUSE
(ul Bałtycka 3; adult/concession 6/4zł; ⊙10am-2pm & 3-7pm Jul & Aug, shorter hours May, Jun & Sep) Through a patch of scrappy woodland at the end of ul Wiejska is the 42m-high octagonal brick lighthouse. It's now a radar station but houses temporary exhibitions.

Museum of Fishery MUSEUM
(Muzeum Rybołówstwa; ☑58 675 0552; www. nmm.pl; Bulwar Nadmorski 2; adult/concession 12/8zł; ⊙10am-6pm daily Jul & Aug, shorter hours rest of year) Hel's Gothic church dates from the 1420s, making it the oldest building in town. Pews and monstrances have given way to recently revamped exhibits on fishing and boat-building, a display of stuffed sea birds and a collection of old fishing boats, all part of the National Maritime Museum (p315). The tower provides views of the peninsula and Gulf of Gdańsk.

Memorial to the Defenders of Hel MEMORIAL
(Pomnik Obrońców Helu; cnr uls Wiejska & Sikorskiego) A park near the train station has a memorial to the 1939 defence of the town during the German invasion. Hel was the last place in Poland to surrender; a garrison of some 3000 Polish soldiers defended it until 2 October. The peninsula became a battlefield again on 5 April 1945 when about 60,000 Germans were caught in a Red Army bottleneck. They lay down their arms on 9 May, making it the last piece of Polish territory to be liberated.

⌨ Sleeping

There are ample beds during summer though few classic hotels or guesthouses. The best place to start if you're looking to stay is the official Hel website (www.gohel. pl), which has lots of listings and an interactive map. Many locals rent out rooms in their homes – look for the many official signs on gates and houses bearing a number – this means the property has been checked by the municipality.

Duna Guesthouse GUESTHOUSE €€
(☑58 351 2063; www.duna.org.pl; ul Morska; d 140-200zł; ☎) This beachside place has fresh, well-tended rooms and apartments in warm colours with flat-pack furniture and modern bathrooms. Some rooms have views of the Bay of Gdańsk and outside high season you can pay as little as 70zł per person.

Cassubia HOTEL €€
(☑69 308 0091; www.hotelewam.pl; ul Boczna 11; s/d from 90/160zł; ℗☎) Take a trip back to Poland's institutional past at this retro relic with furniture from the days of martial law but pleasant-enough staff. The location near the train station is the biggest plus – no dragging heavy bags into town. Another positive is that there is almost always one of 134 beds free.

Eating

★ **Kutter** POLISH €€
(www.kutter.pl; ul Wiejska 87; mains 20-40zł;
⊙9am-11pm daily; 🛜) Hel's top place to eat is
the beautifully done out Kutter where fishing
knick-knacks of yesteryear combine with old
wooden floors, colourful Kashubian motifs,
an entire fishing boat and an aquarium. The
restaurant's speciality is Baltic fish (price per
100g), brought to prettily laid tables by wait-
resses in Kashubian folk costume.

Bar Mewa SEAFOOD €€
(📞72 891 1164; www.mewahel.pl; ul Morska 84;
mains around 20zł; ⊙9am-10pm daily; 🛜) Enjoy
12 types of fish from the Baltic in the tiny
antique-packed interior or out by a set of
fountains in the sea breeze at this popular
spot just steps from the beach.

ℹ️ Information

Post Office (ul Wiejska 55; ⊙9.30am-4.30pm
Mon-Fri, 8am-2pm Sat) Has a currency-
exchange desk.

ℹ️ Getting There & Away

To reach Hel by train, you'll first have to make
your way to Gdynia (from Gdańsk on the SKM,
6zł, 30 minutes) and change there (17.10zł,
two hours, hourly); even in low season there
are fairly regular services. Regular buses also
leave from the lighthouse end of ul Wiejska for
Gdynia (14zł to 22zł, one hour 40 minutes, 10
to 15 daily).

A waterborne option is the **Żegluga Gdańska**
(Map p308; www.zegluga.pl) pleasure boat/hy-
drofoil from May to September from Gdańsk.

KASHUBIA

Stretching for 100km southwest of Gdańsk,
the Kashubia Region is a picturesque area
noted for its small, traditional villages, and
a lack of cities and industry. In contrast to
most of the other groups who gradually
merged to form one big family of Poles, the
Kashubians have managed to retain some
of their early ethnic identity, expressed in
their distinctive culture, dress, crafts, architecture and language. Kashubian, still
spoken in the home by some 50,000, mostly elderly locals, is the most distinct Polish
dialect. It's thought to derive from the old
Slavic Pomeranian language; other Poles
have a hard time deciphering the spoken
language.

The capital of Kashubia is Kartuzy, the
best place to access Kashubia's folk traditions and culture. Hard-to-reach Wdzydze
Kiszewskie and its skansen (open-air museum of traditional architecture) makes for an
interesting day away from Gdańsk.

Kartuzy

POP 14,700

The small town of Kartuzy, 30km west of
Gdańsk, is the capital of Kashubia and hence
the best place to access the Kashubians' folksy culture. It owes its birth and its name to
the Carthusians, a religious order that was
brought here from Bohemia in 1380. Today
Kartuzy is a sleepy provincial centre with
a cosy, semirenovated historical centre and
two huge lakes intruding into the town. Half
a day is about enough to see everything.

WORTH A TRIP

KASHUBIAN ETHNOGRAPHIC PARK

Some 16km south of Kościerzyna, Wdzydze Kiszewskie is a tiny village with a big
attraction, namely the **Kashubian Ethnographic Park** (Kaszubski Park Etnograficzny;
📞58 686 1130; www.muzeum-wdzydze.gda.pl; Wdzydze Kiszewskie; adult/concession 16/11zł;
⊙10am-6pm Tue-Sun Jul & Aug, shorter hours rest of year), an open-air museum (skansen)
displaying the typical rural architecture of Kashubia. Established in 1906 by the local
schoolmaster, this was Poland's first open-air museum of traditional architecture. Many
have followed in its wake.

Pleasantly positioned on the lakeside, it now contains a score of buildings rescued
from central and southern Kashubia, including cottages, barns, a school, a windmill and
an 18th-century church used for Sunday Mass. Some of the interiors feature authentic
furnishings, implements and decorations, showing how the Kashubians lived a century
or two ago.

Reaching Wdzydze is tricky without your own wheels. A few buses a day link the
village with Kościerzyna (8zł, 40 minutes), which has frequent services to/from Gdańsk
(16.50zł, 1½ hours, hourly).

WORTH A TRIP

GNIEW

The small town of Gniew has one big attraction – a red-brick castle housing the local Archaeological Museum. The exhibition is in two rooms, but you will also get to see the chapel and temporary exhibitions in other rooms, and wander through most of the castle. All visits are guided and the tour takes up to 1½ hours.

The first stronghold of the Teutonic order on the left bank of the Vistula, the castle was built in the late 13th century and is a massive, multistorey brick structure with a deep courtyard. In 1464 it came under Polish rule and remained so until the First Partition of 1772. The Prussians remodelled it to accommodate barracks, a jail and an ammunition depot. It was seriously burnt out in 1921, but the 2m-thick walls survived and it was later restored.

Four buses a day run to/from Gdańsk (17zł, one hour 20 minutes) stopping at the bus terminal around 300m northwest of the castle. Otherwise head to Kwidzyn by train and change to a bus there (9zł, approximately hourly, 25 minutes).

⊙ Sights

Kashubian Museum   MUSEUM

(Muzeum Kaszubskie; www.muzeum-kaszubskie. gda.pl; ul Kościerska 1; adult/concession 10/6zł; ⊙9am-6pm Tue-Fri, to 5pm Sat & Sun Jul & Aug, shorter hours rest of year; P) Slavophiles should make a beeline for this surprisingly good and delightfully old-school three-storey museum, south of the train station near the tracks. Amid the inevitable wooden farm implements, kitchen utensils and fishing paraphernalia there are some beautiful toffee-brown and metallic-black pottery so typical of the region, wonderfully embroidered textiles, wood carvings, hefty rural furniture and folksy children's toys.

Church of the Assumption   CHURCH

(Kościół Rzymskokatolicki Pw Wniebowzięcia NMP; ☑69 324 5982; www.kolegiatakartuzy.pl; ul Klasztorna 5) Originally founded in 1084 near Grenoble (France), the Carthusian order was known for its austere monastic rules – its monks passing their days in the contemplation of death, following the motto 'Memento Mori' (Remember You Must Die). In Kartuzy they built a church and, beside it, 18 hermitages laid out in the shape of a horseshoe.

🛏 Sleeping & Eating

Hotel Pod Orłem   HOTEL €€

(☑58 736 6601; www.hotel-podorlem.com; 3 Maja 10; s/d 160/260zł; P🔊) Kartuzy's best place to sleep is this well-run, 29-room hotel in the centre of town. Rooms are mostly business standard with bathrooms of recent vintage. One of Kartuzy's better restaurants adjoins.

Złota Jesień   POLISH €€

(www.grono.gda.pl; Polna 17; mains 15-45zł; ⊙9am-10pm; P🔊) Kashubian dishes can be tricky to track down in Kartuzy, but the food prepared by the chefs at this professional outfit in the far south of town is both traditional and modernly conceived. The duck, trout, *sandacz* (zander) and pierogi are brought to your table by uniformed, polite staff.

ⓘ Information

Tourist office (☑58 684 0201; ul Klasztorna 1; ⊙10am-4pm daily Jun-Sep, 9am-5pm Mon-Fri rest of year) Housed in the Kashubian Culture Centre, this large tourist office is a superb source of information on Kashubian culture throughout the region and sells quality souvenirs, too.

ⓘ Getting There & Away

Gryf buses (not PKS) run from a stop outside Gdańsk bus station to Kartuzy (9.50zł, one hour) every hour or half-hour, depending on the time of day.

Kartuzy's crisply renovated train station is now part of the SKM network with commuter trains making the run to Gdańsk Wrzeszcz (one hour, 8.50zł) where you can change for Gdańsk Główny and Gdańsk Śródmieście.

LOWER VISTULA

The fertile land within the valley of the Lower Vistula, bisected by the wide, slowly flowing river, was prized by invaders for centuries. Flat, open and dotted with green farms, this region developed during the 13th and 14th centuries into a thriving trade centre, via the many ports established along the Vistula's banks from Toruń to Gdańsk.

The history of these towns is intertwined with that of the Teutonic order, the powerful league of Germanic knights who by then occupied much of the valley. Remnants from the order's heyday now comprise some of the most prominent sights in the region.

Though the Lower Vistula suffered much destruction in the closing months of WWII, what survived is a rich cultural inheritance of great depth and interest.

Toruń

POP 202,560

If you've spent your time in Poland jostling with the crowds in Kraków or wandering Warsaw's sprawling boulevards, then Toruń will come as a revelation. This magnificent walled Gothic town on the banks of the Vistula should be high on every traveller's list, especially as its delights seem low on everyone else's, leaving visitors to revel virtually unrestricted in its wealth of historic buildings and city defences, all of which WWII left mercifully untouched. The entire town is listed as a Unesco World Heritage site for being an unusually well-preserved example of a medieval European trading and administrative centre.

Beyond architecture, Toruń is also well known as the birthplace of Nicolaus Copernicus (1473–1543). His name (Mikołaj Kopernik in Polish) is all over the town, and you can even buy gingerbread shaped in his image. This other Toruń icon – its *pierniki* (gingerbread) – is famous across Poland.

History

Toruń was kickstarted into prominence in 1233, when the Teutonic Knights transformed the existing 11th-century Slav settlement into one of their early outposts. The knights surrounded the town, then known as Thorn, with walls and a castle. Rapid expansion as a port meant that newly arriving merchants and craftspeople had to settle outside the city walls and soon built what became known as the New Town. In the 1280s Toruń joined the Hanseatic League, giving further impetus to its development.

Toruń later became a focal point of the conflict between Poland and the Teutonic order, and when the Thirteen Years' War finally ended in 1466, the Treaty of Toruń returned a large area of land to Poland, stretching from Toruń to Gdańsk.

The following period of prosperity ended with the Swedish wars, and the city fell under Prussian domination in 1793, later becoming part of Germany. Toruń didn't return to Poland until the nation was re-created after WWI.

After WWII, Toruń expanded significantly, with vast new suburbs and industries. Luckily, the medieval quarter was unaffected and largely retains its old appearance.

◉ Sights

Old Town Hall   MUSEUM
(Ratusz Staromiejski; Map p334; www.muzeum. torun.pl; Rynek Staromiejski 1; adult/concession 15/10zł, tower 15/10zł, combined ticket 25/18zł; ⊙10am-6pm Tue-Sun May-Sep, to 4pm Oct-Apr) The Old Town Hall dates from the 14th century and hasn't changed much since, though some Renaissance additions lent an ornamental touch to the sober Gothic structure. Today it houses Gothic art (painting and stained glass), a display of local 17th- and 18th-century crafts and a gallery of Polish paintings from 1800 to the present, including a couple of Witkacys and Matejkos. Climb the tower for a fine panoramic view of Toruń's Gothic townscape.

Cathedral of SS John the Baptist & John the Evangelist   CHURCH
(Map p334; www.katedra.diecezja.torun.pl; ul Żeglarska 16; tower 9zł; ⊙9am-5.30pm Mon-Sat, from 2pm Sun, tower closed Nov-Mar) Toruń's mammoth Gothic cathedral was begun around 1260 but only completed at the end of the 15th century. Its massive tower houses Poland's second-largest historic bell, the Tuba Dei (God's Trumpet). On the southern side of the tower, facing the Vistula, is a large 15th-century clock; its original face and single hand are still in working order. Check out the dent above the VIII – it's from a cannonball that struck the clock during the Swedish siege of 1703.

ⓘ JUST THE TICKET

If you're planning to visit all seven attractions affiliated with the Regional Museum in Toruń, why not buy a single pass (adult/concession 50/40zł) valid for two days, but not valid for the Town Hall Tower or the 3D Book of Toruń. A more expensive pass (60/45zł) includes the last two attractions.

Toruń

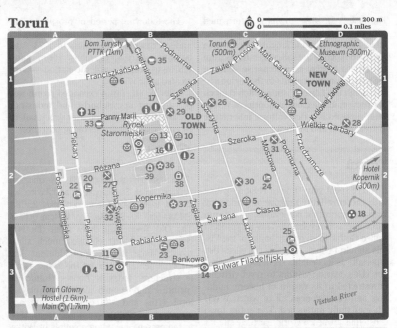

Toruń

House of Copernicus　　　　　　MUSEUM
(Map p334; www.muzeum.torun.pl; ul Kopernika
15/17; museum adult/concession 13/10zł, audiovisual
presentation 15/10zł; ⊘ 10am-6pm Tue-Sun May-Sep,
to 4pm Oct-Apr) While it's not clear if Copernicus was actually born here, this branch of the

Regional Museum is dedicated to the famed
astronomer's life and works. More engaging
than the exhibitions of period furniture and
writing is a short audiovisual presentation
regarding Copernicus' time in Toruń, with a
model of the town.

Explorers' Museum MUSEUM

(Muzeum Podróżników; Map p334; www.muzeum. torun.pl; ul Franciszkańska 11; adult/concession 12/9zł; ☉10am-4pm Tue-Sun Oct-Apr, to 6pm May-Sep) This is usually the last subdivision of the Regional Museum on visitors' mental itineraries, which is a shame as it tells an interesting story. It contains artefacts from the amassed collection of seasoned nomad Tony Halik (1921–98), including his battered suitcases, travel documents, souvenirs of his many journeys and a criminal number of pilfered hotel keys! One of his longest journeys was a 180,000km epic from Tierra del Fuego to Alaska.

More recent additions to the collection have been donated by his wife, Elżbieta Dzikowska, who continues to travel, most notably in Asia. There's also a room dedicated to some of history's greatest explorers (Captain Cook, Marco Polo etc) and another to famous Polish wanderers.

St Mary's Church CHURCH

(Kościół NMP; Map p334; ul Panny Marii; ☉7am-8pm) Toruń's third great Gothic structure in the Old Town (after the Town Hall and Cathedral) is St Mary's Church, erected by the Franciscans at the end of the 13th century. Austere and plain from the outside, the highly strung interior has tall, slender, intricate stained-glass windows, painted Gothic vaulting and a prominent golden altarpiece.

Eskens' House MUSEUM

(Dom Eskenów; Map p334; www.muzeum.torun. pl; ul Łazienna 16; adult/concession 12/9zł, 3D Book of Toruń 12/8zł, combined ticket 19/14zł; ☉10am-6pm Tue-Sun May-Sep, to 4pm Oct-Apr) The impressive Gothic House of the Esken family, set behind the cathedral, was converted into a granary in the 19th century. It contains city history displays on the 1st floor, and a collection of medieval weaponry and archaeological exhibits from the Iron and Bronze Ages on the 2nd floor. Also see the Book of Toruń, a 14-minute 3D film on the city's history.

House Under the Star MUSEUM

(Kamienica Pod Gwiazdą; Map p334; www. muzeum.torun.pl; Rynek Staromiejski 35; adult/ concession 12/9zł; ☉10am-6pm Tue-Sun May-Sep, to 4pm Oct-Apr) The House Under the Star is a chunk of madly stuccoed architectural confectionery embellishing the Main Square. Inside you'll discover an outpost of the Regional Museum, with a small but elegant collection of Asian art, including Japanese swords, Indian statues and Chinese pottery from the Tang dynasty.

Toruń

Gingerbread Museum MUSEUM

(Muzeum Toruńskiego Piernika; Map p334; www. muzeum.torun.pl; ul Strumykowa 4; adult/ concession 12/9zł; ☉10am-6pm Tue-Sun May-Sep, to 4pm Oct-Apr) Not to be confused with the commercial Gingerbread Museum (p336) across town, this branch of the Toruń Regional Museum is housed in a former gingerbread factory and looks at the 600-year-long history of the city's favourite sweet. You also get the chance to make your own gingerbread using dough prepared to the original recipe.

CITY DEFENCES

Lost count of the museum's myriad branches? Teeth aching from too much gingerbread? Could be time to take a break and stroll the remnants of the town's original medieval fortifications, a popular activity with (for the most part) no admission to pay. Take a picnic if the weather's good.

To the east, in a triangle squeezed between the Old and New Towns, are the **ruins of the castle** (Map p334; www.ckzamek.torun.pl; ul Przedzamcze; adult/concession 10/6zł; ☉10am-6pm), built by the Teutonic Knights. It was destroyed by the town's inhabitants in 1454 as a protest against the order's economic restrictions (they must have been really miffed – those Teutonic castles were quite sturdy).

Following the old city walls west from the castle, you'll come to the first of three surviving city gates, the **Bridge Gate** (Brama Mostowa; Map p334; Mostowa). A 700m-long bridge was built here between 1497 and 1500 and survived for over three centuries. Continue along the walls to find the other two gates: the **Sailors' Gate** (Brama Żeglarska; Map p334; Żeglarska) and the **Monastery Gate** (Brama Klasztorna; Map p334; Ducha Świętego). At the far western end are a few gentrified **medieval granaries** (Map p334; ul Rabiańska) and the **Crooked Tower** (Krzywa Wieża; Map p334; Pod Krzywą Wieżą).

STRANGE STATUARY

Toruń's main square is furnished with a number of interesting pieces of statuary, but relatively few locals know the stories behind them.

Starting a few steps from the Old Town Hall entrance, the **statue of Copernicus** (Map p334; Rynek) is one of the oldest monuments dedicated to the stargazer and a regular feature in holiday snaps.

West of the Town Hall, opposite the post office, is an intriguing small **fountain** (Map p334; Rynek) dating from 1914. Bronze-cast frogs sit on its rim, admiring a statue of a violin-playing boy known as Janko Muzykant, Toruń's very own answer to the Pied Piper. Legend has it that a witch once came to the town, but wasn't welcomed by the locals. In revenge, she invoked a curse, and the town was invaded by frogs. The mayor offered a sackful of gold and his daughter to anyone who would rescue the town. A humble peasant boy then appeared and began to play his rustic fiddle and the frogs, enchanted by the melody, followed him to the woods and the town was saved.

On the opposite side of the Rynek, at the corner of ul Chełmińska, you'll find another curious critter-related statue at knee-level, depicting **a dog and an umbrella** (Map p334; ul Chełmińska). The pooch's name is Filus; he starred in a famous long-running Polish comic strip as the pet of brolly-wielding Professor Filutek.

The **bronze donkey** (Map p334; Rynek Staromiejski) in the southeast corner (dubbed the 'brass ass' by some Americans) has a much more sinister story attached. Few tourists straddling its back are aware that this is actually a copy of a wooden donkey that stood here in medieval times, to which criminals were strapped and flogged.

Ethnographic Museum
MUSEUM

(Muzeum Etnograficzne; www.etnomuzeum.pl; Wały Sikorskiego 19; adult/concession 12/7zł; ⊙10am-6pm Tue & Thu-Sun, 9am-4pm Wed Jul & Aug, shorter hours rest of year) The thatched cottages in parkland to the north of the city centre aren't relics from some former age, but belong to this undervisited museum of rural life. It's quite a surreal experience to wander the quiet lanes of barns and windmills, the bustle of the city centre all around a distant murmur.

Gingerbread Museum
MUSEUM

(Muzeum Piernika; Map p334; ☑56 663 6617; www.muzeumpiernika.pl; ul Rabiańska 9; adult/concession 17/12zł; ⊙10am-6pm, tours every hour on the hour) Learn about the history of Toruń gingerbread and create a spicy concoction of your own under the enlightened instruction of a mock-medieval gingerbread master. All of this takes place in a renovated 16th-century gingerbread factory. Tours in English and German at 1pm and 4pm only; best to book in advance on the website.

⚘ Festivals & Events

Jazz Odnowa
MUSIC

(www.jazz.umk.pl; ⊙Feb) One of Poland's top jazz festivals featuring local and international artists.

Probaltica Music & Art Festival of Baltic States
MUSIC

(www.probaltica.art.pl; ⊙May) Classical music and opera festival attracting performers from across the Baltic region.

Toruń Days
CARNIVAL

(www.visittorun.pl) Big city festival that runs throughout June but climaxes on the 24th.

🛏 Sleeping

Toruń Główny Hostel
HOSTEL €

(☑60 656 4600; www.hosteltg.com; Toruń Główny train station; dm/d 39/70zł; 🛜) This hostel is housed in the old post-office building right on the platform at Toruń's main train station with attractive wall paintings of the Old Town. The six- and eight-bed dorms are spacious with suitcase-size lockers and reading lamps; free breakfast is served in the basement kitchen. Downsides include train noise (surprise!) and only one shower per floor.

Fort IV
HOSTEL €

(☑56 655 8236; www.fort.torun.pl; ul Chrobrego 86; dm 30-45zł, s/d from 50/100zł; 🛜) Toruń is encircled by the ruins of 19th-century forts, but this is the only one to house guests for the night in basic rooms. Rooms and dorms come with and without bathrooms; there's also a guest kitchen. Take bus 14 to the end of the line. Due to the location this is often a last resort so bargains are available.

Dom Turysty PTTK　　　　　HOSTEL €

(☑56 622 3855; www.pttk.torun.pl; ul Legionów 24; s/d from 60/90zł; ☎) The 65-bed PTTK hostel is in a residential house, a 10-minute walk north of the Old Town with 24-hour reception and a snack bar. Rooms are simple but clean and functional.

★**Hotel Spichrz**　　　　　HOTEL €€

(Map p334; ☑56 657 1140; www.spichrz.pl; ul Mostowa 1; s/d from 250/310zł; ❄☎) Wonderfully situated within a historic waterfront granary, this hotel's 19 rooms are laden with personality, featuring massive exposed beams above characterful timber furniture and contemporary bathrooms. The location by the river is within walking distance of the sights but away from the crowds. The hotel's Karczma Spichrz restaurant serves traditional Polish cuisine.

Hotel Heban　　　　　HOTEL €€

(Map p334; ☑56 652 1555; www.hotel-heban.com. pl; ul Małe Garbary 7; s/d 150/180zł; P☎) Atmospherically billeted in a prettily gabled townhouse in a quiet street, the Heban has a floral-themed restaurant, a relaxing and stylish lounge in olive green and 22 light and airy rooms dotted with antique reproductions. One of Toruń's most pleasant places to stay and without a hefty price tag.

Hotel Gotyk　　　　　HOTEL €€

(Map p334; ☑56 658 4000; www.hotel-gotyk.com. pl; ul Piekary 20; s/d 180/220zł; ☎) This beautifully restored townhouse hotel is a good choice for those who like some historical character. Passing the suit of armour in the foyer, head up green carpeted stairs to find individually decorated rooms, some with heavy classic antique furniture. Some rooms could do with a bit of an update, but all in all it's a great place to stay.

Hotel Petite Fleur　　　　　HOTEL €€

(Map p334; ☑56 621 5100; www.petitefleur.pl; ul Piekary 25; s/d from 210/270zł; ❄☎) One of the better midrange options in town, this place is full of historic character with an antique lobby, and understated rooms with timber-beam ceilings and elegant prints, though the singles can be small and dark, and there's no lift. The French brick-cellar restaurant is one of Toruń's better dining options and the buffet breakfast is a delight.

Hotel Kopernik　　　　　HOTEL €€

(☑56 659 7333; www.amwhotele.pl; ul Wola Zamkowa 16; r 90-230zł; P☎) This former army hostel has long been a favourite among travellers to Toruń and continues to offer a great deal on the eastern edge of the Old Town. Rooms are basic with pine furniture and cheap carpets, and bathrooms are standard-issue, but staff are superb and the no-frills breakfast taken in the basement provides a filling set-up for the day.

Hotel Pod Orłem　　　　　HOTEL €€

(Map p334; ☑56 622 5025; www.podorlemtorun. pl; ul Mostowa 17; s/d 130/170zł; P☎) The Pod Orłem is one of Toruń's oldest hotels, with a history going back more than a century. Leather-padded doors open onto some pretty spacious rooms; the cheaper ones are strangely like staying in your grandma's spare room. Buffet breakfast is an extra 21zł.

Hotel Pod Czarną Różą　　　　　HOTEL €€

(Map p334; ☑56 621 9637; www.hotelczarnaroza. pl; ul Rabiańska 11; s/d from 180/220zł; ☎) 'Under the Black Rose' has both a historic inn and a newer wing facing the river, though its interiors present a uniformly clean, up-to-date look with the odd antique reproduction. Buffet breakfast included.

✖ Eating

There's a good selection of restaurants and cafes on the main square and in neighbouring side streets. The local speciality is *Toruńskie pierniki* (Toruń gingerbread), made here for 700 years. It is sold in various patterns, the most popular being the six-lobed *Katarzynki*. It also appears as dessert on restaurant menus, usually served with plum sauce *(piernik z sosem śliwkowym)*.

Bar Małgośka　　　　　CAFETERIA €

(Map p334; ul Szczytna 10; meals around 20zł; ☉9am-7pm Mon-Fri, to 4pm Sat & Sun May-Sep, shorter hours weekdays Oct-Apr) Large, cheap and popular milk bar where all of Poland's filling staples are present, correct and ladled out by grumpy dinner ladies. Always a free table, even when invaded by three huge school groups at once. Serves coffee.

Cafe Lenkiewicz　　　　　CAFE €

(Map p334; www.lenkiewicz.net; Wielkie Barbary 14; ☉9am-7pm; ☎) Toruń's top ice-cream and gateau halt, best in summer when things spill out onto the pedestrianised street.

Bar Mleczny　　　　　CAFETERIA €

(Map p334; ul Różana 1; meals around 15zł; ☉9am-6pm Mon-Fri, 10am-5pm Sat & Sun) This very popular milk bar offers substantial Polish stodge for a fistful of złoty amid token gentrification. The outdoor window serves waffles, ice cream and *zapiekanki* (Polish pizza).

Oberża
POLISH €

(Map p334; ☑ 56 622 0022; www.facebook.com/oberzatorun; ul Rabiańska 9; mains 8-17zł; ⊙11am-10pm Mon-Thu, to midnight Fri & Sat, to 9pm Sun; 🗟) This self-service cafeteria stacks 'em high and sells 'em cheap for a hungry crowd of locals and tourists. Find your very own thatched minicottage or intimate hideout amid stained-glass windows, cartwheels, bridles and other rustic knick-knacks and enjoy 11 types of pierogi, soups, salads and classic Polish mains from a menu tuned to low-cost belly-packing.

Sznyt na Winklu
POLISH €€

(Map p334; ☑56 470 8957; www.sznytnawinklu.com; ul Kopernika; mains 24-40zł; ⊙11am-11pm daily; 🗟) Done out like a 19th-century tavern – all bent-wood chairs, old typewriters and analogue phones – this recent addition to Toruń's eating scene offers a meat-heavy menu of Polish favourites plus lots of ethanol-based beverages. Cosy corner setting for dinner and drinks.

Smaki Ukrainy
UKRAINIAN €€

(Map p334; ul Łazienna 26; mains 16-25zł; ⊙11am-9pm Mon-Thu, to 10pm Fri & Sat; 🗟) Not a slap from a burly Gastarbeiter from the east but a neat, central Ukrainian cafe catering for Toruń's numerous Ukrainian community for whom it dishes up staples such as cabbage rolls, *pelmeny* (ravioli), pancakes, *halushki* (dumplings) and filling soups.

Kuranty
INTERNATIONAL €€

(Map p334; Rynek Staromiejski 29; mains 15-40zł; ⊙11am-1am; 🗟) With leathery seating and lots of exposed wood, this place resembles a Victorian British boozer but with flat-screen TVs hanging from the bar. Big burgers, Polish mains and a list of pierogi filled with all types of foodstuffs inhabit the menu card.

★Szeroka 9
INTERNATIONAL €€€

(Map p334; ☑56 622 8424; www.szeroka9.pl; ul Szeroka 9; mains 35-50zł; ⊙noon-11pm Mon-Fri, from 10am Sat & Sun) 🍴 Arguably Toruń's top restaurant, this place offers a changing menu of seasonal gourmet fare ranging from pickled trout with horseradish to pig cheeks with creamed potato and marinated beetroot; the dessert to plump for is local gingerbread in plum sauce. The decor is contemporary urban and the staff are friendly and knowledgeable. Reservations recommended for dinner.

🍷 Drinking & Nightlife

★Jan Olbracht
MICROBREWERY

(Map p334; www.browar-olbracht.pl; ul Szczytna 15; ⊙11am-11pm Mon-Thu, to midnight Fri & Sat, to 10pm Sun) Take a seat in a barrel-shaped indoor booth or at the street-side terrace to sample some of this microbrewery's unusual beers. These include pils, wheat beer, a special ale and, this being Toruń, gingerbread beer, all brewed in the gleaming copper vats at the street end of the bar.

Atmosphera
CAFE

(Map p334; ul Panny Marii 3; ⊙11am-9pm Sun-Thu, to 10pm Fri & Sat) Try a gingerbread-flavoured coffee (*kawa po Toruńsku*) and a hefty wedge of cheesecake at this unassuming and very aromatic caffeine stop littered with odd tables and a jumble of chairs. Over 100 different kinds of tea, plus a global wine list.

Kona Coast Cafe
CAFE

(Map p334; ☑56 664 0049; www.konacoastcafe.pl; ul Chełmińska 18; ⊙9am-9pm Mon-Sat, 11am-6pm Sun; 🗟) Claims to be the only cafe in town that roasts its own beans. The coffee is decent as is the homemade lemonade, chai and various cold drinks. There's also a light-meal menu.

☆ Entertainment

Lizard King
LIVE MUSIC

(Map p334; ☑56 621 0234; www.lizardking-torun.pl; ul Kopernika 3; ⊙6pm-late Mon-Sat; 🗟) Live-music venue with gigs ranging from local tribute bands to major rock acts from Eastern and Central Europe.

Dwór Artusa
CLASSICAL MUSIC

(Map p334; ☑56 655 4929; www.artus.torun.pl; Rynek Staromiejski 6; ⊙box office noon-6pm Mon-Fri) The Artus Court, an impressive late-19th-century mansion overlooking the main square, houses a major cultural centre and has an auditorium hosting musical events, including concerts and recitals.

🔒 Shopping

Sklep Kopernik
FOOD

(Map p334; Rynek Staromiejski 6; ⊙9am-8pm Mon-Fri, from 10am Sat & Sun) *The* place to purchase Toruń's favourite gingerbread, housed in the Artus Court on the southern side of the main square.

Pierniczek
FOOD

(Map p334; ul Żeglarska 25; ⊙9am-8pm) Small shop selling gingerbread creations straight from the factory.

WORTH A TRIP

GOLUB-DOBRZYŃ

Golub's square-set **castle** (Zamek Golubski; ☎ 56 683 2455; www.zamekgolub.pl; Golub-Dobrzyń; adult/concession 12/10zł; ☉ 9am-7pm May-Sep, to 4pm Oct-Apr) overlooks the town from a hill, the prominent structure consisting of a massive Gothic brick base topped with a slightly more refined Renaissance cornice. The original 14th-century castle was converted into a Renaissance palace in the early 17th century during the tenure of its most famous resident, Princess Anna Waza, sister of Polish King Zygmunt III Waza.

The only way to see the castle's rather bare interiors is on an hour-long guided tour. Tagging along with a Polish group, the visit starts with a film then progresses into the various austere rooms housing modest ethnographical and archaeological exhibits. The Gothic architecture is pretty impressive, as are the views out across the town and the forests beyond.

The castle's upper floor houses some of the cheapest fortification accommodation in Poland. There are two standards on offer: one a basic **PTTK hostel** (☎ 56 683 2455; www.zamekgolub.pl; Zamek Golubski, Golub-Dobrzyń; hostel dm 60zł, hotel s/d 169/199zł; P 🛜) with dorm beds, the other consisting of hotel-type rooms. Rates are without breakfast but there's a restaurant and cafe downstairs.

Buses run regularly to/from Toruń (10zł, one hour).

ℹ️ Information

Main Post Office (Map p334; Rynek Staromiejski; ☉ 24hr) One of Poland's grandest post-office buildings stands on the site of a house where Napoleon once stayed.

Tourist Office (Map p334; ☎ 56 621 0930; www.it.torun.pl; Rynek Staromiejski 25; ☉ 9am-6pm Mon-Fri, from 10am Sat & Sun; 🛜) Free wi-fi access, heaps of info and professional staff who know their city.

ℹ️ Getting There & Away

BUS

Toruń bus station (Dworzec Autobusowy Toruń; ul Dąbrowskiego 8-24), close to the northern edge of the Old Town, handles services to the following.

Chełmno 11zł, 1½ hours, hourly
Gdańsk from 20zł, 2½ hours, hourly
Golub-Dobrzyń 10zł, 1¼ hours, hourly
Warsaw from 28zł, three to four hours, at least hourly

TRAIN

Toruń has two stations: Toruń Główny is about 2km south of the Old Town, on the opposite side of the Vistula, while the more convenient Toruń Miasto is on the Old Town's eastern edge. Not all services stop at both stations.

There are direct trains to the following.

Gdańsk 47zł, 2½ hours, four daily
Grudziądz 9.10zł, 1¼ hours, 10 daily
Kraków 62zł, 5¼ hours, one daily
Olsztyn 39zł, two hours, four daily
Warsaw from 50zł, 2¾ hours, hourly

ℹ️ Getting Around

Buses 22 and 27 (2.80zł) shuttle between Toruń Główny and the Plac Rapackiego stop on Aleja Jana Pawła II, just to the west of the historical centre.

Chełmno

POP 20,400

The most worthwhile day trip from Toruń, Chełmno (*heum*-no) is one of those enjoyably forgotten places that seems to lead a provincial life all of its own, with only occasional intrusions from the outside world. Its chipped and faded facades, slightly sooty air and old red-brick institutions belong to the Poland of two decades ago, its churches and impressively beefy ring of defensive walls originating from a medieval golden era.

Chełmno is at its best in summer when the old square and churches come to life. The places closes up over winter.

◎ Sights

Regional Museum　　　　　　　MUSEUM
(Muzeum Ziemi Chełmińskiej; www.muzeum chelmno.pl; Rynek 28; adult/concession 5/3zł; ☉ 10am-4pm Tue-Fri year-round, 10am-4pm Sat, 11am-3pm Sun Apr-Sep, 10am-3pm Sat Dec-Mar) The epicentre of Chełmno's chessboard of streets is the Rynek, in the middle of which stands the compact Renaissance Town Hall, built around 1570 on the site of the previous Gothic structure. It now houses the Regional Museum, whose collection traces the town's history, though the building's interior, including a spectacular courtroom, is equally distracting.

Church of the Assumption
CHURCH

(Kościół Wniebowzięcia NMP; ul Szkolna; ⊙7am-7pm) Just off the Rynek, this massive, Gothic church was commissioned by the Teutonic Knights in the late 13th century. The magnificent interior is crammed with ornate baroque and rococo furnishings, and also holds some supposed relics of St Valentine, patron saint of lovers, locked within the right-hand pillar as you face the altar (this has inevitably spawned an entire miniature tourist industry and a raft of marketing campaigns).

Miniature Castles of the Teutonic Knights
PARK

(Park Miniatur Zamków Krzyżackich; ul Podmurna; ⊙10am-7pm Mon-Sat, from 11am Sun) FREE Head south from the Grudziądz Gate through the park to find this open-air exhibition of nearby Teutonic knights' castles. All nine are depicted in their full glory (not the ruins they are today) with Toruń, Grudziądz and Malbork as well as six minor piles all re-created in medieval miniature.

City Walls
HISTORIC SITE

Chełmno is encircled by 2.2km of defensive walls, which have survived almost in their entirety. Alas, it's not possible to walk around the entire circumference via various gardens and the town's cemetery block the way. Walking along ul Dworcowa from the bus terminal, you'll enter the Old Town through the Grudziądz Gate (Brama Grudziądzka), the only surviving medieval gateway in the town's defences.

Church of SS John the Baptist & John the Evangelist
CHURCH

(Kościół Św Jana Chrzciciela i Jana Ewangelisty; ul Dominikańska; ⊙10am-noon & 1-5pm Mon-Sat, 1-5pm Sun) This church at the far western tip of the Old Town was built between 1266 and 1325 and has a richly gilded high altar with an ornate organ to the side. Underneath the organ is a black-marble tombstone from 1275, one of the oldest in the region. The church is part of the renovated Dominican and Benedictine convent – the nuns have returned, walking through the vista-rich garden behind the church with their rosaries in hand.

Church of SS Peter & Paul
CHURCH

(ul Wodna) Occupying the town's northern corner, the impressive red-brick stepped gable of this 14th-century church fronts an interior containing doored rococo stalls, a huge baroque altar straddled by a star-studded globe and the tomb of the first bishop of Chełmno, Heidenreich. Sadly, it's not open to the public very often.

Sleeping & Eating

Hotelik
HOTEL €

(☑56 676 2030; www.hotelik.info; ul Podmurna 3; s/d 100/150zł; 🛜) Located 60m to the right of the Grudziądz Gate as you enter the Old Town, this well-maintained half-timbered minihotel offers a jumble of good-value en-suite rooms, some small and cosy, others more spacious with antique elements.

Karczma Chełmińska
HOTEL €€

(☑56 679 0605; www.karczmachelminska.pl; ul 22 Stycznia 1b; s/d from 200/240zł; P🛜) This tourist-friendly courtyard hotel, in the southwestern corner of the Old Town, offers Chełmno's best-kept rooms with simple, uncluttered decor and bright, clean bathrooms. The courtyard restaurant, with waiters in traditional garb, serves up tasty fare including interesting seasonal specials. There's a supermarket nearby for room picnickers.

Cukiernia Staropolska
CAFE €

(Rynek 10; snacks from 2zł; ⊙8am-2.30pm Mon, to 4pm Tue-Fri, to 1pm Sat) Tiny bakery cafe on the main square filled with antiques and the aroma of freshly baked pastries and coffee. A lovely place to do breakfast if your hotel doesn't.

Restauracja Spichlerz
POLISH €€

(ul Biskupia 3; mains 8-30zł; ⊙10am-10pm Mon-Sat, from 11am Sun) Ask anyone in Chełmno where to head when it's feeding time and they'll point you in the direction of this pub-restaurant just off the Rynek. The fare is mostly Polish and hearty, the crowd a mix of vodka-swigging old-timers and beer-caressing youths.

ℹ Information

Tourist Office (☑56 686 2104; www.chelmno.pl; Ratusz, Rynek; ⊙8am-4pm Mon-Fri, from 10am Sat, 11am-3pm Sun, closed Mon Nov-May) In the museum entrance within the Town Hall.

ℹ Getting There & Away

Chełmno is 40km north of Toruń. Buses depart roughly hourly to/from Toruń (13zł, 1¼ hours) from the basic station 700m west of the Grudziądz Gate.

Grudziądz

POP 94,400

Grudziądz (*groo*-jonts), located some 30km down the Vistula River from Chełmno, probably doesn't have enough to warrant a special trip, but could be a minor diversion on the way between Toruń and Malbork. Some post-WWII renovation of the Old Town has been attempted and trams still trundle through the now-pretty main square, lending it atmosphere. The remainder of Grudziądz is made up of thundering motorways, communist-era blocks and scrappy streets of 19th-century tenements.

⊙ Sights

Regional Museum   MUSEUM
(www.muzeum.grudziadz.pl; ul Wodna 3/5; adult/concession 10/5zł, free Tue; ⊙10am-6pm Tue & Fri, to 4pm Wed & Thu, to 3pm Sat & Sun May-Sep, shorter hours Oct-Apr) Based in a former Benedictine convent and several granaries at the southern end of the old quarter, the Regional Museum is worth an hour or two's perusal. It provides a general overview of the town's history and also highlights several interesting themes. You will be handed meticulously from one curator to the next during your visit; the ticket is valid for all five sites.

The main building houses contemporary paintings from the region and other historical exhibitions, with further sections in the old granaries on local archaeology, the local Stomil rubber factory, cavalry uniforms and local sports hero, Olympic gold medalist Bronisław Malinowski (steeplechase, Moscow 1980), who died in a car accident on the bridge over the Vistula in 1981. His gold medal and the silver he won in Montreal in 1976 are on display and there's a film about his career.

Castle Hill   HILL
(Góra Zamkowa; ⊙tower 9am-8pm Tue-Sun Apr-Sep) FREE Grudziądz once had a 13th-century castle that stood sentinel high above the Vistula. The remains of this, essentially the 30m Klimek Tower and the results of an archaeological dig, have become the town's latest attraction following extensive renovation work. Climb to the top of the tower for stupendous views of the river, the town and Poland's longest concrete bridge below.

Granaries   HISTORIC BUILDING
(Spichrze; Spichrzowa) The extraordinary row of crumbling granaries was built along the length of the town's waterfront to provide storage and protect the town from invaders. Begun in the 14th century, they were gradually rebuilt and extended until the 18th century, and some were later turned into housing blocks by knocking through windows in the walls. These massive buttressed brick buildings – most of them six storeys high – are an impressive sight rising high above the Vistula.

Church of St Francis Xavier   CHURCH
(Kościół Św Franciszka Ksawerego; ul Kościelna; ⊙8am-8pm Mon-Thu, to 5.30pm Fri-Sun) A few buildings in the centre retain their historical significance, the most impressive of which is this early-18th-century church. Most of the narrow interior is taken up by a beautiful baroque high altar, and the surrounding ornamentation includes some unusual chinoiserie created by a local Jesuit monk in the late 17th century.

⟝ Sleeping & Eating

★**Hotel RAD**   HOTEL **€€**
(☑56 465 5506; www.hotelrad.pl; ul Chełmińska 144; s/d from 140/180zł; P) One of northern Poland's best deals, the plush but cheap RAD is on the Toruń road 2.5km south of the centre. Immaculate business-standard rooms have TV with English channels, superfast wi-fi and desks. The restaurant attracts wedding parties and travelling salespeople alike; the breakfast buffet is as good as anything in Western Europe. Take tram 3 to the Wiejska stop.

★**Kuchnia**   POLISH **€**
(ul Długa 2; mains 10-20zł; ⊙noon-7pm daily;) With its white tiles, bar made of palettes and painted brick walls, this trendy-looking place has a simple menu of well-cooked Polish favourites plus *kompot* (juice from cooked fruit) in jars, brain-reactivating coffee and outdoor seating on the main square. The menu changes daily but usually includes pierogi, soups, *naleśniki* (crêpes) and local *kluski* (dumplings).

ⓘ Information

Post Office (cnr uls Sienkiewicza & Mickiewicza; ⊙8am-8pm Mon-Fri, 10am-3pm Sat) One of Grudziądz's most attractive red-brick edifices.

Tourist Office (☑56 461 2318; www.it.gdz.pl; Rynek 3/5; ⊙8am-5pm Mon-Fri, 10am-2pm Sat May-Sep, 10am-2pm Sun Jul & Aug, shorter hours Oct-Apr)

❶ Getting There & Away

BUS

The bus station is a short walk north of the train station. Buses leave for the following.

Chełmno 10zł, one hour, two daily

Gdańsk 20 to 30zł, 1½ to three hours, three daily

Malbork 17.10zł, two hours, four daily

Toruń 18.50zł, 2½ hours, five daily

TRAIN

The postapocalyptic train station is about 1km southeast of the Old Town. It's a 15-minute walk or a quick trip on tram 1. Grudziądz has the following rail connections.

Toruń 9.10zł, 1¼ hours, seven daily

Kwidzyn

POP 37,800

Kwidzyn is a sleepy town that would be wholly unremarkable were it not for the presence of a mammoth Gothic castle and cathedral. Located 40km downriver from Grudziądz, it's yet another medieval stronghold of the Teutonic order and was formerly known as Marienwerder. Under the rule of German authorities for most of its history, the town became part of Poland after 1945.

◉ Sights

Kwidzyn Castle   CASTLE

(Zamek w Kwidzynie; ☑ 55 646 3780; www.zamek.
kwidzyn.pl; ul Katedralna 1; adult/concession 10/5zł, audio guide 6zł; ⊙ 9am-5pm Tue-Sun May-Sep, to 3pm Oct-Apr) Kwidzyn's 14th-century castle has experienced numerous ups and downs, suffering the most grievous loss in 1798 when the Prussians pulled down two sides (eastern and southern) and the main tower. Unlike many of its red-brick peers, it survived WWII unscathed. Most of the building now houses the Kwidzyn Museum, which has several sections, including displays on medieval sacred art, regional folk crafts and plenty of farming implements, as well as a display in the cellar detailing German-funded archaeological excavations.

Cathedral of St John   CHURCH

(ul Katedralna) The cathedral attached to the castle is the familiar Gothic brick blockbuster, which has a suitably defensive appearance thanks to its 19th-century tower. Look for the interesting ceramic mosaic (from around 1380) in the external wall above the southern porch. However the cathedral's biggest claim to fame is that it houses tombs of three Grand Masters of the Teutonic Order, discovered during excavations in 2007.

▭ Sleeping & Eating

Hotel Maxim   HOTEL €€

(☑ 72 844 0574; www.hotelmaxim.pl; ul Słowiańska 10; s/d 220/260zł; ℗ ⓢ) The pristine Maxim is the area's best hotel by far, offering 21st-century rooms, a very swanky restaurant and little extras such as a sauna and wifi that works. The location is good for both the stations and castle.

Hotel Centrum   HOTEL €€

(☑ 55 613 1366; www.centrumhotel.pl; ul Kopernika 32a; s 260-320zł, d 310-370zł; ℗ ⓢ) Shockingly clean-cut and trendily designed for rural Poland, these digs have 32 en-suite rooms and some of the best facilities you're likely to find outside the big tourist centres, including a better-than-average restaurant.

Bar Mleczny Leniwa Baba   CAFETERIA €

(☑ 60 976 4405; ul Tadeusza Kościuszki 49a; meals around 20zł) Few stick around long in Kwidzyn but for a quick lunch before hopping on the bus elsewhere, this milk bar near the station does the trick. Expect basic staples in a sterile setting and few smiles.

❶ Getting There & Away

The bus station is a 10-minute walk from the castle. Kwidzyn has the following bus services.

Grudziądz 14zł, 45 minutes, three daily

Malbork 8zł, 70 minutes, many daily

Malbork

POP 38,500

Around 30km southeast of Gdańsk, the quiet, rural town of Malbork would be bypassed by 99% of foreigners were it not for its astounding castle, one of the unmissables of any trip to Poland, and a stunning spectacle both inside and out. Top dog among Polish fortifications, the magnificent Unesco-listed structure is a classic example of a medieval fortress and Europe's largest Gothic castle to boot. The fortress is an easy day trip from Gdańsk by train. It's probably not worth overnighting here as there's precious little to Malbork other than its Gothic pile.

◎ Sights

★ **Malbork Castle** CASTLE
(Muzeum Zamkowe w Malborku; ☑ tickets 55 647 0978; www.zamek.malbork.pl; ul Starościńska 1; adult/concession 29.50/20.50zł; ⊙ 9am-7pm May-Sep, 10am-3pm Oct-Apr; P) Malbork's block-buster attraction is its show-stoppingly massive castle sitting on the banks of the sluggish Nogat River, an eastern arm of the Vistula. The construction of Marienburg (Fortress of Mary) was begun by the Teuton-ic Knights in the 13th century and was the headquarters of the order for almost 150 years; its vast bulk is an apt embodiment of its weighty history. Visits are by self-guided tour with audio guide. Allow at least three hours to do the place justice.

The immense castle took shape in stag-es. First was the so-called High Castle, the formidable central bastion that was begun around 1276. When Malbork became the capital of the order in 1309, the fortress was expanded considerably. The Middle Castle was built to the side of the high one, followed by the Lower Castle still further along. The whole complex was encircled by three rings of defensive walls and strength-ened with dungeons and towers. The castle eventually spread over 20 hectares, making it the largest fortress built anywhere in the Middle Ages.

The castle was seized by the Polish army in 1457, during the Thirteen Years' War, when the military power of the knights had started to erode. Malbork then became the residence of Polish kings visiting Pomerania, but from the Swedish invasions onwards it gradually went into decline. After the First Partition in 1772, the Prussians turned it into barracks, destroying much of the decoration and dismantling sections of no military use. In the 19th century the Marienburg was one of the first historic buildings taken under government protection, becoming a symbol of medieval German glory. Despite sustaining damage during WWII, almost the entire complex has been preserved, and the castle today looks much as it did six centu-ries ago, dominating the town and the sur-rounding countryside. The best view is from the opposite side of the river (you can get there via the footbridge), especially in the late afternoon when the brick turns an in-tense red-brown in the setting sun.

The visitor experience has been much improved recently with a new, chattier style of audio guide that works using GPS, a set route (no more getting lost and seeing only half the rooms) and several new exhibitions. The ticket office has left-luggage lockers, toi-lets and refreshments.

The entrance to the complex is from the northern side, through what used to be the only way in. From the main gate, you walk over the drawbridge, then go through five iron-barred doors to the vast courtyard of the **Middle Castle.**

On the western side (to your right) is the **Grand Masters' Palace**, which has some splendid interiors including the kitchen with its 6m-wide fireplace and the **Great Refecto-ry**, the largest chamber in the castle at 450 sq metres. The remarkable ceiling has its orig-inal palm vaulting preserved. Peek into the Grand Master's private loo before heading to the other side of the courtyard where there's a collection of period weapons and armour on display and an excellent **Amber Museum** – the latter would be a major place of interest in its own right, were it anywhere else. Amber was an important source of revenue for the Teutonic Knights – they controlled the entire Baltic coast where it is found. The tour then continues to **St Anne's Chapel** where 12 Grand Masters were buried.

The clever audio guide then leads you to the **High Castle**, over another drawbridge and through a gate to a spectacular arcaded **courtyard** that has a reconstructed well in the middle. This was the monastical part of the castle where monks would sit in session in the **Chapter House** before heading for their meat and mead in the striking **refec-tory**. The mock-up of the monks' **kitchen** is an aromatic affair with nary a potato or tomato in sight. Another memorable halt is the **gdaniska**, the knights' loo perched high atop its own special tower and connected to the castle by a walkway. Perhaps it was one of the order who coined the phrase 'long drop' as he reached for the cabbage leaves they used for toilet paper.

One of the most striking interiors here is **St Mary's Church**, accessed through a beautiful Gothic doorway, known as the **Golden Gate**. This is where the brothers would have met to pray every three hours, 24/7, but it was the part most damaged dur-ing the bombardment of 1945. Renovation ended in 2016, the walls left as bare brick as a powerful reminder of the Red Army shells.

Throughout the castle look out for the interesting **underfloor heating system** in many of the rooms and the little Gothic

GDAŃSK & POMERANIA MALBORK

MALBORK'S OTHER SIGHTS

Tourism in Malbork is dominated by the castle, but there are a couple of other sights worth seeking out. Returned to its original splendour in 2011, the town's **train station** is a riot of wood panelling, embossed ceilings, neo-Gothic broken arches and pseudo-medieval decor.

Skwer Esperanto near the Hotel Stary Malbork isn't much to look at, but around its edge are commemorative stones placed by keen international speakers of Esperanto from as far away as Korea and Congo, in honour of the world language invented by Ludwig Zamenhof. Each one bears the name of a tree in Esperanto, the tree usually planted nearby.

stucco figures pointing the way to the nearest WC. New **exhibitions** along the way examine conservation efforts over the last 200 years, oriental weaponry and Malbork under the Polish Crown.

🛏 Sleeping & Eating

Zajazd Karat   MOTEL €

(🖉55 272 8953; www.karat.malbork.net.pl; ul Boczna 2; s/d from 90/100zł; 🅿🅿❄🛜) The large well-furnished rooms at this motel on the main road heading west are Malbork's best deal and a good choice if you are driving. It's in walking distance of the castle (p343) and the town centre on the other side of the river. Rooms have fridges, breakfast is served at reception and parking is free.

Hotel Stary Malbork   HOTEL €€

(🖉55 647 2400; www.hotelstarymalbork.com.pl; ul 17 Marca 26/27; s 210-250zł, d 330-360zł; 🅿🛜) This graceful if somewhat basically furnished hotel offers airy, relaxing high-ceilinged rooms adorned with faux antique pieces. The singles have double beds and the very spacious deluxe doubles, costing just a fraction more than an ordinary room for two, are a quantum leap in comfort. There's a sauna, cafe and restaurant.

Hotel Grot   HOTEL €€

(🖉55 646 9660; www.grothotel.pl; ul Kościuszki 22d; s/d 199/289zł; 🅿🛜) British and Australian travellers may crack a smirk as they check into the Grot, but there's nothing unhygienic about this place. In fact, it's pretty classy for its price range, with contemporary furniture and spotless bathrooms. On the ground floor you'll find a snazzy restaurant.

Przystanek Patrzałkowie   INTERNATIONAL €

(🖉55 272 3991; ul Kościuszki 25; mains 10-22zł; ⊙11am-9pm Sun-Thu, to 10pm Fri & Sat; 🛜🖶) At the station end of town, this friendly, unpretentious cafe serves helpings of pizza, pasta, salads and an all-day breakfast to a mixed crowd of locals and tourists. The staff speak English and there's a kids' menu.

★**Gothic**   POLISH €€€

(🖉55 647 0889; www.gothic.com.pl; Malbork Castle, ul Starościńska 1; mains around 45zł; ⊙9am-8pm May-Sep, shorter hours Oct-Apr) Malbork's blockbuster castle (p343) also contains one of the area's best restaurants, where the medieval theme continues in commendable authenticity. Taking recipes and ingredients from the Grand Master's cookbook and shopping list (dating to 1399–1409), chef Bogdan Gałązka re-creates dishes the brothers would have enjoyed, with ingredients mainly from the Malbork area.

Bogdan also travels the world seeking out the very ingredients listed by the Grand Master's cooks: Stilton from England, saffron from Iran and dried fruit from the Middle East feature in some dishes. Some concessions are made to modern Polish tastes (yes, some dishes include potatoes and tomatoes). There's mead and excellent local beer to drink, plus a braille and children's menu. Reservations are essential, especially if you don't have a ticket to the castle.

🛈 Information

Tourist Office (🖉55 647 4747; www.visitmalbork.pl; ul Kościuszki 54; ⊙9am-5pm Mon-Fri, 10am-2pm Sat & Sun May-Sep, 9am-3pm Mon-Fri Oct-Apr; 🛜) Large welcome centre with free internet access (plus wi-fi hotspot), free left-luggage service and a library.

🛈 Getting There & Away

BUS

The bus station sits outside the train station. The following services are useful to visitors.

Grudziądz 17.10zł, two hours, four daily

Kwidzyn 6zł, one hour, hourly

TRAIN

The train station and bus terminal are at the eastern end of the town centre, 1km from the castle. Coming from Gdańsk by train, you'll catch a splendid view of the castle; watch out for your right when crossing the river.

Malbork sits on the busy Gdańsk–Warsaw railway route, and has services to the following destinations.

Elbląg 8.20zł, 25 minutes, at least hourly

Gdańsk 13.50zł, 30 to 50 minutes, two hourly

Olsztyn 23.60zł, two hours, every two hours

Warsaw 75 to 147zł, 2½ hours, at least hourly

Elbląg

POP 124,000

Few used to linger longer than a night in Elbląg (*el*-blonk), at one end of the Elbląg–Ostróda Canal, as boats moored long after it was possible to get anywhere else. However, in the 1990s the authorities decided to give canal navigators a reason to stay by rebuilding the Old Town, levelled by the Red Army in 1945. But instead of a painstakingly precise, budget-bustingly expensive rebuild, the new structures are computer-generated versions of what stood here before the shells began to fall. While full marks should be awarded for effort, the old-new streets are a touch sterile, lifeless and unfinished, leaving visitors with the impression that Elbląg is happening elsewhere (don't worry, it isn't). Work on the project seems to have stalled in the last decade but amid the stylised medieval gables in metal tubing and period-faithful plastic windows, some reminders of a more glorious red-brick past do survive.

◉ Sights

St Nicholas' Church   CHURCH

(Kościół Św Mikołaja; Stary Rynek; ☉ tower 10am-5pm Tue-Fri, to 2pm Sat, 2-5pm Sun) One blast from the past amid the evolving rebuild of the Old Town is this sturdy, red-brick island of true oldness, noted for its 95m-high, carefully reconstructed and now ascendable tower. Within, you'll find some of the original woodcarving, including several triptychs, which escaped war damage. On summer mornings the beautiful stained-glass windows speckle the marble floors with ecclesiastical disco light.

Elbląg Museum   MUSEUM

(www.muzeum.elblag.pl; Bulwar Zygmunta Augusta 11; adult/concession 10/8zł; ☉ 10am-6pm Tue-Sun Jun-Oct, 8.30am-3.30pm Tue-Sun Sep-Jun) A five-minute walk south along the riverbank is the Elbląg Museum. Occupying two large buildings, the museum has sections on archaeology and the town's history, plus a photographic record of Elbląg from the 19th century to WWII.

Galeria El   GALLERY

(www.galeria-el.pl; ul Kuśnierska 6; adult/concession 8/4zł; ☉ 10am-6pm Tue-Sat, to 5pm Sun) Some 200m to the north of **Market Gate** (Brama Targowa; Stary Rynek) `FREE` is Galeria El, formerly St Mary's Church. A massive Gothic brick structure, the original church was gutted and now houses a gallery of contemporary art, with occasional concerts and events. It's worth a visit just to see the imposing interior and the large modern-art objects dotting the grounds, including a monster supermarket trolley and some bashed cubes of XXL proportions.

🛏 Sleeping & Eating

Camping Nr 61   CAMPGROUND €

(☏ 55 641 8666; www.camping61.com.pl; ul Panieńska 14; per person/tent 14/6zł; ☉ May-Sep; 🛜) Elbląg's pleasantly shaded campground occupies an unusually convenient spot on the Elbląg River, close to the Old Town.

Hotel Sowa   HOTEL €€

(☏ 55 233 7422; www.sowa.elblag.biz.pl; ul Grunwaldzka 49; s 120-170zł, d 130-200zł; 🛜) This 75-bed option opposite the train and bus stations is basic but handy and inexpensive. There's a restaurant on the premises and a buffet breakfast is usually included.

Hotel Pod Lwem   HOTEL €€

(☏ 55 641 3100; www.hotelpodlwem.pl; ul Kowalska 10; s/d 250/330zł; P ❄ 🛜) Occupying one of Elbląg's old-new reconstructions, this design hotel is a stylish place to sleep after a trip on the canal. Room decor unites cream leather, dark wood and flurries of white punctuated with exclamations of colour, and the dominance of light tones makes some rooms feel bigger than they are. Buffet breakfast is taken in the smart cellar restaurant.

Studnia Smaków   POLISH €€

(☏ 60 622 3864; www.studniasmakow.pl; ul Studzienna 31a; mains 31-43zł; ☉ 9am-11pm Sun-Thu, to midnight Fri & Sat; 🛜 👶) Specialising in meat dishes such as local goose, pork knuckle and duck, this open-all-hours feeding spot tries to cater for everyone with a couple of token vegan options and a children's menu. The dining room is a woody, seasonally decorated affair, portions are on the generous side and the restaurant brews its own beer.

Dom Królów   INTERNATIONAL €€

(☏ 55 611 6695; www.hotelelblag.eu; Stary Rynek 54-59; mains 24-60zł; ☉ 6.30am-11pm Mon-Fri, from 7am Sat & Sun; ❄ 🛜) Within the luxury

GDAŃSK & POMERANIA ELBLĄG

Hotel Elbląg, the town's finest restaurant is overseen by chef Jacek Faltyn who cooks up Polish favourites as well as Argentine steak, Italian pastas and Indian curries to please the hotel's international business clientele. There's an expansive wine list and the inoffensive interior is Elbląg's most contemporary, all metal, greys and blacks with strategic splashes of colour.

ℹ Information

Tourist Office (☑ 55 239 3377; www.ielblag. eu; Stary Rynek 25; ⊙10am-6pm daily May-Sep, 8.30am-4.30pm Mon-Fri Oct-Apr) Inconspicuous office buried well out of sight in the town hall. In front of the entrance is an interesting model of Elbląg in its pre-WWII red-brick glory.

ℹ Getting There & Away

BOAT

Boats heading for the Elbląg–Ostróda Canal depart from the quay next to the Old Town. Information and tickets are available from **Żegluga Ostródzko-Elbląska** (☑ 89 670 9227; www. zegluga.com.pl; ul Wodna 1b), just back from the quay, or buy online.

BUS

The bus terminal is next to the train station 1km southeast of the centre. Buses run to the following.
Frombork 7zł, 40 minutes, several daily

Gdańsk 15zł, one hour, at least hourly
Warsaw 40zł, five hours, three daily

TRAIN
There are services to/from the following.
Gdańsk 17.10zł, 1½ hours, 12 daily or change in Malbork
Malbork 8.20zł, 25 minutes, at least hourly
Olsztyn 19.80zł, one hour 20 minutes, 10 daily

Frombork

POP 2400

Tucked away on the northeast edge of coastal Poland, just a few kilometres shy of Russia's Kaliningrad enclave, Frombork is actually in Warmia (we won't tell if you don't) but has transport links with Pomerania. Its impressive walled complex overlooking the tranquil town and the water beyond is what people come to see, and the town is an enjoyable day trip from Gdańsk.

Alighting from the bus on the main road, what looks like a castle above you is, in fact, a cathedral, established by the Warmian bishops in the 13th century. The complex is the main draw in Frombork, but the icing on the cake is its association with Nicolaus Copernicus. It was here that he spent the latter half of his life and conducted most of the observations and research for his heliocentric theory. Copernicus was buried in the cathedral.

BARGING IN

The rich forests of the Ostróda region have attracted merchants from Gdańsk and Elbląg since medieval times, yet until the 19th century the only way of getting timber down to the Baltic was a long water route along the Drwęca and Vistula Rivers via Toruń. Engineers considered building a canal as a short cut but quickly found that the terrain was rugged and too steep for conventional locks.

In 1836 Prussian engineer Georg Jakob Steenke (1801–82), from Königsberg, produced a sophisticated design for an Elbląg–Ostróda Canal incorporating slipways, but Prussian authorities rejected the project as unrealistic and too costly. Steenke didn't give up, however, and eventually succeeded in getting an audience with the king of Prussia. With typical kingly shrewdness, the monarch approved the plan, not because of its technical or economic aspects but because nobody had ever constructed such a system before.

The part of the canal between Elbląg and Miłomłyn, which included all the slipways, was built between 1848 and 1860, and the remaining leg to Ostróda was completed by 1872. The canal proved to be reliable and profitable, and it cut the distance of the original route along the Drwęca and Vistula almost fivefold. Various extensions were planned, including one linking the canal with the Great Masurian Lakes, 120km to the east, but none were ever built.

The canal was damaged during the 1945 Red Army offensive but was repaired soon after liberation and opened for timber transport in 1946. A year later, the first tourist boat sailed the route. It remains the only canal of its kind in Europe and continues to operate, though the timber boats are a distant memory.

◉ Sights

The Cathedral Hill complex (Wzgórze Katedralne) is today the Nicolaus Copernicus Museum. It covers several sights within the fortified complex, each visited on a separate ticket; the cathedral and the Old Bishops' Palace are the main two sights. The entrance is from the southern side through the massive Main Gate (Brama Główna), where you'll find the ticket office.

Old Bishops' Palace   MUSEUM
(Stary Pałac Biskupi; www.frombork.art.pl; adult/concession 8/4zł; ⊘9.30am-5pm Jul & Aug, 9am-4pm Sep-Jun) The museum's main exhibition space can be found in the southeastern corner of the complex, though the entrance can take a bit of finding. The ground floor is taken up with objects discovered during postwar archaeological excavations, stained glass and ecclesiastical treasures while the other levels are largely devoted to the life and work of Copernicus, along with temporary displays.

The most interesting section is on the 1st floor, where modern artists' interpretations of the great man, in sculpture and oils, are presented, before you pass into the room containing books and other artefacts from his time.

Though Copernicus is essentially remembered for his astronomical achievements (supplanting the old geocentric Ptolemaic system with his revelation that the earth revolves around the sun), his interests extended across many other fields, including medicine, economics and cartography. Apart from an early edition of his famous *De Revolutionibus Orbium Coelestium* (On the Revolutions of the Celestial Spheres), there are copies displayed of his treatises and manuscripts on a range of subjects, together with astronomical instruments and other scientific bric-a-brac. The exhibits are well lit and creatively placed, but English captioning is sadly lacking.

The 3rd floor is occupied by an easily skippable collection of religious art.

Cathedral   CHURCH
(www.muzeum.frombork.pl; adult/concession 9/6zł, during organ recital 13/11zł; ⊘9am-4.15pm, hours vary) Filling the middle of the courtyard with its huge Gothic-brick facade and with a slim octagonal tower at each corner, this impressive building was erected between 1329 and 1388, and was the largest church ever built by the Warmian bishops. So chuffed were they with the result that it

became a blueprint for most of the subsequent churches they founded across the region.

Frombork's cathedral certainly doesn't save the best until last: there it is, right in front of you as you enter the main door – the highlight of a visit for most – the tomb of Nicolaus Copernicus himself. Buried under the floor, his casket is visible through an illuminated glass panel.

The rest of the chilly, elongated main nave is cluttered with a riot of baroque altars and other 18th-century embellishment. Magnificent in powder blue, gold and silver, the organ, dating from 1683, is a replacement for the one nicked by the Swedes in 1626. The instrument is noted for its rich tone, best appreciated during recitals held daily at 11.30am, 1pm and 3pm Tuesdays to Saturdays in July and August and less frequently in May, June and September.

Water Tower   TOWER
(Wieża Wodna; ☑60 443 7500; www.wiezawodna.pl; ul Elbląska 2; adult/concession 7/5zł; ⊘11am-5pm) Across the main road from the cathedral, down in the town, this water tower was built in 1571 making it Europe's oldest. It was used for two centuries to provide Cathedral Hill with water through oak pipes – the pumping mechanism was made by none other than composer Handel's great grandfather! The admission fee gets you to the top and there's a cafe on the ground floor serving Frombork's best cakes.

On the way up the walls are lined with pictures of every castle and mansion in Warmia and Masuria, the jolly music of Handel piped throughout as you ascend slowly.

Planetarium   PLANETARIUM
(www.frombork.art.pl; adult/concession 10/6zł; ⊘9.30am-3pm daily) At the base of the belfry, the planetarium presents half-hour shows in Polish up to nine times daily. Get there at least 10 minutes before the shows start.

Copernicus Tower   TOWER
(adult/concession 9/5zł; ⊘9.30am-5pm) At the northwestern corner of the complex is this 14th-century tower (Wieża Kopernika), believed to be the place from which the astronomer took some of his observations.

Belfry   TOWER
(Dzwonnica; adult/concession 9/5zł; ⊘9.30am-5pm daily) The high tower at the southwestern corner of the defensive walls is the former cathedral belfry, which can be ascended for cracking views of Cathedral Hill, the town, and the Vistula Lagoon and Vistula Spit.

Hospital of the Holy Ghost MUSEUM
(adult/concession 8/4zł; ⊙9.30am-5pm Tue-Sat) The 15th-century Hospital of the Holy Ghost, formerly St Anne's Chapel, contains exhibitions of religious art and medical history. It's a short and well-signposted walk east of the cathedral.

🛏 Sleeping & Eating

Camping Frombork CAMPGROUND €
(📞50 680 3151; www.campingfrombork.pl; ul Braniewska 14; per person/tent 15/10zł, d from 130zł; ⊙May-Oct; 🅿🛜) Privately owned summer campground at the eastern end of town, on the Braniewo road, with comfortable holiday cottages, kayak hire and a games room.

Hotel Kopernik HOTEL €€
(📞55 243 7285; www.hotelkopernik.com.pl; ul Kościelna 2; s/d from 140/180zł; 🅿🛜) The incongruously recent-looking Hotel Kopernik has 42 neat rooms that exude early millennial optimism – all citrus walls and cheap-but-sturdy furniture. Some rooms have cathedral views. There's a budget restaurant occupied most evenings by the mostly German residents of the hotel. The Teutonic guests also guarantee the breakfast spread is a good one. No English spoken.

Restauracja Akcent POLISH €€
(www.restauracja-akcent.com; ul Rybacka 4; fish per 100g 5.60-10.60zł, pierogi 13-15.50zł; ⊙10am-11pm; 🛜) An alternative to the town's hotel restaurants, this decent place offers an honest menu of fish sold per 100g and pierogi. The outdoor summer marquee has views of the cathedral.

❶ Information

Tourist Office (📞55 244 0677; www.frombork. pl; Młynarska 5a; ⊙8.30am-4.30pm Mon-Sat Jul & Aug, 8am-4pm Jun, shorter hours & closed Sat Sep-May) Relatively new municipal office in the town hall.

❶ Getting There & Away

Buses running between Elbląg (7zł, 40 minutes, hourly) and Braniewo stop on the main drag through town, just below Cathedral Hill.

Just north of the station is the marina; from here pleasure boats run by Żegluga Gdańska (www.zegluga.pl) operate daily to Krynica Morska (return adult/concession 42/31zł, 1½ hours).

WORTH A TRIP

WOLIN NATIONAL PARK

Best accessed from the resort of Międzyzdroje, **Wolin National Park** (Woliński Park Narodowy; www.wolinpn.pl) FREE occupies the central section of Wolin Island. With a total area of about 50 sq km, it's one of the smaller Polish parks, yet it's picturesque enough to warrant a day or two's walking.

The park's northern edge drops sharply into the sea, forming an 11km-long sandy cliff nearly 100m high in places.

Back from the coast are a number of lakes, mostly on the remote eastern edge of the park. The most beautiful is the horseshoe-shaped Lake Czajcze. There's Lake Turkusowe (Turquoise), named after the colour of its water, at the southern end of the park, and lovely Lake Gardno close to the seashore, next to the Międzyzdroje–Dziwnów road. The lakes are surrounded by mixed forest, with beech, oak and pine predominating. The flora and fauna is relatively diverse, with rich birdlife. The last wild bison in Pomerania were wiped out in the 14th century, but there's a small bison reserve inside the park, 2km east of Międzyzdroje.

The best way to explore the park is by hiking, and the small area means a good walk needn't be too taxing. Three marked trails wind into the park from Międzyzdroje. The red trail leads northeast along the shore, then turns inland to Wisełka and continues through wooded hills to the small village of Kołczewo. The green trail runs east across the middle of the park, skirts the lake and also ends in Kołczewo. The blue trail goes to the southern end of the park, passing Lake Turquoise on the way. It then continues east to the town of Wolin.

All the trails are well marked and easy. Get a copy of the detailed *Woliński Park Narodowy* map (scale 1:30,000), and consult the park headquarters in Międzyzdroje for further information.

NORTHERN & WESTERN POMERANIA

Stretching northwest from Gdańsk, the Baltic coast is Poland's top summer-holiday strip. It may not be as well known as Spain's Costa del Sol, but this coastline of dunes, pine woods and coastal lakes, fronted by pristine white sandy beaches, is very attractive, especially in summer.

The numerous resort towns extending all the way from Hel to Świnoujście are engaging places to spend some time. Often blessed with historic architecture, they also contain pleasant, green parks and a good mix of restaurants, bars and other diversions. Outside the urban centres, there are also two interesting national parks on the Pomeranian coast.

As you move around, you'll notice that northern and western Pomerania is basically a rural, sparsely populated region, with compact towns and little industry. This blend of natural beauty with the delights of low-key resort towns makes it a pleasing region to explore, whatever the season.

Łeba

POP 3700

Summer in Łeba (weh-bah) brings Polish and German holidaymakers by the busload, who create a relaxed, good-humoured buzz as they stroll the streets, eat out and enjoy the amusements that spring up to keep them diverted. Outside high season, this small fishing port slams the shutters and hunkers down to survive another long Baltic winter.

Most come here for the generous expanse of wide sandy beach and clean water for swimming. The town is also within day-trip distance from Gdańsk, while the attractive Słowiński National Park (p350) is within walking distance.

🛏 Sleeping & Eating

Camping Nr 41 Ambré   CAMPGROUND €
(☑ 59 866 2472; www.ambre.leba.info; ul Nadmorska 9a; per adult/tent 17/14zł, bungalows 280-560zł; 🛜) This camping ground has a handy range of rooms, a restaurant and delicatessen, and neat, cared-for grounds and facilities.

Hotel Gołąbek   HOTEL €€
(☑ 59 866 2175; www.hotel-golabek.com; ul Wybrzeże 10; s/d from 240/360zł; 🅿🛜) It may be named after a cabbage roll (actually the owner's surname), but the Gołąbek exudes

style on the edge of the wharf, with charming old fishing boats and port views. Having undergone a refit in recent years, the bright, cheerful rooms, a sauna, solarium and waterfront restaurant all make this a great deal. Booking ahead in summer is essential.

⭐**Hotel Neptun**   HOTEL €€€
(☑ 59 866 1432; www.neptunhotel.pl; ul Sosnowa 1; s/d from 360/440zł; 🅿🛜🏊) One of the finest places to lay your head by the Baltic, the 32 rooms at this early-20th-century beachside villa are studies in understated elegance, all antique-style furniture, regency wall coverings and multipillowed beds. The highlight is the terrace pool area overlooking the beach, and a bar where sunsets and sundowners can be enjoyed simultaneously. Rates nosedive when temperatures do.

ℹ Information

Tourist Office (☑ 59 866 2565; www.lotleba. pl; ul 11 Listopada 5a; ⏰ 9am-5pm Mon-Fri, 10am-2pm Sat Jul & Aug, shorter hours & closed Sat Sep-Jun)

ℹ Getting There & Away

The usual transit point to/from Łeba is Lębork, 29km to the south, which is well connected to the Tri-City area by SKM services. Trains to/from Lębork (5.50zł, 40 to 50 minutes) depart eight times daily in summer. Buses and minibuses (8zł, 35 minutes) do the run considerably more regularly.

Słowiński National Park

A big attraction for nature lovers on the Pomeranian coast, the 186-sq-km Słowiński National Park extends for 33km between Łeba and Rowy. The park is mostly made up of lakes, the two largest being Łebsko and Gardno, both encircled by peat bog, meadows and woods. All of the lakes are shallow lagoons that started life as bays and were gradually cut off from the sea by the sandbar. With densely overgrown, almost inaccessible marshy shores, they provide a habitat for about 250 species of birds, which live here either permanently or seasonally. Large parts of the lakeshores have been made into strict no-access reserves, safe from human interference. By far the best time to come here is in late spring and summer. In 1977 the park was placed on Unesco's list of World Biosphere Reserves.

⦿ Sights

Shifting Dunes
DUNES

The most unusual feature of the national park is the shifting dunes *(wydmy ruchome)*, which create a genuine desert landscape. They're on the sandbar separating the sea from Lake Łebsko, about 8km west of Łeba. Rommel's Afrika Korps trained in this desert during WWII, and the site was also a secret missile-testing ground from 1940 to 1945.

The dunes are easily reached from Łeba: take the road west to the hamlet of Rąbka (2.5km), where there's a car park and the gate to the **national park** (Słowiński Park Narodowy; www.slowinskipn.pl; adult/concession 6/3zł May-Sep, free Oct-Apr; ⦿7am-9pm May-Sep, 8am-4pm Oct-Apr). Private minibuses, open-sided electric cars and motorised trains ply this road in summer, from a stop on al Wojska Polskiego, north of the canal. It's also an easy walk.

The sealed road continues into the park for another 3.5km to the site of the rocket launcher, now an **outdoor museum**. From here a wide path goes on through the forest for another 2km to the southern foot of the dunes, where half-buried trees jut out of the sand. As you walk round the bend from the woods, it's quite a sight – the pale, immense dunes open up in front of you like a desert dropped into the middle of a forest, with a striking contrast at the line where the trees meet the sand. Continue up the vast dunes for a sweeping view of desert, lake, beach, sea and forest.

No cars or buses are allowed beyond the car park. You can walk to the dunes (45 minutes), buy a ticket on one of the small electric cars or rent a bicycle (per hour/day 10/40zł). Coming back, you can either retrace your steps or walk to Łeba along the beach (8km), perhaps stopping for a swim – something you certainly can't do in the Sahara.

Lake Łebsko
NATIONAL PARK

About 16km long and 71 sq km in area, Lake Łebsko is the biggest in Pomerania and the third largest in Poland, after Śniardwy and Mamry in Masuria. It's steadily shrinking as a result of the movement of the dunes, the growth of weeds and silting.

Kluki Skansen
MUSEUM

(☑59 864 3020; www.muzeumkluki.pl; Kluki 27; adult/concession 16/10zł; ⦿11am-3pm Mon, 10am-6pm Tue-Sun May-Aug, shorter hours Sep-Apr) Set on the southwestern shore of Lake Łebsko, the tiny isolated hamlet of Kluki was the last holdout of Slovincian culture, now showcased in the centrally located skansen, an open-air museum of traditional architecture. It's modest but authentic, comprising original in-situ buildings. The long, two-family, whitewashed houses are fitted with traditional furniture and decorations.

Smołdzino
VILLAGE

West of Kluki, outside the park boundaries, is the village of Smołdzino, with a fine **Natural History Museum** (Muzeum Przyrodnicze; Mostnika 1, Smołdzino; adult/concession 4/2zł; ⦿9am-5pm May-Sep, 7.30am-3.30pm Mon-Fri Oct-Apr) that features flora and fauna from the park's various habitats.

Just 1km southwest of the village is **Mt Rowokół**, the highest hill in the area at 115m above sea level. On its top is a 20m **observation tower**, providing sweeping views over the forest, lakes and sea. The path up the hill begins near the petrol station; you can get to the top in 15 minutes.

ⓘ Getting There & Away

The jumping off points for the national park are the villages of Kluki and Smołdzino, accessible by bus from Słupsk.

Słupsk

POP 91,000

Sometimes it's the anonymous, unpromising names on the map that turn out to be the most charming halts, and that certainly could be said of Słupsk (pronounced 'swoopsk'). A regional service centre with a country town pace, Słupsk has everything that makes a small Polish town just that, with its milk bar, PKP, PKS, PTTK and even a branch of Cepelia all in place. Wide 19th-century avenues lined with mature trees and park benches create an easygoing feel; throw in a touch of architectural and artistic interest and you have a pleasant alternative to the busier centres on the coast, as well as a handy base between Gdańsk and Szczecin for flits to the seaside resorts of Darłowo and Ustka.

⦿ Sights

★ Witkacy Gallery
GALLERY

(www.muzeum.slupsk.pl; Szarych Szeregów 12; ⦿11.30am-3.30pm Mon, 10.30am-6pm Tue-Sun Apr-Sep, 10am-4pm Wed-Mon Oct-Mar) Opened in

2019 in the renovated White Granary building, the 250-piece collection of portraits by Stanisław Ignacy Witkiewicz (1885–1939), aka Witkacy, are the unrivalled highlight of Słupsk's museum. Witkacy was a controversial writer, photographer and painter who specialised in weird-and-wonderful portraits that he produced in a drugged state at his 'portrait company'. Słupsk has no connection to the artist – the museum bought 110 of the pastels from the son of Witkacy's doctor and friend from Zakopane in the 1960s.

Some 40 more were added in the 1970s, this time coming mainly from the artist's dentist. Around 125 are displayed at any one time and the exhibition is changed every few months. The body of work is fascinating, Witkacy having captured the essence of his subjects, sometimes to grotesque effect.

Museum of Central Pomerania   MUSEUM

(www.muzeum.slupsk.pl; ul Dominikańska 5-9; adult/concession 16/10zł, valid for museum & mill; ⊙11am-3pm Mon, 10am-6pm Tue-Sun Jul & Aug, shorter hours & closed Mon Sep-Jun) The Museum of Central Pomerania is housed within Słupsk's main attraction, a commanding 16th-century castle. Beyond its impressive blocky tower are sacral woodcarvings, historic furniture and other exhibits illustrating the town's history. A fascinating exhibition on the ground floor looks at the town's history in drawings, photographs and old postcards from Stolp, its German name. The main building used to house the town's priceless Witkacy exhibition but this was moved to new premises in 2019.

Ticket includes entry to the Mill.

Mill   MUSEUM

(ul Dominikańska; entrance with museum ticket; ⊙10am-3pm Mon, to 6pm Tue-Sun) The building opposite the castle gate is the 14th-century mill, an annex to the museum. Its three floors focus on the folk customs of Pomerania with colourful costumes and chunky kitchenware galore. There's also an exhibition looking at the 1.7 million Poles who arrived in the area from the Polish-speaking territories of the east during the 20th century.

St Mary's Church   CHURCH

(ul Nowobramska; ⊙6.30am-7pm) Fans of red brick and stained glass should check out this chunky Gothic church with its vibrantly coloured, postwar windows and oddly painted vaulting. Come on Sunday to see what a queue to get into a church looks like!

Town Hall   HISTORIC BUILDING

(Plac Zwycięstwa; adult/concession 5/3zł; ⊙10am-3pm Mon-Fri, to 2pm Sat & Sun mid-Jun–Sep, shorter hours & closed Sun rest of year) The elaborate Renaissance-Gothic town hall has an impressive main tower, which can be ascended for a full Słupsk panorama.

Baltic Gallery of Contemporary Art   GALLERY

(www.bgsw.pl; ul Partyzantów 31a; ⊙10am-6pm Mon-Fri) The main building of Słupsk's gallery specialises in short-term exhibits of Polish and international artists. Over 30 exhibitions take place here a year so the chances of seeing something interesting are high.

St Hyacinthus' Church   CHURCH

(Kościół Św Jacka; ul Dominikańska 3) The 15th-century St Hyacinthus' Church, aka St Jack's as the tourist signposting would have it, is usually closed, though you can now peek in through a low glass window in the entrance to see the 20th-century stained glass and Gothic vaulting. Otherwise sneak in during a service or attend a summer organ concert, normally held midweek in July and August.

Witches' Tower   HISTORIC BUILDING

(Baszta Czarownic; Al F Nullo 8; ⊙10am-6pm Tue-Sun) Only three remnants of the 15th-century fortified walls that once encircled the town survive: one of these is the Witches' Tower, which had a sensational career as a 17th-century jail for women suspected of witchcraft; in total, 18 women were executed here up until 1714. Nowadays the tower houses temporary exhibitions for the Baltic Gallery of Contemporary Art.

WISH YOU WERE HERE

Słupsk is the birthplace of Heinrich von Stephan (1831–97), the reputed inventor of the postcard. He was born at former Holstentorstrasse 31, approximately where today's ul Piekiełko meets ul Grodzka. Pause for a moment and pay homage to the creator of an indispensable part of travel culture at the information board that marks the spot.

🛏 Sleeping

Hotel Mikołajek   HOTEL €
(☑59 842 2902; ul Szarych Szeregów 1; s/d 90/120zł; 🛜) The only budget accommodation in town, don't be fooled by the reception's elegant dark-wood panelling and curvaceously grand staircase – this is an old PTTK hotel, sorely in need of an update. The survivable, tobacco-smoke-infused rooms have rickety fittings and time-thinned duvets, but high ceilings and scalding-hot showers lift the mood slightly. It's just across the river from the Old Town.

Hotel Atena   HOTEL €€
(☑59 842 8814; www.hotelatena.slupsk.pl; ul Kilińskiego 7; s 175-198zł, d 210-230zł; 🛜) Słupsk's best deal is this happily non-Greek-themed midrange option with well-groomed rooms, some with balconies and large bathrooms. The superb complimentary breakfast is laid out in the restaurant, a facility that can be a godsend at the end of a long day. Superfast wi-fi, friendly staff and an atmosphere of being generally well run make this a great choice.

Hotel Piast   HOTEL €€
(☑59 842 5286; www.hotelpiast.slupsk.pl; ul Jedności Narodowej 3; s/d 300/350zł; P🛜) Słupsk's top address is this perky, 25-bedroom hotel ensconced in a grand 1897 structure. Options range from comfortable business standard to proper luxury suites. and all rooms are pleasantly light and airy. Breakfast is usually included in the room rate.

Hotel Staromiejski   HOTEL €€
(☑59 842 8464; www.hotel-slupsk.pl; ul Jedności Narodowej 4; s/d from 170/225zł; P🛜) A couple of blocks west of the Stary Rynek, the Staromiejski is a good deal with well-maintained rooms featuring vibrant wallpapers and timber furniture. The fancy in-house restaurant serves quality Polish food.

> **DON'T MISS**
>
> ### SUNDAY FLEA MARKET
> Each summer Sunday a superb **flea market** (ul Dominikańska & around; ⊘11am-2pm Sun) takes place near the castle with everything from commie-era vinyl to Kashubian plates, *Dirty Dancing* videos in Polish and biographies of Piłsudski laid out on blankets and trestle tables.

✕ Eating & Drinking

Bar Mleczny Poranek   POLISH €
(al Wojska Polskiego 46; meals around 10zł; ⊘7.30am-6pm Mon-Fri, 10am-4pm Sat & Sun) Grab a tray and line up for cheap, filling socialist-era fare and glasses of weak *kompot* (boiled fruit drink) in a semi-institutional dining room complete with obligatory potted plants and strip lighting. Unmissable.

Repeta   INTERNATIONAL €€
(☑53 337 0401; www.repeta.eu; Starzyńskiego 11; mains 23-69zł; ⊘noon-10pm Mon-Sat, to 8pm Sun; 🛜) Opposite the tourist office in a brightly muralled strip of buildings, this clean-cut bistro serves pizzas, burgers, salads, pastas and light meat dishes, plus Czech and Polish beers and wildly non-Polish fare such as Eton mess and tortillas. The dining tumbles out into the small adjoining park in summer.

★ Atmosphere   INTERNATIONAL €€€
(☑59 844 4044; www.atmosphere-slupsk.pl; ul Norwida 20; mains 53-72zł; ⊘1-10pm Tue-Sat, noon-6pm Sun; P❄🛜) That Słupsk has one of Poland's best restaurants may come as a surprise – that it's buried in the suburbs 2.3km west of the train station is an even bigger shock. Expect flash decor, impeccably laid tables, Chesterfield-style seating and superpolite waiters serving an eclectic menu combining everything from traditional seasonal Polish fare and Baltic salmon to tuna and crème brûlée.

Everything zings with flavour and can be accompanied by a bottle from one of Pomerania's best stocks of wine. It's a 15-minute walk along uls Szczecińska and Piłsudskiego, a short trip on bus 15 or 19 or a 25zł taxi ride.

Kawodajnia   CAFE
(Al Sienkiewicza 3; ⊘8am-8pm Mon-Thu, to 10pm Fri, from 10am Sat, noon-6pm Sun) Down a set of steps off busy al Sienkiewicza, Caffeteria Retro is one of the town's more characterful spots to grab a cuppa joe.

❶ Information

Post Office (ul Łukasiewicza 3; ⊘8am-8pm Mon-Fri, 9am-2pm Sat)

Tourist Office (☑59 728 5041; www.slupsk. pl; cnr uls Starzyńskiego & Tuwina; ⊘9am-6pm Mon-Fri, to 3pm Sat & Sun mid-Jun–mid-Sep, shorter hours rest of year) This excellent office can arrange walking tours of the town and trips into Słowiński National Park (p350).

ℹ️ Getting There & Away

BUS

No less than three bus companies – PKS, Nordexpress and Ramzes (all bus 500) – take turns to do the run to Ustka (7.50zł, 20 minutes, every 20 minutes) from the first bus stop on the right when heading along al Wojska Polskiego from the train station. Tickets are bought from the driver.

Other destinations include the following.

Darłowo 14.30zł, 1½ hours, seven daily

Kluki 10zł, one hour, six daily

Łeba 13zł, 1¾ hours, three daily

Smołdzino 10zł, one hour, six daily

TRAIN

Słupsk has the following train connections.

Gdańsk 30zł, 2¼ hours, at least hourly (direct or change in Gdynia)

Szczecin 54zł, three to 3½ hours, seven daily

Ustka

POP 16,000

With a leafy, primly maintained centre and streets of graceful architecture, this fishing port is one of the Baltic's more refined resort towns. German sunseekers certainly seem to think so; they've been flocking to Ustka's white-sand beach since the 19th century when 'Iron Chancellor' Otto von Bismarck built an elaborate beach shack here. The town has ample, good-quality digs and an animated seaside promenade, at least in the summer season.

💿 Sights

Beach BEACH
Ustka's main attraction is the dune-backed beach. None of the town is visible from the sand, giving it a wild feel, unless it's carpeted with holidaymakers, that is.

Bunkry Blüchera HISTORIC SITE
(www.bunkryustka.pl; ul Bohaterów Westerplatte; adult/concession 16/9zł; ⏰9am-9pm Jul & Aug, 10am-6pm Mar-Jun & Sep-Oct, 10am-4pm Nov-Feb) Cross the new space-age swing bridge over Słupia River to take a tour of Ustka's extensive network of WWII bunkers, today inhabited by waxwork Nazis. Holds various events throughout the warmer months.

🛌 Sleeping & Eating

V Starym Kinie GUESTHOUSE €
(✆60 277 2575; www.kino.ustka.pl; ul Marynarki Polskiej 82; r 120-160zł; 🛜) They pack them in so tightly in Ustka that even the old cinema has been commandeered to put up guests. Each of the smartly done up, comfortable rooms is named after a Hollywood star, and there's a small kitchen but no breakfast.

⭐**Villa Red** GUESTHOUSE €€
(✆59 814 8000; www.villa-red.pl; ul Żeromskiego 1; r from 280zł; 🅿🛜) A grand old red-brick pile built in 1886 for Otto von Bismarck and recently revamped to make more of its historical character, this is one of the most characterful places to slumber on the Baltic coast. Rooms resemble well-stocked antique emporia, though modern bathrooms and the latest flat-screen TVs puncture the 19th-century illusion. The grand theme continues in the restaurant.

Willa Oliwia GUESTHOUSE €€
(✆50 429 8290; www.willaoliwia24.pl; ul Gombrowicza 1; d from 140zł; 🅿🛜) This guesthouse villa lies 2.7km east of the bus and train stations and within walking distance of the beach. Expect gleaming white rooms with lots of personal touches and perfect contemporary bathrooms. The friendly owners serve a hearty breakfast buffet in their kitchen (20zł extra), will lend you a bike (free), and offer pickups and drop-offs at the stations.

⭐**Dym na Wodzie** POLISH €€
(✆79 343 2403; www.dymnawodzie.pl; ul Żeromskiego 1; mains around 38-47zł; ⏰12.30-10pm) One of the best places to eat on the Baltic, 'Smoke on the Water' is the creation of chef Rafał Niewiarowski. The focus is on local seasonal ingredients with the menu changing at least seven times a year; just steps from the beach, fish feature prominently. The interior is a pleasingly simple, candlelit affair.

Tawerna Portowa POLISH €€
(www.hotel-ustka.pl; bul Portowa 6; mains 27-48zł; ⏰2pm–last customer Tue-Fri, noon-10pm Sat, to 9pm Sun; 🛜) This red-brick warehouse on the waterfront, with old railway lines running past the door and fishing boats bobbing outside, houses one of Ustka's best dining spots. The limited Italian-Kashubian menu features scrumptious dishes such as grilled trout with pumpkin risotto and local herring, all of which can be savoured in the timber-rich, dresser-strewn interior.

ℹ Information

Post Office (ul Marynarki Polskiej 47; ⊘8am-7pm Mon-Fri, 9am-3pm Sat)

Tourist Office (☑59 814 7170; www.ustka.pl; ul Marynarki Polskiej 71; ⊘8am-7pm mid-Jun-Aug, shorter hours & closed Sun rest of year)

ℹ Getting There & Away

The train station is diagonally opposite the tourist office. The bus station is a five-minute walk further north along al Mary-narki Polskiej. Trains to Słupsk depart every hour (8.10zł, 20 minutes) in summer, and there are three buses per hour (7.50zł, 20 minutes). Regular buses also go to Rowy (one hour), on the edge of Słowiński National Park (p350).

Darłowo

POP 14,900

Inland Darłowo and little seaside sister Darłówko on the Wieprza River form an interesting pair of siblings. The former Hanseatic trading port of Darłowo still retains traces of its wealthy medieval past, contrasting starkly with hedonistic Darłówko and its seasonal fish fryers, sandy beach and as-tacky-as-they-come promenade of Chinese-made souvenirs. Inevitably, it's Darłówko that is the main draw for visitors and the town has the lion's share of accommodation and places to eat. Its only 'sight' is a pedestrian drawbridge uniting the western and eastern sides of the river, which opens when boats go into or out of the bay. The two communities are linked by a river taxi and local buses that run along both sides of the river. Otherwise it's around 30 minutes on foot.

◉ Sights

Museum of Pomeranian Dukes MUSEUM
(Muzeum Zamku Książąt Pomorskich; www.zamek darlowo.pl; ul Zamkowa 4; adult/concession 15/13zł, tower 7zł; ⊘10am-6pm Jul & Aug, shorter hours rest of year) South of Darłowo's central Rynek is its well-preserved 14th-century castle, erected in 1352 and renovated in 1988. It was the residence of the Pomeranian dukes until the Swedes devastated it during the Thirty Years' War; the Brandenburgs then took it following the Treaty of Westphalia. The dethroned King Erik, who ruled Denmark, Norway and Sweden from 1396 to 1438, and was known as the 'last Viking of the Baltic', lived in the castle for the last 10 years of his life.

The castle's grand halls and noble quarters are now a museum, but your self-guided tour begins in the claustrophobic brick basement where beer and prisoners were once kept. Amid the impressive interiors, old farming implements, art from the Far East and old postcards from Rügenwalde (the German name for Darłowo), what sticks in the memory is the impressive collection of antique furniture, which includes a late-Renaissance Italian four-poster and some Danzig wardrobes of truly preposterous proportions.

King Erik is believed to have hidden his enormous ill-gotten treasure somewhere in the castle. So far it remains undiscovered, so keep your eyes peeled as you wander! The castle's main tower can be climbed for stupendous views.

St Mary's Church CHURCH
(Kościół Mariacki; ul Kościelna) Behind the baroque Town Hall on Darłowo's Rynek rises this massive brick church. Originally dating from the 1320s it has preserved its Gothic shape well. Worth special attention are the three tombs placed in the chapel under the tower. The one made of sandstone holds the ashes of King Erik, who died in Darłowo in 1459. Two mid-17th-century, richly decorated tin tombs standing on either side contain the remains of the last West Pomeranian duke, Jadwig, and his wife Elizabeth.

St Gertrude's Chapel CHURCH
(Kaplica Św Gertrudy; ul Św Gertrudy; ⊘8am-8pm) A few hundred metres north of the Rynek stands a truly quirky piece of medieval architecture. This 12-sided chapel topped with a high, shingled central spire was once the cemetery chapel but became a church in 1997. The outside is reminiscent of a Carpathian timber church but inside the ceiling is a huge piece of Gothic star vaulting supported by six hefty octagonal columns.

⊨ Sleeping & Eating

Róża Wiatrów CAMPGROUND €
(☑94 314 2127; www.rozawiatrow.pl; ul Muchy 2, Darłówko; site per adult/tent 17/13zł; ⓟ❡❡❡) This multifaceted holiday complex near the sea has space for 100 campers and offers plenty of other accommodation, from plain to glam, as well as a wealth of facilities.

Hotel Irena GUESTHOUSE €€
(☑94 314 3692; www.hotel-irena.pl; Al Wojska Polskiego 64, Darłowo; s/d 110/170zł; ⓟ❡) The best deal in either settlement is this neat little

guesthouse (not a hotel) in central Darłowo, with easy access to the castle and the bus station. The owner speaks no English but can communicate that smokers should go elsewhere. Rooms are quite basic but clean and comfortable and the longer you stay the less you pay per night.

★ **Hotel Apollo**   HOTEL €€€
(☑ 94 314 2453; www.hotelapollo.pl; ul Kąpielowa 11, Darłówko; s 190-410zł, d 290-630zł, apt 580-820zł; P ❋ ☎) Surely one of northern Poland's best places to linger, this tasteful hotel, crafted from a palatial spa house just steps from the Baltic, is welcoming, spacious and crisply luxurious. The 16 contemporary rooms are all the same, just the colour schemes differ, but a bit more cash gets you one with a knockout sea view.

Smażalnia Ryb ATOL   SEAFOOD €€
(☑ 50 953 6102; ul Conrada 22a, Darłówko; meals 20-30zł; ☉ 11am-7pm) Since 1964 tourists have been flocking to this famous self-service fish fryer for finger-licking portions of cod and chips plus many other seafood dishes served on paper plates. The inevitable fishing nets and other maritime paraphernalia adorn the walls and the service is brisk.

ℹ Information

Tourist Office (☑ 51 930 3032; www.darlowko.pl; ul Pocztowa 6; ☉ 10am-7pm Mon-Fri, to 4pm Sat & Sun mid-Jun–mid-Sep, shorter hours & closed Sun rest of year)

ℹ Getting There & Away

The bus terminal is at the southwestern end of Darłowo, a 10-minute walk from the Rynek. A single morning bus runs to Ustka (13.50zł, one hour) and there are seven services to/from Słupsk (15zł, one to 1½ hours).

ℹ Getting Around

Minibuses shuttle between Darłowo and Darłówko but a more interesting way to make the short trip is by **water tram** (☑ 510 216 005; www.darlowko.pl; one-way 12zł; ☉ 9.45am-7.45pm May-Sep), a boat that leaves throughout the day from both places.

Kołobrzeg

POP 46,800

The biggest resort on the Polish Baltic coast, Kołobrzeg (ko-*wob*-zhek) has much more than just its share of the north's pristine white sand. This atmospheric town of seafront attractions, spa traditions and summer crowds of strolling Germans is big enough to offer urban distractions on top of the delights of swimming and sunbathing.

Kołobrzeg was reduced to landfill in 1945 and seven decades since, the town still bears the scars. It was never really rebuilt and the modern 'medieval-style' architecture that now dominates the old centre (in the same ilk as Elbląg) is pretty unconvincing. However, the bombs also created a lot of parkland, and along with the beach and seafront these combine to make this Baltic base a relaxing, if not particularly aesthetically pleasing, place for a couple of days' exploration.

◉ Sights

Not much remains of Kołobrzeg's old quarter, but the odd survivor of WWII can be found among the new imitations.

Cathedral   CHURCH
(ul Katedralna; tower 6zł; ☉ unofficial visiting hours 7am-8pm) The 14th-century cathedral is the most important historic sight in town. Though badly damaged in 1945, it has been rebuilt close to its original form. For such a massive building, it has a surprisingly light-filled interior, illuminated by its extremely tall and narrow windows of beautifully patterned stained glass. Its colossal two conjoined towers occupy the whole width of the building, and the facade is a striking composition of windows placed haphazardly.

No, you haven't had too much vodka, those columns on the right side of the nave really are leaning. But don't worry, you don't have to rush out to avoid being crushed – they've been that way since the 16th century. Still, the impression they create is slightly unnerving.

Old fittings include three 16th-century triptychs and a unique Gothic wooden chandelier (1523) in the central nave. There are some even older objects, such as the bronze baptismal font (1355) featuring scenes of Christ's life; a 4m-high, seven-armed candelabrum (1327); and the stalls in the chancel (1340). The 20th-century stained glass is striking on sunny days and another modern feature in the shape of a monument celebrating 1000 years of Polish Catholicism stands outside.

Despite the time posted at the door (aimed more at huge, disruptive German tour groups), you can actually wander in whenever you like. The views from the tower are just sweeping enough to warrant the admission charged.

DON'T MISS

KOŁOBRZEG'S BEACH

In the seaside sector, the white-sand beach itself is the top attraction, supplemented by the usual seasonal stalls, waffle kiosks, amusement arcades, novelty boat trips, (usually pretty awful) buskers and other street life. At intervals along the sands you can hire a double-seater beach chair, popular among those who've enjoyed too many waffles. Kołobrzeg now has two piers: the old one under which a group of swans gathers on the sand, and a new, industrial-looking structure with a noisy cafe at the end. You can actually walk in the water to the end, it's so shallow. To the west, by the harbour and its constructed cluster of postmillennial waterside apartments, stands the red-brick **lighthouse** (Latarnia Morska; adult/concession 8/6zł; ⊙10am-5pm Apr-Jun, Sep & Oct, to sunset Jul & Aug, 11am-4pm Fri-Sun Nov-Mar), which you can climb for panoramic views.

Polish Arms Museum MUSEUM
(Muzeum Oręża Polskiego; www.muzeum.kolobrzeg.pl; ul Gierczak 5; adult/concession 20/15zł, with History Museum 35/25zł; ⊙9am-2pm Mon, to 6pm Tue-Sun Jul & Aug, shorter hours rest of year, closed Mon Sep-Apr) This large museum isn't as dull as you might expect and is well worth a look if you've time on your hands. The displays cover the history of weaponry across the ages, with examples of swords, armour, halberds and more modern military technology. The huge display of cannonballs are calling cards left by Kołobrzeg's many invaders, and the 1945 destruction is impressively brought to life using war debris arranged against a panorama.

However, the highlight here (visible from outside without paying) is the daunting al fresco display of 20th-century weaponry including a jet fighter, a helicopter, tanks and rocket launchers. If the Russians ever do show up, Kołobrzeg at least is ready.

Amber Museum MUSEUM
(Muzeum Bursztynu; ☎72 701 4869; www.muzeumbursztynu.kolobrzeg.pl; ul Waryńskiego 5; adult/concession 15/12zł; ⊙9am-7pm daily) Kołobrzeg's Amber Museum displays several kilos of prehistoric tree sap in a gleaming white, 21st-century space. It's not a patch on the Malbork or Gdańsk amber museums, but an interesting indoor distraction if the Baltic weather gods decide to spoil your beach day. There's also a small shop and workshop.

History Museum MUSEUM
(www.muzeum.kolobrzeg.pl; ul Armii Krajowej 13; adult/concession 20/15zł, with Polish Arms Museum 35/25zł; ⊙9am-2pm Mon, to 5pm Tue-Sun Jul & Aug, shorter hours rest of year & closed Mon Sep-Apr) Housed in an Empire-style merchant's house called the Braunschweig Palace, the sister institution to the Polish Arms Museum has a neatly presented collection, with an emphasis on weights and scales (metrology). Head downstairs for an interesting audiovisual presentation (in English on request) about the city's history, using images of old postcards from Kolberg (the town's old German name).

Town Hall HISTORIC BUILDING
(ul Armii Krajowej; modern-art gallery adult/concession 5/3zł; ⊙10am-5pm Tue-Sun) The Town Hall, just east of the cathedral, is a neo-Gothic structure designed by Karl Friedrich Schinkel and erected by Ernst Friedrich Zwirner (who also built Cologne Cathedral) in the early 1830s after the previous 14th-century building was razed to the ground by Napoleon's troops in 1807. The area in the front of the main entrance is populated by beer gardens in summer, providing pleasant places to sit and admire the architecture. One wing houses a modern-art gallery.

🛏 Sleeping

Baltic Camping CAMPGROUND €
(☎60 641 1954; www.camping.kolobrzeg.pl; 4 Dywizji WP 1; adult/tent 18/11zł; ⊙mid-Apr–Sep; P@🛜) This 100-pitch campsite by the large park in the western suburbs has a kids' playground, German-standard shower blocks and is close to the beach.

Maximilian Hotel HOTEL €€
(☎94 354 0012; www.hotel-maximilian.pl; ul Borzymowskiego 3-4; r from 159zł; P🛜❄) The splendidly classy Maximilian offers a quiet location and stylishly furnished rooms. The elegant building it occupies stands in stark contrast to the Sand Hotel opposite, which casts a long shadow. A spa, restaurant, sauna and accommodating staff make this a great deal, but book ahead as it fills up before anywhere else. Rates drop by half in winter.

Hotel Centrum
HOTEL €€

(⌨ 94 354 5560; www.ckp.info.pl; ul Katedralna 12; s 110-160zł, d 180-260zł; 🅿🖐) Generously sized rooms behind an unpromising facade often have park or garden views, but it's a bit of a hike to the beach. The hotel and associated restaurants are staffed by students training to work in the hospitality industry, often a guarantee of old-world courtesy, little text-book touches not found in other places and the occasional spillage.

★Sand Hotel
HOTEL €€€

(⌨ 94 404 0400; www.sandhotel.pl; ul Zdrojowa 3; s 429-529zł, d 499-599zł; ✴🖐🏊) Even the economy rooms at this glass-and-steel co-lossus are lessons in elegantly clean-cut retro styling, and more than get you in the mood for all the pampering and pummel-ling available at the hotel's spa. Rooms are pretty spacious, the modern gym is awash with technology and there's not a waffle in sight at the much-lauded restaurant.

 Eating

Bar Syrena
POLISH €

(ul Zwycięzców 11; mains 16-22zł; ⊙ noon-5pm Mon-Sat) The *bar mleczny* (milk bar) brought almost into the 21st century, serving Polish standards in a spick-and-span tiled dining room. You'll forgive the plastic trees when you fork the filling fare shoved through the serving hatch behind the bar – just the ticket after a wind-blasted day by the Baltic. Also does monster mugs of coffee and takeaways.

★Restauracja Pod Winogronami
INTERNATIONAL €€

(www.winogrona.pl; ul Towarowa 16; mains 29-69zł; ⊙ 11am-11pm) Extremely popular among the more discerning of the ambling crowds, 'Un-der the Grapes' has a candlelit rural theme and the meat-heavy menu draws mainly on Polish and German cookbooks. The 'boar with beet-root puree' is delicious and can be followed by desserts such as pear dipped in chocolate with whipped cream or Polish cheesecake. Decent wine list for coastal Poland.

Domek Kata
INTERNATIONAL €€

(ul Ratuszowa 1; mains 36-64zł; ⊙ 11am-11pm Mon-Sat, 10am-10pm Sun) Skip the downstairs over-the-top belle-époque dining space and head upstairs for a more medieval-banquet-hall feel centred around a huge fireplace and capped with a cassette ceiling. The menu is a mixed bag of Polish and international dish-es, all cooked to a high standard and served by friendly, English-speaking staff.

Pergola
INTERNATIONAL €€

(www.pergola.pl; bul Jana Szymańskiego 14; mains 38-58zł; ⊙ 10am-11pm; 🖐) Elevated above the snaffling promenaders and serving a mildly Mediterranean and Polish menu, this is the best of the countless cafes that gather around the lighthouse. Recommended for its fish dishes and grandstand views of the Baltic.

☆ Entertainment

Amphitheatre
CONCERT VENUE

(www.rck.kolobrzeg.eu; ul Fredry) Kołobrzeg's large amphitheatre has been entertaining holidaymakers since 1925 and still puts on around 35 concerts a year. Under renovation at the time of research, it hosts some of the top names in Polish pop and rock over sum-mer. See the website for the program.

ℹ Information

PTTK (⌨ 94 352 2311; www.pttk.kolobrzeg.pl; ul Zwycięzców 5; ⊙ 9am-4pm Mon-Fri, 10am-2pm Sat) Can help find accommodation and has a wealth of information on Kołobrzeg and activities in the surrounding area. Sells tickets to Bornholm, Stralsund and Berlin.

Tourist office (⌨ 94 355 1320; ul Dworcowa 1, train station; ⊙ 10am-6pm Mon-Sat Apr-Nov, 9am-5pm Mon-Fri Dec-Mar) The train station tourist office is in a little unmarked hut opposite the station. Staff speak German and Polish only.

City centre tourist office (⌨ 94 354 7220; www.klimatycznykolobrzeg.pl; Plac Ratuszowy 2/1; ⊙ 8am-5pm Mon-Fri, 9am-4pm Sat, 10am-3pm Sun) Main tourist office within the town hall.

ℹ Getting There & Away

BOAT

Kołobrzeska Żegluga Pasażerska (⌨ 94 352 8920; www.kzp.kolobrzeg.pl; ul Morska 7) operates regular catamaran cruises to Nexø on Bornholm Island, Denmark. The service sails daily in July and August, less often from April to June and September and October.

BUS

Buses head to the following destinations.

Szczecin 20zł, three hours, several daily

Warsaw 75zł, 10 hours, two daily (more in summer)

TRAIN

Kołobrzeg has the following rail connections.

Gdańsk 49zł, four hours, four daily (or change in Białogard)

Szczecin 23.60zł, two hours, four daily (or change in Białogard or Goleniów)

Warsaw 73zł to 179zł, six to eight hours, three daily (or change in Szczecin, Gdynia or Piła)

Świnoujście

POP 41,000

As far northwest as you can get in Poland without leaving the country, Świnoujście (shvee-no-*ooysh*-cheh) is an attractive seaside town occupying the eastern end of Uznam Island. There's a touch of faded grandeur along its waterfront promenade, and it emanates a relaxed atmosphere despite its role as a major port and naval base. There are plenty of green parks and a choice of watery views over sea or river, something that may have inspired its famous literary residents from its 19th-century German past (when it was known as Swinemünde), including Kaiser Wilhelm II and Tsar Nicholas II, who met here in 1907, sparking fruitless hopes that their friendship would avert a European war.

The town remains popular with Germans, mostly elderly day-trippers from the former GDR. Of all the Baltic's resorts, Świnoujście attracts the most sedate crowd and those looking to rave by the sea should move on quickly.

⊙ Sights

★ Beach
BEACH

One of Poland's best beaches, this stretch of sand curves gently along the coast and is backed by out-of-bounds, protected dunes. So high is the sand banked up that none of the town is visible, lending the beach a wild feel. It's the ideal place to laze and the main reason to come to Świnoujście. Kids will love watching ships and ferries sliding in and out of the port at the eastern end.

Take a stroll west along the strand and you will quickly find yourself in Germany.

Lighthouse
LIGHTHOUSE

(Latarnia Morska; Ku Morzu; adult/concession 8/5zł; ☉10am-4pm Jan-Mar, Nov & Dec, to 6pm Apr, May, Sep & Oct, 9am-8pm Jul & Aug) The Baltic's highest lighthouse rises 64.8m into the northern sky on the opposite side of the channel to the main town. Dating from 1857, there are 308 exhausting steps to the top but the view up and down the coast is well worth the climb. There's also an exhibition on the maritime rescue service and lighthouses. The easiest way to reach the lighthouse is to stay on the train to Świnoujście Port.

Museum of Sea Fishery
MUSEUM

(Muzeum Rybołówstwa Morskiego; ☎91 321 2426; Plac Rybaka 1; adult/concession 7/5zł, with aquarium 15/13zł; ☉9am-5pm Tue-Sat, 10am-3pm Sun) If you're keen on stuffed sea life, you'll be delighted by the static displays of albatrosses, sharks and seals, along with fishing paraphernalia, model boats, amber and a few fish in tanks. On the top floor you'll discover an interesting exhibition on the history of Świnoujście using old postcards from Swinemünde, some hefty 18th-century Pomeranian trunks and souvenirs of yesteryear. On the ground floor is a separate section (different ticket needed) that features a coral-reef aquarium.

🛌 Sleeping

Stawa Hostel
HOSTEL €

(☎57 057 0527; www.stawahostel.pl; ul Piłsudskiego 1a, enter from ul Piastowska 9; dm/d from 59/149zł; ☎) This immaculate, bright, 100-bed hostel right in the town centre is the best budget backpacker option on the north coast. It's crammed with facilities, the staff are friendly and there's always a free bed outside July and August.

Camping Nr 44 Relax
CAMPGROUND €

(☎91 321 3912; www.camping-relax.com.pl; ul Słowackiego 1; per adult/pitch 18/16zł; ☎) A large, popular camping ground superbly located between the beach and the spa park.

Willa Paw
GUESTHOUSE €€

(☎91 321 4325; www.willa-paw.pl; ul Żeromskiego 25; r from 200zł; 🅿☎) The seven rooms here are above a relaxing cafe and are big enough to swing a four-pawed animal (actually the name means peacock in Polish). It's a cut above your bog-standard guesthouse with dark-wood furniture and monster bathrooms. Just back from the beach.

Hotel Ottaviano
HOTEL €€

(☎91 321 4403; www.ottaviano.pl; ul Monte Cassino 3; s/d 230/305zł; 🅿☎) Located in the very centre of town, the Ottaviano is a pretty good deal. Rooms are colourful, furnished with imagination and have warm, uncarpeted wood-effect floors. The in-house restaurant has views across the attractive paved street. It's handy for the ferry crossing.

🍴 Eating & Drinking

Kurna Chata
POLISH €€

(☎50 117 7125; ul Piłsudskiego 20; mains 36-59zł; ☉11am-10pm; 🖍) Świnoujście's craziest place to eat is this friendly, rurally themed restaurant, its entire ceiling hung with a meadow's-worth of dried flowers, homemade jams and pickles stacked high at the serving counter and staff in countryside attire. The big portions of hearty Polish-German food are aimed firmly at hungry tourists from over the border.

Rybna Chata
SEAFOOD €€

(📞 505 069 998; ul Piłsudskiego 45; mains 21-54zł; ⊙ 11am-10pm; 🖼) Świnoujście's best seafood restaurant is this simple affair where the main ingredient on your plate is guaranteed to have come from the Baltic. The fisher's hut theme is understated, and the post-it notes stuck all over the walls don't hold back in praising meals that were well enjoyed.

Kaisers Pavillon
POLISH €€

(ul Wybrzeże Władysława IV 34a; mains 26-58zł; ⊙ 11am-10pm; 🏨) Though occupying a modern building, the interior of this popular cafe serving heavy Germano-Polish meat dishes has been convincingly done out as if it were a 1911 spa pavilion, all painted wood, scenes of happy German holidays on panels by the windows and lots of wicker and brass. In summer there's a sunny riverside terrace across the street.

Cafe Wieża
CAFE

(ul Paderewskiego 7; ⊙ 10am-10pm May-Sep, to 6pm Oct-Apr; 🏨) Occupying the ground and 1st floor of a church tower that lost its church in WWII, this tiny cafe has just two tables next to a real fire downstairs and a few more in a cosy parlour upstairs. For 10zł you can climb to the top of the tower for views of commie-era blocks and Prussian-era villas.

ℹ Information

Tourist Office (📞 91 322 4999; www.swinoujscie. pl; Plac Słowiański 6; ⊙ 9am-5pm Mon-Fri, 10am-2pm Sat year-round & Sun Jul & Aug) Very helpful, English-speaking office in the heart of town.

ℹ Getting There & Away

Świnoujście's location makes the city a handy entry point for travellers across the Baltic, via ferry services from Sweden and Denmark; it also has a border crossing with Germany – the most convenient overland crossing is 2km west of town. The first town on the German side, Ahlbeck, handles transport further into the country.

BOAT
Tickets for all boat services are available at the terminals and from most travel agencies around town. All ferries depart from the ferry terminal on Wolin Island, on the right bank of the Świna River (across the river from the main town).

Adler-Schiffe (www.adler-schiffe.de) This German company runs cruises from Świnoujście to Bansin, Ahlbeck and Heringsdorf in Germany, up to four times daily. The tourist office has information on times and prices.

Polferries (www.polferries.pl) Major carrier Polferries operates regular ferries to Ystad (Sweden), and Rönne and Copenhagen (Denmark).

Unity Line (www.unityline.pl) Runs daily ferries from the northwestern port of Świnoujście to Ystad, Sweden. Information and tickets online.

BUS
Świnoujście has the following bus and minibus connections.

Międzyzdroje 6.50zł, 15 minutes, frequent

Szczecin 20zł, 1¾ hours, frequent

CAR & MOTORCYCLE
Cars not belonging to local residents (those not bearing ZSW plates) can only use the shuttle ferry between Uznam and Wolin Islands (between the railway station on one side and the town centre on the other) at weekends and between 10pm and 4am on weekdays; otherwise you'll have to head for the crossing serving Karsibór Island, 7km south of Świnoujście. Passage for both vehicles and passengers is free.

TRAIN
The bus terminal and train station are next to each other on the right bank of the Świna River. Passenger ferries shuttle constantly between the town centre and the stations (free, 10 minutes).

Świnoujście has the following rail connections.

Kraków 86zł, 10 to 12 hours, two daily

Międzyzdroje 5.30zł, 15 minutes, hourly

Poznań 63zł, 4½ to 5½ hours, four daily

Szczecin 17.50zł, 1½ hours, four daily

Warsaw 78zł, 10 hours, daily

SZCZECIN
POP 404,500

Well off any track non-German tourists tread, the western port city of Szczecin (*shcheh*-cheen) is a lively city awash with students and a muddle of architecture inherited from wildly different ages. Crumbly German-era art-nouveau tenements and mansions, some now undergoing renovation, echo a past splendour but historical style is patchy. The authorities seem to have given up on the idea of rebuilding, choosing instead to fill the gaps in the city centre with glass-and-steel malls, sacrificing entire streets in the name of retail. Many of the main thoroughfares have been spruced up, but derelict buildings and overgrown plots are easy to find in the very heart of the city.

It's a busy working port, though you'd never know it wandering the city centre, with just enough to warrant a stopover between Berlin and Gdańsk, to which it has good connections.

History

Szczecin's beginnings go back to the 8th century, when a Slav stronghold was built here. In 967 Duke Mieszko I annexed the town for the newborn Polish state, but was unable to hold or Christianise it. It was Bolesław Krzywousty who recaptured the town in 1121 and brought the Catholic faith to the locals.

Krzywousty died in 1138 and the Polish Crown crumbled; Pomerania formally became an independent principality. Periods of allegiance to Germanic and Danish rulers followed, before Western Pomerania was unified by Duke Bogusław X in 1478, with Szczecin being chosen as the capital.

The next major shift in power came in 1630, when the Swedes conquered the city. Sweden then ceded Szczecin to Prussia in 1720, which as part of Germany held the region until WWII. Under Prussian rule, Szczecin (Stettin in German) grew considerably, becoming the main port for landlocked Berlin. By the outbreak of WWII the city had about 300,000 inhabitants.

In April 1945 the Red Army passed through on its way to Berlin, leaving 60% of the urban area in ruins. Only 6000 souls remained of the former population, most of the others having fled.

With new inhabitants, mostly drawn from territories lost by Poland to the Soviet Union, the battered city started a new life, developing into an important port and industrial centre for the postwar nation. Szczecin played a big part in the strikes that led to the formation of Solidarity; its three shipyards, including Poland's biggest, have survived the transition to capitalism.

◎ Sights

★ Castle of the Pomeranian Dukes CASTLE

(Map p362; www.zamek.szczecin.pl; ul Korsazy 34; castle free, museum adult/concession 6/4zł; ⊙ castle dawn-dusk, museum 10am-6pm Tue-Sun) This castle is the mother of all Szczecin

monuments. This vast, blocky building looms over the Old Town, but the square central courtyard and simple Renaissance-style decoration atop the walls have a certain understated grace (spot the repeated circular pattern that resembles the Yin and Yang symbol). The castle was originally built in the mid-14th century and grew into its current form by 1577, but was destroyed by Allied carpet bombing in 1944 before being extensively restored.

The Castle Museum (Muzeum Zamkowe) allows you to get inside the building where the star exhibits are six spectacular sarcophagi of the Pomeranian dukes. These large tin boxes are decorated with a fine engraved ornamentation and were made between 1606 and 1637 by artists from Königsberg. Following the death of the last Pomeranian duke, Bogusław XIV, the crypt was walled up until the sarcophagi were discovered during restoration work in 1946, after the castle's wartime destruction. The remains of the dukes were deposited in the cathedral, while the least-damaged sarcophagi were restored for display.

Various temporary exhibitions and displays of art take place in other rooms of the castle. In summer, concerts and opera are held in the courtyard (www.opera.szczecin.pl). The castle also houses a restaurant, a cinema and a decent gift shop.

Museum of Technology & Transport MUSEUM

(Muzeum Techniki i Komunikacji; ☑ 91 459 9200; www.muzeumtechniki.eu; Niemierzyńska 18a; adult/concession 10/5zł; ⊙ 10am-3pm Tue, to 4pm Wed, Thu & Sun, to 6pm Fri & Sat) This surprisingly good museum 2.5km north of the centre has a fascinating collection of vehicles, mostly of Polish origin – interesting as today Poland has no car brand of its own. Highlights include a six-wheel amphibious vehicle from the 1970s, clunky communist-era cars such as the inevitable Polski Fiat, Szczecin-produced motorbikes from between the wars and exhibitions on the city's public transport and Polish brands. Well worth taking tram 3 or 10 to see.

Historical Museum of Szczecin MUSEUM

(Muzeum Historii Miasta Szczecina; Map p362; ☑ 91 431 5255; www.muzeum.szczecin.pl; ul Ks Mściwoja II 8; adult/concession 10/6zł; ⊙ 10am-6pm Tue-Thu & Sat, to 4pm Fri & Sun) Szczecin's 15th-century Gothic Town Hall, one of the most architecturally fascinating buildings in the city with its monster red-brick gable, is the only relic of the Old Town, having miraculously survived the near-total destruction of the surrounding streets in WWII. It is home to the Historical Museum, a well-curated exhibit in the light-filled interior.

Cathedral Basilica of St James CHURCH

(Bazylika Katedralna pw Św Jakuba Apostoła; Map p362; ul Wyszyńskiego; 8zł, tower 10zł; ⊙tower 10am-6pm Tue-Sat) Head downhill from the city centre to explore Szczecin's 12th-century cathedral, partially destroyed by Red Army shells in 1945 and reconstructed in 1972. It's the early 1970s renovation you'll notice first, an incongruously modern facade more reminiscent of a derelict factory than a place of worship. As a foreigner you're certain to be cherry-picked to shell out the 8zł admission, then proceed to the nave where a forest of red-brick columns provides perspective to an interior lacking atmosphere.

On the right, almost at the end of the nave, a plaque remembering those who perished in the 2010 Smolensk air disaster sits below another to the Katyń victims they were on their way to honour. Otherwise, possibly the world's tiniest crypt and some impressive stained glass are the only other distractions, along with the tower where a lift winches you up to striking views of the river.

National Museum's Department of Art MUSEUM

(Muzeum Sztuki Współczesnej; Map p362; www.muzeum.szczecin.pl; ul Staromłyńska 1; adult/concession 10/6zł; ⊙10am-6pm Tue-Thu & Sat, to 4pm Fri & Sun) The National Museum's Art Gallery resides in an 18th-century palace that formerly served as the Pomeranian parliament. It displays a collection of religious art, particularly woodcarving from the 14th to 16th centuries, and you can also take a peek at the Pomeranian crown jewels.

★ Szczecin Underground HISTORY

(Map p362; ☑91 434 0006; www.schron.szczecin.pl; ul Kolumba 1; adult/concession tour 25/20zł; ⊙tours noon daily & 1pm Sat) This award-winning attraction near the train station consists of a sprawling set of concrete tunnels beneath the city streets, designated as a bomb shelter in the 1940s and as a fallout shelter thereafter. Tours have a WWII theme (daily) or examine the Cold War (Saturday). Buy tickets from the office at ul Kolumba 15 minutes before the tour begins.

🛏 Sleeping

CUMA Youth Hostel HOSTEL €

(☑91 422 4761; www.ptsm.home.pl; ul Monte Cassino 19a; dm 22-24zł, s/d 80/125zł; 🅿🛜) Everything is pleasant about this place, with simple but bright rooms, located in a leafy neighbourhood. There's a laundry for guest use, and out in the well-kept garden there are concrete table-tennis tables. It's 2km northwest of the centre; take tram 3 from the station to Plac Rodła and change for the westbound tram 1 to the 'Piotra Skargi' stop.

Hotelik Elka-Sen HOTEL €

(Map p362; ☑91 433 5604; www.elkasen.szczecin.pl; al 3 Maja 1a; s/d 120/150zł; 🛜) Sounding like a cure for indigestion, these lodgings have a location almost as strange as their title. A lift acts as the front door and rooms occupy a basement in the incredibly ugly School of Economics, itself next door to the local prison. The foyer is gloomy but the pine-furnished rooms receive natural light from half-moon windows, and bathrooms twinkle.

Hotel Focus HOTEL €€

(Map p362; ☑91 433 0500; www.focushotels.pl; ul Małopolska 23; s/d from 215/230zł; 🅿🛜) If you just want a place to snooze, have breakfast and surf the web, this crisply conceived business hotel overlooking the river is the base for you. High standards throughout, cheery staff, a filling breakfast and an absence of tobacco odour earn this laudable inn glowing reviews. Rooms are standard throughout but tick all 21st-century boxes.

Sztukateria HOTEL €€

(Map p362; ☑91 817 1921; www.sztuka.teria.eu; ul Śląska 4; s 140-180zł, d 200-240zł; 🛜) Don't be fooled by the design-hotel reception here – rooms upstairs are rather austere affairs, though they do have good-quality furniture and pristine bathrooms. They're all pretty spacious, but need an update and the views of Szczecin's soot-streaked backyards from the windows are uninspiring. Breakfast is taken in the cafe on the premises.

Hotel Victoria HOTEL €€

(Map p362; ☑91 434 3855; www.hotelvictoria.com.pl; Plac Batorego 2; s/d 160/240zł; 🛜) Well positioned just uphill from the bus terminal and train station, this well-mannered option, popular with German groups, has cheaply furnished but neatly kept rooms. It's in a quietish location, but has a quite

Szczecin

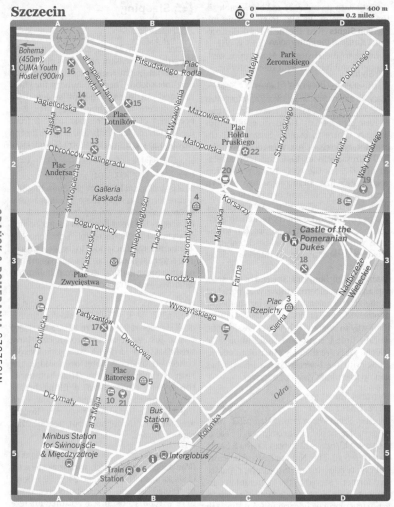

unexpected facility in the shape of the Tango Nightclub, mercifully fired up on weekends only. May win the prize for Poland's grandest hotel restaurant and breakfast room.

Hotel Campanile
HOTEL €€

(Map p362; ☏ 91 481 7700; www.campanile.com; ul Wyszyńskiego 30; r from 155zł; ❀ ☞) Part of a French chain, this modern hotel is in pole position for sightseeing, as it's an easy walk from the castle, the Old Town, the train and bus stations, and the city's main drag. Rooms are compact but pristine and comfortable, with tea- and coffee-making

facilities. There's a bar and restaurant off the foyer.

Hotel Rycerski
HOTEL €€

(Map p362; ☏ 91 814 6601; www.amwhotele.pl; ul Potulicka 1a; s 200-260zł, d 260-300zł; ℗ ☞) Serving a mainly weekday business clientele, this red-brick pile is concealed within its own walled compound off a quiet city-centre street. Receptionists speak little English and communal spaces are a touch too utilitarian, but rooms are well sustained, very comfortable and a nifty deal at the lower end of the price scale. Rates vary at weekends.

Szczecin

✗ Eating

Bar Mleczny Turysta   CAFETERIA €
(Map p362; ul Obrońców Stalingradu 6; meals around 10-15zł; ⊘9am-7pm Mon-Fri) With its chequered tile floor, tiny stools bolted down, time-warped menu boards in 1970s plastic lettering and brusque, ladle-wielding dinner ladies, this is the belly-filling milk-bar experience Szczecin style.

Cafe Koch   BAKERY €
(Map p362; ul Jagiellońska 2/1; snacks from 2zł; ⊘7.30am-5pm Mon-Fri, from 8am Sat, from 9am Sun) There aren't many small businesses here with over 40 years of history, but since 1972 Koch has been supplying the city with exquisite traditional cakes and pastries. Pass through the (fake) stained-glass entrance into this tiny two-table branch for a breakfast of coffee and cheesecake sold by weight.

★ Bohema   INTERNATIONAL €€
(☑91 433 2230; www.bohema.szczecin.pl; ul Wojska Polskiego 67; mains 29-47zł; ⊘noon-11pm Mon-Fri, 1pm-midnight Sat, to 8pm Sun) For a blast of old-world style in sometimes slightly gritty Szczecin, seek out this little-touted restaurant with its romantically aristocratic decor and long menu of excellent Polish and international dishes prepped and plated by a skilful chef. Subscribers to the Slow Food movement, ingredients are as seasonal as possible. The matured beef tenderloin for two comes highly recommended.

Paprykarz Fish Market   SEAFOOD €€
(Map p362; ☑91 433 2233; www.paprykarz.com.pl; al Jana Pawła II 42; mains 39-65zł; ⊘noon-11pm daily; ☏) If fish is your dish, then head for this seafood place on the Jana Pawła II strip which has been done out to look like a traditional fish market. The virtually seafood-only menu covers everything from local trout to exotic octopus to salmon tartare and there's plenty of white wine and beer to choose from.

Karczma Polska Pod Kogutem   POLISH €€
(Map p362; ☑91 434 6873; www.karczmapodkogutem.pl; Plac Lotników 3; mains 30-70zł; ⊘11am-11pm Mon-Sat, noon-10pm Sun; ☏) A lovely spot for a lowlit dinner, this rustic barn inserted into the ground floor of a post-WWII tenement displays its yesteryear knick-knacks with style. The traditional Polish food comes in generous portions, the long menu a veritable zoo of defunct grunters, squawkers and even rutters. The external wooden deck is a great vantage point over the picturesque square opposite.

Ukraineczka   UKRAINIAN €€
(Map p362; ul Panieńska 19; mains 16-29zł; ⊘11am-10pm Mon-Thu, to 11pm Fri-Sun; ☏☀) Serving Szczecin's large Ukrainian Gastarbeiter community, this simple place near the castle offers authentically traditional Ukrainian and Lithuanian dishes, Ukrainian beers and Georgian wines amid photos of old Ukraine, ceremonial towels, sunflowers and other Ukrainian knick-knacks.

Restauracja Bombay   INDIAN €€
(Map p362; www.india.pl; ul Partyzantów 1; mains 22-48zł; ⊘1-11pm; ☏) Possibly the last thing you might expect amid Szczecin's postcommunist cityscape: spicily aromatic Indian food served in subcontinentally adorned surrounds by waiters with impeccable English. It was established by a former Miss India (1973).

Drinking & Entertainment

Stara Komenda
MICROBREWERY

(Map p362; www.starakomenda.pl; Plac Batorego 3; ⊙1-10pm Sun & Mon, to midnight Tue-Thu, to 1am Fri & Sat; 🛜) Szczecin's very own micro-brewery concocts four of its very own beers and has quickly become the city's premier elbow-bending venue for orthodox fans of the hop. First-timers can sample the entire frothy quartet for 14zł including the oh-so Baltic Amber Beer (Burztynowe).

Christopher Columbus
BAR

(Map p362; ul Wały Chrobrego 1; ⊙10am-1am Sun-Thu, to 2am Fri & Sat; 🛜) Pass the large bloody-mouthed plastic shark strung up outside to discover Szczecin's best beer garden wrapped around a wooden pavilion. The place offers drinkers widescreen views of the river, there's lots of cheap food and a band occasionally strikes up in the shade of mature trees. There's even a faint pulse here in winter.

E Wedel Cafe
CAFE

(Map p362; www.wedelpijalnie.pl; Plac Hołdu Pruskiego 1; ⊙10am-10pm daily; 🛜) Housed in the baroque Royal Gate, another fragment of lost history, this franchise hot-chocolate cafe is an authentically historical place to have a drink, either in the barrel-ceilinged interior or outside when the weather is good.

City Hall
CLUB

(Map p362; ☑60 910 4929; www.cityhall.pl; Czerwony Ratusz, ul 3 Maja 18; ⊙6pm-late) This impressive space in the basement of the massive red-brick former Town Hall (Map p362; Plac Stefana Batorego) just off ul Maja packs in up to 400 clubbers for some of the biggest nights in town.

Karłowicz
Philharmonic Szczecin
LIVE MUSIC

(Map p362; ☑91 430 9510; www.filharmonia. szczecin.pl; ul Małopolska 48) Awarded the European Union Prize for Contemporary Architecture in 2015, Szczecin's Philharmonic Hall looks like a misplaced factory, the lack of windows giving the building an unwelcoming look. However, architecture fans might be interested to take an English-language tour of the building (three to five times a month; see the website for details).

ℹ Information

Main Post Office (Map p362; Al Niepodległości 43; ⊙8am-8pm Mon-Fri)

Tourist Office (Map p362; ☑91 489 1630; www.szczecin.eu; ul Korsarzy 34; ⊙10am-6pm daily) Within the castle, this helpful office hands out information and sells tickets for all kinds of events.

Tourist Office (Map p362; ☑91 483 0850; Szczecin Główny, ul Kolumba 2; ⊙9am-5pm Mon-Sat, to 2pm Sun May-Sep, closed Sun Oct-Apr) Branch at the train station.

ℹ Getting There & Away

AIR

The **airport** (☑91 484 7400; www.airport.com. pl) is in Goleniów, about 45km northeast of the city and is served by Wizz Air, Norwegian, LOT and Ryanair from the UK and Ireland. A shuttle bus (15zł) operated by **Interglobus** (Map p362; ☑91 485 0422; www.interglobus.pl; ul Kolumba 1; ⊙9am-5pm Mon-Fri, 10am-2pm Sat) meets major arrivals three or four times a day. Booking a seat on the shuttle online is easy and guarantees you a spot, some reassurance if you are arriving late at night. Alternatively, a taxi should cost around 150zł.

BUS

The **bus terminal** (Map p362; Plac Grodnicki) is uphill from the train station and handles regular summer buses to nearby beach resorts, as well as Świnoujście (20zł, one hour 45 minutes, 15 daily operated by Jomsborg). Alternatively, for Świnoujście take one of the regular minibuses operated by **Emilbus** (www. emilbus.com.pl) that depart from a special stand at the southern end of **al 3 Maja** (Map p362; al 3 Maja).

Berlineks (www.berlineks.com) and **PKS Szczecin** (www.pksszczecin.info) both run comfortable minibuses to Berlin (three hours, frequent), the first from outside the train station, the second from the bus station. Interglobus operates similar services, as well as other trips and transfers. **Flixbus** (www.flixbus.com) runs full-size coaches to Berlin from near the train station.

TRAIN

The ultramodern main train station, Szczecin Główny, is on the bank of the Odra River, 1km south of the centre. As well as domestic connections there are cross-border trains to Berlin (two hours, three daily) and Angermünde (one hour, hourly, change here for Berlin). The city has the following domestic rail connections:

Gdańsk 54zł, 4¾ hours, four daily

Kołobrzeg 23.60zł, 2½ hours, five daily (or change in Goleniów or Koszalin)

Kraków 81zł, nine hours, four daily

Poznań 29.10zł to 40zł, three hours, hourly

Słupsk 54zł, 3½ hours, seven daily

Warsaw 72zł to 130zł, seven to eight hours, four daily

Warmia & Masuria

POP 1.4 MILLION

Best Places to Eat

➡ Podkładka Restobar (p379)

➡ House Cafe (p370)

➡ Cudne Manowce (p370)

➡ Restauracja z Zielonym Piecem (p371)

➡ Przechowalnia Marzeń (p380)

Best Places to Stay

➡ Pensjonat Mikołajki (p380)

➡ Hotel Willa Port (p372)

➡ Hotel Wileński (p369)

➡ Zajazd Pod Zamkiem (p375)

Why Go?

There's something in the water in these two northeast regions bordering the Russian enclave of Kaliningrad – mostly hundreds of sailors, windsurfers and kayakers who come to make a splash in the Great Masurian Lakes, which dominate the landscape. There's more aqua fun to be had here than in the rest of the country put together, and if water sports are your thing, this is your place.

Away from the lakes, one of the world's most intriguing canal trips – the Elbląg–Ostróda experience – and countless rivers, wetlands and swamps mean you're never far from a soaking in these parts. The Łyna and Krutynia Rivers are kayaking bliss, and Warmia even boasts a small stretch of Baltic coastline.

When you've had your fill of water fun, the region has bags of red-brick architecture left by the Warmian Bishops and is home to Hitler's wartime hideout, the Wolf's Lair – one of Europe's most significant WWII sites.

When to Go

Olsztyn

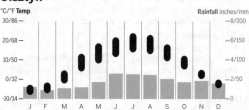

Jan Cross lakes in Masuria on a pair of skis, when the whole region turns to ice.

Aug Join the pilgrimage to Święta Lipka during the Feast of the Assumption.

Oct See the lakes reflect the fiery autumnal shades of the region's many forests.

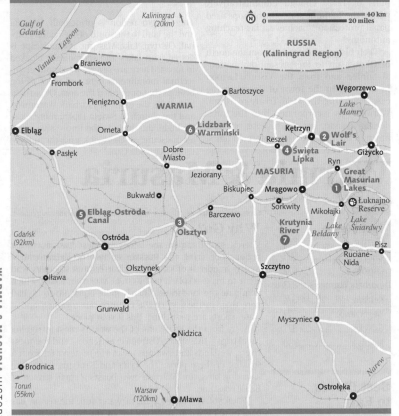

Warmia & Masuria Highlights

1 **Great Masurian Lakes** (p374) Joining the yachting set for a tour of this watery wonderland.

2 **Wolf's Lair** (p376) Scrambling around Hitler's secret wartime bunker.

3 **Olsztyn** (p367) Doing a spot of cobblestone-surfing in the city's rapidly improving Old Town.

4 **Święta Lipka** (p370) Joining the faithful throngs at this major place of Polish Catholic pilgrimage.

5 **Elbląg–Ostróda Canal** (p372) Wondering at the spectacle of boats travelling over dry land via a unique system of slipways.

6 **Lidzbark Warmiński's Castle** (p373) Exploring

the halls of this mammoth Gothic castle, the architectural highlight of the region.

7 **Krutynia River** (p369) Paddling along this 103km scenic river route, Poland's top kayak trip.

History

Despite being lumped together administratively today, Warmia and Masuria have always been separate entities, and their histories, though broadly similar, are largely independent.

Warmia is imaginatively named after its original inhabitants, the Warmians, who were wiped out by the Teutonic Knights in the 13th century, after which the Knights set up a Teutonic province. For more than five centuries this was largely an autonomous ecclesiastical state run by all-powerful Catholic bishops.

The Warmian diocese was the largest of four that were created by the papal bulls of 1243. Though administratively within the Teutonic state, the bishops used papal protection to achieve a far-reaching autonomy.

Their bishopric extended from the north of Olsztyn up to the present-day national border, and from the Vistula Lagoon in the west to the town of Reszel in the east. Following the 1466 Treaty of Toruń, Warmia was incorporated into the kingdom of Poland, but the bishops retained much of their control over internal affairs, answering directly to the pope. When the last grand master adopted Protestantism in 1525, Warmia became a bastion of the Counter-Reformation.

In 1773 the region fell under Prussian rule, along with swathes of western Poland.

In the medieval period, Masuria was dealing with its own upheavals. The Jatzvingians (Jaćwingowie), the first inhabitants, belonged to the same ethnic and linguistic family as the Prussians, Latvians and Lithuanians. For farmers they were unusually warlike, and caused plenty of headaches for the Mazovian dukes, as they ravaged the principality's northern fringes on a regular basis and even pressed as far south as Kraków. In the second half of the 13th century, however, the Teutonic Knights expanded eastwards over the region, and by the 1280s they had wiped them out too.

Both Warmia and Masuria quickly became a bone of contention between the Teutonic order and Lithuania, and remained in dispute until the 16th century. At that time the territory formally became a Polish dominion, but its colonisation was slow. Development was also hindered by the Swedish invasions of the 1650s and the catastrophic plague of 1710.

In the Third Partition of 1795, the region was swallowed up by Prussia, and in 1815 it became a part of the Congress Kingdom of Poland, only to be grabbed by Russia after the failure of the November Insurrection of 1830.

After WWI Poland took over the territory, though not without resistance from Lithuania, but the region remained remote and economically unimportant. Warmia was finally restored to Poland after WWII, and the two halves became a single administrative zone.

THE OLSZTYN REGION

The Olsztyn region is principally Warmia and the land to the south of the region's capital, Olsztyn. Like Masuria, its landscape is dotted with lakes and sporadically cloaked in forest. There are several important architectural monuments here and relics of the bishops that once ruled the area. Of particular note is the castle of Lidzbark Warmiński and the church in Święta Lipka; more secular highlights include the impressive open-air museum at Olsztynek and the unique Elbląg–Ostróda Canal.

Olsztyn

POP 173,700

By far the biggest city in the region, Olsztyn (*ol*-shtin) is the natural jumping-off point and transport hub for many other towns and attractions in Warmia and Masuria. Once a bit of a backwater, no other settlement in northern Poland has improved as much in recent years and it's now worth spending a couple of days to explore the cobblestoned Old Town and enjoy the laid-back feel.

The town was founded in the 14th century as the southernmost outpost of Warmia, and only came under Polish control following the Treaty of Toruń in 1466. With the First Partition of Poland in 1772, Olsztyn became Prussian (renamed Allenstein) and remained so until the end of WWII.

⊙ Sights

Museum of Warmia & Masuria   MUSEUM
(Map p368; www.muzeum.olsztyn.pl; ul Zamkowa 2; adult/concession 12/8zł, with House of the Olsztyn Gazette 20/15zł; ⊙10am-6pm Tue-Sun Jul & Aug, slightly shorter hours rest of the year) A well-rubbed bronze of Copernicus welcomes you to Olsztyn's massive red-brick 14th-century castle, the most important historic building in town. And it's the Copernicus association that makes this the town's top sight, the astronomer as administrator of Warmia having lived in the castle from 1516 to 1520. He made some of his astronomical observations here, and you can still see the diagram he drew on the cloister wall to record the equinox and thereby calculate the exact length of the year.

The rest of the collection is an eclectic mix of rural knickknacks, dubious art and various temporary exhibitions. The tower is hardly worth the climb, though there is some interesting graffiti on the inside of the viewing platform left by visitors from down the decades.

Olsztyn

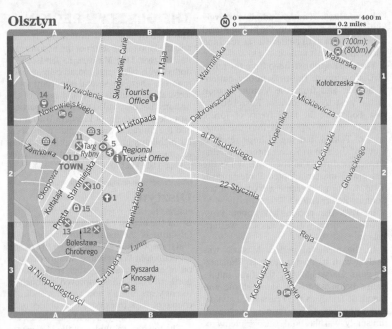

Olsztyn

House of the Olsztyn Gazette   MUSEUM
(Dom 'Gazety Olsztyńskiej'; Map p368; www.
muzeum.olsztyn.pl; Targ Rybny 1; adult/concession
8/6zł, with main branch 20/15zł; ⊙10am-6pm
Tue-Sun Jul & Aug, slightly shorter hours rest of
year) The Museum of Warmia and Masuria's
main annexe is housed in the former *Gazeta
Olsztyńska* newspaper building. The Polish
paper was famed for its outspoken politics
in German Allenstein, so when the Nazis
marched in it was closed down and its editors sent off to Dachau. Half of the building looks at the newspaper's history from
the late 19th century onwards (all sadly in
Polish). The middle floor examines Olsztyn's
history in a jumble sale of varied objects precious and ordinary.

The basement section deals with Polish
schools between 1929 and 1939. Don't miss
the political posters in the entrance, some
communist era denouncing NATO, others
belonging to various Solidarity campaigns.

Cathedral   CHURCH
(Map p368; ul Jana Długosza) This Gothic cathedral dates from the 14th century, though its
huge 60m tower was only added in 1596. As
in Olsztyn's castle, the most impressive architectural feature is the webbed vaulting
in the aisles, reminiscent of Gaudí's Sagra-
da Família in Barcelona. The nave, however,

has netlike arches dating from the 17th century. Among the remarkable works of art are the 16th-century triptych at the head of the left aisle, and a shimmering gold and silver altarpiece of the Virgin Mary.

Lake Ukiel
LAKE

At 4.1 sq km and 43m deep, this is the biggest lake within the city limits and a mecca on hot days for swimmers, boaters and picnickers. You can hire a boat, walk or cycle around the lake or just take it easy on the shore. Take bus 107 or 113.

High Gate
GATE

(Map p368; ul Staromiejska) The High Gate, the historic gateway to the Old Town, is the only remainder of the 14th-century city walls.

🛏 Sleeping

Olsztyn has accommodation in every price range though only a handful are in the old quarter. There's a small private rentals market for those who prefer apartments.

Hotel Wysoka Brama
HOSTEL €

(Map p368; ☑895 273 675; www.hotelwysoka brama.olsztyn.pl; Staromiejska 1; s 65-100zł, d 75-120zł, dm from 23zł; 🛜) It says hostel over the door, but inside this is an inexpensive, basic but well-run hotel used by backpackers and school groups. Decor is cheap and flimsy, some rooms have shared facilities but the location adjoining the High Gate makes it super central. Breakfast is 15zł extra.

★ Hotel Wileński
HOTEL €€

(Map p368; ☑89 535 0122; www.hotelwilenski. com; ul Ryszarda Knosały 5; s/d from 249/289zł; ✴🛜) Installed in a row of knocked-through 19th-century townhouses, this elegant hotel is a real treat. Posh corridors lead to formally furnished quarters with big-print wall coverings and imaginative bathrooms. The downside – some rooms have a view of McDonald's, but bulky curtains black out the golden 'M'. Head instead to the hotel's own restaurant for some of the best fare in town.

Villa Pallas
GUESTHOUSE €€

(Map p368; ☑89 535 0115; www.villapallas.pl; ul Żołnierska 4; s/d 175/210zł; P🛜) This quite sophisticated villa is named after the Greek goddess Athena, whose statue makes up part of the mix 'n' match decor. Negotiate the maze of stairways to find relatively well-furnished, spotless rooms and some decent suites. A smart restaurant and small spa centre complete the picture.

KAYAKING THE KRUTYNIA

The **PTTK Mazury travel agency** (Map p368; ☑89 527 5156; www.mazurypttk. pl; ul Staromiejska 1; 10-day kayaking tour per person 1330zł; ⊙9am-6pm Mon-Fri) runs kayak tours along the country's best rivers in and around the Great Masurian Lakes, including the 10-day Krutynia River route (known as Szlak Kajakowy Krutyni), regarded as Poland's top kayaking trip. Few come away disappointed. Tours depart daily from May to October. Prices include a kayak, food, insurance, lodging in cabins and a Polish-, English- or German-speaking guide.

The 103km trip begins at Stanica Wodna PTTK in Sorkwity, 50km east of Olsztyn, and goes down the Krutynia River and Lake Bełdany to Ruciane-Nida.

Hotel Pod Zamkiem
GUESTHOUSE €€

(Map p368; ☑89 535 1287; www.hotel-olsztyn. com.pl; ul Nowowiejskiego 10; s 150-170zł, d 230-250zł; P🛜) Occupying a large early-20th-century villa, once the home of the influential Sperl family, this stylish guesthouse has character in spades. Wooden beams, murals and lots of pine provide atmosphere, and the park setting puts you right by the castle and the Old Town. Rates include breakfast and supper can be booked for an extra 30zł.

Hotel Warmiński
HOTEL €€

(Map p368; ☑89 522 1400; www.hotel-warminski. com.pl; ul Kołobrzeska 1; s/d from 270/300zł; 🛜) This very well-appointed hotel knows what business travellers need and provides it with a smile. The beige-and-wood-themed rooms are top-notch and rates fall a bit at weekends. The gourmet-style meals in the hotel restaurant can provide a civilised finish to the day.

🍴 Eating & Drinking

The dining scene has come on in leaps and bounds in recent years with many new places to eat sprouting throughout the Old Town.

Lively Targ Rybny is the place to head after dark, the small square lined with bars, restaurants and pubs representing the drinking cultures of the Czech Republic, Poland and Ireland.

WORTH A TRIP

ŚWIĘTA LIPKA

Built between 1687 and 1693, and later surrounded by an ample rectangular cloister, the hugely popular **church** (www.swlipka.pl; Święta Lipka; ☺ 7am-7pm except during Mass) FREE was built around four identical corner towers, all housing chapels. The best artists from Warmia, Königsberg (Kaliningrad) and Vilnius were commissioned for the furnishings and decoration, which were completed by about 1740. Since then the church has hardly changed, neither inside nor out, and is regarded as one of the purest examples of a late-baroque church in the country.

The entrance to the complex is an elaborate wrought-iron gateway. Just behind it, the two-towered cream facade holds a stone sculpture of the holy lime tree in its central niche, with a statue of the Virgin Mary on top.

Once inside (appropriate clothing is required to enter – no shorts or hats for men, covered heads for women), the visitor is enveloped in colourful and florid, but not overwhelming, baroque ornamentation. All the frescoes are the work of Maciej Meyer of Lidzbark, and display trompe l'œil images, which were fashionable at the time. These are clearly visible both on the vault and the columns; the latter look as if they were carved. Of course Meyer also left behind his own image – you can see him in a blue waistcoat with brushes in his hand, in the corner of the vault painting over the organ.

The three-storey, 19m-high altar, covering the whole back of the chancel, is carved of walnut and painted to look like marble. Of the three paintings in the altar, the lowest one depicts the Virgin Mary of Święta Lipka with the Christ child, complete with subtle lighting for effect.

The pulpit is ornamented with paintings and sculptures. Directly opposite, across the nave, is a holy lime tree topped with the figure of the Virgin Mary, supposedly placed on the spot where the legendary tree itself once stood.

The pride of the church is its breathtaking organ, a sumptuously decorated instrument of about 5000 pipes. The work of Johann Jozue Mosengel of Königsberg, it is decorated with mechanical figures of saints and angels that dance around when the organ is played. Short demonstrations are held every hour on the half-hour from 9.30am to 5.30pm, May to September, and at 10am, noon and 2pm in October.

The cloister surrounding the church is ornamented with frescoes, also masterminded by Meyer. The artist painted the corner chapels and parts of the northern and western cloister, but died before the work was complete. It was continued in the same vein by other artists, but without the same success.

★ **House Cafe** CAFE €
(Map p368; Staromiejska 11/16; snacks from 3zł; ☺ 8am-10pm Mon-Fri, from 9am Sat & Sun; ☻) House Cafe has quickly made a name for itself as the place in Olsztyn to meet up and take cake. Stacks of books (in Polish) litter the place, there's a kids corner and piles of colourful, comfy cushions to hug. The coffee is the town's best and the gateau comes stacked high. Understandably always packed out with locals.

Greenway VEGETARIAN €
(Map p368; ul Prosta 10/11; meals around 20zł; ☺ 11am-7pm Sun & Mon, from 10am Tue-Sat; ☻) A branch of the popular Polish chain. Monster portions of the usual offerings, such as Mexican goulash, lasagna and spinach quiche, are great belly fillers and there's a mega-cheap lunch menu for 12zł.

★ **Cudne Manowce** POLISH €€
(Map p368; ☎ 89 535 0395; www.cudnemanowce.pl; Bolesława Chrobrego 4; mains 18-32zł; ☺ noon-10pm Tue-Sat, to 8pm Sun) Lake fish, venison pierogi and a kind of Warmian pizza are the signature dishes at this top restaurant near the cathedral. The eclectic dining room is awash with faded rural colour, recycled furniture and junk-shop odds and ends, the staff are pleasant enough and the drinks menu worth lingering longer for.

Česká Hospoda CZECH €€
(Map p368; Targ Rybny 14; mains 10-30zł; ☺ noon-11pm Mon-Thu, to midnight Fri & Sat, to 10pm Sun) Northern Poland's best Prague-style beer hall is a pretty authentic affair complete with three types of Bohemian lager, a menu of stodgy goulash, potato cakes and sirloin and a large outdoor terrace.

Bar Dziupla
POLISH **€€**

(Map p368; Rynek 9/10; mains 15-27zł; ☺8.30am-7.30pm; 🖥) Choose between the creamy interior or out on the pretty main square to enjoy a mixed menu that pretty much covers all Polish tastes.

★Browar Warmia
BREWERY

(Map p368; 📞89 523 5301; www.browarwarmia.pl; Nowowiejskiego 15; ☺4-11pm Tue-Thu, 3pm-1am Fri & Sat, 1-9pm Sun; 🖥) Possibly the best place in Warmia for a relaxing drink, this purpose-built, 21st-century brewery by the river has an uncluttered, view-rich pub where you can sample around ten beers brewed on site, including the oh-so northern Polish gingerbread beer and the more enticing Baltic Porter. There's a bistro menu when hunger strikes.

🛍 Shopping

Cepelia
ARTS & CRAFTS

(Map p368; cnr Prosta & Staszica; ☺10am-6pm Mon-Fri, to 2pm Sat) Tidy branch of the national handicrafts chain selling a wide range of souvenirs from across Poland.

ℹ Information

Olsztyn has two tourist information offices. The PTTK-affiliated **Regional Tourist Office** (Map p368; 📞89 535 3565; www.mazury.travel; Hotel Wysoka Brama, ul Staromiejska 1; ☺8am-6pm Mon-Fri, 10am-3pm Sat & Sun mid-Jun–Sep, shorter hours rest of year) deals with the wider area, and the municipal **Tourist Office** (Map p368; 📞89 521 03 98; www.olsztyn.eu; plac Jana Pawła II 1, enter from ul 1 Maja; ☺10am-4pm Mon-Sat) based in the town hall that fields questions specifically about the town.

ℹ Getting There & Away

The **bus** and **train stations** (Plac Konstytucji 3 Maja) are both in a big, dilapidated L-shaped building on Plac Konstytucji 3 Maja. Walk to the Old Town (15 minutes) or take one of the frequent city buses that drop off in front of the High Gate.

Buses run from Olsztyn to numerous towns:
Gdańsk 30zł, three hours, many daily
Giżycko 12zł, two hours, five daily
Kętrzyn 14zł, one to two hours, many
Lidzbark Warmiński 9zł, 50 minutes, 10 daily
Olsztynek 5zł, 50 minutes, two or three hourly

Olsztyn has the following regional rail connections:
Elbląg 19.80zł, 1¼ hours, 10 daily
Gdańsk 40zł, 2½ hours, six daily
Kętrzyn 18.60zł, 1¼ hours, seven daily
Toruń 39zł, two hours, four daily

Olsztynek
POP 7600

Around 25km southwest of Olsztyn, Olsztynek is a small town with one big attraction: the Museum of Folk Architecture. It's an easy day trip from Olsztyn with which it has good transport connections and provides a slightly different view of the region away from splashing around on the water.

👁 Sights

Museum of Folk Architecture
MUSEUM

(Muzeum Budownictwa Ludowego; 📞501 416 435; www.muzeumolsztynek.com.pl; ul Leśna 23; adult/concession 16/9zł; ☺10am-6pm Jul & Aug, slightly shorter hours rest of the year; 🅿) Open year-round, this skansen (open-air ethnographic museum) on the northeastern outskirts of Olsztynek features about 70 examples of regional timber architecture from Warmia and Masuria, plus a cluster of Lithuanian houses. There's a variety of peasant cottages complete with outbuildings, various windmills and a thatched-roof church. A number of buildings have been furnished and decorated inside in traditional period manner and the effect is impressive. The museum is best visited in summer when special events take place and demonstrations of local handicrafts can be watched in some of the buildings.

🛏 Sleeping & Eating

Zajazd Mazurski
HOTEL **€**

(📞89 519 2885; www.hotelmazurski.pl; Gdańska 1; s/d from 115/140zł; 🅿🖥) This low-key motel-guesthouse is on the way into town from the motorway and comes with comfortable rooms and efficient staff. Convenient for the Museum of Folk Architecture and good for a one-nighter en-route somewhere else.

★Restauracja z Zielonym Piecem
POLISH **€€**

(📞89 519 1081; www.zielonypiec.pl; Floriana 1; mains 10-35zł; ☺noon-9pm; 🖥) Gathered around a green ceramic stove (the *zielony piec* in question), this is one of Warmia's best restaurants and worth making a detour for. Enjoy home-cooked-style traditional dishes, such as goose breast baked with apple and cranberry, or pork knuckle in beer sauce in the beautiful dining room, all yesteryear knickknacks, lace and candlesticks.

Staff are polite and knowledgeable about the food they plate up and the Polish desserts are to die for.

ℹ Getting There & Away

The train station is 1km northeast of the centre, close to the skansen. Trains run to/from Olsztyn (4zł, 30 minutes) according to the needs of locals meaning lots of services early morning and mid afternoon.

The bus terminal is 250m south of the Rynek, but many regional buses call in at the train station. Buses and minivans run to Olsztyn (5zł, 50 minutes, two or three hourly).

Ostróda

POP 33,200

Drowsy Ostróda (pronounced ostr-*oo*-da) is the southern terminus of the Elbląg–Ostróda Canal, and if you take a boat from the town you might end up spending a night here. Apparently Napoleon once ruled Europe from this quiet corner; he wouldn't look twice at it now, but Polish holidaymakers love the leisurely pace of life here, attracted by its location on placid, swan-studded Lake Drwękie.

WARMIA & MASURIA OSTRÓDA

◉ Sights

Ostróda Castle   CASTLE

(Zamek w Ostródzie; www.muzeumwostrodzie.pl; Mickiewicza 22; adult/concession 5/3zł; ◷ 9am-5pm Tue-Fri Apr-Oct, shorter hours Nov-Mar) Ostróda's blocky red-brick castle was built by the Teutonic Knights in the late 13th century and now houses the town's museum, worth a look if you are into medieval bling. In summer the castle hosts many cultural events.

🛏 Sleeping & Eating

★**Hotel Willa Port**   HOTEL €€

(☎89 642 4600; www.willaport.pl; ul Mickiewicza 17; s/d from 290/350zł; P❄🐾🎵) Perched on the lake edge, this bold hotel is a real treat. Liberally tailored rooms are a delight of funky retro veneer; spots of audacious colour contrasting with beiges and greys, sinks like halved boiled eggs with the yokes removed and all-glass showers. Competition is high for lakeside rooms and the knock-'em-dead views from the balconies are worth the extra.

WORTH A TRIP

ELBLĄG–OSTRÓDA CANAL

The 82km Elbląg–Ostróda Canal is the longest navigable canal still in use in Poland. It's also the most unusual. The canal deals with the 99.5m difference in water levels by means of a unique system of slipways, where boats are physically dragged across dry land on rail-mounted trolleys. It was originally built to transport timber to the Baltic but is now used almost exclusively by tourist boats.

The canal follows the course of a chain of six lakes, most of which are now protected conservation areas. The largest is Lake Drużno near Elbląg. It was left behind by the Vistula Lagoon, which once extended deep into this region.

The five slipways are on a 10km stretch of the northern part of the canal. Each slipway consists of two trolleys tied to a single looped rope, operating on the same principle as a funicular. They are powered by water, a quite unique mechanism not found anywhere else in Europe.

The part of the canal between Elbląg and Miłomłyn, which included all the slipways, was built between 1848 and 1860, and the remaining leg to Ostróda was completed by 1872. The canal proved to be reliable and profitable, and it cut the distance of the original route along the Drwęca and Vistula almost fivefold. Various extensions were planned, including one linking the canal with the Great Masurian Lakes, 120km to the east, but none were ever built.

From June to September, Żegluga Ostródzko-Elbląska pleasure boats sail the most interesting parts of the canal between Ostróda and Elbląg. Sadly they no longer do the entire route which was, you have to admit, a rather long day. There are two tours to choose from – Elbląg to Buczyniec (4½ hours) which includes all five slipways, and Ostróda to Miłomłyn (2½ hours); both can be done in the opposite direction. Buses transfer passengers to their starting points. For timetables and prices see the website.

Regular services run throughout the summer and on hot summer days it may be an idea to book ahead. Outside this period there are fewer services. It's worth ringing Żegluga Ostródzko-Elbląska a couple of days in advance to find out about the availability of tickets and the current timetable status. Boats have snack bars on board, which serve some basic snacks and drinks.

Staff fluent in English, innovative design throughout and a trendy restaurant make this one of northeast Poland's finest sleeps.

Tawerna POLISH €€
(☑89 640 5293; www.tawerna.ostroda.pl; ul Mickiewicza 21; mains 15-30zł; ⊘noon-11pm; 🛜) Tawerna occupies a lovely spot on a small lake inlet at the northern end of town. Its large wooden deck is the perfect place for an aperitif or a hearty Polish meal. Kayak hire available for burning off any excesses.

ℹ Information

Tourist Office (☑89 642 3000; www.mazury-zachodnie.pl; Plac 1000-lecia Państwa Polskiego 1a; ⊘9am-6pm Mon-Fri, 10am-4pm Sat, to 2pm Sun Jun-Aug, shorter hours rest of year)

ℹ Getting There & Away

BOAT

Ostróda is the terminus of the **Żegluga Ostródzko–Elbląska** (☑89 670 9217; www.zegluga.com.pl; Mickiewicza 9a) and many people arrive here on one of their boats. See the website for the current timetable.

BUS

Elbląg 21zł, 1¼ hours, approximately hourly
Olsztynek 14zł, 35 minutes, 11 daily

TRAIN

Olsztyn 10.60zł, 30 to 40 minutes, at least hourly
Toruń 24zł to 34zł, 1½ to two hours, 10 daily

Lidzbark Warmiński

POP 16,400

Lidzbark Warmiński, 46km north of Olsztyn, is a rough and ready town with a massive Gothic castle. Its past is certainly more glorious than its present; it was the capital of the Warmian bishopric for over four centuries. In 1350 the bishops chose it as their main residence; a castle and a church were built and the town swiftly became an important religious and cultural centre. The astronomer Copernicus lived here between 1503 and 1510, serving as doctor and adviser to his uncle, Bishop Łukasz Watzenrode.

Today there's little trace of the town that was reputedly the richest and most cultured in Warmia, but the castle alone is enough to justify a day trip.

◉ Sights

Castle CASTLE
(www.muzeum.olsztyn.pl; Plac Zamkowy 1; adult/concession 14/10zł; ⊘10am-6pm Tue & Sat, to 5pm Wed, 9am-5pm Thu, Fri & Sun May-Sep) This stocky, square-set red-brick fortress, adorned with corner turrets, is probably Warmia's most significant cultural gem. Enter from the south through the palatial, horseshoe-shaped building surrounding Plac Zamkowy, which was extensively rebuilt in the 18th century. A wide brick bridge runs up to the main castle gate. Most of the interior, from the cellars up to the 2nd floor, now houses a branch of the Museum of Warmia.

The castle was commissioned in the late 14th century on a square plan with a central courtyard, the whole area surrounded by a moat and fortified walls. When the bishops' era ended with the 18th-century Partitions, the castle fell into decline and served as a variety of purposes, including use as barracks, a warehouse, a hospital and an orphanage. In the 1920s, restoration was undertaken and within 10 years the castle had been more or less returned to its original form. Miraculously, it came through the war unharmed, and today it is easily one of Poland's best-preserved medieval castles.

The first thing you'll notice is a beautiful courtyard with two-storey arcaded galleries all round it. It was constructed in the 1380s and has hardly been altered since then. The castle's two-storey vaulted cellar, cool on even the hottest of days, is largely empty aside from a few marble fireplaces and cannon barrels. The cannons once belonged to the bishops, who maintained their own small army.

Most of the attractions are housed on the 1st floor, which holds the main chambers; the vaulted Grand Refectory (Wielki Refektarz) is quite remarkable. The chessboard-style wall paintings, dating from the end of the 14th century, feature the names and coats of arms of bishops who once resided here. In stark contrast is an adjoining tiny room centred on a dank, dark pit, which was once used as a prison cell. Exhibitions on this floor include medieval art from the region, such as some charming Madonnas and fine silverware. The adjoining chapel was redecorated in rococo style in the mid-18th century and is quite overbearing compared to the rest of the castle.

The top floor contains several exhibitions, including cubist and surrealist 20th-century Polish painting, a collection of icons dating from the 17th century, and army uniforms and evening gowns from the early 1800s.

WARMIA & MASURIA LIDZBARK WARMIŃSKI

ⓘ Getting There & Away

The bus terminal occupies the defunct train station, about 500m northwest of the castle. There are 10 buses a day to Olsztyn (9zł, 50 minutes), supplemented by private minibuses.

THE GREAT MASURIAN LAKES

The Great Masurian Lake district (Kraina Wielkich Jezior Mazurskich), east of Olsztyn, is a verdant land of rolling hills dotted with countless lakes, healthy little farms, scattered tracts of forest and small towns. The district is centred on **Lake Śniardwy** (114 sq km), Poland's largest lake, and **Lake Mamry** and its adjacent waters (an additional 104 sq km). Over 15% of the area is covered by water and another 30% by forest.

The lakes are well connected by rivers and canals to form an extensive system of waterways. The whole area has become a prime destination for yachters and canoeists, and is also popular among anglers, hikers, bikers and nature-lovers.

The main lakeside centres are Giżycko, Mikołajki and Węgorzewo. All the lake towns burst into frenetic life in July and August, take it easy in June and September, and retire for a long snooze the rest of the year.

⌂ Sleeping

Accommodation in the region is aimed primarily at the summer holiday crowds, and consists mainly of campsites, pensions, holiday cottages and privately rented rooms, many let by the week, and most only open in July and August. Giżycko, Mikołajki and Węgorzewo are the main centres, while Kętrzyn has a handful of year-round hotels and is a useful out-of-season base.

ⓘ Getting There & Away

Trains run only to Kętrzyn and Giżycko (from Olsztyn and Białystok), but there are frequent buses to and between all the main towns. Nonetheless, exploring the region is much faster and easier with your own transport.

ⓘ Getting Around

Yachties can sail most of the larger lakes, all the way from Węgorzewo to Ruciane-Nida. These larger lakes are interconnected and form the district's main waterway system. Kayakers will perhaps prefer more intimate

surroundings alongside rivers and smaller lakes. The best established and most popular kayak route (p369) in the area originates at Sorkwity and follows the Krutynia River and Lake Bełdany to Ruciane-Nida.

If you're not up for doing everything yourself, you can enjoy the lakes in comfort from the deck of one of the pleasure boats operated by the **Żegluga Mazurska** (www.zegluga mazurska.com.pl). Theoretically, boats run between Giżycko, Mikołajki and Ruciane-Nida daily from May to September, and to Węgorzewo from June to August. In practice, trips can be cancelled if fewer than 10 passengers turn up, so the service is most reliable from late June to late August. Schedules are clearly posted at the lake ports.

The detailed *Wielkie Jeziora Mazurskie* map (scale 1:100,000), produced by Copernicus, is a great help for anyone exploring the region by boat, kayak, bike, car or on foot. The map shows walking trails, canoeing routes, accommodation and much more.

Kętrzyn

POP 27,500

Busy Kętrzyn (*kent*-shin) is the best base for daytrips to both the Wolf's Lair and Święta Lipka, though the town itself has little to offer visitors. It was founded in the 14th century by the Teutonic Knights and for most of its history was known as Rastenburg. Though partly colonised by Poles, it remained Prussian until WWII, after which it became Polish. The name derives from Wojciech Kętrzyński (1838–1919), a historian who documented the history of the Polish presence in the region.

◎ Sights

Castle   CASTLE

(www.muzeum.ketrzyn.pl; Plac Zamkowy 1; adult/concession 5/3zł; ⊙9am-6pm Tue-Sun May-Sep, 8am-4pm Oct-Apr) Kętrzyn's Teutonic past lives on in its mid-14th-century brick castle on the southern edge of the town centre. Today the building is home to the disappointingly scrappy Regional Museum, which displays exhibits tracing the town's history in very un-castle-like interiors. Highlights include a Prussian standing stone reminiscent of Central Asia's Scythian figures, old photos of Rastenburg and some beautiful old trunks.

St George's Church   CHURCH

(Bazylika Św Jerzego; www.bazylika.ketrzyn.pl; ul Zamkowa 5; tower adult/concession 5/3zł; ⊙9am-5pm) With its squat, square tower, the Gothic church looks like the town's second fortress

The Great Masurian Lakes

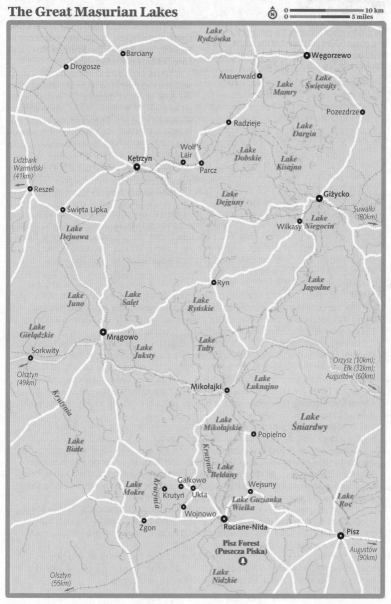

N
0 — 10 km
0 — 5 miles

WARMIA & MASURIA KĘTRZYN

from a distance. Its interior has furnishings and decoration dating from various periods, indicating a number of alterations over time.

Sleeping & Eating

★ **Zajazd Pod Zamkiem** GUESTHOUSE €
(☏89 752 3117; www.zajazd.ketrzyn.pl; ul Struga 3; s/d 110/140zł; ☒☜) Sitting pretty above a superb Polish restaurant and the town's best beer garden, the four generously cut rooms (sleeping up to four) all have identical layouts but different decor and colour schemes, with antiques thrown into the mix here and there. The 19th-century villa setting, proximity to the castle and filling breakfasts make this Kętrzyn's top choice. Book ahead.

WOLF'S LAIR

Hidden in thick forest near the hamlet of Gierłoż, 8km east of Kętrzyn, **Wolf's Lair** (Wilczy Szaniec; ☑ 89 741 0031; www.wilczyszaniec.olsztyn.lasy.gov.pl; Gierłoż; adult/concession 15/10zł, parking 5zł; ⊙ 8am-8pm Apr-Sep, to 4pm Oct-Mar; P) is one of Poland's eeriest historical relics – 18 overgrown hectares of huge, partly destroyed concrete bunkers. This was Hitler's main headquarters during WWII, baptised with the German name of Wolfsschanze. A famous attempt to assassinate the Führer took place here in July 1944.

The location was carefully chosen in this remote part of East Prussia, far away from important towns and transport routes, to be a convenient command centre for the planned German advance eastwards. The work, carried out by some 3000 German labourers, began in autumn 1940; about 80 structures were finally built, including seven bombproof bunkers for the top leaders. Martin Bormann (Hitler's adviser and private secretary), Hermann Göring (Prussian prime minister and German commissioner for aviation) and Hitler himself were among the residents. Their bunkers had walls and ceilings up to 8m thick.

The whole complex was surrounded by multiple barriers of barbed wire and gun emplacements, and a sophisticated minefield. An airfield was built 5km away and there was an emergency airstrip within the camp. Apart from the natural camouflage of trees and plants, the bunker site was further disguised with artificial vegetation-like screens suspended on wires and changed according to the season of the year. The Allies did not discover the site until 1945.

Hitler arrived at the Wolf's Lair on 26 June 1941 (four days after the invasion of the Soviet Union) and stayed there until 20 November 1944, with only short trips to the outside world. His longest journey outside the bunker was a four-month stint at the Ukraine headquarters of the Wehrmacht (the armed services of the German Reich) in 1942, overseeing the advancing German front.

Having survived an assassination attempt within the complex in July 1944, Hitler left the Wolf's Lair as the Soviet Red Army approached a few months later. The German army prepared the bunkers to be destroyed, should the enemy have attempted to seize them. The complex was eventually blown up on 24 January 1945 and the Germans retreated. Three days later the Soviets arrived, but the extensive minefield was still efficiently defending the empty ruins. It took 10 years to clear the 55,000 mines within the complex.

Today, the site has succumbed to Mother Nature; bunkers are slowly disappearing behind a thick wall of natural camouflage, and mosquitos are a pest. It's best to pick up a site map or booklet sold from stands in the parking area. If you're in a group, organise a guide to show you around; English-, German- and Russian-speaking guides charge 60zł for a 1½-hour tour. All structures are identified with numbers and marked with big signs telling you not to enter the ruins, advice that many people ignore, including some guides (bunker 6 appears to be the most popular one to enter).

Of Hitler's bunker (13) only one wall survived, but Göring's 'home' (16) is in relatively good shape. A memorial plate (placed in 1992) marks the location of Colonel Claus von Stauffenberg's 1944 assassination attempt on Hitler and a small exhibition room houses a scale model of the original camp layout.

You can also continue 200m past the entrance towards Węgorzewo, and take a small road to the right signposted 'Kwiedzina (5km)'. On either side of this narrow path is a handful of crumbling bunkers that can be explored free of charge.

Hotel Koch
HOTEL €€

(☑ 89 751 1093; www.hotelkoch.pl; ul Sportowa 1; s/d 220/270zł; P✷☎) The 29 bog-standard rooms with large bathrooms are a touch overpriced at this central option, but there's a decent restaurant (a rarity in these parts) and cycle hire available. Staff can help with trips out of Kętrzyn to local attractions.

Restauracja Kardamon
POLISH €€

(☑ 89 751 1022; www.kardamonketrzyn.pl; Plac Piłsudskiego 1; mains 15-48zł; ⊙ 10am-10pm Mon-Thu, to 11pm Fri & Sat, 11am-10pm Sun; ☎⑩) The Kardamon is quite a treat with its period, beige-and-white antique-style dining room in Kętrzyn's old town hall. The fare on offer is quite Polonia-centric, though pizzas and

Italian seafood pastas bookend the menu. Hosts regular high-brow concerts throughout the summer.

ℹ️ Information

Tourist Office (☎ 89 751 4765; www.it.ketrzyn. pl; Plac Piłsudskiego 10; ⊗ 9am-6pm Mon-Fri, 10am-3pm Sat & Sun Jun-Aug, 8am-4pm Mon-Fri rest of the year)

ℹ️ Getting There & Away

BUS

For the Wolf's Lair, take a service heading for Węgorzewo via Radzieje and alight at Gierłoż. At weekends it's advisable to take a taxi (40zł) from the large ul Szkolna rank in the town centre, as buses operate a why-bother-at-all kind of service. Otherwise buses run to the following towns:

Giżycko 8zł, 45 minutes, at least hourly
Olsztyn 14zł, one to two hours, many
Święta Lipka 2zł, 20 minutes, hourly
Węgorzewo 11.60zł, one hour, four daily

TRAIN

Kętrzyn has the following train services:

Gdańsk 50zł, four hours, two daily
Giżycko 8.20zł, 30 minutes, seven daily
Olsztyn 18.60zł, 1¼ hours, seven daily

Węgorzewo

POP 11,400

The small but busy town of Węgorzewo (ven-go-*zheh*-vo) on **Lake Mamry** is the northernmost lakeside centre for both excursion boats and independent sailors. The main town itself isn't quite on the lake shore but is linked to it by a 2km river canal. In summer it's less overrun by tourists than its southern cousins and has a slightly more rural feel.

🛏️ Sleeping

Camping Rusałka CAMPGROUND €
(☎ 87 427 2191; www.cmazur.pl; ul Leśna 2; per adult/tent 19/14zł; ⊗ May-Sep) With its pleasant wooded grounds, a restaurant, and boats and kayaks for hire, Rusałka is a good, well-run base with 200 pitches. It's on Lake Święcajty, 4km from Węgorzewo, off the Giżycko road. Infrequent PKS buses go here in season; if you don't want to wait, take any Giżycko-bound bus to the lake turn-off, then walk the last 1km.

Pensjonat Nautic GUESTHOUSE €€
(☎ 87 427 2080; www.nautic.pl; ul Słowackiego 14; s 120-160zł, d 220-240zł, apt 160-400zł; 🅿 🛜) An excellent and versatile family guesthouse near

the canal and the boat wharf. Rooms range from comfortable standard en suites with blue wood fittings to five superb apartments with their own kitchenettes and terraces.

ℹ️ Information

Tourist Office (☎ 87 427 4009; www.wegorzewo.pl; Bul Loir-et-Cher 4; ⊗ 8am-6pm Mon-Fri, 9am-5pm Sat, 10am-5pm Sun Jul & Aug, shorter hours and closed Sat & Sun rest of year)

ℹ️ Getting There & Away

BOAT

From July to August, a single **Żegluga Mazurske** (www.zeglugamazurska.pl) boat sails from the wharf at Lake Mamry for Giżycko at 3pm.

BUS

There are no trains, so head for the bus terminal 1km northwest of the centre, from where there are services to the following towns:

Giżycko 7.50zł, 35 minutes, hourly (change here for Olsztyn)
Kętrzyn 11.60zł, one hour, four daily

Giżycko

POP 29,700

Positioned on the northern shore of **Lake Niegocin**, Giżycko (ghee-*zhits*-ko) is the largest sailing centre in the lakes, and the focal point of the seasonal tourist trade. It's not an aesthetically pleasing town, with a lake frontage more tacky than tasteful, but it's one of the few Masurian towns with a buzz and its huge fortress is worth at least an hour of your time.

The town started life under the Teutonic Knights but was destroyed on numerous occasions by Lithuanians, Poles, Swedes, Tatars, Russians and Germans in turn. Today it's essentially a transport hub and provisions base for the holiday homes and water-sports centres that have grown up outside the town, and for the hordes of lake-bound holidaymakers who arrive en masse in the short summer season.

👁️ Sights

Boyen Fortress FORTRESS
(Twierdza Boyen; www.boyen.gizycko.pl; ul Turystyczna 1; adult/concession fortress & museum 12/7zł; ⊗ 9am-7pm Jul & Aug, slightly shorter hours Apr-Jun & Sep-Oct) The Boyen Fortress was built between 1844 and 1856 to protect the kingdom's border with Russia, and was named after the then Prussian minister of war, General

Hermann von Boyen. Since the frontier ran north–south along the 90km string of lakes, the stronghold was strategically placed in the middle, on the isthmus near Giżycko, situated by the lake to the west of the town centre.

The fortress, which consists of several bastions and defensive towers surrounded by a moat, was continually modified and strengthened, and successfully withstood Russian attacks during WWI. In WWII it was a defensive outpost of the Wolf's Lair, given up to the Red Army without a fight during the 1945 offensive. The fortifications have survived in surprisingly good shape, and some of the walls, bastions and barracks can safely be explored. Inside the museum you'll find a scale model of the fortress and a few odd items, such as a section of wall with a Russian soldier painted on it, used as target practice by the Prussians.

Rotary Bridge
BRIDGE

(Most obrotowy; ul Moniuszki) Giżycko's working rotary bridge was built in 1889 and is the only one of its kind in the country. Despite weighing more than 100 tonnes, it can be turned by one person, and is opened up to seven times daily to allow boats through, closing to traffic for between 20 minutes and 1½ hours each time. If you're travelling by car, circumvent the wait and take the long way round via ul Obwodowa. Pedestrians can take the footbridge a little further up the canal.

Water Tower
HISTORIC BUILDING

(Wieża Ćiśnień; www.wieza-gizycko.pl; cnr ul Warszawska & Wodociągowa; adult/concession 12/6zł; ⊙10am-10pm Jul & Aug, shorter hours May, Jun & Sep) Built in 1900 in neo-Gothic style, Giżycko's seven-storey Water Tower supplied the city with running water until 1997. Today the red-brick structure houses a cafe and memorabilia exhibition, but the main attraction is of course the views from the top, accessed by lift. The tower is located a short walk along ul Warszawska from the main Plac Grunwaldzki.

🏃 Activities

Yacht Charters

Giżycko has the largest number of yacht-charter agencies in the area, and accordingly offers the widest choice of boats. The town is also a recognised centre for disabled sailors, with regular national regattas, and many companies provide specialist equipment, advice and training.

The tourist office is likely to have a current list of agents (sometimes up to 40) and can provide advice. Finding anything in July and August without advance booking can be difficult. Securing a boat in early June or late September is much easier, but shop around, as prices and conditions vary substantially.

In July and August, expect to pay somewhere between 250zł and 500zł per day for a sailing boat large enough to sleep around four to five people. Prices depend on the size of cabins, toilet and kitchen facilities and so on, and are significantly lower in June and September – often half of the high-season prices. You pay for your own petrol.

Check the state of the boat and its equipment carefully, and report every deficiency and bit of damage in advance to avoid hassles on return. Come prepared with your own equipment, such as a sleeping bag, sturdy rain gear and torch.

Bełbot
BOATING

(☑87 428 0385; www.marina.com.pl) Yacht hire company with six vessels available.

Grzymała
BOATING

(☑87 428 6276; www.czarter.mazury.info.pl) Family company with six yachts for hire.

Interjacht
BOATING

(☑660 222 880; www.interjacht.pl) Large company with many yachts and low/last minute prices.

Osmolik Romuald
BOATING

(☑602 702 524; www.osmolik.com.pl) Small operation with prices around 300zł per day per yacht.

Ice Sailing

The Masurian Lake district is one of Poland's coldest regions in winter; lake surfaces often freeze over from December to April. During this time the lakes support ice sailing and ice windsurfing, mostly on crisp, clear days. The tourist office has a list of operators renting boats and giving lessons.

Cross-Country Skiing

Skiing on and around the frozen lake is a popular cold-weather activity. Ask the tourist office about where to hire the necessary gear.

Diving

CK Diver (☑602 718 580; www.ckdiver.pl; ul Mickiewicza 9) offers scuba-diving courses for all levels throughout the year, in groups or on an individual basis. Prices start at 100zł for a taster session, going up to 1600zł for advanced tuition. To find the office, walk north from Plac Grunwaldzki along al 1 Maja for around 150m, then take a left into ul Mickiewicza.

🛌 Sleeping & Eating

Gościniec Jantar
GUESTHOUSE €

(📞734 440 291; www.jantar-gizycko.eu; ul Warszawska 10; s 80-160zł, d 110-160zł; P 🛜) Stacked above its own traditional restaurant in the centre of town, this is a decent, cheap little guesthouse with 12 pine-filled rooms, thick rugs and polite staff. All rooms are en-suite and there's a pulse here even in the depths of winter.

Hotel Wodnik
HOTEL €€

(📞87 428 3871; www.cmazur.pl; ul 3 Maja 2; s 130-175zł, d 180-295zł; P 🛜) From the outside this looks like the worst kind of Socialist-era slab but the renovated rooms inside have only occasional reminders of Poland's yesteryear hospitality industry. Chunky radios and the odd noisy fridge aside, the small rooms are well maintained. Book ahead as this place fills up even in midwinter. It's located just off the main Plac Grunwaldzki.

Hotel Cesarski
HOTEL €€

(📞87 732 7670; www.cesarski.eu; Plac Grunwaldzki 8; s 130-180zł, d 195-310zł; P 🛜) This long-established hotel, Giżycko's oldest in fact, couldn't be more central, located as it is on the main town square near the tourist office. Rooms vary in standard but all are comfortable with recently updated bathrooms and dark furniture. Best of all there is the large roof terrace where breakfast can be taken.

★ Podkładka Restobar
INTERNATIONAL €€

(📞87 441 1606; www.podkladkarestobar.pl; Pasaż Handlowy, ul Kolejowa; mains 15-39zł; ⊘noon-midnight; 🛜) Urban, chic and hip, this large restaurant-bar hangout with its exposed lightbulbs and ventilation tubes and bare-brick walls is one of the best places in the lakes for a relaxing meal and a beer. The menu covers everything from pizzas and fajitas to Caesar salads and pho soup and lots in between and portions are big.

Kuchnia Świata
INTERNATIONAL €€

(📞87 429 2255; www.kuchnieswiata.pl; Plac Grunwaldzki 1; mains 22-39zł; ⊘10am-10pm; 🛜) One of the best year-round places to eat in town, the 'Cuisines of the World' certainly lives up to its name, with countless reminders of the culinary world you've left behind, such as Thai green curry, Greek salads and king prawns, populating the huge menu.

Grota
INTERNATIONAL €€

(ul Nadbrzeżna 3a; mains 15-30zł; ⊘11am-midnight Jul & Aug; 🛜) Restaurants on the marina may draw crowds with their lake-front views, but Grota gets the locals' vote for its food. Wood-oven-baked pizzas and a mix of Polish and German cuisine fill the menu, and there's canalside seating in summer. To find Grota, head to the Rotary Bridge from Plac Grunwaldzki, but turn left before crossing the river; it's on the left-hand side about 150m along.

Bar Hornet
POLISH €€

(www.barhornet.pl; ul Unii Europejskiej 3; mains 12-39zł; ⊘10am-10pm Sun-Fri, to 11pm Sat; 🛜) The suitably yellow Hornet splits itself into two sections: a self-service cafeteria and a smarter sit-down restaurant. The only difference between them is the waiters, but it's nice to have a choice! The food's decent value, with a fine selection of quick eats and a salad bar, and the wooden deck is good for warm evenings.

ℹ Information

Main Post Office (ul Pocztowa 2; ⊘8am-7pm Mon-Fri, to 2pm Sat) Three hundred metres north of Plac Grunwaldzki.

Tourist Office (📞87 428 5265; www.gizycko. turystyka.pl; ul Zajączka 2; ⊘9am-6pm Mon-Fri, 10am-4pm Sat & Sun Jul & Aug, shorter hours Sep-May, closed Sun Jan-Apr; 🛜) Friendly, award-winning office with loads of info on the region and free internet access. Enter from Plac Grunwaldzki.

ℹ Getting There & Away

BOAT

Żegluga Mazurska (www.zeglugamazurska. com) boats operate from May to September, with extra services in July and August. Services run to Mikołajki and Węgorzewo, among other destinations; check the website or the timetable at the wharf (near the train station) for sailing times and prices.

BUS

On the southern outskirts of town next to the train station, the bus terminal handles services to the following towns:

Kętrzyn 8zł, 45 minutes, at least hourly

Mikołajki 15zł, 45 minutes, every two hours

Olsztyn 12zł, two hours, five daily

Warsaw 45zł, 3¾ hours to 5½ hours, hourly (most services summer only)

Węgorzewo 7.20zł, 35 minutes, many daily

TRAIN

The train station is on the southern edge of town near the lake. Trains run to the following towns:

Ełk 13.50zł, 45 minutes, eight daily

Gdańsk 54zł, 4½ hours, two daily

Kętrzyn 8.20zł, 30 minutes, seven daily

Olsztyn 22zł, two hours, six daily

Warsaw 65zł, 5¾ hours, daily

WARMIA & MASURIA GIŻYCKO

Mikołajki

POP 3800

More intimate and scenic than Giżycko, lively lakeside Mikołajki (mee-ko-*wahy*-kee) perches on narrows crossed by three bridges. Tourism has all but taken over here, and its spruced up waterfront is filled to overflowing with promenading families and pleasure boats in summer. Like most of its neighbours, Mikołajki is a big hit with German tourists, especially those from the former GDR.

◉ Sights

Łuknajno Reserve　　NATURE RESERVE
(www.lukajno.pl) The shallow 700-hectare Lake Łuknajno, 4km east of Mikołajki, shelters Europe's largest surviving community of wild swans and is home to many other birds – 128 species have been recorded here. The 1200- to 2000-strong swan population nests in April and May but stays at the lake all summer. A few observation towers beside the lake make swan viewing possible. A rough road from Mikołajki goes to the lake, but there's no public transport. Walk 3.5km until you get to a sign that reads '*do wieży widokowej*' (to the viewing tower), then continue for 10 minutes along the path to the lake shore. The track can be muddy in spring and after rain, so choose your shoes wisely. Depending on the wind, the swans may be close to the tower or far away on the opposite side of the lake.

🏃 Activities

As in Giżycko, yacht hire is big business here in summer, and several well-established companies vie for the seasonal trade.

Szekla Czartery　　BOATING
(☑ 880 045 779; www.motorowka.eu; ul Kowalska 3) Hires out motorboats large and small at the marina for between 170zł and 900zł per hour.

Port Rybitwa　　BOATING
(☑ 87 421 6163; www.portrybitwa.pl) For short-term excursions, Port Rybitwa hires out low-powered motorboats from near the town's swimming beach. The owner can suggest plenty of excursions on the connecting lakes.

🛌 Sleeping & Eating

Camping Wagabunda　　CAMPGROUND €
(☑ 503 300 141; www.wagabunda-mikolajki.pl; ul Leśna 2; pitch per person/tent 18/16zł; ⊙ May-Sep; 🛜) The town's main camping ground. It's across the bridge from the centre and a 600m walk southwest. In addition to the camping area, it has plenty of small cabins that vary in standard and price, and bicycles, boats and canoes are available for hire.

★ Pensjonat Mikołajki　　GUESTHOUSE €€
(☑ 87 421 6437; www.pensjonatmikolajki.pl; ul Kajki 18; d from 180zł; P 🛜) In this part of Poland, accommodation is all about lake views, and if you book early here that's precisely what you'll get. But the other surprisingly contemporary rooms aren't bad either – all are fragrant with new furniture and boast well-maintained bathrooms. Small discounts for stays of four nights.

Hotel Mazur　　HOTEL €€
(☑ 87 428 2899; www.hotelmazur.pl; Plac Wolności 6; s/d 260/390zł; P 🛜) Occupying Mikołajki's grandest edifice, the former town hall on the main square, the Mazur is the town's finest digs, with liberally sized rooms and pristine bathrooms, though for these prices some of the pine furniture feels cheap. The wood-panelled salon and brick cellar restaurant are Mikołajki's swankiest dining nooks.

★ Przechowalnia Marzen　　BISTRO €€
(☑ 608 865 459; Osiedle na Górce 29; mains from 12zł; ⊙ 9am-noon & 2-8pm May-Sep; 🛜) 🍴 Books and blackboards and herbs gardens, this seasonal bistro (The Dream Storage Room!) provides a wonderful hideaway from the yachties. Most shun the tiny interior for the straggling garden where folding chairs find spots under apple trees. The breakfasts and afternoon bistro menu is a cut above the lake's normal standards with vegetarian options.

ℹ Information

Tourist Office (☑ 87 421 6850; www.mikolajki. eu; Plac Wolności 7; ⊙ 10am-6pm Mon-Sat, to 5pm Sun Jun-Aug, to 6pm Mon-Sat May & Sep)

ℹ Getting There & Away

BOAT

From May to September, **Żegluga Mazurska** (www.zeglugamazurska.com) boats connect Mikołajki with Giżycko – check the website for exact sailing times.

BUS

There are no trains serving Mikołajki, so that just leaves the tiny bus station on small plac Kościelny near the church at the top of the main street (ul 3 Maja) near the bridge, which handles services to the following towns:
Giżycko 15zł, 45 minutes, every two hours
Olsztyn 20zł, 2¼ hours, three daily (or change in Mrągowo)

Understand
Poland

Poland Today

In recent years, politics has sharply divided Polish society. There appears to be a chasm between the two major parties: liberal, left-of-centre Civic Platform (PO), once led by Donald Tusk, and Law & Justice (PiS), who espouse highly conservative, nationalistic values. In the firing line have been the country's media, judges, immigrants and the LGBT+ community.

Best on Film

Cold War (Paweł Pawlikowski; 2018) Oscar-nominated film that follows a tempestuous, tragic love story in and out of Poland during the post-WWII years.

Katyń (Andrzej Wajda; 2007) Moving depiction of the mass murder of over 22,000 Polish military officers and POWs by the Soviets in 1940.

The Pianist (Roman Polański; 2002) Highly acclaimed film about life in Warsaw's WWII Jewish ghetto.

Three Colours: White (Krzysztof Kieślowski; 1994) This 'anti-comedy' captures the free-wheeling capitalism of post-communist Warsaw.

Best in Print

Flights (Olga Tokarczuk; 2007) Winner of the the Man Booker International Prize, it includes a story of how Chopin's heart made its secret journey from Paris to Warsaw.

God's Playground: A History of Poland (Norman Davies; 1979) Highly readable two-volume set that covers 1000 years of Polish history.

The Painted Bird (Jerzy Kosiński; 1965) Page-turner on the travails of an orphan boy on the run during WWII.

Survival in Auschwitz (Primo Levi; 1947) Classic of Holocaust literature that hasn't lost a drop of impact.

Murder of a Mayor

On the evening of 13 January 2019, Gdańsk mayor Paweł Adamowicz suffered a brutal attack. He had been attending a charity gala, when his assailant, a 27-year-old man recently released from prison, stabbed the politician in the chest. Adamowicz, mayor of Poland's sixth-largest city since 1998, died the following afternoon. The day of his burial was one of national mourning and tens of thousands of Poles marched in silent tribute to him through the country's major cities.

It remains moot whether the murder was politically motivated. At the time of the crime, the attacker shouted that he had been wrongly imprisoned under a previous national government led by Civic Platform (PO), of which Adamowicz was once a member. However, officials have also described the assailant as mentally disturbed with a history of violence.

Nevertheless, in Poland's tense social climate, it has proved difficult to separate the killing from the toxic strain of politics in the country. Adamowicz was well known for his liberal, Eurocentric views. He declared Gdańsk a city open to refugees in 2017, going against the populist policies of the Law & Justice party (PiS), who have led the national government since 2015.

Traditional Values Rule?

While Poland's economy has been booming in recent years, not everyone has been swept along on the growing tide of prosperity. Among the economic policies that made PiS popular with less affluent Poles are a cut in the retirement age, additional housing benefits, and a monthly payment of 500zł per child to encourage women to have more babies. However, at the same time, under the conservative, Catholic-leaning PiS, funding for IVF treatment was scrapped in 2016, and there was an attempt to introduce stricter rules on abortion – the proposed changes failed when there were mass public rallies in protest.

In the run-up to the May 2019 EU elections, PiS chairman Jarosław Kaczyński had repeatedly painted the LGBT+ community as the No 1 enemy of traditional family values. While over half of Poles support civil partnerships, less than 50 per cent are in favour of same-sex marriage or allowing adoption by gay couples. In the capital, however, it's a different story to the rest of the country, with Warsaw's mayor promising to create an LGBT hostel and community centre, as well as a local crisis intervention system, plus access to anti-discrimination and sex education at schools.

Poland vs the EU

The vast majority of the population – 70% in one survey – consider EU membership positively, despite the current government's anti-EU stance. PiS has not seen eye to eye with the EU over several issues. First there was a clash over immigration policy, and then the new media laws allowing the government more control of state TV and radio – this was deemed a threat to freedom of expression in Poland by the EU.

There is also continued conflict over planned reforms of the judicial system, which PiS says are needed to purge vestiges of communism. The EU is concerned that the reforms will bring Poland's courts under tighter political control.

2019 Elections

At the time of research, Poland had yet to fix a date for its next parliamentary or presidential elections, although the former have to happen by no later than November 2019 and the latter during 2020. Opinion polls place the ruling PiS party way ahead of PO, the main opposition.

With this in mind, all eyes are on Donald Tusk, the former PO prime minister who has distinguished himself as President of the European Council and for his handling of the EU's side in the Brexit negotiations with the UK. Tusk's term of office at the EU expires in November 2019, and while he has yet to confirm his return to Polish politics, the pugnacious politician has also been unafraid to criticise PiS.

GDP (PER HEAD): **US$15,430**

INFLATION: **1.96%**

UNEMPLOYMENT: **3.7%**

LAKES: **AROUND 10,000**

WILD BISON: **1873**

WWII DEATHS AS % OF POPULATION: **21.4%**
(UK 3%; USA 0.9%)

if Poland were 100 people

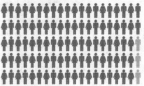

97 would be Polish
1 would be Silesian
2 would be other

belief systems
(% of population)

88
Catholic

2
none

1
other

9
no answer

population per sq km

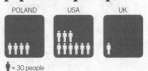

POLAND   USA   UK

≈ 30 people

History

Polish history is characterised by a series of epic climbs, cataclysmic falls and back-from-the-brink recoveries. The country that we would recognise today got its start around the first millennium, with the conversion to Christianity of Duke Mieszko I in 966. Once Europe's largest nation, it was carved up in the 18th century and disappeared from maps entirely until after the end of WWI. Survivor of WWII and communism in the 20th century, Poland is now a star EU performer.

Slavic Origins & the Piast Dynasty

Although the exact date of the arrival of the first Slavic tribes is unknown, historians agree Slavs began settling the area between the 5th and 8th centuries. From the 8th century onwards, smaller tribes banded together to form greater conglomerations, thus establishing themselves more fully on the lands of the future Polish state.

The country's name derives from one of these tribes, the Polanie (literally, 'the people of the fields'), who settled on the banks of the Warta River near present-day Poznań. Their tribal chief, the legendary Piast, managed to unite the scattered groups of the surrounding areas into a single political unit in the 10th century, and gave it the name Polska (later Wielkopolska, meaning Great Poland). It wasn't until the coming of Piast's great-great grandson, Duke Mieszko I, that much of Poland was united under one dynasty, the Piast.

Christianity & Conquering

The Ottoman Empire, though an ancient enemy of the Poles, was the only European power that never recognised the partition of Poland.

After Duke Mieszko I converted to Christianity, he did what most early Christian rulers did and began conquering the neighbours. Soon the entire coastal region of Pomerania (Pomorze) fell under his sovereignty, along with Śląsk (Silesia) to the south and Małopolska (Little Poland) to the southeast. By the time of his death in 992, the Polish state was established within boundaries similar to those of Poland today, and the first capital and archbishopric were established in Gniezno.

By that time, towns such as Gdańsk, Szczecin, Poznań, Wrocław and Kraków already existed. Mieszko's son, Bolesław the Brave, continued

TIMELINE	700 BC	Before AD 500	966
	During the Iron Age, the Lusatian tribe, present on the territory of modern-day Poland, builds a remarkable fortified settlement in the town of Biskupin.	Establishment of the first Polish town, Gniezno, by Lech, one of three mythical brothers who in legend founded the three Slavic nations (Poland, Ruthenia and Bohemia).	Poland's first recorded ruler, Duke Mieszko I, converts to Christianity, possibly as a political move against Otto the Great. It marks the formal birth of the Polish state.

his father's work, even pushing the Polish border as far east as Kyiv. The administrative centre of the country was moved from Wielkopolska to the less vulnerable Małopolska, and by the middle of the 11th century Kraków was established as the royal seat.

When pagan Prussians, from the region that is now the northeastern tip of Poland, attacked the central province of Mazovia in 1226, Duke Konrad of Mazovia called for help from the Teutonic Knights, a Germanic military and religious order that had made its historic mark during the Crusades. The knights soon subjugated the pagan tribes but then bit the hand that fed them, building massive castles in Polish territory, conquering the port city of Gdańsk (and renaming it Danzig), and effectively claiming all of northern Poland as their own.

They ruled from their greatest castle of all, at Malbork, and within a matter of decades became a major European military power.

The Reign of Casimir III the Great

Under the rule of Kazimierz III Wielki (Casimir III the Great; 1333–70), Poland gradually became a prosperous and powerful state. Kazimierz Wielki regained suzerainty over Mazovia, then captured vast areas of Ruthenia (today's Ukraine) and Podolia, thus greatly expanding his monarchy in the southeast.

Kazimierz Wielki was an enlightened and energetic ruler on the domestic front. Promoting and instituting reforms, he laid down solid legal, economic, commercial and educational foundations. He also passed a law providing privileges for Jews, thus establishing Poland as a safe house for the Jewish community for centuries to come. Over 70 new towns were founded, and the royal capital of Kraków flourished.

In 1364 one of Europe's first universities was established at Kraków, and an extensive network of castles and fortifications was constructed to improve the nation's defences. There is a local saying that Kazimierz Wielki 'found Poland built of wood and left it built of stone'.

The Defeat of the Knights

The close of the 14th century saw Poland forge a dynastic alliance with Lithuania, a political marriage that increased Poland's territory fivefold overnight and would last for the next four centuries. The union benefited both parties – Poland gained a partner in skirmishes against the Tatars and Mongols, and Lithuania received help in the fight against the Teutonic Knights.

Under Władysław II Jagiełło (1386–1434), the alliance finally defeated the Knights in 1410 at the epic battle of Grunwald and recovered eastern Pomerania, part of Prussia and the port of Gdańsk. For 30 years the Polish empire was Europe's largest state, extending from the Baltic to the Black Sea.

Norman Davies' two-volume *God's Playground: A History of Poland* is beautifully written, easy to read and perfect for understanding 1000 years of the Polish nation. *Heart of Europe: A Short History of Poland* is a condensed version, with a greater emphasis on the 20th century.

HISTORY SLAVIC ORIGINS & THE PIAST DYNASTY

1038	1226	1241–42	1333
Under the rule of Piast Kazimierz I, the Polish capital is moved from Gniezno to Kraków. The city would remain the seat of royal Poland for the next 550 years.	Duke Konrad of Mazovia calls in the Teutonic Knights to help him subdue a band of pagan Prussians, allowing the Knights to gain a firm foothold on Polish soil.	As Mongol invasions leave much of Europe in ruin, German settlers move east into Poland, at the same time as the country expands eastwards into modern day Ukraine.	Kazimierz III Wielki (Casimir III the Great) assumes the throne; under his near-40-year rule, Poland gradually becomes a prosperous and powerful state.

But it was not to last. Towards the end of the 15th century attacks on the country were launched by the Ottomans from the south, the Tatars of Crimea from the east, and the tsars of Moscow from the north and east. Independently or together, they repeatedly invaded and raided the eastern and southern Polish territories, and on one occasion managed to penetrate as far as Kraków.

The Golden Age & Royal Republic

The early 16th century brought the Renaissance to Poland and during the reigns of Zygmunt I Stary (Sigismund I the Old; 1506–48) and his son Zygmunt II August (Sigismund II Augustus; 1548–72), the arts and sciences flourished. This is traditionally viewed as the kingdom's 'golden age'.

The bulk of Poland's population at this time was made up of Poles and Lithuanians but included significant minorities from neighbouring countries. Jews constituted an important and steadily growing part of the community.

On the political front, Poland evolved during the 16th century into a parliamentary monarchy, with most of the privileges going to the *szlachta* (the feudal nobility), who comprised roughly 10% of the population. In contrast, the status of the peasants declined, and they gradually found themselves falling into a state of virtual slavery.

The Sejm (an early form of parliament reserved for the nobility) convened in Lublin in 1569, unified Poland and Lithuania into a single state, and made Warsaw the seat of future debates. When Zygmunt II August died without an heir it was the Sejm that also decided to established the 'Royal Republic' - the practice of 'electing' the kings by the nobility.

But the decision to allow foreign candidates would prove fatal as other European countries vied to promoted their candidates by bargaining and bribing voters. During this period, no fewer than 11 kings ruled Poland; only four were native Poles.

The first elected king, Henri de Valois, retreated to his homeland to take up the French crown after only a year on the Polish throne. His successor, Stefan Batory (Stephen Bathory; 1576–86), prince of Transylvania, was a much wiser choice. Batory, together with his gifted commander and chancellor Jan Zamoyski, conducted a series of successful battles against Tsar Ivan the Terrible and came close to forming an alliance with Russia against the Ottoman threat.

After Batory's premature death, the crown was offered to the Swede Zygmunt III Waza (Sigismund III Vasa; 1587–1632), and during his reign Poland achieved its greatest extent ever, more than three times the size of present-day Poland.

1493	1541	1569	1570s
Poland's lower house of parliament, or Sejm, is established. The first Sejm consists of bishops and noblemen, and is largely present to keep an eye on the monarchy.	Nicolaus Copernicus proposes that the earth orbits the sun and changes the course of science forever. Poles say that Copernicus 'stopped the sun and moved the earth'.	The Kingdom of Poland and the Grand Duchy of Lithuania unite as a single state to counteract the rising threat of the Moscow tsars. The union lasts until 1791.	Poland uniquely establishes a parliamentary monarchy, with most of the privileges going to the feudal nobility. This eventually proves a disaster when the nobles cannot agree on many key issues.

Poland Under Partition

The partition of Poland refers to the period at the end of the 18th century when the country was carved up between its more-powerful neighbours, Prussia, Russia and Austria. The partition period lasted all the way to the end of WWI. For 123 years Poland disappeared from world maps.

The partition initially led to immediate reforms and a new, liberal constitution, and Poland remained relatively stable. Catherine the Great could tolerate no more of this dangerous democracy, though, and sent Russian troops into Poland. Despite fierce resistance, the reforms were abolished by force.

Enter Tadeusz Kościuszko, a hero of the American War of Independence. With the help of patriotic forces, he launched an armed rebellion in 1794. The campaign soon gained popular support and the rebels won some early victories, but Russian troops, stronger and better armed, defeated the Polish forces within a year.

Despite the partition, Poland continued to exist as a spiritual and cultural community, and a number of secret nationalist societies were created. Since revolutionary France was seen as their major ally in the struggle, some leaders fled to Paris and established their headquarters there.

> The French general Napoleon Bonaparte was revered by many Poles as a potential national saviour. Speaking in Italy in 1797, he personally vowed to reverse the Polish partition that had been imposed on the country by Russia.

WWI & the 'Second Republic'

Though most of the fighting in WWI, at least on the eastern front, was staged on Polish land and caused staggering loss of life and livelihood, paradoxically, the war led to the country's independence.

On the one side were the Central Powers, Austria-Hungary and Germany (including Prussia); on the other, Russia and its Western allies. Since no formal Polish state existed, there was no Polish army to fight for the national cause. Even worse, some two million Poles were conscripted into the Russian, German or Austrian armies, and were obliged to fight one another.

After the October Revolution in 1917, Russia plunged into civil war and no longer had the power to oversee Polish affairs. The final collapse of the Austrian empire in October 1918 and the withdrawal of the German army from Warsaw in November brought the opportune moment for Poland to remerge as a sovereign state.

Rise & Fall of the Second Republic

The Treaty of Versailles in 1919 that formally ended WWI called directly for the creation of a newly independent Poland, and thus the 'Second Republic' was born.

1596–1609	1655–60	1683	1764
King Zygmunt III Waza (Sigismund III Vasa) moves the capital to Warsaw from Kraków because of its central location and closer proximity to Vilnius.	During the 'Deluge', Poland loses a quarter of its territory, cities are plundered and the economy is destroyed. From a population of 10 million, four million succumb to war, famine and plague.	Jan III Sobieski leads a Polish force in a battle against the Ottoman Turks at the gates of Vienna. His victory saves the city, but weakens Poland's own military defences.	King Stanisław August Poniatowski assumes the throne. He is a popular but weak ruler who allows Russia's Catherine the Great to exercise direct intervention in Poland's affairs.

PIŁSUDSKI: PATRIOT, SOLDIER, STATESMAN

Across Poland, you'll see statues bearing the stern, moustached visage of Marshal Józef Piłsudski, a controversial political figure in the 1920s and '30s who is nevertheless revered as a Polish patriot and superb military commander.

Piłsudski was born in 1867 in what is now Lithuania, then a part of the Russian empire. He joined the anti-tsarist movement while a teenager and spent many of his early years in prison: five years in Siberia, a brief stint in Warsaw's Citadel, and more jail time in St Petersburg, before returning to Poland to lead the Polish Legions in WWI.

Declaring the birth of a new Polish state in Warsaw on 11 November 1918 Piłsudski declared launched a massive offensive to the east, capturing vast territories that had been Polish before the 18th-century partitions. In the Battle of Warsaw in August 1920, the Polish army, under Piłsudski's command, outmanoeuvred and defeated the Red Army.

With an independent Poland safely back on the map and a modern democratic constitution adopted in 1921, Piłsudski stepped down in 1922. However, four years later, he declared an effective coup d'état in order to rescue the country from what he saw as a political stalemate and economic stagnation. Piłsudski's sudden return spurred three days of street fighting that left 400 dead and over 1000 wounded.

After the government resigned, the National Assembly elected Piłsudski as president. He refused to take that post and opted instead for the office of defence minister, which he maintained until his death. There are few doubts, though, that it was Piłsudski who ran the country behind the scenes until he died in 1935 and was buried with ceremony among Polish kings in the crypt of Kraków's Wawel Cathedral.

The treaty awarded Poland the western part of Prussia, providing access to the Baltic Sea. The city of Gdańsk, however, was omitted and became the Free City of Danzig. The rest of Poland's western border was drawn up in a series of plebiscites, which resulted in Poland acquiring some significant industrial regions of Upper Silesia. The eastern boundaries were established when Polish forces defeated the Red Army during the Polish–Soviet war of 1919–20.

Marshal Józef Piłsudski's most famous quotation is: 'To be defeated and not to submit, that is victory; to be victorious and rest on one's laurels, that is defeat'.

When Poland's territorial struggle ended, the Second Republic covered nearly 400,000 sq km and had a population of 26 million. One third was of non-Polish ethnic background, mainly Jews, Ukrainians, Belarusians and Germans.

After Piłsudski retired from political life in 1922, the country experienced four years of unstable governments until the great commander seized power once again in a military coup in May 1926. Parliament was gradually phased out but, despite the dictatorial regime, political repression had little effect on ordinary people. The economic situation was relatively stable, and cultural and intellectual life prospered.

1772	3 May 1791	1793	1795
First Partition of Poland at the instigation of Catherine the Great. Russia, Prussia and Austria annex substantial chunks of the country, amounting to roughly 30% of Polish territory.	The world's second written constitution (the first was in the USA) is signed in Warsaw. It places peasants under direct protection of the government, and attempts to wipe out serfdom.	Second Partition of Poland, with Russia and Prussia grabbing over half the remaining Polish territory. Poland shrinks to around 200,000 sq km and a population of four million.	The Third Partition of Poland. The country ceases to exist completely, and will only again become a republic after the end of WWI in 1918.

WWII

If Poles had been asked in the 1930s to sketch out a nightmare scenario, many would likely have said 'Germany fighting the Soviet Union over Poland', and that's more or less what happened. On 23 August 1939 a pact of nonaggression between Germany and the Soviet Union was signed in Moscow by their respective foreign ministers, Ribbentrop and Molotov. This pact contained a secret protocol in which Hitler and Stalin planned to carve up the Polish state.

The war that would vastly reshape the country started at dawn on 1 September 1939 with a massive German invasion. Fighting began in Gdańsk (at that time the Free City of Danzig) when German forces encountered a stubborn handful of Polish resisters at Westerplatte. The battle lasted a week.

Simultaneously, another German line stormed Warsaw, which finally surrendered on 28 September. Despite valiant resistance, there was simply no hope of withstanding the numerically overwhelming and well-armed German forces; the last resistance groups were quelled by early October.

Hitler's policy was to eradicate the Polish nation and Germanise the territory. Hundreds of thousands of Poles were deported en masse to forced-labour camps in Germany, while others, primarily the intelligentsia, were executed in an attempt to exterminate the spiritual and intellectual leadership.

The Jews were to be eliminated completely. At first they were segregated and confined in ghettos, then shipped off to extermination camps scattered around the country. Almost the whole of Poland's Jewish population (three million) and roughly one million other Poles died in the camps. Resistance erupted in numerous ghettos and camps, most famously in Warsaw.

Books on Poland in WWII

Rising '44: The Battle for Warsaw, by Norman Davies

Bloodlands: Europe between Hitler and Stalin, by Timothy Snyder

Between Two Evils, by Lucyna B Radlo

Soviet Invasion

Within a matter of weeks of the German invasion, the Soviet Union moved into Poland and claimed the country's eastern half. Thus, Poland was yet again partitioned. Mass arrests, exile and executions followed, and it's estimated that between one and two million Poles were sent to Siberia, the Soviet Arctic and Kazakhstan in 1939–40. Like the Germans, the Soviets set in motion a process of intellectual genocide.

Government-in-Exile & Homegrown Resistance

Soon after the outbreak of war, a Polish government-in-exile was formed in France under General Władysław Sikorski, followed by Stanisław Mikołajczyk. It was shifted to London in June 1940 as the front line moved west.

1807	1810	1815	Late 19th Century
Napoleon Bonaparte establishes the Duchy of Warsaw after crushing the Prussians on Polish soil. After Napoleon's defeat at the hands of the Russians, the duchy returns to Russia and Prussia.	The birth year of Frédéric Chopin, Poland's most beloved musician and a perennial favourite around the world. Until the age of 20 he lives in Poland.	Congress Kingdom of Poland is established at the Congress of Vienna. The Duchy of Warsaw is swept away and Poland once again falls under the control of the Russian tsar.	At the end of the century around four million Poles, from a total population of 20 to 25 million, emigrate to avoid harsh Russian rule. Most go to the USA.

Acclaimed Polish director Andrzej Wajda's 2007 film *Katyń* is a powerful and moving piece of work about the massacre of Polish officers in the Soviet Union on Stalin's orders during WWII. It's given added emotional impact by the fact that Wajda's own father was one of those officers.

The course of the war changed dramatically when Hitler unexpectedly attacked the Soviet Union on 22 June 1941. The Soviets were pushed out of eastern Poland by the onslaught and all of Poland lay under Nazi German control. The Führer set up camp deep in Polish territory, and remained there for over three years.

A nationwide resistance movement, concentrated in the cities, had been put in place soon after war broke out to operate the Polish educational, judicial and communications systems. Armed squads were set up by the government-in-exile in 1940, and these evolved into the Armia Krajowa (AK; Home Army), which figured prominently in the Warsaw Rising.

The Tide Turns

Hitler's defeat at Stalingrad in 1943 marked the turning point of the war on the eastern front, and from then on the Red Army successfully pushed westwards. After the Soviets liberated the Polish city of Lublin, the pro-communist Polish Committee of National Liberation (PKWN) was installed on 22 July 1944 and assumed the functions of a provisional government. A week later the Red Army reached the outskirts of Warsaw.

MASSACRE AT KATYŃ

In April 1943, German troops fighting Soviet forces on the eastern front came across extensive mass graves in the forest of Katyń, near Smolensk, in present-day Russia. Exploratory excavations revealed the remains of several thousand Polish soldiers and civilians who had been executed. The Soviet government denied all responsibility and accused the Germans of the crime. After the communists took power in Poland the subject remained taboo, even though Katyń was known to most Poles.

It wasn't until 1990 that the Soviets admitted their 'mistake', and two years later finally made public secret documents showing that Stalin's Politburo was responsible for the massacre.

The full horror of Katyń was finally revealed during exhumations of the mass graves by Polish archaeologists in 1995–96. Here's what happened: soon after their invasion of Poland in September 1939, the Soviets took an estimated 180,000 prisoners, comprising Polish soldiers, police officers, judges, politicians, intellectuals, scientists, teachers, professors, writers and priests, and crammed them into various camps throughout the Soviet Union and the invaded territories. On Stalin's order, signed in March 1940, about 21,800 of these prisoners were transported from the camps to the forests of Katyń and other areas, shot dead and buried in mass graves. The Soviet intention was to exterminate the intellectual elite of Polish society.

No one has been brought to trial for the atrocity, as Russia states that Katyń was a military crime rather than a genocide, war crime, or crime against humanity.

1903	1914	11 November 1918	28 June 1919
Warsaw-born Marie Curie is awarded the Nobel Prize for physics. The first woman so honoured, she becomes the first person to win two when she gets a second in 1911, for chemistry.	Start of WWI. The occupying powers – Germany and Austria to the west and south, Russia to the east – force Poles to fight each other on Polish soil.	The date of the founding of the Second Republic, so named to create a symbolic bridge between itself and the Royal Republic that existed before the partitions.	The Treaty of Versailles that formally ends WWI awards Poland the western part of Prussia and access to the Baltic Sea, but leaves Gdańsk a 'free city'.

Warsaw at that time remained under Nazi German occupation. In a last-ditch attempt to establish an independent Polish administration, the AK attempted to gain control of the city before the arrival of the Soviet troops, with disastrous results. The Red Army continued its westward advance across Poland, and after a few months reached Berlin. Germany capitulated on 8 May 1945.

At the end of WWII, Poland lay in ruins. Over six million people, about 20% of the prewar population, had lost their lives, and out of three million Polish Jews in 1939, only 80,000 to 90,000 survived the war. The cities were no more than rubble; only 15% of Warsaw's buildings survived. Many Poles who had seen out the war in foreign countries opted not to return to their devastated homeland.

Communist Poland

Poland emerged from WWII to find itself falling within the Soviet-dominated Eastern bloc. The problems started at the Yalta Conference in February 1945, when the three Allied leaders, Roosevelt, Churchill and Stalin, agreed to leave Poland under Soviet control. They agreed that Poland's eastern frontier would roughly follow the Nazi Germany–Soviet demarcation line of 1939. Six months later Allied leaders set Poland's western boundary along the Odra (Oder) and the Nysa (Neisse) Rivers; in effect, the country returned to its medieval borders.

The radical boundary changes were followed by population transfers of some 10 million people: Poles were moved into the newly defined Poland, while Germans, Ukrainians and Belarusians were resettled outside its boundaries. In the end, 98% of Poland's population was ethnically Polish.

As soon as Poland formally fell under Soviet control, Stalin launched an intensive Sovietisation campaign. Wartime resistance leaders were charged with Nazi German collaboration, tried in Moscow and summarily shot or sentenced to arbitrary prison terms. A provisional Polish government was set up in Moscow in June 1945 and then transferred to Warsaw. After rigged elections in 1947, the new Sejm elected Bolesław Bierut president.

In 1948 the Polish United Workers' Party (PZPR), the country's communist party, was formed to monopolise power, and in 1952 a Soviet-style constitution was adopted. The office of president was abolished and effective power passed to the first secretary of the Party Central Committee. Poland became an affiliate of the Warsaw Pact.

Bread & Freedom

Stalinist fanaticism never gained as much influence in Poland as in neighbouring countries, and soon after Stalin's death in 1953 it all but

You can find a library of wartime photographs chronicling the horror and destruction of the Warsaw Rising at www.warsawuprising.com.

A Surplus of Memory: Chronicle of the Warsaw Ghetto Uprising, by Yitzhak Zuckerman, is a detailed narrative of this heroic act of Jewish resistance.

Learn more about the communist years at www.ipn.gov.pl, the website of the Institute of National Remembrance.

August 1920	12–14 May 1926	1 September 1939	17 September 1939
Poland defeats the Soviet Red Army in the Battle of Warsaw. The battle helps to secure large portions of land in what is now Belarus and Ukraine.	Poland's postwar experiment with democracy ends when Marshal Józef Piłsudski seizes power in a military coup, phases out parliament and imposes an authoritarian regime.	Nazi Germany uses a staged attack on a German radio station by Germans dressed as Poles as a pretext to invade Poland. WWII starts.	The Soviet Union fulfils its side of the Molotov-Ribbentrop Pact, a blueprint for the division of Eastern Europe between it and Nazi Germany, and invades eastern Poland.

THE WARSAW RISING

In early 1944, with German forces retreating across Poland, the Polish resistance (Armia Krajowa; AK) in Warsaw was preparing for the liberation of its city. On 1 August 1944, orders were given for a general anti-German uprising, with the intention of establishing a Polish command in the city before the Red Army swept through.

The initial 'rising' was remarkably successful and the AK, creating barricades from ripped-up paving slabs and using the Warsaw sewers as underground communication lines, took over large parts of the city. It hoped to control the city until support came from both the Allies and the Soviets. But none arrived. The Allies were preoccupied with breaking out of their beachhead in Normandy after the D-Day landings, and the Red Army, which was camped just outside the capital, didn't lift a finger. On learning of the rising, Stalin halted the offensive and ordered his generals not to intervene or provide any assistance in the fighting.

The Warsaw Rising raged for 63 days before the insurgents were forced to surrender; around 200,000 Poles were killed. The German revenge was brutal – Warsaw was literally razed to the ground, and, on Hitler's orders, every inhabitant was to be killed. It wasn't until 17 January 1945 that the Soviet army finally marched in to 'liberate' Warsaw, which by that time was little more than a heap of empty ruins.

disappeared. The powers of the secret police declined and some concessions were made to popular demands. The press was liberalised and Polish cultural values were resuscitated.

In June 1956 a massive industrial strike demanding 'bread and freedom' broke out in Poznań. The action was put down by force and soon afterwards Władysław Gomułka, a former political prisoner of the Stalin era, was appointed first secretary of the Party. At first he commanded popular support, but later in his term he displayed an increasingly rigid and authoritarian attitude, putting pressure on the Catholic Church and intensifying persecution of the intelligentsia.

It was ultimately an economic crisis, however, that brought about Gomułka's downfall; when he announced official price increases in 1970, a wave of mass strikes erupted in Gdańsk, Gdynia and Szczecin. Again, the protests were crushed by force, resulting in 44 deaths. The Party, to save face, ejected Gomułka from office and replaced him with Edward Gierek.

1980 Strikes

Another attempt to raise prices in 1976 incited labour protests, and again workers walked off the job, this time in Radom and Warsaw. Caught in a downward spiral, Gierek took out more foreign loans, but, to earn hard currency with which to pay the interest, he was forced to divert

---

Books on the '89 Revolution

The Magic Lantern: The Revolution of '89, by Timothy Garton Ash

1989: The Struggle to Create Post–Cold War Europe, by Mary Elise Sarotte

The Year That Changed the World, by Michael Meyer

---

22 June 1941	1942	19 April 1943	1 August 1944
Nazi Germany abrogates the Molotov-Ribbentrop Pact and declares war on the Soviet Union. This creates an uneasy alliance between Poland and the Soviet Union against their common foe.	Nazi Germany establishes 'Operation Reinhard', the name given to its plan to murder the Jews in occupied Poland, and builds secret extermination camps in Poland's far eastern regions.	The date of the start of the Ghetto Uprising in Warsaw. The Jewish resistance fighters hold out against overwhelming German forces for almost a month.	Start of the Warsaw Rising. The entire city becomes a battleground, and after the uprising is quelled, the Germans decide to raze Warsaw to the ground.

consumer goods away from the domestic market and sell them abroad. By 1980 the external debt stood at US$21 billion and the economy had slumped disastrously.

By then, the opposition had grown into a significant force, backed by numerous advisers from the intellectual circles. When, in July 1980, the government again announced food-price increases, the outcome was predictable: fervent and well-organised strikes and riots spread like wildfire throughout the country. In August, they paralysed major ports, the Silesian coal mines and the Lenin Shipyard in Gdańsk.

Unlike most previous popular protests, the 1980 strikes were nonviolent; the strikers did not take to the streets, but stayed in their factories.

When God Looked the Other Way, by Wesley Adamczyk, is a gripping and terrible tale of a Polish family deported to southern Siberia in WWII.

Solidarity & the Collapse of Communism

The end of communism in Poland was a long and drawn-out affair that can be traced back to 1980 and the birth of the Solidarity trade union.

On 31 August of that year, after protracted and rancorous negotiations in the Lenin Shipyard, the government signed the Gdańsk Agreement. It forced the ruling party to accept most of the strikers' demands, including the workers' right to organise independent trade unions, and to strike. In return, workers agreed to adhere to the constitution and to accept the Party's power as supreme.

Workers' delegations from around the country convened and founded Solidarity (Solidarność), a nationwide independent and self-governing trade union. Lech Wałęsa, who led the Gdańsk strike, was elected chair.

It wasn't long before Solidarity's rippling effect caused waves within the government. Gierek was replaced by Stanisław Kania, who in turn lost out to General Wojciech Jaruzelski in October 1981.

The trade union's greatest influence was on Polish society. After 35 years of restraint, the Poles launched themselves into a spontaneous and chaotic sort of democracy. Wide-ranging debates over the process of reform were led by Solidarity, and the independent press flourished. Such taboo historical subjects as the Stalin–Hitler pact and the Katyń massacre could, for the first time, be openly discussed.

Not surprisingly, the 10 million Solidarity members represented a wide range of attitudes, from confrontational to conciliatory. By and large, it was Wałęsa's charismatic authority that kept the union on a moderate and balanced course.

Martial Law & Its Aftermath

In spite of its agreement to recognise the Solidarity trade union, the Polish government remained under pressure from both the Soviets and local hardliners not to introduce any significant reforms.

27 January 1945	February–August 1945	8 May 1945	1947
The Soviet Red Army liberates Germany's Auschwitz-Birkenau extermination camp. Some of the first photos and film footage of the Holocaust are seen around the world.	Poland's borders are redrawn. The Soviet Union annexes 180,000 sq km to the east, while the Allies return 100,000 sq km of Poland's western provinces after centuries of German rule.	WWII officially ends with the surrender of Nazi Germany. There's great joy throughout Poland, but also apprehension as the war's end finds the country occupied by the Soviet Red Army.	Despite Stanisław Mikołajczyk – the government-in-exile's only representative to return to Poland – receiving over 80% of the vote in elections, 'officials' hand power to the communist government.

Books on the '89 Revolution

The Magic Lantern: The Revolution of '89, by Timothy Garton Ash

....

1989: The Struggle to Create Post–Cold War Europe, by Mary Elise Sarotte

....

The Year That Changed the World, by Michael Meyer

This only led to further discontent and, in the absence of other legal options, more strikes. Amid fruitless wrangling, the economic crisis grew more severe. After the unsuccessful talks of November 1981 between the government, Solidarity and the Church, social tensions increased and led to a political stalemate.

When General Jaruzelski unexpectedly appeared on TV in the early hours of the morning of 13 December 1981 to declare martial law, tanks were already on the streets, army checkpoints had been set up on every corner, and paramilitary squads had been posted to possible trouble spots. Power was placed in the hands of the Military Council of National Salvation (WRON), a group of military officers under the command of Jaruzelski himself.

Solidarity was suspended and all public gatherings, demonstrations and strikes were banned. Several thousand people, including most Solidarity leaders and Wałęsa himself, were interned. The spontaneous demonstrations and strikes that followed were crushed, military rule was effectively imposed all over Poland within two weeks of its declaration, and life returned to the pre-Solidarity norm.

In October 1982 the government formally dissolved Solidarity and released Wałęsa from detention, but the trade union continued underground on a much smaller scale, enjoying widespread sympathy and support. In July 1984 a limited amnesty was announced and some members of the political opposition were released from prison. But further arrests continued, following every public protest, and it was not until 1986 that all political prisoners were freed.

The Gorbachev Impact

The election of Mikhail Gorbachev as leader in the Soviet Union in 1985, and his *glasnost* and *perestroika* programmes, gave an important stimulus to democratic reforms throughout Central and Eastern Europe.

By early 1989, Jaruzelski had softened his position and allowed the opposition to challenge for parliamentary seats.

These 'semifree' elections – semifree in the sense that regardless of the outcome, the communists were guaranteed a number of seats – were held in June 1989, and Solidarity succeeded in getting an overwhelming majority of its candidates elected to the Senate, the upper house of parliament. The communists, however, reserved for themselves 65% of seats in the Sejm.

Jaruzelski was placed in the presidency as a stabilising guarantor of political changes for both Moscow and the local communists, but a non-communist prime minister, Tadeusz Mazowiecki, was installed as a result of personal pressure from Wałęsa.

June 1956	1970	1978	November 1980
Poland's first industrial strike, in Poznań. Around 100,000 people take to the streets; the Soviet Union crushes the revolt with tanks, leaving 76 dead and over 900 wounded.	West German chancellor Willy Brandt signs the Warsaw Treaty that formally recognises the country's borders. Brandt famously kneels at a monument to the victims of the Warsaw Ghetto Uprising.	Karol Wojtyła, archbishop of Kraków, becomes Pope John Paul II. His election and triumphal visit to his homeland a year later dramatically increases political ferment.	Solidarity, the first non-communist trade union in a communist country, is formally recognised by the government. One million of the 10 million members come from Communist Party ranks.

This power-sharing deal, with the first non-communist prime minister in Eastern Europe since WWII, paved the way for the domino-like collapse of communism throughout the Soviet bloc. The Communist Party, losing members and confidence, historically dissolved itself in 1990.

The Rise & Fall of Lech Wałęsa

In November 1990, Solidarity leader Lech Wałęsa won the first fully free presidential elections and the Third Republic of Poland was born. For Wałęsa it marked the high point of his career and for Poland the start of a very rocky rebirth.

In the first few months of the new republic, the government's finance minister, Leszek Balcerowicz, introduced a package of reforms that would change the centrally planned communist system into a free-market economy almost overnight. His economic plan, dubbed 'shock therapy' for the rapid way that it would be implemented, allowed prices to move freely, abolished subsidies, tightened the money supply, and sharply devalued the currency, making it fully convertible with Western currencies.

The effect was almost instant. Within a few months the economy appeared to have stabilised, food shortages evaporated and shops filled up with goods. On the downside, prices skyrocketed and unemployment exploded. The initial wave of optimism and forbearance turned into uncertainty and discontent, and the tough austerity measures caused the popularity of the government to decline.

As for Wałęsa, while he was a highly capable union leader and charismatic man, as president he proved markedly less successful. During his statutory five-year term in office, Poland witnessed no fewer than five governments and five prime ministers, each struggling to put the newborn democracy back on track. His presidential style and accomplishments were repeatedly questioned by practically all of the political parties and the majority of the electorate.

Poland Joins the EU

Wałęsa was defeated in the 1995 presidential election by Aleksander Kwaśniewski – a former communist. Though the election was close, it marked quite a comedown for Solidarity and for Wałęsa, its anti-communist folk hero.

With the post of prime minister in the hands of another former communist, Włodzimierz Cimoszewicz, and parliament moving to the left as well, the country that had spearheaded the anti-communist movement in Central and Eastern Europe oddly found itself with a firmly left-wing government – a 'red triangle' as Wałęsa himself had warned.

The website www.polishroots.org shows how Poland's borders have shifted over the past 200 years since the country's partition.

13 December 1981	April 1989	1990	1995
Martial law is declared in Poland. It is debatable whether the move is Soviet driven or an attempt by the Polish communists to prevent Soviet military intervention. It lasts until 1983.	Poland becomes the first Eastern European state to break free of communism. In so-called round-table negotiations, Poland's opposition is allowed to stand for parliament and Solidarity is re-established.	Not a great year for Polish communists. The Party dissolves, the first democratic presidential election takes place and the country becomes a free-market economy.	Former communist Aleksander Kwaśniewski defeats Lech Wałęsa for the presidency in what ends up being a humiliating climb-down for the former leader of the Solidarity trade union.

SMOLENSK TRAGEDY

On 10 April 2010 a Polish air-force jet carrying 96 people, including president Lech Kaczyński, his wife and a high-level Polish delegation of 15 members of parliament, crashed near the Russian city of Smolensk. There were no survivors. The plane had been flying in from Warsaw for a memorial service to mark the 70th anniversary of the WWII-era massacre of Polish officers at Katyń Forest.

The pilot attempted to land the plane in heavy fog at a military airport, struck a tree on the descent and missed the runway. An initial high-level Russian commission placed the blame on pilot error, though an official Polish government report, released in 2011, assigned fault to both the Polish side and to air-traffic controllers on the Russian side.

Initially, all political sides were united in Poland after the crash as the country mourned at a procession of high-level funerals. While many leading officials were killed, there was no ensuing succession crisis and the country's government speedily got back on track, proving the strength of Poland's democracy.

However, the tragedy has since become a bone of contention between the left and right of Polish politics. In 2018, PiS, led by Jarosław Kaczyński, Lech's twin, claimed control of Warsaw's Piłsudski Square, so as to erect a memorial to the crash. This takeover of Warsaw's largest square from the city has been challenged as unlawful, and Warsaw's mayor, Rafał Trzaskowski, has refused to rule out the possibility of a referendum on whether the Smolensk monument should stay or be moved elsewhere.

The Catholic Church, much favoured by Wałęsa during his term in the saddle, also lost out and didn't fail to caution the faithful against the danger of 'neopaganism' under the new regime.

President Kwaśniewski's political style proved to be much more successful than Wałęsa's. He brought much-needed political calm to his term in office, and was able to cooperate successfully with both the left and right wings of the political establishment. This gained him a degree of popular support, and paved the way for another five-year term in office in the presidential election in October 2000. Wałęsa, trying his luck for yet another go, suffered a disastrous defeat, collecting just 1% of the vote this time around.

A referendum on EU membership in June 2003 resulted in a huge majority voting in favour, allowing Poland, on 1 May 2004, to fulfil one of its biggest post-communist foreign-policy objectives – joining the EU, along with seven other countries from Central and Eastern Europe.

1999	1 May 2004	July 2006	April 2010
Poland becomes a member of NATO. The country has come full circle, moving from the Warsaw Pact with the former Soviet Union to an alliance with the West.	Poland joins the EU. Despite massive support, there is fear that the country is swapping one foreign governing power for another, and EU membership will spark a wave of emigration.	Twin brothers Lech and Jarosław Kaczyński occupy the presidential and prime minister seats respectively. Their nationalistic and conservative policies alienate many people.	President Lech Kaczyński, his wife and more than 90 others die in a tragic plane crash near the Russian city of Smolensk. The country unites in grief.

Right vs Left

Polish politics in the first two decades of the 21st century has been polarised by the ideological tussle between the two main parties: Europhile, liberal Civic Platform (PO) and populist, conservative Law & Justice (PiS). During the 2000s these parties alternately held national power in various coalition governments.

Following the 2010 death of president Lech Kaczyński in the tragic Smolensk plane crash, the presidency fell to parliamentary speaker Bronisław Komorowski, who promptly called for early elections. Komorowski, representing PO, won in a run-off against PiS' Jarosław Kaczyński (twin brother of Lech Kaczyński), and served as president until the elections of 2015, when he was defeated by the right-of-centre Andrzej Duda. In parliamentary elections that same year, PiS won a simple majority, allowing it to form the first single-party government since the fall of communism in 1989.

Current prime minister Mateusz Morawiecki serves as the head of government and shares power with Duda. As both of them belong to PiS, it is party leader Jarosław Kaczyński who is said to exercise the most influence over policy decisions, which have veered sharply to the right. Opposition has come from Poland's major cities, including Warsaw and Kraków, where the citizens have elected PO-affiliated mayors. Additionally, citizens groups, such as Stop Abortion, have helped organised mass protests that led to a government climbdown over plans to ban abortion.

Acclaimed Polish director Andrzej Wajda's 2007 film *Katyń* is a powerful and moving piece of work about the massacre of Polish officers in the Soviet Union on Stalin's orders during WWII. It's given added emotional impact by the fact that Wajda's own father was one of those officers.

2015	2017	2018	2019
In the closest presidential race in Polish history, right-of-centre Law & Justice (PiS) candidate Andrzej Duda defeats incumbent Bronisław Komorowski.	Tens of thousands of people march in Warsaw in protest against the potential curbs on democracy imposed by the governing PiS.	Poland is referred to the EU's top court over its controversial Supreme Court reforms, which could force 40 per cent of its judges out via early retirement.	The nation grieves over the murder of Pawel Adamowicz, the liberal-leaning mayor of Gdańsk, who is stabbed to death at a public event.

Jewish Heritage

For centuries up until WWII, Poland was home to Europe's biggest population of Jews. Then came WWII, which saw the nation's Jewish citizens almost totally eradicated by Nazi Germany during the Holocaust. Communist Poland was also, at times, very anti-Semitic, driving away the few Jews that had survived and remained in the country. Recently though, Polish Jewish history and culture has been rediscovered and the community embraced.

Early Days & Kazimierz

Jews in Poland: A Documentary History, by Iwo Cyprian Pogonowski, provides a comprehensive record of half a millennium of Polish-Jewish relations.

Jews began arriving in what is now Poland around the turn of the first millennium, just as the Polish kingdom was being formed. Many of these early arrivals were traders, coming from the south and east along established trading routes.

From the period of the early Crusades (around 1100), Poland began to develop a name for itself as a haven for Jews, a reputation it would maintain for centuries. At least some of the early Jewish inhabitants were coinmakers, as many Polish coins from the period bear Hebrew inscriptions.

The Polish ruler most often associated with the growth of Poland's Jewish population is Kazimierz III Wielki (Casimir III the Great; 1333–70), an enlightened monarch who passed a series of groundbreaking statutes that expanded privileges for Jews. It's no coincidence that the Kazimierz district near Kraków and Kazimierz Dolny, both important Jewish centres, bear his name.

All was not a bed of roses and the good times were punctuated by occasional deadly pogroms, often as not whipped up by the clergy. At the time, the Catholic Church was not as fond of Jews as were the king and nobility, who relied on Jewish traders as middlemen and financiers.

The Golden Age

Cities with Important Jewish Heritage

Warsaw

Kraków

Lublin

Łódź

Kazimierz Dolny

The 16th century is considered the 'golden age' of Poland's Jews; the century saw a dramatic leap in the kingdom's Jewish population, driven in part by immigration. It was during this century that the Jewish population of the Kraków district of Kazimierz began to grow. It was an independent town at the time, with a significant Catholic population. Over the centuries, it would evolve into one of Poland's most important concentrations of Jewish culture and scholarship.

Much of Europe was then an intolerant place, and Jews were being forced out of neighbouring countries. Many new arrivals were Sephardim, descendants of Spanish Jews who'd been tossed out of Spain by King Ferdinand and Queen Isabella in 1492. By the end of the 16th century, Poland had a larger Jewish population than the rest of Europe combined.

Pogroms & Partition

If the 16th century was good, the 17th century was an unprecedented disaster, both for the country and its Jewish population.

The Cossack insurrection of the 1650s in neighbouring Ukraine, led by Bohdan Chmielnicki, resulted in massive pogroms and the slaughter of tens of thousands of Jews in the southeastern parts of the Polish kingdom.

The war with Sweden, the 'Deluge', laid waste to much of the kingdom. Jews found themselves caught in the middle, ruthlessly hunted by Swedes on one side and Poles on the other.

After the partitions of the 18th century, conditions for Jews differed greatly depending on what area they found themselves in. In the southern and eastern parts of the country that went to Austria, Jews enjoyed a gradual move towards religious tolerance – a trend that began in 1782 under Austrian Emperor Joseph II with his 'Edict of Tolerance'. The edict formally allowed Jewish children to attend schools and universities and permitted adults to participate in various jobs outside of traditional trades, as well as to own and operate factories. These freedoms were expanded slowly, in fits and starts, to other areas of the former Polish kingdom over the 19th century.

Industrialisation in the 19th century led to higher living standards for Jews and non-Jews alike. Many Jews chose to leave the *shtetl* (small Jewish villages in the countryside) for greater opportunities in rapidly growing cities such as Łódź and Warsaw. Urbanisation accelerated the process of assimilation, and by the 20th century, urban-dwelling Jews and Poles had much more in common than they had apart.

Any existing legal distinctions between Jews and Poles vanished after WWI with the establishment of an independent Poland, which declared everyone equal under the law regardless of religion or nationality.

A 1931 census showed Poland's Jews numbered just under three million people, or around 10% of the population.

> The Statute of Kalisz, enacted in 1264 by Bolesław the Pious, invited Jewish settlement in Polish lands and granted Jews legal rights that were unprecedented in Europe at that time.

JEWISH HERITAGE POGROMS & PARTITION

Historic Synagogues

Kraków (Kazimierz)

Warsaw

Zamość

Nowy Sącz

READING UP ON THE HOLOCAUST

Books about the Holocaust are numerous and it's not possible to cover all of the excellent titles, many written by Holocaust survivors and rich with detail. A few recommendations:

Auschwitz: A New History by Laurence Rees combines excellent scholarship with personal anecdote to explain how the changes in official Nazi policy during the war were felt at camps like Auschwitz-Birkenau. It sounds dry; however, it's anything but.

The novel *Fatelessness* by Hungarian Nobel laureate Imre Kertész tells the Auschwitz story through the eyes of a 15-year-old boy separated from his family in Budapest.

Primo Levi, an Italian Jew who survived the death camps, is the author of the classic *Survival in Auschwitz* (published in some countries under the name *If This is a Man*). Levi continued writing for several decades before his death in 1987 of an apparent suicide. He returned to the theme of the Holocaust again and again in books such as *The Reawakening*, *If Not Now, When?* and *The Drowned and the Saved*.

To see the camps from a Polish author's perspective, pick up a copy of Tadeusz Borowski's *This Way for the Gas, Ladies and Gentlemen*. Borowski was not a Jew, but a political prisoner. His Auschwitz-Birkenau is a madhouse of boxing matches and brothels and filled with unlucky souls willing to risk everything simply for the chance to steal a potato.

Holocaust Memorial Sites & Camps

Auschwitz-Birkenau

Majdanek

Bełżec

Treblinka

Sobibór

WWII & the Holocaust

When it comes to the near-total slaughter of Poland's Jewish population by Nazi Germany, starting in 1939, the numbers speak for themselves: of around three million Jews living in Poland in 1939, fewer than 100,000 survived the war. Whole communities, large and small, were wiped out.

In the early stages of the war, in 1940 and '41, the German occupiers forced Jews to live in restricted ghettos, such as in Warsaw, Łódź, Kraków's Podgórze neighbourhood, and scores of smaller cities around the country. In some cases, these were de facto internment camps; in others, like at Łódź, they were labour camps, harnessed directly to Germany's war effort. Living conditions were appalling and thousands died of disease, exhaustion and malnutrition.

After Germany declared war on the Soviet Union in the summer of 1941, Nazi policy towards the Jews shifted from one of internment to that of full-scale extermination. For many, death would come quickly. By the end of 1942 and early 1943, the majority of Poland's Jewry was gone. Most of the victims were shot in the fields and forests around their villages, or deported to hastily erected extermination camps at Auschwitz-Birkenau, Treblinka, Sobibór and Bełżec.

The extermination camps at Auschwitz-Birkenau and some other places would continue on through 1944, but by then most of the victims were European Jews from outside Poland.

Disillusionment & Emigration

In the aftermath of WWII, many surviving Jews opted to emigrate to Israel or the USA. A small percentage decided to try to rebuild their lives in Poland, with decidedly mixed results.

It seems hard to believe now, but in the immediate years after the war, there was not much sympathy in Poland for Holocaust survivors. Poland was a ravaged country, and every person had been made a victim by the war. Adding to this vitriolic atmosphere, after the war many impoverished Poles had simply asserted ownership of the homes and apartments of Jews who had been forcibly evacuated by the Nazis. In many cases, they were not prepared to give the properties back (even in the rare instances when the original owners actually survived the Holocaust).

Auschwitz: The Nazis and the Final Solution is a six-episode BBC documentary that attempts to deal with the horrific events at Auschwitz-Birkenau.

While it must be stated that most Poles acted honourably during the war – and many gave shelter to their Jewish neighbours – this ugly strain of Polish anti-Semitism has attracted its own share of scholars and books. Among the best-known of these is Jan T Gross' *Fear: Anti-Semitism in Poland After Auschwitz*. The low point came in Kielce in July 1946, when around 40 Jews were attacked and killed by an angry mob. The origins of the pogrom are unclear – some believe the attack was instigated by communist authorities – but for many Jews it marked a watershed in Polish attitudes. Emigration rates rose and few Jews chose to stay.

Additionally, Poland's position within the Soviet-controlled Eastern bloc greatly complicated the way the Holocaust was taught and commemorated. The Soviet Union had waged a mighty struggle to defeat Nazi Germany and the official line was to milk that effort for all it was worth. To that end, the suffering of the Jews was politicised, viewed as part of a greater struggle of the working class over fascism. Even today, many Holocaust memorial sites – such as Majdanek near Lublin – remain marred by wildly overblown communist-era statuary that appear to cast the Holocaust as part of an epic battle, instead of more appropriately being memorials to honour the lives lost.

State-sanctioned anti-Semitic campaigns during Poland's later communist years also saw big waves of forced Jewish emigration, in 1956 and 1968.

JEWISH TOURS

Apart from the following, local tourist offices can provide information on a particular area's Jewish sights and history.

Jarden Tourist Agency (p136) Based in Kraków, this tour operator specialises in Jewish heritage tours around town, including a popular two-hour driving tour of places made famous by the film *Schindler's List*.

Momentum Tours & Travel (☑in the USA 305 466 0652; www.momentumtours.com) Offers specialised tours of Jewish heritage sites in Poland. Its 10-day Poland tour starts and finishes in Warsaw and includes Łódź, Kraków, Rzeszów, Łańcut and Zamość.

Menora Info Punkt (p65) Can advise on all aspects of Jewish Warsaw. It also organises Jewish cooking classes and runs culinary tours of Poland in conjunction with the Taube Center for the Renewal of Jewish Life in Poland (www.taubephilanthropies.org).

Jewish Revival

The years since the collapse of the communist regime have seen a marked improvement in local attitudes towards Jewish culture and history. Even though Poland's conservative government has sought to silence criticism of Polish complicity in the Holocaust, the country is home to one of the fastest-growing Jewish communities in the world. Poles are now generally unafraid to discover their Jewish ancestry and those with Polish Jewish family roots are beginning to return to the country. It's estimated there are now 30,000 Jews among Poland's 38.5 million citizens, a threefold increase since 2007.

Kraków, especially the former Jewish quarter of Kazimierz, has led the way. The city's annual Jewish Culture Festival is filled with theatre, film and boisterous klezmer music. The festival has emerged as one of the city's – and the country's – cultural highlights. In 2010, Kraków opened the doors to an impressive museum covering the Nazi German occupation of the city during WWII, housed in the former enamel factory of Oskar Schindler, of *Schindler's List* fame.

Kazimierz itself is a mixed bag of serious Jewish remnants and cheesy-but-fun Jewish restaurants, where the *Fiddler on the Roof* theme is laid on so thick that even Zero Mostel would probably blush. Still, the energy is infectious and has exerted a positive influence on other cities, including Warsaw, Lublin and Łódź, to embrace their own Jewish heritage.

In Łódź there is an important Jewish landmarks trail that you can follow through the city's former Jewish area, in the process learning the tragic but fascinating story of what was the country's longest-surviving ghetto during the war. Lublin, too, now has a self-guided tour that highlights that city's rich Jewish heritage. In Tarnów you can eat at a kosher cafe, while the synagogue in Nowy Sącz is once more a place of worship.

Warsaw, home to the biggest Jewish population and thus the largest wartime ghetto, had long been a laggard in the effort to embrace the country's Jewish past. That changed in 2014 with the opening of the award-winning POLIN Museum of the History of Polish Jews. The Nożyk Synagogue, the only Warsaw synagogue out of some 440 to survive WWII, has been beautifully restored and holds regular services. Much has been done to preserve the city's two major Jewish cemeteries. JCC Warszawa offers a variety of Jewish cultural classes and activities, including Hebrew courses, and there's a busy programme of annual events such as Jewish music, food and film festivals. Set to open in 2023 is the Warsaw Ghetto Museum, located within the confines of the former ghetto.

Best Jewish Festivals

Jewish Culture Festival, Kraków

Jewish Cultural Festival, Białystok

Four Cultures Festival, Łódź

Singer's Warsaw Festival, Warsaw

The Arts

The Polish have long been a highly cultured people. Literature and cinema are where the country excels. Poland has produced five Nobel Prize winners in literature and several household names in film, such as Andrzej Wajda, Roman Polański and Krzysztof Kieślowski. The performing arts, including classical music, theatre and dance, are alive and kicking across the country, with concerts and festivals throughout the year.

Literature

In Poland, as in many Central European countries, literature holds a special place in the hearts of citizens. It has served as the only outlet for resentment against foreign rule during occupation, and has often captured the spirit of a struggling country.

The Polish Way: A Thousand-Year History of the Poles and their Culture (1987), by Adam Zamoyski, is one of the best accounts of Polish culture from its birth to the recent past. It is fully illustrated and exquisitely written.

Late-19th & Early-20th-Century Novelists

In 1905 Henryk Sienkiewicz (1846–1916) became the first of five Polish writers to be awarded the Nobel Prize for literature. His most famous work is *Quo Vadis?*, an epic novel chronicling the love affair between a pagan Roman and a young Christian girl in ancient Rome.

Władysław Reymont (1867–1925), who bagged the Nobel in 1924, is best known for *The Peasants* (Chłopi), a novel about Polish village life written in four parts between 1904 and 1909, and *The Promised Land* (1899), set in Łódź during the Industrial Revolution.

Between the wars, several brilliant avant-garde writers emerged, who were only fully appreciated after WWII. They included Bruno Schulz (1892–1942), Witold Gombrowicz (1904–69) and Stanisław Ignacy Witkiewicz (also known as Witkacy; 1885–1939).

Despite penning only a handful of books, Schulz is regarded as one of Poland's leading literary lights; his *The Street of Crocodiles* is a good introduction to his ingenious, imaginative prose.

The Post-WWII Generation

The postwar period presented Polish writers with a conundrum: adopt communism and effectively sell out, or take a more independent path and risk persecution or expulsion.

Czesław Miłosz (1911–2004), who broke with the communist regime, offered an analysis of this problem in *The Captive Mind* (Zniewolony Umysł). Miłosz, a long-time émigré, spent the last 40 years of his life in the USA. He won the Nobel Prize in 1980 in recognition of his achievements.

Novelist, screenwriter and film director Tadeusz Konwicki (1926–2015) is another remarkable figure of the postwar literary scene. Konwicki was a teenage resistance fighter during WWII, and his pre-1989 works had communist censors tearing their hair out. He wrote more than 20 novels; among the best known are the brilliant *A Minor Apocalypse* (Mała Apokalipsa) and *The Polish Complex* (Kompleks Polski).

Stanisław Lem (1921–2006) excelled at science fiction. Around 45 million copies of his books, translated into 41 languages, have been sold around the world. The most famous is *Solaris*, which has been made into a feature film three times.

Contemporary Writers

In 2018, Olga Tokarczuk became the first Polish winner of the the the Man Booker International Prize for her novel *Flights,* a book that is themed around travel in the modern age. Tokarczuk's novel *Drive Your Plow over the Bones of the Dead* (originally published in 2009 and more recently translated by Antonia Lloyd-Jones) was also shortlisted for the Man Booker International Prize in 2019.

Zygmunt Miłoszewski has penned a series of entertaining crime fiction novels featuring the world-weary state prosecutor Teodor Szacki. *Entanglement* is set in modern-day Warsaw and shines a light on the murderous operations of the shady state services during Poland's communist era, while *A Grain of Truth* tackles issues of anti-Semitism.

Married couple Jacek Dehnel and Piotr Tarczyński collaborate under the pen name Maryla Szymiczkowa on a historical mystery series set in turn-of-the-19th-century Kraków. The first of their translated books *Mrs Mohr Goes Missing*, featuring their housewife-turned-detective Zofia Turbotyńska, is very much in the Agatha Christie mould.

> Culture.pl (www.culture.pl) promotes all aspects of Polish culture, with features in Polish, English and Russian on literature, design, visual arts, music, film and more.

THE ARTS LITERATURE

Poetry

The 19th century produced three exceptional Polish poets: Adam Mickiewicz (1798–1855), Juliusz Słowacki (1809–49) and Zygmunt Krasiński (1812–59). Known as the Three Bards, they captured a nation deprived of its independence in their romantic work.

The greatest of the three, Mickiewicz, is to the Poles what Shakespeare is to the British, and is as much a cultural icon as a historical and creative figure. Born in Navahrudak, in what is now Belarus, he was a political activist in his youth and was deported to central Russia for five years. He left Poland in the 1830s, never to return, and served as a professor of literature in Lausanne and Paris.

Mickiewicz' most famous poem, known to all Polish schoolchildren, is the epic, book-length 'Pan Tadeusz' (1834). It is a romantic evocation of a lost world of 18th-century Polish-Lithuanian gentry, torn apart by the Partition of 1795.

Poet, essayist and translator Maria Wisława Anna Szymborska (1923–2012) was the Nobel Prize recipient in 1996. Her poem 'Love At First Sight' inspired Krzysztof Kieślowski's movie *Three Colours: Red.* For those wanting to sample her work in English, a good introduction is the volume entitled *View with a Grain of Sand,* published in 1995.

POLISH WRITERS ABROAD

One of the most famous Polish émigré writers is Joseph Conrad. He was born Józef Teodor Konrad Nałęcz Korzeniowski (1857–1924) in Berdichev, in what is now in western Ukraine. After 20 years travelling the world as a sailor, he settled in England where he dedicated himself to writing in English, adopting his pen name in 1895. His novels (*Heart of Darkness* and *Lord Jim*, to name but two) are considered classics of English literature.

Polish-born Nobel Prize–winner Isaac Bashevis Singer (1902–91) spent his formative years in Poland before moving to the USA in 1935. Singer originally wrote in his native Yiddish, before translating his work into English for an American audience. Two of his most memorable stories are *Enemies, a Love Story* and *Yentl*; the latter was made into a film starring Barbra Streisand.

Cinema

Though the invention of the cinema is attributed to the Lumière brothers, some sources claim that a Pole, Piotr Lebiedziński, should take some of the credit; around the same time the French brothers were holding their first private screening of projected motion pictures in 1895, Lebiedziński had also developed his own cine camera.

The earliest surviving Polish movie is from 1908, but large-scale film production only took off after WWI. Little work produced between the wars reached international audiences; the country's greatest contribution to world cinema at the time was actress Pola Negri (1897–1987), a star of Hollywood's silent flicks of the 1920s.

The Polish School

Polish cinema came to the fore from 1955 to 1963, the period known as the Polish School. The school drew heavily on literature and dealt with moral evaluations of WWII – its three greatest prodigies, Andrzej Wajda (1926–2016), Roman Polański (b 1933) and Jerzy Skolimowski (b 1938), all attended the Łódź Film School and went on to international acclaim.

Check out the Polish Film Institute's website (www.pisf.pl) for up-to-date information on the Polish film industry.

Wajda produced arguably his best work during this time, the famous trilogy *A Generation* (Pokolenie), *Canal* (Kanał) and *Ashes and Diamonds* (Popiół i Diament). Among his other best works are *Man of Marble* (Człowiek z Marmuru), its sequel *Man of Iron* (Człowiek z Żelaza), *The Promised Land* (Ziemia Obiecana), which was nominated for an Oscar, and his deeply moving *Katyń,* about the massacre of Polish officers by the Soviet Union in the Katyń Forest during WWII.

Polański and Skolimowski began their careers in the early '60s; the former made only one feature film in Poland, *Knife in the Water* (Nóż w Wodzie), before continuing his career in the West. The latter shot four films, of which the last, *Hands Up* (Ręce do Góry), made in 1967, was kept from the public until 1985. Skolimowski also left Poland for more receptive pastures, and while he gained an international following, it was nothing compared to the recognition Polański received. Polański's body of work includes the classics *Cul-de-Sac, Revulsion, Rosemary's Baby, Chinatown* and *The Pianist.*

After the Polish School

After the 1960s, Polish filmmakers continued to create exemplary works. The communist era produced a string of important directors, including Krzysztof Zanussi, Andrzej Żuławski and Agnieszka Holland, and in 1970 Marek Piwowski shot *The Cruise* (Rejs), Poland's first cult film, a quasi-documentary comedy that parodies life in the communist-run nation.

Jakub Żulczyk's Warsaw-set neo-noir thriller *Blinded by the Lights* has been turned into a six-part HBO TV series that debuted to general acclaim in 2019.

Krzysztof Kieślowski (1941–96) is the director of the extraordinary trilogy *Three Colours: Blue/White/Red*. He started in 1977 with *Scar* (Blizna), but his first widely acclaimed feature was *Amateur* (Amator). His ambitious 1988 project *Decalogue* (Dekalog), a 10-part TV series of one-hour films based on the Ten Commandments, was broadcast all over the world.

In 2015 the film *Ida,* by director Paweł Pawlikowski, became the first Polish feature to win the Oscar for Best Foreign Film. It's a moving story – filmed in black and white – of a young girl in training to become a nun in 1960s as she discovers her Jewish roots and the wartime fate of her family. Pawlikowski's superb 2018 feature *Cold War* was also nominated for an Oscar.

Music

Classical

The foremost figure in the history of Polish music is Frédéric Chopin (1810–49), who crystallised the national style in classical music, taking inspiration from folk or court dances and tunes such as *polonez* (polonaise), *mazurek* (mazurka), *oberek* and *kujawiak*. No one else in the history of Polish music has so creatively used folk rhythms for concert pieces, nor achieved such international recognition.

Chopin was not the only composer inspired by folk dances at the time. Stanisław Moniuszko (1819–72) used his inspiration to create Polish national opera; two of his best-known pieces, *Halka* and *Straszny Dwór*, are staples of the national opera-house repertoire. Henryk Wieniawski (1835–80), another remarkable 19th-century composer, also achieved great heights in the world of Polish music.

By the start of the 20th century, Polish artists were beginning to grace the world stage. The first to do so were the piano virtuosos Ignacy Paderewski (1860–1941) and Artur Rubinstein (1886–1982); the latter performed right up until his death. Karol Szymanowski (1882–1937) was another musical personality of the first half of the 20th century; his best-known composition, the ballet *Harnasie,* was influenced by folk music from the Tatra Mountains, which he transformed into the contemporary musical idiom.

Jazz

Jazz retains a passionate following in Poland - possibly owing something to the fact that the genre was officially frowned upon by the former communist government for nearly 40 years.

Krzysztof Komeda (1931–69), a legendary pianist, became Poland's first jazz star in the postwar decades and an inspiration to many who followed, including Michał Urbaniak (violin, saxophone), Zbigniew Namysłowski (saxophone) and Tomasz Stańko (trumpet), all of whom became pillars of the scene in the 1960s. Urbaniak opted to pursue his career in the USA, and is perhaps the best-known Polish jazz musician on the international scene.

Of the younger generation, Leszek Możdżer (piano) is possibly the biggest revelation thus far, followed by several other exceptionally skilled pianists such as Andrzej Jagodziński and Włodzimierz Pawlik, who in 2014 was the first Polish jazz musician to receive a Grammy. Other jazz talents to watch out for include Piotr Wojtasik (trumpet), Maciej Sikała (saxophone), Adam Pierończyk (saxophone), Piotr Baron (saxophone) and Cezary Konrad (drums). Singers include Aga Zaryan, the first Polish singer to sign with Blue Note Records.

Visual Arts

The country's first major painter was no Pole at all. Bernardo Bellotto (c 1721–80) was born in Venice, the nephew (and pupil) of that quintessential Venetian artist, Canaletto. He specialised in *vedute* (town views) and explored Europe thoroughly, landing the job of court painter in Warsaw during the reign of King Stanisław August Poniatowski (1764–95). An entire room in Warsaw's Royal Castle is devoted to his detailed landscapes of the city, which proved invaluable as references during the reconstruction of the Old Town after WWII. Bellotto often signed his canvases 'de Canaletto', and as a result is commonly known in Poland simply as Canaletto.

Chopin Locations

Fryderyk Chopin Museum (Warsaw)

Church of the Holy Cross (Warsaw; Chopin's heart is buried here)

Warsaw University (where Chopin studied)

Żelazowa Wola (Chopin's birthplace)

Development of Polish Artists

By the middle of the 19th century, Poland was ready for its own paint-ers. Born in Kraków, Jan Matejko (1838–93) created stirring canvases that glorified Poland's past achievements. He aimed to keep alive in the minds of his viewers the notion of a proud and independent Polish na-tion, at a time when Poland had ceased to exist as a political entity. His most famous work is *The Battle of Grunwald* (1878), an enormous paint-ing that took three years to complete. It depicts the famous victory of the united Polish, Lithuanian and Ruthenian forces over the Teutonic Knights in 1410 and is displayed in Warsaw's National Museum.

The likes of Józef Brandt (1841–1915) and Wojciech Kossak (1856–1942) also contributed to the documentation of Polish history at this time; Kos-sak is best remembered as co-creator of the colossal cycloramic painting *Racławice Panorama,* which is on display in Wrocław.

Post-WWII Art & Design

From the end of WWII until 1955 the visual arts were dominated by so-cialist realism – canvases and sculptures of tractors, heroic peasants and epic landscapes dotted with factories.

This was also a time when graphic poster art came to the fore, build-ing on a tradition dating back to the turn of the last century. One of the most influential artists was Tadeusz Trepkowski (1914–54), who produced his best posters after WWII. His works, and those by other more contemporary poster artists such as Ryszard Kaja (1962–2019) can be seen at Warsaw's Poster Museum and various commercial galleries around the country.

From 1955 onwards, Poland's painters began to experiment with a va-riety of forms, trends and techniques. Zdzisław Beksiński (1929–2005) is considered one of the country's best contemporary painters; he created a mysterious and striking world of dreams in his art. Also look out for works by Wojciech Fangor (1922–2015), particularly his 'E series' of paint-ed circles, which pulsate with their dynamic colour ranges.

Folk Arts, Crafts & Music

Folk culture is strongest in the mountains, especially in the Podhale at the foot of the Tatras, but other relatively small enclaves, such as Kurpie and Łowicz (both in Mazovia), help to keep traditions alive.

The distinctive Polish pottery decorated with an indigo pattern on a white background, often seen in homeware and gift shops across the country, comes from in and around the Silesian town of Bolesławiec. The region is rich in natural clay deposits and pottery has been made here since at least the 14th century. A professional ceramics school was founded in Bolesławiec in 1897 and today there are more than 20 com-panies in the area making hand-crafted and hand-decorated tableware and decorative objects.

Poland's many open-air ethnographic museums, called *skansens*, are the best places to see traditional arts and crafts – good ones to visit in-clude those in Sanok and Nowy Sącz.

Folk music has been kept alive by groups such as the Śląsk Song and Dance Ensemble (www.slask.art.pl), formed in 1953, and the Warsaw Vil-lage Band (www.warsawvillageband.net), who have been gathering old music traditions since 1977 to create a more contemporary sound.

Landscape & Wildlife

With primeval forest, wind-raked sand dunes, reedy islands, caves, craters, a desert, a long chain of mountains and even a peninsula called Hel, it's fair to say that Poland has one of Europe's most diverse collections of ecosystems, which support thousands of species of flora and fauna. The country enjoys a long stretch of the Baltic coast and has countless lakes and rivers, popular with yachties, anglers, swimmers and divers.

A Varied Landscape

Poland's bumps and flat bits were largely forged during the last ice age, when the Scandinavian ice sheet crept south across the plains and receded some 10,000 years later. This left five identifiable landscape zones: the Sudetes and Carpathian Mountains in the south, the vast central lowlands, the lake belt, the Baltic Sea coast and the north-flowing rivers.

Mt Rysy was climbed by Nobel laureate Marie Curie and her husband in 1899, and possibly by Russian revolutionary Lenin in either 1910 or 1913.

Southern Mountains

The southern mountains stretch from the Sudetes range in the southwest to the Tatras in the south and the Beskids in the southeast. The Sudetes are geologically ancient hills, their rounded peaks reaching their highest point at the summit of Śnieżka (1602m) in the Karkonosze range. Poland's highest point is Mt Rysy (2499m) in the Tatras, a jagged, alpine range shared with Slovakia. Indeed, the hiking trails in Tatras are integrated with those on the other side of the ridge in Slovakia, meaning you can hike across the border and pick up the same trails on the other side.

To the north of the Tatras lies the lower (but much larger) densely forested range of the Beskids, with its highest peak at Babia Góra (1725m). The southeastern extremity of Poland is occupied by the Bieszczady, part of the Carpathian arc and arguably the most picturesque and lonely procession of peaks in the country.

Central Lowlands

The central lowlands stretch from the far northeast all the way south to around 200km shy of the southern border. The undulating landscape of this, the largest of Poland's regions, comprises the historic areas of Lower Silesia, Wielkopolska, Mazovia and Podlasie. Once upon a time, streams flowing south from melting glaciers deposited layers of sand and mud that helped produce some of the country's most fertile soils. As a result, the central lowlands are largely farmland and Poland's main grain-producing region. In some places, notably in Kampinos National Park to the west of Warsaw, fluvioglacial sand deposits have been blown by wind into sand dunes up to 30m high, creating some of the largest inland natural sand structures in Europe.

Poland is Europe's fourth most forested country, with woodlands covering about 30% of the land area. The forests are an important habitat for animals, such as red deer, roe deer and wild boars.

Fuel for the 19th-century Industrial Revolution was extracted from the vast coal deposits of Upper Silesia in the western part of the lowlands. The close proximity of this relatively cheap fuel encouraged the eventual growth of giant steel mills in industrial plants in this part of the country, leaving a legacy of air and water pollution that the country is still coping with.

Lakelands

The lake zone includes the regions of Pomerania, Warmia and Masuria. The last contains most of Poland's 10,000-plus lakes, which more than in any other European country except Finland. The gently undulating plains and strings of post-glacial lakes were formed by sticky clay deposited by the retreating ice sheet. The lake region boasts the only remaining *puszcza* (primeval forest) in Europe, making Białowieża National Park and the wildlife inhabiting it among the highlights of a visit to Poland.

Baltic Coast

The sand-fringed Baltic coast stretches across northern Poland from Germany to Russia's Kaliningrad exclave. The coastal plain that fringes the Baltic Sea was shaped by the rising water levels after the retreat of the Scandinavian ice sheet and is now characterised by swamps and sand dunes. These sand and gravel deposits form not only the beaches of Poland's seaside resorts but also the shifting dunes of Słowiński National Park, the sand bars and gravel spits of Hel, and the Vistula Lagoon.

Northern Rivers

Polish rivers drain northwards into the Baltic Sea. The largest is the mighty 1090km-long Vistula (Wisła), originating in the Tatra Mountains. Along with its right-bank tributaries – the Bug and the Narew – the Vistula is responsible for draining almost half of the country and is known as the 'mother river' of Poland, given its passage through both Kraków and Warsaw. The second-largest river, the Odra (along with its major tributary, the Warta) drains the western third of Poland and forms part of the country's western border. Rivers are highest when the snow and ice dams melt in spring and are prone to flooding during the heavy rains of July.

Wildlife

There is a rich bounty of zoological and ornithological treasure in Poland. Its diverse landscapes provide habitats for mammal species such as wild boar, red deer, elk and lynx in the far northeast, and brown bears and wildcats in the mountain forests of the south. Rare bird species found in Poland include thrush nightingales, golden eagles, white-backed and three-toed woodpeckers, and hazel grouses, among 200 other species of nesting birds.

Bison

The European bison (*Bison bonasus; żubr* in Polish) is the largest European mammal, its weight occasionally exceeding 1000kg. These large cattle, which can live for as long as 25 years, might look pretty clumsy but can move at 50km/h when they need to.

Bison were once found all over the continent, but the increasing exploitation of forests in Western Europe pushed them eastwards. In the 19th century, the last few hundred bison lived in freedom in the Białowieża Forest. In 1916 there were still 150 animals, but three years later they were gone, hunted to extinction. At that time only about 50 bison survived in zoos across the world.

It was in Białowieża that an attempt to prevent the bisons' extinction began in 1929, by taking several animals from zoos and breeding them in their natural habitat. The result is that today around 900 bison live in freedom in the Białowieża Forest, and several hundred more have been sent to a dozen other places around Poland. Many bison from Białowieża have been distributed among European zoos and forests, and their total worldwide population is now around 6,600.

Various programmes are underway in the Oder Delta, spanning the northwestern border of Poland and Germany, to help protect and enhance the area's rich ecosystems. For more information see www.rewildingeurope.com/areas/oder-delta.

In addition to their baby-delivery service, *bociany* (storks) are also known in Poland to bring good luck. Poles will often place wagon wheels and other potential nesting foundations on their roofs to attract the white stork.

Wolves

Grey wolves are the largest members of the canine family and were once a common feature of the Polish landscape. In the days of old, wolf hunting was a favourite pastime of Russian tsars. This, and diminishing habitats, drove their numbers down until wolves had all but disappeared in the 1990s. After specialised legislation to protect them was passed in 1998, recent wolf counts have revealed that the numbers have once again begun to climb and are now around 2000.

Horses

Poland has a long tradition of breeding Arabian horses and the Polish plains were once home to wild horses. Several species of wild horse have been preserved in zoos, including the tarpan, which is extinct out of captivity. Luckily, Polish farmers used to crossbreed tarpans with their domestic horses and the small Polish konik horse is the result of this mix, keeping the tarpan genes alive. Konik horses are now being used to breed the tarpan back. The hucul pony is a direct descendant of the tarpan, living in the Carpathians.

Bird Life

The diverse topography of Poland is home to a diverse range of bird species. The vast areas of lake, marsh and reed beds along the Baltic coast, as well as the swampy basins of the Narew and Biebrza Rivers, support many species of waterfowl and are also visited by huge flocks of migrating geese, ducks and waders in spring and autumn. A small community of cormorants lives in the Masurian Lakes.

Storks, which arrive from Africa in spring to build their nests on the roofs and chimneys of houses in the countryside, are a much-loved part of the rural scene. The expression 'every fourth stork is Polish' is based on the fact that Poland welcomes around 30,000 white storks each year (around one third of the total European population), most of which make their summer homes in Masuria and Podlasie in the northeast.

The *orzeł* (eagle) is the national symbol of Poland and was adopted as a royal emblem in the 12th century. Several species can be seen, mostly in the southern mountains, including the golden eagle and short-toed eagle, as well as the rare booted eagle, greater spotted eagle and lesser spotted eagle. The white-tailed eagle, supposedly the inspiration for the national emblem, lives in national parks along the Baltic coast.

Josepha Contoski's prize-winning children's book *Bocheck in Poland* is a beautifully rendered story of the relationship between white storks and Polish people.

LANDSCAPE & WILDLIFE WILDLIFE

Environmental Organisations

Polish Green Network (www.zielonasiec.pl)

Polish Ecological Club (www.zb.eco.pl)

ClientEarth (www.clientearth.org/poland)

TACKLING AIR POLLUTION

Poland has made some strides in environmental protection in recent years, but continues to cope with legacy issues, including the massive deforestation that occurred during WWII and the rapid build-up of industrial output – particularly in Upper Silesia – during the communist period.

A major ongoing problem is the country's reliance on coal for heating and electricity generation. Europe's largest coal-fired power plant, in Bełchatów, is the continent's largest carbon emitter. Poland has some of the most polluted air in all of the EU, and 33 of its 50 dirtiest cities. Some 48,000 Poles are estimated to die annually from illnesses related to poor air quality.

The national government is devoting resources and has plans to combat pollution, though at the same time it continues to champion the politically powerful coal industry, allowing the development of new coal mines in Silesia and even importing coal from the US.

Local administrations are tackling the issues more directly. In March 2019, Poland's Supreme Court upheld the Kraków government's decision to ban coal and wood burning across the city, an action that environmental groups believe will pave the way for similar anti-smog resolutions to be passed across the country.

Plant Life

Many visitors will probably be surprised to hear that Poland contains the only surviving fragment of original forest that once covered much of prehistoric Europe. This old-growth forest of Białowieża National Park is still home to majestic five-centuries-old oak trees and a range of flora that is, quite literally, ancient.

The most common plant species in Poland is the pine, which covers 70% of the total forested area, but the biological diversity and ecological resilience of forests are increasing thanks to the proliferation of deciduous species such as oak, beech, birch, rowan and linden. The forest undergrowth hosts countless moss and fungus species, many of the latter suitable for rich sauces or to be fried in breadcrumbs.

In the highest mountain regions, coniferous forests of dwarf mountain pines are capable of resisting harsher climates, while the lowlands and highlands are hospitable for dry-ground forests and marsh forests. Distinctly Polish plants include the Polish larch *(Larix polonica)* and the birch *(Betula oycoviensis)* in the Ojców region.

Conservation Areas in Poland

Around 23% of the country is under some sort of protection as a national park, landscape park or other type of conservation area. Entry into national parks, as well as some regional and landscape parks, normally requires an admission fee, payable at kiosks located near trailheads. Fees vary by park but typically range from 5zł to 10zł per day.

Poland's oldest national park, Białowieża, was established in 1932. There are now 23 *parki narodowe*, covering about 3200 sq km – about 1% of the country's surface area. Outside of a group of six in the Carpathian Mountains, they are distributed fairly evenly and therefore exhibit the full range of landscapes, flora and fauna the country possesses.

There are also 121 *parki krajobrazowe* (landscape parks), covering a total area of approximately 25,000 sq km. These also play a key role in conservation efforts. As well as their aesthetic contribution, landscape parks are often of key historical and cultural value.

Finally there are around 1470 *rezerwaty* (protected nature reserves), usually small areas containing a particular natural feature such as a cluster of old trees, a lake with valuable flora or an interesting rock formation. Ten biosphere reserves have been recognised by Unesco for their innovative approach to sustaining various ecological elements.

Information on local initiatives for environmental protection and sustainable development can be found on the website of the Partnership Fund Foundation (www.ffp.org.pl), the Polish branch of a regional foundation that promotes ecology and ecoresponsible tourism.

The WWF notes that Poland's forests are particularly vulnerable to acid rain and other forms of air pollution, especially from the emissions of coal-fired plants.

Survival Guide

Directory A-Z

Accessible Travel

When it comes to accessible travel in Poland the general consensus is it's difficult, but doable.

Medieval town centres with cobblestones, stairs and high curbs present challenging mobility issues, and many older buildings, including hotels and museums, are not wheelchair friendly. However, all new buildings, including modern museums, art galleries, shopping malls and train stations, are designed to be accessible, and an increasing number of older buildings are being retrofitted with ramps, lifts and wider doors.

In terms of public transport, most trains, buses and trams have ramps and are designed to accommodate wheelchairs.

Download Lonely Planet's free Accessible Travel guides from http://lptravel.to/AccessibleTravel.

Accessible Poland Tours (☏22 518 7983; www.accessibletour.pl) Specialises in organising tours for travellers with disabilities and mobility problems.

ZTM (Zarząd Transportu Miejskiego; Municipal Transport Authority; ☏19 115; www.ztm.waw.pl) Information on public transport in the capital (on the English-language website, click on Information and Travel Without Barriers).

Nie Pełno Sprawni (www.niepelnosprawni.pl) Polish language only; up-to-date information on the current situation for people with disabilities in Poland.

Accommodation

Poland has a wide choice of accommodation to suit all budgets. Advanced booking is recommended for popular destinations such as Kraków, Zakopane and Gdańsk.

➜ Warsaw is the most expensive place to stay, followed by Kraków, Gdańsk and Wrocław. The further away from the big cities you go, the cheaper accommodation gets.

➜ Watch for seasonal fluctuations in rates. Summer resorts, particularly on the Baltic coast or in the mountains, have higher prices in July and August. Ski centres increase prices in winter, particularly over the Christmas and New Year holidays.

➜ Hotels in large cities often offer discounts on the weekend. Similarly, resort properties may offer lower room rates during the week.

PRACTICALITIES

Newspapers & Magazines Catch up on Polish current affairs at the Warsaw Voice website (www.warsawvoice.pl). Foreign newspapers can be found at Empik stores, bookshops and news stands in the lobbies of upmarket hotels.

Radio State-run Polskie Radio (www.polskieradio.pl) is the main radio broadcaster, operating on AM and FM in every corner of the country; all programmes are in Polish.

TV The two main state-run, countrywide TV channels are TVP1 and TVP2, the latter of which is more educational and culture focused. There are several private channels, including the countrywide PolSat.

Smoking Smoking and vaping are banned in all public indoor spaces, including hotels, bars and restaurants, on public transport and at transport stops and stations. Some restaurants, bars and clubs have a separate, closed-off room for smokers.

Weights & Measures Poland uses the metric system.

➡ Prices normally include breakfast but not parking, which can range from 10zł a night in smaller properties to 100zł a night for garaged parking in Warsaw and Kraków.

➡ Room rates include VAT and should be the final price you pay. A small number of municipalities levy a tourist tax on lodging, but this seldom costs more than around 2zł a night per room.

➡ Prices are quoted in złoty, though some larger hotels geared to foreign clients may also quote rates in euros. All hotels accept złoty as payment.

Types of Rooms

Polish hotels offer a standard mix of rooms, including singles, doubles, and apartments or suites. Often hotels will also have rooms for three or four people. Hotels normally display a sign at the reception desk, listing the types of rooms and prices. Look for the following:

single room	*pokój 1-osobowy*
double room	*pokój 2-osobowy*
with bathroom	*z łazienką*
without bathroom	*bez łazienki*
basin in room only	*z umywalką*

➡ Prices for double rooms may vary depending on whether the room offers twin beds or one full-sized bed, with the latter generally more expensive.

➡ Some properties do not have dedicated single rooms, but may offer a double at a reduced rate. It never hurts to ask.

Hotels

Hotels account for the majority of accommodation options in Poland, encompassing a variety of old and new places, ranging from basic to ultra-plush.

BOOK YOUR STAY ONLINE

For more accommodation reviews by Lonely Planet authors, check out http://lonelyplanet.com/hotels/. You'll find independent reviews, as well as recommendations on the best places to stay. Best of all, you can book online.

At the top end are various international and Polish hotel chains that offer high-standard accommodation to a mostly business-oriented clientele. Going down the chain, there are plenty of smaller, privately owned hotels that cater to the mid-range market. Many are very nice and represent excellent value, but it always pays to check the room before deciding whether to stay.

Pensions

Pensjonaty (pensions) are small, privately run guesthouses that provide breakfast and occasionally half or full board. By and large, these are clean, comfortable and good value.

While prices vary depending on the location and comfort, they are usually cheaper than comparable hotels. Note that breakfast buffets can sometimes lack imagination (mostly simple ham and cheese plates) and they often have only instant coffee.

Hostels

Polish hostels include both the newer breed of privately owned hostels and the older, publicly run or municipal hostels. There are big differences. There are also simple, rustic mountain lodges operated by PTTK (Polish Tourist & Sightseeing Society).

PRIVATE HOSTELS

You will usually only find these in cities such as Kraków, Warsaw, Zakopane, Wrocław, Poznań and Łódź. Standards are often higher than in basic youth hostels and prices are roughly the same. They typically offer shared dorm-room accommodation, with higher prices charged for rooms with fewer bunks.

➡ Private hostels usually provide group kitchens, laundry facilities and sometimes a lounge and bar.

➡ Beds normally come with sheets included, and rooms should have lockers to guard your things when you're not around.

➡ Free wi-fi and computers are often available to surf the net, and friendly multilingual staff can help answer questions.

➡ Although marketed toward backpackers, there are no age restrictions or curfews.

PUBLIC HOSTELS

Poland has around 600 *schroniska młodzieżowe* (youth hostels), which are operated by the **Polskie Towarzystwo Schronisk Młodzieżowych** (PTSM; Polish Youth Hostel Association; www.ptsm.org.pl), a member of Hostelling International (HI). Of these, around 20% are open year-round; the rest are open in July and August only.

➡ Hostels are normally marked with a sign featuring a green triangle with the PTSM logo inside, placed over the entrance.

➡ Curfew is normally 10pm, and almost all hostels are closed between 10am and 5pm.

➡ Facilities and conditions of public hostels differ markedly. Some hostels are in poor shape, while others are pleasant and modern.

SLEEPING PRICE RANGES

The following price ranges refer to an average double room in high season, with private bathroom and breakfast.

Warsaw & Kraków:

€ less than 170zł

€€ 170zł–600zł

€€€ more than 600zł

Elsewhere:

€ less than 150zł

€€ 150zł–400zł

€€€ more than 400zł

➡ Seasonal hostels are normally located in schools while pupils are on holidays, and conditions are much more basic, with some lacking showers, kitchens and hot water. Bed sheets may not be available, so bring your own.

➡ Youth hostels are open to all, members and non-members alike, and there is no age limit.

PTTK & MOUNTAIN HOSTELS

PTTK (Polish Tourist & Sightseeing Society, Polskie Towarzystwo Turystyczno-Krajoznawcze; ☎ 22 826 2251; www.pttk.pl) has built up a network of its own hostels, called *dom turysty* or *dom wycieczkowy*. They are aimed at budget travellers, providing basic accommodation for hikers and backpackers. Single rooms are a rarity, but you'll always have a choice of three- and four-bed rooms, usually with shared facilities, where you can often rent just one bed (not the whole room) for around 45zł.

PTTK also runs a network of *schroniska górskie* (mountain hostels). Conditions are simple, but prices are low and hot meals are usually available. The more isolated mountain hostels will usually try to take in all-comers, regardless of how crowded they get, which means that in high summer beds can be scarce.

Many hostels are open all year, though it's best to check at the nearest regional PTTK office before setting off.

Private Rooms

Many private homes offer rooms to let for the night. These are particularly prevalent in mountain areas or places that draw large amounts of visitors. Look for signs reading '*pokoje*', '*noclegi*' or '*zimmer frei*' in the window.

Private rooms are a lottery: you don't know what sort of room you'll get or who your hosts will be. It's therefore a good idea to take the room for a night or two and then extend if you decide to stay longer.

➡ Private rooms may or may not offer their own bathrooms.

➡ Breakfast and other meals may be available but not included in the basic room rate. It's best to sort this out at the beginning, before taking the room.

➡ Hosts are unlikely to speak English well, but will be used to accommodating guests, so communication is usually not a problem.

➡ Expect to pay around 45zł for singles and 100zł for doubles, depending on the standard.

Short-Term Apartment Rental

A short-term apartment rental can make sense for longer stays (three days or more) in big cities such as Warsaw and Kraków. They range from simple studios to two-bedroom luxury establishments, and are often centrally located.

➡ Expect apartments to be fully equipped with towels and bed sheets. Better places may have a washing machine as well as kitchen appliances.

➡ Note that payment is usually made in cash upfront or by credit card transfer over the internet. It's always a good idea to look at the property first before surrendering any money.

➡ Rental websites such as Airbnb are good places to hunt for accommodation in major cities.

Camping

Poland has over 500 camping and bivouac sites registered at the **Polish Federation of Camping & Caravanning** (22 810 6050; www.pfcc.eu). The sites are distributed throughout the country and can be found in all the major cities (usually on the outskirts), in many towns and in the countryside.

About 40% of registered sites are camping grounds with full facilities, including lighting, electricity, running water, showers, kitchen and caravan pitches. The remaining 60% are bivouac sites, the equivalent of very basic camp sites, usually equipped with toilets and not much else.

➡ Many places also have wooden cabins for rent, which are similar to very basic hotel rooms.

➡ Most camping grounds are open from May to September, but some run only from June to August.

➡ Fees are usually charged per tent site, plus an extra fee per person and per car. Some camping grounds levy an additional fee for electricity use.

Children

Poland is a strongly family-oriented place and travelling with children doesn't create any specific problems.

For general suggestions on how to make a family trip easier, pick up a copy of Lonely Planet's *Travel with Children*.

Practicalities

➜ Almost all city buses and trams have special areas to accommodate prams and pushchairs.

➜ Many restaurants cater for children with play areas, high chairs, and children's menus *(menu dla dzieci* or *menu dziecięce)*.

➜ Children get discounts on local transport, accommodation and museum admission fees; museums often have child-friendly play areas.

➜ Nappies and toddlers' supplies are readily available in pharmacies, corner shops and supermarkets.

➜ Most hotels and pensions are child-friendly and can supply cots and high chairs.

➜ Child seats are available for rental cars, but should be requested at the time of booking.

Custom Regulations

➜ Travellers arriving from non-EU countries can bring in up to 200 cigarettes, 50 cigars or 250g of pipe tobacco; and up to 2L of alcoholic drink (of 22% ABV or less), and up to 1L of spirits (above 22% ABV).

➜ Travellers arriving from an EU member state can import up to 800 cigarettes, 200 cigars or 1kg of pipe tobacco; and up to 110L of beer, 90L of wine and 10L of spirits. This is seldom checked.

➜ The export of most items of an age exceeding 50 years and of a value exceeding 16,000zł is prohibited without an export permit *(pozwolenie eksportowe)*. Official antique dealers may offer to help you out with the paperwork, but the procedure is bureaucratic and time-consuming.

Discount Cards

A handful of Polish cities, including Warsaw, Kraków and Gdańsk, offer short-term 'tourist' cards. These usually provide discounted or free admission to museums, galleries and cultural institutions. Some also provide free public transport. Cards are normally available at tourist information offices and other sales points. Check online for details.

Hostel Cards

A HI membership card can get you a 10% to 25% discount on youth-hostel prices, though some hostels don't give discounts to foreigners. Bring the card with you, or get one issued in Poland at the provincial branch offices of the **PTSM** (Polish Youth Hostel Association; www.ptsm.org.pl) in the main cities. Visit the website to find an office.

Student Cards

Students receive great discounts in Poland, including price reductions on museum entry, as well as on some public transport. To qualify you need to be under the age of 26 and have a valid **International Student Identity Card** (ISIC; www.isic.pl). The website has a list of hostels and establishments that honour the card.

Electricity

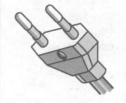

Type C
220V/50Hz

Type E
220V/50Hz

Food

For in-depth coverage of Polish cuisine, see Eat & Drink Like a Local (p37).

Health

Tick-borne encephalitis is a risk for hikers in forested areas during summer. For more information, see www. tickalert.org.

The European Health Insurance Card (EHIC) entitles EU citizens to the same emergency health-care benefits that local citizens receive from their national health care; therefore, most emergency care in Poland will be free for EU citizens. However, transporting you to your home country if you fall ill will not be covered.

Citizens from other countries should find out if their personal insurance policy covers them abroad. Doctors expect cash if you do not have a national or European health-insurance card; make sure your insurance plan will reimburse your expenses.

Regardless of whether or not you carry an EHIC card, it's always wise to bring cash, a credit card and a valid passport to any hospital or emergency clinic.

The level of health care in Poland is high and all cities and large towns will have a hospital offering emergency medical treatment. Costs are reasonable and generally lower than in Western Europe, and much lower than in the US.

Tap Water

Tap water is generally safe to drink, though bottled water is cheap and readily available.

Insurance

Insurance can cover you for medical expenses, theft or loss, and also for cancellation of, or delays in, any of your travel arrangements. There are a variety of policies and your travel agent can provide recommendations.

Always read the small print of a policy carefully and make sure the policy includes health care and medication in Poland. Some policies specifically exclude 'dangerous activities' such as scuba diving, motorcycling, skiing, mountaineering and even trekking.

Worldwide travel insurance is available at www. lonelyplanet.com/travel-insurance. You can buy, extend and claim online anytime – even if you're already on the road.

Internet Access

Poland is well wired, and wi-fi (pronounced vee-fee in Polish) is ubiquitous. Most hotels, pensions and youth hostels offer it free of charge to guests, though more expensive properties sometimes charge (or offer free wi-fi only in the lobby). Many bars, cafes and restaurants offer free wi-fi (usually marked on the door with the international wi-fi sign). Free public wi-fi is also available in many city centres.

Legal Matters

Foreigners in Poland, as elsewhere, are subject to the laws of the host country. While your embassy or consulate is the best stop in any emergency, bear in mind that there are some things it can't do for you, like getting local laws or regulations waived because you're a foreigner, investigating a crime, providing legal advice or representation in civil or criminal cases, getting you out of jail and lending you money.

➡ A consul can usually issue emergency passports, contact relatives and friends, advise on how to transfer funds, provide lists of reliable local doctors, lawyers and interpreters, and visit you if you've been arrested or jailed.

➡ In Poland the legal blood-alcohol content for drivers is 0.02.

➡ Buying, selling and possession of drugs of any kind, including cannabis, is illegal.

➡ Jaywalking is illegal, and can result in an on-the-spot fine of up to 500zł.

LGBT+ Travellers

Homosexuality is legal in Poland. However, the ruling Law & Justice (PiS) party is very anti-LGBT+ in its policies, reflecting the generally conservative, highly religious nature of many Poles. This said, in the major cities such as Warsaw, Kraków and Gdańsk, you'll encounter a much more liberal attitude.

All up this means the Polish LGBT+ scene is fairly discreet. Warsaw and Kraków are the best places to find bars, clubs and gay-friendly accommodation, and Sopot is noted as gay-friendly compared to the rest of Poland. The best sources of information are the Warsaw and Kraków city guides on www.queerintheworld.com, and www.queer.pl (in Polish only).

Money

The Polish currency is the złoty, abbreviated to zł and pronounced zwo-ti. It is divided into 100 *groszy*, which are abbreviated to gr. Banknotes come in denominations of 10zł, 20zł, 50zł, 100zł and 200zł, and coins in 1gr, 2gr, 5gr, 10gr, 20gr and 50gr, and 1zł, 2zł and 5zł. The złoty is a relatively stable currency, holding at around 4zł to €1 since 2010.

Keep some small-denomination notes and coins for shops, cafes and restaurants – it can be a problem getting change for the 100zł and 200zł notes that ATMs often spit out.

ATMs

ATMs are ubiquitous in cities and towns, and even the smallest hamlet is likely to have at least one. The majority accept Visa and MasterCard.

➡ Polish ATMs require a four-digit PIN code.

➡ Inform your bank before travelling abroad, to avoid having your card blocked by bank security when overseas transactions start appearing on your account.

➡ You'll often be given the choice to convert your ATM transaction to your home currency on the spot, but you'll get a better rate if you decline the option and choose 'Polish złoty'.

➡ Avoid Euronet ATMs, which give a much poorer rate of exchange than bank ATMs.

Cash

The best exchange rates are obtained by changing money at banks, or by taking cash out of bank ATMs.

Kantors (private currency-exchange offices) are found in town centres as well as travel agencies, train stations, post offices and department stores. Rates vary, so it's best to shop around.

➡ *Kantors* are usually open between 9am and 6pm on weekdays, and to 2pm on Saturdays, but some open longer and a few stay open 24 hours.

➡ *Kantors* normally exchange cash only against major world currencies and neighbouring countries' currencies. The most common and easily changed are US dollars, euros and UK pounds.

➡ There's usually no commission on transactions – the rate you get is what is written on the board (every *kantor* has a board displaying their exchange rates).

Credit Cards

Visa and MasterCard are widely accepted. American Express cards are usually accepted at larger hotels and restaurants, though they are not as widely recognised as other cards.

Credit cards can also be used to get cash advances from banks and ATMs.

International Transfers

Have money sent to you through the money-transfer service **Western Union** (www.westernunion.com), which is generally quick and reliable, though fees can add up. Western Union outlets can be found in all Polish cities and most large towns.

Taxes

Poland's VAT (PTU in Polish) is calculated at 23%, 8% or 5% depending on the product. The tax is normally included in the prices of goods and services as marked.

Tipping

Tipping is customary in restaurants and at service establishments such as hairdressers; optional everywhere else.

➡ **Hotels** Essentially restricted to top-end establishments, which usually have decent room-service staff and porters, who all expect to be tipped.

➡ **Restaurants** At smaller establishments and for smaller tabs, round the bill to the nearest 5zł or 10zł. Otherwise, 10% is standard.

➡ **Taxis** Drivers won't expect tips, but round the fare up to the nearest 5zł or 10zł for good service.

Opening Hours

Most places adhere to the following hours. Shopping centres generally have longer hours and are open from 10am to 10pm on weekends. Many (but not all) museums are closed on Mondays, and have shorter hours outside high season.

Banks
9am–5pm Monday to Friday, to 1pm Saturday (varies)

Offices
8am–4pm Monday to Friday (varies)

Post Offices
8am–8pm Monday to Friday, to 1pm Saturday (cities)

Restaurants
11am–11pm daily

Shops
8am–6pm Monday to Friday, 10am–8pm Saturday

Post

Postal services provided by **Poczta Polska** (www.polish-post.pl) are generally reliable. In large cities there will be a dozen or more post offices, of which the *poczta główna* (main post office) will have the widest range of facilities, sometimes including poste restante and currency exchange.

Public Holidays

New Year's Day
1 January

Epiphany
6 January

Easter Sunday
March or April

Easter Monday
March or April

State Holiday
1 May

Constitution Day
3 May

Pentecost Sunday
Seventh Sunday after Easter

Corpus Christi
Ninth Thursday after Easter

Assumption Day
15 August

All Saints' Day
1 November

Independence Day
11 November

Christmas
25 and 26 December

Safe Travel

→ Poland is a relatively safe country, but it pays to be alert around major train stations such as Warszawa Centralna and Kraków Główny, which are favourite playgrounds for thieves and pickpockets. There is also a small risk of theft on overnight trains, especially on international routes. Try to keep your luggage in sight, and share a compartment with other people if possible.

→ Theft from cars is common, so leave your vehicle in a guarded car park (*parking strzeżony*) whenever possible.

Telephone

Domestic & International Calls

All telephone numbers, land line and mobile, have nine digits. Landlines are written 12 345 6789. Mobile-phone numbers are written 123 456 789.

To call abroad from Poland, dial the international access code (00), then the country code, then the number. To dial Poland from abroad, dial your country's international access code, then 48 (Poland's country code) and then the unique nine-digit local number.

Mobile Phones

Poland uses the GSM 900/1800 system, the same as Europe, Australia and New Zealand. It's not compatible with most cell phones from North America or Japan (though many mobiles have multi-band GSM 1900/900 phones that will work in Poland).

If your mobile phone is unlocked, a cheaper and often better option is to buy a prepaid local SIM card, available from any mobile-phone shop. Prepaid SIMs allow you to make local calls at cheaper local rates. In this case, of course, you can't use your existing mobile number.

Before leaving home, it's a good idea to contact your home provider to consider short-term international calling and data plans appropriate to what you might need.

There's also the option of using an internet phone service such as Skype.

Phonecards

Most payphones in Poland require a phonecard, which you can buy from post offices and newspaper kiosks. Alternatively, buy a calling card from a private telephone service provider, such as **Telegrosik** (www. telegrosik.pl), whose international rates are even cheaper.

BORDER CROSSINGS

Poland is a member of the EU's common border zone, the Schengen Area, and frontier crossings to neighbouring EU countries, including Germany, the Czech Republic, Slovakia and Lithuania, don't involve checks of passports or visas.

Belarus A 30-day visa-free regime is in place for most visitors as long as they arrive in and depart from Minsk National Airport. If arriving or departing by land, everybody needs a visa – unless you are targeting either Brest or Hrodna, the two visa-free zones, or if you're hiking into Belarus from Białowieża National Park. For stays longer than 30 days, everybody needs a visa.

Ukraine Citizens of the EU, USA and Canada do not need a visa for stays of up to 90 days in a 180-day period, but citizens of South Africa, Australia and New Zealand need to get a visa in advance. Check the Ukrainian Foreign Ministry website (www.mfa.gov.ua) for details.

Kaliningrad Most travellers need a Russian visa to enter Kaliningrad. Apply at the Russian embassy in your home country, and allow at least four weeks for processing.

Time

Poland lies in the same time zone (GMT/UTC plus one hour) as most of continental Europe, which is one hour ahead of London and six hours ahead of New York.

Poland observes daylight saving time (DST), and moves the clock forward one hour at 2am on the last Sunday in March, and back again at 3am on the last Sunday in October.

Toilets

➡ Toilets are labelled '*toaleta*' or 'WC'.

➡ Men should look for '*dla panów*' or '*męski*', or a door marked by a downward-pointing triangle.

➡ Women should head for '*dla pań*' or '*damski*', or a door marked with a circle.

➡ Public toilets often charge a fee of 2zł, collected by a toilet attendant sitting at the door. Have small change ready.

Tourist Information

The **Polish Tourism Organisation** (www.poland.travel) is a trove of useful information. Many towns have local tourist information offices that vary greatly in terms of usefulness and language ability, though they should be able to provide a free map of the city and practical advice on places to stay and eat.

Visas

EU citizens do not need visas and can stay indefinitely. Citizens of the USA, Canada, Australia, New Zealand, Israel, Japan and many other countries can stay in Poland for up to 90 days without a visa.

Other nationalities should check with their local Polish embassy or on the Polish Ministry of Foreign Affairs website (www.gov.pl/web/diplomacy).

Volunteering

The main opportunity for volunteering in Poland is teaching English as a second language; check online for various programmes.

Work

Without a high standard of Polish, most people will need to arrange a job in Poland through an international company or be prepared to teach English. Teaching standards are high, however, and you'll probably need a TEFL (Teaching English as a Foreign Language) certificate to secure a job.

Transport

GETTING THERE & AWAY

Flights, cars and tours can be booked online at lonely planet.com/bookings.

Entering the Country/Region

Poland is an EU member state and part of the Schengen Area.

Passport

EU citizens need only a valid ID to travel in Poland. For everyone else, a passport is required. Note some airlines may deny travel to passengers whose passports are within six months of expiration from the date of departure.

Air

Airports & Airlines

Most international flights to Poland arrive at **Warsaw Chopin Airport** (Lotnisko Chopina Warszawa; ☑22 650 4220; www.lotnisko-chopina. pl; ul Żwirki i Wigury 1, Włochy; ⓡWarszawa Lotnisko Chopina). Warsaw has a second, smaller airport, **Warsaw**

Modlin Airport (Modlin Lotnisko; ☑22 315 1880; www. modlinairport.pl; ul Generała Wiktora Thommée 1a, Nowy Dwór Mazowiecki; ⓡModlin), 39km north of the city, which handles budget flights.

Other international airports include the following.

➡ **Gdańsk Lech Wałęsa Airport** (☑801 066 808, 52 567 3531; www.airport.gdansk. pl; ul Słowackiego 210)

➡ **Katowice Airport** (Port Lotniczy Katowice; ☑32 392 7000; www.katowice-airport. com; ul Wolności 90, Pyrzowice; ⓡ)

➡ **Kraków John Paul II International Airport** (KRK; ☑12 295 5800, 801 055 000; www.krakowairport. pl; ul Kapitana Mieczysława Medweckiego 1, Balice; ⓡ)

➡ **Łódź Airport** (www.airport. lodz.pl; ul Maczka 35)

➡ **Lublin Airport** (www. airport.lublin.pl)

➡ **Rzeszów Airport** (www. rzeszowairport.pl)

➡ **Wrocław Airport** (☑71 358 1100; www.airport.wroclaw.pl; ul Graniczna 190)

Poland's national airline is **LOT** (www.lot.com). Several budget carriers serve the Polish market, usually landing at smaller airports such as Warsaw Modlin, Łódź, Katowice and Rzeszów, though some fly to Kraków as well.

Land
Border Crossings

As a member of the EU, Poland has open borders (and plenty of rail and road crossings) on its western and southern frontiers with Germany, the Czech Republic and Slovakia. Crossings with EU-member Lithuania, on the northeastern end of the country, are also open.

It's a different story crossing into Ukraine, Belarus and Russia's Kaliningrad exclave, which form part of the EU's external border and may require visas and advance planning (p418).

The main border crossings into Poland's non-EU neighbours are.

Belarus (south to north): Terespol, Kuźnica

Russia (Kaliningrad) (east to west): Bezledy-Bagrationowsk, Gronowo

Ukraine (south to north): Medyka, Hrebenne-Rawa Ruska, Dorohusk

Bus

Eurolines (www.eurolines.pl), **Ecolines** (www.ecolines.net) and **FlixBus** (https://global. flixbus.com) all run services linking Poland with its immediate European neighbours and beyond. Check online timetables for current routes and prices.

BELARUS, LITHUANIA, UKRAINE & RUSSIA

Sample fares and travel times from Warsaw:

Minsk From €20, 10 hours

Vilnius From €16, eight hours

Kyiv From €34, 18 hours

Kaliningrad From €38, nine hours

CZECH REPUBLIC & SLOVAKIA

➡ FlixBus offers daily bus service between Warsaw and Prague (from €18, 10 hours) via Wrocław.

➡ From Kraków, **Leo Express** (www.leoexpress.com) services run to Prague (from €16.50, seven hours), as well as to Slovak cities such as Košice (€26, five hours).

➡ From Zakopane, **Strama** (www.strama.eu) runs regular coaches to Poprad in Slovakia (26zł, two hours, two to four daily) from mid-June to mid-October.

UK

Sindbad (www.sindbad.pl) coaches run between London and most Polish cities, including Warsaw (one way from £80, 25 hours, four per week); the frequency of the service varies depending on the season.

WESTERN EUROPE

As a rough guide only, average one-way fares and journey times between some Western European cities and Warsaw are as follows.

TO	FARE (€)	TIME (HR)
Amsterdam	from 70	20
Brussels	from 70	20
Cologne	from 71	18
Frankfurt	from 68	16
Hamburg	from 44	14
Munich	from 71	17
Paris	from 79	24
Rome	from 74	29

Train

Poland is well served by international rail routes. Journeys to and from EU countries are straightforward, but if heading east, you'll need to check visa requirements. Passengers travelling from Poland to Moscow may need a Belarus transit visa.

Border crossings can be slow, but do not normally mean leaving the train – customs personnel work their way through the carriages checking passports and visas.

The following websites provide useful information on international train travel to/from Poland.

➡ **The Man in Seat Sixty-One** (www.seat61.com)

➡ **Polrail Service** (☑52 332 5781; www.polrail.com)

Belarus, Lithuania, Ukraine & Russia

Ukraine There are daily trains from Warsaw to Kyiv (from 200zł, 17 hours) and from Kraków to Lviv (from 120zł, nine hours).

Overnight trains have sleeping cars, for which there is an extra charge.

Belarus & Russia There is a daily (daytime) train service from Warsaw to Minsk (from 276zł, 10 hours). The overnight *Polonez* sleeper train passes through Brest and Minsk on its way to Moscow (from 126zł, 19 hours, three a week).

Lithuania Until the completion of the Rail Baltica project (www.railbaltica.org) in 2026, there are no direct trains from Warsaw to Vilnius. However, you can make the journey via Białystok, with another change at Kaunas (total fare around €24, 11 hours, Friday to Sunday only).

Czech Republic & Slovakia

➡ Express trains run from Prague (from €28, eight hours, three daily) and Bratislava (from €80, eight hours, four daily) to Warsaw.

➡ There's one direct train each day between Prague and Kraków (from €40, seven hours), a further three services daily require a change in Katowice, and sometimes Ostrava too.

Germany

The Berlin–Warsaw Express runs via Poznań and Gdańsk (from €30, 6½ hours, three to four daily).

There is a daily direct sleeper train between Berlin and Kraków (from €39 in a three-berth cabin, 11 hours).

CLIMATE CHANGE & TRAVEL

Every form of transport that relies on carbon-based fuel generates CO_2, the main cause of human-induced climate change. Modern travel is dependent on aeroplanes, which might use less fuel per kilometre per person than most cars but travel much greater distances. The altitude at which aircraft emit gases (including CO_2) and particles also contributes to their climate change impact. Many websites offer 'carbon calculators' that allow people to estimate the carbon emissions generated by their journey and, for those who wish to do so, to offset the impact of the greenhouse gases emitted with contributions to portfolios of climate-friendly initiatives throughout the world. Lonely Planet offsets the carbon footprint of all staff and author travel.

UK

There is no direct train route
from London to Warsaw –
you will have to overnight and
change trains either in Brussels or Berlin (from €99.80
on either route) – see www.
seat61.com for details.

Sea

Ferry services connect the
Baltic coast ports of Gdańsk,
Gdynia and Świnoujście to
destinations in Scandinavia.

Polferries (☎94 355 2102;
www.polferries.com) Operates
car ferries from Gdańsk to
Nynäshamn (near Stockholm)
in Sweden (foot passenger/car
with driver from Skr620/1470,
19 hours, up to seven a week),
and from Świnoujście to Ystad
(foot passenger/car with driver
from 226/458zł, eight to nine
hours, two or three daily).

Every Saturday from 29 June
to 31 August you can travel
with Polferries from Świnoujście in Poland to the Danish
island of Bornholm.

Stena Line (☎58 660 9200;
www.stenaline.pl) Operates
ferries between Gdynia and
Karlskrona in Sweden (foot
passenger/car with driver from
160/340zł, 10½ to 12 hours,
two or three daily). Services
depart from the ferry terminal
5km northwest of central
Gdynia.

Unity Line (☎91 880 2909;
www.unityline.pl; ⏰7am-8pm
Mon-Fri, 9am-3pm Sat) Runs
ferries from Świnoujście to
Ystad in Sweden (foot passenger/car with driver 228/446zł,
six to seven hours, two a day).

TT-Line (www.ttline.com)
Runs a daily crossing between
Świnoujście and Trelleborg in
Sweden (foot passenger/car
with driver from €34/86, six
hours).

GETTING AROUND

Air

Poland is a big country, and
domestic flights can be
time-saving if you have to get
from one end to the other.

LOT (www.lot.com; ☎22 577
7755) Operates a comprehensive
network of domestic routes.
Many flights between regional
cities travel via Warsaw and
connections aren't always
convenient.

Ryanair (www.ryanair.com;
☎+44 871 246 0000 in the UK)
Operates direct flights between
Warsaw and Szczecin, and from
Gdańsk to Wrocław and Kraków.

Bicycle

Poland has great potential
as a place to tour by bicycle
– most of the country is
flat and you can throw your
bike on a train to cover long
distances quickly. Camping
equipment isn't essential, as
hotels and hostels are usually no more than a day's ride
apart, although carrying your
own camping gear will give
you more flexibility. Check
out www.poland.travel/en/
experience/cycling.

There are cycling shops
and repair centres in large
cities and major tourist resorts, and you'll be able to
hire a bike in most cities.
The going rate for rentals is
about 10/40zł per hour/day.

Road Conditions

➡ Major roads carry heavy
traffic and are best avoided.
Instead, plan your route
along minor roads, which are
usually much less crowded
and in reasonable shape.

➡ Stock up on detailed hiking
maps, which normally show
bike trails as well as walking
trails.

➡ Some drivers hug the
side of the road to give cars
and trucks more room to
overtake, passing perilously
close to cyclists. Note that

in Poland cyclists are not
allowed to ride two abreast.

➡ Cities are often not the
most pleasant places to
cycle, though many now
have dedicated cycle paths
and more are planned. The
main problem is drivers
who often don't have much
regard for two-wheeled
travellers.

Taking Your Bike on the Train

Many – but not all – trains
allow you to transport bikes.

➡ When buying your ticket
at the station, inform the
ticket seller you have a bike
and they will let you know
whether it's allowed on
board. Online timetables
usually note whether bikes
are permitted.

➡ Bikes require a separate
ticket costing 9.10zł (flat fee
regardless of distance).

➡ Many trains have special
carriages equipped to carry
bicycles and these will be
marked. Other times you'll
have to stow the bike in a
baggage car. If the train has
no baggage car, bikes are
only permitted in the first
and last carriages of the
train. If you have to stow
your bike there, try to sit
near it and keep it out of the
way of other passengers.

➡ Bikes cannot be taken on
sleeping cars.

Security

➡ Bike theft is common.
Always firmly lock your
bike to a stationary object
and try not to leave the bike
unattended for too long.

➡ Many hotels have secure
luggage rooms, which are
normally fine for overnight
storage; if in doubt, take your
bike with you into your room.

➡ Trains pose a particular
risk of theft. If you have to
leave your bike in a baggage
car, try to sit near the car
and check on your bike
periodically. Lock your bike
to a fixed part of the rail car if
possible.

Boat

Poland has a long coastline and lots of rivers and canals, but passenger-boat services are limited and operate only in summer. There are no regular boats running along the main rivers or along the coast.

➡ Several cities, including Szczecin, Gdańsk, Toruń, Poznań, Wrocław and Kraków, have local river cruises in summer, and a few coastal ports (Kołobrzeg and Gdańsk) offer sea excursions. There are also trips out of Elbląg to Frombork and Krynica Morska.

➡ Tourist boats are available in the Augustów area, where they ply part of the Augustów Canal.

Bus

Poland has a comprehensive bus network (far greater than the rail network) covering nearly every town and village accessible by road. Buses are often more convenient than trains over short distances, and occasionally over longer ones, when, for instance, the train route involves a long detour.

The frequency of service varies greatly: on the main routes there may be a bus leaving every 15 minutes or so, whereas some small remote villages may get only one bus a day. Ticket prices also vary due to fierce competition between bus companies, so shop around.

Bus Companies

There are hundreds of regional and private operators. Most cities have a main bus station (dworzec autobusowy), often located close to the train station. Bus stations usually have only basic facilities (no left-luggage service or even a place for coffee), but most do have some sort of information counter or at least a posted timetable.

Shorter local routes, especially in rural areas, are served by privately owned minibuses. Minibus stops are usually in the vicinity of the main bus station; there is rarely any sort of information counter, but destinations are displayed on the vehicles. Buy tickets from the driver.

FlixBus/Polski Bus (https://global.flixbus.com) The main nationwide coach operator, running services between major cities and towns using modern coaches with free wi-fi. You can buy tickets online using the company's smartphone app; real-world ticket outlets are listed on the website.

PKS Polonus (✆703 403 403; www.pkspolonus.pl) Warsaw-based company, with bus services mostly to northern Poland, but also to Silesia, Częstochowa, Opole and Tarnów in the south.

Costs

Buses are generally cheaper than trains, but slower. For example, a coach from Warsaw to Kraków can cost as little as 30zł and takes five hours, while the fastest express train takes 2½ hours but costs 126zł.

Tickets

➡ The only place to buy local bus tickets is at the bus station itself, either from the ticket counter or the bus driver. If you get on the bus somewhere along the route, you buy the ticket directly from the driver.

➡ Tickets for FlixBus and other intercity bus companies can be bought online. In this case, simply print out the ticket, or save the online ticket to your smartphone or tablet and show the driver when you board the bus.

Timetables

➡ For comprehensive timetable information, use the online journey planner at www.en.e-podroznik.pl.

➡ Printed timetables are posted on boards at bus terminals. The list of odjazdy (departures) includes kierunek (destinations), przez (the places passed en route) and departure times.

➡ Check any symbols that accompany the departure time. These symbols can mean that the bus runs only on certain days or in certain seasons. They're explained in the key at the end of the timetable but can be difficult to decipher.

Car & Motorcycle

While driving in Poland is mostly trouble-free, and having a car makes exploring rural areas more spontaneous, there are some drawbacks. The highway network is still in the process of being upgraded, and there will be long stretches of construction works, detours and delays for several years to come.

Poland straddles major east–west and north–south transit routes, and long lines of heavy trucks are the norm on many highways. Also, despite some improvement in recent years, the country has one of the poorest road-safety records in Europe – speeding and dangerous overtaking are commonplace.

Bringing Your Own Car

Many tourists bring their own vehicles into Poland. There are no special formalities: all you need is your passport (with a valid visa if necessary), driving licence, vehicle registration document and proof of third-party insurance (called a Green Card). Fines are severe if you're caught without insurance. A nationality plate or sticker must be displayed on the back of the car.

ROAD DISTANCES (KM)

	Białystok	Bydgoszcz	Częstochowa	Gdańsk	Katowice	Kielce	Kraków	Łódź	Lublin	Olsztyn	Opole	Poznań	Rzeszów	Szczecin	Toruń	Warsaw	Wrocław
Bydgoszcz	389																
Częstochowa	410	316															
Gdańsk	379	167	470														
Katowice	485	391	75	545													
Kielce	363	348	124	483	156												
Kraków	477	430	114	565	75	114											
Łódź	322	205	121	340	196	143	220										
Lublin	260	421	288	500	323	167	269	242									
Olsztyn	223	217	404	156	479	394	500	281	370								
Opole	507	318	98	485	113	220	182	244	382	452							
Poznań	491	129	289	296	335	354	403	212	465	323	261						
Rzeszów	430	516	272	642	244	163	165	306	170	516	347	517					
Szczecin	656	267	520	348	561	585	634	446	683	484	459	234	751				
Toruń	347	46	289	181	364	307	384	159	375	172	312	151	470	313			
Warsaw	188	255	222	339	297	181	295	134	161	213	319	310	303	524	209		
Wrocław	532	265	176	432	199	221	268	204	428	442	86	178	433	371	279	344	
Zielona Góra	601	259	328	411	356	422	427	303	542	453	245	130	585	214	281	413	157

Driving Licences

EU driving licences are valid in Poland. Non-EU licences can be used for up to six months, and non-EU-licence holders also require an International Driving Permit.

Fuel

Benzyna (petrol) is readily available at petrol stations *(stacja benzynowa* or *stacja paliw)* throughout the country. There are several different kinds and grades available, including 95- and 98-octane unleaded and diesel. The price of fuel can differ from petrol station to petrol station, with the highest prices typically found on major highways. Nearly all petrol stations are self-serve and accept cash, debit and credit cards.

Car Hire

Car-hire agencies require a passport, valid driving licence and credit card. You need to be at least 21 or 23 years of age (depending on the company).

One-way hire within Poland is possible with most companies (usually for a fee), but most will insist on keeping the car within Poland. No company is likely to allow you to take its car beyond the eastern border.

As a rough guide, economy models offered by reputable local companies cost around 185/695zł per day/week (including insurance and unlimited mileage). Rates at the big international agencies are higher. It's usually cheapest to book your car online before you travel.

MOTORWAYS

Poland's motorways (called *autostrady*) are so far limited to one north–south route (A1 Gdańsk–Łódź–Katowice) and two west–east routes (A2 Poznań–Łódź–Warsaw and A4 Wrocław–Kraków–Rzeszów). They are mostly only four-lane highways (ie two lanes in each direction).

Parts of these are toll roads, where you either collect a ticket at the beginning of the toll section and pay at the end, or just pay the cashier as you pass through (cash and bank cards accepted). As an example of costs, the section of the A4 from Kraków to Wrocław costs 36.20zł in total for a car. For more info see www.tolls.eu/poland.

Road Conditions

➡ Driving for long distances in Poland is no fun. Roads may be crowded, while road building and repair can lead to many detours and delays.

➡ Poland has an abundance of two-lane (ie single-carriageway) national highways. These vary greatly in condition. Main roads often pass directly through the centres of towns and villages.

➡ Drive carefully on country roads, particularly at night; there are still horse-drawn carts on Polish roads. The further off the main routes you wander, the more elderly cyclists and carts, tractors and other agricultural machinery you'll encounter.

Road Rules

Road rules are similar to much of the rest of Europe. A vehicle must be equipped with a first-aid kit, a red-and-white warning triangle, and a nationality sticker on the rear; the use of seat belts is compulsory.

Police can hit you with on-the-spot fines for speeding and other traffic offences (be sure to insist on a receipt).

➡ Drinking and driving is strictly forbidden – the legal blood-alcohol level is 0.02% (one drink can put you over the limit!).

➡ Use of handheld mobile phones while driving is prohibited.

➡ Speed limits are 50km/h in urban areas (60km/h between 11pm and 5am), 90km/h outside urban areas, 120km/h on dual carriageways and 140km/h on motorways.

➡ Headlights must be on at all times, even on a sunny day.

➡ Trams must be overtaken on the right. At tram stops where there are no pedestrian islands, drivers should stop to allow

passengers to walk safely between the tram and the pavement.

➡ Motorcyclists should remember that both rider and passenger must wear helmets.

Hitching

➡ *Autostop* (hitching) is never entirely safe, and we don't recommend it. Travellers who hitch should understand that they are taking a small but potentially serious risk.

➡ That said, hitching does take place in Poland; locals can often be seen thumbing a ride from one small village to the next. Car drivers rarely stop though, and drivers of large commercial vehicles (which are easier to wave down) expect to be paid the equivalent of a bus fare.

➡ Those who choose to hitch will be safer when travelling in pairs and when letting someone know where they are planning to go.

Local Transport

Bus, Tram & Trolleybus

Polish cities offer excellent public transport. Every large and medium-sized city will have a comprehensive *autobus* (bus) network, while some cities will also have *tramwaj* (tram) and *trolejbus* (trolleybus) systems. Warsaw is the only city with a metro.

➡ Public transport normally operates daily from around 5am to 11pm. Service is less frequent on weekends.

➡ Trams and buses are likely to be crowded during rush hour (7am to 9am and 4.30pm to 6.30pm Monday to Friday).

➡ Timetables are usually posted at stops, but don't rely too much on their accuracy.

TICKETS & FARES

Each city has a slightly different system of ticketing and fares, so be prepared to watch what the locals do and do likewise.

Most cities have a fare system based on the duration of the ride, with a standard 60-minute ticket costing around 3zł. There may be slightly cheaper tickets available for shorter rides (20 or 30 minutes) and more expensive tickets for longer ones (90 minutes).

There are many common features across Polish buses and trams.

➡ In most cities you can buy tickets from machines inside buses and trams (*automat biletów*) using contactless card payment. You don't get a paper ticket; if an inspector asks, allow them to scan the card you used for payment.

➡ There are also ticket machines on the street at major bus and tram stops. These accept cash (coins and notes) as well as cards, and issue paper tickets.

➡ You can also buy paper tickets from newspaper kiosks such as Ruch or Relay or from street stalls around the central stops.

➡ Paper tickets should be validated in one of the little machines installed near the doors when you enter the bus or tram.

➡ Plain-clothed ticket inspectors are always on the prowl and foreigners are not exempt from checks.

Taxi

Taxis are widely available and not too expensive. Daytime fares are generally based on an 8zł flagfall and around 2zł per kilometre. Prices are higher at night (10pm to 6am), on Sunday and outside city limits. The number of passengers (usually up to four) and the amount of luggage doesn't affect the fare.

➡ Avoid unmarked pirate taxis (called 'mafia' taxis by Poles), which usually have just a small 'taxi' sign on the roof, with no name or phone number.

➡ You can flag down cabs on the street or order them by phone. It's best to book by phone if possible, as it cuts down the chance you'll get a rogue driver.

➡ Apps such as Taxify and Uber are highly popular ways of booking taxis.

➡ Remember to carry small denomination banknotes, so you'll be able to pay the exact fare. If you don't, it may be hard to get change from a driver who's intent on charging you more.

Train

Poland's train network is extensive and reasonably priced. It's likely to be your main means of transport for covering long distances.

That said, service to many smaller cities is poor or nonexistent, which means you may find yourself relying more on buses or a combination of bus and train.

Train Companies

Since the demise of the state monopoly **Polskie Koleje Państwowe (PKP)** the Polish rail network has been broken up into around 10 different operators that manage different routes and trains.

PKP InterCity (IC; ☑from Poland 703 200 200, from abroad +48 22 391 9757; www.intercity.pl) runs all of Poland's express trains, including ExpressInterCity Premium (EIP), ExpressInterCity (EIC), InterCity (IC), EuroCity (EC) and TLK trains.

A second main operator, **PolRegio** (www.polregio.pl), takes care of most other trains, including relatively fast InterRegio (IR) trains and slower Regio trains.

A handful of other private operators provide regional services.

You can buy international and domestic train tickets in advance from outside Poland through **Polrail Service** (☑52 332 5781; www.polrail.com). Its website is a very useful source of information on Polish train travel.

Timetables & Information

Rozkład jazdy (train timetables) are posted on the walls of most stations, with *odjazdy* (departures) written on yellow boards and *przyjazdy* (arrivals) on white.

In addition to departure and arrival times, timetables also include initials beside the destinations to let you know what type of train is running: EIP, EIC, TLK, IR or Regio. Faster trains are marked in red and slower trains in black.

The letter 'R' in a square indicates a train with compulsory seat reservations. There may also be some small letters and/or numbers following the departure times that show whether a train runs on holidays or weekends (there should be a key at the bottom of the timetable to help you figure it out).

ONLINE TIMETABLES

There are several useful online timetables that show schedules, and also usually display prices and allow you to purchase tickets online.

www.rozklad-pkp.pl Shows information for all Polish trains.

www.rozklad.sitkol.pl Another general timetable with easy-to-use instructions in English.

www.intercity.pl Displays information for high-speed express and TLK trains.

Timetables normally require Polish spelling for cities (diacritical marks are not necessary).

Tickets

There are several options for buying tickets. Most of the time you'll purchase them at train-station ticket windows.

Plan to be at the station at least half an hour before the departure time of your train.

➡ Most ticket windows, but not all, accept payment with a credit card (look for the credit-card symbol).

➡ Don't expect ticket sellers to speak English. Write down the relevant details on a piece of paper.

➡ Seat reservations (5zł) are compulsory on EIP, EIC, IC, EC and TLK trains; you'll automatically be sold a *miejscówka* (reserved-seat ticket) on these services.

➡ Except on EIP trains, you can board a train without a ticket if the ticket line's not moving and the departure is imminent. Buy from the conductor (there's a supplement of 10zł).

➡ Private travel companies can help organise travel times and book tickets online. One of the best of these is **Polrail Service** (☑52 332 5781; www.polrail.com).

Costs

➡ Costs for Polish trains vary greatly depending on the type of train and the distance travelled.

➡ It pays to shop around online before buying. Generally, 1st class is around 50% more expensive than 2nd class.

➡ The most expensive trains are InterCity EIP/EIC trains. Prices for these include the basic ticket price, as well as a mandatory seat reservation.

➡ As a guideline, the approximate 2nd-class fare (including compulsory seat reservation) on an EIP train from Warsaw to Kraków is 150zł for the three-hour journey. The trip from Warsaw to Gdańsk also costs 150zł for the similar-length journey.

➡ TLK trains are slower but usually cost much less. The journey from Warsaw to Kraków costs 60zł and takes three to five hours. The journey from Warsaw to Gdańsk costs 60zł and takes four to five hours.

TYPES OF TRAIN

Poland's rail network has several different types of train that differ primarily by speed, cost and level of comfort. Identify the train type by the initials on station and online timetables.

ExpressInterCity Premium (EIP) High-speed 'Pendolino' trains that travel between major cities, such as Warsaw, Kraków, Katowice, Wrocław and Gdańsk. Both 1st- and 2nd-class seats are available, and reservations are mandatory for both.

ExpressInterCity (EIC) One step down from EIP trains, the modern, comfortable EIC trains also run between major cities, such as Warsaw–Kraków and Warsaw–Gdańsk, but are slightly less expensive. There's seating in both 1st and 2nd class, and reservations are compulsory in both.

InterCity (IC) As with EIC, but generally offering a slightly slower service with more stops than EIC trains.

EuroCity (EC) International express trains linking Polish cities with cities in other European countries.

TLK (*Pociąg Twoje Linie Kolejowe;* TLK) Low-cost express trains that run between major cities at speeds approaching EIP trains, but at fares that are around 40% cheaper. TLK trains are a step down in comfort and can be crowded. There's seating in both 1st and 2nd class; both classes require reservations. Bicycle carriage on TLK trains may be limited.

InterRegio (*Pociąg InterRegio;* IR) These are the standard Polish 'fast' trains running between regions, with stops at most medium-sized cities along the route. IR trains normally don't offer 1st-class seating, and no seat reservations are required.

Regio (*Pociąg Regio;* Regio/Osob) These trains are much slower as they stop at all stations along the way. These may be 2nd-class only and reservations are not required.

Discounts

➡ Children under four travel for free. Older children and students up to age 26 are usually entitled to some form of discount, but the system is complicated and seems to change year by year. Your best bet is to ask whether you qualify for a cheaper fare when you buy your ticket.

➡ If you're over 60 and planning to do a lot of travelling, ask about the *Bilet dla Seniora* (senior ticket) that provides a 30% discount on 1st- and 2nd-class seats. You'll need photo ID that confirms your age.

Train Passes

If you're planning on travelling a lot, consider buying an InterRail pass. Passes are only available if you're a resident in Europe for at least six months, and they're priced according to your age, whether you choose to go 1st or 2nd class, and the amount of time you plan to spend travelling by train within one, two or three months.

See www.interrail.net for more information.

Train Stations

Many Polish train stations have undergone major renovations since 2010, and those in Kraków, Poznań and Warsaw are now attached to gleaming shopping malls. Others, such as those in Wrocław or Tarnów, are historic buildings in their own right. Most larger stations have left-luggage desks and lockers (fees are around 12zł to 16zł per bag per 24 hours).

Station platforms (*peron*) are numbered, but there are usually also track (*tor*) numbers if there is a line on either side of the platform – check you have the right one.

If there are no overhead signs displaying the destination of the next train, look for the signboards on the sides of the carriages.

Language

Poland is linguistically one of the most homogeneous countries in Europe – more than 95% of the population has Polish as their first language. Polish belongs to the Slavic language family, with Czech and Slovak as close relatives. It has about 45 million speakers.

Polish pronunciation is pretty straightforward, as each Polish letter is generally pronounced the same way wherever it occurs.

Vowels are generally prounounced short, giving them a 'clipped' quality. Note that a is pronounced as the 'u' in 'cut', ai as in 'aisle' and ow as in 'cow'. Polish also has nasal vowels (pronounced as though you're trying to force the air through your nose), which are indicated in writing by the letters ą and ę. Depending on the letters following these vowels, they're pronounced either as an m or an n sound following the vowel, ie ą as om or on and ę as em or en.

Most Polish consonant sounds are also found in English. Note that kh is pronounced as in the Scottish *loch*, r is rolled and zh is pronounced as the 's' in 'leisure'. Consonants are sometimes grouped together without vowels between them, eg in *pszczoła* pshcho·wa – with a bit of practice they will roll off your tongue with ease. In our pronunciation guides the apostrophe (eg in *kwiecień* kfye·chen) indicates that the preceding consonant is pronounced with a soft y sound.

If you read the coloured pronunciation guides in this chapter as if they were English – and not worry too much about the intricacies of Polish pronunciation – you'll be understood just fine. Note that stressed syllables are indicated with italics.

In the following phrases the masculine/feminine, polite and informal options are included where necessary and indicated with 'm/f', 'pol' and 'inf' respectively.

> **WANT MORE?**
>
> For in-depth language information and handy phrases, check out Lonely Planet's *Polish Phrasebook*. You'll find it at **shop.lonelyplanet.com**.

BASICS

Hello.	*Cześć.*	cheshch
Goodbye.	*Do widzenia.*	do vee·dze·nya
Yes./No.	*Tak./Nie.*	tak/nye
Please.	*Proszę.*	pro·she
Thank you.	*Dziękuję.*	jyen·koo·ye
You're welcome.	*Proszę.*	pro·she
Excuse me./ Sorry.	*Przepraszam.*	pshe·pra·sham

How are you?

Jak pan/pani się miewa? (m/f pol)	yak pan/pa·nee shye mye·va
Jak się masz? (inf)	yak shye mash

Fine. And you?

Dobrze.	dob·zhe
A pan/pani? (m/f pol)	a pan/pa·nee
Dobrze. A ty? (inf)	dob·zhe a ti

What's your name?

Jak się pan/pani nazywa? (m/f pol)	yak shye pa·na/pa·nee na·zi·va
Jakie się nazywasz? (inf)	yak shye na·zi·vash

My name is ...

Nazywam się ...	na·zi·vam shye ...

Do you speak English?

Czy pan/pani mówi po angielsku? (m/f pol)	chi pan/pa·nee moo·vee po an·gyel·skoo
Czy mówisz po angielsku? (inf)	chi moo·veesh po an·gyel·skoo

I don't understand.

Nie rozumiem.	nye ro·zoo·myem

ACCOMMODATION

Where's a ...?	*Gdzie jest ...?*	gjye yest ...
campsite	*kamping*	*kam·peeng*
guesthouse	*pokoje gościnne*	po·ko·ye gosh·chee·ne
hotel	*hotel*	ho·tel
youth hostel	*schronisko młodzieżowe*	skhro·nees·ko mwo·jye·zho·ve

Do you have a ... room?	*Czy jest pokój ...?*	chi yest po·kooy ...
single	*jedno-osobowy*	yed·no·o·so·bo·vi
double	*z podwójnym łóżkiem*	z pod·vooy·nim woozh·kyem

How much is it per ...?	*Ile kosztuje za ...?*	ee·le kosh·too·ye za ...
night	*noc*	nots
person	*osobę*	o·so·be
air-con	*klimatyzator*	klee·ma·ti·za·tor
bathroom	*łazienka*	wa·zhyen·ka
window	*okno*	ok·no

DIRECTIONS

Where's a/the ...?
Gdzie jest ...? gjye yest ...

What's the address?
Jaki jest adres? ya·kee yest ad·res

Could you please write it down?
Proszę to napisać. pro·she to na·pee·sach

Can you show me (on the map)?
Czy może pan/pani mi pokazać (na mapie)? (m/f) chi mo·zhe pan/pa·nee mee po·ka·zach (na ma·pye)

at the corner/ traffic lights	*na rogu/ światłach*	na ro·goo/ shfyat·wakh
behind ...	*za ...*	za ...
in front of ...	*przed ...*	pshet ...
left	*lewo*	le·vo
near ...	*koło ...*	ko·wo ...
next to ...	*obok ...*	o·bok ...
opposite ...	*naprze-ciwko ...*	nap·she-cheef·ko ...
straight ahead	*na wprost*	na fprost
right	*prawo*	pra·vo

EATING & DRINKING

I'd like to reserve a table for ...	*Chciałem/am zarezerwować stolik ... (m/f)*	khchow·em/am za·re·zer·vo·vach sto·leek ...
(two) people	*dla (dwóch) osób*	dla (dvookh) o·soob
(eight) o'clock	*na (ósmą)*	na (oos·mom)
I don't eat ...	*Nie jadam ...*	nye ya·dam ...
eggs	*jajek*	yai·ek
fish	*ryb*	rib
(red) meat	*(czerwonego) mięsa*	(cher·vo·ne·go) myen·sa
poultry	*drobiu*	dro·byoo

What would you recommend?
Co by pan/pani polecił/poleciła? (m/f) tso bi pan/pa·nee po·le·cheew/po·le·chee·wa

What's in that dish?
Co jest w tym daniu? tso yest v tim da·nyoo

I'd like the menu, please.
Proszę o jadłospis. pro·she o ya·dwo·spees

That was delicious!
To było pyszne. to bi·wo pish·ne

Cheers!
Na zdrowie! na zdro·vye

Please bring the bill.
Proszę o rachunek. pro·she o ra·khoo·nek

Key Words

bottle	*butelka*	*boo·tel·ka*
bowl	*miska*	*mee·ska*
breakfast	*śniadanie*	*shnya·da·nye*
cold	*zimny*	*zheem·ni*
cup	*filiżanka*	*fee·lee·zhan·ka*
dinner	*kolacja*	*ko·la·tsya*
fork	*widelec*	*vee·de·lets*
glass	*szklanka*	*shklan·ka*
grocery	*sklep spożywczy*	*sklep spo·zhiv·chi*
hot	*gorący*	*go·ron·tsi*
knife	*nóż*	*noosh*
lunch	*obiad*	*o·byad*
market	*rynek*	*ri·nek*
menu	*jadłospis*	*ya·dwo·spees*
plate	*talerz*	*ta·lesh*
restaurant	*restauracja*	*res·tow·rats·ya*
spoon	*łyżka*	*wish·ka*
vegetarian	*wegetariański*	*ve·ge·ta·ryan'·skee*
with ...	*z ...*	*z ...*
without ...	*bez ...*	*bes ...*

Meat & Fish

beef	*wołowina*	*vo·wo·vee·na*
chicken	*kurczak*	*koor·chak*
cod	*dorsz*	*dorsh*
duck	*kaczka*	*kach·ka*
fish	*ryba*	*ri·ba*
herring	*śledź*	*shlej*
lamb	*jagnięcina*	*yag·nyen·chee·na*
lobster	*homar*	*ho·mar*
mackerel	*makrela*	*ma·kre·la*
meat	*mięso*	*myen·so*
mussels	*małże*	*mow·zhe*
oysters	*ostrygi*	*os·tri·gee*
prawns	*krewetki*	*kre·vet·kee*
pork	*wieprzowina*	*vyep·sho·vee·na*
salmon	*łosoś*	*wo·sosh*
seafood	*owoce morza*	*o·vo·tse mo·zha*
trout	*pstrąg*	*pstrong*
tuna	*tuńczyk*	*toon'·chik*
turkey	*indyk*	*een·dik*
veal	*cielęcina*	*chye·len·chee·na*

Fruit & Vegetables

apple	*jabłko*	*yabw·ko*
apricot	*morela*	*mo·re·la*
bean	*fasola*	*fa·so·la*
cabbage	*kapusta*	*ka·poos·ta*
carrot	*marchewka*	*mar·khef·ka*
cauliflower	*kalafior*	*ka·la·fyor*
cherry	*czereśnia*	*che·resh·nya*
cucumber	*ogórek*	*o·goo·rek*
fruit	*owoc*	*o·vots*
grapes	*winogrona*	*vee·no·gro·na*
lemon	*cytryna*	*tsi·tri·na*
lentil	*soczewica*	*so·che·vee·tsa*
mushroom	*grzyb*	*gzhib*
nut	*orzech*	*o·zhekh*
onion	*cebula*	*tse·boo·la*
orange	*pomarańcza*	*po·ma·ran'·cha*
peach	*brzoskwinia*	*bzhosk·fee·nya*
pear	*gruszka*	*groosh·ka*
pepper (bell)	*papryka*	*pa·pri·ka*
plum	*śliwka*	*shleef·ka*
potato	*ziemniak*	*zhyem·nyak*
strawberry	*truskawka*	*troos·kaf·ka*
tomato	*pomidor*	*po·mee·dor*
vegetable	*warzywo*	*va·zhi·vo*
watermelon	*arbuz*	*ar·boos*

Other

bread	*chleb*	*khlep*
cheese	*ser*	*ser*
egg	*jajko*	*yai·ko*
honey	*miód*	*myood*
noodles	*makaron*	*ma·ka·ron*
oil	*olej*	*o·ley*
pasta	*makaron*	*ma·ka·ron*
pepper	*pieprz*	*pyepsh*
rice	*ryż*	*rizh*
salt	*sól*	*sool*
sugar	*cukier*	*tsoo·kyer*
vinegar	*ocet*	*o·tset*

Drinks

beer	*piwo*	*pee·vo*
coffee	*kawa*	*ka·va*
(orange) juice	*sok (pomarańczowy)*	*sok (po·ma·ran'·cho·vi)*
milk	*mleko*	*mle·ko*

red wine	wino czerwone	vee·no cher·vo·ne
soft drink	napój	na·pooy
tea	herbata	her·ba·ta
(mineral) water	woda (mineralna)	vo·da (mee·ne·ral·na)
white wine	wino białe	vee·no bya·we

EMERGENCIES

| Help! | *Na pomoc!* | na po·mots |
| Go away! | *Odejdź!* | o·deyj |

Call the police!
Zadzwoń po policję! zad·zvon' po po·lee·tsye

Call a doctor!
Zadzwoń po lekarza! zad·zvon' po le·ka·zha

There's been an accident.
Tam był wypadek. tam biw vi·pa·dek

I'm lost.
Zgubiłem/am się. (m/f) zgoo·bee·wem/wam shye

Where are the toilets?
Gdzie są toalety? gjye som to·a·le·ti

I'm ill.
Jestem chory/a. (m/f) yes·tem kho·ri/ra

It hurts here.
Tutaj boli. too·tai bo·lee

I'm allergic to (antibiotics).
Mam alergię na (antybiotyki). mam a·ler·gye na (an·ti·byo·ti·kee)

SHOPPING & SERVICES

I'd like to buy ...
Chcę kupić ... khtse koo·peech ...

I'm just looking.
Tylko oglądam. til·ko o·glon·dam

Can I look at it?
Czy mogę to zobaczyć? chi mo·ge to zo·ba·chich

How much is it?
Ile to kosztuje? ee·le to kosh·too·ye

That's too expensive.
To jest za drogie. to yest za dro·gye

Can you lower the price?
Czy może pan/pani obniżyć cenę? (m/f) chi mo·zhe pan/pa·nee ob·nee·zhich tse·ne

There's a mistake in the bill.
Na czeku jest pomyłka. na che·koo yest po·miw·ka

ATM	bankomat	ban·ko·mat
credit card	karta kredytowa	kar·ta kre·di·to·va
internet cafe	kawiarnia internetowa	ka·vyar·nya een·ter·ne·to·va
mobile/cell phone	telefon komórkowy	te·le·fon ko·moor·ko·vi
post office	urząd pocztowy	oo·zhond poch·to·vi
tourist office	biuro turystyczne	byoo·ro too·ris·tich·ne

SIGNS

Wejście	Entrance
Wyjście	Exit
Otwarte	Open
Zamknięte	Closed
Informacja	Information
Wzbroniony	Prohibited
Toalety	Toilets
Panowie	Men
Panie	Women

DRINKS

TIME & DATES

What time is it?
Która jest godzina? ktoo·ra yest go·jee·na

It's one o'clock.
Pierwsza. pyerf·sha

Half past (10).
Wpół do (jedenastej). fpoow do (ye·de·nas·tey)
(lit: half to 11)

morning	rano	ra·no
afternoon	popołudnie	po·po·wood·nye
evening	wieczór	vye·choor
yesterday	wczoraj	fcho·rai
today	dziś/dzisiaj	jeesh/jee·shai
tomorrow	jutro	yoo·tro
Monday	poniedziałek	po·nye·jya·wek
Tuesday	wtorek	fto·rek
Wednesday	środa	shro·da
Thursday	czwartek	chfar·tek
Friday	piątek	pyon·tek
Saturday	sobota	so·bo·ta
Sunday	niedziela	nye·jye·la
January	styczeń	sti·chen'
February	luty	loo·ti
March	marzec	ma·zhets
April	kwiecień	kfye·chyen'
May	maj	mai
June	czerwiec	cher·vyets
July	lipiec	lee·pyets
August	sierpień	shyer·pyen'
September	wrzesień	vzhe·shyen'
October	październik	pazh·jyer·neek
November	listopad	lees·to·pat
December	grudzień	groo·jyen'

NUMBERS

1	jeden	ye·den
2	dwa	dva
3	trzy	tshi
4	cztery	chte·ri
5	pięć	pyench
6	sześć	sheshch
7	siedem	shye·dem
8	osiem	o·shyem
9	dziewięć	jye·vyench
10	dziesięć	jye·shench
20	dwadzieścia	dva·jyesh·chya
30	trzydzieści	tshi·jyesh·chee
40	czterdzieści	chter·jyesh·chee
50	pięćdziesiąt	pyen·jye·shont
60	sześćdziesiąt	shesh·jye·shont
70	siedemdziesiąt	shye·dem·jye·shont
80	osiemdziesiąt	o·shem·jye·shont
90	dziewięćdziesiąt	jye·vyen·jye·shont
100	sto	sto
1000	tysiąc	ti·shonts

TRANSPORT

Public Transport

When's the ... (bus)?	Kiedy jest ... (autobus)?	kye·di yest ... (ow·to·boos)
first	pierwszy	pyerf·shi
last	ostatni	os·tat·nee
next	następny	nas·temp·ni
boat	statek	sta·tek
bus	autobus	ow·to·boos
plane	samolot	sa·mo·lot
taxi	taksówka	tak·soof·ka
ticket office	kasa biletowa	ka·sa bee·le·to·va
timetable	rozkład jazdy	ros·kwad yaz·di
train	pociąg	po·chonk

A ... ticket (to Katowice).	Proszę bilet ... (do Katowic).	pro·she bee·let ... (do ka·to·veets)
one-way	w jedną stronę	v yed·nom stro·ne
return	powrotny	po·vro·tni

What time does it get to ...?
O której godzinie przyjeżdża do ...? — o ktoo·rey go·jee·nye pshi·yezh·ja do ...

Does it stop at ...?
Czy się zatrzymuje w...? — chi shye za·tshi·moo·ye v ...

Please tell me when we get to ...
Proszę mi powiedzieć gdy dojedziemy do ... — pro·she mee po·vye·jyech gdi do·ye·jye·mi do ...

Please take me to (this address).
Proszę mnie zawieźć pod (ten adres). — pro·she mnye za·vyeshch pod (ten ad·res)

Please stop here.
Proszę się tu zatrzymać. — pro·she shye too za·tshi·mach

Driving & Cycling

I'd like to hire a ...	Chcę wypożyczyć ...	khtse vi·po·zhi·chich ...
4WD	samochód terenowy	sa·mo·khoot te·re·no·vi
bicycle	rower	ro·ver
car	samochód	sa·mo·khoot
motorbike	motocykl	mo·to·tsikl

Is this the road to ...?
Czy to jest droga do ...? — chi to yest dro·ga do ...

Where's a service station?
Gdzie jest stacja benzynowa? — gjye yest sta·tsya ben·zi·no·va

How long can I park here?
Jak długo można tu parkować? — yak dwoo·go mozh·na too par·ko·vach

I need a mechanic.
Potrzebuję mechanika. — po·tshe·boo·ye me·kha·nee·ka

I've had an accident.
Miałem/am wypadek. (m/f) — myow·em/am vi·pa·dek

diesel	diesel	dee·zel
leaded	ołowiowa	o·wo·vyo·va
petrol/gas	benzyna	ben·zi·na
unleaded	bezołowiowa	bes·o·wo·vyo·va

QUESTION WORDS

What?	Co?	tso
When?	Kiedy?	kye·di
Where?	Gdzie?	gjye
Which?	Który/a/e? (m/f/n)	ktoo·ri/ra/re
Who?	Kto?	kto
Why?	Dlaczego?	dla·che·go

GLOSSARY

The following is a list of terms and abbreviations you're likely to come across in your travels through Poland. For other food and drink terms, see page 434.

aleja or Aleje – avenue, main city street; abbreviated to al in addresses and on maps
apteka – pharmacy

bankomat – ATM
bar mleczny – milk bar; a sort of basic self-service soup kitchen that serves very cheap, mostly vegetarian dishes
bazylika – basilica
bez łazienki – room without bathroom
biblioteka – library
bilet – ticket
biuro turystyki – travel agency
biuro zakwaterowania – office that arranges private accommodation
brama – gate
britzka – horse-drawn cart

Cepelia – a shop network selling artefacts made by local artisans
cerkiew (cerkwie) – Orthodox or Uniat church(es)
cukiernia – cake shop

Desa – chain of old art and antique sellers
dom kultury – cultural centre
dom wycieczkowy – term applied to PTTK-run hostels; also called *dom turysty*
domy wczasowe – workers' holiday homes
dwór – mansion

góra – mountain
gospoda – inn, tavern, restaurant
grosz – unit of Polish currency, abbreviated to gr; plural groszy; see also *złoty*

jaskinia – cave

kancelaria kościelna – church office
kantor(s) – private currency-exchange office(s)
kawiarnia – cafe
kemping – camping
kino – cinema
kolegiata – collegiate church
komórka – literally, 'cell'; commonly used for cellular (mobile) phone
kościół – church
księgarnia – bookshop
kwatery agro-turystyczne – agrotourist accommodation
kwatery prywatne – rooms for rent in private houses

miejscówka – reserved-seat ticket
muzeum – museum

na zdrowie! – cheers!; literally, 'to the health'
noclegi – accommodation

odjazdy – departures (on transport timetables)
ostrów – island
otwarte – open

park narodowy – national park
parking strzeżony – guarded car park
pchać – pull (on door)
pensjonat(y) – pension or private guesthouse(s)
peron – railway platform
piekarnia – bakery
PKS – Państwowa Komunikacja Samochodowa; former state-run company that runs most of Poland's bus transport
Plac – Sq
poczta – post office
poczta główna – main post office
pokój 1-osobowy – single room
pokój 2-osobowy – double room
przechowalnia bagażu – left-luggage room

przez – via, en route (on transport timetables)
przyjazdy – arrivals (on transport timetables)
PTSM – Polskie Towarzystwo Schronisk Młodzieżowych; Polish Youth Hostel Association
PTTK – Polskie Towarzystwo Turystyczno-Krajoznawcze; Polish Tourist & Countryside Association

rachunek – bill or check
riksza – bicycle rickshaws
rozkład jazdy – transport timetable
Rynek – Town/Market Sq

sanktuarium – church (usually pilgrimage site)
schronisko górskie – mountain hostel, providing basic accommodation and meals, usually run by the PTTK
schronisko młodzieżowe – youth hostel
Sejm – the lower house of parliament
skansen – open-air ethnographic museum
sklep – shop
stanica wodna – waterside hostel, usually with boats, kayaks and other water-related facilities
stare miasto – old town/city
Stary Rynek – Old Town/Market Sq
stołówka – canteen; restaurant or cafeteria of a holiday home, workplace, hostel etc
święty/a (m/f) – saint; abbreviated to Św
szopka – Nativity scene

teatr – theatre
toalety – toilets

ulica – street; abbreviated to ul in addresses (and placed before the street name); usually omitted on maps
Uniat – Eastern-rite Catholics

GLOSSARY

wódka – vodka; the number one Polish spirit

z łazienką – room with bathroom

zajazd – inn (sometimes restaurant)

zamek – castle

zdrój – spa

złoty – unit of Polish currency; abbreviated to zł; divided into 100 units called grosz

Food Glossary

bażant – pheasant

befsztyk – beef steak

befsztyk tatarski – raw minced beef accompanied by chopped onion, raw egg yolk and often chopped dill, cucumber and anchovies

botwinka – soup made from the stems and leaves of baby beetroots; often includes a hard-boiled egg

bryzol – grilled beef (loin) steak

budyń – milk pudding

chłodnik – chilled beetroot soup with sour cream and fresh vegetables; served in summer only

ciastko – pastry, cake

ćwikła z chrzanem – boiled and grated beetroot with horseradish

dorsz – cod

dzik – wild boar

gęś – goose

gołąbki – cabbage leaves stuffed with minced beef and rice, sometimes also with mushrooms

grochówka – pea soup, sometimes served *z grzankami* (with croutons)

indyk – turkey

kaczka – duck

kapuśniak – sauerkraut and cabbage soup with potatoes

karp – carp

knedle ze śliwkami – dumplings stuffed with plums

kopytka – Polish 'gnocchi'; noodles made from flour and boiled potatoes

kotlet schabowy – a fried pork cutlet coated in breadcrumbs, flour and egg, found on nearly every Polish menu

krupnik – thick barley soup containing a variety of vegetables and small chunks of meat

kurczak – chicken

leniwe pierogi – boiled noodles served with cottage cheese

łosoś wędzony – smoked salmon

melba – ice cream with fruit and whipped cream

mizeria ze śmietaną – sliced fresh cucumber in sour cream

naleśniki – crepes; fried pancakes, most commonly *z serem* (with cottage cheese), *z owocami* (with fruit) or *z dżemem* (with jam), and served with sour cream and sugar

pieczeń cielęca – roast veal

pieczeń wieprzowa – roast pork

pieczeń wołowa – roast beef

pieczeń z dzika – roast wild boar

placki ziemniaczane – fried pancakes made from grated raw potato, egg and flour; served *ze śmietaną* (with sour cream) or *z cukrem* (with sugar)

polędwica po angielsku – English-style beef; roast fillet of beef

pstrąg – trout

pyzy – ball-shaped steamed dumplings made of potato flour

rosół – beef or chicken (*z wołowiny/z kury*) bouillon, usually served *z makaronem* (with noodles)

rumsztyk – rump steak

ryż z jabłkami – rice with apples

sałatka jarzynowa – 'vegetable salad'; cooked vegetables in mayonnaise, commonly known as Russian salad

sałatka z pomidorów – tomato salad, often served with onion

sarna – deer, venison

schab pieczony – roast loin of pork seasoned with prunes and herbs

serem i z makiem – dumplings with cottage cheese/ poppy seeds

śledź w oleju – herring in oil with chopped onion

śledź w śmietanie – herring in sour cream

stek – steak

surówka z kapusty kiszonej – sauerkraut, sometimes served with apple and onion

sztuka mięsa – boiled beef with horseradish

zając – hare

zrazy zawijane – stewed beef rolls stuffed with mushrooms and/or bacon and served in a sour-cream sauce

zupa grzybowa – mushroom soup

zupa jarzynowa – vegetable soup

zupa ogórkowa – cucumber soup, usually with potatoes and other vegetables

zupa pomidorowa – tomato soup, usually served either *z makaronem* (with noodles) or *z ryżem* (with rice)

zupa szczawiowa – sorrel soup, usually served with hard-boiled egg

Behind the Scenes

SEND US YOUR FEEDBACK

We love to hear from travellers – your comments keep us on our toes and help make our books better. Our well-travelled team reads every word on what you loved or loathed about this book. Although we cannot reply individually to your submissions, we always guarantee that your feedback goes straight to the appropriate authors, in time for the next edition. Each person who sends us information is thanked in the next edition – the most useful submissions are rewarded with a selection of digital PDF chapters.

Visit **lonelyplanet.com/contact** to submit your updates and suggestions or to ask for help. Our award-winning website also features inspirational travel stories, news and discussions.

Note: We may edit, reproduce and incorporate your comments in Lonely Planet products such as guidebooks, websites and digital products, so let us know if you don't want your comments reproduced or your name acknowledged. For a copy of our privacy policy visit lonelyplanet.com/privacy.

OUR READERS

Many thanks to the travellers who used the last edition and wrote to us with helpful hints, useful advice and interesting anecdotes:

Marcia Anton, David Bourchier, Rebecca Bramlett, Nicolas Combremont, Mark Czerkawski, Jalle Daels, Peter Divine, Alyssa Donald, Reinhart Eisenberg, Paul Gallagher, Gillian Gardiner, Mathieu Gendaj, Stefan Görke, Debbie Greenlee, Marcus Hinske, Kingsley Jones, Elliot Leader, Aneta McNally, Brian Mooney, Marie Neumann, Łukasz Patejuk, Rhonda Penny, Robyn Quaintance, Bob Read, Theo Roell, Elaine Silver, Robert Srodulski, Mikolaj Stasiewicz, Lucas Szymansk, Assen Totin, Arie van Oosterwijk, Lars Walter, Mark Wenig, Emlyn Williams, Daniëlle Wolbers, David Zaitegui

WRITER THANKS

Simon Richmond

A particular thanks to locals Konrad Pyzel, Noam Silberberg and Micheal Moran; and to Sarah Johnstone for keeping me company. In memory of members of my family and my dear departed friend Dora Grynberg, all of whom had the good fortune to escape – and to the many, many others who sadly did not and whose ghosts will forever haunt Warsaw.

Mark Baker

I'd like to thank the staff at the InfoKraków tourist offices for their information and recommendations. Special thanks to my friend Olga Brzezińska and her friend, Anna Szybist, formerly of Kraków City Hall, for their tips and assistance. Thanks as well to my friends throughout Poland for their support, and to my co-writers on the Poland project. One last thanks to my Destination Editor Gemma Graham, who offered me the project in the first place.

Marc Di Duca

Huge thanks to my wife for holding the fort during my long absences, to all the staff at the Polish National Tourist Office and to all those helpful tourist offices across Pomerania, Warmia and Masuria, especially those in Toruń, Świnoujście, Szczecin, Malbork and Olsztyn.

Anthony Haywood

I'd like to thank the very helpful staff at visitor information centres and the myriad of other places – those who patiently and professionally answered my very many questions. Especially notable was Andrzej Ajchstet and colleagues at Informacja Turystyczna in Poznań for helping to unearth some of the more obscure information I sought.

Hugh McNaughtan

Thanks to Stanislaw, Marek, Jacek and the other kind people who helped me come to terms with Poland. Thanks also to my excellent editor and friend Gemma, and as always to Tasmin, Maise and Willa for their patience and support.

Ryan Ver Berkmoes

Better than a pot full of pierogis was the team of brilliant people who helped me along the way: in Bailystyok, Poland's best guide, Sylwia Bućko; in Suwałki, Karol Szulc; in Płock, Małgosia Szymczak; in Lublin, Maciej Zbarachewicz; in Łódź, Milena Kozik and Hubert Koperin; in Kielce, Magdalena Osełka; and a blessed source in Częstochowa, Daniel Zalejski. In New York City, Magdalena Zelazowska offered great insight from the start. Meanwhile back home, Alexis Ver Berkmoes was my pierogi of love.

ACKNOWLEDGEMENTS

Climate map data adapted from Peel MC, Finlayson BL & McMahon TA (2007) 'Updated World Map of the Köppen-Geiger Climate Classification', *Hydrology and Earth System Sciences*, 11, 1633–44.

Cover photograph: Young woman in traditional local dress from Zamosc, Lubin. Frans Sellies/ Getty Images ©

THIS BOOK

This 9th edition of Lonely Planet's *Poland* guidebook was researched and written by Simon Richmond, Mark Baker, Marc Di Duca, Anthony Haywood, Hugh McNaughtan and Ryan Ver Berkmoes. The previous two editions were written by Mark Baker, Marc Di Duca and Tim Richards.

This guidebook was produced by the following:

Destination Editor Gemma Graham

Senior Product Editors Genna Patterson, Sandie Kestell

Regional Senior Cartographer Valentina Kremenchutskaya

Product Editor Claire Rourke

Book Designers Fergal Condon, Gwen Cotter

Assisting Editors Andrew Bain, Judith Bamber, Nigel Chin, Michelle Coxall, Kate Daly, Samantha Forge, Carly Hall, Gabrielle Innes, Kate James, Kellie Langdon, Lauren O'Connell, Kristin Odijk, Rosie Nicholson, Tamara Sheward, Gabrielle Stefanos

Cover Researcher Meri Blazevski

Thanks to Elizabeth Jones, Catherine Naghten, Kathryn Rowan, Victoria Smith

Index

Map Legend

Sights

- Beach
- Bird Sanctuary
- Buddhist
- Castle/Palace
- Christian
- Confucian
- Hindu
- Islamic
- Jain
- Jewish
- Monument
- Museum/Gallery/Historic Building
- Ruin
- Shinto
- Sikh
- Taoist
- Winery/Vineyard
- Zoo/Wildlife Sanctuary
- Other Sight

Activities, Courses & Tours

- Bodysurfing
- Diving
- Canoeing/Kayaking
- Course/Tour
- Sento Hot Baths/Onsen
- Skiing
- Snorkelling
- Surfing
- Swimming/Pool
- Walking
- Windsurfing
- Other Activity

Sleeping

- Sleeping
- Camping
- Hut/Shelter

Eating

- Eating

Drinking & Nightlife

- Drinking & Nightlife
- Cafe

Entertainment

- Entertainment

Shopping

- Shopping

Information

- Bank
- Embassy/Consulate
- Hospital/Medical
- @ Internet
- Police
- Post Office
- Telephone
- Toilet
- Tourist Information
- Other Information

Geographic

- Beach
- Gate
- Hut/Shelter
- Lighthouse
- Lookout
- Mountain/Volcano
- Oasis
- Park
- Pass
- Picnic Area
- Waterfall

Population

- Capital (National)
- Capital (State/Province)
- City/Large Town
- Town/Village

Transport

- Airport
- Border crossing
- Bus
- Cable car/Funicular
- Cycling
- Ferry
- Metro station
- Monorail
- Parking
- Petrol station
- S-Bahn/Subway station
- Taxi
- T-bane/Tunnelbana station
- Train station/Railway
- Tram
- U-Bahn/Underground station
- Other Transport

Routes

- Tollway
- Freeway
- Primary
- Secondary
- Tertiary
- Lane
- Unsealed road
- Road under construction
- Plaza/Mall
- Steps
- Tunnel
- Pedestrian overpass
- Walking Tour
- Walking Tour detour
- Path/Walking Trail

Boundaries

- International
- State/Province
- Disputed
- Regional/Suburb
- Marine Park
- Cliff
- Wall

Hydrography

- River, Creek
- Intermittent River
- Canal
- Water
- Dry/Salt/Intermittent Lake
- Reef

Areas

- Airport/Runway
- Beach/Desert
- Cemetery (Christian)
- Cemetery (Other)
- Glacier
- Mudflat
- Park/Forest
- Sight (Building)
- Sportsground
- Swamp/Mangrove

Note: Not all symbols displayed above appear on the maps in this book

Anthony Haywood
Wielkopolska

Born in the port city of Fremantle, Western Australia, Anthony first pulled anchor in the late 1970s to travel Europe, North Africa and the US. Later, he studied comparative literature and Russian language at university. Anthony works as a freelance journalist and writer based in Germany. Publications include Lonely Planet guidebooks, *Siberia – A Cultural History* (Signal Books/Oxford University Press), travel articles, short stories and translations.

Hugh McNaughtan
Silesia; Carpathian Mountains

A former lecturer and history geek, Hugh has a long-standing fascination with Central and Eastern Europe and their impossibly complex stories. Silesia and the Carpathians were every bit as interesting as he hoped and the dumplings were always welcome.

Ryan Ver Berkmoes
Mazovia & Podlasie; Małopolska

Ryan has written more than 110 guidebooks for Lonely Planet. He grew up in Santa Cruz, California, which he left at age 17 for college in the Midwest, where he first discovered snow. All joy of this novelty soon wore off. Since then he has been travelling the world, both for pleasure and for work, which are often indistinguishable. He has covered everything from wars to bars - though he definitely prefers the latter. Ryan calls New York City home. Read more at ryanverberkmoes.com and at @ryanvb. His byline has appeared in scores of publications, and he's talked travel on the radio and TV.

OUR STORY

A beat-up old car, a few dollars in the pocket and a sense of adventure. In 1972 that's all Tony and Maureen Wheeler needed for the trip of a lifetime – across Europe and Asia overland to Australia. It took several months, and at the end – broke but inspired – they sat at their kitchen table writing and stapling together their first travel guide, *Across Asia on the Cheap*. Within a week they'd sold 1500 copies. Lonely Planet was born.

Today, Lonely Planet has offices in Franklin, London, Melbourne, Oakland, Dublin, Beijing and Delhi, with more than 600 staff and writers. We share Tony's belief that 'a great guidebook should do three things: inform, educate and amuse'.

OUR WRITERS

Simon Richmond
Warsaw

Journalist and photographer Simon Richmond first worked for Lonely Planet in 1999 on their *Central Asia* guide. He's since researched and written guidebooks to many countries, including Australia, China, Greece, India, Indonesia, Iran, Japan, Malaysia, Mongolia, Myanmar (Burma), Russia, Singapore, South Africa, South Korea and Turkey and the USA. He's penned features for Lonely Planet's website on topics from the world's best swimming pools to the joys of Urban Sketching – follow him on Instagram (simonrichmond) to see some of his photos and sketches. His travel features have been published in many publications, including in the UK's *Independent*, *Guardian*, *Times* and *Daily Telegraph* newspapers, and the *Royal Geographical Society Magazine*; and Australia's *Sydney Morning Herald* and *Australian* newspapers, and *Australian Financial Review Magazine*.

Simon also wrote the Plan & Understand chapters

Mark Baker
Kraków

Mark Baker is a freelance travel writer with a penchant for offbeat stories and forgotten places. He's originally from the United States, but now makes his home in the Czech capital, Prague. He writes mainly on Eastern and Central Europe for Lonely Planet as well as other leading travel publishers, but finds real satisfaction in digging up stories in places that are too remote or quirky for the guides. Prior to becoming an author, he worked as a journalist for *The Economist*, *Bloomberg News* and Radio Free Europe, among other organisations.

Instagram: @markbakerprague Twitter: @markbakerprague
Blog: www.markbakerprague.com

Mark Di Duca
Gdańsk & Pomerania; Warmia & Masuria

A travel writer for over a decade, Marc has worked for Lonely Planet in Siberia, Slovakia, Bavaria, England, Ukraine, Austria, Poland, Croatia, Portugal, Madeira and on the Trans-Siberian Railway, as well as writing and updating tens of other guides for other publishers. When not on the road, Marc lives near Mariánské Lázně in the Czech Republic with his wife and two sons.

OVER PAGE MORE WRITERS

Published by Lonely Planet Global Limited
CRN 554153
9th edition – Mar 2020
ISBN 978 1 78657 585 2
© Lonely Planet 2020   Photographs © as indicated 2020
10 9 8 7 6 5 4 3 2 1
Printed in China

Although the authors and Lonely Planet have taken all reasonable care in preparing this book, we make no warranty about the accuracy or completeness of its content and, to the maximum extent permitted, disclaim all liability arising from its use.